SEPARATIST MOVEMENTS
a global reference

CQ Press
2300 N Street, NW, Suite 800
Washington, DC 20037

Phone: 202-729-1900; toll-free, 1-866-4CQ-PRESS (1-866-427-7737)

Web: www.cqpress.com

Cover design: Naylor Design, Inc., Washington, D.C.
Maps: International Mapping Associates
Composition: C&M Digitals (P) Ltd.

⊗ The paper used in this publication exceeds the requirements of the American National Standard for Information Sciences—Permanence of Paper for Printed Library Materials, ANSI Z39.48-1992.

Printed and bound in the United States of America

15   14   13   12   11   1   2   3   4   5

Library of Congress Cataloging-in-Publication Data

Beary, Brian.
    Separatist movements: a global reference / Brian Beary.
        p. cm.
    Includes bibliographical references and index.
    ISBN 978-1-60426-569-9 (cloth: alk. paper) 1. Autonomy and independence movements. I. Title.
    JC312.B43 2011
    320.01'5—dc22

                                                                                2010048216

Contents

Australasia and East Asia   135

South and West Asia   193

List of Countries

Alphabetical List of Movements

List of Biographies

List of Maps

About the Author

BRIAN BEARY is a freelance journalist based in Washington, D.C., who specializes in international political relations. Since 2007 Beary has been a frequent contributor to CQ Press, authoring issues for CQ Press's *Global Researcher* on the New Europe, Turkey, Separatism, Religious Fundamentalism, and The Arctic.

Originally from Dublin, Ireland, Beary lived in Brussels from 1999 to 2006, where he worked as a reporter for the European Union affairs daily newspaper *Europolitics*. As an EU reporter, his main policy beats were justice and home affairs and internal trade. A fluent French speaker, he has been featured as a guest EU analyst on *PBS NewsHour*, the Arabic television channel Al Jazeera, and the francophone Belgian public radio channel RTBF. In 2006 he moved to Washington, D.C., to become the first U.S. correspondent for *Europolitics*. He is also a Washington correspondent for the European Parliament's *Parliament Magazine* and is a regular contributor to *The Globalist*, a Washington-based magazine on global politics, economics, and society.

Preface

Separatist Movements: A Global Reference provides readers with a solid grasp of the major separatist movements ongoing around the world. The book uses a template model in which the reader is presented with concise, fact-laden summaries of movements, with a focus on concrete manifestations of separatism rather than theories related to it. I include only current, active movements, which proved helpful in formulating a definition of separatism, as the notion of what constitutes a country today differs from what it was in 1800 or 1900.

The book features fifty-nine movements, making it a truly global reference and the first such work to feature so many movements in such detail. All of the well-known movements—roughly twenty-five—are covered, such as those of the Kurds, Tamils, and Tibetans. More off-the-radar movements, such as those of the Oromo in Ethiopia, Maori in New Zealand, and Saami in northern Scandinavia, are also covered. The various models of autonomy that different movements seek are described and form useful points of comparison. As the book goes to press, it appears as though the South Sudanese are set to secede, following an internationally approved referendum on independence. They are still included, however, because a split would not take effect until July 2011.

The movements are arranged by region, with twelve from Africa, eleven from the Americas, eleven from Australasia and East Asia, eight from South and West Asia, nine from East Europe, and eight from West Europe. The Table of Contents also lists movements alphabetically and by country to help readers find the movement most relevant to their field of study. Each region is accompanied by a map indicating where relevant groups live. I have also included individual maps for the Kurds and North Caucasians, given how fragmented those movements are, split among various political borders.

Each of the fifty-nine movement essays begins with a description of the people and a summary of their core aspirations—political, cultural, and economic. This is followed by a section charting the movement's history, stretching back decades and, in some cases, centuries. Then the movement's leadership—political parties, individuals, and militant groups—is outlined. There follows a current status section in which recent political developments are mentioned, with 2008 generally used as a chronological dividing line demarcating the current from the historical. A further reading section at the end of each essay lists the source material I used when researching the movement and provides additional sources for the reader.

Interspersed throughout the book are twenty-four succinct biographies of separatist leaders. In selecting profile subjects, I underscored the sharp contrasts that exist among different separatist leaders' ideologies. Thus, a hard-core militant secessionist such as Iratxe Sorzabal, leader of the Basque group ETA, is featured alongside the Dalai Lama, political and spiritual leader of the Tibetans, who opposes violence and is not secessionist. I have also included an appendix with excerpts from key international legal texts pertaining to the right of self-determination.

The Introduction provides an analysis of all the movements covered and includes a table summarizing their core elements. Often several movements from the same region show similar features. For example, the struggle by indigenous, or "First Nation," peoples to gain control over how their natural resources are exploited is prominent in the Americas and Australasia. Religion is a hot-button issue across Asia, with several movements exhibiting a strong Islamist element. In Africa, many of the movements are traceable to the political borders drawn up by colonial powers without due consideration for the tribal or ethnic makeup of inhabitants. In Europe, protecting and promoting native languages is a recurring theme.

About this book

To make each essay as self-contained as possible, I reduce to a minimum comparisons among movements within individual essays. I cross-reference other movements only where I feel there is a clear link of which the reader should be aware. For the table within the Introduction, I strove to create fields that are as fact-based as possible.

The use of terminology is a sensitive issue when writing about separatism. Indeed, the term *separatist* is pejorative, tending to be used more by opponents of separatists rather than by separatists themselves. Throughout the book, a reference to a "country" generally implies that the political entity in question is a member of the United Nations, which is perhaps the best indicator of statehood that exists today. Thus, none of the movements covered are UN member states. Many of the populations/groups, including the Scots and Welsh in the United Kingdom, Catalans of Spain, and Quebecois of Canada, describe themselves as distinct nations. Such a designation is often a source of friction between the populations/groups and their government.

In selecting source material for the book, I sought as broad a mix as possible. I read hundreds of academic and journalistic articles and studied dozens of reports from government agencies such as the U.S. State Department and from non-governmental organizations such as the International Crisis Group and Human Rights Watch. I attended academic conferences and seminars. With each essay, I tried to conduct at least one personal interview. The fact that I am based in Washington, D.C., the world capital of political activism, helped enormously. Thus, I was able to set up face-to-face interviews with, for example, a Baluch pro-independence activist, a Syrian Kurdish journalist, and an Iranian Azerbaijani minority rights campaigner. Where face-to-face interviews were not possible, I did telephone interviews and email exchanges with activists, politicians, academics, and journalists from Chile to New Zealand, from Japan to Greenland.

For facts and figures, I relied mostly on global databases. CQ Press's annual *Political Handbook of the World* was a good source for the leadership section of each essay. The CIA's *World Factbook* was a solid reference for up-to-date figures on population and religious and ethnic makeup. For the history of peoples covered, a database from Minority Rights Group International, which is a London-based non-governmental organization, proved invaluable.

Acknowledgments

For their general advice and support, I would like to thank my editors, Linda Dziobek, Sarah Fell, and January Layman-Wood. I also thank my CQ Press colleague and friend Darrell Dela Rosa. Andrew Swan at the Unrepresented Nations and Peoples Organization deserves special thanks for sharing with me his wealth of knowledge on the peoples covered and for helping to connect me with many activists and experts. And I thank CQ Press interns Andrea Bradley, Daniel Katz, and Katrina Overland for their help with researching and writing the biographies.

In terms of help on individual essays, I wish to acknowledge Patricio Abinales, Mindanao expert and professor at the Center for Southeast Asian Studies at Kyoto University; Mattias Ahren, Norway-based president of the Saami Council; François Alfonsi, Corsican autonomy advocate and member of the European Parliament; Arturo Arias,

Guatemalan novelist and critic; Kristin Bakke, lecturer in politics and international relations at University College London; Louise Beaudoin, member of the Quebec parliament for the Parti Quebecois; Pastor Norman Bent, indigenous and ethnic groups advocate from the Moravian Church of Nicaragua; Jacqueline Balfour, Belgium-based South African translator; Iain Campbell Smith, former Australian diplomat and peace monitor; Gunther Dauwen, Flemish independence activist for the European Free Alliance group; Lynette Clark, Alaskan Independence Party Chair; Andres Doernberg, Chilean retired development economist; Jill Evans, member of the European Parliament for the Welsh independence party Plaid Cymru; Martin Evans, international development studies lecturer at University of Chester; Farzin Farzad, Iranian ethnic minority rights activist; Ergun Fikri, U.S.-based Turkish Cypriot; Eduardo Gamarra, professor and director of the Latin American and Caribbean Center at Florida International University; Dr. Fai Ghulam Nabi, executive director of the Kashmiri American Council; Anne Hagood, U.S.-based media analyst of French Basque ancestry; Susan Hammond from The Forum on Cambodia, Laos and Vietnam, a non-governmental organization; Selig Harrison, author and journalist specializing in South Asian politics; Vicki Hykes-Steere, Inupiaq sovereignty activist; Sirwan Kajjo, Syrian Kurdish political activist and journalist; Seth Kaplan, author and expert on different countries' models of government; Buket Kop at the Turkish Republic of Northern Cyprus's Washington office; T. Kumar at Amnesty International; Menna Machreth, chair of Welsh Language Society; Joseph Mariampillai, Tamil relief agency worker; Gene Martin, peace worker at the United States Institute of Peace; Ardeth Maung Thawnghmung, associate professor at the University of Massachusetts; Russell Means, Lakota Indian independence activist; Cesar Millahueique, Mapuche cultural rights activist and artist; Ahmar Mustikhan, Baluch pro-independence activist, writer, and poet; Margaret Mutu, professor and head of the Maori Studies Department at University of Auckland; Ibrahim Nasar, Pashtun journalist for Voice of America; Daniel Ntoni-Nzinga, Baptist minister and peace activist in Angola; Martin Ottenheimer, professor of anthropology at Kansas State University and expert on the Comoros Islands; Marie Pace, Nigeria expert at the United States Institute of Peace; Anthony Regan, expert on the Bougainville conflict; Amy Reger, researcher at the Uyghur American Association; Luis Rivera-Pagan, Ecumenics Professor Emeritus at Princeton Theological Seminary; Aaron Running Hawk from the Black Hills Sioux Treaty Council; Tim Rowse, professor at the Center for Citizenship and Public Policy at University of Western Sydney; Erika Schlager at the U.S. Congress's Helsinki Commission in Washington, D.C.; David Short, Anglophone Canadian and attorney at FedEx; Dr. Pritam Singh, senior lecturer at Oxford Brookes University Business School; Isabelle Smets, Francophone Belgian journalist for *Europolitics;* Dennis Smith from the Central American Evangelical Center for Pastoral Studies in Guatemala; Philip Smith, Hmong advocate at the Center for Public Policy Analysis in Washington, D.C.; Tibor Szendrei, Hungarian journalist for *Europolitics* in Brussels; Bo Tedards, director at the Taiwan Foundation for Democracy; Rosa Thorsen, press officer for the Premier of Greenland; Tink Tinker, professor of American Indian cultures and religious traditions at Iliff Theological Seminary in Denver; Mililani Trask, Hawaiian sovereignty activist; Bhuchung K. Tsering, director of the International Campaign for Tibet in Washington, D.C.; Christophe Wilcke, Yemen expert at Human Rights Watch; Bill Wilson, member of the Scottish Parliament for the pro-independence Scottish National Party; Stefan Wolff, self-determination expert and professor of International Security at University of Birmingham; and William Zartman, professor of International Organizations and Conflict Resolution at Johns Hopkins University's School of Advanced International Studies.

Brian Beary
January 2011

Introduction

The value of these collected essays lies in their providing readers with in-depth analyses of the major separatist movements around the world without their having to seek out multiple sources. Each of the fifty-nine essays describes a particular group of people, in a particular place, who are dissatisfied with how they are governed. For all separatists, the principle of self-determination—that is, the right to decide how and by whom one is governed—is paramount. Separatists espouse various forms of self-government. Some are content with devolution, where the central government devolves power to certain regions, or autonomy, where they are granted a self-governing statute. Others would like to establish a separate country through secession, asserting complete sovereignty and declaring independence. In some instances, a neighboring country encourages a group of people to secede with the ultimate aim of annexing that seceding territory. This phenomenon is known as irredentism. To quell separatism, governments may try to integrate a people by encouraging them to identify more with their country. Other governments go further and adopt assimilation policies where a group of people is expected to shed its distinct identity entirely. In extreme cases, governments try to resolve the problem by physically removing the people from their territory—a phenomenon known as ethnic cleansing.

Separatist movements vary greatly in size. The most-populous of these movements is that of the Pashtuns of Afghanistan and Pakistan, who number forty million. The next largest is that of the Northern Italians of Italy, who number thirty million, with the movements of the Kurds of Iraq, Iran, Syria, and Turkey and the Oromo of Ethiopia, each with a population numbering twenty-five million, following. Other large movements include the Taiwanese of China (23 million); Azerbaijanis of Iran (16–24 million); Baluch of Afghanistan, Iran, and Pakistan (15 million); Kashmiris of India and Pakistan (15 million); Uyghurs of China (9–16 million); and Mayans of Guatemala and Mexico (10–15 million). The least populous movement covered is that of the Greenlanders of Denmark, who number 56,000. Other small movements include the Inuit of Canada and South Ossetians of Georgia (70,000 each), Abkhazians of Georgia (50–100,000), and the Saami of Finland, Norway, Russia, and Sweden (100,000).

A movement's size is not necessarily a good indicator of its geopolitical importance. Some of the smallest movements attract the most attention. The movement of the South Ossetians, despite being the second least populous, has been the focus of major diplomatic and military efforts by Russia and the United States since 2008. By contrast, some of the largest movements have been largely forgotten. The twenty-five million Oromo in Ethiopia are scarcely known outside of Africa, despite having waged a violent insurgency since the 1990s. The fifteen million Baluch live in south Asia, a region where the global spotlight is constantly fixed. Yet their independence struggle has been largely eclipsed by the militant insurgencies waged by another ethnic group in the neighborhood, the Pashtuns, who are the dominant group leading the Islamist Taliban movement.

The decision to exclude certain peoples from the book merits some explanation. Kosovo's Albanians, who declared independence from Serbia in 2008, have been omitted because Kosovo's independence is recognized by seventy-two countries (September 2010), including most of its European neighbors and by the United States. Moreover, Kosovar Albanians control most of their territory and function as an independent country in practice. In July 2010, the International Court of Justice ruled that Kosovo's declaration of independence did not violate international law. In the United Kingdom, Northern Ireland's Catholics were excluded because their political goal is to unify with southern Ireland, not to transform Northern Ireland into an independent country. A third difficult decision involved the situation of the Palestinian people. They were excluded because while the Palestinian Territories are partly occupied by Israel, the Israeli government does not claim sovereignty over them. Thus, if and when an independent country called Palestine is created, the Palestinians would not be seceding from Israel because they are not now legally a part of Israel.

Regional comparison

To help draw conclusions about how extensive separatism is, what causes it, and what impact it has internally and internationally, there is a table summarizing core elements of each of the fifty-nine movements. For fifty-six of the fifty-nine movements covered, or 95 percent, the people form a minority of their country's overall population. In many such cases, desire for autonomy or independence is fueled by resentment at having been deprived of political power because of minority status. In the case of ten of the movements, or 17 percent, the people form a minority of less than 1 percent. Four of these are indigenous American peoples—Hawaiians, Inuit, Lakota, and Mapuche—and a fifth—Alaskans—has a strong indigenous element to it. In thirty-two of the movements, or 54 percent, the people form a minority of between 1 and 10 percent. For sixteen of the movements, or 27 percent, they form a minority of between 10 and 50 percent.

The three movements where the people constitute 50 percent or more of the population are the Flemings of Belgium (58 percent), Mayans of

Guatemala (40–60 percent), and Northern Italians of Italy (50 percent). The Flemings and Northern Italians buck the general trend of separatist movements in that they are not in some way underprivileged or marginalized. The Flemings are on average wealthier than Francophone Belgians, and Northern Italians are wealthier than their southern neighbors. Indeed, this wealth gap is a significant motivating factor: many Flemings and Northern Italians resent having to support their poorer compatriots financially. Given their majority status in the total population, were a clear majority of Flemings or Northern Italians to demand it, secession would likely result.

By coincidence, the number of countries covered, fifty-nine, equals the number of movements covered. For forty-seven of the fifty-nine movements, or 80 percent, the people in question are based in a single country. Eight movements, or 14 percent, are based in two countries: Basques (France, Spain), Hmong (Laos, Vietnam), Kashmiris (India, Pakistan), Mapuche (Argentina, Chile), Mayans (Guatemala, Mexico), Pashtuns (Afghanistan, Pakistan), Serbs (Bosnia, Kosovo), and Somalis (Ethiopia, Kenya). Two are spread across three countries: Baluch (Afghanistan, Iran, and Pakistan) and Hungarians (Serbia, Slovakia, and Romania). And two are dispersed among four countries: Kurds (Iraq, Iran, Syria, and Turkey) and Saami (Finland, Norway, Russia, and Sweden).

Separatist movements divided between political boundaries generally find it more difficult to forge a unified leadership. The cases of the Kurds and Saami underscore, however, how this challenge can be affected by the political situation in the countries involved. The Kurds, who number twenty-five million, have a very fragmented leadership. Different factions occasionally fight against, rather than with, one another. Turkish Kurdish leader Abdullah Ocalan may have used Syria as a base for launching an insurgency against Turkey in the 1980s and early 1990s, but he did not support the Syrian Kurds' campaign for autonomy. Ocalan knew that if he had, the Syrian government would not have allowed him to stay. The Saami, by contrast, who number 100,000, are politically united despite having been divided across four countries between the 1700s and 1905. Their representative body, the Saami Council, adopts common positions on issues such as land rights and autonomy. The Saami are in a stronger position politically than the Kurds: they enjoy full political freedoms in three of the four countries where they live (Finland, Norway, and Sweden). The Kurds live in a more politically repressive part of the world. Their freedom to assemble and organize politically is especially curtailed in Syria.

Even where a movement is concentrated in a single country, it can lack strong leadership or be torn over what its goals and methods should be. The Aboriginals in Australia, for example, do not have a country-wide political party to advance their interests. The Hawaiians in the United States are split between those advocating autonomy for "truebloods"—people of majority Native Hawaiian ancestry—and those favoring autonomy for all Hawaiian residents. The Karen of Myanmar have been badly affected by internal feuding between the Christian- and Buddhist-dominated factions of their movement. The Moros in the Philippines are split between two militant Islamic groups, Abu Sayyaf and the Moro Islamic Liberation Front. With the Zanzibaris of Tanzania, the political fault line runs between Zanzibaris of African ancestry and those of Arab ancestry, with the latter tending to be more secessionist-oriented.

Where a movement is spread across two countries, it is often stronger in one than the other. The Pashtuns in Afghanistan have held political power at various times, whereas the Pashtuns in Pakistan have struggled to assert themselves in a Pakistani government dominated by Punjabis, a rival ethnic group. The Basques in Spain have a strong autonomous government, whereas the Basques in France are politically weak and are struggling to preserve their culture. Population size may be a factor here: there are 2.1 million Basques in Spain but only 70,000 in France. The Serbs of Bosnia have been more successful in enshrining a unitary, geographically contiguous, autonomous government than the Serbs in Kosovo. In Bosnia, Serbs constitute 31 percent of the population; in Kosovo, they account for just 7 percent of the population. By contrast, the Mayans account for a smaller share of the population in Mexico (5 percent) than in Guatemala (40–60 percent), yet Mexican Mayans have been the more successful in securing self-government.

The Baluch are split among three countries. In Pakistan, many Baluch resent the way in which Pakistan has grown more Islamic under the Punjabi-dominated government. In Iran, the Baluch are more Islamist, with the militant group Jundallah spearheading an anti-government insurgency. In Afghanistan, the Baluch are not as politically well-organized.

Countries that are having to contend with several movements at once include Afghanistan, Canada, China, Ethiopia, France, Georgia, India, Iran, Kenya, Pakistan, Russia, Spain, the United Kingdom, and the United States. The countries that face the greatest threat of breaking up due to secessionism tend to be the most hostile to it. China and Iran are good examples. Both operate autocratic models of government where separatists have few legal or democratic avenues to advance their goals. In both cases, separatist movements have turned violent: in China with the Tibetan and Uyghur riots of 2008 and 2009, respectively, and in Iran with long-standing insurgencies waged by disaffected Baluch and Kurds.

The United States, where a bloody war was fought from 1861–1865 to prevent the southern U.S. states from seceding, marks a sharp contrast with China and Iran. The many separatist movements are allowed to form political parties and field candidates in elections. Especially in recent times, they have been overwhelmingly peaceful. Indeed, none of the four U.S.-based movements covered poses a serious threat to the country's unity, which is not the case with China and Iran.

Summary of movements

Movement	Population	Proportion of overall population in country of residence (percent)	Primary motivating factor*				Violence involving at least one fatality since 1990	Reasonable possibility of gaining independence by 2020***
			Language or ethnicity	Control of natural resources	Religion	Historical political borders**		
Abkhazians	50–100,000	1–2	x			x	x	•
Aboriginals and Torres Strait Islanders	420,000	2	x	x				
Acehnese	4,000,000	1.7	x	x	x	x	x	
Afrikaners	3,000,000	6	x				x	
Afro-Caribbean and Amerindians	1,200,000	20	x					
Alaskans	700,000	0.25	x	x				
Anjouanais	280,000	37		x			x	
Azerbaijanis	16–24,000,000	25–40	x					
Baluch	15,000,000	Afghanistan: 2 Iran: 2 Pakistan: 4	x	x	x	x	x	
Basques	2,200,000	France: 0.1 Spain: 5	x	x			x	
Bougainvilleans	180,000	3		x			x	x
Cabindans	400,000	3		x		x	x	
Casamançais	1,400,000	10	x	x	x	x	x	
Catalans	7,000,000	17	x					
Corsicans	300,000	0.5	x	x			x	
Crimeans	2,700,000	4 (Russians) 1 (Tatars)	x	x	x	x	x	
Flemings	6,000,000	58	x			x		x
Greenlanders	56,000	1	x	x				x
Hawaiians	1,300,000	0.4	x	x				
Hmong	1,500,000	Laos: 8 Vietnam: 1	x				x	
Hungarians	3,000,000	Romania: 7 Serbia: 4 Slovakia: 10	x			x		
Inuit	70,000	0.2	x	x				
Karabakh Armenians	138,000	1.5	x			x	x	•
Karen	4,000,000	7	x		x		x	
Kashmiris	15,000,000	Pakistan: 2 India: 1	x		x	x	x	
Kurds	25,000,000	Iran: 7 Iraq: 15–20 Syria: 5–10 Turkey: 18	x	x		x	x	x (in Iraq)
Lakota	155,000	0.04	x	x				
Lowlanders	2,835,000	34	x	x				
Malays	3,300,000	5	x		x	x	x	
Maori	630,000	15	x	x				

Summary of movements

Movement	Population	Proportion of overall population in country of residence (percent)	Primary motivating factor*				Violence involving at least one fatality since 1990	Reasonable possibility of gaining independence by 2020***
			Language or ethnicity	Control of natural resources	Religion	Historical political borders**		
Mapuche	615,000	Argentina: 0.2 Chile: 3.2	x	x			x	
Mayans	10–15,000,000	Guatemala: 40–60 Mexico: 5	x	x			x	
Moros	4,500,000	5	x	x	x	x	x	
North Caucasians	6,000,000	4	x		x	x	x	
Northern Italians	30,000,000	50						
Ogoni	500,000	0.3	x	x			x	
Oromo	25,000,000	33	x	x			x	
Pashtuns	40,000,000	Afghanistan: 40 Pakistan: 14	x		x	x	x	
Puerto Ricans	4,000,000	1.3	x					
Quebecois	7,000,000	20	x					
Saami	100,000	Norway: 1.3 Fin. , Russ., Swe.: <1	x	x		x		
Scots	5,000,000	9	x	x				x
Serbs	1,830,000	Bosnia: 31 Kosovo: 7	x		x	x	x	x (in Bosnia)
Sikhs	22,000,000	2			x		x	
Somalilanders	3,500,000	33				x	x	•
Somalis	4,500,000	Ethiopia: 7 Kenya: 2	x		x	x	x	
South Cameroonians	3,000,000	15	x			x		
South Ossetians	70,000	1.5	x			x	x	•
South Sudanese	8,000,000	20	x	x	x	x	x	x
South Yemenis	5,000,000	20		x	x	x	x	x
Taiwanese	23,000,000	1.7	x					•
Tamils	3,700,000	18	x		x		x	
Tibetans	5–6,000,000	0.5	x	x	x		x	
Transnistrians	537,000	13	x			x	x	•
Turkish Cypriots	264,000	24	x	x	x			•
Uyghurs	9–16,000,000	1–2	x		x		x	
Welsh	3,000,000	5	x					
Western Saharans	400,000	1				x	x	
Zanzibar and Pemba Islanders	1,100,000	3	x		x		x	

* The absence of an "x" in a field does not signify that this issue is not relevant to the movement but rather that other factors tend to play a more prominent role in motivating the movement.

** The way in which countries' political borders were constructed historically.

*** • = Movement has succeeded in establishing a de facto independent entity but one that is not recognized as such by the United Nations.

Sources for population data: Minority Rights Group International, World Directory of Minorities and Indigenous Peoples, www.minorityrights.org/directory; CIA, The World Fact Book, www.cia.gov/library/publications/the-world-factbook.

Quantifying how much support separatist movements have from their people can be difficult. In some cases—for example, the Hmong in Laos and Tibetans in China—they are legally barred from establishing their own political party. Moreover, in these countries there are no free and fair elections in which to field candidates and thereby accurately judge the degree of support. In other cases—for example, the Basques in Spain and Kurds in Turkey—separatists have political parties that compete in elections. However, they are regularly banned by the courts and forced to reincarnate under different names. In still other cases—for example, the Malays in Thailand and Moros in the Philippines—the leadership of the separatist movement is very fragmented. Finally, some factions are militant groups that do not compete in elections.

Where separatists do compete in elections, parties that are overtly secessionist tend to attract the support of only a minority of their people. This is the case with the Afrikaners in South Africa, Alaskans and Puerto Ricans in the United States, and Welsh in the United Kingdom. In a few cases, secessionist parties are close to obtaining majority support from their people. In Belgium, the two pro-independence Flemish parties won 40.8 percent of the Flemish vote in the June 2010 general elections. In Danish-owned Greenland, the pro-independence Inuit Ataqatigiit party scored 43.7 percent in the May 2009 elections. Since 2008 Greenlanders have controlled most of their affairs, including control over their oil and gas reserves, while Denmark is still responsible for foreign policy and defense. The Danish government has indicated it will not oppose full independence for Greenland should the Greenlanders desire this. It is unusual for a government to adopt such a tolerant stance on the issue of secession.

Eight of the movements covered enjoy de facto independence but are not recognized by the United Nations as independent countries. For the secessionist enclaves of Abkhazia, Nagorno Karabakh, South Ossetia, and Transnistria, it is hard to gauge how much popular support for independence there is given the tense political and security environments. It does seem, however, that these populations have little desire to be reintegrated into the countries they split from. The Turkish Cypriot government is participating in talks to reunify Cyprus in a decentralized federation, but it is far from clear these talks will lead to the island's reunification. In Taiwan the situation hangs in the balance. Of the two dominant political parties, one advocates unifying with China while the other supports independence for Taiwan.

Causes of separatism

Turning to the most common causes of separatism, for fifty-one of the fifty-nine movements, or 86 percent, language or ethnicity is a primary motivating factor. Notable cases include the Basques and Catalans in Spain; Flemings in Belgium; Hungarians in Romania, Serbia, and Slovakia; Quebecois in Canada; South Cameroonians in Cameroon; and Welsh in the United Kingdom. The right to educate one's children through the medium of one's native tongue is a major battleground. For indigenous communities in the Americas and East Asia and Australia, including the Aboriginals and Torres Strait Islanders of Australia, Maori of New Zealand, and Hawaiians of the United States, the threat is existential; they are trying to prevent their language from becoming extinct. Language is not as prominent a motivating factor in the African movements covered.

Closely linked to language is ethnicity. A sharp cultural divide between ethnic groups can lay the foundation of a separatist conflict. Examples include the clash between Aboriginal and white Australians and between Afrikaners (South Africans of Dutch ancestry) and black South Africans. In Nicaragua, two ethnic minorities, the American Indian and Afro-Caribbean peoples on the Atlantic coast, tend to speak either an indigenous language or English. They have resisted the integration policies of

Nicaragua's Spanish-speaking majority, which lives mostly on the Pacific coast.

There are cases where language and ethnicity are not primary motivating factors. These movements include the Anjounais in the Comoro Islands, Northern Italians in Italy, Somalilanders in Somalia, South Yemenis in Yemen, and Western Saharans in Morocco. This does not mean that there are no linguistic or ethnic variations in these places; rather, these issues are not what is currently driving the separatist movement. For example, there are many dialects of the Italian language that help to differentiate northern from southern Italians, but this is not a dominant factor in the Northern Italian separatist movement.

Control of natural resources is a primary motivating factor in thirty (51 percent) of the movements. How to share revenues from oil and gas reserves in an equitable manner is the single biggest cause of conflict within this category. A good example is that of the Ogoni people of Nigeria. The Nigerian economy relies heavily on oil, and much of this comes from the Ogoni homelands in the Niger Delta. Other such cases involve the Acehnese in Indonesia, Baluch in Pakistan, Cabindans in Angola, Greenlanders in Denmark, Kurds in Iraq, Lowlanders in Bolivia, South Sudanese in Sudan, and South Yemenis in Yemen.

In Papua New Guinea (PNG), it was copper, not oil, that provoked a secessionist conflict on the island of Bougainville in the 1990s. Locals rebelled against a situation that involved an Australian company extracting copper and the PNG government reaping much of the profit, while the Bougainvilleans' environment suffered major pollution from the mining activities. In Chile, forests are a source of conflict; the indigenous Mapuche people would like to restrict commercial logging on their ancestral lands. For the Saami, the contested resource is renewable energy. In the 1970s and 1980s, the Saami tried in vain to stop Norway from building a hydroelectric dam on their river. More recently, they have had concerns about the construction of electricity-generating windmills on their lands.

Religion is a primary motivating factor in twenty movements, or 34 percent. Islamic fundamentalism plays a prominent role in the separatist movements of the Acehnese in Indonesia, Kashmiris in India, Moros in the Philippines, Malays in Thailand, and North Caucasians in Russia. In the case of the Turkish Cypriots of Cyprus, the separatists are Muslims who are dissatisfied with a Christian-dominated government, although they are not Islamic fundamentalists. With the South Yemenis of Yemen, divisions among Muslims play a role. Southerners are Shafist, a branch of Sunni Islam, while most northerners are Zaidist, a branch of Shia Islam. The Baluch of Pakistan are a relatively secular Muslim people who have become alienated by a government that has grown increasingly Islamic.

Religious differences among separatists can be a factor, too. In Myanmar, the leading Karen rebel group, the Karen National Union (KNU), is Christian-dominated; however, most of the Karen people are Buddhist. A group of disaffected Buddhist Karen formed a rival faction called the Democratic Karen Buddhist Army (DKBA), which is fighting on the side of the government against the KNU. Much of the leadership of the Tamil Tigers, the leading Tamil separatist militant group in Sri Lanka, is Christian, though most Tamils are Hindu.

The Serbs in Bosnia and Kosovo, and the South Sudanese in Sudan, are examples of Christian peoples trying to secede from Muslim-dominated governments. The Bosnian and Kosovo governments, it should be noted, are much less Islamic than the Sudanese government. With the Sikhs of India—given that their religion is their primary identifier—it is not surprising that religion is a primary motivating factor in the Sikh separatist movement. India is majority Hindu, although officially it is secular. The Muslim Uyghurs and Buddhist Tibetans are examples of religious peoples rebelling against an atheist government—China.

For twenty-five of the peoples covered, or 42 percent, the circumstances under which their political borders were constructed is a primary motivating factor in their movement. Typically, major powers established borders that were not based on the ethnic makeup of the territory, or merged two territories that historically were ruled separately. Examples of this include the Cabindans in Angola and Casamançais in Senegal, who were transferred to Portuguese and French colonial rule, respectively, in 1885. Following World War I (1914–1918), the borders of Europe and western Asia were drastically changed. The Hungarians and Kurds fared badly in this process. Hungary was forced to cede two-thirds of the territory it had historically governed, an area that contained one-third of its population. The Kurds were denied a country of their own.

Western colonial powers have contributed to separatist disputes as well. The United Kingdom in the case of the Baluch, Kashmiris, and Pashtuns; the United States in the case of the Moros; and Spain in the case of the Western Saharans ignited separatist movements because of the way they constructed political boundaries upon relinquishing colonies. Two movements are mainly the result of a local power's expansion of its territories: Ethiopia's annexation of Oromo lands in the late 1800s and the annexation by Siam (now Thailand) of three Muslim Malay provinces in 1902. The sudden disintegration of the Soviet Union in 1991 was a primary motivating factor in six movements: Abkhazians, Crimeans, Karabakh Armenians, North Caucasians, South Ossetians, and Transnistrians. Soviet leader Joseph Stalin in the 1920s deliberately split nationalities between administrative regions to try to weaken their sense of national identity. Despite his and his successors' efforts, there has been a major resurgence of nationalist sentiment in the areas of the former Soviet Union since the 1990s. The Serb separatist movements in Bosnia and Kosovo are a consequence of the bloody breakup in the 1990s of Yugoslavia, which was a multi-ethnic country.

A motivating factor in some movements can be traced to the actions of a former colonial ruler who favored one ethnic minority over another; when the colonial power left, the favored minority lost its privileged position, sparking resentment. The U.K.'s privileged relationship with the Karen of Burma (now Myanmar) and Tamils of Ceylon (now Sri Lanka) are cases in point. When the Burmese and Sinhalese majorities came to power in 1947, the Karen and Tamils, respectively, lost power and became marginalized. Another factor driving some movements is support from the diaspora community—that is, from emigrants from their historical homeland. The diaspora influence is evident among the Acehnese in Sweden, Hmong in the United States, Sikhs in Canada, and Tamils in the United Kingdom. The diaspora often has greater financial resources and political freedoms than do the people in the home countries.

Divergences in political ideology may play a role. The communist government in Laos has historically viewed its Hmong minority with suspicion because some Hmong fought alongside the anti-communist United States in the Vietnam War of the 1960s and early 1970s. In South Africa, some Afrikaners still support the racist apartheid system in place from 1948 to 1994 and therefore oppose the majority rule system introduced in 1994 that in practice has resulted in governments dominated by black South Africans. In Mexico, many Mayans are fighting to retain their traditional system of communal land ownership. The Mexican government has eroded this tradition through its privatization policies. The lowlanders in Bolivia, many of whom are of European ancestry, fear that Bolivia's first indigenous president, Evo Morales, will redistribute their wealth to poorer regions.

The issue of immigration—specifically, of "ethnic flooding"—merits a mention as a motivating factor. Sometimes governments try to repress a separatist movement by encouraging outsiders to emigrate. This is done to weaken the cohesion among the locals and to turn them into a minority in their homeland. Examples include Han Chinese moving en masse to Tibetan and Uyghur areas and Filipinos moving to Mindanao, the island where most Moros live. Ethnic flooding often further inflames, rather than reduces, separatist sentiment, however, as indigenous peoples view such policies as an attempt at cultural genocide. A separatist movement can itself promote ethnic flooding to bolster its people's numbers. More than 100,000 Turks from mainland Turkey have settled in the Turkish-occupied part of Cyprus since Turkey invaded the island in 1974; as a result, the Turkish Cypriot population has doubled.

Violence

To determine whether or not a separatist movement can be described as violent, the following standard is in place: if there has been at least one fatality directly linked to the movement since 1990 then a movement is deemed violent. Thus, a separatist-inspired protest involving clashes with authorities where no person was killed would not meet this standard. Thirty-seven of the fifty-nine movements, or 63 percent, can be considered violent by this standard. Movements that have been particularly violent include those of the Acehnese, Cabindans, Karen, Kashmiris, Kurds, Moros, North Caucasians, Serbs, and South Sudanese. Asia, Africa, and Europe are the continents where movements are most likely to be violent, with fifteen, ten, and eight violent movements, respectively. Only two of the eleven movements in the Americas—the Mapuche of Argentina and Chile and Mayans of Guatemala and Mexico—are violent. Of the three separatist movements in Australasia, just one, Bougainvilleans of PNG, is violent. Of the twenty-two movements, or 37 percent, that can be considered peaceful, nine are in the Americas, seven in Europe, two in Australasia, and one in Asia.

When a movement reaches resolution

The ultimate political goal of separatist movements varies considerably. Some are focused on the most basic first step: simply being recognized as a distinct people. For example, in the North Caucasus region of Russia, an ethnic group called the Circassians has, since the 1990s, tried to put themselves on the contemporary world map by stressing a common identity and promoting greater use of the term *Circassian.* Since Soviet times, Circassians have been split among various multi-ethnic administrative regions and, as a result, are often named after these regions rather than called Circassians.

Attaining cultural autonomy is the priority for some movements, with strong emphasis on the right to communicate in public life and educate oneself and one's children through the medium of one's own language. This is frequently the priority of movements in countries where the government is dominated by people who speak a different language. The Mayans of Guatemala, for example, despite constituting half of that country's population, struggle to receive Mayan-language public services, such as court interpreters, as Spanish dominates public life. In Eastern Europe, the ethnic Hungarian minority in Slovakia is trying to defend the Hungarian language in the face of a concerted effort by the Slovak government to bolster the use of Slovak. Slovakia passed a law in July 2009 that restricts the use of Hungarian in state institutions. In Ukraine, the Tatars, who make up 13 percent of Crimea, are trying to revive their language, which was suppressed in the Soviet era. Their campaign is viewed with unease by ethnic Russians, who account for 62 percent of Crimea's population. The Tatars were expelled from their homeland in Crimea in 1944. They began returning in large numbers in the 1980s, which has triggered tensions with Crimea's ethnic Russian majority.

In many instances, a movement is seeking territorial autonomy, meaning a designated area of land where they enjoy self-government. There are many different forms of territorial autonomy. With the Zanzibaris in Tanzania, such autonomy came about in a somewhat ad hoc manner. In 1964 the presidents of two independent countries, Zanzibar and Tanganyika, agreed between themselves to unify their countries while permitting Zanzibar to retain a large degree of autonomy. In Ethiopia, the Oromo were granted their own state within a federal structure in 1995. The state of Oromo constitutes 30 percent of Ethiopian territory. While this has satisfied some Oromo, for others it is not enough, and a militant pro-independence insurgency continues. The Moros in the Philippines gained territorial autonomy in 1990 with the creation of the Autonomous Region of Muslim Mindanao. One faction of separatists, the Moro National Liberation Front, has accepted this arrangement for now, but other factions, Abu Sayyaf and the Moro Islamic Liberation Front, have not and are leading a militant insurgency.

In Aceh, a peace agreement was signed in 2005 between militant separatists and the Indonesian government. Aceh's autonomous government appears to be functioning reasonably well. It has a generous budget, funded in part by revenues from the region's abundant oil and gas supplies. Aceh, which tends to be more devout than other parts of Indonesia, is allowed to apply a stricter form of Islamic law than elsewhere in Indonesia, including caning and whipping as punishment for alcohol consumption. On the island of Bougainville, residents seem largely content with the autonomy they were granted by the PNG government in 2001. However, some Bougainvilleans are thought to favor full independence. A referendum on independence is due to be held between 2015 and 2020. The Kurds in Iraq have, since 2003, enjoyed an autonomous regional government. One major challenge the Kurdish government in Iraq faces is agreeing with the central Iraqi government on how to divide up revenues from Iraq's oil and gas reserves, much

of which is in the Kurdish region. In Canada, the Inuit were granted an autonomous territory called Nunavut in 1999. It covers a huge area, larger than Western Europe, but is home to a population of just 32,000. The tensions between the Inuit and the central Canadian government often relate to the right to exploit natural resources—notably water, oil, and gas—in Inuit-populated regions.

Another form of self-government is community autonomy, where power is devolved to a people rather than a place. The Spanish government has instituted such autonomy throughout Spain, with its Basque and Catalan communities enjoying particularly high degrees of autonomy since 1979. The Basques and Catalans differ in one notable respect: there is a prominent militant strand to Basque separatism, whereas Catalan separatism has been peaceful. The Lakota in the United States are legally considered a distinct nation. They enjoy a form of community autonomy that involves tribal governments administering U.S. government–designated Indian lands called reservations. The largest Lakota reservation is Pine Ridge in South Dakota. Many Lakota are dissatisfied with how their autonomy functions in practice. Separatist Lakota leaders allege that the tribal government's law enforcement system is woefully inadequate and that the U.S. government, through manipulation, keeps its hands on the levers of power.

For some separatist movements, the goal is full independence. Seven of the movements, or 12 percent, fall into a gray zone of operating as independent states but not being recognized as such by the UN. This de facto-but-unrecognized status applies in the case of Abkhazians, Karabakh Armenians, Somalilanders, South Ossetians, Taiwanese, Transnistrians, and Turkish Cypriots. The Taiwanese have lived in this legal limbo for the longest time—since 1947. The present Taiwanese government is forging closer links with China, the "mother country." The separatist Turkish Cypriot government is officially committed to reunifying with the official Cypriot government in the southern part of the island where the Greek Cypriots live. Cyprus' joining of the European Union in 2004 gave Greek—but not Turkish—Cypriots access to a market of five hundred million people in twenty-seven countries. This functions as a major incentive for Turkish Cypriots to reunify with Greek Cypriots and end their present economic isolation. The people who are probably closest to attaining international recognition are the Somalilanders. Since seceding from Somalia in 1991, they have transitioned from military to civilian rule and have created a functioning economic and political system, in sharp contrast to Somalia, which has been a failed state for two decades. The de facto independence of three peoples—Abkhazians, South Ossetians, and Transnistrians—is heavily reliant upon military support from Russia. The Karabakh Armenians receive similar support from the government of Armenia.

Western Saharans maintain a unique status. While they have their own government, it controls only 15 percent of Western Sahara's territory and is based in neighboring Algeria. Morocco controls 85 percent of Western Sahara. Some countries support Morocco's efforts to annex Western Sahara, while others support Algeria, which recognizes Western Sahara as an independent country. The key regional inter-governmental organization, the African Union, accepted Western Sahara as a member in 1984. Ever since the territory's colonial ruler, Spain, departed in 1975, the UN has considered the region's status to be undetermined.

Once a separatist movement's independence is recognized by the UN, it can no longer be classified as separatist and thus is no longer a subject of this book. There are eight movements covered, or 14 percent, where there is a reasonable possibility of UN recognition occurring by 2020: Bougainvilleans of PNG, Flemings of Belgium, Greenlanders of Denmark, Kurds of Iraq, Serbs of Bosnia, Scots of the United Kingdom, South Sudanese of Sudan, and South Yemenis of Yemen. Four are in Europe, three in Asia, and one in Africa.

Relevance to global politics

Separatist movements often have an impact extending beyond the borders of the countries where they are based. World superpowers or other powers operating in a separatist region may use the movement to conduct a proxy war. A good example of this is the Georgia–South Ossetia conflict. Since becoming independent in 1991, Georgia, a former Soviet republic, has oriented itself firmly in the Western camp, becoming a close ally of the United States and applying to join NATO. In parallel, Georgia's separatist enclave, South Ossetia, has oriented itself toward Russia. Moscow has given military support to South Ossetia; without it, Georgia may well have retaken control of the enclave. The United States has, for its part, supported Georgia diplomatically and financially, although it has not encouraged Georgia to retake South Ossetia by force. When a war between Georgian and South Ossetian forces broke out in August 2008, Russia, which has the advantage of a physical border with South Ossetia, tightened its control over the area.

A historical example of the proxy war phenomenon is the covert U.S. military support, via the CIA, of Tibetan independence fighters in the 1950s. Similarly, the Soviet Union in 1944 helped the Uyghurs of China set up an independent republic, though one that was crushed by the Chinese communist army in 1949. An example of a separatist movement becoming a battleground for rival regional powers involves the Western Saharans. Algeria's decision to allow the Western Saharan government to base itself in Algeria has soured its relations with its neighbor Morocco, which wants to annex Western Sahara.

Sometimes separatist movements can cause a domino effect that may destabilize an entire country, especially if that country has many ethnic or linguistic communities. This is probably the single biggest reason why national governments tend to be hostile to separatist movements. In Spain, for example, the government does not want the Basques to establish their own country because it fears the Catalans, Galicians, and other communities of Spain may follow suit. Belgium is dominated by two communities, Flemings and Francophones, so if the Flemings were to secede, Belgium would most likely cease to exist. Fear of disintegration is what drives the Indonesian government's opposition to an independent Aceh and the Chinese government's refusal to countenance an independent Tibet.

Sometimes governments concede autonomy to peoples in the hope that secessionist sentiment will dissipate. The generous degree of autonomy enjoyed by the Quebecois in Canada is a good example. As to whether such a concession truly helps to stem secessionism or simply further whets a movement's appetite for independence, the evidence points in both directions. In some instances, there are subgroups living in the separatists' homeland who are vehemently opposed to splitting from the home country. For example, the Inuit in Quebec may have campaigned for autonomy for the Inuit, but they have also voted overwhelmingly against independence for Quebec in two referenda. In Indonesia, the Gayo ethnic minority in Aceh has a tense relationship with the Acehnese government. In Ukraine, the Tatars oppose efforts by some Crimean Russians to secede from Ukraine.

The colonial era may be over, with former African and Asian colonies having mostly gained independence since 1945, but this has not stopped some former colonial rulers from exploiting separatist movements to preserve long-standing interests. In the Comoro Islands in Africa, for example, the French government covertly sponsored a separatist movement on the island of Anjouan in order to maintain a foothold in the islands. France ruled all of the islands until 1975. Australia sought to preserve its economic interests in Bougainville, the island in PNG that it administered from 1920 until 1975. An Australian company ran Bougainville's highly lucrative Panguna copper mine from 1972 to 1989. When Bougainvilleans tried to secede from PNG in the 1990s, largely in protest over the Panguna mine, Australia opposed the move.

Developed countries tend not to involve themselves quite so readily in separatist movements in other developed countries. For example, Spain's militant Basque separatists have not received support from neighboring European governments. Instead, these governments have helped Spain to arrest Basque militants. One instance of a developed country meddling in another's internal politics was French president Charles de Gaulle's support for Quebec independence. Franco-Canadian diplomatic relations took years to recover from de Gaulle having uttered, while on a visit to Canada in 1967, the phrase *Vive le Québec libre* ("Long live free Quebec"). In the North Caucasus, Western governments criticized Russia's heavy clampdown on Chechen separatists in the 1990s. Such criticism has grown muted since 2000. European governments are keen to avoid antagonizing Russia given Europe's dependence on Russian gas. The United States has distanced itself from the Chechens since the September 11, 2001, Islamist terrorist attacks, in light of the strong Islamist orientation of many Chechen separatists. Since China emerged as an economic superpower in the 1990s, the United States and Europe have grown more cautious in commenting on China's human rights abuses against Tibetans.

Many separatist movements turn to nongovernmental or regionally based organizations for support. The European Parliament has become a champion of marginalized peoples, including the Kurds, Tatars, Tibetans, and Uyghurs. A political group, the European Free Alliance (EFA), was established in the European Parliament made up of parliamentarians from pro-autonomy or pro-independence parties. The EFA's membership includes Catalan, Corsican, Flemish, and Welsh parliamentarians.

One of the most prominent non-governmental organizations (NGOs) supporting autonomy movements around the world is the Unrepresented Nations and Peoples Organization (UNPO). Founded in 1991, this organization has offices in Brussels, the EU's capital, and The Hague, seat of many international courts. The UNPO supports peaceful autonomy movements by raising public awareness of their members' plight. It also educates its approximately sixty members on how different models of autonomy work, the aim being to provide them with knowledge they can use in negotiations with governments.

In cases of violent separatist conflicts, international mediators often try to broker a peace agreement between a government and separatist group, while NGOs provide relief for those regions affected by the fighting. The Casamançais in Senegal, Karabakh Armenians in Azerbaijan, and Tamils in Sri Lanka are such cases. International involvement in separatist conflicts can be controversial. Some governments do not want separatists to be elevated to the status of equal negotiating partners. Others allege that peace promotion and war relief efforts inadvertently prolong conflicts by hampering government efforts to score a decisive military victory against separatist militants. For example, when Sri Lankan government forces comprehensively crushed the Tamil Tigers in 2009, it effectively rendered the peace process obsolete.

The fifty-nine movements covered in the book show remarkable diversity in size, geopolitical importance, root causes, goals, and levels of popular support. While most of the movements covered exhibit elements of violence, a sizeable minority—39 percent—are peaceful. In responding to separatism, many governments are willing to make some concessions, notably by granting greater self-government; however, very few are willing to countenance full secession. Consequently, only a handful of "new" countries—Flanders, Greenland, Somaliland, and South Sudan being major candidates—can be anticipated within the next decade.

Africa

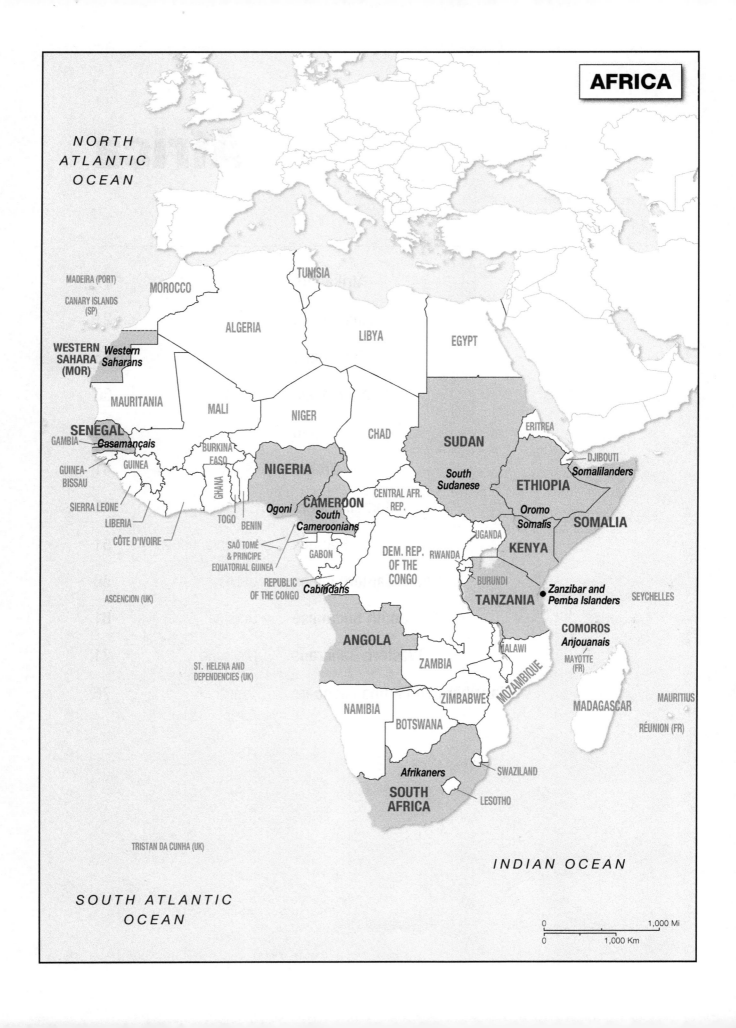

AFRIKANERS
(South Africa)

Afrikaners are white South Africans of mostly Dutch origin. Numbering about three million, they are best known internationally as the architects and staunchest defenders of South Africa's apartheid policy that separated blacks and whites from 1948 until 1994. Their language, Afrikaans, is derived from Dutch. Afrikaners were traditionally farmers and the land remains at the core of their national identity, even though many have since moved out of farming. This sets them apart from the approximately two million South Africans of British ancestry and the one million of Indian ancestry, who gravitated toward commerce and who speak English. Among South Africa's roughly fifty million inhabitants, there are several million black and mixed race people who speak Afrikaans but are not considered Afrikaners because they are not white.

Once the backbone of the South African government, Afrikaners have become alienated from the government since they lost political power in the early 1990s. *Washington Post* journalist Karin Brulliard, reporting from the country in 2009, wrote that "a white pastor spoke of the 'tremendous amount of hurt' his fellow Afrikaners feel in black-ruled South Africa. A man complained that racial quotas keep white children off school sports teams. Another fretted about dwindling education in Afrikaans." More than 50 percent of the schools that used Afrikaans as a medium of instruction have been dismantled since 1994, and many town and street names honoring Afrikaners have been changed. English has replaced Afrikaans as the official language of government.

Alienation, coupled with pride in their unique cultural heritage, has convinced some Afrikaners they would be better off living in an independent homeland, or *Volkstaat.* Various political groups have sketched out such a territory, usually locating it in the western part of the country where the Afrikaners have their deepest roots. A group of about six hundred Afrikaners tried to realize this dream in 1991 by purchasing a five-hundred-acre plot of land in a deserted town, Orania, and converting it to a whites-only separatist enclave. Although Orania residents see themselves as sowing the seeds for the *Volkstaat,* the enclave is perceived today more as a curiosity—one increasingly popular with tourists—than a threat to South Africa's unity.

Separatism is not the dominant force among Afrikaners today. The largest overtly separatist Afrikaner party, the Freedom Front Plus (VF Plus), typically garners 15 percent of the Afrikaner vote. Most Afrikaners support the Democratic Alliance, the white-dominated, pro-union, largest opposition party.

Since black rule came in 1994, many Afrikaners have joined the roughly one million, or one in five, white South Africans who have emigrated, mostly to Australia, Canada, New Zealand, the United Kingdom, and the United States. Some see this as evidence of Afrikaners abandoning their country because they have lost political power. However, the country's former (white) president, Frederik Willem de Klerk, has insisted this is not so. Speaking at the Woodrow Wilson International Center for Scholars in Washington, D.C., in February 2009, de Klerk suggested this so-called white flight was only temporary, motivated by a hunger to see the world, as South Africa was shut out of the international community throughout the apartheid era.

History

The year 1652 is significant to Afrikaners as it was the year that Dutch traders first landed at the southern tip of Africa and founded Cape Town. The early settlers were later joined by French Huguenots and Germans. In 1788 the Afrikaners lost their Dutch citizenship when the Prince of Orange, ruler of the Netherlands, ceded control of the Cape Colony to the British. In order to escape British domination, many of the Dutch settlers' descendants, called Boers from the Dutch word for farmer, moved north from 1835 to 1837 and founded their own republics: Orange Free State and Transvaal.

The discovery of diamonds in 1867 and gold in 1886 triggered further northward migration. The Afrikaners resisted British encroachments on their territory but were ultimately defeated, with the British conquering the Boer republics of Orange Free State and Transvaal during the Boer War (1899–1902). These republics, along with the neighboring colonies of Cape and Natal, broke free from British rule in 1910 and immediately merged to form the Union of South Africa. In 1948 South Africa introduced apartheid following the election to power of the Afrikaner National Party. Apartheid resulted in whites, who made up about 10 percent of the population, governing the country, and the Afrikaners, who outnumber the Anglophones roughly sixty to forty, were in the ascendant. South Africa was largely boycotted at this time by the international community, which opposed its racist system of government.

When apartheid began to crumble in 1989 after de Klerk's election, separatism among Afrikaners grew stronger. Some urged de Klerk to partition the country along racial lines, but he refused to do this. Instead, within five years de Klerk had dismantled apartheid and ushered in majority-rule government, with the multi-racial elections of 1994 won by the black-dominated African National Congress (ANC). Competing in the elections on a platform of creating a *Volkstaat*, the Afrikaner political leader Constand Viljoen won 14 percent of the white vote. Various separatist parties (see leadership section) have made similar demands since then but have so far remained a minority voice among white South Africans.

Leadership

The strongest voice advocating an independent Afrikaner state in 2010 is the VF Plus, which has four seats in the four-hundred-seat national parliament. VF Plus was formed in 2004 as a merger of three Afrikaner parties. It takes its name from one of these parties, the Freedom Front (VF), which was set up in 1994 by Viljoen. VF won 2.2 percent nationally in the 1994 elections, but since then its support has leveled off to about 1 percent nationwide. Pieter Mulder has been party leader since 2001. VF Plus has identified a territory straddling South Africa's Northern Cape and Western Cape provinces, situated between the west coast and the

Eugène Terre'Blanche (1941–2010)

AP Photo/Greg English

EUGÈNE TERRE'BLANCHE grew up in a South Africa dominated by apartheid, and he fought to keep it in place. Legalized in 1948, the apartheid system classified citizens by race and then forcibly segregated residential areas. As a young man, Terre'Blanche served as a police officer. However, he became disillusioned with the politicians he worked to protect, especially then–prime minister John Vorster, who was in power from 1966–1978. Terre'Blanche's distrust of the South African government prompted him to leave the police force and take up farming.

In 1973 a group of seven white separatists, including Eugène Terre'Blanche, founded the Afrikaner Weerstandsbeweging, or the Afrikaner Resistance Movement (AWB), the purpose of which was to establish a separate Boer state for white Boer-Afrikaner people. As the conservative movement expanded in response to growing opposition to apartheid, more people joined the AWB. In 1979 Terre'Blanche became nationally known for tarring and feathering a professor at the University of South Africa for implying that God did not bless Afrikaners in their battle against Zulus in 1838.

In the 1980s Terre'Blanche became a critic of right-wing South African president P. W. Botha as Botha began to make small concessions, such as granting political rights to Indians and "colored" persons. Terre'Blanche traveled the country, speaking to large groups and gathering support. At his public appearances, he spoke mostly in Afrikaans, calling for the creation of an Afrikaner homeland or an independent Boer Republic separate from South Africa.

His extreme white supremacist views, coupled with personal charisma, compelled critics to compare Terre'Blanche to Adolf Hitler. Similarities between the AWB flag and that of Nazi Germany were noted. As leader of the AWB, his handle became *die Leier*, Afrikaans for "the leader," and he traveled protected by bodyguards dubbed "the Iron Guard." Terre'Blanche challenged such comparisons, instead portraying himself as an Afrikaner nationalist rather than a white supremacist.

Terre'Blanche's image was not always fierce, and his prominence was marred by buffoonish events: falling off his horse at an AWB parade and rumors of an affair with South African journalist Jani Allen. The affair was also noted in the 1991 British documentary *The Leader, His Driver and the Driver's Wife*. The film, directed by Nick Broomfield, detailed the last days of apartheid and presented an unflattering portrait of Terre'Blanche.

On August 9, 1991, pro-apartheid militants affiliated with the Afrikaner separatist movement, led by Terre'Blanche, entered a hall in Ventersdorp in the North West province and tried to prevent President F. W. de Klerk from speaking. As hundreds of policemen and protesters fought, over fifty people were wounded and three were killed in what later became known as the Battle of Ventersdorp.

On June 25, 1993, Terre'Blanche led an armed invasion of the World Trade Centre in the city of Kempton Park, where negotiations to end apartheid through multi-racial elections were taking place. The invaders, many of them members of the AWB, threatened to kill all the black leaders in the building. No one was injured, but the building suffered extensive damage.

Such incidents of violence, coupled with the AWB's Nazi-esque behavior and rhetoric, led other right-wing conservative Afrikaner groups to distance themselves from the AWB, labeling it an extremist fringe group.

In 2000 Terre'Blanche served a six-month sentence for allowing his dogs to attack a gas station attendant. Terre'Blanche and his supporters sought and received amnesty for their violent acts from the Truth and Reconciliation Commission, a post-apartheid tribunal that was created to help with the transition to democracy. In 2001 he was sent to jail again for a 1996 assault on a black worker he employed that left the man brain-damaged. Terre'Blanche was released from prison in 2004.

In 2004 he was also voted the twenty-fifth greatest South African in a contest held by a South African public television network. In 2006 a follow-up documentary to *The Leader, His Driver and the Driver's Wife,* entitled *His Big White Self,* was released.

After his release from prison Terre'Blanche claimed to have moderated his racist views; he nevertheless worked to restart the AWB and gave speeches advocating for a free Afrikaner republic and Boer liberation. He announced a revival of the AWB in 2008 and continued to push for secession.

In April 2010, Terre'Blanche was murdered at the age of 69, allegedly by two black farm workers, aged 28 and 15. It was reported that the workers had not been paid since December 2009. His death sparked racial tensions in Ventersdorp. The AWB claimed that the murder of Terre'Blanche brought in some three thousand membership applications.

Orange River, where it says Afrikaners "can become a sustainable majority and eventually enjoy territorial freedom." Likening this homeland to Israel for the Jews, the party insists that not all Afrikaners would have to move there.

A more marginal separatist Afrikaner political group is the Refounded National Party (Herstigte Nasionale Party, or HNP), a right-wing Calvinist party with a racist doctrine, established in 1968 by Dr. Albert Hertzog. The HNP fought with the VF in the 1990s. In 1993 the Afrikaner movements briefly banded together to form the Afrikaner Volksfront (AVF), an alliance of twenty groups that discussed options for self-determination. However, by 1996 the AVF had collapsed as a result of infighting and defections.

Afrikaner separatism has also manifested itself in militant form. In 1973 the Afrikaner Resistance Movement (Afrikaner Weerstandsbeweging, or AWB) was established by Eugène Terre'Blanche, who was murdered on April 30, 2010. Racist and supremacist in ideology, the AWB also seeks to create an independent Boer homeland. It fought in the early 1990s to prevent the demise of white rule, occupying a building in 1993 where talks on creating a multi-racial system of government were taking place. Other militant groups include the Warriors of the Boer Nation, who carried out a wave of bomb blasts in the black township of Soweto on October 30, 2002, and the Boer Freedom Action, whose plot to poison a township's water supplies was foiled in November 2002.

Current Status

South Africa's robust economic growth and relative political stability since 2000 has weakened the separatist movement somewhat because black rule has not ruined the country, as some Afrikaners predicted it would. In addition, South Africa's

president, Jacob Zuma, has reached out to Afrikaners, praising their strong attachment to the land and making VF Plus leader Pieter Mulder Deputy Agriculture Minister in May 2009. Zuma is from the ruling ANC party, which has governed since 1994 with a large majority, winning 65.9 percent of votes in the April 2009 elections.

Yet many Afrikaners have doubts about their future. They are especially fearful they will have their land "grabbed" from them, as happened to white farmers in neighboring Zimbabwe when that country switched to majority (i.e., black) rule. They are anxious about the dramatic rise in crime: there have been over two thousand attacks on white-owned farms since 1994.

The government's affirmative action policies, which pushed many whites out of government jobs, continue to cause resentment among whites, as former leader de Klerk has noted. Yet de Klerk, who alongside ANC leader Nelson Mandela was awarded the Nobel Prize in 1993 for peacefully steering the country toward multi-racial democracy, was optimistic about his country's prospects. "The pendulum is beginning to swing towards a more balanced policy" on affirmative action, de Klerk said, adding that "the government needs to make all South Africans feel wanted, needed, and appreciated."

Further Reading

Brulliard, Karin. "White Afrikaners in S. Africa Hear Inclusive Voice from ANC Leader," *Washington Post*, April 13, 2009, www.washingtonpost.com/wp-dyn/content/article/2009/04/13/AR2009041302994.html.
Freedom Front Plus political party Web site, www.vryheidsfront.co.za.
Giliomee, Hermann. *The Afrikaners: Biography of a People*. Charlottesville: University of Virginia Press, 2005.
Griggs, Richard A. "The Boundaries of Afrikaner Self-Determination," *IBRU Boundary and Security Bulletin*, Summer 1995, www.dur.ac.uk/resources/ibru/publications/full/bsb3–2_griggs.pdf.

ANJOUANAIS
(Comoro Islands)

The inhabitants of Anjouan, an island in the Indian Ocean between Mozambique and Madagascar, have long had difficult relations with the government of the Comoro Islands, the archipelago of which they form a part. In 1997 and 2007 political leaders in Anjouan tried to secede, only to be reintegrated, first by a peace agreement and subsequently by military force. That the seat of the Comorian government is on the neighboring island of Grand Comore has been at the root of much of Anjouanais secessionism, with many islanders feeling they do not get a fair deal from the union.

The Comoros has a third island, Mohéli, that is smaller, poorer, and more remote than Anjouan; a fourth island, Mayotte, is ruled by France, the colonial power that governed all the islands until 1975. Anjouanais number about 280,000 and make up over a third of the estimated Comorian population of 750,000. Many Anjouanais support the union. For example, the Comorian president, Ahmed Abdallah Sambi, is from Anjouan, and yet in 2009 he successfully pushed to scrap the federal structure introduced in 2002 that installed four presidents, parliaments, and armies. Sambi replaced this with a more centralized form of government.

The Anjouanais have a rich mosaic of Arab and African ancestry, with Persian, Indian, and European elements mixed in, and a particularly strong Malagasy (the people of Madagascar) influence (see separate biography). They, like the other Comorian islanders, speak a language similar to Swahili, the dominant language in East Africa; the more educated also speak French and Arabic, the official languages. The Comorian people are overwhelmingly Muslim, but the Anjouanais tend to be more traditional than other islanders. Women, for example, are more likely to dress in Islamic attire.

The island is notably poorer than French-ruled Mayotte, as is Grand Comore and Mohéli. The Anjouanais' main crop for export is ylang-ylang, a yellow flower used to produce perfume, although this trade is no longer as lucrative as it once was. Their other sustaining industries are tourism, offshore banking (especially since a secessionist coup in 1997), shipping, and gambling. They operate the only deepwater port in the Comoros, giving them control over international trade.

The African Union (AU), in the past dismissed as politically weak, surprised many by playing a decisive role in suppressing Anjouanais secessionism in 2007–2008 by helping President Sambi regain control of Anjouan. The Arab league also supported Sambi, as did Iran, which has forged close ties to the Comorian government, helping set up schools and giving financial support to pay civil servants' wages. French interests in the region, by contrast, aligned themselves more closely to the separatist regime in Anjouan led by Mohamed Bacar, in part because of French disapproval of Sambi's close ties to the Islamist regime in Iran. The French helped to arm Bacar in the early 2000s, in a bid to prevent President Sambi from clamping down on the use of Anjouan as a tax and money-laundering haven.

History

Arab sultans ruled the Anjouanais for centuries until Europeans began arriving in the sixteenth century. Anjouan became a French protectorate in 1886, as did Grand Comore and Mohéli; Mayotte had come under French rule in 1843. The colonial era ended in the 1970s when Anjouan, Mohéli, and Grande Comore voted for independence in a referendum on December 22, 1974, proclaiming a Federal Islamic Republic of the Comoro Islands on July 6, 1975. Mayotte, where French influence was more deeply rooted, chose to remain part of France.

Ahmed Abdallah, an Anjouanis, led the Comoros for most of the late 1970s and 1980s, assisted by a French mercenary, Bob Denard. Separatist tendencies were kept at bay while Abdallah held power but grew after he was assassinated in December 1989 and was replaced by a Grand Comorian president. In 1997 Anjouan, along with Mohéli, declared its independence. The island's name was officially changed to Nzwani—the traditional name the locals have always used—and its inhabitants expressed a wish to reunite with France. The French government rejected this request and did not recognize the secession, nor did the Organization for African Unity, the precursor to the AU.

The breakaway states were brought back into the Comorian fold in 2001 after a peace agreement was signed on February 17. Anjouan renounced secessionism in return for a new constitution in which each island formed a semi-autonomous government, with the Comoro Islands' presidency rotating from one to another of the islands, while each island also had its own president. This failed to satisfy some Anjouanais, who complained that the union's revenue-sharing arrangement only benefited the corrupt elite on Grand Comore. Secession reared its head again in June 2007, following a disputed Anjouanais presidential election in which outgoing president Bacar refused to step down at the end of his five-year term. The AU imposed United Nations–endorsed sanctions against the Anjouan political and business elite, restricting their free movement and freezing financial assets. In March 2008, Bacar was deposed after President Sambi dispatched four hundred Comorian and six hundred AU troops (mostly Tanzanians and Sudanese) to Anjouan, causing Bacar to flee first to Mayotte and then to Réunion, a French-ruled island in the Indian Ocean.

Leadership

The most prominent secessionist movement to emerge in the late 1990s was the Anjouan People's Movement, called the MPA (Mouvement des Peuple d'Anjouan). On August 3, 1997, the MPA declared Anjouan an independent country and named Abdallah Ibrahim president two days later. In 1999 Ibrahim transferred power to Colonel Said Abeid, who in turn was overthrown by Mohamed Bacar, a French-trained policeman, in August 2001, following a bloodless coup. Bacar signed on to the 2001 peace treaty that gave Anjouanais autonomy within a Comorian union, but many MPA members opposed that agreement and remained staunchly secessionist.

Chrysantus Ayangafac, a researcher at the Institute for Security Studies in Addis Abba, wrote of Bacar, two months before President Sambi drove

Robert "Bob" Denard (1929–2007)

AP Photo/Francois Muri

ROBERT DENARD was born Gilbert Bourgeaud in Bordeaux, France, and is best known for his skill as a hired mercenary for the French government. Denard took orders from Jacques Foccart, who served as chief advisor for African policy under Presidents Charles de Gaulle and Georges Pompidou. Foccart was in charge of *Françafrique*, or the policy and relationship between France and Africa. The word started out with positive connotations, pointing to the close relationship between France and Africa, but gradually came to stand for shadowy and secretive politics. According to François-Xavier Verschave, founder of the NGO *Survie*, the term today is defined as "the secret criminality in the upper echelons of French politics and economy, where a kind of underground Republic is hidden from view," and serves as a good summation of the neocolonialism that plagued former French colonies.

Denard carried out his orders as a mercenary well, gaining infamy for his exploits. He led coups d'états and failed coups d'états all across the continent of Africa and parts of Asia, in North Yemen, Congo, Zimbabwe, Iran, Nigeria, Benin, Gabon, Angola, and the Comoro Islands. He is believed to be the inspiration for the 1974 Frederick Forsyth novel *The Dogs of War*.

Denard's favorite place to work became the Comoro Islands, where he eventually settled for a stretch of years. France first began colonizing the islands in 1841, officially declaring them colonies in 1914. One island of the archipelago, Mayotte, remains under French rule. Its residents voted in March 2009 to become a French overseas department in 2011.

Ahmed Abdallah's declaration of unilateral independence for the islands and assumption of the presidency in July 1975 (though Mayotte rejected leaving French rule) did not mark the end of Denard's influence in the sphere of Comoros politics. In fact, by August 1975 Denard had succeeded in deposing Abdallah and replacing him with Prince Said Mohammed Jaffar.

Jaffar did not manage to rule for long, and was himself deposed by his minister of defense, Ali Soilih, in January 1976. Soilih was devoted to Comoros independence and instituted isolationist policies in his effort to ensure it, but he also became known for increasingly eccentric rule, exhibited by his selection of a fifteen-year-old chief of police. He faced seven coup attempts, the last occurring on May 13, 1978. Denard returned to the archipelago, and President Soilih was shot and killed. After personally delivering the body to Soilih's sister, Denard orchestrated the return to power of Abdallah.

Under Abdallah's rule, the islands were renamed the Federal and Islamic Republic of Comoros. Denard stayed on and became the leader of the presidential guard. He delved into business, gained citizenship, and converted to Islam, taking the name Said Mustapha Mahdjoub. He had multiple wives.

Abdallah ruled for eleven years, at the end of which he was shot by a member of his presidential guard. This coup was rumored to have been organized by Denard, though he denied it vehemently. Denard fled to South Africa, aided by French paratroopers, and Said Mohammed Djohar, the half-brother of Soilih, then assumed the presidency.

Djohar ruled until September 1995, when Denard returned with a "miniflotilla of inflatable dinghies" and captured Djohar in the presidential palace with the aid of thirty mercenaries. He had by this time lost the support of the French government, and France proceeded to send three thousand troops to defeat his band of mercenaries and to free the president, who the French then pressured out of office. French officials threw their support behind the presidential candidacy of Mohamed Taki Abdoulkarim, who won.

Denard was arrested in 1995 for his attempted coup and spent ten months in prison. Many politicians spoke in his favor at his trial, and he evaded serious consequences. In fact, this was only the first of many trials he would eventually face for his mercenary activities. Denard again faced the prospect of prison in May 1999 when he was put on trial for the murder of Abdallah. Although he was acquitted due to lack of evidence, President Abdoulkarim declared that he was not to return to the islands.

In 2006 Denard was again tried for the 1995 coup. During the trial Denard claimed to have had implicit support from Jacques Foccart and the French government. At the conclusion of the trial Denard received a suspended five-year jail sentence, due to his advancing Alzheimer's disease. He died in October 2007. Denard, who had been married six times, had eight children.

him out of power, "though he is considered to be an Anjouan nationalist who prefers to remain within the union, he is undoubtedly playing the nationalist card as a means of bolstering his eroding support base." After the disputed June 2007 elections, Bacar became increasingly repressive, detaining and imprisoning critics, including journalists, intellectuals, politicians, and teachers, many of whom were tortured. Bacar's departure with about thirty of his followers in 2008 greatly weakened the MPA.

Also registering its presence as a separatist group in Anjouan from 1996 was the Organization for the Independence of Anjouan (OPIA). Linked to many anti-government demonstrations, the OPIA's leader was Mohamed Ahmed Abdou. References to its activity have been limited since 2000.

Current Status

Separatism on Anjouan suffered a setback on May 17, 2009, when a referendum was passed revising the constitution, this time re-concentrating power in the union government, based in Moroni on Grand Comore. Under the new framework, the presidents of each island have been downgraded to governors and the Comorian president has been empowered to dissolve parliament. Popular support for these changes is difficult to gauge because, while 93.8 percent of those who voted backed them, fewer than half the electorate voted.

In his efforts to quell separatism, President Sambi has been supported by the political leaders of the other two islands, Grand Comore and Mohéli. Sambi is due to step down in November 2011 and be replaced by a candidate from Mohéli, in accordance with the new constitution. The international community is more supportive of maintaining Comorian unity than it is of encouraging Anjouanais separatism. For example, the AU, averse to separatism

generally, was willing to flex its military muscle to support Sambi's bid to recapture Anjouan. Pakistan has helped bolster the Comorian government, too, by setting up schools, while China has financed construction of a new airport in Moroni.

France officially supports keeping the three islands unified but is widely accused of tacitly promoting Anjouanais separatism to create instability. This deflects focus away from Mayotte, which it still governs—illegally, argues the Comorian government. The Mayotte people voted overwhelmingly in a referendum in March 2009 to become further integrated into France, motivated by the higher standard of living on Mayotte and possession of the European Union passport that being part of France confers.

According to researcher Ayangafac, the economic and political rivalry between Anjouan and Grand Comore lies at the heart of the Anjouanais' efforts to distance themselves from the union and the Comorian government's refusal to countenance secession. "Beneath the rhetoric of self-determination and the need to put an end to inter-island fighting and instability, the Comorian crisis is a contest over the sources of wealth; a contest for power and resources through control of Anjouan, the island with the most viable economy."

Further Reading

Ayangafac, Chrysantus. "Situation Critical: The Anjouan Political Crisis," Institute for Security Studies, 2008, Addis Abba, www.iss.co.za/dynamic/administration/file_manager/file_links/SITREPANJOUANMAR08.PDF?link_id=3&slink_id=5593&link_type=12&slink_type=13&tmpl_id=3.

Ottenheimer, Martin, and Harriet Ottenheimer. *Historical Dictionary of the Comoro Islands.* Metuchen: The Scarecrow Press, Inc., 1994.

U.S. State Department. "2008 Country Report on Human Rights Practices—Comoros," February 25, 2009, http://paei.state.gov/g/drl/rls/hrrpt/2008.

CABINDANS
(Angola)

The Cabindan people live in an exclave called Cabinda, one of Angola's eighteen provinces, but one that is totally detached from the rest of country. Much of the terrain is rainforest and most of the people are farmers, hunters, and fishers. However, the vast majority of the province's wealth comes from Cabinda's abundant oil supplies, found both on and off shore. Major foreign oil corporations, including Chevron from the United States and Elf from France, have for decades operated oil concessions. Oil—more specifically, questions about how to distribute the wealth derived from it—is one of the main causes of the separatist tensions.

One hundred miles long and twenty-five miles wide, Cabinda is bordered by the Democratic Republic of Congo (DRC) to the east, the Republic of the Congo to the north, and the Atlantic Ocean to the west. Cabindans make up some 400,000 of the total Angolan population of thirteen million. They have a similar ethnicity to other Angolans, coming mostly from the Bakongo ethnic group, who are a Bantu people like most of the rest of the country's inhabitants. A small minority of Cabindans come from a different ethnic grouping, Mayombe. The Bakongo people speak Kikongo, while the Mayombe speak a dialect of Kikongo. Cabinda is predominantly Catholic, which sets it apart from the rest of Angola, where approximately 47 percent are adherents of indigenous religions, 38 percent are Catholic, and 15 percent are Protestant.

Cabindan separatists stress that their region has a very different history from the rest of Angola. The area was under Portuguese colonial rule for just ninety years (1885–1975). This is in marked contrast to other parts of Angola, which hosted colonial settlement as far back as the late fifteenth century, when Portuguese navigators seeking trade routes to India first appeared. The separatists maintain that Cabinda has its own distinct identity and culture and that it was illegally occupied by Angolan troops when Portugal gave it independence in 1975. The Angolan government counters that any ethnic distinctions that may have once existed have long since been blurred by intermarriage and mixing.

The Angolan economy is heavily dependent on oil; the country is the second biggest oil producer in Africa after Nigeria. Oil accounts for 85 percent of the gross domestic product, and about 60 percent of the oil revenue is generated from the Cabindan oil fields, which churn out about 700,000 barrels of crude per day. The U.S. relationship with Angola is dominated by the oil industry, with Angola its fifth largest oil supplier.

A violent secessionist struggle against the Angolan government, sometimes called "the forgotten war" as it was less reported on than the Angolan civil war (1975–2002), has been raging for thirty-five years in Cabinda. The primary group fighting for independence is the Front for the Liberation of the Cabinda Enclave, or FLEC (Frente de Libertação do Enclave de Cabinda). Over the years the Angolan government has accused many countries in the region of helping the Cabindan separatists, including Togo, Burkina Faso, Cameroon, and Zambia. FLEC has launched attacks in Cabinda from bases in both the DRC and the Republic of Congo, which led the Angolan government to step up its security presence in these two countries. The non-governmental organization Human Rights Watch (HRW), in a February 2009 report, noted that "aside from FLEC, the independence movement has been based on civil society, rather than political parties, as locally- and regionally-based parties and calls for secession are prohibited by Angolan law."

A shaky truce has existed since 2006 when a peace agreement between FLEC and the Angolan government, which the Catholic Church helped to mediate, was signed. According to Lisa Rimli, a researcher at HRW speaking at a May 2009 seminar on Angola at the Center for Strategic International Studies in Washington, "the problem is that the government only signed the agreement with one faction and sidelined the rest, but the separatist movement in Cabinda is very heterogeneous." Negotiations between Cabindans and the Angolan authorities are difficult because the Angolan constitution does not provide a path to independence, leaving Cabinda little room for negotiation. Neither does it make a clear distinction between peaceful and armed movements calling for succession, instead defining Angola as a "unitary and indivisible state" that will "fight against any separatist attempt."

HRW has criticized this and noted that under international law governments should not ban parties that peacefully advocate greater autonomy or secession. However, the Angolan government is afraid that if it allows Cabinda to secede, other regions—in particular, those where most of the country's natural resources are found—will be inspired to push for greater autonomy too, said HRW's Rimli. Meanwhile, on the military side the Angolan government remains frustrated because low-level violence continues despite the peace agreement. It finds it hard to comprehend how it could win a large-scale civil war that lasted almost thirty years and yet remain unable to defeat a few hundred guerrillas.

History

Before the European colonial powers arrived, Cabinda was ruled by old African kingdoms such as Makongo, Mangoyo, and Maluangu. The Europeans competing for influence in Cabinda during colonial times were France, the Netherlands, Germany, and Portugal. In 1885 Cabinda was definitively placed inside the Portuguese sphere of influence when European powers meeting in Berlin with the intention of carving up Africa among them established the boundaries of modern-day Angola. The Portuguese initially governed Cabinda separately from the rest of Angola, in accordance with the 1885 Treaty of Simulambuco signed with local leaders. Under this treaty, Portugal promised not to allow Cabinda to be annexed by King Leopold II of Belgium, who was the absolute ruler of neighboring Congo. But in the 1950s the Portuguese began tightening their control, with Portuguese dictator Antonio de Oliveira Salazar making Cabinda, along with the rest of Angola, an overseas Portuguese province rather than a protectorate.

Various Angolan independence movements emerged. One of these, the Popular Movement for the Liberation of Angola (MPLA), which established itself in 1956, took control of Cabinda. The other movements were the National Front for the Liberation of Angola (FNLA), the National Union for the Total Independence of Angola (UNITA), and FLEC, which was the only Cabinda-based group. In the 1960s, while most European countries were in the midst of ceding independence to their colonies, Portugal continued asserting its sovereignty over Angola. This only served to provoke further guerrilla attacks from the independence movements. Ultimately, the Portuguese, keen to avoid additional military losses, negotiated independence with the Angolans in the early 1970s. During these talks, Cabinda became consolidated into the rest of Angola, despite the historic differences in how the two regions had been governed.

Angola gained independence on November 11, 1975, but civil war broke out almost immediately between the two biggest Angolan parties competing for power: the MPLA, led by Jose Eduardo Dos Santos, and UNITA, led by Jonas Savimbi. Up to 1.5 million people were killed and 4 million people displaced in the subsequent war that was to stretch over three decades. There was heavy interference from outside powers. Cuba sent eighteen thousand troops, along with armored vehicles and rocket launchers from the Soviet Union, to help the MPLA, which was then Marxist in ideology. For its part, the United States funded an anti-communist FNLA, and U.S. oil interests arrived too, with Gulf Oil Corporation operating a large oil concession in Cabinda. At one point troops from communist Cuba were protecting Gulf Oil's employees and installations, though Cuba eventually withdrew its troops.

During this turbulent period, the status of Cabinda was not considered a high priority for the warring groups. FLEC appealed to the former colonizer, Portugal, for help, but Portugal did not wish to get involved. The MPLA ruled Angola under a one-party system from 1979 until the first multiparty elections took place in September 1992, when MPLA leader Dos Santos defeated UNITA's Savimbi, 49.6 percent to 40.1 percent. Savimbi died in 2002. A peace treaty was signed shortly thereafter that brought an end to the civil war and further bolstered MPLA power.

With more military resources now available, the government in late 2002 dispatched thirty thousand troops to Cabinda to repress the separatist insurgency. Widespread human rights abuses were reported in the clampdown. Additional efforts to quell Cabinda's separatist tendencies included the settling of Angolans in Cabinda and the appointment by the MPLA and UNITA of Cabindans to leadership positions in their parties. In August 2006, the Angolan government signed a Memorandum of Understanding with certain Cabinda separatist factions that officially ended the thirty-one-year war. Cabinda rebels were granted an amnesty under the peace deal.

Leadership

FLEC has long been the dominant movement advocating independence for Cabinda. It was established in 1963 when three groups merged together. When Angola became independent in 1975, FLEC switched its energies from fighting the colonial ruler, Portugal, to resisting the newly independent government in Angola, whose capital was Luanda. FLEC then split into three factions, one led by Luis Ranque Franque, another by Henriques Tiago Nzita, and a third by Francisco Xavier Lubota.

The party's goals were the expulsion of the Angolan military, the holding of a referendum on self-determination, and the installation of a parliament and government in Cabinda. One major obstacle to these goals was a chronic inability to forge unity among the separatists' disparate elements. For example, a separate movement, the Popular Movement for the Liberation of Cabinda (MPLC), was established in 1979. In the 1980s two South African–backed groups were operating; both ceased functioning when South Africa stopped providing them with aid. And in the early 1990s, two more groups linked to separatism, the National Union for the Liberation of Cabinda and the Communist Committee of Cabinda, emerged.

While militarily FLEC has at various times controlled parts of Cabinda's interior, it is unclear exactly how much popular support it has because FLEC has never contested elections in Cabinda. In 1992 the party, supported by the Catholic Church, urged Cabindans to boycott the election, which they mostly did. But when the next elections took place in 2008 and FLEC demanded another boycott, the people did not follow its instructions and voter turnout in Cabinda was high.

The 2006 peace agreement was signed by Antonio Bento Bembe, a former FLEC leader who claimed to be representing the various secessionist movements. FLEC was officially disbanded in January 2007, and many of its members were drafted into the Angolan police and army. But the legitimacy of the negotiating process remained in doubt because the coalition of Cabindan groups called the Cabinda Forum For Dialogue, which led the talks, included only some FLEC factions. Most notably, the veteran FLEC leader Nzita Tiago, in exile in Paris, was not involved in the process. He complained that Bembe had no authority to negotiate. In 2008 the MPLA appointed Bembe a minister in the new government.

Current Status

It is widely believed that most Cabindans, if given the option, would choose either greater autonomy or independence; however, for the time being Cabinda continues to be governed as a province of Angola, with government officials appointed directly from Luanda. The main opposition party in Angola, UNITA, has promised to consider granting autonomy to Cabinda in a form similar to that which the Portuguese island of Madeira in the Atlantic Ocean enjoys. But UNITA is in no position to deliver on such a promise, having been heavily defeated in the 2008 elections. Notably, it received its highest level of support from Cabinda.

While greater autonomy remains a possibility, the Angolan government, regardless of which party is in power, is highly unlikely to allow Cabinda to secede because of the exclave's abundant supply of the backbone of the country's economy—oil. Because of this resource, Angola's economy is thought to be the fastest growing in Africa. It has become China's number one oil supplier, and Luanda has overtaken Tokyo as the most expensive city in the world for foreigners. With oil exploration set for further expansion onshore in Cabinda, tensions are unlikely to diminish, and Cabindans can be expected to demand a fair share of the oil revenue that is now filling the government's coffers.

Since the 2006 truce, many Cabindan separatists have been returning to Cabinda from neighboring states and Europe; however, guerrilla attacks continue, and there remains a very high concentration of Angolan military in the exclave. HRW has reported that the Angolan government is trying to repress the insurgency and prevent the local society from campaigning for self-determination. This has been accomplished through restriction of freedom of expression, assembly, and association. For example, HRW has noted that a correspondent for the Voice of America news service, Fernando Lelo, was sentenced to twelve years in prison for "crimes against the security of the state," and a Catholic priest, Pedro Sevo Agostinho, had his passport confiscated temporarily without any explanation after he made a trip to Spain.

The still-fragile state of democracy in Angola has not helped inspire confidence among Cabindans in their country. The MPLA may have won the 2008 general elections by a landslide, securing 82 percent of the vote compared to just 10 percent for UNITA, but European Union election monitors in Cabinda alleged numerous irregularities there. For example, it was reported that the MPLA transported over fifteen hundred people from neighboring Republic of Congo to vote in Cabinda on polling day. HRW reported that the MPLA-run provincial government distributed large sums of money, between $100,000 and $200,000, as well as cars, motorcycles, and corrugated sheet roofs to at least twenty churches to secure their support. The human rights watchdog added that there was a high degree of intimidation in rural areas, though not much violence. Freedom of expression in Angola continues to be restricted. An April 2010 article by the United Nations' IRIN news service reported that while Angolan officials claim the separatist war is over, opposition politicians deny this. There remained sporadic violence, the article said, such as a January 2010 ambush in Cabinda of a bus carrying the soccer team of Togo to the Africa Cup, in which two people were killed.

The Angolan government has strong support from the international community, which may help it to keep the country unified. Despite the decades-old secessionist conflict, Cabinda remains an internationally recognized part of Angola, and that appears unlikely to change. On the U.S. side, apart from Angola's strategic importance as a major oil supplier at a time when the United States is trying to become less reliant on Arab oil, there is also appreciation that Angolan troops have helped to stabilize the perennially tense situation in the neighboring Democratic Republic of the Congo. Moreover, despite flaws in the 2008 elections, there is a feeling among the international community that at least Angola is moving in the right direction and should therefore be supported.

Further Reading

Human Rights Watch. "Democracy or Monopoly: Angola's Reluctant Return to Elections," chap. VIII, February 23, 2009, www.hrw.org/en/reports/2009/02/23/democracy-or-monopoly-0.

IRIN News (United Nations–sponsored news agency). "ANGOLA: The death of one man does not end a war," April 26, 2010, www.irinnews.org/report.aspx?Reportid=88933.

———. "Angola: Cabinda, one of Africa's longest, least reported conflicts," October 2003, www.irinnews.org/IndepthMain.aspx?IndepthId=25&ReportId=66282.

Porto, Joao Gomes. "Cabinda: Notes on a soon-to-be Forgotten War," Institute for Security Studies Situation Report—Paper 77, August 2003, www.iss.co.za/pubs/papers/77/Paper77.pdf.

Vines, Alex. "Angola: Looking Beyond Elections," European Union Institute for Security Studies Opinion (2008), www.iss.europa.eu/uploads/media/Angola_looking_beyond_elections.pdf.

CASAMANÇAIS
(Senegal)

The Casamançais live in a swathe of territory stretching three hundred miles east-west and fifty miles north-south, wedged on the western tip of Africa. They are governed by Senegal, even though geographically they are mostly separated from it by Gambia, a sliver of a country that traces its borders along the River Gambia on Casamance's northern border. Casamance was named by its former colonizer, Portugal, who based it on the traditional name *cassamoukou*, which means "paddy country," as it is the main rice-producing area of Senegal. The Casamançais are flanked to their south by the two Guineas, Guinea-Bissau and Guinea, and to the west by the Atlantic Ocean. There are approximately 1.4 million Casamançais, compared to the total population in Senegal of 14 million. The largest city in Casamance is Ziguinchor, which has 230,000 residents.

A secessionist insurgency has been waged in Casamance since 1982, led by the Movement of Democratic Forces in Casamance, or MFDC (Mouvement des Forces Démocratiques de la Casamance). There have been many short-lived cease-fires and peace deals since hostilities began. According to the United Nations, between three and six thousand civilians have died in the conflict, including hundreds of victims of landmines, and up to sixty thousand people have been displaced.

As the MFDC is an outlawed organization and does not take part in elections, it is difficult to gauge how much popular support it has. But according to Martin Evans, a lecturer in international development at the University of Chester who has written about the region and lived there, in a July 2009 email exchange, most Casamançais "are just sick to death of the whole business and want to get on with developing Casamance—trade, family life, etc." For the Senegalese government, the conflict has been a major blemish in an otherwise relatively positive track record in comparison with other African countries. Since gaining independence half a century ago, Senegal has been more consistently stable than most of its neighbors, with a functioning democracy and civilian leadership, as well as a long history of deploying troops to international peacekeeping missions.

The Casamançais have a different ethnic makeup than the northern Senegalese. The Diola form a majority in the Ziguinchor region of Casamance, whereas the Mandinga are the largest ethnic group in Casmance's other two regions, Sédhiou and Kolda. Other Casamance-based ethnic groups include the Balanta and Bainouk. The dominant ethnic group in northern Senegal are the Wolofs, who make up just under half the Senegalese population. According to the University of Chester's Evans, Diola society is notable for having a more egalitarian structure than other Senegalese groups.

The Casamançais mainly speak local languages, such as Diola and Mandingo. Many of them, in particular the MFDC separatists and the Diola, resent the growing dominance in the country of the Wolof language. French is spoken in Senegal as the language of the elite and of officialdom. The people of Casamance differ somewhat in their religious makeup, too. Whereas the country is overwhelmingly Muslim—94 percent—Casamance has a larger non-Muslim minority than elsewhere in the country. This minority is mostly Christian—especially Catholic—and animist, the indigenous religion that stresses belief in spirits and fetishes.

Economically, in contrast to other separatist movements in Western Africa, such as the Ogoni in Nigeria or the Cabindans in Angola (see separate essays), oil does not play a role in the conflict. This is because Senegal has no oil that is economically exploitable for now, the crude from an oilfield on the Senegal–Guinea Bissau border being considered too low a grade to be worth extracting. Casamance remains predominantly agricultural, with cashew nuts, peanuts, cotton, rice, mangoes, and citrus fruits the main crops grown. Most of the country's food is produced in Casamance because it is the wettest and most fertile part of the country.

Senegal as a whole is a poor state, relying heavily on foreign aid and suffering from high levels of unemployment and emigration. Casamançais separatists accuse the northern Senegalese of misappropriating their lands and doing little in the way of providing them with decent infrastructure, education, or economic support. They also complain of being underrepresented in the Wolof-dominated government. The separatist conflict has spawned a war economy in which Senegalese soldiers compete with Casamance militants to illegally trade in low-income, high-volume resources like timber, cashews, orchard fruits, and cannabis, some of the profits of which fund the war effort.

As for the Casamançais' neighbors, the one with the most documented involvement in the separatist conflict is Guinea-Bissau to the south. The Gambian government of President Yahya Jammeh, an ethnic Diola, is suspected of arming the MFDC and trafficking in timber and cannabis, yet it hosted peace talks in 2001 between the warring sides.

History

The Casamançais' colonial history differs from that of the northern Senegalese, as the former were originally ruled by Portugal whereas the latter came under French influence as early as the seventeenth century. At the Berlin conference of 1885, when Africa was divided up among European governments, the Portuguese ceded Casamance to France in return for receiving other lands, which Portugal then grafted onto its Portuguese Guinea colony. The presence of a British colony, Gambia, ensconced between northern Senegal and Casamance, limited French influence somewhat. But France did gradually integrate Casamance into Senegal, especially after 1920 when Senegal was formally established as a French colony.

Soldiers from Casamance were incorporated into the French Senegalese legion and fought with France during World War I and II. In January 1959, Senegal formed a short-lived union with Mali, then known as French Sudan. The two nations became a single independent country on April 4, 1960. But Senegal, including Casamance, broke away from this federation on August 20, 1960, and founded modern-day Senegal as a unitary state of eleven regions, each one headed by a governor appointed by the president. Casmance's southerly neighbor, Portuguese Guinea, gained its independence from Portugal in 1974 and renamed itself Guinea-Bissau.

In February 1982, the Casamançais were merged with the Gambians when the Senegalese and Gambian governments formed a confederation called Senegambia. Differences in political cultures and agendas caused this experiment to fail, and the confederation was dissolved on September 30, 1989. This failure adversely affected the Casamançais by making it harder for them to forge closer trade links with Gambia. The Gambian capital, Banjul, was a preferred trading port for the Casamançais because it was closer to them geographically than the Senegalese capital, Dakar.

Discontent with how the Senegalese authorities were administering Casamance began to bubble up in the late 1970s. While initial protests were peaceful, by the early 1980s the conflict began to turn violent as the Senegalese government adopted a policy of repression toward protesters. Meanwhile, the Senegalese authorities began to appropriate lands in Casamance and give them to non-Casamançais for patronage. Ethnic Wolofs, Serers, and Toucouleurs from northern Senegal were notable beneficiaries. The violence continued intermittently, and the Senegalese government accused other countries in the region of promoting it, including Libya, Guinea-Bissau, and Mauritania (this last was accused of selling Iraqi weapons to the MFDC). In December 1992, Senegalese forces bombed bases that Casamance separatists had set up in Guinea-Bissau. The leader of the MFDC's political wing, Father Augustin Diamacoune Senghor, was expelled from Guinea-Bissau several days later.

Guinea-Bissau continued to be used by militant Casamance separatists in the 1990s as a staging post for attacks on Senegalese forces in Casamance. The situation became even more complicated in 1998 and 1999 when Guinea-Bissau itself became embroiled in a civil war. The Senegalese government and the MFDC extended their hostilities against one another to a new battlefield by supporting opposing sides in the Guinea-Bissau civil war. The MFDC's favored side in Guinea-Bissau

briefly prevailed before being forced out of power following a November 2000 coup. The new Guinea-Bissau president, Kumba Yala, was pro-Senegalese and made a serious—and largely successful—effort to stop the flow of arms from Guinea-Bissau to the MFDC. He also flushed the hard-line guerrillas out of the country. According to Casamance expert Evans, "there is not the constant supply of arms to and threat from MFDC guerrillas in Guinea-Bissau." Evans told the United Nations–sponsored news agency IRIN in March 2009 that "calm in the Guinea-Bissau border area has been the biggest factor in allowing people to return to their home villages."

Leadership

The MFDC, the main secessionist movement in Casamance, attracts most of its support from the ethnic Diola. The organization was founded not as a pro-independence movement, but rather as a regional political party, by Emile Badiane and Ibou Diallo. It ceased to exist in the 1950s after being absorbed into the Senegalese Democratic Bloc party. Casamance separatists resurrected the name in the early 1980s, although, according to Professor Evans, there was no direct historical connection between the two organizations.

On December 26, 1982, the MFDC in its separatist reincarnation organized a peaceful march demanding independence, which the government repressed using force. In 1986 the authorities arrested 152 people for attending an MFDC secret meeting. The MFDC developed a military wing, ATTIKA, that became fully mobilized in 1990. ATTIKA waged a low-level campaign of violence interspersed with sporadic cease-fires. For example, the MFDC stopped militant activities in July 1993 on condition that the government release MFDC prisoners. The spiral of violence continued, however, and both sides were accused of committing human rights abuses.

The leading light in the MFDC's political wing from the 1980s until his death in January 2007 was Father Diamacoune. An eager promoter of Casamance culture on his radio broadcasts, the Catholic priest was drawn toward a peaceful separatist movement early on. He originally urged full independence but became progressively more moderate. According to Professor Evans, "he never had much control over the military wing and was constantly frustrated trying to keep them in check." More hard-line and militant elements began to dominate the MFDC, such as a pro-independence group led by Leopold Sania that resumed guerrilla activities in July 1995 after Diamacoune and fifty others were arrested. Other notable hard-liners included Mamadou Nkrumah Sane, Sidi Badji (who died in 2003), and Salif Sadio.

The MFDC became involved in economic activities, too. According to the news agency IRIN, militants in 2008 and 2009 profited from collecting cashew nuts grown in Casamance and selling them in Ziguinchor and Guinea-Bissau. This has become something of a racket, IRIN reported, with the MFDC involved in an episode in May 2008, for example, where the ears of up to twenty farmers were sliced off for not heeding warnings to stop selling cashews. MFDC member Damien Manga told the news agency the money from the cashew business was used to pay the rebels' living expenses, not to buy weapons.

Current Status

Decades of fighting in what has become West Africa's longest-running civil conflict has caused many Casamançais to flee their villages. By early 2009 there were about ten thousand displaced persons in Casamance and several thousand more in Gambia and Guinea-Bissau, according to the U.S. State Department's "2008 Country Reports on Human Rights Practices" for Senegal, published in February 2009. Thousands of refugees returned home to areas where the conflict had abated, but some of these met with hostility from MFDC combatants in rural communities south of Ziguinchor. Most of the conflict's violence has taken place in the Ziguinchor region in western Casamance.

The MFDC and a splinter group called the Movement for the Liberation of the People of the Casamance meanwhile killed civilians, committed robberies, and harassed the local population, the report alleged. There have also been many landmine explosions in Casamance. The non-governmental organization Handicap International has been working with the Senegalese government to de-mine the region since 1999 and receives funds from the United States, the European Union, and France. A May 2010 report from the UN news service IRIN said many Casmançais were suffering from post-traumatic stress disorder brought on by atrocities they had witnessed or by injuries sustained during the twenty-eight-year secessionist conflict.

According to Gert-Jan Stads, a researcher for the Rome-based Food and Agriculture Organization of the UN who has traveled to Senegal regularly for work, the northern Senegalese people are largely detached from the conflict. "Most of those I meet in Dakar have no idea what is really happening in Casamance. As far as they are concerned, it is another country," he said in a July 2009 phone interview. From his personal conversations, Stads felt that rather than resenting the Casmançais, "the Wolof people in Dakar do feel some sympathy for the Casamance cause."

Already geographically remote from the rest of Senegal, the secessionist conflict has exacerbated Casamance's isolation. "With currently no air link and one of the ferries down for repairs, plus violent robberies on both the trans-Gambian highway and the Bignona-Diouloulou road, the options for travel between northern Senegal and Casamance, and within Bignona department particularly, are limited," said University of Chester's Evans. This is hindering Casamance's economic development, as the people cannot move freely, food and manufactured goods cannot be transported easily, and tourists are discouraged from visiting.

The international community has pumped considerable resources into Casamance to try to improve the situation. However, Evans warned there was paradoxically a danger of this prolonging rather than shortening the conflict because local actors have become dependent on foreign aid: "Since 2000 there's been a lot of multilateral and bilateral money coming in to support the peace process, return of the displaced and reconstruction. . . . [I]t can be a bit of a gravy train for everyone." Political instability in countries adjacent to the Casamance is not helping. On March 3, 2009, Guinea-Bissau's president, Joaò Bernardo Vieira, was assassinated, placing it in the same category as Mauritania and Guinea, both of whose civilian governments were upended by their military in 2008.

The Casamance conflict has been a constant embarrassment for the Senegalese government internationally. While Senegal president Abdoulaye Wade has tried to broker peace in the Sudan and Chad conflict and mediated talks with Zimbabwe, he has been unable to secure peace at home. MFDC hard-liners are refusing to negotiate with the government. The Senegalese government has been criticized for treating the conflict as an internal matter instead of involving Gambia and Guinea-Bissau in peace talks. And while most agree that reform of the land ownership system in Casamance needs to be part of the solution, this is very hard to achieve because the region is so heavily mined that whole villages have had to be abandoned.

Further Reading

Boas, Morten, and Kevin Dunn, eds. *African Guerrillas: Raging against the Machine.* Boulder, Colo.: Lynne Rienner, 2007. See chap. 10, "The Resilient Weakness of Casamançais Separatists," by Vincent Foucher.

Evans, Martin. "Senegal: Mouvement des Forces Démocratiques de la Casamance (MFDC)," Briefing Paper—Chatham House Africa Programme, December 2004, www.chathamhouse.org.uk/files/3208_bpm edec04.pdf.

———. "Ni paix ni guerre: the political economy of low-level conflict in the Casamance," Background Paper—Overseas Development Institute, February 2003, www.odi.org.uk/resources/download/321.pdf.

IRIN News (United Nations–sponsored news agency). "Guinea-Bissau-Senegal: Assassinations breed uncertainty in neighbouring Casamance," March 5, 2009. Available at www.irinnews.org/Report.aspx?ReportId=83320.

———. "Senegal: Fresh violence in Casamance," June 12, 2009, www.irinnews.org/Report.aspx?Report Id=84832.

———. "Senegal: Tackling Trauma in Casamance," May 20, 2010, www.irinnews.org/Report.aspx?Report Id=89196.

OGONI
(Nigeria)

"This is a contest between the fly and the lion. The lion cannot fly and the fly cannot deliver a knockout blow," Nigeria's foreign minister, Chief Ojo Maduekwe, said in June 2009, speaking at the Center for Strategic and International Studies (CSIS) in Washington, D.C. The minister was describing the worsening conflict between Nigerian authorities and ethnic groups living in the Niger Delta region of the country. The Ogoni, one such group, has attracted particular attention globally because of its fight for greater autonomy. This has come largely in response to half a century of seeing their land exploited by major oil corporations the government has allowed to operate there. Nigeria is Africa's most populous state, with some 150 million people. The Ogoni, numbering 500,000 and living in the densely populated swamps and waterways of the eastern Niger Delta, constitute a tiny fraction of that population.

The Ogoni have a history of poor relations with the government and multinational companies such as Shell Oil. However, while the Ogoni would like more autonomy to govern their affairs, they are not looking for an independent Ogoni state. They continue to lobby for compensation for the damage inflicted on their environment by Shell and other oil companies such as Chevron, Mobil, and Texaco. The Ogoni say they can no longer successfully farm the land or fish in the rivers because of oil industry–related events, such as leaking pipelines and gas flares. Since petroleum was first discovered there in 1958, the oil companies have pumped tens of billions of dollars worth of oil away and given precious little back to the community in the way of schools, roads, hospitals, electricity or housing, they complain.

The economic dimension to this separatist conflict cannot be overstated. Oil accounts for 95 percent of Nigeria's foreign exchange earnings, and the Niger Delta is the source of 90 percent of that oil. Under the 1999 Nigerian federal constitution, 13 percent of the country's oil revenue is supposed to be returned to the state from which it was derived, but government critics say it has consistently failed to honor this commitment. Although the Ogoni, like most southern Nigerians, are predominantly Christian and live in a country where there is considerable conflict between Muslims and Christians, religion is not a factor driving this conflict.

Apart from the Ogoni, the Niger Delta is inhabited by many other ethnic groups, including the Ijaw, Itsekiri, Ikwere, Annang, Efik, Isoko, and

Urhobo. These groups have similar grievances concerning the oil companies and the government's exploitation of their lands. The government often links all opposition emanating from the Niger Delta together and labels the militants thugs and criminals. However, the leader of the dominant Ogoni political group, the Movement for the Survival of the Ogoni People (MOSOP), has strongly rejected both the link and the tag. In an interview with the Nigerian newspaper *Vanguard* in June 2009, Goodluck Diigbo insisted that "the Ogonis are not Niger Deltans, we are just neighbors with the Niger Delta people." He said the government lumped them together in order "to overshadow our non-violent struggle and our demands."

The government downplays the separatist dimension to the conflict. "This is not a quest for autonomy or secession. It is merely a hijack of a just cause, arising from many years of neglect of that part of the country by oil majors, local politicians, and federal government," said Foreign Minister Maduekwe. Most observers agree—while admitting their evidence is mostly anecdotal—that the majority of violence in the Niger Delta today is perpetrated for financial gain by organized criminals. The extent of Ogoni involvement in such activity is hard to decipher because, while MOSOP claims to be peaceful, at least one peace worker who has spent time in the region said the Ogoni's record is not clean on this front. Some peace workers have urged the government to engage in a political process with the politically motivated groups, but the government has been reluctant to do so.

Foreign Minister Maduekwe has warned, "if you confer legitimacy to this struggle, others will follow." He cited as a case in point the Ibo people, who live in southeastern Nigeria and who constitute about 18 percent of the Nigerian population. The Ibo established a short-lived independent state called Biafra in the late 1960s. "Biafran flags are still in my village. If the separatists there see the Niger Delta groups getting international respect and attention

they will think that violence pays and you will have neo-Biafranism," he said. An Ibo secessionist organization called the Movement for the Actualization of the Sovereign State of Biafra (MASSOB) remains active. There is also a militant secessionist organization representing the Yoruba, an ethnic group to which 21 percent of the population belongs, called the O'odua People's Congress (OPC), which has been accused of carrying out violent attacks in 1999 and 2000.

History

Ogoni nationalists stress that prior to colonization, their people were not conquered by any other ethnic group of present-day Nigeria. For centuries, the Ogoni remained a tightly knit, isolated ethnic unit of six kingdoms. The dense forests where they lived helped to shield them from attacks by slave traders. The dominant colonial power to exert influence over them was the United Kingdom. Initially present for commercial reasons, by the end of the nineteenth century the British began exerting political control, too. In 1884 they bought out French interests on the lower Niger and in 1885 established a protectorate around the Niger Delta. In 1914 the British merged various territories they controlled into a single British colony and protectorate that broadly corresponded to modern-day Nigeria.

To help govern their colony, the British tended to put power in the hands of the larger ethnic groups such as the Ibo, Hausa, and Yoruba. This sowed the seeds for later inter-ethnic tensions, as smaller groups such as the Ogoni were overlooked and ultimately began to feel colonized by the bigger groups. The British divided up the Ogoni lands administratively from 1908–1947, but following protests from the Ogoni, they established an Ogoni Native Authority in 1947. However, this only lasted until 1951, after which the Ogoni were integrated into the eastern Nigeria regional government. In 1954 Britain made Nigeria a self-governing federation, and on

October 1, 1960, the country, including the Ogoni lands, gained full independence.

After independence, Nigeria faced a severe threat to its territorial integrity—not from the Ogoni, but from the Ibo, who on May 30, 1967, seceded and declared an independent Biafra. There followed an extremely destructive four-year war. By the time the Ibo surrendered on January 15, 1970, some 100,000 people had been killed directly from the conflict and between 500,000 and two million had starved to death due to a government-imposed blockade. This experience traumatized the country deeply and made future governments ultra-sensitive and hostile to pro-autonomy or secessionist movements. At the same time, considerable political power has been devolved to Nigeria's thirty-six state governments.

In the 1980s and 1990s, tensions among southern ethnic groups such as the Ogoni and the government grew as the balance of power shifted to northern Nigerians, who were mostly Muslim and who introduced Islamic law, or *sharia,* to some northern states. Confidence in the government was further eroded by chronic political instability, as the country vacillated between civilian rule and repressive military regimes. During the rule of General Sani Abacha (1993–1998), there was a major crackdown on the Ogoni. Human Rights Watch and other human rights organizations reported that the government carried out widespread extrajudicial killings, internment of civilians, arbitrary detentions, torture, burnings, and rapes. When four Ogoni pro-government officials were killed in 1994, the Nigerian authorities responded by arresting nine Ogoni leaders, most notably MOSOP leader Kenule Saro-Wiwa, who they later executed (see separate biography).

In the fall of 1999, ethnic tensions among the Ogoni and other Niger Delta groups escalated once more. To counteract the threat, the government dispatched troops in 2000 to Bayelsa, one of Nigeria's states. However, the military buildup failed to stem the violent attacks that persisted throughout the decade by Niger Delta militants, most of whom were not thought to be Ogoni. Although a peace agreement was signed in September 2004 between the government and the Niger Delta's People's Volunteer Force (NDPVF), an ethnic Ijaw-based militia, the truce fell apart six months later. According to Stephen Davis, Canon Emeritus at Coventry Cathedral, Britain has been a peace facilitator in the conflict. However, noted Davis, "each time the peace fails, the conflict resumes with more intensity and the militant groups get more organized than they were before."

Leadership

MOSOP is the leading voice campaigning for greater autonomy for the Ogoni. The organization was established in 1990 after Ogoni chiefs, meeting in the traditional Ogoni capital of Bori, adopted a bill of rights. The bill said the Ogoni wanted to stay part of Nigeria but that their lands should be made into a distinct unit and that they should have the right to control and use the economic resources there. MOSOP demanded compensation for damage done to the environment by the oil industry, plus a greater share of oil revenues. It led a non-violent campaign from the early 1990s, as part of which it demanded $10 billion compensation from Shell, Chevron, and the Nigerian Petroleum Corporation. In 1993, 300,000 Ogoni marched peacefully against Shell; the company subsequently withdrew from Ogoni lands.

The world became familiar with the Ogoni's plight largely because of the high-profile trial and execution of MOSOP leader Saro-Wiwa. Author, television producer, environmentalist, and minority rights activist, Saro-Wiwa was arrested in 1994 by the Nigerian authorities on murder charges, which he strenuously denied. He and eight others were found guilty in late October 1995; Saro-Wiwa was hanged on November 10, 1995. The case sparked international outrage stemming from serious doubts about the fairness of the trial. As a result, the United

Kenule "Ken" Beeson Saro-Wiwa (1941–1995)

"KEN" SARO-WIWA was born in the city of Bori in the Niger Delta. His father was a chieftain of the Ogoni tribe, which consisted of about a half-a-million people living in a four-hundred-square-mile area in the delta of the Niger River. The area was under lease to oil companies for mining rights, and those companies, primarily Shell, had extracted $30 billion worth of oil from Ogoniland over thirty years, degrading soil, polluting water, and generating gas flares. Shell paid royalties to the Nigerian federal government, but this money was not used to improve the infrastructure of Ogoniland, and the area had no roads, schools, clinics or facilities.

Saro-Wiwa was an adept student and received a scholarship to the Government College at Umuahia, where he received a classical British education in English. After he completed his studies, he became a university English teacher for a short time.

A secessionist war in Nigeria began in 1967, during which Saro-Wiwa became a high-ranking federal civil servant. He was the Civilian Administrator for the city of Bonny, and then became the Regional Commissioner for Education in the Rivers State Cabinet in the 1970s. During the war, he was a supporter of the Nigerian government over the Biafrans, who were trying to secede, but his support for Ogoni autonomy led to his dismissal in 1973.

At the end of the war and after his dismissal from the government, Saro-Wiwa went into business as a grocer to support himself. While working, he self-published novels, essays, short stories, plays, and poems. Saro-Wiwa's financial success grew, and in 1985 he financed, wrote, directed, and produced Nigeria's most popular television series, "Basi and Company," which ran for five years and was watched by over thirty million people.

Many of his written works were inspired by the Nigerian Civil War, including his best known novel, *Sozaboy: A Novel in Rotten English*, a first-person narrative of a young man who becomes a "sozaboy" (soldier boy). He also published his war diaries, *On a Darkling Plain*, describing his own experiences in the war.

As time passed Saro-Wiwa became more and more concerned with the situation in Ogoniland and the political climate in Nigeria. In 1990 he helped found the Movement for the Survival of the Ogoni People (MOSOP). Saro-Wiwa sought a voice in government for each ethnic group in Nigeria and control of the mineral resources of each group's own land. Saro-Wiwa was imprisoned by the government for several months without trial in 1992, but was then released.

MOSOP had its largest demonstration in 1993, a peaceful protest that mobilized 300,000 Ogoni to demand a share of Shell's revenues and more political autonomy. Over half of the Ogoni population marched through four Ogoni cities, bringing international attention to the Ogoni plight of having their land destroyed by oil companies without any direct compensation. MOSOP wanted the oil companies to begin paying restitution for the environmental damage caused by oil extraction, including oil spills and acid rain. The Nigerian government responded by sending in military forces to occupy the area.

The year 1993 also saw Saro-Wiwa become vice president of the Unrepresented Nations and Peoples Organization (UNPO), a position he held until his death in 1995. UNPO works to give indigenous people in unrecognized and/or occupied territories an international voice, since they have none in the United Nations. He was arrested and detained by the Nigerian authorities, but again released.

Several Ogoni elders set up a meeting in Giokoo, Ogoniland, on May 21, 1994. Although Saro-Wiwa was due to attend, he was turned away by soldiers. Some of his supporters became enraged, killing four of the elders and burning their bodies. Saro-Wiwa and fourteen others were charged with murder and imprisoned for over a year before a specially convened tribunal found Saro-Wiwa and eight others guilty and sentenced them to death. At least two witnesses later recanted their statements against Saro-Wiwa, saying they had been bribed by Shell to give false testimony.

Although the trial was widely renounced by human rights organizations, the Ogoni Nine were hanged by military personnel on November 10, 1995. Saro-Wiwa was the last to be hanged, forced to watch his colleagues' executions.

In 1995, six months after the trial, Saro-Wiwa was awarded the Goldman Prize, an international prize for grassroots environmental activists, for his leadership in MOSOP, as well as the Right Livelihood Award.

Many books about his life have been published posthumously, including *In the Shadow of a Saint: A Son's Journey to Understanding His Father's Legacy*, authored by Saro-Wiwa's son, journalist Ken Saro-Wiwa.

States and the European Union implemented modest sanctions against the Nigerian government from 1996 until the Nigerian leader, General Sani Abacha, died in 1998. Ledum Mitee took over from Saro-Wiwa as leader of MOSOP, but in 2000 Mitee, too, was arrested. The leader of MOSOP since 2009 has been Goodluck Diigbo, a former associate of Saro-Wiwa.

While MOSOP says it is pursuing its goals through peaceful means, other groups in the Niger Delta region have espoused armed resistance. The two main militia groups are the Movement for the Emancipation of the Niger Delta (MEND), formed in 2005, and the NDPVF, which was established in 2004. The latter has a political arm called the Niger Delta People's Salvation Front. Drawing their ranks mainly from the Ijaw ethnic group, these groups are responsible for numerous attacks on pipelines and kidnappings of government officials and oil company employees. In June 2006, MEND, a loose alliance of various factions, declared a cease-fire after a Nigerian court ordered Shell to pay $1.5 billion in environmental reparations. MEND resumed its attacks the following month.

Current Status

Life for the Ogoni remains precarious. Local pollution has caused a preponderance of health problems and lowered life expectancy. Government repression has killed many (at least two thousand between 1993–1999), and the Ogoni homeland remains heavily militarized. In recent years, armed insurgency—most of which has been perpetrated by neighboring ethnic groups—has mushroomed. Often taking the form of "bunkering" (that is, stealing) oil and "shut-in" (blockading oil supplies) operations, these activities have cost the Nigerian government billions of dollars in lost revenue. There has also been a sharp rise in kidnappings: five hundred between January 2006 and June 2009. Illegal weapons, mostly small arms, have flooded into the Niger Delta region,

usually via the port of Lagos and imported mostly from Turkey, Liberia, Cameroon, South Africa, Ukraine, and Côte d' Ivoire .

In May 2009, a new military offensive against militant groups in the Niger Delta was launched. Foreign Minister Maduekwe defended the offensive at the June 2009 CSIS conference, saying, "our military cannot go and eat ice cream when they are being attacked and having their boats sunk by bandits. There is an existential threat to the integrity of the Nigerian state." The government offered the militants an amnesty if they called a cease-fire and laid down their weapons. Speaking at the Council on Foreign Relations in Washington, D.C., in August 2010, Nigeria's foreign minister Henry Odein Ajumogobia said that 20,000 militants had availed themselves of this amnesty and disarmed, adding that the challenge now was to find gainful employment for them. But according to peace activist Davis, "you have to have more than just returning guns for money. You need a long-term plan to develop the region." He said a Truth Commission needed to be established to help bridge the credibility gap that existed between the government and the militias. He said that militia leaders with whom he was in contact were willing to negotiate in independently mediated talks. The conflict has become more political in nature, he said, noting that whereas in 2004 most oil seized by militias was simply stolen, by 2009 most was being shut in or blockaded.

Economically, the violence has hurt the whole country as oil production, Nigeria's primary source of income, has fallen. After years of ignoring the Ogoni and other groups' concerns, the Nigerian government seems to finally be trying to address them. In November 2008, the first-ever Minister for Niger Delta Affairs, Chief Ufot Ekaette, started work, tasked with implementing a plan to develop the Delta. The government hopes this effort will help curb dissent from the Ogoni and other ethnic groups. Construction of roads, railways, a seaport, and decent housing to lift the locals out of poverty has been announced. The minister has pledged to clean up the oil spillages, introduce a waste disposal scheme, and—aware how unemployment has aggravated the conflict—employ more locals in the oil and gas industry. Until the Ogoni and others in the area see wealth flowing back into their communities in the form of better health and education, improved infrastructure, and more jobs, separatist violence is unlikely to disappear.

In June 2009, Shell agreed to pay $15.5 million in compensation to the son and relatives of executed Ogoni leader Saro-Wiwa. Some of this money will go into a trust for social programs in the Ogoni region. Shell made the settlement to avoid an embarrassing trial in which its environmentally damaging practices would have been aired, along with evidence of Shell's collusion with the Nigerian authorities in the 1990s in bribing witnesses to give false testimony against Saro-Wiwa and his colleagues. Nigeria's president, Umaru Yar'Adua, in June 2009 announced that Shell would have to abandon its Niger Delta oilfields (it had already left the Ogoni lands) because of a loss of confidence between the corporation and the local population. President Umaru Yar'Adua

died in May 2010; however, MOSOP continues to advocate for enhancement of the rights of the Ogoni people, with the clean-up of their environment the focus of its campaign.

Further Reading

"A conversation with Henry Odein Ajumogobia," Council on Foreign Relations, August 4, 2010, www.cfr.org/publication/publication_list.html?type=audio.

Davis, Stephen. "The Potential for Peace and Reconciliation in the Niger Delta," Coventry Cathedral (religious-based center for reconciliation), February 2009, www.coventrycathedral.org.uk/downloads/publications/35.pdf.

Maier, Karl. *This House has Fallen.* New York: Public Affairs Press, 2000. See chap. 4, "The Ogoni Wars."

Minorities At Risk Project, Center for International Development and Conflict Management, University of Maryland (database). "Assessment for Ogoni in Nigeria," www.cidcm.umd.edu/mar/assessment.asp?groupId=47504 (accessed June 2009).

Movement for the Survival of the Ogoni People (MOSOP) Web site, www.mosop.org.

Onah, George. "Ogonis are not Niger Deltans and we want our own state out of Rivers State—MOSOP," *Vanguard* (Nigerian newspaper), June 14, 2009, www.vanguardngr.com/2009/06/14/ogonis-are-not-niger-deltans-and-we-want-our-own-state-out-of-rivers-state-%e2%80%94-mosop.

OROMO
(Ethiopia, Kenya)

The Oromo are the single largest ethnic group in Ethiopia, accounting for a third of the overall population and numbering at least 25 million people. Oromo separatism has long been a potent force in the country, fuelled by a strong sense among the Oromo people that they have been inadequately represented and their interests inadequately addressed by the political leadership of Ethiopia. The Ethiopian government has traditionally been dominated by two rival ethnic groups, the Amhara, who make up about 30 percent of the population, and the Tigray, who account for just 6 percent of the population. The political party system in Ethiopia is largely ethnically-based.

The Oromo live predominantly in the west and south of Ethiopia, with a small minority—about 200,000—living in neighboring Kenya to the south and Somalia to the east. They speak their own language, called Oromoo or Oromiffa. The Oromo are the dominant ethnic group in southern Ethiopia, whereas the Amhara and Tigray live mainly in the central and northern highlands. About 40 percent of the Oromo are Christian, their denominations a mix of Orthodox and Protestant; 40 percent are Muslim; and a small minority adhere to the indigenous Oromo religion called Waaqa. Oromo society is overwhelmingly rural; only about 15 percent of the population lives in urban areas. Unlike their neighbors to the east, the Somalis, who are mostly nomadic herders, the Oromo grow crops such as coffee, wheat, barley, and oil seeds, and trade in hides and skins. Whereas the Somalis mostly inhabit the more arid lowlands, the Oromo tend to live in the fertile and cooler highlands, which are nourished by many rivers, providing them with plentiful water resources.

Despite being a multi-ethnic country, Ethiopia had retained a unitary state structure from the late nineteenth century to the late twentieth century. However, in 1995, following the approval of a new constitution, it moved to a federal system. In theory, this meant that the Oromo were granted political autonomy. The area where they live was designated Oromia and formed one of the nine new states created under the new system. Oromia is by far the largest of the states, occupying 30 percent of Ethiopian territory. It is also the most populous, containing about 30 million people, or 35 percent of the Ethiopian population. The capital of Ethiopia, Addis Ababa, and the city of Dire Dawa are physically located within Oromia but are not part of it politically, as they have their own autonomous, city-state governments.

The new constitution supposedly allows Oromia to secede and become a new country, provided it follows the prescribed procedure, which includes the federal government's agreeing to let Oromia hold a referendum on independence. But Oromo separatists say that in practice it is impossible to exercise their right of self-determination. The most important separatist group is the Oromo Liberation Front (OLF), which, since the 1990s, has carried out a campaign of armed resistance that it insists is simply an act of self-defense against the repressive Ethiopian government. The goal of the OLF, which has been outlawed by the Ethiopian authorities, is to establish a secular, independent Oromia. They stress that the non-Oromo ethnic minorities who live in Oromia would have the right to develop their culture and govern their affairs.

According to a May 2009 report by Human Rights Watch (HRW), which has sent research missions to the Oromo region, the Ethiopian government has used the OLF's guerrilla campaign as a pretext for clamping down on any political dissent among the Oromo. This repression has included the targeting of teachers, students, and politicians. "Since 1992 the regional authorities in Oromia have cultivated a climate of fear and repression," Human Rights Watch said. For example, teachers have been forced to provide information about their students to the school administrators or else face transfer to remote areas away from their home and family. The human rights group cited Oromo farmers, who alleged they were made to perform forced labor on projects that they had no hand in designing, as well as having had their freedom of movement restricted. HRW said that such abuses "seriously call into question the Ethiopian government's claim that it is making real progress in putting in place democratic forms of governance."

This clampdown on the Oromo is not unlike the Ethiopian government's policy toward the approximately four million ethnic Somalis living in Ethiopia. Many of these are, despite in theory having an autonomous state just like the Oromo, also waging a violent struggle to split from Ethiopia. The separatist-minded Somalis would like either to become independent or unite with Somalia to the east (see separate essay).

The Oromo-Ethiopian conflict has received scant attention from the surrounding countries and from Western powers such as the United States and Europe. There is one country to Ethiopia's north—Eritrea—that has given refuge and aid to the OLF separatists since the late 1990s. The Eritreans fought their own war for independence with Ethiopia in the early 1990s; Eritrea became an independent nation in 1993.

History

The issue of when the Oromo first settled in Ethiopia is one that is hotly contested. The separatist OLF insists that the Oromo arrived thousands of years ago from the Nile region to the north. They refute the claims of Amharic Ethiopian historians who say that the Oromo arrived from the fourteenth to sixteenth centuries from Asia and Madagascar. The Oromo say this is a fabrication used to justify the colonization of the Oromo by the Amhara.

Traditionally, the Oromo had their own political system, called the *gadaa*, under which leaders were elected for eight-year, nonrenewable terms. The Oromo continued to govern themselves until the late 1800s, when Emperor Menelik II of Ethiopia (1889–1913) expanded his domains southward into Oromo territory. Because they were colonized by another black African nation, the Oromo's experience differed from that of their neighbors, the Kenyans, Somalis, and Sudanese, who were colonized either by Europeans or Arabs. The Ethiopians, who had been Christianized as early as the third century C.E., had by the thirteenth century established a powerful kingdom. Following several centuries of decline due to clan infighting coupled with invasions by the Oromo, Somalis, and Turks, the Ethiopians reemerged as a regional power under Menelik II.

Oromo nationalists claim that colonization brought with it a succession of non-Oromo autocratic leaders, who have suppressed their culture and language and tried to divide the Oromo people by region and religion. They claim that the Oromo population was halved from ten to five million people between 1870–1900, as a result of killings by the colonial army, famine, and disease; those that survived were reduced to the status of serfs to Amharic and Tigraen landlords. In 1935, Italy, which had colonies to Ethiopia's north (Eritrea) and east (South Somalia), invaded Ethiopia, then called Abyssinia. While Ethiopian Emperor Haile Selassie I loudly protested, many of the Oromo viewed the Italian invasion as a liberation.

In 1974 Selassie was toppled by a military junta led by Mengistu Haile Mariam, which in contrast to Selassie's Christian, pro-Western regime, was Soviet-sponsored and communist-leaning. But this regime change did little to improve the plight of the Oromo, who remained the underclass. The Mengistu government began to crumble in the late 1980s following attacks both from the OLF and militant Eritrean separatists. In May 1991, a group dominated by the Tigray minority—the Ethiopian People's Revolutionary Democratic Front (EPRDF)—seized power.

The EPRDF replaced the unitary state with a federal structure consisting of nine states with borders drawn up largely along ethnic lines. The new regions were Afar, Amhara, Benishangul-Gumuz, Gambela, Harari, Oromia, Somalia, Southern Nations, Nationalities and People's, Tigray, and the city states Addis Ababa and Dire Dawa. Each state was granted a parliament, president, and judiciary. States were allowed to secede if a two-thirds majority of their state parliament plus a majority of the people voted for a referendum on independence authorized by the federal government.

The introduction of federalism did not succeed in quelling Oromo separatism. Many Oromo continued to feel excluded from power as the central Ethiopian government remained dominated by another ethnic group, the Tigray. While some Oromo have accepted the new federal structure and have competed in the state elections for Oromia, others have not, and both political and militant groups have remained active throughout the 1990s and since 2000.

Leadership

The goal of the leading Oromo separatist group, the banned OLF, was initially an independent country, Oromia. However, it has increasingly shown signs that it might accept autonomy within Ethiopia, provided it involves genuine self-rule and not just the trappings, which it says is the case now. The OLF was established in 1974, the same year that a military junta called the Derg toppled the Ethiopian monarchy. Initially concentrated in the east of Ethiopia, the OLF soon expanded westward and southward. The OLF fought to overthrow the Mengistu dictatorship in the 1980s, eventually toppling it in 1991, with the help of various other Ethiopian groups.

The OLF did not ascend to power in the aftermath of Mengistu's overthrow, and in 1992 withdrew from the political process following clashes with Ethiopia's new ruling coalition, the EPRDF. The OLF opposed the new federal system; by 1995 it was carrying out a low-level guerrilla campaign. In 1996 the OLF allied itself with the Ogaden National Liberation Front (ONLF), which since being founded in the 1980s has been fighting for independence for Ethiopia's Somalis. In 2004 the OLF chairman, Gelasa Dilbo, was forced by the Ethiopian authorities into exile in Kenya; other OLF leaders have also been driven out and have based themselves in Asmara, the capital of Eritrea.

The party that actually governs in Oromia is the Oromo People's Democratic Organization

(OPDO), which is not a separatist group. OPDO is allied with the Tigray People's Liberation Front (TPLF), the main party representing the Tigray, which also dominates the EPRDF, the governing coalition in Ethiopia. Established in 1990, some OPDO members defected to the OLF in 1992. OPDO won about 99 percent of the seats in the May 2000 regional elections in Oromia. It still controls the regional government, having won the 2005 parliamentary elections, too, albeit with a less overwhelming majority in the 537-seat parliament (the *caffee*).

The largest opposition party is the Oromo Federalist Democratic Movement (OFDM), led by Bulcha Demeksa, which supports the constitutional status quo. Another party, the Oromo National Congress, was founded in 1998 by a political science professor, Merera Gudina, to promote the right of self-determination for the Oromo people. It won 39 seats in the 2005 elections, but soon after there was a split in the party, causing Merera to form a new party, the Oromo People's Congress.

Current Status

Despite the Ethiopian government's efforts to curb separatism by decentralizing the country in the 1990s, Oromo separatism remains a potent force. There is particular resentment among the Oromo that the Ethiopian government is dominated by the Tigray. The Tigraens have tried to placate the discontented Oromo by gestures such as installing, by a unanimous parliamentary vote in 2001, an Oromo—Girma Wolde Giorgis—as Ethiopia's president, a post that wields little political power. The OLF dismisses such gestures as "cosmetic changes intended to affect the momentum of our just struggle."

Violent attacks in Oromia have been on the rise, and the Ethiopian government blames the OLF. On May 20, 2008, a bomb exploded on a public

minibus, killing six people and wounding five. Just six days later two hotels in Oromia were bombed, killing three people. In October 2008, the Ethiopian authorities arrested fifty-three ethnic Oromo, including university lecturers, businessmen, and housewives, accusing them of supporting the OLF, which remains an illegal organization. In March 2009, it arrested over eighty Oromo students at Bahir Dar University, located in the capital of the Amhara state in northwestern Ethiopia, after the students protested over derogatory remarks made about the Oromo people.

In a November 2008 report, Georgette Gagnon, deputy director of Human Rights Watch's Africa division, stated that "Ethiopia has well-founded fears of terrorist attacks, but has often manipulated those fears to suppress dissent." Gagnon said the mass arrests bore "all the hallmarks of the 'imprison first, investigate later' tactics used to arbitrarily detain peaceful critics."

Meanwhile, the government has been stepping up its campaign to defeat the OLF militarily. In March 2009, it announced that it had recently eradicated a contingent of OLF rebels who had been regrouping in the southeast of the country. The government claimed that the OLF leader, Dawud Ibsa, had been giving instructions to this OLF unit by telephone from his headquarters in Eritrea. The conflict has spilled over into neighboring Somalia, too. Early in 2009 leaders of the Oromo expatriate community in the Somali capital, Mogadishu, called on the Ethiopian authorities to release some two hundred Oromo arrested when Ethiopian troops occupied Mogadishu from 2006 to 2008. The detainees were being held in deteriorating conditions in the town of Hawasa in Ethiopia.

Journalists, academics, and non-governmental organizations (NGOs) have accused Ethiopia of having one of the worst human rights records in Africa. The government repressed media reporting for a period in early 2008 and banned a traditional

Oromo religious group, Waka-Feta, for supposed links to the OLF. In January 2009, the government passed a law that Human Rights Watch says has effectively criminalized most human rights work. The law forbids NGOs that receive more than 10 percent of their funds from abroad from doing human rights and governance work. Very few NGOs can meet this requirement in practice as there is little domestic funding of NGOs, given Ethiopia's extreme poverty.

The authorities continue to subject opposition leaders—including non-OLF ones—to harassment and abuse. In November 2008, for example, Bekele Jirata, Secretary General of the OFDM, was arrested. Despite this, Ethiopia remains one of the United States' closest allies, and the European Union rarely criticizes it. The African Union, whose attitude to separatist movements is quite hostile generally, has not intervened in the conflict thus far.

Given the repressive political climate domestically, coupled with the absence of international pressure on the government to better integrate the Oromo into Ethiopia's political structure, it seems unlikely that Oromo separatism will disappear in the near future.

Further Reading

Human Rights Watch. "Suppressing Dissent: Human Rights Abuses and Political Repression in Ethiopia's Oromia Region," May 9, 2005, www.hrw.org/en/node/11759/section/1.

Melbaa, Gadaa Oromia. *An Introduction to the History of the Oromo People.* Minneapolis: Kirk House Publishers, 1999.

Oromia State Government Web site, www.oromiagov.org.

Oromo Liberation Front Web site, www.oromoliberation front.org.

Oromsis (news blog on politics, human rights, and social justice issues affecting the Oromo people) Web site, www.opride.com.

Pausewang, Siegfried. *The Oromo and the Coalition for Unity and Democracy.* Bergen: Chr. Michelson Institute, 2007.

Wiren, Robert. "Interview with Bulcha Demeksa, Chairman of the Oromo Federalist Democratic Movement (OFDM)," lesnouvelles.org (Ethiopian online journal), April 4, 2005, www.lesnouvelles.org/P10_magazine/16_analyse03/16152_electionseth/022_bulcha_eng.html.

SOMALILANDERS
(Somalia)

Somaliland is a secessionist territory in northwestern Somalia. It has been an oasis of relative peace in a region ravaged by conflict for decades and in many ways disproves an oft-cited argument of governments that separatist movements invariably lead to disharmony and violence. Somaliland contains a third of the population of Somalia and covers a fifth of its territory. Situated on the eastern tip of Africa, it is bordered by the Gulf of Aden, the Indian Ocean, Djibouti, and Ethiopia. Its population of 3.5 million is made up mainly of ethnic Somalis. They are Sunni Muslims who speak the Somali language.

Somaliland's status as a de facto independent country came about when a rebel group that had taken control of northern Somalia, the Somali National Movement (SNM), on May 18, 1991, declared an independent Republic of Somaliland. At the same time, rival groups were fighting for control of the rest of the country. After a decade of autonomous rule, its independent status was confirmed by a referendum on May 31, 2001, in which 97 percent of the voters endorsed a new constitution. That constitution introduced a strong executive branch of government, enshrined multi-party democracy including universal suffrage, and established Islam as the country's national religion. It also guaranteed freedom of the press, though in practice the government still exercises considerable control over journalists.

Although still not recognized by the international community, Somaliland is, according to author Seth Kaplan, who used it as a case study in his 2008 book *Fixing Fragile States,* "arguably the healthiest democracy between Israel and Tanzania." According to Kaplan, Somaliland's success can be attributed to three main elements: "it has a fairly homogenous population, it does not have the type of massive disparities in wealth and access to resources that can create severe social cleavages, and other countries have not interfered much in its affairs."

This harmony has been somewhat disrupted since 2002 as a result of clashes with the neighboring region of Puntland on its eastern borders. The people of Puntland, like the Somalilanders, are ethnic Somalis and Muslims but have allegiance to different clans. Though Puntland is still part of Somalia and does not aim for independence, it declared itself an autonomous state in 1998 and does not participate in the government of Somalia. Puntland and Somaliland have been engaged in conflict since 2007 over the disputed regions of Sanaag and Sool, which they both claim. These disputes have arisen in part because the borders were drawn up by colonial powers, with little attention paid to where the various clans were living. A third breakaway region emerged in April 2002 when one of the many groups competing for power and influence in Somalia declared an autonomous "State of Southwestern Somalia." This was not an attempt to create another country but rather a protest against both the government in Mogadishu and the activities of other rival southern factions.

Having held several violence-free elections, which foreign observers have described as generally fair and free, Somaliland is relatively peaceful and stable. It stands in stark contrast to the rest of Somalia where the government is struggling to assert control, life expectancy is just forty-one to forty-three years, and adult literacy is about 20 percent. Somaliland has its own currency—the Somaliland shilling—flag, army, government, and airline. Refugees who had fled to neighboring Ethiopia have returned home since the 1990s; immigrants from surrounding states have also settled in Somaliland. A substantial portion of the territory's wealth comes from remittances that are sent home from Somali emigrants living abroad. The Somaliland government also relies heavily on duties collected from the port of Berbera, which is used by landlocked Ethiopia.

The government of Somaliland has tried to establish relations with its neighbors, including Israel, the Arab League, and Ethiopia. The European Union has sent delegations there, and Sweden is also interacting with it. However, the lack of formal international recognition for the territory has been a major drawback. For example, Somaliland cannot receive grants from the International Monetary Fund or World Bank, and foreign investment is limited. It is not a member of any inter-governmental organization, most notably the United Nations. While the African Union (AU) is still a relatively minor player, its influence is growing. The AU has not been able to adopt a common policy on Somaliland, though the general orientation of most of its members is to oppose secessionist movements.

The debate over whether to recognize Somaliland often focuses on the impact this action might have on the surrounding region, but a key issue sometimes overlooked is whether recognition would promote stability in Somaliland itself. Somalilanders are currently unified in their campaign for international recognition; should they attain this goal, however, this common purpose would no longer exist. The danger here is that Somaliland would become afflicted with the same type of factional splits that have caused chaos and bloodshed in the rest of Somalia.

History

The territory known as Somaliland was first colonized by the United Kingdom in the 1880s and became a protectorate in 1887. It was governed as a separate colonial entity throughout the colonial era. Ethnic Somalis in neighboring areas came under Italian and French domination during this period. The Somalis under British occupation were given relative autonomy to govern their affairs, unlike in Italian Somaliland where the Italians installed a ruling political class. These quite different experiences of colonialism may explain why Somaliland later succeeded in forging a functioning government supported by the general population, while neighboring Somalia failed to do so. During World War II the Italians captured Somaliland, but the British quickly retook it in 1941.

In the wave of decolonization that swept through Africa after World War II (1939–1945), Somaliland gained its independence on June 26, 1960, the first of the Somali-populated colonies to do so. However, five days later it joined itself to the newly independent South Somalia—the former Italian Somaliland—to form the unitary state of Somalia. At this time a main goal of the new regime was to create a "greater Somalia" that would also encompass ethnic Somalis living in the neighboring countries of Kenya and Ethiopia. The ethnic Somalis living in a smaller colony, French Somaliland in the northwest (also known as the French territory of the Afars and the Issas), gained their independence in 1977 and formed their own state, Djibouti.

The 1960s were a turbulent time for Somalia. In 1969 a socialist coup elevated Siad Barre to the leadership of the country. Barre held his grip on power by placing members of his clan in high office—an approach that alienated other Somalis from government. In 1981 opposition to Barre led to the establishment of the Somali National Movement (SNM), which over the next decade mounted a campaign to overthrow the Barre regime. By the late 1980s, Somalia had begun to fall apart; the Barre regime finally collapsed in 1991. On May 18, 1991, Somaliland announced its secession, and the SNM, formerly an enemy of the state, became the civil authority in Somaliland.

Meanwhile, the situation continued to deteriorate in Somalia. In 1992 the United States sent troops to open up corridors to allow delivery of humanitarian aid, as warlords blocked off access. But the mission, which subsequently became a United Nations force (UNOSOM), failed to restore peace or stability to the region. Things went from bad to worse after twenty-three Pakistani peacekeeping soldiers were murdered in June 1993 by forces loyal to General Mohamed Farah Aidid, a Somali military leader. The United States decided to pursue General Aidid and launched an offensive in which over a thousand Somalis were killed or injured. Many Somalis viewed this action negatively, believing the United States was taking sides in a civil war, and attacks on U.S. soldiers began to increase. Already scant in resources, the UN mission was discontinued in 1995.

Amid this chaos, and despite other obstacles such as clan infighting and a lack of support from other governments, the Somalilanders, with the support of a large Somali diaspora, managed to create a viable state. Yet neither the UN nor any of its neighbors recognized it as such. In 2005 an AU fact-finding mission determined that Somaliland did indeed have a legitimate claim to independence and concluded that its case was "unique and self-justified" and not likely to lead to the "opening of Pandora's Box." Despite this finding, there has been little follow-up on the part of African governments to recognize or establish formal ties with Somaliland.

Leadership

The SNM is the group mainly responsible for bringing about Somaliland's de facto independence. Established in London in 1981 by exiles who sought to overthrow the Barre regime, the SNM allied itself neither with the United States nor the Soviet Union. The SNM soon moved its headquarters to Ethiopia after the Ethiopian government offered it military support; however, it lost this backing in 1988 when Somalia and Ethiopia signed an agreement to normalize relations. That same year the SNM mounted an offensive against the government in the Somali capital, Mogadishu, and by 1989 it had succeeded in driving the government out of rural areas and had captured the city of Hargeisa (population 500,000), which has since become the capital of Somaliland.

The president of the SNM when Somaliland seceded in 1991 was Abdurahman Ahmed Ali, who became the first president of Somaliland. In May 1993, the SNM central committee named Mohamed Ibrahim Egal president, and Egal won reelection in May 1995. After the 2001 referendum confirming independence, the SNM ceased to function when political parties were formed. On May 3, 2002, Egal died in office and Vice President Dahir Riyale Kahin took over. In a popular vote in April 2003, Kahin was reelected for five years by a margin of just eighty votes (out of the 490,000 that were cast). Kahin's main challenger, Ahmed Mohamed Mohamoud, initially protested, but after the constitutional court ruled the election valid Mohamoud urged his supporters to accept it. Mohamoud had been chair of the SNM from 1984–1990.

The Somaliland parliament consists of a House of Elders and House of Representatives, each of which has eighty-two members. The largest political party is the United Democratic People's Party (UDUB), which rules the country. The second largest is the Solidarity Party (Kulmiye), led by Mohamoud. The smallest of the three parties is the nationalist Justice and Welfare Party (UCID), led by Farah Ali.

Current Status

The leaders of Somaliland occasionally express their willingness to consider reuniting with Somalia; however, the absence of a stable and well-functioning central government in Somalia makes it difficult for any concrete steps to be taken toward reunification. Instability in Somalia has tended to have the effect of strengthening the voices of those who feel that Somaliland is better off on its own. Somaliland has a strong legal argument in support of independence. It meets the three criteria for statehood set out in the 1933 Montevideo Convention on the Rights and Duties of States: a permanent population, a defined territory, and a functioning government. Ethiopia and Djibouti already accept passports from Somaliland.

The economy continues to function reasonably well, with trade in livestock—especially sheep, cattle and camels—forming the backbone of economic activity. The territory contains an estimated twenty-four million livestock and has developed a strong industry in exporting livestock to Middle Eastern countries. Crops are less important to the economy, as only 10 percent of the land is suitable for agriculture and only 3 percent is under cultivation. The government has been trying to promote domestic industry, in particular the production of frankincense and myrrh, and has supported offshore oil exploration.

Neighboring governments remain unwilling to recognize Somaliland, for fear that to do so would lead to the fragmentation of their own countries. This concern stands in contrast to their fears during the initial years of Somalia's independence, when they worried that ethnic Somalis throughout east Africa would band together and form a "greater Somalia." The pan-Africanist philosophy of some African leaders, such as Uganda's president, Yoweri Museveni, made them hostile to the idea of recognizing Somaliland, as they prefer to see a politically united Africa. Were major African countries or the AU to recognize Somaliland independence, Western powers such as the United States and Europe would likely quickly follow suit. In February 2010, Israel broke ranks with the international community by announcing it was ready to recognize Somaliland.

There are signs that Somalia's central government in Mogadishu is regaining control, a development that could have an impact on the future of Somaliland. In January 2009, Sheikh Sharif Sheikh Ahmed, a moderate Muslim, was elected president of Somalia. Many Somalis have high hopes that he will restore stability. Others have grown cynical, after the many failed attempts in the past decade to restore some kind of political order. If he is successful, the international community may become more reluctant to recognize Somaliland's independence.

Somaliland itself has experienced some political turmoil, notably due to the emergence of a new party, Qaran, which tried to form in April 2007 with the goal of establishing an independent, democratic Somaliland and a free market economy. The government suppressed the party on the grounds that it was unconstitutional, arrested its leaders, and detained them for several months. It eventually released them but not before barring them from seeking public office for five years. Territorial disputes with Puntland continue, too, in the disputed areas of Sool and Sanaag, creating an estimated twenty thousand refugees. The Somaliland defense minister, Adan Mine Mohamed, was dismissed from government in 2007 for failing to prevent the fighting in Sanaag.

In October 2008, the relative peace in the region was disturbed when twenty-nine people were killed in coordinated car bombings in Somaliland, which officials in Somalia blamed on Al Shabab, an Islamist militant insurgency. There is growing debate about what role Islam should play in public life, partly as a reaction to the rise of Islamist leaders in neighboring Somalia. President Kahin had announced in October 2006 that Somaliland would be governed according to Islamic law, or *sharia*, but the specifics of what this would mean in practice are not clear.

In presidential elections on June 26, 2010, President Kahin was defeated by Ahmed Silanyo, who won 50 percent of the vote as compared to Kahin's 33 percent. According to a July 2010 article in *The Economist*, "international elections observers reported, with some qualifications, a well-organized and fair vote." The poll took place on the fiftieth anniversary of Somaliland's independence from British colonial rule. The new president immediately pledged to continue the campaign for international recognition of Somaliland.

Further Reading

AllAfrica.com (online African news service based in Mauritius), http://allafrica.com.

"Deadly car bombs hit Somaliland," BBC News, October 29, 2008, http://news.bbc.co.uk/2/hi/africa/7696986.stm.

Kaplan, Seth. *Fixing Fragile States: A New Paradigm for Development*. Westport: Praeger Security International, 2008.

"Not so failing; Somaliland's elections," *The Economist*, July 3, 2010, www.economist.com/node/16488840?story_id=16488840.

Rift Valley Institute (independent, non-profit research and educational association established in 2001 and based in Kenya, the United States, and the United Kingdom) at www.riftvalley.net.

Somaliland Forum (diaspora-based think-tank for Somalilanders), http://somalilandforum.org/sl/contact.

Somaliland government Web site, www.somalilandgov.com.

Somaliland Times (English language Somaliland newspaper), http://www.somalilandtimes.net.

Thompkins, Gwen. "Somaliland Struggles For Recognition," National Public Radio, May 27, 2009, www.npr.org/templates/story/story.php?storyId=104620217.

SOMALIS
(Ethiopia, Kenya)

The Somali people are among the more homogenous ethnic groups in Africa, united by a common language, religion, and culture, yet they are also among the most divided politically. When the colonial powers of France, Italy, and the United Kingdom departed the region in the 1960s and 1970s, they left the Somali people dispersed among four countries—Djibouti, Ethiopia, Kenya, and Somalia. Their decision to divide ethnic Somalis across political borders has caused great resentment; many Somalis accuse the colonial powers of having presided over the "balkanization" of the Somali nation.

The Somalis living in modern-day Ethiopia and Kenya have been especially critical. Unlike Somalis in Djibouti and Somalia, Ethiopian and Kenyan Somalis are ethnic minorities in their own countries and face a constant struggle to ensure they are properly represented in their states' political structures. This has led to major tensions that for decades have regularly escalated into violent conflict. It has also greatly hindered economic development in these regions.

The four million Somalis in Ethiopia constitute about 7 percent of the overall population of Ethiopia, while an estimated half a million Somalis live in Kenya and constitute about 2 percent of the Kenyan population. In terms of economic subsistence, the Somalis are mostly livestock farmers. They are overwhelmingly Muslim but are living in countries where the ruling elite are mostly Christian.

In Ethiopia, the strongest secessionist movement is in the Ogaden region in the east, where a separatist group, the Ogaden National Liberation Front (ONLF), has been mounting an insurgency campaign for over two decades. According to Human Rights Watch (HRW) in a June 2008 report, fighting between the Ethiopian government and ONLF rebels has affected tens of thousands of people and resulted in grave abuses, including arbitrary detention and torture, committed by both sides.

The ONLF is dominated by one particular Somali clan, the Ogaden, who make up about half of the ethnic Somali population living in Ethiopia. The Ogaden are regularly in conflict with other Somali clans in the region, including the Darood, Isaaq, Dir, Hawiye, Bantu, and Rahaweyn. The ethnically-based separatism of the ONLF has been challenged since 2000 by the emergence of a religiously-based insurgency led by Islamist militants who are fighting the Ethiopian government. Although many of these Islamist fighters are ethnic Somalis, the ONLF considers them more foe than friend because the ONLF is officially secular. Muslims account for nearly half the population of Ethiopia, but only a fraction of them are Somali.

The ONLF is not clear about whether it wants to create an independent "Ogedania" or to unite the Somali region of Ethiopia with neighboring Somalia. The government in Somalia, from its inception in 1960, has supported the creation of a "greater Somalia." For example, the flag of Somalia has a five-pointed star representing each of the five Somali regions. This irredentist ideology, which advocates the annexation of the Ogaden to Somalia, has made Somalia's neighbors, Ethiopia and Kenya, hostile to the government of Somalia and distrustful of their own Somali population.

Human rights organizations have criticized Western powers such as the United States and the United Kingdom for doing little to help resolve the long-standing conflicts and tensions in the region. In a September 2007 article for the New York–based Social Science Research Council, Tobias Hagmann, a Human Geography lecturer at the University of Zurich and an expert on the Ogaden conflict, said the prevailing attitude of the big powers was one of chronic indifference tinged with a resigned "the Somalis are always fighting" mentality. HRW has said that the United States and the European countries view Christian-dominated Ethiopia as a staunch ally and are therefore reluctant to criticize the Ethiopian government's brutal clampdown on the insurgency. Indeed, the United States has tacitly supported the Ethiopian government's counter-insurgency efforts, it said. The International Committee of the Red Cross was forced to suspend operations for a period in 2007 after the Ethiopian government accused it of aiding the ONLF. Most African countries have sided with Ethiopia, while the Arab states have generally supported the Somalis.

Somali separatism in Kenya is concentrated in the northeast, an area once known as the Northern Frontier District but now called the North Eastern Province. Somalis are one of the four main ethnic groups in Kenya, but the Somalis are in an especially precarious situation. According to the U.S. State Department, in 2008 Somalis in Kenya were routinely stopped by the police, and some were deported on the assumption that they were potential terrorists. The Somali region remains one of the most insecure in Kenya. The large-scale buildup of Kenya's military, coupled with restrictions imposed by the Kenyan government, have had a negative impact on the daily lives of Kenya's Somalis. Meanwhile, the growth in Islamist violence in neighboring Somalia has caused some fifty thousand Somali refugees to flee Somalia and seek refuge in Kenya, further destabilizing the region.

History

Somalis and Ethiopians have been fighting for centuries to control the Ogaden region. In the thirteenth century the Ethiopians invaded from the highlands, in the fifteenth century the Somalis invaded, and in the late nineteenth century Emperor Menelik II (ruled 1889–1913) reclaimed it for Ethiopia. There has always been a strong religious dimension to the conflict; historically, Ethiopia was a Christian empire while Somalis were Muslim. For example, Somali leader Sayid Mohammed Abdullah Hassan in the late nineteenth and early twentieth centuries declared his campaign to eject the Ethiopians from the Ogaden a *jihad* against Christian invaders. Hassan's fighters were defeated by colonial British forces in 1921.

In 1935 Italy invaded Ethiopia (or Abyssinia as it was then known). The British defeated the Italians in 1941 and briefly ruled the Ogaden before giving it back to Ethiopia in 1948—a move resented by Somalis. In 1960, when the British and Italians departed the Horn of Africa and several new countries were created, ethnic Somalis were split between Somaliland (see separate essay), South Somalia, Ethiopia, and Kenya. The former British colony of Somaliland immediately united with the former Italian colony of South Somalia to form Somalia. Somalis living in French Somaliland to the north formed their state, Djibouti, in 1978.

In the Ogaden a struggle for independence among Somalis began in 1963 with an uprising called *Nasrullah,* an Arabic term meaning "sacrifice for Allah." Troops from Somalia invaded Ethiopia in July 1977 and seized control of a large portion of the Ogaden before being driven out in 1978 by the Ethiopians, who were aided by eleven thousand Cuban troops and weapons from the Soviet Union. Ethiopia had allied itself with the communist bloc countries after a revolution in 1974, in which the pro-Western Emperor, Haile Selassie, was replaced by a socialist military regime led by Mengistu Haile Mariam.

In Somalia the collapse of the government of Siad Barre, Somalia's ruler from 1969 to 1991, ushered in an era of conflict, chaos, and statelessness out of which three ethnic Somali-dominated separatist entities emerged: Somaliland, Puntland, and South West Somalia. Of the three, only Somaliland aims to become an independent country.

Neighboring Kenya was colonized by the British in the late nineteenth century. When the British were preparing to hand over power to the Kenyans in the early 1960s, they conducted a survey of public opinion that took the form of a series of town hall–style meetings. From this they concluded that the Somalis wanted to either form their own country or unite with Somalia. Nevertheless, at the constitutional conferences of 1963 that led to Kenyan independence, the British authorities and Kenyan leaders decided to create a Somali-region within Kenya rather than allow it to secede. The Somali delegates walked out in protest, supported by the government in Somalia, which broke off relations with the United Kingdom.

There followed a four-year *shifta* (Somali word for "bandit") war, which began in 1963 when Somali secessionists assassinated the commissioner of the Isiolo District, Daudi Wabera. The Kenyan government ultimately crushed the Somali rebels and in 1967 signed a peace agreement with the government of Somalia. Somali militants carried out sporadic killings in Kenya in the 1980s, triggering harsh retaliation. In 1984, for example, Kenyan authorities carried out the Wagalla massacre, in which six hundred people were killed.

In 1992 Ethiopia tried to defuse its separatist tensions by decentralizing the country. A form of ethnic federalism was introduced, with the country divided into nine regions, including a Somali one, and two city states. All the while Ethiopia has had to contend with another major separatist movement, the Oromos (see separate essay).

Leadership

A pro-independence party for Ethiopian Somalis, the Western Somalia Liberation Front (WSLF), first emerged in the early 1970s. Based in the cities of Mogadishu, the capital of Somalia, and Hargeisa in Somalia, it was supported by disgruntled pastoral farmers from the Ogaden clan who suffered heavily from Ethiopian military campaigns and the famine of 1974–1975. The WSLF helped the troops from Somalia who invaded the Ogaden in 1977. By the late 1980s the WSLF had been eclipsed by the ONLF, a group that had emerged several years earlier out of a split within the WSLF. The ONLF is the most significant Ethiopian-based Somali separatist group.

According to independent lawyer Mohammed Mealin Seid, who has studied the role of religion in the Ogaden conflict, in a January 2009 essay for the Social Science Research Council, a Horn of Africa-focused web forum, "despite portraying itself as secular when communicating with the international community, buzzwords such as *jihad* and fighting for the Muslim nation against invader 'infidels' characterize ONLF's strategies for mobilizing supporters." In a June 2008 report outlining human rights abuses committed by the Ethiopian government and the ONLF, HRW stressed how "the ONLF, which claims to be seeking self-determination for the region, represents only a segment of the divided Ethiopian Somali community." The ONLF rebels do not seem to have a single vision for what the region's future political or economic system should be, vacillating between independence and uniting with Somalia. Most of the ONLF's top officers live abroad where they canvass for support from the Somali diaspora by stressing Somalis' common identity as Muslims.

While the ONLF "has been unable to overcome its parochial clan basis," according to Tobias Hagmann, an Islamist group called the United Western Somali Liberation Front (UWSLF) has emerged that does transcend the Somali clan structure. It is also fighting the Ethiopian government, but unlike the ONLF it does not have a secular nationalist ethos.

With the introduction of ethnic federalism to Ethiopia in 1992, the Somali region has its own parliament and president. The ONLF won the first regional elections and formed the new government. But in the intervening years its dominance has been challenged by rival parties representing non-Ogaden Somali clans, such as the Ethiopian Somali Democratic League (ESDL). A Somali People's Democratic Party was formed in 1998 under the leadership of Abdul Mejid Hussein when the ESDL joined forces with an ONLF splinter group.

Current Status

Separatist tendencies remain strong among Somalis in Kenya and even more so in Ethiopia. By contrast, given the virtual collapse of a functioning government in Somalia, the Mogadishu-led irredentist campaign to incorporate the Ethiopian Ogaden and Kenyan Somali regions into Somalia has weakened. According to Nureldin Satti, an ex-Sudanese and United Nations diplomat involved in peace-building efforts in the Horn of Africa, in a March 2009 talk at the Woodrow Wilson International Center for

Scholars in Washington, "the Greater Somalia campaign has cost Somalia dearly. Instead of focusing on building up the state where they live, the Somalis have been distracted by this movement."

In April 2007, there was a marked escalation of the conflict in the Ogaden in Ethiopia when the ONLF attacked a Chinese-operated oil field in Degehabur, killing more than seventy Chinese and Ethiopians. A brutal clampdown by the government of Ethiopian prime minister Meles Zenawi followed. According to HRW, thousands of people have been displaced and hundreds or thousands have been held in barracks on suspicion of aiding the ONLF; there have also been reports of widespread torture, rape, and assault. Ethiopian soldiers carried out over 150 executions in 2007 and 2008, often singling out relatives of suspected ONLF members, the human rights organization reported. Meanwhile, the Ethiopian government has severely restricted the ability of independent media to report from the Ogaden. The Ethiopian government also continues its dispute with Somalia over where their mutual border lies.

Both the ONLF and government forces have pressured civilians to collaborate by providing information about enemy activities and mobilize for its cause. The Ethiopian administration, wrote Tobias Hagmann in September 2007, has "lost Somalis' 'hearts and minds' by dishonoring the region's constitutionally guaranteed autonomy, by meddling in its internal decision-making, and by the ruthless conduct of its security forces." Hagmann said this experience "forcefully demonstrates that national identity cannot be decreed or engineered by financial subsidies, political quotas or the holding of elections." The standard of living based on education, healthcare, roads, and security is worse in the Ogaden region than in the rest of Ethiopia, and what resources the region has are concentrated among a Somali-Ethiopian elite based in the regional capital of Jijiga. While Ethiopia's Somalis have been given autonomy in the form of a regional government, they remain in practice largely excluded from national institutions, Hagmann wrote.

Governmental and academic observers believe that Eritrea, Ethiopia's neighbor to the north, has been providing material support both to the nominally secular ONLF and to Somali Islamist insurgents in Ethiopia. Eritrea itself seceded from Ethiopia in 1993 following a war of independence and subsequent referendum and is now recognized internationally as an independent country. In September 2010, a Somali online news service, Garoweonline, reported that several hundred ONLF rebels, allegedly trained in Eritrea, had entered neighboring Somaliland. Ethiopian forces responded by crossing into Somaliland, hunting down the rebels, and forcing them to flee to Ethiopia. The African Union, whose powers remain limited, though they are growing, has not played a substantial role in trying to resolve the conflict.

The persistent clan infighting in neighboring Somalia led to a significant influx of refugees into Kenya's Somali-populated region in 2008. After years of neglect, Western powers began to focus on the wider Somali region once more due to the surge in piracy operations off the coast of Somalia, where Western ships are increasingly targeted. Although still reluctant to mandate a major international peace-keeping mission, given the failure of a UN mission to restore peace and stability in the early 1990s, both the United States and the European Union have come to realize that lawlessness around the Horn of Africa has created the conditions that have allowed piracy to thrive. In December 2008, the EU decided to deploy a modest-sized naval mission to clamp down on piracy. By July 2010, the mission, which also helps the United Nations deliver food aid to Somalis displaced by conflict, consisted of eighteen hundred military personnel and twenty vessels. Its mandate has been extended until December 2012.

Further Reading

BBC Monitoring Africa, "Ethiopian forces arrive in Somaliland to hunt down ONLF rebels," September 15, 2010 (original source: Garoweonline news service, September 14, 2010).

Hagmann, Tobias. "The Political Roots of the Current Crisis in Region 5," Social Science Research Council, September 21, 2007, http://hornofafrica.ssrc.org/Hagmann.

Human Rights Watch. "Collective punishment: war crimes and crimes against humanity in the Ogaden area of Ethiopia's Somali regional state," June 12, 2008, www.hrw.org/en/reports/2008/06/12/collective-punishment.

Oyugi, Walter. "Politicized Ethnic Conflict in Kenya: A Periodic Phenomenon," United Nations Public Administration Network, 2000, http://unpan1.un.org/intradoc/groups/public/documents/CAFRAD/UNPAN010963.pdf.

Seid, Mohammed Mealin. "The Role of Religion in the Ogaden Conflict," Social Science Research Council, January 26, 2009, http://hornofafrica.ssrc.org/mealin/index.html.

U.S. State Department, "2008 Country Reports on Human Rights Practices: Kenya, Ethiopia," February 22, 2009, http://paei.state.gov/g/drl/rls/hrrpt/2008.

SOUTH CAMEROONIANS
(Cameroon)

Cameroon, a country in western Africa lying just north of the equator and slightly larger in size than California, is not an obvious candidate for a separatist movement. Relatively stable and peaceful by African standards, it has been spared the ethnic strife that has plagued so many of its neighbors. Nevertheless, a sizable minority of the population, namely English-speaking Cameroonians who live in two provinces in the western part of the country, continue to harbor grievances about their minority status in this majority French-speaking nation. Their case is notable in that language is the driving force behind the movement rather than race, ethnicity, tribe, or religion. But while language may be the main cause, history and economics are underlying factors, too. For example, much of Cameroon's natural resources, including oil, are located in the Anglophone region, yet many Anglophones feel they have not reaped the benefits of these resources since Cameroon became independent in 1961.

Cameroon, in addition to the linguistic divide, is an extremely culturally diverse nation, with some 240 ethnic groups that can be divided into five broad regional-cultural groups. In terms of religion,

the northern part of the country is mostly Muslim, while the south—where the Anglophones live—is predominantly Christian. A large proportion of Cameroonians adhere to indigenous African religious beliefs. The two colonial languages, French and English, are spoken predominantly in the areas that came respectively under French and English rule in the first half of the twentieth century. Cameroonians, who number about nineteen million, typically speak English or French as well as one of the 240 local languages. The Anglophones are thought to number between 15 and 20 percent of the population, or some three million people.

Legally, Anglophone Cameroonians have a solid case for self-determination. The 1961 referendum that led to the establishment of independent Cameroon did not give English-speakers the option of their own country. They were only allowed to choose between joining with Nigeria or with French Cameroon, both of whom had recently become independent. Anglophone separatists wish to create an independent country, to be called Southern Cameroons, the name applied to the area when governed by Britain under an international mandate from 1916 until 1961.

Cameroon has had only two presidents since the end of colonial rule, Ahmadou Ahidjo (1960–1982) and Paul Biya (1982–present). Both Francophone, Ahidjo, and later Biya, did make some efforts to prevent the Anglophone minority from feeling marginalized, notably by appointing vice presidents and premiers from the English-speaking region. Biya has tried to ensure that all linguistic as well as ethnic, regional, and religious groups are represented in the government, which is based in Yaoundé in the Francophone region. Like his predecessor, however, Biya has employed repressive measures to stifle secessionism. In 1966, for example, President Ahidjo required all political parties, which had previously been organized along linguistic lines, to be merged into a single party, the Cameroon National Union. For the next twenty-five years this remained the only legal political party. In the 1990s President Biya reacted to the emergence of Anglophone separatism by choosing to repress it rather than engage it in dialogue. The main group advocating secession for the Anglophone provinces, the Southern Cameroons National Council (SCNC), was outlawed in 2001, and its leaders are regularly detained. For example, Chief Ayamba Ette Otun from the SCNC, who is in his eighties, was arrested in October 2008 in the town of Tiko.

Economically, many English-speaking Cameroonians feel they have not fared well under majority Francophone rule. They claim that corporations formerly administered by the Anglophones, such as the Cameroon Bank, are now poorly managed by the Francophone-led government in Yaoundé. They complain that their road infrastructure has been neglected by the central government and that their regional airports, such as that in the coastal town of Tiko, have been abandoned. Cameroon is the only country in Africa where both English and French are official languages, but the Anglophones complain that French dominates in practice in the education system, in government, and in private commerce. As an example, they note that former president Ahidjo never addressed the nation in English.

They also allege that when President Biya changed the country's name in 1984 from the United Republic of Cameroon to the Republic of Cameroon, he was distorting history in an effort to obscure the country's origins as a federal state in which the English-speaking region enjoyed considerable autonomy. Anglophone-rights activist Albert Mukong characterized what happened as follows: "Two states came together to form one nation. They are distorting everything to look as if Cameroon was only one country from the beginning." Indeed the separatists say the Anglophone provinces never voluntarily united with French Cameroons but rather were annexed by it.

History

The divide between Anglophone and Francophone Cameroonians is a relatively recent phenomenon. The British and French only established authority over Cameroon in 1916 when their armies defeated German troops stationed there. Cameroon had been a German protectorate since 1884. The Portuguese were present long before that, arriving in the fifteenth century and naming the area Rio dos Cameroes (*cameroes* is Portuguese for "prawn," which is abundant in the region).

After France and Britain gained control during World War I, they partitioned the area, with Britain taking about a fifth of the land and France taking the remainder. This division was enshrined at war's end in the 1919 Treaty of Versailles, which turned the two Cameroons into League of Nations–mandated territories. "This artificial boundary that divided the country into two distinct political and cultural traditions has left an indelible mark on the country's political landscape," the Pretoria-based Institute for Security Studies (ISS) concluded.

Political groups slowly developed along linguistic lines. For example, in order to counter the threat from Nazi dictator Adolf Hitler, who sought to retake Cameroon for Germany, France sponsored the establishment in 1938 of the Jeunesse Camerounaise Française, the first Francophone-based political movement in Cameroons. By the late 1950s the two Cameroons—like much of the rest of Africa—were in flux, as colonial powers attempted to set the borders of the new countries they were creating from their former empires. French Cameroons gained full independence on January 1, 1960, with Ahmadou Ahidjo as prime minister (he subsequently became president of the unified state formed from British and French Cameroons).

Meanwhile, the United Nations in 1959 invited the people in British-ruled Cameroons to choose between joining Nigeria or French Cameroons. "The third option of an independent state of south Cameroons did not get a majority opinion, both within Cameroon and from the British, who thought it was not economically viable," according to the ISS. In a referendum in February 1961 most people living in the northern part of British Cameroons voted to join Nigeria. This area then became the Sardauna province of Nigeria.

The majority in the southern part, by contrast, voted to join French Cameroons, so in October 1961 the French and remaining British areas were unified. English-speaking Cameroonians, whose territory was now called West Cameroon, were initially given autonomy to run their affairs under a federal structure. But this came to an end following a referendum on May 20, 1972, in which a majority of Cameroonians voted to scrap federalism and make Cameroon a unitary state.

Despite their loss of autonomy, discontent among Anglophone Cameroonians was not vocal in the 1970s and early 1980s, possibly because the country was doing comparatively well economically by trading in its oil, cocoa, and coffee resources. But when the economy went through a slump in the late 1980s, voices within the Anglophone community began demanding a review of the union, claiming they were marginalized despite being in possession of the bulk of the country's resources. In 1990 a group of Anglophones drew up a 156-page manifesto cataloging abuses suffered under majority Francophone rule, which helped spawn a full-fledged separatist movement by the mid-1990s.

Partly as a bid to assuage Anglophone discontent, President Biya agreed to revise the constitution in 1996, giving extra autonomy through the introduction of local and regional elections. However, he did not return Cameroon to a federal system, and the central government retained strong control by appointing delegates to the local councils. The Anglophone separatist movement has continued to simmer ever since, never rising to the level of all-out armed conflict, but causing considerable domestic tension as the government has sought to clamp down on various separatist groups.

Leadership

The SCNC is the leading secessionist group representing English-speaking Cameroonians. The SCNC's goal, an independent Southern Cameroons, is one that most analysts believe is not shared by the majority of Anglophone Cameroonians, who may feel marginalized but do not wish to secede. The SCNC evolved out of the All Anglophones Conference (AAC), a movement launched in April 1993. The Cameroonian government quickly tried to suppress the AAC, notably deploying troops in 1994 to try—unsuccessfully—to stop a meeting of leaders that included Ekontang Elad, Simon Munzu, and Carlson Anyangwe.

The government blamed the SCNC for a series of armed attacks in March and April 1997. These attacks, in which ten people were killed, targeted local administrative officials and military police in the Northwest region, one of the two Anglophone areas (the other being the Southwest). Its ongoing clampdown against the SCNC has led most of the leaders to leave the country to escape arrest. The Cameroonian newspaper *La Nouvelle Expression* reported in October 2008 that Anyangwe, a university professor, went to Zambia and was doing world tours to raise awareness of the cause, while Munzu had become a UN official and was based in Western Africa. Another leader, Gorji Dinka, set up headquarters in Nigeria and was traveling frequently to London. SCNC youth leader Ebenezer Akwanga was reported to be in the United States. The SCNC has tried to attract members from the large Cameroonian expatriate community, for example, by setting up a European branch in 2008 in Brussels, Belgium. It claims to have support from within the European Parliament, which is based in Brussels, specifically from the Alliance of Liberals and Democrats, which is the third largest group in the parliament.

Other secessionist groups to have emerged since the 1990s include the Southern Cameroons People's Organization (SCAPO), the Southern Cameroons Youth League (SCYL), and the Southern Cameroons Restoration Government. In 1999 Justice Fred Ebong aligned himself with the separatist cause by proclaiming an independent state of Southern Cameroons in a local radio broadcast.

The first Anglophone Cameroon political group to be established was the Cameroons Youth League (CYL), founded in 1940 by Peter M. Kale and Dr E. M. L. Endeley when the British were still administering the area. The CYL's main demand was that the British govern Cameroons separately from Nigeria, Britain's neighboring colony, and not as an appendage, as was happening. The British responded in 1954 by granting the Cameroonians their own assembly and allowing them to send six representatives to the Nigerian parliament.

Current Status

Though the separatist movement remains active, there seems little likelihood of Cameroon breaking apart in the near future. Despite the substantial shortcomings of its democratic system, Cameroon's relative stability has helped to keep the country united. "Cameroon is one of those rare African countries that has never experienced a regime change by means of a coup d'état," noted Paul-Simon Handy, head of the ISS African Security Analysis Program in an August 2007 report. But Handy added that corruption remains widespread and that the state structures are extremely centralized—a legacy of the French Jacobin model. Given this political environment, the sense of marginalization among the English-speaking Cameroonian minority has not disappeared. A possible solution that might help ease tensions would be to recreate a two-state federation, effectively a return to the pre-1972 situation, but the government has given no indication thus far it wants to go down this path.

The party that has governed Cameroon since 1966, President Biya's Cameroon People's Democratic Movement (CPDM), is staunchly pro-unity. It was formed from a merger of French and British Cameroon parties and called itself the Cameroon National Union until 1985. No other political parties were allowed to function until 1990 when Biya, under pressure from other countries—notably France, which still exercises considerable influence over its former colony—agreed to multiparty elections. In the August 2007 elections, the CPDM won 152 out of 180 seats in the parliament. Francophone Biya, who was reelected in 2004 with 70.9 percent of the vote, is due to remain in office until October 2011, by which time he will have ruled the country for almost thirty years. ISS scholar Handy reported that there is "a widespread sense of popular resignation at the inability of elections to produce significant change," and that "Cameroon's political life is still characterized by immobility and stagnation."

Despite widespread dissatisfaction with the political system among Anglophones, journalist Kini Nsom has reported that the Anglophone separatist movement has actually lost momentum due to internal squabbles among its leaders. "Until the SCNC leaders reunite themselves under one umbrella clearly stating their objectives, they will remain a group of clowns, self-seeking schemers who are acting a play of the grotesque," Nsom wrote in an October 2008 opinion article for the Cameroon newspaper *The Post.*

An SCNC leader Chief Ayamba, in 2008, accused the Cameroonian authorities of committing serious human rights violations. He said the government was responsible for the death of thirteen SCNC activists tortured to death while imprisoned by the authorities for supporting the pro–South Cameroons independence movement. The British newspaper the *South Wales Echo,* in an August 2008 article by James McCarthy, reported that a Cameroonian refugee in the United Kingdom, Jean-Pierre Gueutchue, claimed he had been arrested, beaten, and whipped for giving out SCNC leaflets.

Reacting to the repression at home, Anglophone separatist leaders have taken their campaign abroad. In late 2008 they petitioned the African Commission for Human and People's Rights, a quasi-judicial body that reports to the African Union (AU), which was meeting in Abuja, Nigeria. The leader of Libya, Muammar Qaddafi, invited SCNC leaders to Addis Ababa, where the AU has its headquarters, to make their case to the commission. On the other side, the Cameroonian government has maintained generally good relations with its neighbors: the Central African Republic, Chad, the Republic of Congo, Equatorial Guinea, and Gabon, and in 2008 resolved a border dispute with Nigeria. By giving neighboring governments no reason to aid separatist groups in order to destabilize the country—something often seen in Africa, as with Eritrea's support for ethnic Somali separatists in Ethiopia (see separate essay)—the Cameroonian government has helped contain secessionism.

Further Reading

Dicklitch, Susan. "Failed Democratic Transition in Cameroon: A Human Rights Explanation," *Human Rights Quarterly* 24, no. 1 (2002), http://muse.jhu.edu/login?uri=/journals/human_rights_quarterly/v024/24.1dicklitch.html.

Handy, Paul-Simon. "Cameroon's Parliament and Council Elections: Plus ça Change . . . ," Institute for Security Studies, August 3, 2007, www.iss.co.za/pgcontent.php?UID=6984.

Institute for Security Studies, "Cameroon—Country File," http://www.iss.co.za/countries.php (accessed June 2009).

Konings, Piet, and Francis B. Nyamnjoh. *Negotiating an Anglophone Identity: A Study of the Politics of Recognition and Representation in Cameroon.* Leiden-Boston: Brill Academic Publishers, 2003.

Nsom, Kini. "Cameroon: The Anglophone Struggle—Going Down Memory Lane," *The Post Online,* October 3, 2008, http://allafrica.com/stories/200810030642.html.

Southern Cameroons National Council Web site, www.scncforsoutherncameroons.net.

SOUTH SUDANESE
(Sudan)

Africa's largest country, Sudan, has been traumatized for over half a century by a separatist conflict between the north and south in which the south has gradually edged toward forming its own country. Apart from a hiatus between 1972 and 1983, southern militants have been fighting the northern-dominated central government in a bid to prevent the northerners from imposing their culture, language, and religion. Indeed, since 1820 south Sudan has only had three or four decades of peace. The south Sudanese campaign has been led since the 1980s by the Sudan People's Liberation Movement (SPLM) and its military wing, the Sudan People's Liberation Army (SPLA). The SPLM has been the governing party of an autonomous government created in south Sudan in 2005, as part of a north-south peace accord that took years to broker. In January 2011, as part of that agreement, southerners held a referendum on independence. International observers endorsed the vote and a resounding Yes vote was widely forecast. Official results will be announced in February. South Sudan looks set to become an independent country in July 2011, when the 2005 peace accord expires.

The southern Sudanese people make up about eight million of Sudan's population of roughly forty million. Relations between north and south have historically been difficult, as there are real and substantial differences between the populations. Ethnically, southerners derive from scores of black African tribes, which are themselves often divided by language and culture. The most prominent ethnic group in the south is the Dinkas; other prominent tribes include the Nuers, Aruaks, Shilluks, and Latukas. Northerners, by contrast, speak Arabic and have sought to establish closer ties to the Arab world. Southerners have long resisted the efforts of the north Sudanese to Arabize them. English is the official language in the south, Arabic in the north. The southerners are a mix of Christian and adherents of indigenous religious beliefs, whereas the northerners are predominantly Muslim. In recent decades, an increasing number of south Sudanese have become Christian, possibly in reaction to the sporadic efforts of the north to forcibly convert southerners to Islam. The south has a tropical climate, while the north is arid desert. The south Sudanese are a mix of sedentary farmers and nomadic pastoralists; the north Sudanese tend to be nomadic. Sudan has abundant oil reserves, though they lie overwhelmingly in the south: 75 percent of oil production takes place in southern regions, and a further 15 percent from the Abyei region on the north-south border, which the south claims.

The northerners occupy two thirds of Sudanese territory and have, since Sudan gained independence in 1956, been the political ruling class. Not surprisingly, this has caused great discontent among southerners. A northerner, Omar Hassan Al-Bashir, has led Sudan since 1989, while a southerner, Salva Kiir Mayardit from the SPLM, is Sudan's first vice president. This governing coalition was put in place by the 2005 peace accord.

While the north-south tensions and unresolved issues continue to attract considerable international attention, since 2003 the world has focused equally intensely on another bloody conflict in Sudan: the conflict in Darfur. This is a region in the northwest of Sudan that the Sudanese government has struggled to maintain control over. Darfur consists of three states—north, south, and west—all in northern Sudan. Darfur is about the size of France and has a population of seven million. The Darfur conflict is not a classic separatist movement, in part because the Darfurians are neither cohesively organized politically or militarily nor secessionist-leaning. However, there are similarities between the two conflicts: as with the north and south, there are significant ethnic and historical differences between Darfurians and north Sudanese. In the case of Darfur, these differences are the driving force behind the conflict. Darfurians share a common religion with the northerners, Islam, but they are black Africans, not Arabs. They come predominantly from three ethnic groups—the Fur (hence the name, Darfur), the Masalit, and the Zaghawa—though for centuries they have intermarried with Sudanese Arabs. Until the twentieth century Darfurians were ruled independently from the rest of Sudan, and even when they were placed under Sudanese rule they were given considerable autonomy to run their affairs. Darfurians tend to be farmers, whereas Sudanese Arabs tend to be nomadic. Darfurians speak a distinctive form of Arabic.

The Sudanese army has allied itself with militias, called the Janjaweed, who have carried out widespread atrocities against Darfurians. In 2004–2005, when the violence in Darfur was at its bloodiest, coverage of the conflict eclipsed that of the north-south conflict. However, since 2009 the spotlight has shined again on the north-south conflict as the likelihood that the south will secede has increased. The United States feels a particular attachment to Darfur, which some attribute to a transferred feeling of guilt for having failed to prevent the genocidal slaughter of a million people in Rwanda, to the south of Sudan, in 1994. When reports of slaughter emerged from Darfur, determination crystallized in the United States as well as other parts of the world to prevent a Rwanda-scale genocide from happening on their watch.

The impact of the north-south and Darfur conflicts has been devastating on Sudan. From 1983–2005 four million people, or 80 percent of the south Sudanese population, were displaced, and two million were killed as a result of military hostilities, drought, and famine. In the Darfur conflict from 2003–2008, some 2.4 million people were displaced and 400,000 killed.

Meanwhile, the south Sudanese people have grown increasingly impatient with the northerners for failing to implement the 2005 north-south Comprehensive Peace Agreement (CPA). For example, in October 2007 the SPLM pulled out of the unity government created by the CPA in protest over lack of implementation, though it rejoined the government in December 2007. The CPA requires that profits from the country's oil resources, which are concentrated in the south, be split fifty-fifty between north and south. It allows the SPLM to keep troops in the south but requires them to withdraw troops from the east. In practice, the SPLM and the Sudanese government each have posted troops along the border regions, both because this is where the oilfields are located and because the actual boundaries have not yet been agreed on.

The publication in May 2009 of a nationwide census, as required by the CPA, has been another political hot potato. The SPLM rejected as too low the estimation of south Sudanese as 20 percent of the population, or eight million people. In fact, determining these figures is extremely difficult because the country has witnessed massive population displacement as a result of the Darfur and north-south wars. For example, the SPLM disputed the estimate that there were just 500,000 southerners living in the north. The figures are significant because they will influence discussions on how to divide up the country's oil revenue.

The CPA set up a system of central government in which southerners were granted greater powers than previously enjoyed. The SPLM was allotted a 28 percent share of representation in the national institutions, which translates into 9 of the 30 cabinet seats in the central government. The dominant political party in the north, the National Congress (NC), was allocated 52 percent of the seats in the national assembly and 15 cabinet seats in government, while 6 seats were reserved for other northern and southern opposition groups. Both the NC and SPLM have consolidated their power through the CPA, garnering 80 percent of the seats on the national legislature between them. The CPA also created an autonomous government for the South Sudan region, which is based in the city of Juba in the deep south of Sudan. The first cabinet of South Sudan region was appointed on October 21, 2005, and is made up of 16 SPLM members, 3 seats for the NC and 3 for other south Sudanese groups.

Relations between north and south remained tense in the run-up to the January 2011 referendum. Foreign diplomats and politicians have been encouraging the two sides to resolve their differences. Of all the foreign powers, the one with greatest diplomatic leverage is China because it is by far the biggest economic investor in Sudan. Since the 1990s, the Chinese have been selling small arms, anti-personnel mines, tanks, and helicopters to Sudan in return for access to Sudan's generous oil supplies. The Sudanese, who only began exporting crude oil in 1999, have, since 2004, directed 60 percent of their exports to China; the Chinese, for their part, have built many oil refineries in Sudan.

China has been criticized in the past for not using its influence to promote peace or human rights, notably when standing idly by as the Sudanese government committed atrocities in the south and in Darfur. In the run-up to the Beijing Olympics in 2008, the Chinese government, keen to ward off any international criticism that might cast a pall over the games, did in fact begin to apply some pressure on the Sudanese government to improve its human rights record. But the Chinese have been much less forceful in raising the issue than the United States and other Western nations. Because of the veto that China wields in the UN Security Council, Beijing's support has shielded Khartoum from damaging UN sanctions.

Despite their peace-making efforts in the north-south conflict and in Darfur, the United States, European Union, United Nations, and Sudan's neighbors have not been immune from criticism. The international community has been accused of compartmentalizing its policies for the two conflicts, the consequence of which has been to undermine progress in both. U.S. involvement has been at times inconsistent. For example, in late 2006 U.S. president George W. Bush appointed Andrew Natsios as an envoy to Sudan, but Natsios resigned in late 2007, complaining of lack of support from the U.S. State Department. In March 2009, U.S. president Barack Obama appointed a retired major general Scott Gration special envoy to resolve the north-south conflict and the Darfur humanitarian crisis.

History

The south Sudanese live in an area historically known as the land of Kush. From the middle ages to the modern era, their Muslim Egyptian neighbors to the north were the dominant influence, though the Christian Byzantine Empire did send a proselytizing mission in the sixth century and Christian kingdoms existed periodically. In the nineteenth century the Sudanese came under the control of two colonial powers: Egypt and the United Kingdom. The Egyptians unified and conquered northern Sudan in 1820–1821, and in the intervening decades amassed wealth by making raids into the south to kidnap black Africans and sell them as slaves in the north. The southerners still feel great resentment over this lucrative slave trade.

The British involvement began in 1882 when the British occupied Egypt. Sudanese Muslims rebelled against Anglo-Egyptian domination in 1885 and briefly established an independent Islamic theocracy. However, the British re-established control over Sudan in the late 1890s and then administered the whole country as a colony from 1899–1956. The British were especially dominant in south Sudan, where Christianity spread; the Egyptians maintained their influence over the northern half, which retained its Muslim identity. The south of the colony was ruled separately from the north, with the British even imposing travel restrictions. Darfur, which had governed itself as a separate kingdom or sultanate from 1650, became incorporated into the rest of Sudan in 1916.

In 1923 the borders of modern-day Sudan were established by two British district commissioners. When World War II ended in 1945 the British began to withdraw from Sudan and reconnect the south, which they governed, with the north. The British handed over power to the northern Arab elites in Khartoum, the Sudanese capital that lies in the north of the country. Given the broad cultural, ethnic, linguistic, and religious differences between north and south, the southerners at a conference in Yuba in 1947 raised the possibility of establishing Sudan as a federation rather than as a unitary state. However, the British colonial rulers rejected this suggestion; the concept of a federal colony was alien to them and they feared it would lead to secession.

On January 1, 1956, Sudan gained independence from Egypt and the United Kingdom. The north seized the opportunity to consolidate power over the whole country, which triggered a rebellion in the south that would last, with intermittent lulls, for fifty years. There were a series of coups in the 1950s and 1960s that resulted in the Sudanese government's alternating between civilian and military rule. All the while, southerners continued to resent the Arab-dominated government in Khartoum.

A resistance movement called *Anyanya* ("scorpion"), led by Joseph Lagu and aimed at ending Arab-Muslim domination, emerged in 1955. The Sudanese authorities responded with a brutal military clampdown that caused thousands of south Sudanese to flee to neighboring countries. Those in exile became more radical in pushing for full independence than those who remained who were more willing to accept unity with Sudan provided they were given more autonomy. In 1967 a prominent exiled leader, Aggrey Jaden, established a Provisional Government of Southern Sudan.

In 1972 Sudan's leader, General Jaafar Nimeiri, who had seized power in 1969 in a coup, signed a peace agreement with the south that gave the south autonomy. A new constitution was adopted that provided for a 250-member parliament for the south, which was elected in May 1974. But north-south tensions resurfaced once more in the late 1970s when oil was discovered in the south and the northerners moved to keep the profits. In 1981 the government advanced a plan to split the south into three regions based on the historical provinces: Bahr al Ghazal, Equatoria, and Upper Nile. Some southerners, notably Abel Alier from the numerically dominant Dinka tribe, opposed this division, while former *Anyanya* rebel leader Lagu from the Wahdi tribe supported it. In 1983 General Nimeiri began implementing this tripartite division and renounced the 1972 accord that gave the south autonomy. He also began to impose strict Islamic law, or *sharia,* effectively turning Sudan into an Islamic state. These moves provoked the SPLM, under the leadership of John Garang, to renew its military campaign.

Nimeiri was toppled in 1985, but soon after a new leader, Omar Hassan Al-Bashir, emerged who continued laying the government's Islamic foundations. Bashir even provided a safe haven for extremist Osama bin Laden, leader of the radical Islamist movement al Qaeda, until international pressure led him to expel bin Laden. The suffering of the southerners caused by the north-south conflict was compounded by a massive drought in the mid-1980s that led to a further 200,000 deaths from starvation. Many southerners fled northward to Khartoum. In May 1989, Garang announced a cease-fire, and peace talks commenced in the Ethiopian capital Addis Ababa, mediated by former U.S. president Jimmy Carter.

Sudan's neighbors tried to promote north-south peace, too, by setting up the Intergovernmental Authority on Development (IGAD) in 1993, which launched a peace process and which remains a key peace facilitation framework for Sudan. Although that process stalled in 1997, north-south contacts were kept up, which helped to soften negotiating positions. Meanwhile, Ethiopia, Eritrea, and Uganda were providing military support to the SPLM's military wing, the SPLA. Peace talks were re-launched in 2002 in the Kenyan capital Nairobi, with the Kenyan government acting as mediator and the United States, United Kingdom, Norway, and Italy as facilitators. Garang was the lead negotiator for the south, while his northern counterpart was Vice President Ali Osman Taha. In January 2005, the north and south signed the CPA, bringing an end to the twenty-two-year conflict.

As southerners were gaining political autonomy, the Darfurians were reeling from the 2003–2005 conflict. The international community's focus on securing a north-south peace agreement had resulted in an initially slow response to the escalation of the Darfur conflict. But the focus gradually shifted toward Darfur as the situation there worsened. By 2004 the U.S. House of Representatives was labeling the killings in Darfur genocide. On May 5, 2006, a peace agreement for Darfur was signed in Abuja, the Nigerian capital. As more diplomatic energy shifted to Darfur, the SPLM grew resentful, believing that their concerns were being ignored. In late 2007 the party withdrew from the Sudanese legislature.

Sudan's relations with its neighbors, Ethiopia, Eritrea, Chad and Uganda, have see-sawed between warm and hostile as the governments have sporadically accused one another of funding rebels on each other's territory. Relations have been similarly rocky with its Arab neighbors to the north, Egypt and Libya. In the early 1970s moves to establish a common federation among Egypt, Libya, and Sudan failed due to mutual mistrust. Egypt has been wary of letting the south secede because it fears this might have a negative impact on Egypt's water rights on the River Nile, which flows through Sudan. Egypt currently benefits from generous access, under a 1959 treaty. Relations with the United States, never particularly good, worsened in the 1990s as the Khartoum government grew increasingly Islamist and decided to harbor bin Laden, who in 1998 declared holy war on the West. The United States bombed a pharmaceutical factory in Sudan in 1998 that it said was producing chemical weapons.

Leadership

The SPLM/SPLA has for almost three decades been the dominant group representing the south Sudanese people. It was formed in 1983 by Colonel John Garang, a U.S.-educated former officer in the Sudanese army. Garang had been sent by Sudan's leader, General Nimeiri, to negotiate with rebellious soldiers in the south. He subsequently switched sides and became leader of the rebels. Libya's leader,

John Garang de Mabior (1945–2005)

AP Photo/Virginia Mayo

JOHN GARANG was born into the southern Dinka ethnic group to a poor Christian family. After the death of his parents by age ten, a relative paid for his primary education. The first Sudanese civil war began in 1955. At age seventeen Garang joined the southern Sudan–based Anyanya movement. In light of his youth, the leaders of the movement encouraged him to first educate himself. Garang attended school in Tanzania due to the fighting in the Sudan.

Garang eventually earned a scholarship and traveled to the United States, where in 1969 he earned a Bachelor of Arts in economics from Grinnell College in Iowa. He then received the Thomas J. Watson Fellowship, which enabled him to return to Tanzania and study East African agricultural economics at the University of Dar es Salaam. He also joined the University Students' African Revolutionary Front. Before completing his master's degree, however, he returned to Sudan to fight.

At the end of the first Sudanese civil war in 1972, Garang was inducted into the Sudanese military, which he served in for eleven years. As a career soldier, he returned to the United States, where he attended the Infantry Officers Advanced Course at Fort Benning, Georgia. This training helped him rise to the rank of colonel in the Sudanese military.

While in the United States, he took a period of academic leave and earned a master's degree in agricultural economics and a Ph.D in economics from Iowa State University. There, he wrote his thesis on the agricultural development of southern Sudan.

In 1983 Garang was serving as an instructor in a military academy in Khartoum when he was sent to quell a mutiny of five hundred southern troops. When he arrived, rather than ending the rebellion, he joined it and encouraged other garrisons to mutiny. He then proceeded to organize the rebellious soldiers into the Sudan People's Liberation Army. The group of five hundred grew to sixty thousand by the early 1990s, and the fighting erupted into a long civil war between the Christian and animist south Sudanese and the Muslim north Sudanese. Garang's goal was the establishment of a democratic Sudan, with the Sudan People's Liberation Movement as the southern area's leading party. Oil had also been recently found in south Sudan, which spurred additional fighting as the factions fought for control of this key resource.

Garang, once described as an "ultimate survivor," traveled with heavy security and thwarted numerous assassination attempts. Under his leadership the SLPA fought a long and hard guerrilla war. During the 1980s and 1990s, he and his ever-increasing garrison of fighters fought for years in their efforts to achieve their goal. Two million people were killed during a war that spanned two decades and ended only after the SPLA and its political faction forced a negotiated settlement. This settlement was signed in Kenya in January 2005. After the peace deal was concluded, Garang transitioned from First Lieutenant General to Vice President of Sudan.

Garang held this title for just three weeks. He died in a helicopter crash on July 30, 2005. Garang's death sparked riots that resulted in the deaths of 100 people.

Muammar Qaddafi, initially supported the SPLM because of its bad relations with General Nimeiri. But in 1985 he withdrew this support when Nimeiri was toppled. The SPLM originally espoused a Marxist ideology and received support from Ethiopia's communist military dictator, Mengistu Haile Mariam.

By the late 1980s the SPLM had amassed a force of over twenty thousand troops and had taken control of most of the non-urban areas in south Sudan. In 1991 Garang, who came from the numerically dominant Dinka ethnic group from which he derived most of his support, successfully suppressed a revolt from within SPLM ranks that had been instigated by leaders from a different ethnic group, the Nasir-Nuer. Thousands of people were killed in the feud. In 2004 there were rumors of another revolt aimed at replacing Garang with Salva Kiir Mayardit, but it never materialized as Kiir moved to prevent it. Garang was still the SPLM leader when he was killed in a helicopter crash on July 30, 2005, an event that triggered rioting in which 100 people were killed. Garang personally leaned toward keeping Sudan unified, so his death was seen as a blow to the SPLM's pro-unity faction. His successor, Kiir, focused his efforts on uniting the south, and in January 2006 he concluded deals with dissident SPLA factions.

The SPLM's goals have shifted over the years from increased autonomy to outright independence. In 1983–1984 it fought against the southern pro-independence movement, Anyanya II. Around 1986 it supported a unified Sudan, one in which the south would have a larger say in national affairs. By 1992 it was advocating that the south remain in Sudan as part of a confederation, with the north governed by Islamic law and the south consisting of secular states. Subsequently, the SPLM has grown more separatist-minded. Today, most members are thought to favor the independence of south Sudan; however, a significant minority remains willing to stay united with the north, provided the south retains real political autonomy. The pro-unity faction stresses how the south Sudanese can help reform the manner in which Sudan is governed and address grievances of marginalized regions. For example, a leading SPLM figure, Abdel Aziz al-Hilu, who is half Darfurian, half Nuba, is promoting a national agenda rather than a southern one. The separatists, by contrast, focused on the 2011 independence referendum.

A splinter group of the SPLM, which calls itself SPLA-United, was created in April 1993 in the Kenyan capital Nairobi, but divisions soon emerged from within. In 1995 a secessionist wing formed the Southern Sudan Independence Movement (SSIM), led by Raik Machar from the Nuer tribe. In 1997 SPLA-United and SSIM renounced the goal of seceding from Sudan. By 2002 SSIM leader Machar had reintegrated into SPLA-United. The leader of SPLA-United, Lam Akol, was made foreign minister of Sudan in the 2005 government of national unity. He was replaced in October 2007 by the SPLM's Deng Alor after the SPLM accused Akol of becoming too close to the dominant north Sudanese party, the NC, which has been in power since 1989. Another south Sudan–based party is the United Democratic Salvation Front (UDSF), which emerged out of Machar's SSIM as a splinter group. Led by Eng Joseph Malwal, the UDSF holds a cabinet post in the national unity government.

There is also the Sudan National Party (SNP), which officially registered in 1999 and whose core supporters are the Nuba tribes in the state of South Kordofan on the northern side of the north-south border. The Nuba are a conglomerate of fifty groups ethnically distinct from northerners and southerners. Since the 1980s the Nuba have repeatedly clashed with the Misseriya Humr tribe in South Kordofan, who are Arabic-speaking pastoralists. The Nuba have allied themselves with southern separatists, motivated by their common experience of having been subjected to severe pressure from the Arab-dominated northerners to culturally assimilate. The SNP, led by Father Philip Abbas Ghaboush, has criticized the 2005 peace agreement, saying it does not benefit the Nuba people, and says it will call for self-determination for the Nuba should the south Sudanese secede.

In eastern Sudan, an amalgamation of separatist groups emerged in 2005 calling itself the Eastern Front. Its members claimed that the central Sudanese government had ignored their issues and concerns for years. A peace agreement was signed with the Eastern Front on October 14, 2006.

Current Status

The situation in the south has improved since the peace accord was signed in 2005. After the devastation inflicted from decades of war, the southerners are anxious to avoid a return to war. Progress has been made in implementing the CPA. For example, an electoral law was adopted in July 2008 and a border demarcation report was submitted to the president in November 2008.

This relative calm has encouraged many people to return to their homes in the south, though there are still 130,000 refugees in Egypt, Ethiopia, Kenya, and Uganda. Low-level conflict continues. In May 2008 northern troops stationed in the oil rich, Dinka-dominated Abyei area on the north-south border clashed with the SPLA. Eighty-nine people were killed and fifty thousand displaced. The United Nations peacekeeping mission (UNMIS) was criticized for not protecting the civilians, but UNMIS countered that it had neither the mandate nor the capacity to do so. The CPA gives the people in Abyei the right to call a referendum on whether to remain part of the north or to join an independent south, though this is problematic as Abyei's borders still have to be demarcated. Home to three major oil fields whose revenues from 2005–2007 totaled $1.8 billion, neither side is likely to easily cede Abyei.

In refugee camps in the north, Sudanese forces have been accused of persecuting south Sudanese women—for example, by imprisoning them for up to six months for producing and selling home-brewed alcoholic drinks. Although Islamic law is not supposed to apply in south Sudan, south Sudanese women have been arrested for adultery. The SPLA is also reported to have committed serious human rights abuses, including extrajudicial killings, raping of women, arbitrary arrests, and use of child soldiers. From 1983–1999 the SPLA abducted roughly fifteen thousand women and children, many of whom remain unaccounted for. Approximately fifty south Sudanese civilians were killed in 2008 by exploding landmines. The south has been destabilized by an outside force as well. The Lord's Resistance Army (LRA), a Christian fundamentalist militia fighting to seize power in neighboring Uganda, uses south Sudan as a base and regularly abducts Sudanese and Ugandan children.

In March 2009, the world's spotlight shone again on Sudan when the International Criminal Court (ICC), based in The Hague, issued an arrest warrant for Sudan's President Bashir for war crimes committed in Darfur. Regional experts criticized the ICC for pursing the case at such a delicate time, warning it would only polarize political leaders and make a peaceful settlement harder to secure. The ICC indictment did not cover war crimes in the north-south conflict. However, according to Andrew Natsios, former U.S. presidential envoy to Sudan, "the southerners have taken the ICC's message on board and are demanding the arrest of 20,000 janjaweed." The latter are accused of carrying out massacres, rapes, and displacement of whole villages.

In contrast to the neglect displayed toward other African separatist conflicts like the ethnic Somalis and Oromo in Ethiopia (see separate essays), the international community devotes considerable attention to Sudan. The first contingents of the 26,000-strong UN peacekeeping force arrived in January 2008.

In the April 2010 Sudanese presidential and parliamentary elections, the SPLM won 22 percent of the vote. International observers, including those from the United States, criticized the election, claiming that it did not meet international standards. Concerns were also expressed about persistently high levels of violence in the south. After years of painstaking efforts to bring peace to the region, the international community made a major diplomatic effort to ensure that the January 2011 referendum passed off smoothly. The United States, backed by the European Union, led this well-coordinated campaign throughout 2010 and early 2011, through generous funding and by deploying hundreds of observers to verify the complex voter registration and voting process.

Nureldin Satti, a former Sudanese diplomat and Fellow at the Wilson International Center for Scholars in Washington, D.C., in a March 2009 talk at the Wilson Center opposed secession because he believed it would destabilize the country. "I do not want to see Sudan go the way of Somalia," Satti commented. He was referring to the collapse of the Somali government in 1991 that triggered two decades of violent conflict, lawlessness, the secession of Somaliland to the north (see separate essay), and the emergence of a self-declared autonomous region, Puntland, in the northeast. The north's strategy, Satti said, was "to make unity more attractive. However, this message has unfortunately not trickled down to the people of the south who historically have seen the northerners as their oppressors."

One danger posed by the partitioning of the country is the creation of new marginalized minorities—be it southerners in north Sudan or northerners in south Sudan. Past experience—for example, the India-Pakistan split in 1947 and the breakup of Yugoslavia in the early 1990s—offer a stark warning. The division of Sudan could actually cause rather than prevent further bloodshed. Many northerners believe that the southerners will not be capable of governing themselves as an independent country and that any "South Sudan" will quickly be torn asunder by ethnic or tribally-based conflicts.

The disputed border areas cover some 20 percent of the total border, including the Nuba Mountain and Blue Nile areas between the north and south. With the Nuba dispersed between north and south, their future remains unclear in the event of secession. The Nuba and the people living in the Blue Nile state are allowed under the CPA to have a "popular consultation" on their future status, but this does not give them a clear right of self-determination and could therefore sow the seeds of further conflict. Secession will also require the north and south to come to an arrangement on what the citizenship rights are of the many southerners who have immigrated to northern Sudan. And the south would also have to reach an agreement with Ethiopia and Kenya on exactly where their mutual borders lie.

A system for dividing up southern oil revenues should the south secede is also necessary. This could take the form of an "oil for land" deal, whereby northerners are given access to oil in return for the granting of enhanced land ownership rights for southerners. Under the CPA the south is only entitled to a share in oil revenues from oil from south Sudan, not from the whole country. One thing that is clear is that oil will play a key role in the country's future: 50 percent of the Sudanese government's revenue and fully 95 percent of the south Sudanese regional government's revenue is derived from oil. And while most of the country's oil reserves are located in the south, the oil pipelines run through the north, leaving it vulnerable if the northerners are dissatisfied with the disagreement with the south.

In a November 2010 seminar at the Center for Strategic and International Studies (CSIS), a Washington D.C. think tank, CSIS researcher Brian Kennedy stressed how insecurity was likely to remain a problem in the months ahead. He noted that most south Sudanese carried guns as the SPLA did not provide enough security and that disarming the population would be a key challenge in the future. The situation is especially volatile in border regions.

Further Reading

Carney, Timothy. "Some Assembly Required: Sudan's Comprehensive Peace Agreement," United States Institute of Peace, Washington, D.C., November 2007, www.usip.org/resources/some-assembly-required-sudans-comprehensive-peace-agreement.

Eggers, Dave. *What Is the What?* New York: Vintage, 2007. [Novel based on the experiences of a south Sudanese child refugee who fled the north-south conflict and was ultimately resettled in the United States.]

Felton, John. "Aiding Refugees: Should the U.N. Help More Displaced People?" *CQ Global Researcher* 3, no. 3 (March 2009).

Foerstel, Karen. "Crisis in Darfur: Is There Any Hope for Peace?" *CQ Researcher* 2, no. 9 (September 2008).

Guillaume Lavallee (AFP), "Observers approve South Sudan vote," *Agence France Presse,* January 17, 2011.

International Crisis Group. "Sudan's Comprehensive Peace Agreement: Beyond The Crisis," March 13, 2008, www.crisisgroup.org/library/documents/africa/horn_of_africa/b50_sudan_cpa_beyond_the_crisis.pdf. www.cmi.no/sudan/doc/?id=930.

Natsios, Andrew. "Waltz with Bashir: Why The Arrest Warrant Against Sudan's President Will Serve Neither Peace nor Justice." *Foreign Affairs,* March 23, 2009, www.foreignaffairs.com/articles/64904/andrew-natsios/waltz-with-bashir.

Thomas, Edward. "Against the Gathering Storm: Securing Sudan's Comprehensive Peace Agreement," Chatham House Report, January 2009, www.chathamhouse.org.uk/publications/papers/view/-/id/688. [See page 9 for political map of Sudan.]

U.S. State Department, "2008 Country Report on Human Rights Practices: Sudan," February 22, 2009, http://paei.state.gov/g/drl/rls/hrrpt/2008.

WESTERN SAHARANS
(Morocco)

In northwest Africa, about 400,000 people live in a Colorado-sized territory called Western Sahara, also known as the Sahrawi Arab Democratic Republic (SADR), which since 1975 has been a legal no-man's land. SADR is a rather exceptional example of a separatist movement because most of the people living there have in practice been governed by Morocco since 1980, and yet most countries do not recognize that Morocco has sovereignty over the territory. Indeed, many recognize SADR as an independent country and have diplomatic relations with its Algerian-based government-in-exile. On world maps, it tends to be drawn in with unique shading to indicate this unusual status of being neither a functioning independent country nor an integral part of Morocco.

The Sahrawi ("people of the Sahara") are ethnically a mix of Arab, Moor, Berber, and black African. They speak a form of Arabic and are Sunni Muslims. Their land is sparsely populated, with the largest city, Laayoune on the northwest coast, having a population of just 200,000. The other ports are Ad Dakhla and Cabo Bojador. The Sahrawi inhabit a hot, dry, desert terrain that is mostly lowland, with small mountains in the south and northeast. Their neighbor to the south and east is Mauritania; they share a twenty-five-mile border with Algeria to the northeast, while to the west lies the Atlantic Ocean and Spain's Canary Islands, which are less than a hundred miles offshore.

Sahrawi separatists were engaged in a guerrilla war—first against Spain and then Morocco and Mauritania—from 1974 until 1991, in pursuit of independence. A cease-fire was put in place in 1991 that brought an end to the hostilities; however, the political stalemate continues, with the Sahrawi political leadership in complete disagreement with the Moroccan government over who should govern the territory. The United Nations appointed former U.S. secretary of state James Baker special envoy in 1997 to mediate an agreement, but after seven years of efforts Baker ultimately failed to broker a deal. The UN is still heavily involved in mediation efforts. In 2008 it persuaded the parties to continue negotiations, and in January 2009 Christopher Ross was appointed envoy in an effort to rejuvenate the process.

Morocco controls about 85 percent of Western Sahara, while Polisario, the dominant Sahrawi independence group, controls about 15 percent. The Moroccan government allows all Western Saharan residents to take part in local and national elections, but the region does not have special autonomy. The

UN has retained a strong physical presence in Western Sahara since the 1991 cease-fire through its peace-keeping mission, MINURSO (Mission for the Referendum in Western Sahara). But the price has been high: from 1991–2004 some $600 million was spent to maintain the mission. MINURSO's mandate was renewed in April 2009. For twenty years massive diplomatic efforts have been expended in an effort to come to an agreement on the terms of a referendum that would determine how the territory should be governed. The biggest obstacle to organizing this referendum has been the failure of Polisario and the Moroccan government to agree on who should be allowed to vote in it.

Internationally, both sides have their champions. Polisario has consistently been supported by Algeria, where it is headquartered. The Algerians have succeeded in securing it considerable international recognition. Cuba has been another longtime ally. One of Morocco's most powerful supporters has been France. SADR is recognized as a member of the African Union (AU). This is unusual in that generally the AU has been unsupportive of separatist movements on the grounds that they often further fragment already fragile states. Major African nations, including South Africa, Nigeria, and Kenya, recognize SADR, though Morocco's diplomatic counter-offensive has succeeded in persuading others, such as Togo and Senegal, to withdraw recognition.

The territory's principal natural resources are fish and phosphates. A 2006 report by the Nordiska Afrikainstitutet, a Swedish-based research center, said the Moroccan government has been increasingly exploiting Western Sahara's coastal waters for its fish resources because over-fishing has depleted stocks in Moroccan waters. The report criticized the European Union for concluding a fishing agreement with Morocco in 2006 that allows European vessels to fish in Western Saharan waters, calling it "backdoor recognition of the status quo." The center also alleged that Morocco was keen to annex the

territory because of its potential as a source of oil and noted that the Moroccan government in 2001 granted research licenses to the French-based Total and U.S.-based Kerr McGee oil companies.

Were independence to became a practical reality, Western Sahara, by virtue of its small population, would be "one of the smallest non-island states in the world," noted a March 2009 report from the Johns Hopkins University. Given how potentially weak it would be as a state, the authors of the report concluded that it "could fall prey to subversion and terrorist groups" and endure as a source of tension in Algerian-Morocco relations.

History

The people of the Western Sahara descend from nomadic tribes that came there from the Arabian Peninsula during the tenth and eleventh centuries. In 1884 the coastal part of Western Sahara became a colony of Spain, when European powers divided up the African continent among themselves at a conference in Berlin. France, which was the colonial ruler in neighboring Morocco and Algeria, confirmed the borders of Western Sahara with Spain in 1912. Spain had another protectorate just north of Western Sahara called Tarfaya. In the late 1950s Sahrawi resistance fighters stepped up their campaign against French and Spanish colonization. The ensuing hostilities ultimately led the Spanish to hand over Tarfaya to Morocco in 1961.

On December 16, 1965, the UN General Assembly adopted a resolution calling on Spain to end its colonial rule in the Western Sahara. A UN commission concluded in 1975 that most Sahrawis favored independence—both from Spain and Morocco. In addition, Sahrawis disputed the territorial claims of neighboring Mauritania. Morocco had gained its independence in 1956, while Mauritania had gained its in 1960. The Moroccans suffered a setback in October 1975 when the International Court of Justice ruled that Morocco did not have sovereignty over Western Sahara. On November 6, 1975, King Hassan II of Morocco called for a "Green March" against the ruling, and in response to his appeal some 350,000 unarmed civilians crossed from Morocco to Western Sahara.

By this time the Spanish had decided to give up their African colony. They had even pledged to hold a referendum to ascertain what the Sahrawis wanted, but they failed to follow through on this promise. Instead, when they left in early 1976, in the midst of domestic political turmoil surrounding the death of fascist dictator General Francisco Franco, who had died in November 1975, the future status of Western Sahara had not been determined. The withdrawal of Spanish forces opened the door for both Morocco and Mauritania to press their territorial claims by military means, which they did. Morocco annexed and occupied two thirds of the disputed territory while Mauritania did the same with the remaining one third. Fierce Sahrawi resistance flared, and in the 1980s the UN became involved in trying to end the conflict. It submitted a settlement proposal in 1988 that gave Sahrawis the choice between becoming integrated into Morocco or becoming independent. International peace-making efforts succeeded in brokering a cease-fire, which took effect on September 6, 1991, and was monitored by the UN's MINURSO mission.

In the subsequent UN-mediated talks on the self-determination referendum, Polisario demanded that the electorate be based on the 1974 Spanish census. By contrast, Morocco wanted to include tens of thousands of Sahrawi who had moved to Morocco before 1974 when it was still a Spanish protectorate. Morocco submitted a list of 181,000 voters, Polisario proposed 39,000, and Mauritania proposed a further 10,000. In September 1997 UN envoy James Baker made a breakthrough by facilitating the signing of the "Houston Agreements," which enabled the process of identifying eligible voters to be completed. In February 2000, 86,386 voters were identified out of 198,469 applicants, with 79,000 rejected applicants appealing the decision.

Morocco realized by 2000 that it was likely to lose the independence referendum if the UN-proposed electorate stood, so it began to consider granting autonomy to the Sahrawi instead of full independence. However, Polisario refused to countenance this option. In January 2003, Baker proposed giving Western Sahara autonomy within Moroccan jurisdiction for five to six years, after which there would be a referendum on independence. This time Polisario accepted the plan but Morocco did not, so the stalemate continued.

Leadership

One of the earliest Sahrawi leaders to resist colonial rule was Ma El Ainin, who, in 1898, established himself in Smara, a town in the Spanish-ruled north. Ma El Ainin led a resistance campaign against the colonizers. Sahrawi opposition to both Spanish and French colonial rule escalated into armed resistance in the early 1930s, which France and Spain clamped down on in 1934. Spain subsequently annexed the Western Saharan interior. In 1957 Sahrawi fighters attacked Spanish bases, triggering Operation Ecouvillon—a crackdown by French and Spanish troops in which thousands of Sahrawis were displaced to the Tarfaya strip in southern Morocco. In 1969 the group Harakat Tahrir was formed to campaign for Sahrawi independence, only to be crushed a year later by Spain. Its leader, Muhammad Basiri, disappeared while in Spanish custody.

Sahrawi resistance to foreign rule culminated with the establishment in 1973 of Polisario (Frente Popular para la Liberacion de Saguia el-Hamra y del Rio de Oro). Polisario initially fought against Spain, but when the Spanish pulled out it re-directed its energies against Morocco, which had annexed Western Sahara. In February 1976, Polisario declared the establishment of the Sahrawi Arab Democratic Republic and named Mohamed

Abdelaziz president. The declaration was made in Algerian refugee camps where tens of thousands of Sahrawis had fled from Moroccan forces.

Polisario has been a government-in-exile ever since, basing itself since the mid-1970s in Algeria. In 1981 Morocco began to build fortified sand walls, or berms, to consolidate the areas over which it had control. But while Morocco has succeeded in largely defeating Polisario militarily, the latter scored a significant diplomatic victory in 1984 when the Organization of African Unity, the precursor of the AU, agreed to seat the Polisario government-in-exile as a member. This decision prompted Morocco to leave the AU.

Although it was originally Marxist in ideology, since the 1990s Polisario has adopted promarket policies. It continues to preside over a one-party system of government for SADR, though according to its 1999 constitution it plans to eventually move to a multi-party democracy. There have been numerous defections of high-level Polisario officials to Morocco, including in August 1992 SADR foreign minister Brahim Hakim. The president of SADR is Mohamed Abdelaziz, and the prime minister is Abdelkader Taleb Oumar.

Current Status

The phrase "seemingly intractable" tends to appear frequently in analyses of the Western Sahara conflict. Talks between the two sides were ongoing as of late 2010. Morocco had in 2007 offered Western Sahara special status within Morocco, but Polisario refused to accept this, preferring to hold out for full independence. In April 2008, the UN envoy to Western Sahara said that independence was unrealistic. Although the 1991 cease-fire continues, Polisario has threatened a return to hostilities unless its preferred solution is enforced. There has been no substantial shift in positions regarding the referendum of self-determination. Polisario insists independence must be an option on the ballot, and Morocco

says it cannot. And just as before, they disagree over who should be allowed to vote in a referendum. A fifth round of UN-sponsored talks to break the deadlock is under way.

In the meantime, the UN classifies Western Sahara as a "non self-governing territory" pending determination of its final status. In a July 2009 telephone interview, Johns Hopkins University professor William Zartman, who is an expert on self-determination generally and on Western Sahara specifically, said the general trend among the international community is to accept the status quo of Moroccan occupation. The reasons for this are twofold: countries see that formal recognition of SADR has not, in reality, led to independence, and the issue is no longer a "top burner" on the global stage. That said, Algeria has remained very pro-Polisario, partly because it wishes to keep Morocco "on the edge of stability."

The territory remains heavily militarized, with some 160,000 Moroccan and up to 6,000 Polisario troops stationed there. In addition, there are thought to be well over 100,000 Moroccans who have settled in Western Sahara since the Moroccan occupation began. There is also a humanitarian element to the conflict as there are an estimated 100,000 Sahrawi refugees, most of whom live in camps near Tindouf in southwest Algeria that are governed by Polisario. Claims of human rights abuses inside the camps have spurred controversy. In June 2009, an Australian documentary, *Stolen*, alleged that slavery existed in the camps. The film maintained that the camps were divided ethnically into a white Arab majority and a black African minority, and that some black Africans had complained of being subjected to slavery by white Arabs. Polisario strongly rejected these allegations, and the main subject of the documentary, a woman called Fetim Sallem, flew to the premier in Sydney to protest the claim as well.

The situation in the camps led some 1,500 refugees to leave in 2010 and move to the Moroccan-occupied part of Western Sahara, according to a December 2010 article in the

Washington Post newspaper. Journalist Alison Lake charted how their return has caused tensions both among Western Saharans and between them and the Moroccan authorities. "On November 8, outside the Moroccan-administered town of Laayoune, pro-Polisario militants attacked police with rocks, machetes and knives, killing 11 and wounding 70 others," Lake reported. The violence was sparked by "a demonstration against Moroccan favoritism toward those who have moved back from the Algerian camps," the article said.

The uncertainty surrounding Western Sahara's status has hindered both trade and investment ties with the world's major economies. However, some see the 2006 EU-Morocco fishing agreement, whereby EU vessels gained access to Western Saharan waters without Polisario's consent, as a sign that this is changing. The pressure to do business with Morocco in Western Sahara is likely to increase further if substantial oil deposits are discovered, either onshore or offshore.

According to a March 2009 Johns Hopkins University report issued by the Potomac Institute for Policy Studies and Conflict Management Program, the conflict in Western Sahara has hindered prosperity throughout the wider North Africa region. The so-called Maghreb nations—Algeria, Libya, Mauritania, Morocco, and Tunisia—have been discouraged from promoting integration with each other because of their disagreements concerning Western Sahara's status. Algeria and Morocco have, for example, spent large amounts of money on increasing the size of their armies and purchasing arms, in part because they are on opposite sides of the conflict. Furthermore, the chronic lack of cooperation between Algeria and Morocco has permitted terrorism, illegal immigration, and drug smuggling to flourish.

Further Reading

Lake, Alison. "Decades later, refugees return to a land still divided," *The Washington Post*, December 5, 2010, www.washingtonpost.com/wp-dyn/content/article/2010/12/04/AR2010120403324.html.

Olsson, Claes, ed. "The Western Sahara Conflict: The Role of Natural Resources in Decolonization," Nordiska Afrikainstitutet, *Current African Issues*, no. 33 (2006), www.nai.uu.se/publications/books/book.xml?id=25191.

Potomac Institute for Policy Studies and The Conflict Management Program. "Why the Maghreb Matters: Threats, Opportunities, and Options for Effective American Engagement in North Africa," Johns Hopkins University School for Advanced International Studies—Special Report, March 2009.

Shelley, Toby. *Endgame in the Western Sahara, What Future for Africa's Last Colony.* London and New York: Zed Books, 2004.

Theofilopoulou, Anna. "The United Nations and Western Sahara—A Never-ending Affair," United States Institute of Peace—Special Report, July 2006, www.usip.org/files/resources/sr166.pdf.

Zartman, William. *Ripe for Resolution.* New York: Oxford University Press, 1989.

ZANZIBAR AND PEMBA ISLANDERS (Tanzania)

The people of Zanzibar, an archipelago twenty miles off the coast of Tanzania, have long thought of themselves—and been seen by outsiders—as distinct from mainland Tanzanians. An internationally recognized country for four months, Zanzibar's union with mainland Tanzania, which came about in 1964 following a popular revolt against the ruling elite in Zanzibar, has been far from harmonious. Tensions have bubbled away for decades, even though Zanzibaris have throughout this time enjoyed a great deal of autonomy to govern their own affairs.

Zanzibar consists mainly of two islands: Unguja, sometimes also known as Zanzibar, the larger of the two where the state capital is located, and Pemba, which is just over half the size of Unguja and lies fifty kilometers to its north. About 60 percent of the Zanzibari population lives on Unguja and 40 percent on Pemba. Pemba is the more fertile of the islands, with about 85 percent of Zanzibar's cloves—the islands' main industry—grown there. With its 1.1 million people, Zanzibar is much more densely populated than mainland Tanzania, where some 38 million people live. Zanzibar has a more hectic, commercial, even exotic feel to it, due in large part to the huge influence Arab culture

has had there. For many centuries, Arabs—in particular from Oman—have been trading with Zanzibaris and even settling in Zanzibar. Zanzibaris speak the same language as mainland Tanzanians, Swahili, which is the lingua franca throughout central and eastern Africa. Swahili is indigenous in structure but its vocabulary borrows heavily from Arabic and English. Arabic is widely spoken in Zanzibar too.

The islands are distinguishable from the mainland as well by the prominence of Islam. Fully 98 percent of Zanzibaris are Muslim. In contrast, the mainland hosts a mix of Christians, Muslims, and adherents of indigenous religions. As with many other Muslim-dominated regions around the world, Islamist activism has become more prevalent in Zanzibar since the 1990s.

The people of Zanzibar are majority African-origin and minority Arab- or mixed-origin. Separatist sentiments are felt strongest among the Zanzibaris of Arab extraction; the Arab influence is more prevalent in Pemba than in Unguja. Many Pemba islanders feel resentment toward the African-dominated Zanzibari administration in Unguja and allege that they are discriminated against for government appointments. In 2009 only 26 of the 192 top government positions in Zanzibar were held by Pemba islanders. Consequently, a pro-autonomy movement has been on the rise in Pemba. There is a history of self-rule on the island, which governed itself as an island state for many centuries until it fell under Omani sovereignty about 1750. In the midst of the 1964 revolution that led Zanzibar to merge with Tanganyika to form Tanzania, a People's Republic of Pemba was declared, although the attempted secession only lasted a few days.

The origins of the tensions between the Unguja and Pemba islanders can be traced back to when they were both ruled by the sultan of Oman. The sultan was more repressive to the Unguja islanders, who were mainly slaves and clove pickers, than to the Pemba islanders. Some people of Unguja accuse the Pemba islanders of pretending to be Arab and of only employing people from Pemba.

Ever since the 1964 union, the autonomous government of Zanzibar has supported unity with the mainland. That said, the Zanzibari authorities have been keen to retain as much autonomy as possible within the union. They have no intention of giving up their own parliament or president, and they continue to operate special Islamic courts, called *kadhi,* in which cases concerning family and related matters are heard. In external relations, they have acted independently too, most notably by trying to join the Organization of the Islamic Conference (OIC), a pro-Muslim intergovernmental organization whose other members are sovereign states. That bid failed, however, after a Tanzanian parliamentary commission deemed it unconstitutional and membership was withdrawn in August 1993.

Despite strong kinship ties between the Zanzibaris and mainlanders, there are strong resentments, too. The mainlanders complain that Zanzibar is over-represented in the Tanzanian administration, which is based in the city of Dodoma. Zanzibaris counter that they are a sovereign state and are entitled to equal representation. They also have strong reservations about the way that the 1964 union was imposed on them—through a

gentleman's agreement between the presidents of Tanganyika and Zanzibar. Neither a unitary state nor a federation or confederation, it remains unclear what the precise legal status of Tanzania is. Amid this uncertainty, calls for constitutional reform continue to grow louder.

History

Zanzibar began forging its unique blend of Afro-Arab identity in the seventh century when it emerged as the main center of Arab trade on the East African coast. It gradually fell under the control of the sultan of Oman, leading to Arab domination of trade and politics, although the Arabs remained a minority of the overall population. In 1832 Sultan Seyyid Said of Oman transferred his capital from Muscat to Zanzibar and established a permanent physical presence there. The Omani sultans placed Arabs in positions of authority over the black African majority. Omani influence began to wane in 1890, however, when the British arrived and quickly seized control of political life, turning Zanzibar into a British protectorate while leaving the sultan as the titular head of state. A Zanzibari parliament was formed in 1926. After World War II, two new political parties, each with a strong nationalist ethos, were formed: the Arab-dominated Zanzibar Nationalist Party (ZNP) in 1955 and the African-dominated Afro-Shirazi Party (ASP) in 1957. British gerrymandering of electoral constituencies left the ZNP in a dominant position in the parliament.

The wave of decolonization sweeping through Africa in the 1950s and 1960s touched Zanzibar, too, and on December 19, 1963, it was granted independence. An Arab-dominated government was installed under Sultan Seyyid Jamshid bin Abdullah bin Khalifa. However, independence proved short-lived. African Zanzibaris joined with opposition Arab Zanzibari leaders to overthrow the ZNP government on January 12, 1964, in a revolution in which thousands, mostly Arabs, were killed and many more fled, including the sultan, who went into exile. The ASP's Sheikh Abeid Amani Karume was installed as president.

On April 26, 1964, Karume entered into an agreement with the president of Tanganyika, Julius Nyerere, to unify their countries and form a new state, to be called Tanzania. On July 1, 1964, foreign embassies in Zanzibar were downgraded to consulates, and in September 1965 a popular vote on the islands and mainland endorsed the union. The mainland had been colonized by Germany in 1884 but was administered by Britain from 1919, when Germany lost its colonies after being defeated in World War I. The British governed under a League of Nations and later, United Nations, mandate until Tanganyika became independent on December 9, 1961.

Karume, who stayed on as president of Zanzibar after the union, was assassinated in April 1972 and succeeded by Aboud Jumbe. In 1979 a new Zanzibari constitution was introduced that provided for a House of Representatives with law-making powers and direct election of the president. Secessionist agitation bubbled up in 1984 and forced the resignation on January 27 of President Jumbe, who had begun to draft a Zanzibari constitution with a national flag and currency. As the 1990s progressed the union looked increasingly fragile, especially after October 1999 when Tanzania's founding father, Nyerere, died. Nyerere had been a widely respected, charismatic figure who had helped to keep the country unified. Both the 2000 and 2005 elections in Zanzibar were marred by violent clashes between the Zanzibari authorities, who were broadly pro-union, and the more separatist-leaning opposition. Dozens of people were killed and hundreds injured.

The appetite for constitutional reform continued to grow. A fact-finding mission sent to Zanzibar in 2003 by the East Africa Centre for Constitutional Development, a Uganda-based non-governmental organization (NGO) that promotes constitution-making and democratic governance, concluded that "according to the vast majority of views heard by the mission, while Zanzibaris definitely want a union and accept the original articles as the legal basis for the union, they are dissatisfied with several aspects of its current operation." The report, entitled "Constitutionalism and Political Stability in Zanzibar: The Search for a New Vision," also found that there was "a widespread conviction that Zanzibar is a state."

Leadership

After Zanzibar merged with Tanganyika in 1964, the separatist forces effectively lost their political voice because the only two political parties allowed to compete in the elections were both pro-union. These were the African-dominated ASP in Zanzibar and TANU, the dominant party on the mainland. These two parties merged in 1977 to form the Revolutionary Party of Tanzania (CCM). A political opposition emerged in the early 1990s when the president of Tanzania, Ali Hassan Mwinyi—the former president of Zanzibar—allowed other parties to form. The Civic United Front (CUF) established itself in 1992 and became the dominant group advocating greater autonomy for Zanzibar, although it did not call for outright secession. The CUF is a Tanzania-wide party but attracts most of its support from Zanzibar and has its stronghold in Pemba.

The CUF participated in the first multi-party elections in Zanzibar in 1995 and in the two subsequent elections of 2000 and 2005. It won seats in parliament on each occasion, but not enough to form the government. Indeed, the CUF has grown increasingly frustrated with the political system and consistently alleges that the ruling CCM party rigs the elections. There have been signs that the CUF is becoming more pro-independence in its ideology. In August 2008, the CUF Secretary General, Seif Sharif Hamad, said the 1964 union was "just like a coat, which you can put on and take off according to the weather." According to Hamad, when Presidents Karume and Nyerere merged the two countries together, they did not have a detailed vision for the new state and that they acted "without the input of other leaders."

The CUF's nemesis in resisting Zanzibari separatism has historically been the CCM. The latter has been accused of exploiting differences between Pemba and Unguja in order to weaken the campaign for a unified, independent Zanzibar. For its part, the CUF has been accused of exaggerating the differences between Pemba and Unguja, although the goal in its case is to maintain its strength in Pemba. There have been efforts to improve relations between the CCM and CUF. Two agreements, called *Muafaka*, were signed in 1999 and 2001 aimed at easing tensions following electoral violence, but they failed to resolve the underlying conflict. In January 2007, the CCM and CUF started talks aimed at formulating a power-sharing agreement, but these talks broke down in April 2008.

Current Status

The archipelago continues to operate as a largely self-governing entity within Tanzania. Under an agreement from the early 1990s, Zanzibar, whose population is about 3 percent that of mainland Tanzania, receives 4.5 percent of the revenue collected by the Tanzanian government. Zanzibar continues to have its own president, Amani Abeid Karume from the CCM, which is the dominant party throughout Tanzania. Karume's father was the revolutionary leader who, along with President Nyerere, brought about the 1964 union.

There is strong support among Zanzibaris for a reform of the constitutional setup. Some have suggested that there should be three governments: regional authorities for both Tanganyika (the mainland) and Zanzibar plus a federal-type

administration, Tanzania, made up of representatives of both the mainland and the islands. Currently, the country has just two governments: Tanzania and Zanzibar. But pro-union forces are resistant, fearing that a three-government framework would ultimately lead to the secession of Zanzibar. The CUF continues to call for Zanzibar to become a member of the intergovernmental Islamic association, the OIC. But the prime minister of Zanzibar, Mizengo Pinda, a member of the CCM, has rejected such as idea, insisting that Zanzibar is not a sovereign state and that such a move would breach the 1964 union agreement.

In addition to the political divisions, relations between the mainland and island have grown increasingly fraught for economic reasons. This is due in large part to the strong possibility that large quantities of oil will soon be identified off the Zanzibari coast. Zanzibar's minister for natural resources, Mansour Yossuf Himid, caused a stir in July 2008 when he announced that his government did not intend to share with the mainland future revenues it might earn from oil extracted from Zanzibari waters. The oil issue could well end up forging unity among the deeply fractured political leadership in Zanzibar, as both parties are keen to secure Zanzibar's right to issue licenses for oil exploration and to manage any resulting revenues. The Tanzanian government on the mainland is countering that it should be in charge of regulating oil exploration because it has sovereignty over the waters surrounding Zanzibar. This is something of a grey area legally because the 1964 articles of union did not specifically address the issue. Prior to the emergence of oil as a potential source of revenue, Zanzibar's prospects for going it alone seemed not at all promising as its main industry, cloves, had been collapsing and it remains heavily dependent on mainland Tanzania for its electricity supply.

In Pemba, which is the more pro-independence–leaning of the two islands, the Elders of Pemba (Wazee wa Pemba) in 2008 called for the formation of a separate authority for Pemba Island. According to an April 2009 report from the Legal and Human Rights Center, a Tanzanian NGO, "they were arrested and interrogated and some government officials started to suggest that they be prosecuted for treason." The organization alleges that the right to freedom of association is being hampered in Pemba due to the requirement that all NGOs be registered in the Zanzibar town on Unguja Island where the Zanzibari government and parliament is based. The report also notes that an organization calling itself the National Reconstruction Alliance held a demonstration in 2008 in support of an independent Zanzibar. In a May 2008 report, Global Insight, a company that provides financial, economic and political analysis, warned there was a danger that Pemba would try to secede from Zanzibar. The report compared the situation to the efforts of secessionists in Anjouan, south of Zanzibar, who tried to split from the Comoro Islands, another archipelago on the Indian Ocean (see separate essay).

Further Reading

Burgess, Thomas. *Race, Revolution, and the Struggle for Human Rights in Zanzibar: The Memoirs of Ali Sultan Issa and Seif Sharif Hamad.* Athens: Ohio University Press, 2009.

Center for International Development and Conflict Management—Minorities at Risk Project, "Assessment for Zanzibaris in Tanzania," University of Maryland, www.cidcm.umd.edu/mar/assessment.asp?groupId=51001 (accessed May 2009).

Legal and Human Rights Center, "Tanzania Human Rights Report 2008: Progress through Human Rights," Dar-es-Salaam, 2009, http://alpha.web2-netshine-hosting.co.uk/~lhrc/index.php?option=com_docman&task=cat_view&gid=28&Itemid=56. (See pages 175–223 for Zanzibar.)

Nassali, Maria, and Joseph Oloka-Onyango. "Constitutionalism and Political Stability in Zanzibar: The Search for a New Vision," The Friedrich Ebert Stiftung, Kampala, 2003, http://library.fes.de/pdf-files/bueros/tanzania/02112.pdf.

Said, Salma. "Seif Fans Flames of Union Debate," *The Citizen*, August 31, 2008. http://hakinaumma.wordpress.com/2008/09/11/maalim-fans-flame-on-union.

Selassie, Gus. "Opposition Blames Zanzibar President for Breakdown of Reconciliation Talks, Threatens to Impeach Him," *Global Insight*, May 27, 2008.

Americas

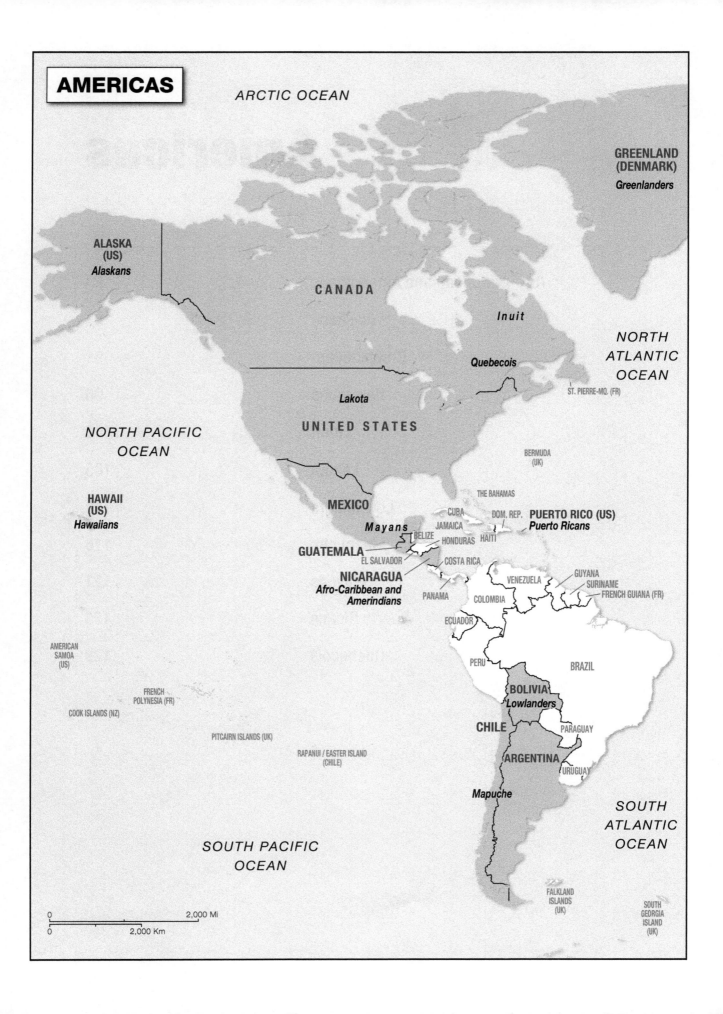

AFRO-CARIBBEAN AND AMERINDIANS
(Nicaragua)

The Afro-Caribbean and Amerindian people living along the Atlantic coast of Nicaragua have, since 1894, been campaigning for greater autonomy. Their core demands are a genuine devolution of political power to their region, secure land ownership rights, and the right to promote their culture and educate themselves in their own languages rather than Spanish. Their distinctness from Pacific coast Nicaraguans is a consequence of divergent histories and ethnic origins plus a geographical separation, by a mountain range, from the Pacific coast.

Self-governing for centuries until Nicaragua annexed them in the late 1800s, the Atlantic coast people saw autonomy restored in the 1980s when two regions, Atlantico Norte (north) and Atlantico Sur (south), were created. The north is populated predominantly by Amerindian peoples, the south by Afro-Caribbean. Most people would be satisfied with genuine autonomy. However, in April 2009 a fringe movement emerged calling itself the Council of Elders of the Miskito People and held an assembly at which it declared independence for the Atlantic coast. Historically, the

Nicaraguan government, which is based in Managua on the Pacific side, has been dominated by Spanish-speaking Pacific Ladinos who are a mix of whites and Amerindians.

The Amerindian and Afro-Caribbean Atlantic coast population accounts for about 20 percent of Nicaragua's six million inhabitants. Among the Amerindians, the numerically and politically dominant group is the Miskito, whose language is still widely spoken and written. The Miskito are predominantly Protestant and have been strongly influenced by the Moravian Church, whose missionaries first arrived in 1849 from England, Germany, and Sweden, and whose pastors are key community leaders. The other two main Amerindian groups are the Rama and Mayagna. The Afro-Caribbean people speak English or English-based Creole. They are the descendents of slaves of African ancestry brought over by the British from nearby Caribbean islands, such as Jamaica and Saint Lucia, in the eighteenth and nineteenth centuries.

According to Reverend Norman Bent, an Atlantic coast native and Moravian Church preacher, the relationships between Afro-Caribbean and Amerindian communities are generally good and intermarriage between the communities is common. By contrast, there is long-standing mistrust between these two groups and the Ladinos. One element distinguishing Pacific and Atlantic coast Nicaraguans, Bent noted, was that ecumenicalism—the movement to unite diverse Christian denominations—was markedly stronger among Atlantic coast communities.

The Atlantic autonomy movement has been mostly peaceful in recent years, although in previous decades violence had occasionally erupted. The communities' main grievances include a perceived failure on the part of the government to help the Atlantic region recover from the severe damage it suffered during Hurricane Felix in 2007. There is also resentment over the heavy presence of the Nicaraguan army—there primarily to clamp down on drug-trafficking—as it is dominated by Ladinos. And the Atlantic coast people have concerns about a government plan to build a corridor of pipelines, railways, and highways across their territory to the Pacific, fearing it will threaten their environment and undermine their land ownership rights.

History

The Atlantic-Pacific cultural divide has its origins in the Spanish conquistadors' decision in the early 1500s to settle the Pacific rather than Atlantic coast. In 1687 the English, arriving from their nearby colony in Jamaica, established a settlement along the Atlantic coast of modern-day Nicaragua. The indigenous Miskito entered into an alliance with the English, who allowed them to exist as an autonomous kingdom that was gradually expanded southward. When Nicaragua gained independence from Spain in the 1820s, the Atlantic coast was still an autonomous British protectorate and was ceded in 1860 only on condition that it would remain self-governing. Centuries of self-rule ended in 1894, however, when Nicaraguan troops occupied and annexed the region, prompting Miskito and Creole resistance, which the government, helped by the United States and the United Kingdom, repressed.

The Nicaraguan government extended its economic grip over the Atlantic coast in the 1950s and 1960s during the dictatorial rule of the Somoza dynasty by developing large industries such as forestry and fishing. Some indigenous people supported the Somoza regime as they gained employment in these industries. However, by the late twentieth century concerns had grown over the rapid growth in Ladino migration to the Atlantic, which was putting increasing strain on the environment and urban infrastructure.

A new threat emerged in 1979 when the Marxist Sandinista guerrillas came to power. The Sandinistas launched Spanish literacy programs along the Atlantic coast and nationalized untitled lands. They threatened to undermine Moravian Church community leaders, believing—according to Reverend Bent—they were CIA agents because of the church's links to the United States. The United States was vehemently anti-Sandinista. By the early 1980s disaffected Amerindian militants were launching attacks from neighboring Honduras and Costa Rica. In the ensuing Sandinista clampdown, some twenty thousand indigenous Nicaraguans fled the country. The Sandinistas, to gain support from the locals, then changed policy by successfully pursuing peace talks and agreeing to introduce autonomy to the Atlantic coast. By the late 1980s Amerindian refugees were returning and regional parliaments had been set up. However, some Atlantic coast residents grew frustrated with the slow pace of the autonomy process.

Leadership

The establishment in 1985 of two regional governments, RAAN in the north and RAAS in the south, each with its own governor and forty-five-member legislature, has provided a legal framework for Atlantic coast autonomy. In theory, RAAN and RAAS jointly govern with the Managua-based central government the Atlantic region's economic, cultural, and environmental affairs.

Regionally based political parties also exist. The strongest Amerindian party is the Miskito-dominated Yatama, which wants to strengthen communal land claims and promote indigenous culture. However, Yatama is not in favor of an independent Atlantic coast state. Yatama was previously incarnated as the Alliance for the Progress of Miskitos and Sumus, established in 1974 by Steadman Fagoth and Brooklyn Rivera. In 1979 it changed its name to Misurasata. Smaller indigenous parties include Misatán, a pro-Sandinista movement led by Rufino Lucas Wilfred; the Multiethnic Indigenous Party, led by Carla White Hodgson; and the right-wing Coastal Democratic Alliance, led by RAAS coordinator Alvin Guthrie.

There is no specific political party that represents the Afro-Caribbean community. Many support and are members of the Sandinista party, the FSLN. Many Afro-Caribbean people also support the transnational Black People's Movement, which campaigns for better representation of blacks in governments across Latin America and is especially strong in Brazil, Honduras, and Nicaragua. The Atlantic coast communities are also reasonably well represented in the central government in Managua. Several Atlantic coast Amerindians and Creoles serve as government deputy ministers, and they have several representatives in the ninety-two-member legislature.

Current Status

The April 2009 independence declaration was made by a group fronted by a local Pentecostal pastor, Hector Williams. Widely dismissed as fringe extremists, they garnered support from Miskito lobster drivers protesting over a drop in their wages, according to a *New York Times* report. They were only lightly armed and Yatama, the ruling regional party, quickly responded by retaking control of the building they occupied. A top Sandinista leader accused the U.S. ambassador to Nicaragua of encouraging the movement, but the ambassador denied this. According to Reverend Bent, who met with the leaders, "they say independence would be the best thing but do not understand what that means. Really, they are just frustrated with the slow pace of the autonomy process."

Unlike many former leaders, Daniel Ortega, a Pacific coast Ladino reelected president for the Sandinistas in November 2006 (the Sandinistas were out of power from 1990–2006), supports the autonomy process, and the country is moving in that direction. There have been advances in cultural rights, for example, with two indigenous universities set up, including one with English-language classes. While the Atlantic communities mostly own the land on which they live, the government has strengthened ownership rights by passing a law that reserves 40 percent of Atlantic coast lands for indigenous communities. Despite this, a February 2009 U.S. State Department human rights report noted that President Ortega was accused in 2008 of ordering the police to ignore court orders to evict migrants from the Pacific coast who had invaded indigenous lands. The land is used mostly for agriculture, notably grain cultivation, although there are forests, and this has caused divisions among Atlantic coast residents over whether these should be exploited commercially. The Nicaraguan government was notably one of the four countries to recognize the independence of Georgia's breakaway republics, Abkhazia and South Ossetia, following the August 2008 Russia-Georgia war (see separate essays).

The emergence of a more democratic and decentralized system of government has helped to improve inter-community relations, as has the lack of serious armed conflict in neighboring countries. While tensions persist, large-scale conflict or secession looks unlikely.

Further Reading

Lacey, Marc, and Blake Schmidt. "List of Grievances Grows into Independence Claim," *New York Times*, June 10, 2009, www.nytimes.com/2009/06/10/world/americas/10nicaragua.html.

Minority Rights Group International. "World Directory of Minorities and Indigenous Peoples—Nicaragua," 2008, www.minorityrights.org/?lid=2579 (accessed August 2009).

University of Maryland Center for International Development and Conflict Management. "Minorities at Risk—Assessment for Indigenous Peoples in Nicaragua," 2006, www.cidcm.umd.edu/mar/assessment.asp?groupId=9302 (accessed August 2009).

U.S. State Department. "Human Rights Report 2008—Nicaragua," February 25, 2009, http://paei.state.gov/g/drl/rls/hrrpt/2008/.

ALASKANS
(United States)

Separatist sentiment in the United States' state of Alaska has been considerably stronger than in most other U.S. states since Alaska gained statehood in 1959. Alaska's wealth of natural resources, including oil and gas, and Alaskan residents' desire to exert control over those resources, is a major contributor to this sentiment. U.S. government restrictions on resource development have caused widespread resentment that in some instances has spilled over into secessionism, although it has not so far been accompanied by violence.

Alaska is separated geographically from the rest of the United States, situated in the remote Arctic regions where the sun never sets in summer and never rises in winter. It is the largest U.S. state and its most sparsely inhabited, with a population of about 700,000. The state has the highest proportion of residents who have native ancestry in the country: 20 percent, compared to the U.S. average of 1.5 percent. Alaska Natives are a diverse mix of Inuit—both Inupiat (40,000) and Yupik (15,000)—Aleut, and Athabascan Indian, whose languages are not always mutually intelligible. The U.S. government initially classified Alaska Natives in the same category with American Indians when compiling the census. Beginning in 1940 they were counted separately. In the 2000 and 2010 censuses, however, the government reverted to its original system of grouping Alaska Natives with American Indians.

Six Alaska Native communities have set up forms of local government authorized by the U.S. administration under which the tribe owns the land. An example of this is Arctic Village in northeastern Alaska where several hundred Gwich'in, an Athabascan people, live by fishing, hunting wild animals, and collecting berries. Other Natives have taken a different approach, establishing government-recognized village corporations to manage their resources. Natives enjoy special rights to hunt marine mammals, notably seals, walruses, and whales, for subsistence and small-scale trade.

Alaska Natives are a key support base within the autonomy movement. Victoria Hykes-Steere, an Inupiat Alaska Native advocate, said in an October 2009 telephone interview that she favored a model of self-government for Natives similar to what Greenlanders have with Denmark (see separate essay). "We do not want to cut our ties completely with the U.S. We just want to undo the damage done by colonization," she said. Lynette Clark, chair of the Alaskan Independence Party (AIP), who has

Cherokee Indian ancestry, claimed in an October 2009 telephone interview that Natives formed a majority of AIP members.

The AIP contests elections, usually attracting no more than 5 percent of the vote, although it has scored higher in past decades, the most impressive performance coming in 1990 when Walter Hickel (1919–2010) was elected governor of Alaska on an AIP ticket after winning 38.8 percent of the vote. As governor (1990–1994) Hickel disavowed secession, but he did file lawsuits to try to wrest control of Alaska's natural resources from the U.S. government—suits that ultimately failed. The AIP's supporters are divided on what Alaska's status should be: some want Alaska to become fully independent; others, including Clark, think becoming a commonwealth would be enough to secure control of the land and resources; still others want it to remain a U.S. state.

History

Natives had been living in Alaska for twenty thousand years before Europeans started arriving. Initially, European contact came in the form of Russian fur traders, but in 1784 Russian Orthodox Church missionaries established a permanent settlement. Alaska's borders were fixed in 1825 when an Anglo-Russian treaty was signed. Russia sold Alaska to the United States in 1867 for $7.2 million—a move Alaska Natives claim was illegal, as they insist Russia never had dominion over the territory in the first place. Under U.S. rule, Alaska's natural resources were increasingly exploited, with development focusing on the gold-mining, salmon, and reindeer industries.

In January 1959, Alaska was fully integrated into the United States after voters approved a constitution that paved the path to statehood. The AIP's Clark said this plebiscite was deeply flawed—even illegal—because many Alaska Natives were excluded from voting by a requirement that voters be able to read and write English. Moreover, forty

thousand U.S. military personnel and their families stationed in Alaska were allowed to vote by a special act of Congress, which skewed the vote in favor of statehood.

In 1971 the U.S. Congress passed the Alaska Native Claims Settlement Act under which the U.S. government gave Alaska Natives forty-four million acres of land and $962.5 million. Clark maintained that this act was designed to encourage Alaska Natives to "sell out" to the white people. Despite this, she admitted that some successful Native-run corporations have sprung up, such as Doyon, which owns and manages vast oil and gas fields.

In 1993 the Alaskan independence movement suffered a blow when the AIP's charismatic founding father, Joe Vogler, was murdered (see biography). Vogler was buried in Canada's Yukon Territory in observance of his wish not to be buried on U.S. soil. A fellow secessionist, Manfred West, was later convicted of the killing. Vogler, a high-profile figure who was largely responsible for the growth of the AIP's membership to twenty thousand, threatened armed insurrection against the United States. As reported in an October 2008 article in *The Toronto Star*, Vogler once said, "I hope we don't have to take human life but if they go on trampling on our property rights, look out, we're ready to die."

Leadership

The AIP is the dominant separatist voice in Alaska. It has a libertarian, anti-government ethos and has, since the 1980s, consistently fielded candidates in statewide and U.S. elections. Its membership fell in the late 1990s and early 2000s, but party chair Clark said she has pushed it back up from eleven to fourteen thousand. One of the AIP's primary goals is to rerun the 1958 referendum, this time with four options on the ballot instead of two: (1) remaining a state; (2) becoming a commonwealth; (3) becoming a territory; or (4) becoming independent. The AIP has elaborated policies

Joseph Vogler (1913–1993)

JOSEPH VOGLER was born in Barnes, Kansas, where he was raised on a farm, as one of five children. He attended the University of Kansas on a scholarship at the age of sixteen and graduated with a law degree in five years. At twenty-one he was admitted to the Kansas State Bar.

In 1945 Vogler moved to Alaska, his reputation in Kansas diminished by his unpopular political views, including his harsh criticism of President Franklin D. Roosevelt. After a year in Kodiak, he moved to Fairbanks and began working for the U.S. Army Corps of Engineers at Ladd Air Field. He worked there until 1951, after which he began a mining operation. Although he owned some four hundred acres of property, he did not farm, preferring to work as a miner and developer. Vogler was often at odds with U.S. officials over access to his gold claims, which lay on federally managed lands—a not uncommon complaint among Alaskan miners.

While in Fairbanks, he earned a reputation for feuding with Alaskan businessman Paul Greimann Sr. over a traffic stand-off on the Cushman Street Bridge—the men were in separate vehicles going in opposing directions when the altercation caused a traffic jam. He also threatened to give the mayor of Fairbanks two black eyes, saying, "Get ready to look at this town for the last time, because I'm going to close your left eye with one fist and your right eye with the other."

Though his rhetoric often included violent imagery, his politics were surprisingly non-violent. His political views included an idolization of Thomas Jefferson and a belief that the federal government had long overstepped constitutional boundaries. He maintained that the federal government had no claim to property outside the original thirteen states, aside from "forts, arsenals, dockyards and other needful government uses." He used a pocket-sized Constitution as his calling card.

The 1970s saw Vogler rise to prominence on the Alaskan political scene. In 1973 he began a petition calling for Alaska to secede from the Union, and he claimed to have garnered over twenty-five thousand signatures in just three weeks.

Vogler founded both the Alaskan Independence Party (AIP) and Alaskans for Independence (AFI) in the 1970s. The AIP focused on the legality of the 1958 vote for Alaskan statehood while the AFI pursued secession for Alaska. The AIP, always more popular and exhibiting better staying power, became Vogler's dominant vehicle for his separatist ideals. In 1984 the AIP was officially recognized as a political party by the Alaskan government.

Vogler ran for governor of Alaska in 1974, 1982, and again in 1986. His 1986 running mate was former Alaska state trooper Al Rowe. The AIP received 5.1 percent of the vote, acting as a spoiler for the two main parties. Vogler's bold, anti-federal government views turned him into a larger-than-life Alaskan folk hero, known for colorful speeches and memorable turns-of-phrase.

Vogler married twice. He had two children by his first wife, though he was estranged from them. He married his second wife, Doris, in the 1960s, and they stayed together until her death from cancer in the 1990s.

Vogler vanished in May 1993 at the age of eighty, just a few weeks before he was scheduled to give a speech on Alaskan independence to the United Nations. Manfred West, a convicted thief, confessed in the summer of 1993 to having murdered Vogler during an illegal sale of plastic explosives. He wrapped the body in a tarp and buried Vogler in a gravel pit. Vogler's remains were found on October 15, 1994. He was buried in Canada in observance of his oft-stated wish not to be buried under the American flag.

The AIP endures as Alaska's third largest political party and the oldest active third party in the United States.

---

on a wide range of sovereignty-related issues. It has even formulated rebuttals to Alaskans who fear the negative fallout from giving up statehood. Were Alaska to become independent, the party maintains, it could achieve a solid financial underpinning by fully developing its oil and gas industry unfettered by U.S. government limitations. It favors retention of a U.S. military presence, however, given the state's strategically sensitive location with Russia's coastline just across the

Bering Strait. The AIP supports home-schooling, the right of individuals to keep and bear arms, the abolition of property taxes, an extension of mining operations, and an end to a U.S. ban on the exportation of Alaskan oil to foreign countries.

There is another sovereignty movement with a narrower agenda: The Second Amendment Task Force. It is trying to strengthen gun ownership rights. Alaska Native leadership is dispersed among various community-based groups seeking greater autonomy, with various models advocated.

Current Status

The U.S. spotlight shone on Alaskan separatism in August 2008 when Alaska governor Sarah Palin became the running mate of the Republican Party's presidential candidate, Sen. John McCain. Palin's husband, Todd, who is one eighth Yupik, had been an AIP member for seven years, and Palin herself had sent a video message to the party saying "keep up the good work." As governor, Palin supported Alaska Native efforts to allow oil exploration in the Arctic National Wildlife Refuge, a huge chunk of Alaskan land that the U.S. government has kept out of bounds for commercial development. Palin resigned as governor unexpectedly in July 2009.

Control of the land remains a pivotal issue in the sovereignty debate in Alaska. The vast majority of Alaskan territory is owned by the U.S. or Alaskan governments, and this continues to be the source of great resentment. "My husband and I were fined $50,000 in the 1980s for setting up a 660-x-1330-ft gold mine—all because the authorities said we were polluting the U.S. in breach of the Clean Water Act," Clark noted by way of example. The AIP is demanding that the government return the Alaskan lands to Alaskans and no longer refuse locals permission to cross U.S. government–owned areas. The state produces large quantities of oil today, keeping 12 percent of the revenues. Sovereignty activist Vicki Hykes Steere, who is Inupiat, said the state's licensing regulations for hunting animals should be changed to favor rural hunters, who tend to be Alaska Natives.

In May 2009, the Alaska legislature adopted a sovereignty resolution similar to the one passed by several state legislatures across the United States. The AIP's Clark predicted that the resolution would catch on across the country as more and more Americans rebelled against the federal government's intrusions into their lives. Hykes-Steere said the time had come to "reinvent colonization in a way that benefits the Natives for a change." However, given the current political and constitutional setup in the United States, it is unlikely that the resolution will lead to special autonomous status for Alaska within the next five years.

Further Reading

Alaskan Independence Party Web site, www.akip.org.
Cole, Terence. *North to the Future.* Kenmore: Epicenter Press, 2008.
Lee, Jeannette. "Alaska Natives Mixed on Palin," *National Journal,* September 20, 2008.
Talbot, David. "Where's the uproar on Palin links to anti-U.S. group?" *The Toronto Star,* October 9, 2009, www.thestar.com/News/USElection/article/514503.

GREENLANDERS
(Denmark)

The people of Greenland—which, at more than three times the size of Texas, is the largest island in the world—have achieved a large degree of political autonomy since 1979. They remain a part of Denmark, but given the current political situation it is very possible they will achieve independence in the coming years.

The island, situated in the Arctic Ocean and known as Kalaallit Nunaat in Greenlandic, is one of the most sparsely populated places in the world, with 56,000 inhabitants. The island's population accounts for just 1 percent of Denmark's total population. About 51,000, or 88 percent, are Inuit, an Arctic people formerly known as Eskimos. Some 7,000, or 12 percent, are of Danish origin. They have a regional government in the town of Nuuk, formerly known by its Danish name Godthab, where about a quarter of the islanders live. Nuuk is located on the more populated, western side of the island. Greenlanders' head of state is the Danish Queen, Margrethe II, who is represented by an appointed high commissioner, a position currently filled by Soren Hald Moller.

Greenlanders speak Greenlandic, an Inuit language closely related to the language spoken by Inuit peoples in Canada, the United States, and Siberia. There are three Greenlandic dialects, which are spoken in the west (Kalaalliit), north (Inughuit), and east (Lit) of the island. Unlike many other indigenous languages, which are under threat of extinction, Greenlandic is not in danger of dying out and is the dominant language in schools, homes, the media, and the church. Danish still prevails in administration, however, and most residents also speak Danish. Due to the vast distances involved and difficult terrain, there is no network of roads connecting Greenland's towns. Instead, air and sea are the principal forms of town-to-town transportation. Greenlanders are overwhelmingly Christian, having been converted by the Evangelical Lutheran Church of Denmark from the eighteenth century. They use the Danish Krone as their currency. The average temperature in the warmest month does not exceed ten degrees Celsius.

The Greenlandic autonomy movement is largely an effort to decolonize the country after three centuries of Danish influence. It is notable for being both remarkably successful and non-violent. Greenland's premier, Kuupik Kleist, said in June 2009 at a celebratory event commemorating the introduction of enhanced autonomy: "It has cost great suffering for many societies to achieve recognition, but our self-governance has been earned through negotiation, mutual understanding, and mutual respect." At the same event, the head of the Greenlandic parliament, Josef Motzfeldt, said that self-government was "a symbol of the dreams of the Greenlandic people." He added that "we have achieved the right of control of our subsoil, and we expect in the years to come that this will be a supplement to lay the foundation for an economically independent Greenland."

Motzfeldt was referring to the fact that the new self-government framework, which Greenlanders approved in a November 2008 referendum, grants them the exclusive right to decide how their natural resources can be exploited. The Greenland Home Rule government, which was first established in 1979, had previously shared control over natural resources with the Danish government. The change is significant because Greenland is thought to possess large quantities of oil and gas offshore. The Greenland government in 2004 began awarding offshore exploration and exploitation licenses to oil companies. Drilling is expected to begin off the western coast in 2011. Onshore oil exploration has not begun yet. Onshore reserves are more difficult to access because over four-fifths of the land is covered by up to three kilometers of ice, most of which is frozen year round.

An abundance of accessible oil and gas would make an independent Greenland a more economically viable prospect. At present, Greenlanders rely heavily on subsidies from the Danish government, which are worth about $700 million a year, or over $10,000 per inhabitant. Greenland has other mineral resources, too, with gold, olivine, zinc, and lead already exploited, while rubies, diamonds, iron, and other minerals may be exploited in the future.

Fishing is the backbone of the economy and accounts for 95 percent of exports. Most of the fish exports go to Denmark; other key markets include Germany, Japan, Norway, Thailand, the United Kingdom, and the United States. Cold-water prawn is Greenland's single biggest export, followed by halibut, crab, and cod. Global warming is meanwhile enabling Greenlanders to grow more food as warmer temperatures permit market gardening in the south, including the cultivation of turnips, broccoli, cauliflower, lettuce, and strawberries. However, one of global warming's negative consequences has been dramatic: melting ice caps in the north are shortening the winter hunting season as hunting requires hard ice for dog sleds. Greenlanders are allowed to hunt seals—about 170,000 are killed each year—walruses, and whales for local trading. Those whose primary occupation is hunting are also permitted to hunt polar bears.

History

The inhabitants of Greenland are descended from nomadic hunters of land mammals who first arrived 4,500 years ago, crossing from Canada via the Davis Strait. Waves of Inuit migration from North America to Greenland occurred sporadically, with the most recent wave taking place around 1870. European settlement did not begin until 985 C.E., when Icelandic Vikings arrived during a period of climate warming. The Vikings stayed until about 1450 and left, it is widely believed, because the climate cooled down again. The Europeans returned in the 1600s to hunt whale, ultimately decimating the stocks as a result of over-hunting.

Danish colonization began in 1721 when a Danish-Norwegian priest, Hans Egede, settled in Greenland and introduced Christianity. Trade links were cemented in 1776 after the Danish government established the Royal Greenland Trade Company, which marked the beginning of a trade monopoly that would last until 1950. A Danish naval officer, R. R. J. Hammer, mapped out many of Greenland's glaciers and fjords in expeditions in 1879, 1880, and 1883. Sheep farming was introduced in 1906 and commercial fishing in 1908, the same year that

Greenland's first local elections took place. Danish sovereignty over northeastern Greenland was contested by Norway in the 1930s; the International Court of Justice (ICJ) ruled in 1933 that the whole island belonged to Denmark. Greenlanders supported the Danish government in this dispute because they did not want the island partitioned.

During World War II Greenlanders lost contact with the Danes after Denmark was invaded and occupied by Nazi Germany. The Danish authorities invited the United States to protect Greenland in the event that the Nazis invaded the island. While there was no major Nazi invasion, the request had lasting consequences because the United States used Greenland as a hub for its bombers during the war and in the early 1950s built a permanent U.S. Air Force base in Thule on the northwestern Greenlandic coast. The U.S. presence has caused some local resentment over the years. There was, for example, anger over the forcible removal in 1953 of a group of Inuit to make way for the base, an episode the Danish government apologized for in 1999. Another controversy developed as a result of a crash in 1968 of a U.S. B-52 bomber near Thule after it emerged that the plane had been carrying nuclear weapons, even though Denmark had officially banned nuclear weapons from its territory. A Danish parliamentary investigation revealed in 1995 that the United States had in fact notified the Danish government of the weapons in 1957. An agreement was signed in 2003 between the Greenlandic, Danish, and U.S. authorities under which the United States was granted permission to upgrade a radar station it had installed at Thule on condition it consulted with the Greenlandic authorities.

Greenland's colonial status officially ended in 1953 when it became fully integrated into Denmark. The Inuit were encouraged to move to the western coastal towns at this time. In 1979 home rule was introduced following a referendum. Greenlanders were given a parliament, or *landsting*, while continuing to send two members to the Danish parliament. In 1985 Greenland left the European Economic Community (EEC), the precursor of today's European Union (EU), following a referendum. The island had entered the EEC automatically in 1973 when Denmark joined, despite the objections of most Greenlanders at the time. The decision to leave stemmed from Greenlanders' desire not to be confined by EEC fishing quotas. Greenland renegotiated its relationship with the EU in 2006, granting permission to some EU fishing vessels to fish in Greenlandic waters in return for the EU's providing $30 million (€25M) in subsidies, notably intended to raise education standards.

Leadership

Greenland has its own political party system, one that is quite distinct from the rest of Denmark. The party platforms are distinguishable in part by where they stand on the issue of greater autonomy. One party, Inuit Ataqatigiit (IA), which means "Inuit who stand together" in Greenlandic, would like the island to become an independent country. The IA emerged as the biggest party in the May 2009 Greenland elections, securing 43.7 percent of the vote and fourteen seats in the thirty-one-seat parliament. It is now the ruling party, having formed a coalition government with two smaller parties, Demokraatit and Kattusseqatigiit. The IA's victory was a milestone in Greenlandic politics because the home rule government had, since its inception thirty years earlier, been dominated by a party that sought greater autonomy within Denmark. This party, Siumut, meaning "forward," is led by Aleqa Hammond. In a further indication that pro-independence sentiment in Greenland is on the rise, the party that supports retaining close ties with Denmark, Atassut, came in fourth place in the elections, its support dropping to 10.9 percent.

Greenlanders do not have formal diplomatic representation in foreign countries; however, they are increasingly registering their presence on the global stage through various international forums.

For example, they are members of the Inuit Circumpolar Council (ICC), the body that represents the 160,000-strong Arctic Inuit community, of which Greenlanders make up about a third. The ICC in turn is a member of the Arctic Council, an intergovernmental body set up in 1996 whose mission is to bolster cooperation among Arctic states. The Arctic Council's member states are Canada, Denmark, Finland, Iceland, Norway, Russia, Sweden, and the United States (Alaska being in part an Arctic region).

The president of ICC Greenland, Aqqaluk Lynge, has argued that the Inuit could become a unifying force throughout the Arctic by helping to prevent and resolve disputes between governments who exert control over the Arctic's vast natural resources. "We can be the glue that stops this from disintegrating into a territorial fight," Lynge said in a 2008 interview for *CQ Global Researcher.* Lynge stressed that the Inuit have shared the Arctic's resources for thousands of years without resorting to conflict. In May 2008, Greenland's glacier town of Ilulissat was notably chosen as the venue for a meeting of ministers and senior officials from Arctic states to discuss how to improve cooperation on issues including territorial claims, transportation, fishing, and mineral exploitation rights.

Current Status

On November 25, 2008, Greenlanders entered a new era after 76 percent of voters approved a self-government framework to extend their autonomy. The Act on Greenland Self-Government recognizes Greenlanders as a distinct people under international law and provides a path to full independence. Danish prime minister Lars Lokke Rasmussen indicated in June 2009 at the ceremony inaugurating the new framework that his government would not stand in the way of Greenland cutting the cord completely. "The question of independence is not the issue today, but it is totally up to the Greenlandic people," he said.

The new framework was jointly devised by the Greenlandic and Danish parliaments and approved by both governments. The part dealing with natural resources stipulates that if oil revenue starts to flow, Greenlanders should pay back the subsidies they receive from the Danish government but should keep everything beyond that. The plan is for the subsidies, which provide 60 percent of the Greenland government's revenue, to be phased out as the island becomes economically self-sufficient.

Cited in a June 2009 *Washington Times* article, Greenlandic clothing designer Mette Krinstensen suggested that the new framework would mean that Greenlanders could no longer attribute present problems to their colonial past. "People will have to be responsible for their own situation now," she said, calling the island's colonial status "a crutch we've been relying on too long. If you're independent you have to solve your problems yourself." However, while Greenlanders have made great gains on the autonomy front, they still have many of the same social problems that tend to afflict indigenous peoples who have been colonized. These include high rates of alcoholism and drug abuse, high suicide and infant mortality rates, and an over-reliance on government subsidies.

Economically, the island is trying to diversify and become less reliant on fishing. Oil and gas, found predominantly on the west and east coasts, respectively, are seen as the key to future development, especially since foreign oil companies are increasingly looking to Greenland, given that oil production in the North Sea is on the decline. In November 2010, the Greenland government awarded licenses to explore and exploit oil and gas in the seas off Greenland's western coast to various companies, including ConocoPhillips, Shell, Statoil and Maersk Oil. Eco-tourism, specifically cruise ships from Europe, Asia, and the United States, is another growth industry that could help to make Greenland economically independent.

The United States has a stake in Greenland through its air base in Thule, the status of which was not called into question by the new self-government framework. Greenlandic premier Kleist has indicated that he is content with the status quo. "We've had a long relationship with the U.S., sometimes troublesome, but we've renewed our agreement between Denmark, the U.S., and Greenland, and it is a positive one," he said, as cited in a 2009 *Washington Times* article. Greenlanders have no independent military capacity and would thus more than likely be unable to fend off any unfriendly foreign incursion. The Danish government retains control over their foreign policy, and Denmark remains a staunch U.S. ally and member of the North Atlantic Treaty Organization defense pact. For these reasons, the U.S. base is likely to stay. The Danes, if anything, are expected to raise their military presence on the island, as they are embroiled in an ongoing dispute with Canada and Russia to gain sovereignty over the North Pole area. Denmark argues that this vast maritime territory is an extension of Greenland's continental shelf; Canada and Russia claim this potentially resource-rich area for themselves. A United Nations panel will ultimately decide.

Further Reading

Beary, Brian. "Race for the Arctic," *CQ Global Researcher* 2, no. 8 (August 2008). See sidebar on Greenland.

Fortson, Danny. "Oil giants zero in on untapped Greenland; The high price of crude and rising demand make exploration of the coastline viable," *The Sunday Times*, September 13, 2009, http://business.timesonline.co.uk/tol/business/industry_sectors/natural_resources/article6832247.ece.

Greenland Home Rule government Web site, http://uk.nanoq.gl.

Kucera, Joshua. "Danish island fueled for independence; Control of oil reserves could build up economy," *The Washington Times*, June 22, 2009, www.washingtontimes.com/news/2009/jun/22/danish-island-fueled-for-independence/print.

Woodard, Colin. "In Greenland, an Interfaith Rally for Climate Change," *Christian Science Monitor*, September 12, 2007, www.csmonitor.com/2007/0912/p06s01-woeu.html.

HAWAIIANS
(United States)

The 1.3 million people living on the archipelago of Hawaii have had a tense relationship with the United States ever since the U.S. government invaded and annexed Hawaii in the late 1800s. Awarded U.S. statehood in 1959, the likelihood of Hawaii seceding today is remote. However, there is much residual tension caused by the failure to install some type of self-government that would meet the aspirations of the Native Hawaiians. Given the manner in which the United States took control, Hawaiians—or Kanaka Maoli in their native language—have a solid legal case for such a framework. While the U.S. government seems open to accommodating their wish, there is disagreement among Hawaiians over what form autonomy should take.

There are three basic alternatives to the status quo under discussion: autonomy as part of the United States for all Hawaiians; independence for a narrowly defined subset of islanders deemed "Native Hawaiians"; or independence for all islanders. Mililani Trask, a longtime and leading pro-sovereignty activist, is adamant that all Hawaiians, not just a select minority, should be granted autonomy. "There has never been any definitive data to quantify how many Hawaiians

are so-called purebloods," she noted in a September 2009 telephone interview. Because of massive immigration and widespread intermarriage, not many Hawaiians are actually pure-blooded today, although about 400,000 claim Hawaiian ancestry, according to U.S. census figures. "Pureblood" in Hawaii was historically interpreted to mean at least 50 percent native.

The U.S. government tried to apply a pure-blood rule from the 1920s in order to limit the numbers applying for native homesteads under the 1921 Hawaiian Homes Commission Act, but it scrapped the policy when Hawaii became a U.S. state. About eight thousand such homesteads have been granted in total, mostly small residential plots in recent years; in the past, larger rural estates were awarded. Most U.S. and Hawaiian officials and lawmakers continue to favor going beyond this by installing self-government for Native Hawaiians, but no details have been fleshed out.

The islands were created by volcanic activity in the Pacific Ocean and are spread across fifteen hundred miles. While English is the dominant language, the Native Hawaiian language has undergone a major revival since the 1970s, after having being driven to near extinction. Noted Trask, "We teach Hawaiian at all schooling levels now. You can hear Hawaiian being spoken in homes and in shops."

Whereas many, if not most, separatist struggles around the world have had some element of violence, according to Trask Hawaiians are "fiercely proud" that their pursuit of sovereignty has been largely peaceful. Before being taken over by the United States, the islanders had a long history of building relations with foreign nations, having entered into "friendship" treaties with France, Japan, Russia, and Switzerland. Relations were especially well-developed with the United Kingdom, with Queen Victoria acting as godmother to the Hawaiian Crown Prince, Albert, and Britain raising formal objections when the United States overthrew the Hawaiian monarchy.

History

Western influence over Hawaiians began in 1778 when the British explorer Captain James Cook landed there. In 1840 Hawaiians adopted a new, Western-style constitution with a two-chamber legislature, and in 1848 they introduced the Western concept of land ownership and began giving out private plots of land. A defining moment in Hawaiian history came in 1893 when U.S. marines, supported by U.S. and European businessmen, invaded the islands, marched up to the royal palace, and forced Queen Liliuokalani to abdicate her throne. The United States formally annexed Hawaii in 1898 and moved quickly to pass laws that required that both business and government record-taking be done in English, precipitating a decline in the Hawaiian language.

Given its strategically significant location in the Pacific Ocean, the United States began installing major naval bases there, notably at Pearl Harbor, which Japan bombed in December 1941, causing the United States to enter World War II (1939–1945). When, in a 1959 referendum, Hawaiians were asked to choose between becoming a U.S. state or remaining a U.S. territory, 94 percent opted for statehood. Full independence was not included as an option on the ballot. While statehood was initially met with euphoria, discontent with government slowly grew, leading to the emergence of sovereignty movement by the 1970s.

A campaign to revive the Hawaiian language began, inspired by the model adopted by a fellow-Polynesian people, the Maori of New Zealand (see separate essay). In 1993 the United States formally apologized for the 1893 invasion in a resolution adopted by the U.S. Congress and signed by President Bill Clinton that acknowledged the "illegal overthrow" of the Hawaiian kingdom. The Hawaiian state government organized a referendum in 1996, with the electorate limited to eighty thousand Native Hawaiians, 73 percent of whom voted for sovereignty.

How to implement sovereignty has been a source of considerable division among the islanders. In 2006 pro–United States and pro-Hawaiian sovereignty advocates clashed at Iolani palace, the official residence of the last queen and the site where Hawaii's statehood was declared. A shouting match ensued, with those in support of the United States singing the U.S. national anthem, "The Star-Spangled Banner," and those in support of Hawaiian sovereignty trying to drown them out.

Leadership

Hawaii does not have a full-fledged pro-independence political party, nor does it have a single, strong unified organization that speaks for all pro-sovereignty advocates. Instead, it fields an array of movements and groups campaigning for sovereignty, autonomy, or self-determination that often have competing visions of how to achieve it. One of these, the Ka Lahui Hawaii (Sovereign Hawaiian Nation), was established in 1987 and maintains that independence should be one of a number of options from which Hawaiians are allowed to choose. Prominent member Mililani Trask said, "We are not separatists. We are for self-determination." Trask said she personally would not vote for independence, nor would most Hawaiians, because they depend heavily on U.S. financial aid. There are some two hundred thousand Hawaiians living on the U.S. mainland, and there remains some fear of being invaded.

Other sovereignty activists and groups include Puuohonua "Bumpy" Kanahele from the Nation of Hawaii organization; Henry Noa, whose Restored Hawaiian Kingdom group supports restoration of the monarchy; Ka Pakaukau; the Native Hawaiian Legal Corporation; and the Ohana Council. An important pro–Native Hawaiian organization is the Council for Native Hawaiian Advancement. Established in 2001 as a corporate nonprofit, the council acts as an umbrella body, representing the interests of 150 member organizations and agencies whose goal is to enhance the Native Hawaiian culture, economy, and community. The current president is Robin Danner. There is also the State of Hawaii's Office of Hawaiian Affairs, created in 1978 in order to represent the interests of Native Hawaiians in administering Native Hawaiian homesteads.

Current Status

In May 2009, U.S. senator for Hawaii, Daniel Akaka (D), introduced a bill to grant Native Hawaiians self-government. U.S. president Barack Obama, who, although born in Hawaii is not Native Hawaiian, spoke in favor of the legislation as it was being debated, indicating he would sign it if passed. Cited in a February 2010 article from the Fox News media organization, President Obama said, "Hawaii has always acknowledged and celebrated diversity, and an important part of Hawaii's culture is the Native Hawaiian people."

The Akaka bill has been met with stiff opposition from the U.S. Commission on Civil Rights, which wrote a letter to congressional leaders in August 2009 saying, "We don't believe Congress has the constitutional authority to reorganize racial and ethnic groups into sovereign nations unless those groups have a long and continuous history of separate self-governance." The bill would badly affect Hawaiians of African, Asian, European, or other heritage who would not have the special benefits given to ethnic Hawaiians, the commission noted. Trask said the bill—or versions of it—was backed primarily by so-called pureblood Hawaiians and by the Hawaiian and U.S. governments. The bill would establish a register of Native Hawaiian voters who would elect a governing council that would negotiate transfers of lands and natural resources with the U.S. government. In February 2010, the U.S. House of Representatives passed the bill; the following month the Senate Committee on Indian Affairs sent it to the full Senate floor for approval.

The sovereignty debate has not escalated into sustained or serious violence, but there are sporadic scuffles. In 2008, for example, twenty-three Hawaiian pro-sovereignty protesters were arrested for breaking into the Iolani palace and posting signs that read "Property of the Kingdom of Hawaiian Trust." "There's a very vibrant and vocal Hawaiian community that's well-versed in the history. They know statehood was a product of the overthrow," Dean Sarillo, a student of Hawaiian political history, told the Associated Press. Some descendents of Queen Liliuokalani claim the throne, but Trask said that "while most Hawaiians respect the monarchy, they do not want it returning to power." Moreover, restoration would be difficult because there are various branches of the family who are potential candidates to be the monarch, she added. While the campaign for autonomy is set to continue, equally prominent will be the debate among Hawaiians over what form that autonomy should take.

Further Reading

Hawaii Nation pro-independence Web site, www.hawaii-nation.org.

Lajeunesse, William. "Bill to Grant Native Hawaiians Sovereignty Passes House," FOXNews.com, February 24, 2010, www.foxnews.com/politics/2010/02/24/grant-native-hawaiians-sovereignty-passes-house.

Niesse, Mark. "Protests planned for Hawaiians 50th anniversary," Associated Press, August 21, 2009.

Trask, Haunani-Kay. *From a Native Daughter—Colonialism and Sovereignty in Hawaii.* Honolulu: University of Hawaii Press, 1999.

Wood, Daniel B. "Hawaii's Search for Sovereignty," *Christian Science Monitor,* October 17, 1994, www.hawaii-nation.org/csmgif.html.

INUIT
(Canada)

The Inuit people living in Canada are a striking example of how a small and economically insignificant but politically cohesive community can secure autonomy not by force, but by assiduously negotiating with a government that is willing to make concessions. The Inuit are equally remarkable in that they form a majority in about 40 percent of the territory of Canada—itself the second largest country in the world—even though they make up a tiny portion, just 0.2 percent, of Canada's overall population of thirty-three million. This unusual situation is a consequence of the very uneven distribution of Canada's population. The bulk of the population lives in the south, with huge swathes of land in the north virtually uninhabited.

Formerly know as Eskimos, a term that has fallen out of favor over the past two decades, most Inuit speak one of four Canadian Inuit dialects in addition to English and/or French. Perhaps their greatest achievement in their decades-long campaign for sovereignty was the establishment on April 1, 1999, of an autonomous Inuit Territory in northern Canada called Nunavut, which means "our land" in Inuit. Made up of an 85 percent Inuit population and formed following a decision to split in two Canada's enormous Northwest Territory, Nunavut has a population of just thirty-two thousand living in twenty-six communities spread across an area larger than Western Europe. The largest city and the capital of Nunavut is Iqaluit, meaning "place of many fish," which has a population of 6,500.

Nunavut does not include the northwestern part of Canada within its borders, even though there are some Inuit living there. This is in part because the region is populated by many other indigenous peoples, often called Aboriginal, or "First Peoples," including the Yukon, Athabascan, and Innu Indians. They have a different history, culture, and language from the Inuit, which the Inuit seek to emphasize to Canadian officials responsible for setting aboriginal policies. The other First Peoples, such as the fifteen thousand–strong Mohawk Indian community in Quebec that straddles the Canadian-U.S. border, have negotiated their own self-government treaties with the federal and provincial governments of Canada.

Separatism among Canadian Inuit has been predominantly peaceful. In their dealings with different tiers of government, the Inuit's most tense and difficult relationship has been with the authorities in Quebec. Unlike the rest of the country, which is predominantly Anglophone, the province of Quebec is majority French-speaking. Quebec has a long history of antagonism toward the Canadian government. The Inuit are a significant obstacle to the Quebecois separatists fulfilling their goal of splitting entirely from Canada and creating an independent French-speaking country (see separate essay). Fearful that they will lose the concessions they have fought long and hard for from the Canadian authorities, the Inuit have consistently voted overwhelmingly against Quebec secession: 87 percent in the 1980 independence referendum.

Quebec's Inuit population, which numbers about 9,500, lives mainly in a northern part they call Nunavik, which constitutes about one third of the province's territory. The Quebecois provincial government signed a land claims agreement with Nunavik in 2008 that provides for an Inuit regional government accountable to the Quebec parliament. There are a further two thousand Inuit living in Nunatsiavut in the provinces of Labrador and Newfoundland in eastern Canada; three thousand in the Inuvialuit Settlement Region in the Northwest Territories; and eleven thousand dispersed throughout other parts of Canada.

As with many aboriginal peoples in the Americas, the Inuit have above-average alcoholism, drug abuse, infant mortality, and suicide rates, and lower life expectancy, dying on average about fifteen years younger than other Canadians. However, the Inuit are faring better than some other American Indian nations socioeconomically. According to the government of Nunavut, the employment rate in their territory is about 50 percent and unemployment 15 percent. One major challenge Inuit communities across the country face is a higher-than-average cost of living. This is a consequence both of their remoteness, with their towns mostly accessible only by plane or sealift rather than by road or rail, and the sparseness of their population. For example, purchasing essentials like milk can be three or four times more expensive than elsewhere in Canada.

Inuit authorities are trying to improve the situation by persuading the Canadian government to invest more in transport infrastructure in their regions.

Inuit lands contain some of the largest oil and gas reserves in the world—and they have yet to be fully tapped. Inuit leaders are debating among one another, and with the Canadian government, the pros and cons of further development of the petroleum industry. While exploitation of these resources could make the Inuit more self-sufficient and provide welcome income, it could also do lasting damage to the environment.

History

Canada's Inuit are predominantly Inupiat, one of two broad subgroups of Inuit, the other being Yupik, who live mainly around coastal Alaska in the United States (see separate essay). First called Sivullirmiut and then Thule, they have lived in Canada for about five thousand years. Their traditional livelihoods were hunting, fishing, and whaling. In the late sixteenth century European explorers began arriving and claiming Inuit homelands. From the early eighteenth century, European whalers, notably the Dutch, and fur traders came, and by 1850 they had set up year-round whaling shore stations. The first Christian missionaries arrived in 1771—Moravians who settled in Nain in eastern Canada. These missionaries had a major impact on Inuit communities, converting many to Christianity and providing education and health services. According to the Web Site of Inuit Tapiriit Kanatami (ITK), an association representing Canadian Inuit, "We often hear non-Inuit talk about how missionaries were not good for us. When Inuit talk about this, they usually give another opinion and tell of their respect for the religious teachings."

Meanwhile, British and French immigrants had been settling in southern Canada from the seventeenth century. The British gained the upper hand politically in 1763 after Great Britain defeated

France in the Seven Years' War and took over the formerly French-ruled province of Quebec. Several British-ruled provinces in Canada were merged to form a federation in 1867 with the passage of the British North America Act. They gradually became more independent from the United Kingdom, although the British monarch remained head of state, their authority exercised via an appointed governor general. In 1903 the Royal Canadian police, anxious to secure control of access routes to Arctic lands and waters, established their first posts in Inuit territories.

The Inuit's plight grew increasingly perilous from the late 1800s when whaling, an important part of their culture, became more difficult as a result of over-fishing, and many Inuit died from exposure to European diseases. Predictions that the Inuit would soon become extinct were commonplace. As whaling declined, the fox fur industry flourished from the early 1900s, and Inuit were often employed to set steel traps and then typically paid with guns and ammunition.

In 1953 and 1955 Canadian authorities relocated seventeen Inuit families in Nunavik to a remote, uninhabited area in Ellesmere Island in the High Arctic. This operation was described in a July 1994 report by a panel set up by the Canadian government as "illegal, dishonest, and inhumane." It was ostensibly done to assert Canadian sovereignty, although the report claimed the government's true motivation was to remove them from welfare and social programs. The families were left stranded without enough food or housing in a region no Inuit had lived in for five hundred years.

In 1975 Quebec Inuit won greater autonomy through the James Bay Agreement, under which the Quebec government gave the Inuit $90 million in return for their consenting to the installation of huge hydroelectric dams in their territory. In 1976 the Inuit Tapirisat of Canada (ITC), the main representative body for Canadian Inuit at the time, proposed creating a self-governing region called Nunavut in

the Northwest Territories as part of a comprehensive land claims settlement. By 1987 tentative agreement to create Nunavut had been reached, and the plan was gradually implemented in subsequent years. The establishment of Nunavut was approved by 54 percent of Northwest Territories voters and 96 percent of Inuit voters in referenda held in May and November 1992, respectively. In 2002 the Quebec provincial government granted $450 million to Quebec Inuit in exchange for allowing the construction of a hydropower facility in the Inuit area. The funds were used to build parks and roads and to provide housing.

Leadership

The most visible manifestation of Inuit sovereignty today is the territorial government of Nunavut. The government includes a premier and a nineteen-member, popularly elected legislative assembly. The Nunavut political system is unusual in that there are no political parties. It operates a form of government known as Inuit Qaujimajatuqangit, which is grounded in traditional Inuit knowledge and values. Inuit who live elsewhere in Canada are recognized as a distinct group, but they are not in quite as strong a position politically because they must negotiate with both the provincial or territorial and Canadian governments, whereas the Nunavut Inuit only have to deal with the Canadian government.

The ITK is the main non-governmental representative body for Canadian Inuit. Established in 1971 as the ITC, which later evolved into the ITK, the organization's current president is Mary Simon from northern Quebec. Its policy is to promote Inuit autonomy while remaining part of Canada, an approach that involves "self-reliance and full participation in all aspects of Canadian society." The ITK devoted much of their efforts from the 1970s to 1990s to campaigning for self-government and to land claim settlement negotiations. With these goals now in large part achieved, a growing priority for the ITK today is to raise the

Inuit's living and educational standards, which are currently below the Canadian average. For example, 61 percent of Inuit aged 25–64 have not completed high school; this compares to 23 percent of non-Aboriginal Canadians. The organization presses the Canadian government to recognize that Inuit have needs and concerns that differ from other aboriginal peoples in Canada.

In addition to the ITK, a country-wide body, four regional Inuit associations came together in 1994 to form the Canadian Inuit Business Development Council in a bid to further promote the Inuit economy and culture. As a follow-up to the 1975 James Bay Agreement, Quebec Inuit established the non-profit Makivik Corporation to promote Inuit interests.

Canadian Inuit have strong links with Inuit in other countries via the Inuit Circumpolar Council (ICC), a non-governmental association representing 150,000 Inuit in Canada, Greenland (see separate essay), Russia, and the United States. The body meets every four years and has consultative status on the United Nation's Economic and Social Council. It formulates common positions on the pressing issues of the day.

Current Status

There are about fifty thousand Inuit in Canada today living for the most part in fifty-three Arctic communities. While they enjoy considerable autonomy in their homelands, since 2008 the Canadian government has moved to strengthen Canada's sovereignty in the Arctic region. In a bid to claim new territory, it has submitted scientific evidence to a United Nations adjudicating panel in an effort to prove that Nunavut's continental shelf extends to the North Pole. Denmark, which owns Greenland, and Russia are in turn filing competing claims to this region, which is known as the Lomonosov Ridge and includes an area as large as California, Indiana, and Texas combined.

Since 2008 the Canadian military has been boosting its presence in Inuit areas, including launching a space satellite, Polar Epsilon, to provide land and sea surveillance. Some Inuit fear the Canadian government will hinder Inuit sovereignty plans. "We have occupied these lands for millennia. The prime minister is not giving us due credit," complained Inuit leader John Amagoalik in an August 2009 *Economist* article.

The Canadian government is more interested than ever before in extracting oil and gas from Inuit lands. This is causing concern among Inuit, who fear that they will lose out in a future scramble for resources. The Inuit could try to block or delay plans to construct oil and gas pipelines on environmental grounds, but it is far from certain they will take such an approach. Indeed, the ITK had expressed "cautious interest" in oil and gas development and has argued that the Inuit are in a strong negotiating position because of their land claims agreements with Canada. The Inuit rely heavily on imported oil for diesel power and are, as a result, trying to shift to use of renewable energy sources like hydro, wind, and solar power.

Seal meat remains a staple of the Inuit diet. In August 2009, Canada's prime minister, Stephen Harper, showed his solidarity with the Inuit by being photographed eating seal meat after touring Nunavut in response to the European Union's decision in July to ban imports of seal products. In January 2010, the ITK filed a lawsuit challenging the ban. ITK president Mary Simon said in a press release, "Inuit have been hunting seals and sustaining themselves for food, clothing, and trade for many generations. No objective and fair-minded person can conclude that seals are under genuine conservation threat." The government of Nunavut in October 2009 protested a U.S. government proposal to impose an international ban on trade in polar bears. *The Toronto Star* reported that sport hunters were paying up to $30,000 for the opportunity to hunt polar bears, and that Inuit hunters earned up to $150 a foot for bear hide.

The Inuit are also involved in mining diamonds, gold, and uranium, and derive income from tourism, notably cruise ships. Small-scale projects to promote Inuit artwork, in particular carvings and prints, have generated employment while many Inuit work in the municipal, regional, and federal governments. Average Inuit income now stands at about two-thirds the national average.

Global warming has had a bigger impact on Inuit territories than in most parts of the world, but that impact has not necessarily been a negative one. For example, the warmer temperatures are enabling them to cultivate new food sources. The melting icecaps are making Inuit waters more navigable, although they are still relatively treacherous and inaccessible. The famed and fabled Northwest Passage that connects the Atlantic and Pacific Oceans, which traverses Inuit homelands, was ice-free for the first time in recorded history in summer 2007. If warming continues, the passage could become a major waterway for transporting goods or people between continents because it is shorter than most existing routes. The United States contests Canada's sovereignty over the passage, arguing it is an international strait through which all ships should have right of free passage.

While Canada's Inuit have made great strides in establishing an autonomous government, there is little indication of a desire to create an independent country.

Further Reading

Beary, Brian. "Race for the Arctic," *CQ Global Researcher* 2, no.8 (August 2008).

Government of Nunavut Web site, www.gov.nu.ca.

"Harper of the melting North," *The Economist*, August 29, 2009, www.economist.com/world/americas/displaystory.cfm?story_id=14313727.

Inuit Circumpolar Conference Web site, www.inuit.org.

Inuit Tapiriit Kanatami Web site, www.itk.ca. Includes "Inuit Statistical Profile," October 2008, www.itk.ca/sites/default/files/InuitStatisticalProfile2008_0.pdf; and "5000 Years of Inuit History and Heritage," www.itk.ca/sites/default/files/5000YearHeritage.pdf (accessed October 2009).

Joseph, Ralph. "Analysis: Quebec reaches out to Inuits," United Press International, April 10, 2002.

Krauss, Clifford. "Quebec Offers $450 Million to Inuit Villages," *New York Times*, April 10, 2002, www.nytimes.com/2002/04/10/world/quebec-offers-450-million-to-inuit-villages.html.

Weber, Bob. "U.S. efforts to abolish bear trade anger Inuit; Nunavut group asks Ottawa to help defend key aboriginal industry," *The Toronto Star*, October 17, 2009, www.thestar.com/news/canada/article/711778—u-s-efforts-to-abolish-bear-trade-anger-inuit.

LAKOTA INDIANS
(United States)

The Lakota nation—also known as the Great Sioux Nation—is a confederation of Lakota, Nakota, and Dakota American Indians living mainly in the northwestern United States. On December 17, 2007, a disaffected group of Lakota leaders from Pine Ridge Reservation in South Dakota traveled to Washington, D.C., to inform the U.S. State Department they were seceding. They declared a large swathe of continuous territory straddling the states of Nebraska, North Dakota, South Dakota, Montana, and Wyoming an independent Indian country called "Republic of Lakotah." Although the U.S. government never responded to the declaration and elected Lakota leaders distanced themselves from it, the dissidents continued to pursue their claim.

There are approximately 120,000 Lakota living in the United States, the greatest concentration of them at Pine Ridge Reservation; a further 35,000 live in Canada. English is the dominant spoken language among them, with only a few thousand fluent Lakota speakers left, mostly elderly people. The Lakota are perhaps better known as "Sioux Indians," but this term has fallen out of favor due to its negative connotations, having been originally coined by the Lakota's adversaries to mean "snake" or "cutthroat." The Lakota are just one nation among the much wider American Indian population, which numbers about 2.5 million in the United States, most of whom live on 314 federally recognized reservations.

The Lakota, like other Indian nations, have officially enjoyed autonomy since 1934, when the U.S. Congress passed the Indian Reorganization Act that was supposed to enable Indian tribes to establish self-rule on designated reservations. Theoretically, they were permitted to write their own laws, operate their own local justice system, collect taxes, and own the lands reserved for them, with the U.S. government officially "managing" them in a trust capacity. But in practice U.S. authorities are more involved in Indian affairs than many would like. In the case of the Lakota, this is in large part due to the fact that the Lakota are extremely poor and thus heavily reliant on government grants. According to Tink Tinker, a professor of American Indian Culture at Iliff Theological Seminary in Denver, this has caused the U.S. government to interfere in Lakota internal politics and has corrupted the tribal leadership.

A milestone in the Lakota independence movement came in 1973 when charismatic leader Russell Means helped organize the occupation of the town of Wounded Knee, South Dakota, where, in 1890, three hundred Indians were massacred by U.S. government forces. Means remains a central figure in the movement. Interviewed by telephone in September 2009, he called the United States "the most vile country in the history of the human race," and accused it of having committed genocide on the Indians by stealing their land and slaughtering their food supply, notably the buffalo. His priorities, as listed on his "Republic of Lakotah" Web site, include building a school to preserve Lakota culture and Lakota language, which is in danger of becoming extinct, and constructing wind energy turbines and locally made solar panels to make the Lakota energy independent.

History

The Lakota were independent in the early years of European colonization of North America because the area where they lived was not settled by "white men" initially. Tensions began to increase in the nineteenth century, however, as the United States expanded its boundaries westward and tens of thousands migrated into Lakota-populated areas. According to Professor Tinker, in the early years the United States treated the Lakota and other Indians as independent nations—the U.S. Constitution deemed them as such—and signed border treaties with them, notably in 1851 and 1868. But in 1871 the U.S. Congress decided to no longer sign such treaties. Then, under the General Allotment Act of 1887, the Lakota communal land system was dismantled as reservations were split into individual allotments, resulting in the loss of much of their land. In the twentieth century cohesion among the Lakota was further eroded by the U.S. policy of assimilation, whereby Indians were relocated from reservations to cities.

In the 1960s many Lakota featured prominently in the nascent American Indian civil rights movement and were involved in highly publicized protests that were a catalyst for the Indian self-determination movement. From 1969 to 1971 Indians occupied the tiny island of Alcatraz in San Francisco Bay, California. In 1972 they took over the Washington, D.C., headquarters of the U.S. Bureau of Indian Affairs. In 1973 they occupied Wounded Knee. These actions encouraged the U.S. government to change its policy by officially advocating self-determination for Indians, although in practice it never accepted Indians' right to establish their own country.

The Lakota meanwhile successfully sued the U.S. government for seizing lands illegally. In 1980 the U.S. Supreme Court awarded the Lakota $122 million in compensation for the loss of the Black Hills of South Dakota, which the United States took in breach of the 1868 Treaty of Fort Laramie. The Lakota refused the settlement, however, because the Court did not return the land. The *Rapid City Journal*, a South Dakota newspaper, reported in December 2007 that the compensation is now worth about $1 billion with interest accrued.

Leadership

Russell Means is a leading light in the Lakota independence movement. Asked how many Lakota supported his campaign, Means noted he won 45 percent of the votes in the Pine Ridge tribal elections in November 2008 campaigning on his freedom ticket. While it is not clear that all who voted for him would also support independence, Professor Tinker said that Means "commands a lot of support among the Lakota" and stressed that his campaign was "not a fringe movement."

In a June 2008 article for the *Washington Post*, writer Bill Donahue reported that many other

Russell Means (1939–)

AP Photo/Marcy Nighswander

RUSSELL MEANS, an American Indian activist and actor, was born on the Pine Ridge Reservation in South Dakota on November 10, 1939. His family, all full-blooded Yankton Lakota, moved to California in 1942, and he graduated from San Leandro High School in 1958. He continued his education at Oakland City College and Arizona State University.

Means first began working for American Indian rights when he became the director of Cleveland's American Indian Center in 1969. Through this position, he encountered Dennis Banks, co-founder of the American Indian Movement (AIM), and they began to work together.

Also in 1969, Means joined AIM in its takeover of Alcatraz Island; over five thousand American Indians participated in the occupation. The federally owned property was held for nineteen months while the American Indians lived in the guard barracks and reclaimed the land for themselves.

In 1970 Means was appointed AIM's first national director, a position he used to encourage protests and occupations nationwide. For example, he was involved in an AIM protest on Thanksgiving of the same year, during which Plymouth Rock was painted red and members seized a replica of the Mayflower. Also, Means led three hundred AIM affiliates in a 1972, six-day occupation of the Washington, D.C., Bureau of Indian Affairs building, where they smashed windows and repossessed artifacts.

The takeover of the sacred grounds of Wounded Knee might be Means' most famous activist initiative. On February 27, 1973, Means, in the company of AIM and several other Oglala Lakota of the Pine Ridge Indian Reservation, seized the area and proceeded to secure control for seventy-one days. The U.S. military and FBI wasted no time in responding and had the town surrounded within twenty-four hours. The takeover was a protest designed to place a spotlight on the deplorable living conditions and crippling poverty at the Pine Ridge Reservation; in addition, Means and his allies were critical of the sale of grazing rights on tribal lands.

Both the AIM activists and government forces traded fire over the course of three months. Several occupiers were killed, and a U.S. marshal was paralyzed from the waist down. On May 5, after the fatalities that had marred April, both sides agreed to disarm, and the government took control of the village. Means was arrested in Los Angeles a few hours after the surrender of the AIM occupiers.

The next year, Means ran against Richard "Dick" Wilson for the presidency and chairmanship of the Oglala Lakota nation. Though Means lost, an investigation by a federal court concluded that there had been voting fraud and ordered a new election. However, the government run by Wilson refused.

The 1980s saw AIM split into several factions, one of which was adamantly opposed to Means, his tactics, and his support for Native Americans in Nicaragua. In 1984 he was the vice-presidential candidate for the Libertarian party.

In 1992 Means began to pursue a film career. His first major role was that of Chingachook in the film *The Last of the Mohicans*. He was awarded the role following an audition that put him up against another AIM leader, Dennis Banks. Means has appeared in several other films, including *Natural Born Killers, Into the West*, and *Pathfinder*, and voiced Chief Powhatan in Disney's Pocahontas. More recently, he has had a reoccurring guest role on the HBO show "Curb Your Enthusiasm."

Thirty years after he first ran, Means received 46 percent of the vote in his 2004 bid for the Pine Ridge tribal chair election. Although he did not win, he could point to a significant following in support of his goal of an independent Lakota nation. Many tribal leaders are critical of Means' radical stance, as well as the fact that he has not consulted with the tribe's elders. Means plans to institute a matriarchal government in Lakota and is building a "Total Immersion School" on the Pine Ridge Reservation where children will be immersed in the Lakota way of life.

His most recent film, an independent venture titled *Rez Bomb*, was filmed on the reservation of his youth, Pine Ridge. He has produced two CDs of protest music and is a printmaker and painter. Means has been married four times and has ten children.

Lakota leaders resented Means for having made his declaration of independence without consulting with them. Donahue wrote that there had been internal splits, too. Means was originally backed by Duane Martin Sr., a Pine Ridge Lakota Indian who has led a paramilitary force that responds to crimes—a force that is necessary, Martin says, because the Indian police are ineffective. However, Martin has since fallen out with Means and formed a breakaway independence movement called Lakota Oyate. Martin has issued over 150 Lakota identity cards.

Another pro-sovereignty group is the Black Hills Sioux Nation Treaty Council, which is trying to reinstate traditional forms of government in the Black Hills and revive the Lakota language. The Lakota are officially represented at the local level by elected tribal councils and at the national level by the two umbrella associations for American Indians: the American Indian Movement and National Congress of American Indians.

Current Status

The current framework for local autonomy has not resolved the Lakota's growing list of social and environmental problems. The Lakota have below-average life expectancy rates—forty-four years for men—and well above-average poverty, unemployment, alcoholism, suicide, and infant mortality rates. Uranium mining, which began in the region after World War II (1939–1945), has left a legacy of abandoned pits, polluted waters, and high radiation levels. The Lakota "have the lowest life expectancy in the whole world if you exclude deaths caused by AIDS," noted Means.

Lakota reservations are being badly hit by a surge in organized crime. According to John Mousseau, chair of the Sioux Tribal Judicial Council in Pine Ridge, which has a population of fifty thousand, there are thirty-nine identified gangs attracting five thousand gang members on Pine Ridge. Mousseau told a U.S. Senate hearing in July 2009 that the lack of cultural and education programs was leaving kids idle and more prone to join gangs.

Lakota leader Russell Means has focused his recent energies on establishing the T.R.E.A.T.Y. schools concept on Pine Ridge. Inspired by the Maori in New Zealand, it aims to revive the Lakota nation and culture through a "total immersion" education and skills-training system that will make the Lakota self-sustaining. Despite the many obstacles to securing independence, Means has remained optimistic about the long-term prospects. "At first they ignore you, then they laugh at you, then they fight you, then you win," he told the *Washington Post* in 2008.

The Black Hills Council in August 2009 sent an "amended declaration" to the United Nations and U.S. governments aimed at invoking rights inherent in the 1851 and 1868 Fort Laramie treaties the Council claims the Sioux have been denied. One of its main grievances is the U.S. government's failure to hand over lands in South Dakota to the Lakota. There was little response to the declaration, one of its drafters, Bill Bielecki, said in a June 2010 telephone interview. In November 2009, U.S. president Barack Obama organized a conference in Washington, D.C., with Indian tribal leaders. He was urged by the representative of the Lakota, Theresa Two Bulls, to honor existing treaties and help Indians to exercise sovereignty and self-determination. Bielecki dismissed the conference as a "political smokescreen," saying the U.S. president was uninterested in American Indian issues as Indians account for such a small fraction of the electorate. It remains highly unlikely that an Obama or future U.S. administration would allow the Lakota to establish an independent country.

Further Reading

American Indian Movement Web site, www.aimovement
.org.

Donahue, Bill. "Ways and Means . . ." *Washington Post,*
June 29, 2008, www.washingtonpost.com/wp-dyn/
content/article/2008/06/24/AR2008062401162
.html.

Eckholm, Erik. "Gang Violence Grows on an Indian Reservation," *The New York Times,* December 14, 2009,
www.nytimes.com/2009/12/14/us/14gangs.html.

Harlan, Bill. "Lakota group secedes from U.S.," *Rapid
City Journal,* December 21, 2007, www.rapidcity
journal.com/articles/2007/12/21/news/local/
doc476a99630633e335271152.txt.

National Congress of American Indians Web site, www
.ncai.org.

Reinhardt, Akim D. *Ruling Pine Ridge: Oglala Lakota
Politics from the IRA to Wounded Knee (Plains Histories).* Lubbock: Texas Tech University Press, 2009.

Republic of Lakotah official Web site, www.republicofla
kotah.com.

LOWLANDERS
(Bolivia)

Since the early 1990s, there has been a marked surge in separatist sentiment in the lowlands of Bolivia, a landlocked country in South America with a population of 8.3 million.

The Camba—the Bolivian term for lowlanders—live in the eastern departments of Santa Cruz, Beni, Pando, and Tarija, and account for 34 percent of the Bolvian population. The rising separatism there is most pronounced among so-called white Bolivians (that is, people of non-indigenous, mostly European ancestry) and among Mestizo, or mixed race, Bolivians. These two groups form a majority of the lowland population, although there are numerous indigenous groups there as well, such as the Guarani, Arawaks, and Chiquitanos, who are also seeking greater autonomy. The majority of Bolivia's indigenous population lives in the highlands, in the western departments of La Paz, Cochabamba, Chuquisaca, Potosi, and Oruro, where the dominant groups are the Aymara and Quechua.

The lowlanders have grown more powerful, in particular economically, since the 1950s as a result of large-scale immigration from the highlands and beyond Bolivia's borders, coupled with the development of a lucrative gas industry. The economic growth has been most pronounced in the Santa Cruz department. Many lowlanders have grown concerned about the future of this prosperity, particularly since 2005, the year Bolivians elected Evo Morales, a former coca grower of Aymara Indian ancestry, to be the country's first-ever indigenous president. The populist, pro-indigenous policies pursued by Morales have triggered a striking escalation in the lowlanders' campaign for autonomy. According to author Seth Kaplan, who devoted a chapter to Bolivia in his 2008 book *Fixing Fragile States*, the current unrest is "the culmination of a long history of antagonistic inter-group relations and elite domination of the state, brought to a climax by a dispute over how to manage the country's gas reserves" and by "competing visions about how to organize the state." Pro-autonomy campaigners are for the most part concerned about economic self-governance and do not wish their departments to secede from Bolivia. However, there are fringe factions pushing for political independence, too, and they often depict their struggle in terms of a clash between European and indigenous values.

A major factor driving the autonomy campaign is the fact that most of Bolivia's hydrocarbon resources are found in the lowlands. Gas is now the biggest earner for the country, accounting for a third of all exports in 2008 and netting the government $2 billion in royalties. This is a relatively new situation; historically, the mining of minerals such as tin and silver, most of which were found in the highlands, was the dominant source of income for Bolivia. Agriculture accounts for a sixth of Bolivia's gross domestic product, with the main crops being soybeans, rice, cotton, coffee, sugar, wheat, barley, and corn. Bolivia is also the world's third largest cultivator of coca after Colombia and Peru. The crop is grown mainly by indigenous peoples for medicinal and ceremonial uses, although some is illicitly diverted for cocaine production.

Despite an abundance of resources, Bolivia remains one of the poorest countries in Latin America, with a national per capita income of $4,700 (CIA World Factbook, 2009 estimate). There are huge disparities in wealth between the regions, with the western highlands poorer than the eastern lowlands, and this has further exacerbated the regional split. Bolivian law requires a sizable chunk of the revenue derived from gas exports to be returned to the department where the gas was produced. As a result, the Tarija and Santa Cruz lowland departments receive 65 percent of state royalties despite accounting for only 29 percent of the population. The pro-autonomy lowlanders are worried that President Morales, who espouses a brand of socialism that emphasizes the rights of indigenous communities, will seize the natural resources they have historically controlled. This includes large agricultural estates mostly owned by non-indigenous Bolivians of diverse backgrounds, including Mestizo, white Bolivian, Brazilian, German, Serbian, and Croatian. The Morales government is planning to redistribute large portions of arable land in a bid to change the status quo, in which 90 percent of the nation's land is in the hands of just 10 percent of the country's farmers.

Given the sweeping nature of the changes the government would like to make to the country's economic structure, it is not surprising that one of the strongest supporters of the autonomy movement has been the lowland business community. Many in the community believe that the capitalist system that has helped them to amass considerable wealth—especially after the government liberalized the economy and encouraged more private investment in the 1980s—is threatened by Morales, who is concerned more with collective rights than individual rights. Morales' supporters insist the government is only redressing historical injustices and discrimination against indigenous peoples. According to Seth Kaplan, "There is little or no national consensus on the overall nature, purpose, and conduct of the state."

History

When Bolivia won independence from Spain in 1825, the highlands were in the ascendancy politically and economically. Most Bolivians lived there, and the mining industry, which formed the backbone of the economy, was based there. In the late 1800s, the power struggle was not between highlander and lowlander but rather between the silver mining industry magnates of largely Spanish ancestry and the tin mining elite of mostly Mestizo descent. The latter ultimately gained the upper hand, which led to the relocation of the capital in 1898 from Sucre to La Paz. Both cities are located in the highlands.

For most of the twentieth century, Bolivia remained a unitary, highly centralized state, with all key government decisions made in La Paz. Spanish, the language of the colonizer, was and has remained the dominant language. The indigenous languages of Aymara and Quechua were not recognized as official languages until 1977. Bolivia began to decentralize in the 1990s with the passage of laws in 1994 and 1995 that divided the country into 311 municipalities and provided for the direct election of mayors; prior to this, mayors were placed in office via appointment.

Morales, who is from the Movement Toward Socialism (MAS) party, was elected president in December 2005, winning 53 percent of the vote. He immediately went to work forging a new type of populist democracy that marked a clear break from the past. Morales' actions caused considerable consternation among the wealthy elite, who are mainly of European and Mestizo ancestry. They became even more concerned when Morales announced in May 2006 that he was nationalizing the oil and gas industry and followed up by quickly renegotiating agreements with foreign firms that had invested in that sector, making them pay more royalties to the state. While this was politically popular and led to a rise in state revenues, it also caused foreign investment to fall, with Brazilian state-owned Petrobras, for example, selling two refineries to the Bolivian government for $112 million. Many lowlanders were also opposed to Morales' foreign policy, as he strengthened relations with countries that were anti–United States and anti-capitalist, notably Venezuela, Cuba, and Iran.

In December 2005, the prefects (governors) of Bolivia's nine departments were directly elected for the first time. Armed with a popular mandate and supported by robust business communities, lowland prefects began pushing for greater autonomy. The Bolivian constitution was rewritten to grant greater autonomy to all the departments—not just those in the lowlands—but the revised draft was rejected in a referendum on July 2, 2006, with 57 percent voting against. Lowlanders were frustrated with the outcome because while each of the four lowland departments voted yes, they were not given autonomy. Relations with the Morales government continued to deteriorate.

Lowlanders accused the central administration of trying to intimidate them. In August 2007, the government decided to move the annual military parade from the usual venues of La Paz or Sucre in the highlands to Santa Cruz in the lowlands. The *Washington Times* newspaper reported that

"eastern leaders charge that Mr. Morales is implementing 'Plan Vinto,' a strategy calling for Indians to encircle lowland cities that was drafted more than a decade ago by an indigenous highland group called Tupac Katari." The government denied this was an act of intimidation and insisted it had no plans to militarize the region. The lowland regions decided to hold pro-autonomy referenda in May and June 2008; in every region the referenda passed overwhelmingly, albeit with high abstention rates. However, Morales declared the votes illegitimate and instead called a referendum on his leadership in August 2008, which he won with 67 percent of Bolivians supporting him.

Leadership

Camba Nation (Nación Camba) is the main political group calling for greater autonomy for Santa Cruz as well as the three other lowland departments. Set up in the early 2000s, it is led by Sergio Antelo and claims to have forty thousand members. The group says it is peaceful, but the Bolivian government has accused it of accumulating arms. Many local politicians have been demanding greater autonomy and acting independently of the Camba Nation party. For example, Mario Cossio, Prefect of Tarija, where 85 percent of Bolivia's gas reserves are found, has tried to wrench control of the department's gas revenues from the central government. A coalition of lowlander prefects formed an "Autonomy Junta" in 2007 and proposed a package of laws concerning government services, land, revenues, and immigration that has not thus far been adopted.

The pro-autonomy movement has a militant side, too, notably through a group called the Santa Cruz Youth Union of the Pro–Santa Cruz committee (*Union Juvenil Crucena*). Its supporters have had violent clashes with government forces in recent years. The Bolivian authorities have meanwhile been accusing human rights groups, local politicians, and business leaders of trying to establish a military organization or terrorist cell to further

Eduardo Rozsa-Flores (1960–2009)

EDUARDO ROZSA-FLORES was born March 31, 1960, in Santa Cruz, Bolivia. Rozsa-Flores had an international background, being the son of a Hungarian father and Spanish mother. His father was a passionate communist, and in 1972 the family moved to Chile in order to escape the right-wing dictator of Bolivia, Hugo Banzer. From Chile the family sought political asylum in Sweden in 1973, before eventually settling down in Hungary in 1975. It was in Hungary that Rozsa-Flores attended the Eötvös Loránd University, graduating with a degree in Liberal Arts in 1991.

© IMRE FOELDI/epa/Corbis

In 1991 Rozsa-Flores travelled to Croatia on assignment with the Spanish newspaper *La Vanguardia*. Croatia at that time was a constituent republic within the country of Yugoslavia, although it was on the verge of seceding. Rozsa-Flores was supposed to cover the impending Balkan wars that were triggered by the breakup of Yugoslavia, but instead he became committed to the Croatian independence movement. Rozsa-Flores joined the Croatian National Guard, the precursor to the Croatian army, as its first international volunteer in 1991, and later created the First International Unit, known by its initials PIV. Rozsa-Flores was well-suited to combat and rose quickly through the ranks of the Croatian army. During the Croatian War of Independence (1991–1995), the PIV proved controversial for its use of foreign nationals, who were condemned by the United Nations as "mercenaries."

Rozsa-Flores himself proved controversial. He was well-regarded for his military prowess; however, his unit was accused of massacring Serbian civilians and torturing suspected spies. Rozsa-Flores was linked to the murder of a Swiss national, Christian Wurtemburg, as well as to the alleged murder of Paul Jenks, a British national and war photographer. On the battlefield Rozsa-Flores' ruthless style was often likened to that of Kurtz, the character made famous by Joseph Conrad's *Heart of Darkness*.

In 1994 Rozsa-Flores left the Croatian army with a rank of colonel and was granted Croatian citizenship by the president of Croatia, Franjo Tudjman. He then returned to Hungary and his original vocation of journalism. He became one of the editors of the literary magazine *Kapu* and published several volumes of poetry. Rozsa-Flores also wrote a book about his experiences in Croatia entitled *The Filthy War*. During his years in Croatia Rozsa-Flores was exposed to Islam, eventually converting and becoming a prominent member of the Hungarian Muslim community. In 2001 his life story was made into a feature film, *Chico*, in which he played himself. In Hungary Rozsa-Flores continued to affiliate himself with political movements outside of the mainstream. He maintained close personal connections with the Hungarian far right and in 2003, after his conversion to Islam, became a spokesperson for the Iraqi Independent Government, an Iraqi splinter group.

In December 2005 Bolivia saw the election of a socialist president of indigenous heritage, Evo Morales. Morales' wealth redistribution plans sparked concern and calls for secession from the Bolivians living in the oil-rich lowlands who were predominantly of European ancestry. Born in Santa Cruz to European parents, Rozsa-Flores was sympathetic to their cause, and in May 2008 he returned to the land of his birth in order to help the lowlanders in their struggle for autonomy. Rozsa-Flores' presence in Bolivia sparked concern in the government; he and two associates, Hungarian national Magyarosi Arpak and Irish national Michael Dwyer, were suspected of plotting to assassinate the president. In April 2009, Rozsa-Flores and his companions were gunned down in an apparent firefight with Bolivian police. His death, and the death of twenty-four-year-old Dwyer, sparked an international controversy between Bolivia and Ireland, prompting the latter to call for further investigation.

their goals. On April 16, 2009, government forces conducted a sting on a Santa Cruz–based international cell that the authorities alleged was linked to the Santa Cruz autonomy movement. Three men were shot dead in the operation, including Eduardo Rozsa Flores, a journalist-turned-revolutionary of Bolivian-Hungarian parentage who had announced in a television interview in Hungary in late 2008 that he was putting together a militia to fight for low-lander independence. Rozsa first became famous in the early 1990s after leaving his job as a reporter covering the wars in crumbling Yugoslavia in order to fight for the Croatian independence movement. Pro-autonomy business and political groups have denied any connection to Rozsa, and some have accused the government of mounting a politically motivated investigation aimed at discrediting the lowland autonomy movement.

While most of the lowlanders demanding self-government are not of indigenous descent, there are indigenous lowlanders seeking greater auton-omy as well. Historically, the indigenous lowlander groups were not as well organized as the indigenous highland groups such as the Aymara and Quechua. However, the indigenous lowlanders have increas-ingly been coordinating their positions, especially since 1982 when an umbrella organization called the Confederation of Indigenous People of Bolivia (CIDOB) was set up to represent them.

Current Status

The Morales government's policies continue to fuel lowland separatism. Land ownership is a key battle-ground as lowlanders oppose government plans to redistribute the land. At a seminar at George Wash-ington University in Washington, D.C., in March 2008, Bolivia's Vice Minister for Lands, Alejandro Almarez, insisted that land redistribution was nec-essary to prevent indigenous people from being per-petually condemned to the role of worker on large estates owned by others. His government intended restricting the future sale of these lands to avoid speculation. Ninety percent of lands slated for redis-tribution were forested areas where indigenous com-munities had lived for thousands of years, he added.

While Almarez claimed "the east of Bolivia is ready to secede and cause a civil war," many lowland-ers contest such claims. According to Eduardo Paz Vargas, president of the Business Chamber of Santa Cruz, "There is no risk of the country splitting up, although calls for decentralization are increasing." Speaking at the Hudson Institute in Washington, D.C., in April 2009, Paz accused Morales of trying to further centralize power, while admitting that "50–60 percent of Bolivians support [Morales]." Paz said rural areas were now over-represented in Boliv-ian elections and that this helped Morales' MAS party. Santa Cruz, with a population of 1.5 million, is Bolivia's biggest and wealthiest urban area, with a rapidly growing population and economy.

Control of the gas sector is the other key bat-tleground. Former Bolivian finance minister Javier Comboni, now a professor at Wheaton College in Illinois, argued at the Hudson Institute seminar that the government's efforts to take control of the coun-try's natural resources had heightened the regional tensions. "The government has succeeded in getting control over all branches of government. But with absolute power comes absolute corruption," Com-boni said.

On January 25, 2009, 61.6 percent of Bolivi-ans voted in favor of a new 411-article constitution, which boosted the central government's pow-ers, although an article that would have enhanced its ability to expropriate lands was not voted on. Underscoring the country's regionally based divi-sions, the lowlands—and cities—voted against the new constitution while the highlands voted for it. The new constitution heralds a shift away from a strictly European-centered legal code by giving official recognition to community justice rooted in indigenous culture, and by requiring judges to be popularly elected.

According to a January 2009 article in The Economist magazine, supporters of the new legal system say it "reverses centuries of injustice since the Spanish conquest, and ensures that a 'white' minor-ity can no longer boss Indians around." However, the magazine also reported that the constitution's oppo-nents claim it "will politicize justice, create jurisdic-tional conflicts and uncertainty for the police, and legitimize mob justice in the form of lynchings and stonings, which have become more common over the past two years." Prior to the new constitution, Bolivia's legal system was based on a combination of Spanish law and the Napoleonic code.

In the general elections of December 2009, President Morales won reelection in both houses of Congress, taking 63 percent of the vote. His main opponent, Manfred Reyes, whose stronghold was in Santa Cruz, home of the lowlanders' separatist movement, won just 27 percent.

According to author Kaplan, the personality of President Morales has been a major factor in the rise of the autonomy movement in the Bolivian lowlands. Morales' "confrontational and centralizing style has weakened Bolivia's institutions and strengthened the extremists on both sides of the country's east-west divide," he wrote. Kaplan asserted that in order for Bolivia to remain united, the more capitalist-oriented lowlands needed to be given greater control over their economy, but he said they in return needed to distribute more of the wealth they generate to the poorer highland areas.

Further Reading

Arostegui, Martin. "Morales shifts parade site; Bolivian lowlands call move an 'Andean invasion,'" *The Washington Times,* July 31, 2007, www.washingtontimes.com/news/2007/jul/31/morales-shifts-parade-site/print.

"Bolivian leaders clash over 'plot,'" *Irish Times,* May 14, 2009, www.irishtimes.com/newspaper/breaking/2009/0514/breaking60.htm.

Confederation of Indigenous People of Bolivia (CIDOB) Web site, www.cido-bo.org.

Gamarra, Eduardo. "Bolivia on the Brink," Council on Foreign Relations, CSR No. 24, 2007, www.cfr.org/content/publications/attachments/BoliviaCSR24.pdf.

Kaplan, Seth. *Fixing Fragile States: A New Paradigm for Development.* Westport: Praeger Security International, 2008. See chapter 9.

Mabblog (Blog on Bolivian politics), www.mabb.blogspot.com.

"A passport to Utopia; Bolivia's new constitution," *The Economist,* January 24, 2009, www.economist.com/displayStory.cfm?story_id=12974135.

MAPUCHE
(Argentina, Chile)

The Mapuche are an indigenous people in South America known for having one of the most vibrant autonomy movements across the continent. Deriving their name from the words *mapu*, meaning "land," and *che*, meaning "people," there are an estimated 540,000 Mapuche in Chile and 75,000 in Argentina. They live in Chile's south central regions of Araucania, Bio-Bio, Los Lagos, Los Rios, and in the Argentine provinces of Neuquén, Rio Negro, Buenos Aires, and Santa Cruz. Their language, Mapudungun, is spoken by about 18 percent of Chilean Mapuche and a smaller proportion of Argentine Mapuche.

Many Mapuche live on reservations that were established by governments in the 1800s; between a third and a half reside in urban areas. In religious affiliation, they mostly blend their indigenous traditions, including a ceremony known as *Guillatun*, with Catholic or Protestant beliefs. They use indigenous medicines provided by a *machi*, who often also serves as a spiritual leader, performing prayer ceremonies, overseeing feast day celebrations, and officiating at funerals. Rural Mapuche subsist mainly from grain and cattle farming, hunting game, and gathering edibles, including pine nuts, which they

trade for other goods. In cities, they have historically been employed in housekeeping, construction, and the food industry. During the period of Spanish colonial rule from the sixteenth to the nineteenth centuries, the Mapuche population dropped sharply but then recovered substantially in the twentieth century. There are other indigenous groups in Chile and Argentina, such as the Aymara and Quechua, with similar grievances to those of the Mapuche, but they are not as numerous or as well organized.

At the root of the Mapuche autonomy movement in Chile is a demand for the return of ancestral lands lost to the Chilean government in the late 1800s. Under Spanish rule, the Mapuche had enjoyed considerable autonomy; later, an independent Chile followed a policy of subjugation of its indigenous peoples. Many Mapuche today are deeply unhappy with how the natural resources of their homelands have been sold, exploited, and depleted of their natural resources. For example, since the 1990s large forestry companies have replaced much of the old Mapuche forests—once a diverse mix of trees and plants—with non-native mass pine and eucalyptus plantations. These trees are cultivated mainly to produce pulp and paper, much of which is exported to North America, Asia, and Europe. There is also discontent over the Chilean government's sale of concessions, often to foreign consortia, to extract minerals, and over the government's promotion of an industrial-scale salmon sector. The tensions regularly spill over into violent clashes between radical Mapuche groups and landowners, industrialists, or police.

In Argentina, the Mapuche grapple with similar issues. Evicted by the government from ancestral lands, they could only stand by and watch as their land was sold to multinational companies operating in the petroleum, mining, and soy industries, or see it developed for tourism. Those who resisted faced police brutality, as documented by the human rights organization Human Rights Watch (HRW) in an October 2004 report. Women, old people, and the Mapuche spiritual healers, the *machi*, were mistreated, HRW noted. Although the Argentine government recognized them as a distinct group in 1983, and Argentine law provides for some ancestral lands to be returned and for bilingual education, these rights have not been systematically enforced. For example, in 1997 the Italian fashion brand Benetton bought 2.2 million acres (900,000 hectares) of land in the southernmost region of Patagonia where the Mapuche have historically lived; once bought, the company proceeded to enclose the property with a fence.

In Chile, a long-standing grievance is the Mapuche's lack of representation in the upper echelons of government. One first-generation Chilean, raised in the capital, Santiago, but now living in Washington, D.C., who did not wish to be named, noted in a July 2009 email interview that former Chilean president, Salvador Allende, "had a Mapuche minister that was the brunt of many racist jokes." He added, "It is very hard in Chile to get ahead unless you look European." The Mapuche have numerous related social problems, including above-average levels of poor housing, malnutrition, illiteracy, alcoholism, and infant mortality. According to HRW, "While the living standards of the rest of the country continue to improve, Mapuche in the south live in an impoverished enclave. On top of the discrimination from which they have suffered for years, many now feel the additional weight of political persecution."

That said, the Mapuche have succeeded since the 1990s in asserting themselves on the political stage. They have gained official recognition of their distinct cultural identity and their right to ancestral lands. For example, following the election of Michele Bachelet as Chilean president in 2006, the government transferred 40,000 acres (16,000 hectares) of indigenous lands, benefiting one thousand Mapuche families. Their strategy has been to forge alliances, not so much with neighboring governments as with civil society groups and international organizations. For example, in 1993 environmentalists joined with the Mapuche in opposing the construction of the Pengue hydroelectric system on the Bio-Bio River. The World Bank withdrew from the project in response, although the Chilean government was able to continue with the project by finding alternative funding sources. In 1993 the Mapuche joined the Hague-based Unrepresented Nations and Peoples Organization, which promotes their interests internationally.

History

Since their arrival in their current homeland some twelve thousand years ago, the Mapuche have had a recurring history of resisting colonial subjugation. In the twelfth century, this resistance was directed toward the Incas, who were then expanding their empire southward. From the sixteenth century on, the colonial threat came from the Spanish conquistadors. In 1641 the Mapuche won autonomy from Spain by signing the Treaty of Quillin, which gave them sovereignty over a large swathe of territory stretching from the Bio-Bio River southward to the Archipelago de los Chonos.

After Chile and Argentina became independent from Spain in the early 1800s, the Mapuche gradually lost their autonomy as these newly independent nations sought to forge a homogenous national identity. By 1845 Chile was encouraging Europeans to migrate into indigenous lands without Mapuche consent. This triggered clashes that culminated in a war from 1881–1883, in which Chilean and Argentine armies defeated—or "pacified," in their words—the Mapuche. As a result, much of the Mapuche's land was confiscated. Subsequently, many Mapuche found employment as tenant farmers or sharecroppers on large estates owned by European immigrants, which led to chronic poverty and economic marginalization.

For much of the twentieth century, the authorities did not recognize past injustices, much less make amends. According to the U.S.-based Chilean émigré, urban Chileans in the 1950s and 1960s had limited awareness of the Mapuche and many prejudices towards them. "In my school, any hint of a teacher telling the kids how bad the Spaniards or Chileans may have behaved towards 'Indians' and they would have been attacked by irate parents as a Communist." However, he added that "Chilean society did actually have some good things to say about the Mapuche—hard working and honest. Having a Mapuche maid in Santiago was considered quite a coup." He said that Mapuche in Santiago were not separated culturally from other Chileans of mixed ancestry, with no explicitly Mapuche restaurants or neighborhoods. The Mapuche influenced Chilean culture mainly through their legends and superstitions, and through their artwork, notably silver jewelry.

A tripling of the Mapuche population between 1927 and 1961 exacerbated poverty and disease, leading about a quarter of them to migrate to the cities. Chilean president Allende, elected in 1970 with Mapuche support, pushed through reforms that allowed indigenous peoples to reclaim some lands and created a Directorate of Indigenous Affairs. But when Allende was deposed in a military coup in 1973, his successor, General Augusto Pinochet, confiscated much of the land Allende had reclaimed, returning it to large estate owners. Severe political repression of the Mapuche continued through the 1970s and 1980s under the Pinochet dictatorship.

In the post-Pinochet era of the 1990s, political repression of the Mapuche declined. After consulting and concluding a pact with a coalition of Mapuche leaders in 1989, the government passed a law in 1993 recognizing the Mapuche as one of eight indigenous communities. The law established a government agency, the National Corporation of Indigenous Development, or CONADI, to promote their social development and culture. But a new threat emerged when the government embraced neoliberal economic policies, which caused a rapid expansion of industries such as forestry and hydroelectric energy onto the Mapuche's ancestral lands. Massive commercial plantations sprang up, encircling communities and harming the ecosystems on which the Mapuche depended for their livelihood. Militant resistance grew, and violent clashes with police and attacks on private property were commonplace by the end of the 1990s. The government prosecuted protesters using an anti-terrorist law dating from the Pinochet era. Human Rights Watch complained that Mapuche leaders were kept in pre-trial detention for months and that evidence was admitted from witnesses whose identities were withheld from the defense.

Leadership

As well as being the most numerous of the indigenous groups in Chile, the Mapuche are also one of the best organized. However, according to Cesar Millahueique, a Mapuche artist and performer, in an August 2009 email exchange, there is no single political group representing the interests of all Mapuche. Instead, they operate through an alliance of local, regional, and national organizations. These include Wallmapuwen, launched in February 2006; the

Mapuche Inter Regional Council, an umbrella organization based in Temuco City uniting six groups established in 1993; and Agrupación de Mapuche, established in 1984 as an umbrella body for thirteen hundred groups. Leading Mapuche figures include Pedro Gustavo Quilaqueo, Pedro Mariman, and Claudio Curihuentru. The Mapuche leadership includes both poor farmers and traditional leaders, as well as younger Mapuche who have lived in urban areas, studied in universities, and then returned to mobilize their community. In Argentina, the Indigenous Federation of Neuquén was established in 1973 to represent the Mapuche. It is demanding autonomy in order to unite with the Mapuche in Chile.

Of the more militant Mapuche pro-autonomy groups, one of the best-known is the All Lands Council (Consejo de Todas Las Tierras). Established in 1990, its goal is to see the formation of a completely autonomous Mapuche region. It focuses much of its energy on the campaign to reclaim Mapuche ancestral lands, including by force. Its leader is Aucan Huilcaman.

Around 2000, a more radical group emerged, the Coordinadora Arauco Malleco (CAM). It sets forth a pro-autonomy platform with nationalist undertones. CAM is led by Mapuche who felt excluded from the discussions between the Chilean government and other Mapuche tribal leaders in the late 1980s and early 1990s that culminated in the 1993 law enhancing indigenous community rights. CAM believes that the Mapuche people are a nation with the right to self-determination. Like the All Lands Council, CAM advocates confrontational methods, such as occupying the estates of the big landowners who acquired their property during the Pinochet era; blocking roads; firebombing houses, trucks, and warehouses; and burning lands owned by forestry industry consortia. About 2.4 percent of the Mapuche are involved in such illegal acts. HRW noted that most of the weapons used in these attacks are rudimentary—slingshots, sticks, and stones, along with a few shotguns. The regions of Chile most affected by the violence include Araucania, where estates have been seized, and the city of Concepción, the capital of the Bio-Bio region, where a rebel parliament has been established.

Current Status

The Bachelet government in Chile (2006–2010) continued to take steps recognizing a distinct Mapuche identity. In April 2008, it launched a Social Pact for Multiculturalism, and in September 2008 it ratified the International Labor Organization's 1989 Convention on Indigenous and Tribal Peoples (Convention 169). It has also begun to implement a plan to introduce bilingual education in regions where many Mapuche live. Poverty rates remain higher and education levels lower among Mapuche than among non-indigenous Chileans, but the gap is narrowing.

Reforms aside, Chile remains a centralized state, and many Mapuche, eager for greater autonomy, resent this. Tensions with the government center on land ownership and use. The state's efforts to restore some ancestral lands to indigenous communities have run into obstacles that have delayed the process. By choosing to buy properties from private owners and then hand them over to the Mapuche and other indigenous communities, the government has inadvertently encouraged rampant property speculation.

In early 2008, violence erupted in the Araucania region, with Mapuche militants setting fire several times to equipment owned by logging and agribusiness firms on lands the Mapuche claimed they owned. At least one Mapuche was killed in the clashes. In late 2007 and early 2008, a Mapuche female prisoner, Patricia Troncoso, staged a 111-day hunger strike that brought international attention to the Mapuche cause. Troncoso had been serving a ten-year prison sentence after being prosecuted under anti-terrorist legislation for setting fire to 250 acres (100 hectares) of land belonging to the Forestal Mininco Company.

One of Troncoso's demands was for the government to de-militarize the Mapuche areas—something that remains a pressing concern for the Mapuche. In 2009 there were more clashes with the government and more arrests of Mapuche militants. In April 2009, Mapuche activists staged a protest in the municipality of Curarrehue in Araucania triggered by concerns about pollution from a planned mining exploitation. Other projects the Mapuche have raised objections to include a gold mine in Pascua Lama, the megadam project, HidroAysen, and the Maqueo hydropower plant, which a Norwegian company, SN Power, is set to construct. According to a November 2009 article in *The Economist* magazine, the land restitution process launched in 1993, "far from satisfying the Mapuche . . . has ended up generating uncertainty and spreading conflict."

There have been similar clashes in Argentina. In October 2008, Mapuche families occupied land in the Nahuel Huapi National Park in the Neuquén province in order to secure 123,000 acres (50,000 hectares) for other Mapuche communities.

The Mapuche autonomy movement continues to receive strong support from environmentalists, in whom they have found a natural ally. Mapuche artist Millahueique stressed that the environmentalists were just one of a wide range of actors with whom the Mapuche have forged links in order to further their goals. "The Mapuche do not count on a single organization to represent them all," he added. "What exists is a great set of organizations, independent of one another that form alliances depending on the political and historical moment." He said that the mass media, in its depiction of the Mapuche autonomy movement, had erred by "ignoring these internal dynamics."

A former Chilean minister, Francisco Huenchumilla, who is of Mapuche ancestry, commented in July 2009 about the upsurge in Mapuche attacks: "It is less a matter of ill will or trying to damage the state than it is an ongoing feeling of unfairness." Huenchumilla criticized the Chilean government for failing to look at the ongoing conflicts with a broader, historical perspective: "The real dimensions of the conflict remain unknown by the Chilean authorities." He said the solution to the conflict should "start with revealing the historical truth instead of committing the mistake of believing it is only a matter of public order or poverty." While the Mapuche stand a reasonable chance of gaining greater control over how their natural resources are utilized, the prospects look slim that an autonomous Mapuche region will be created.

Further Reading

Center for International Development and Conflict Management, University of Maryland. "Minorities At Risk—Assessments for Indigenous Peoples in Chile," 2003, www.cidcm.umd.edu/mar/assessment.asp?groupId=15501.

Human Rights Watch, "Terrorism trials, military courts, and the Mapuche in Southern Chile," October 26, 2004, www.hrw.org/en/reports/2004/10/26/undue-process.

Mapuche International Link (Web site that provides information on Mapuche history and culture), www.mapuche-nation.org/english/frontpage.htm.

"The people and the land," *The Economist,* November 5, 2009, www.economist.com/node/14816728.

Unrepresented Nations and Peoples Organization Web site, entry on the Mapuche, www.unpo.org/content/view/7895/127.

Zibechi, Raúl. "Historical Mapuche Hunger Strike Ends in Success," Americas Program Special Report, Center for International Policy, February 26, 2008, http://americas.irc-online.org/am/5021.

MAYANS
(Guatemala, Mexico)

The Mayans, an indigenous American people living mainly in Guatemala and southern Mexico, have in recent years stepped up their campaign for greater cultural, judicial, and local autonomy. Neither the Guatemalan nor Mexican governments have granted self-government to Mayan communities, responding instead by enhancing Mayan cultural rights—for example, to educate themselves in their own language.

The Mayans make up between 40 and 60 percent of Guatemala's population of 13.5 million. Precise estimates are difficult to ascertain, in part because for centuries the Ladino peoples of European—mostly Spanish—ancestry have intermixed with the Mayans. In addition, Mayans were, until the late 1990s, wary of declaring themselves as such to officials taking the census for fear of being persecuted by the government. The Mayans live predominantly in the central highland areas stretching from the capital, Guatemala City, northward to the border with Mexico. There are about twenty distinct ethnic Mayan groups; the major ones include the K'iche,' Kaqchikel, Mam, and Q'eqchi.' Each group has its own language, many of which are not mutually intelligible. Mayans in the Q'eqchi' region and in rural areas are most likely to speak a Mayan language, whereas city-dwelling Mayans are more likely to speak Spanish. In religion, some are Catholic, some Protestant (mostly Evangelical), and many follow indigenous Mayan beliefs.

One of their biggest grievances with the Guatemalan state is the massacres perpetrated on them during a thirty-six-year civil war that raged from 1960 to 1996, in which 200,000 people either disappeared or were killed. Those responsible for the killings have not been brought to justice, and many still live among the Mayans, which has left a great deal of hostility toward the government. Though the civil war did not originate as a Mayan rebellion against repression or discrimination, as it dragged on the cultural and economic divide between Mayans and Ladinos became increasingly central to the conflict.

Guatemalan Mayans continue to face challenges in asserting their political rights and remain underrepresented in the Ladino-dominated administration, further heightening a sense of estrangement from the Guatemalan state. For example, only 14 percent of the Guatemalan police are of indigenous ancestry. Other grievances include having to work as migrant farm laborers on large Ladino-owned estates, receiving well-below-average wages, enduring substandard working conditions, and being unable to communicate with their government in their own language. The Minorities at Risk database of the University of Maryland's Center for International Development and Conflict Management noted "legislation and funding passed in 2004 to promote and protect indigenous languages and provide money for bilingual education." However, it added, "legal strides have yet to make a significant difference in quality of life. Indigenous are still drastically disadvantaged when it comes to education, wealth and political strength."

Mexican Mayans number several million out of Mexico's total population of 112 million. Separatism among Mexican Mayans is most visible along the Yucatan peninsula and in Chiapas, Mexico's southernmost state. Historically, the Mayans have had fewer opportunities to advance themselves economically than white or mixed-race Mexicans. Some still speak the indigenous Mayan languages, especially in rural areas and in the Yucatan. The main Mexican Mayan subgroups are the Maya, Tzeltal, Tzotzil, Chol, Tojolabal, and Zoque, with each possessing its own language. Mexican Mayans are predominantly Catholic. There are many non-Mayan indigenous Mexicans who live further north in the country, stretching up to the U.S. border.

Mexican Mayan separatism has manifested itself most obviously in the emergence in the mid-1990s of self-declared autonomous municipalities in Chiapas led by a movement called the Zapatistas, named after Emiliano Zapata, a famed revolutionary leader. The Mexican government has taken a nuanced approach to the Zapatistas, not recognizing them officially yet not clamping down on them using brute force either. The Zapatistas have thus been able to introduce cultural autonomy—for example, schooling in their own languages and practicing traditional medicines. However, they do not have the financial resources to develop the region economically—for example, constructing roads or health clinics.

According to Felipe Arizmendi, the Catholic bishop of San Cristobal de Las Casas who has been closely aligned with the Zapatistas, "the Indians are reclaiming their dignity. They are becoming more conscious of their history." Arizmendi, cited in a January 2004 *Boston Globe* article, said "they are now promoters of their rights. But Mexican society has also become more conscious that they exist and that they are people with rights." In the same article Xochitl Galvez, an Otomi Indian who headed the National Council for Indian Peoples, rejected the Mexican government's oft-stated mantra that devolution of power could lead to a "balkanization" of Mexico. "I don't see any risk in granting autonomy, nor that it could fragment the country," she said.

History

The Mayans have a long and illustrious history, with Mayan civilization flourishing in Central America in the first millennium C.E. From the early 1500s, their position became increasingly perilous after Spanish colonists arrived, seized lands, and forced Mayans onto the highlands or onto privately held estates to work as indentured labor. The Mayan population was also decimated by diseases such as influenza and smallpox brought over by the Europeans. After three hundred years of Spanish rule, Mayans between 1810 and 1821 fell under the authority of newly independent Mexico and Guatemala. The Mexican government in particular struggled for over a century to exert control over the rebellious Mayans.

In Guatemala the origins of today's tensions over land use can be traced to the 1870s when the government gave large plots of Mayan communal lands to European and U.S. investors, who grew coffee intended mainly for export. A century later, the Guatemalan civil war, from 1960 to 1996, proved highly destructive. The war began when a faction of the military revolted in protest over the government's having permitted U.S. troops to use Guatemala as a launch pad for the failed Bay of Pigs invasion in Cuba. The rebels were brutally repressed in 1965–1966, and some fled to the mountains and took refuge in regions populated by Mayans, with whom they began to forge close links. Mayans joined the guerrillas in growing numbers when, after a devastating earthquake in 1976, the government's response to their plight proved, in their view, grossly inadequate. By 1980 Mayan militant groups, like the Guerrilla Army of the Poor, had emerged. The Guatemalan government clamped down on them by setting up civilian self-defense patrols, which harassed, threatened, and sometimes killed Mayan leaders with impunity. The worst massacres took place from 1981–1983 when government troops destroyed hundreds of Mayan villages that had supported the guerrillas. About a million people were made refugees during the civil war, with many fleeing to Mexico. On December 29, 1996, a peace agreement was signed. In February 1999, the United Nations–sponsored Commission for Historical Clarification concluded that the Guatemalan government had committed acts of genocide against the Mayans during the civil war and confirmed that the U.S Central Intelligence Agency had aided the government.

The Mayans in Mexico were not brought under the full political control of the Mexican government until the early twentieth century, with the last village falling to the Mexican army in April 1933. Soon after, the traditional *ejido* system of communal land ownership was threatened when the Mexican government began privatizing lands from the 1940s. Culturally, the Mexican government's policy was to assimilate Mayans into Mexican society. In 1940 a Department of Indigenous Affairs was established to oversee this policy. The department was reincarnated in 2003 as the National Commission for the Development of Indigenous Peoples.

On January 1, 1994, the Zapatistas in eastern Chiapas revolted against the Mexican government by issuing the Declaration of the Lacandon Jungle and instituted a "parallel government" led by Amado Avendano. Two years of conflict ensued, which were interspersed with negotiations that ultimately led to the signing of a peace agreement with the Mexican authorities in 1996. On March 28, 2001, Zapatista leaders marched from Chiapas to the nation's capital, Mexico City, and addressed the Mexican Congress to demand passage of a bill bolstering indigenous rights. A law was passed in April 2001, but the Zapatistas rejected it because it did not give them sufficient autonomy or land rights. They instead proceeded to introduce autonomy in thirty municipalities in Chiapas, using ancestral forms of government and promoting communal land ownership, indigenous education, and traditional medicine. In 2003 they created a new justice system rooted in Mayan tradition.

Leadership

An independent country is not likely in the future for either the Mayans of Mexico or those of Guatemala. Their political leaders are focused instead on securing recognition of their culture and increasing local autonomy. The Zapatistas' official name is the Zapatista National Liberation Army (EZLN). Armed with about a thousand men, it has a leftist political ideology and an agenda of providing economic relief for indigenous Mexicans. According to *Boston Globe* journalist Marion Lloyd, their leader, known by the alias Subcomandante Marcos, has inspired a cult following, in part as a result of poetic letters he penned from the jungle. Marcos has lost some of his support in recent years, however, due to his long silences as well as diatribes against a Spanish judge for trying to outlaw the political wing of ETA, the Basque separatist militant group in Spain (see separate essay). The EZLN's political wing, the Zapatista National Liberation Front (FZLN), does not compete in elections and is not formally constituted as a political party. According to journalist Lloyd, "even if the Zapatistas have achieved little in the way of concrete changes, many observers credit them with putting indigenous rights on the national political agenda." A non-governmental group fighting for indigenous community rights in Mexico, the Organization of Indigenous Me'phaa People, is based in Guerrero state.

In Guatemala there is no political party that is committed exclusively to advancing Mayan interests. According to Arturo Arias, Guatemalan novelist and literature professor at the University of Texas in Austin, in an August 2009 telephone interview, this is because Mayans wish to avoid accusations of inverted racism. Local autonomy is their goal, and there are a growing number of Mayan mayors being elected. Mayan-based associations include the National Assembly of Representatives of the Mayan Peoples, the National Council of Mayan Peoples, the National Federation of Peasant Organizations (CNOC), the Equality Committee on Indigenous People's Land Rights, and Families of Guatemalan Disappeared (FAMDEGUA). Militant Mayan groups include the Guerrilla Army of the Poor, the Organization of the People in Arms, and the Rebel Armed Force.

A political party called the Center of Social Action (CASA) was launched in 2003 to represent all indigenous peoples of Guatemala. In the 2007 elections it won four legislative seats, and its presidential candidate, Eduardo Suger, came in fourth place, winning 7.4 percent of the vote. Suger and Rigoberto Queme are the party's leading forces. Rigoberta Menchu, who won the Nobel Peace Prize in 1992, established an indigenous group in 2005 called Winaq, which means "wholeness of being."

Current Status

In Guatemala, Mayans continue to eke out a difficult existence as migrant workers on large coffee and sugar plantations. In addition, there is increasing resentment over the presence of foreign companies that are extracting the area's natural resources. For example, a Canadian firm operates an open pit gold mine in San Marcos, while an international consortium operates a small-scale petroleum plant in Lake Izabal. Language rights continue to be a sensitive subject. While a law has existed since 2002 to guarantee Mayan speakers the right to be heard before a bilingual judge, a Human Rights Commission report found in 2004 that Mayan speakers, in practice, often appear in court with few, if any, translators. Mayans are still generally much poorer than Ladinos, and many Mayan children are malnourished.

Guatemalan president Alvaro Colóm, who took office in January 2008, has taken steps to build bridges with Mayans. He has increased the number of compensation payments, ranging from $1,500 to $2,500, to the survivors of the civil war, many of whom are Mayan. According to journalist Anne-Marie O'Connor, in a May 2009 *Washington Post* article, Colóm has even sent letters asking forgiveness. Eight hundred houses have been built for war victims.

Mayans are making progress in their campaign for justice over previous human rights abuses committed against them. On August 31, 2009, a former military commissioner was sentenced to 150 years in prison for the forced disappearances of members of a Mayan indigenous group from 1982–1984. Their campaign is not without risk: in August 2009 the president of the Guatemalan Association of Mayan Lawyers, Amilcar Pop, received a death threat. On October 18, 2009, a human rights lawyer and advocate for Mayan community rights, Fausto Leonel Otzin Poyon, was attacked and killed.

According to University of Texas' Arias, provisions in the 1996 peace agreement to allow Mayans to educate themselves in the Mayan language are slowly being implemented, with Mayan textbooks and primary schools now operating. So too are the accord's provisions to allow cases to be judged under traditional Mayan law. The U.S. State Department noted in March 2010, in its annual human rights report on Guatemala, that Mayan-language court interpreters were, despite being legally mandated, still rarely available in practice. There was also a shortage of Mayan-speaking judges.

In Mexico there has been no large-scale conflict between Mayans and the Mexican government since the late 1990s. Foreign observers are stationed in each Zapatista municipality to report any acts of aggression committed by the Mexican army against the Fray Bartolome Center for Human Rights in the city of San Cristobal in Chiapas. Discontent with the Mexican government's failure to implement the 1996 peace agreement has led thousands of Zapatista supporters to renounce government aid and rely on international donations. Such aid, which is also channeled to Guatemalan Mayans, comes from various European sources, including Scandinavian governments and churches, Spanish NGOs, labor groups, and German and Dutch left-leaning political parties. According to Dennis Smith, a U.S.-born, Guatemalan-based community worker for the Central American Evangelical Center for Pastoral Studies, the aid is used to finance cultural exchange programs, education and healthcare projects, and leadership training scholarships. The Mexican and Guatemalan governments accept this situation, he said, because it provides a "safety valve," helping to ease tensions triggered by Mayan resentment of their own governments' lack of services.

The Mexican government has enhanced Mayan cultural rights somewhat. In 2003 it created a National Council for Indian Peoples and gave it a budget of $320 million to improve infrastructure, healthcare, and education in Indian communities. Aid was also set aside to resolve land conflicts where a fundamental philosophical clash remains. For example, when Vicente Fox was elected president in 2000, he promoted further privatization of land, which goes against the traditional Mayan value of communal land ownership.

Further Reading

Center for International Development and Conflict Management, University of Maryland. "Minorities At Risk—Assessments for Indigenous Peoples in Guatemala and Mexico," 2003, www.cidcm.umd.edu/mar/assessments.asp?regionId=7.

Lloyd, Marion. "Zapatistas Endure A Decade Of Struggle," *The Boston Globe*, January 2, 2004, www.boston.com/news/world/articles/2004/01/02/struggle_endures_for_zapatistas.

O'Connor, Anne-Marie. "Payments and Apologies for Victims of Guatemala's Civil War; Under Colom, State Steps Up Program," *Washington Post*, May 6, 2009, www.washingtonpost.com/wp-dyn/content/article/2009/05/05/AR2009050503809.html.

Wilkinson, Daniel. *Silence On The Mountain: Stories of Terror, Betrayal, and Forgetting in Guatemala*. Durham, N.C.: Duke University Press, 2004.

U.S. Department of State. "2009 Human Rights Reports: Guatemala," March 11, 2010, www.state.gov/g/drl/rls/hrrpt/2009/index.htm.

PUERTO RICANS
(United States)

The people of Puerto Rico, a small Caribbean island with a population of four million, live in one of the last remaining colonies in the world. A small and occasionally violent minority has fought for Puerto Rico's independence since the United States seized it from Spain during the 1898 Spanish-American War, but most Puerto Ricans are reasonably content with the large degree of self-government they currently enjoy. Others are campaigning to further cement ties with the United States by making Puerto Rico the fifty-first U.S. state.

Most Puerto Ricans are of Spanish ancestry, with a strong mix of African blood dating from earlier centuries, when slaves were brought after the community and culture of the island's original inhabitants, the Taíno, had been wiped out. Puerto Rico is roughly three-quarters Catholic and one-quarter Protestant, with Pentecostalism the fastest growing group. Though over a century of U.S. political, economic, and cultural dominance has "Americanized" the people, it has also fostered anti-Americanism, which manifests itself through Puerto Ricans' strong identity with Spanish culture. Fuelling anti-Americanism is the fact that Puerto Ricans have no voting representative in the U.S. Congress and cannot vote in the U.S. presidential elections despite being U.S. citizens who pay social security taxes. Cultural nationalism is similarly strong among the three-and-a-half million people of Puerto Rican ancestry living on the U.S. mainland.

The islanders are sharply divided over whether to remain a commonwealth, become a U.S. state, or become fully independent. They have never had the chance to determine their status through a legally binding referendum, although there have been nonbinding plebiscites in 1967, 1993, and 1998. Typically, only about 5 percent of the electorate has voted for independence in these plebiscites, with the other 95 percent tending to split evenly between the pro-statehood and pro–status quo faction. The main political party advocating independence is the Puerto Rican Independence Party (PIP). Of the two largest parties on the island, one—the Popular Democratic Party (PPD)—favors remaining a commonwealth while the other—the New Progressive Party (PNP)—favors statehood.

Internationally, the issue of Puerto Rico's status is discussed regularly within the United Nations. The UN Decolonization Committee passed a resolution on June 9, 2008, calling for self-determination for Puerto Rico. That resolution was introduced by Cuba and Venezuela, two countries that have a strongly anti–U.S. foreign policy. Countries that spoke in favor of Puerto Rican independence on the UN panel included Ecuador, Bolivia, Nicaragua, Panama, Dominica, Syria, Iran, and Saint Vincent and the Grenadines. Under the U.S. political framework, the U.S. Congress has the lead on the status question. It has struggled to formulate a consistent line, with many representatives wary of making Puerto Rico a U.S. state while Spanish remains the dominant language there. What the long-term status of Puerto Rico will be remains unclear.

History

Not since before Spanish colonization in the early 1500s has Puerto Rio enjoyed independence. The first anti-colonial revolt, "El Grito de Lares," took place on September 23, 1868, and was quickly suppressed. In 1897 Spain gave autonomy to Puerto Rico, but it proved short-lived as the U.S. army invaded on July 25, 1898. Spain ceded the island, along with Cuba, Guam, and the Philippines, on December 10, 1898, under the Treaty of Paris. With the advent of U.S. rule, English replaced Spanish as the language of instruction in public schools. A governor was appointed by the U.S. president, a thirty-five-member Congress established, the Puerto Rican currency replaced by the dollar, and public funds for the Catholic Church curbed, enabling Protestant churches to grow. U.S. corporations gained control over the island's economy and resources, notably taking over the sugar plantations and making Puerto Rico increasingly dependent on the United States economically.

From 1900 Puerto Ricans could travel to the United States without restrictions, and in 1917 they were granted U.S. citizenship. However, they did not enjoy all the rights of mainland U.S. citizens and notably were not empowered to elect a voting representative to Congress. In the 1940s, encouraged by the U.S. government, many Puerto Rican farm workers migrated to the eastern U.S. states. Congress passed a law in 1947 establishing direct election of the governor of Puerto Rico. In 1948 Congress passed a gag law persecuting those who advocated independence that remained in force until the 1970s. In 1952, in its new constitution, Puerto Rico was designated a commonwealth, effectively allowing the U.S. Congress to continue legislating in many policy areas.

In 1989 U.S. senator John Bennett Johnston introduced a bill to give Puerto Ricans the right to determine their status. The bill included independence as one of their options, but it failed to muster enough support for passage. In May 2003, the U.S. Navy departed the Puerto Rican island of Vieques in response to intense local opposition, with residents having voted in 2001 by a two-to-one margin in favor of the base's closure. In 2004 a U.S. airbase in the town of Ceiba, the last significant U.S. military presence on the island, was closed.

Leadership

Established in 1946, the PIP's goal is a fully independent country where Puerto Ricans are permitted to retain U.S. citizenship and continue to receive U.S. social security, pension, and health benefits if they have contributed to the U.S. system. It wants a complete U.S. military withdrawal and a treaty to allow free trade and continuation of U.S. financial support to Puerto Rico. Another pro-independence political group is the Puerto Rican Socialist Party; together with the PIP it attracts about 5 percent of the vote.

Militant Puerto Rican separatist groups include the Armed Forces for National Liberation (FALN), the Volunteers of the Puerto Rican Revolution, the Boricua Popular Party, and the Armed Forces of Popular Resistance. Low level militant violence peaked in the early 1950s, late 1970s, and early 1980s, and included the killing of U.S. military personnel.

The first pro-independence group was the Nationalist Party, formed by lawyer Pedro Albizu Campos in the 1920s, who rose to prominence after defending a 1934 strike by sugar workers called in response to wage cuts imposed by U.S. sugar corporations. On March 21, 1937, Puerto Rican police fired on an independence march in the city of Ponce, killing twenty-one and wounding two hundred. In 1950 there was an uprising in the town of Jayuya that was brutally suppressed. On November 1, 1950, Nationalist Party militants tried to assassinate U.S. president Harry Truman, and on March 1, 1954, they wounded five members of Congress after entering the Capitol and opening fire.

Current Status

The pro-independence faction cites the examples of the Bahamas, Cyprus, Malta, and Singapore as proof that small islands can survive and thrive on their own. However, most Puerto Ricans remain unconvinced, fearful that independence will make them give up their U.S. passports and worsen poverty levels as U.S. financial aid dries up. The abandoned U.S. naval base at Vieques is now administered by the U.S. Fish and Wildlife Service, which is clearing it of unexploded munitions and hopes to convert it into a wildlife refuge. Spanish is now the dominant language in public and private life in Puerto Rico, having gradually regained its dominance from the 1940s. Young people today are likely to speak English as well.

There are ongoing campaigns for the release of imprisoned pro-independence militants, called *macheteros*. One former such prisoner, Alberto Rodriquez, was cited in a September 2009 *Chicago Tribune* article as saying, "When the powerful wage terrorism, they call it war. When the weak wage war, they call it terrorism." In May 2009, Puerto Rico's non-voting representative in Congress, Pedro Pierluisi, introduced the latest in a long line of self-determination bills. The bill provided for the holding of a non-binding referendum in which independence would be included among the options presented to Puerto Rican voters. It was approved by the U.S. House of Representatives on April 29, 2010, by 223 votes to 169 but the bill fell after the U.S. Senate failed to approve it by the end of 2010.

Historically, few Puerto Ricans have attained high office in the U.S. administration. That changed when, in August 2009, Judge Sonya Sotomayor was appointed to the Supreme Court. Although Sotomayor herself was born and raised in New York, both her parents were born in Puerto Rico. She has not voiced her opinion on Puerto Rico's status recently, but she did have strong views in her student years, which were recalled in the press during her Senate confirmation hearings. As a Princeton undergraduate, Sotomayor argued against integrating Puerto Rico into the United States. "The experiences of Alaska and Hawaii since statehood with cultural destruction has been indicative of the cultural loss Puerto Rico would eventually face if statehood for the island was chosen," she wrote.

Further Reading

Avila, Oscar. "Former Puerto Rico radicals celebrate 10 years of freedom," *Chicago Tribune*, Sept. 15, 2009, www.chicagotribune.com/news/nationworld/la-na-faln-clemency10-2009sep10,0,5403986.story.

Fernández, Ronald. *The Disenchanted Island: Puerto Rico and the United States in the 20th Century.* Westport: Praeger, 1996.

Grody, Arienna. "Puerto Rican Nationalism and the Drift Towards Statehood," Council on Hemispheric Affairs, 2006, www.coha.org/2009/07/puerto-rican-nationalism-and-the-drift-towards-statehood.

Puerto Rico Independence Party Web site, Independencia.net.

Skiba, Katherine. "Puerto Rican statehood? No thanks, Gutierrez says," *Chicago Tribune*, May 2, 2010, http://articles.chicagotribune.com/2010-05-02/news/ct-met-gutierrez-puerto-rico-0501-20100501_1_puerto-rican-statehood-puerto-rico-democracy-act-island-s-political-status.

QUEBECOIS
(Canada)

Separatism in the mostly French-speaking province of Quebec has for almost half a century constituted the single biggest threat to the unity of Canada. The high watermark of the secessionist movement came in 1995 when the francophone Quebeckers, or Quebecois, came within a hair's breadth of splitting away from Canada in a referendum.

Today, the issue is no longer as pressing, in part because the Quebecois already enjoy extensive autonomy that is exercised through a provincial government with control over sensitive areas, including language and culture policy. Quebeckers employ a unique legal system too. They apply the Canadian criminal law code but use the French-based Napoleonic code for civil law matters, unlike the rest of the country which applies a civil code based on English law. The United Kingdom monarch, Queen Elizabeth II, remains the titular head of state for Quebec, as she is for all Canadians. In practice, the British monarch is not involved in Canadian politics. The Queen is represented by a Governor General, who is appointed for five years, and Lieutenant Generals for each province. Their roles are largely ceremonial.

French Canadians are a relatively cohesive force politically, due in large part to their high territorial concentration. Numbering about seven million, or roughly one fifth of Canada's population of thirty-four million, about 90 percent of French Canadians live in Quebec, with 400,000 living in the province of Ontario and 250,000 in the province of New Brunswick. Eighty-two percent of Quebec residents are French-speaking. Of the 18 percent non-Francophone Quebeckers, English-speakers account for 10 percent, with Italian, Portuguese, and Arabic-speakers constituting the other principal linguistic communities. Quebec City, the provincial capital, has a population of 700,000 and is overwhelmingly francophone. However, Quebec's largest city, Montreal, which has a population of 3.6 million, has a much slimmer francophone majority, about 60 percent. Outside of Quebec, English is the dominant language throughout Canada.

The Quebecois have historically had strained relations with non-French speakers, including with Canada's indigenous Indian and Inuit peoples, most of whom are Anglophone. The Quebec Inuit—formerly known as Eskimo—live mostly in the north in a sparsely inhabited region called Nunavik, which makes up about a third of the province and has a population of just 9,500. Both the Inuit and other aboriginal, or "First Nation," people have tended

129

to be hostile to Quebecois separatism. They voted overwhelmingly against Quebec independence in referenda in 1980 and 1995, including the French-speakers among them who are called "Montagnais." Recent immigrants, including those from francophone North Africa and Haiti, similarly tend to be anti-separatist, with their allegiances directed more toward the Canadian state.

The issues of independence and sovereignty continue to generate heated debate in Canadian politics, even though Quebec separatism has not manifested itself in violence since the 1970s. And while many Quebecois are ardent secessionists, others passionately support a continued union with Canada. For example, two of Canada's longest-serving prime ministers in recent years have been French-speaking Quebeckers who were among the fiercest campaigners against Quebec separatism. These were Pierre Trudeau, prime minister for the Liberal party from 1968–1979 and 1980–1984, and Jean Chrétien, who was premier from 1993–2003.

Economically, Quebec has performed reasonably well in recent decades and has developed strong hydroelectricity, biotechnology, and service industries. This has helped to change the perception that persisted until the 1960s of Quebeckers as a rural, economically backward, and not very business-minded people. Their nearest neighbor is the United States, with most Quebeckers living relatively close to the U.S. border. The United States has avoided taking a position in the secession debate, although from a trade perspective it would prefer to have to deal with only one country. Were Quebec to go it alone, it is uncertain how this would impact the 1989 Canada-U.S. Free Trade Agreement or the 1994 North American Free Trade Agreement between Canada, Mexico, and the United States. Those pacts have greatly helped to integrate the U.S. and Canadian economies.

One country, France, has spoken out on the Quebec sovereignty question. In 1967 French president Gen. Charles de Gaulle entered the fray when he gave a speech while visiting Montreal that concluded with the controversial words, *"Vive le Québec libre,"* or "Long live free Quebec." As this phrase was already being used by the separatists, it was seen as a clear endorsement of their agenda and helped to embolden them at home while raising their profile around the world. Unsurprisingly, the comment went down very badly among pro-union Canadians, and de Gaulle departed early after Canada's prime minister cancelled a scheduled meeting in Ottawa. The incident caused a rift in relations between Canada and France that did not fully heal until the 1980s. The French government has never again spoken out so forcefully, and diplomats from other countries have tread lightly, keen not to antagonize the Canadian government.

History

French settlers first arrived in Quebec in 1608, just as English settlers were starting to migrate to North America. The French-speaking community came under British rule in 1763 after France lost the Seven Years War to Great Britain. The new British rulers initially tried to integrate the francophone community into the English-speaking colony before reversing policy and recognizing Quebec's francophone culture and legal system, a division formalized in 1791 by the British parliament. The Quebecois rebelled against British rule in 1837, but the uprising was quashed. In 1867 Quebec and three other British-ruled provinces—Ontario, Nova Scotia, and New Brunswick—were merged into a single federation following an act passed by the British parliament. Other provinces subsequently joined the federation.

The Quebec independence movement developed from the 1960s and became known as the "Quiet Revolution." The French language was progressively bolstered, with Canada's parliament passing a law in 1969 providing for linguistic equality. The Quebec government granted local autonomy to the Inuit in 1975 when it signed the James Bay Agreement, which included a $90 million compensation payment to the Inuit in return for the latter's agreeing to the installation of huge hydroelectric dams. In 2002 the Quebec authorities gave fourteen Inuit villages $450 million for projects related to infrastructure and the environment, in return for allowing the expansion of hydropower capacity in Inuit areas.

The Quebec independence movement gathered steam in the 1970s. A watershed moment for French Canadians came in 1976 when the separatist Parti Quebecois (PQ) won the provincial elections for the first time and entered government. It called a referendum on independence in 1980, but 60 percent of the voters rejected secession. In 1982 Canada adopted a new constitution formalizing the long-standing reality of Canada's political independence from the United Kingdom. Despite this "repatriation" of the constitution, Canada chose not to become a republic, and the British monarch remained Canada's head of state. Quebecois separatists refused to endorse the new constitution, however, because it deprived them of the right to veto future changes to the constitution and did not give them the powers they wanted in setting their own education and immigration policy. In 1987, to try to persuade Quebec to ratify the constitution, the Canadian government signed the Meech Lake Accord in which Quebec was recognized as a "distinct society," but the accord was never ratified as some English-speaking provinces opposed it.

The distinct society concept was supposed to have been enshrined in the constitution by a nationwide referendum in October 1992, giving further autonomy to Quebec as well as to First Nation Canadians. But that referendum was rejected due to opposition on two fronts: hard-liner Quebecois who felt it did not go far enough and federalist Canadians, notably in the west, who felt that Quebec was being given too much autonomy. The election of the separatist PQ to the provincial government in 1994 precipitated another referendum on independence in October 1995. This also failed, albeit by a much smaller margin, with 50.6 percent voting against independence on a turnout of 93 percent.

The ensuing years saw the fortunes of the Quebecois separatists wax and wane. In August 1998 Canada's Supreme Court ruled that Quebec could secede if it wished, but it needed the consent of the federal government and other provinces on specific issues such as the national debt and the common currency. The Quebecois received a blow in March 2000 when the Canadian parliament passed a law empowering it to determine whether the wording in any future independence referendum was sufficiently clear. In November 2006, the Canadian parliament recognized Quebec as "a nation within a united Canada."

Leadership

As it is legal to campaign for peaceful secession, French Canadian separatists have mostly channeled their energies into the democratic political system. The main Quebec separatist party has two branches: PQ at the regional level and the Bloc Québecois (BQ) at the national level. While independence is the long-term goal, in the short term the two parties are pushing for Quebec's provincial government to be given greater control over its language, immigration, and cultural policy; they want French to become even more dominant in the province; and they want to boost Quebec's presence on international bodies such as UNESCO, the United Nations culture agency, and the International Labor Organization.

The PQ was established in 1968 by journalist Rene Levesque. The BQ was established in 1991 by Lucien Bouchard, reaching its zenith in national politics from 1993–1997 when it was the second largest party in Canada and the official opposition to the Canadian government. Bouchard, one of the strongest advocates for full independence in the

Lucien Bouchard (1938–   )

LUCIEN BOUCHARD was born December 22, 1938, in Saint-Coeur-de-Marie, Quebec, Canada. He is well known in Canada as a former politician on both the national and provincial levels. Bouchard attended Université Leval, where he received a Bachelor of Social Science and Law in 1964. Bouchard practiced law in the public sector, working mostly in the public interest in corporate and trade union law.

Bouchard's separatist sympathies led him to become politicized in the 1970s as separatist sentiment among the Quebecois grew. Bouchard first came to public prominence in Canadian politics in the 1980 referendum on Quebec independence, in which he served as chair of the "Oui" (Yes) side. Although the Oui side was defeated 60 percent to 40 percent, the result served to show the rest of Canada the depth of Francophone discontent within Quebec. In 1984 Brian Mulroney, an old friend of Bouchard's from Université Leval, became prime minister of Canada as a member of the Progressive Conservative party. Mulroney asked Bouchard to join his government, and Bouchard agreed, although he remained a staunch Quebec nationalist. Mulroney and Bouchard thought that they could improve the status of Quebec within Canada.

Bouchard served as Ambassador to France from 1985–1988. In 1988 he was elected to the House of Commons as a Progressive Conservative, representing his home electoral district of Lac-Saint-Jean. Prime Minister Mulroney appointed Bouchard to his cabinet, where he served first as Secretary of State and later as Minister of the Environment.

In 1990 the Canadian political establishment was shocked—nobody more so than Prime Minister Mulroney—when Bouchard abruptly resigned as Minister of the Environment and left the Progressive Conservative party. Bouchard was joined by several other Quebecois legislators who left their parties after the failure of the Meech Lake Accord. Meech Lake was an effort by Canadian lawmakers to bring Quebec more fully in line with the Canadian Constitution. It would have provided Quebec a great deal of autonomy within Canada as well as providing special rights for francophones. Several of the anglophone provinces felt that Meech Lake went too far in providing for the francophone population of Canada and was in fact anti-anglophone. The combined resistance of these provinces killed the Meech Lake Accord.

In 1991 Bouchard founded a new political party at the national level that was explicitly separatist—the Bloc Quebecois. Its first major success was in 1993 when it won fifty-four seats in the House of Commons, and Bouchard became the head of the opposition. At this time, separatist sentiments in Quebec were once again on the rise. In 1994, at the provincial level, the Parti Quebecois, or PQ (the provincial sister party to the Bloc Quebecois, which is a national party), won a large enough majority to begin pressing for a second referendum on Quebec sovereignty. Bouchard once again became a prominent advocate for the "Oui" side, despite the loss of a leg due to necrotizing fasciitis (flesh-eating bacteria). Although the "Oui" side lost the referendum vote again, this time the outcome was much closer, with 50.6 percent voting "Non" and 49.4 percent voting "Oui".

After the 1995 referendum, the PQ premier of Quebec, Jacques Parizeau, announced his retirement from politics, and Bouchard announced that he would be leaving the House of Commons in order to seek the premiership of Quebec. Bouchard became premier of Quebec in 1996 and promised that there would be no more referenda "for the time being." Instead, Bouchard focused on fixing the province's financial problems. In 2001 Bouchard stepped down as premier of Quebec, resuming his life as a private citizen. He was succeeded as premier by Bernard Landry. Bouchard is married to Audrey Best, although they are currently separated. They have two children.

early 1990s, decided to redirect his energies toward building up the Quebec economy after the 1995 independence referendum failed. In 2001 Bouchard was replaced as Quebec premier by the more separatist-minded Bernard Landry, but by then public opinion in Quebec had shifted away from demanding full independence. In the 2008 provincial elections, the PQ scored second place. The parties' current leaders are Gilles Duceppe (BQ) and Pauline Marois (PQ).

A smaller pro-independence party, Québec Solidaire, was set up in 2006 and typically attracts about 5 percent support. A party was established in 1994, the Democratic Action of Quebec (ADQ), which advocates greater autonomy for Quebec within a more loosely configured Canadian state or confederation. Support for the ADQ rose steadily in Quebec elections, from 6.5 percent in 1994 to 30.8 percent in 2007, but slipped back to 16.4 percent in 2008.

Various militant Quebecois groups have emerged since the 1960s, although there has not been a major outbreak of separatist-related violence in recent years. The best-known of these is the Quebec Liberation Front (FLQ), which carried out hundreds of bombings in the 1960s and 1970s. The FLQ lost most of whatever popular support it had after a notorious operation in October 1970, when the group kidnapped and murdered Quebec's Minister of Labor, Pierre Laporte. Other militant separatist groups to have emerged since 2000 include the Young Patriots of Quebec (JPQ) and the Quebec Resistance Network (RRQ).

Current Status

The Quebecois have succeeded in their goal of preserving French culture in Canada. French is now the required language for commerce, the workplace, education, and government in Quebec. Indeed, some of the non-French speaking Quebeckers feel that government policies have swung too far in favor of the francophone community. For example, there is resentment over a 1978 Quebec law that makes it difficult for parents—especially immigrants—to send their children to English schools that receive public funds. The law requires at least one of the parents to have attended an English school in Canada for a child to be able to go. The Quebecois' relations with the Inuit community have recently improved. The Quebec government in February 2008 signed a land claims agreement with the Inuit of Nunavik,

out of which an Inuit-controlled regional government was created.

Relations between French- and English-speaking Canadians remain patchy. Tensions bubbled up in 2009 during the commemorations of the 250th anniversary of the Battle of the Plains of Abraham, in 1759, when British forces defeated the French military on Canadian soil. The battle was a pivotal moment in Canada's history as it ushered in British rule in Quebec. Patrick Bourgeois, leader of the radical RRQ party, threatened to disrupt a re-enactment of the battle planned for summer 2009, which caused the event's cancellation.

In September 2009, much to the irritation of the Canadian federalists, Quebec artists recited writings of famous Quebec separatists, including the 1970 manifesto of the militant FLQ, at a ceremony attended by the leaders of the PQ and BQ. A February 2009 article in *The Economist* magazine noted how the Plains of Abraham battle continues to be interpreted very differently by the two sides: "for many sovereigntists [Quebecois separatists] it was the beginning of domination by the wretched English, and of the struggle for cultural survival. Federalists, however, both Francophone and Anglophone, argue that after the Conquest the French of New France got rights they could only dream of under the exploitative, authoritarian ancien régime."

There is a considerable element of bluff in the secession debate. Federalists claim that the Canadian government will sever all ties with Quebec in the event of independence. The secessionists believe this to be hyperbole and a federalist scare tactic aimed at keeping the Quebecois a part of Canada. The Inuit continue to be a small but significant element in the equation. Inuit leaders insist that if Quebec does separate, the Inuit in turn will secede from a newly independent Quebec. The Inuit are not the only aboriginal group likely to make it difficult for the Quebecois to secede. There is a Mohawk Indian population of fifteen thousand in Quebec that opposes Quebecois separatism. The Mohawks also refuse to recognize Canadian or U.S. sovereignty.

Speaking at the Woodrow Wilson International Center for Scholars in Washington D.C. in October 2010, BQ leader Gilles Duceppe insisted "the question of Quebec's political future is by no means settled." He claimed the public was "evenly split" on the independence question and stressed how in the past, once a referendum is actually called, popular support for independence has increased. Duceppe said that if his party returns to power—an election is due by 2013—the referendum issue will be on the table again. Quebec, albeit not quite as wealthy as the neighboring Canadian province of Ontario, would still be among the more affluent countries in the world if it became independent. But Canada's English-speakers are likely to continue to vigorously oppose secession, in part for strategic reasons. Given its geographic location, an independent Quebec would divide English-speaking Canada in two, potentially threatening the country's viability. The eastern provinces of New Brunswick, Newfoundland and Labrador, Nova Scotia, and Prince Edward Island would be completely cut off from the western part. Canada would lose prestige on the global stage, possibly having to give up its seat in major political forums such as the G-8 world leaders summit. Moreover, an independent Quebec would create new, discontented linguistic minorities, given that 18 percent of Quebec is non-French-speaking.

Further Reading

Bauch, Hubert. "Sovereignty debate passé, poll shows," *The Gazette* (Montreal), May 19, 2010, www.montreal gazette.com/technology/Sovereignty+debate+pass% C3%A9+poll+shows/3044717/story.html.

Bloc Quebecois Web site, www.blocquebecois.org.

Cooper, Mary H. "Québec Sovereignty," *CQ Researcher* 5, no. 37 (October 1995).

"Fighting old battles; Quebec," *The Economist,* February 28, 2009, www.economist.com/world/americas/ displaystory.cfm?story_id=13185508#.

Macpherson, Don. "Only in Quebec, you say?" *The Gazette,* September 15, 2009, www.montrealgazette .com/news/Only+Quebec/1994223/story.html.

Murphy, Michael. *Quebec and Canada in the New Century: New Dynamics, New Opportunities.* Kingston: Queens University, 2005.

Parti Quebecois Web site, www.pq.org.

Australasia and East Asia

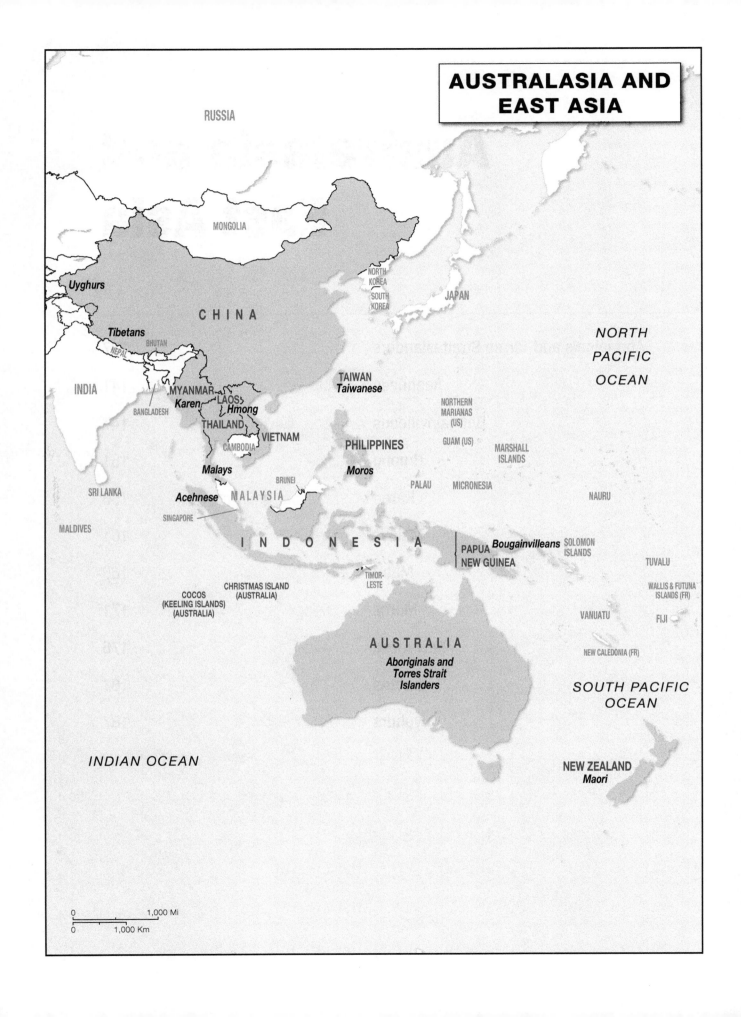

AUSTRALASIA AND EAST ASIA

RUSSIA

MONGOLIA

Uyghurs

CHINA

Tibetans

NEPAL BHUTAN

INDIA

NORTH KOREA

SOUTH KOREA

JAPAN

NORTH PACIFIC OCEAN

TAIWAN
Taiwanese

MYANMAR
Karen LAOS
Hmong

BANGLADESH

THAILAND

VIETNAM

CAMBODIA

PHILIPPINES

NORTHERN MARIANAS (US)

GUAM (US)

MARSHALL ISLANDS

Malays

Moros

Acehnese

MALAYSIA

BRUNEI

PALAU MICRONESIA

NAURU

SINGAPORE

SRI LANKA

MALDIVES

I N D O N E S I A

PAPUA NEW GUINEA

Bougainvilleans SOLOMON ISLANDS

TUVALU

TIMOR-LESTE

WALLIS & FUTUNA ISLANDS (FR)

COCOS (KEELING ISLANDS) (AUSTRALIA)

CHRISTMAS ISLAND (AUSTRALIA)

VANUATU

FIJI

NEW CALEDONIA (FR)

AUSTRALIA

Aboriginals and Torres Strait Islanders

SOUTH PACIFIC OCEAN

INDIAN OCEAN

NEW ZEALAND
Maori

0   1,000 Mi
0   1,000 Km

ABORIGINALS AND TORRES STRAIT ISLANDERS (Australia)

Accounting for 2 percent of the Australian population of twenty-one million, the Aboriginals are still struggling to adjust to the impact of European colonization. They gained considerable autonomy in the 1970s but have seen much of this erode since 2007, as internal problems in their communities have triggered greater government intervention. After fifty millennia of undisturbed subsistence, they now live in the sixth largest country in the world in terms of land area, where English is the dominant language, the political elite is overwhelmingly of European ancestry, and their head of state is the British monarch.

Most Aboriginals—also called Aborigines—live in cities, but they are more numerically dominant in remote areas in northern and central Australia, notably in Queensland and in the Northern Territory. There are also 50,000 indigenous Australians who are culturally distinct from the Aborigines who come from the Torres Strait Islands located between the northern tip of Australia and Papua New Guinea. There are many different Aboriginal languages, some of which have become extinct since colonization; there are only about 10,000 speakers of Aboriginal languages left. The Aboriginal population shrank from about 750,000 when European colonization began in 1788 to 102,000 by 1966. By 2006 their numbers had risen to half a million, although this was partly due to a revised definition of "Aboriginal" in the census.

The pro-autonomy movement in the Aboriginal community has focused on claiming ancestral lands and seeking compensation for past abuses committed by the government. Great bitterness remains over the government policies that were in place from 1901 until the mid-1960s, policies that sought to dilute Aboriginal identity and further the goal of assimilation into white Australian society. Those policies changed in the late 1960s, after which the government granted autonomy to the Aboriginals on tribal reservations and supported "self-determination," although this concept has never been clearly defined. In the late 1990s, the government changed direction again and assumed a more direct role in governing Aboriginal communities. This came in response to a growing feeling among Australians that previous policies had only made Aboriginals more dependent on welfare and worsened social problems such as alcoholism, poverty, and inadequate education.

Some prominent Aboriginal leaders are still campaigning for greater self-government, while others feel the model of autonomy introduced in the 1970s and 1980s has failed. Few advocate a return to the kind of assimilation policies that led authorities from the late 1800s to the 1960s to remove up to 100,000 Aboriginal children from their parents and place them with white Australians in foster homes. This policy, which resulted in the so-called Stolen Generations, was highlighted in a 1997 report from a national Commission of Inquiry. Australian prime minister Kevin Rudd made a formal apology for it before parliament on February 13, 2008, something his predecessor, John Howard, had refused to do. The federal government has not yet offered financial compensation to the victims, although one state government, Tasmania, which has a relatively small Aboriginal population, has done so.

History

The Aboriginals first arrived in Australia about fifty thousand years ago, subsisting on foods acquired through hunting, gathering, and fishing. Europeans did not make any formal claim of ownership until 1770, the year Captain James Cook claimed it for Great Britain, marking the beginning of British rule. Six British colonies were created. These colonies came together on January 1, 1901, to form the Commonwealth of Australia. The Australian government's initial policy toward the Aboriginal population was to integrate it into the white community, sometimes forcibly.

The political and economic rights of Aboriginals as a distinct people were bolstered after a referendum passed in 1967 enabling the federal government to adopt laws specifically for Aboriginals and requiring that Aboriginals be counted in the census for the first time. Aboriginal representative structures were set up aimed at giving them a role in setting policy. The National Aboriginal Consultative Committee operated from 1973–1977; it was succeeded by the National Aboriginal Conference from 1977–1985 and the Aboriginal and Torres Strait Islanders Commission from 1989–2005. Each of these bodies was disbanded following criticisms that they were either dysfunctional or not truly representative of Aboriginal interests.

Following a strike initiated in 1966 by Aboriginal workers at a cattle station in Gurindji in the Northern Territory, Aboriginals grew more assertive in demanding land rights. While the federal government did establish Aboriginal reservations and land councils, it did not have the legal authority to install a country-wide land rights system. Some state governments, like that of South Australia, supported land rights claims; others, like those of Queensland and Western Australia, were more reticent. Aboriginal land rights were greatly enhanced in June 1992 when the Australian High Court rejected the long-established *terra nullius* principle, which claimed Australian land had been owned by no one until European settlement began. The Mabo judgment—named after plaintiff Eddie Mabo, a Torres Strait Islander—led the government in December 1993 to pass the Native Title Act, which allowed Aboriginals to file claims to up to 10 percent of Australian territory. There have been many court rulings since then, with Aboriginals scoring both successes and defeats.

Leadership

There is no country-wide Aboriginal government or political party. The most effective bodies operate at the regional level, and most of these either represent Aboriginal landowners or have a specific policy focus. For example, the National Aboriginal Community Controlled Health Organization is a coalition that lobbies the government on health policy. Indigenous groups like the Australian Aborigines League and the Aborigines Progressive Association first formed in the 1930s, while bodies like Aboriginal Health Services and Aboriginal Legal Services were set up in the 1970s.

The leaders of the Aboriginal autonomy movement tend to be well-educated lawyers and academics. Lawyer Noel Pearson, once a leading land rights campaigner who helped to negotiate the 1993 Native Title Act, has since the late 1990s focused on ending Aboriginal dependency on welfare. Mick Dodson, a law professor at Australian National University, has lobbied the United Nations to boost Aboriginals' right to self-determination. Marcia Langton, a professor at the University of Melbourne, also has a national presence. Eddie Mabo's land claim case—he died five months before the ruling was delivered—made him an icon of the land rights movement.

Prominent Aboriginal politicians are scarce. As of January 2011, there was only one person of Aboriginal ancestry in the national parliament, Ken Wyatt, who was elected in August 2010, and only a few in state parliaments. The first Aboriginal elected at the national level was Neville Bonner, a senator from Queensland from 1971–1983. Aden Ridgeway, from New South Wales, was the only Aboriginal member of the federal parliament from 1999–2005. Given this underrepresentation in state and federal parliaments, it has fallen to Aboriginal athletes such as Olympic gold-medalist runner Catherine Freeman to provide leadership role models, but Aboriginal athletes typically have not promoted a particular political agenda.

Current Status

The autonomy movement is on the defensive, undermined by the dire social problems Aboriginal communities face. These include an alcoholism epidemic, widespread abuse of Aboriginal women and children, substandard health conditions, and a life expectancy seventeen years below that of other Australians. Only 20 percent of Aboriginals participate in the labor market, and most of those who do work in low-skilled jobs. Approximately 50 percent rely on government welfare, and Aboriginals account for a disproportionately high share of the prison population.

The government since 2007 has been more interventionist, restricting sales of alcohol in townships, requiring Aboriginal children to undergo medical checks, and restricting how Aboriginals can spend their welfare. Land ownership claims continue. On April 25, 2008, a federal court rejected a claim to a large chunk of southwestern Western Australia, including the city of Perth. A bright spot in Aboriginal efforts to become more economically independent has been a boom in sales of their artwork, which in 2008 accounted for 50 percent of all Australian art sales.

The autonomy debate often focuses on life on Aboriginal reservations. Helen Hughes, a professor and author of a book on indigenous policy, argued in a September 2008 article in *The Australian* that "communal property rights have prevented development. Dismal shops and public housing are reminiscent of communist Russia." Echoing a view common among Australians, she lambasted former separatist policies, saying they had denied Aboriginal children basic schooling and that "bilingual education has been an excuse for no education at all." Only about 20 percent of Aboriginals actually live on reservations today, with most now residing either in or near urban centers. Many of them also reject cultural separatism, communal land rights, and traditional subsistence living.

Internationally, the autonomy movement scored a victory in September 2007 when the United Nations General Assembly passed the Declaration on the Rights of Indigenous Peoples, which enshrined their right to self-determination and autonomy. Australia, along with Canada, New Zealand, and the United States—each of which are contending with indigenous movements—were the only four countries to vote against the declaration.

Further Reading

"Bringing them Home," National Inquiry into the Separation of Aboriginal and Torres Strait Islander Children from Their Families (Australian government report), April 1997, www.hreoc.gov.au/social_justice/bth_report/report/index.html.

Hooley, Neil. "Aboriginal children need teaching that respects their culture," *The Age*, April 15, 2008, www.theage.com.au/news/opinion/aboriginal-children-need-teaching-that-respects-their-culture/2008/04/14/1208025085406.html.

Hughes, Helen, and Mark Hughes. "Gap worse for remote indigenous," *The Australian*, September 3, 2008, www.theaustralian.com.au/politics/opinion/gap-worse-for-remote-indigenous/story-e6frgd0x-1111117374575.

Maddison, Sarah. *Black Politics.* Crows Nest: Allen and Unwin, 2009.

Pearson, Noel. *Up from the Mission.* Melbourne: Black Inc., 2009.

Rothwell, Nicolas. "Giving it back: a revolution in the bush." *Weekend Australian,* October 31, 2009, www.theaustralian.com.au/news/giving-it-back-a-revolution-in-the-bush/story-e6frg6po-1225792734396.

ACEHNESE
(Indonesia)

Separatists in Aceh, a province on the northern tip of Sumatra, one of Indonesia's four main islands, fought a bloody war of independence against Indonesian authorities from 1976 until 2005. A peace agreement was signed in August 2005 that granted them a large degree of autonomy, which seems to have quelled their secessionist aspirations. The Acehnese number four million and account for 2 percent of Indonesia's total population of 240 million.

The province, which includes 119 islands, is 99 percent Muslim. The residents are renowned for strict adherence to Islam—more so than elsewhere in Indonesia, a country that is 86 percent Muslim, 9 percent Christian, 2 percent Hindu, and 1 percent Buddhist. The Indonesian government, which is secular, has since 1999 permitted Aceh to apply Islamic laws in an effort to curb secessionism. Thus, women in Aceh must wear headscarves, and corporal punishment, including caning and whipping, is meted out to residents convicted of drinking alcohol or gambling.

The Acehnese language is written in Arabic script and is more closely related to Malay than Javanese, the most widely spoken language in Indonesia. The number of Acehnese-speakers dropped from 67.5 percent in 1980 to 57.4 percent in 1995, according to census figures. Most residents identify themselves as "Acehnese"—82.7 percent a 2003 survey found—although there is no clear definition of this term. In the twentieth century many people from other parts of Indonesia immigrated to Aceh, including workers on colonial Dutch coffee and rubber plantations, and Javanese were encouraged to move there by the Java-based government. Aceh also has two indigenous minorities, the Gayo and Alas, who live in the central highlands.

The separatist conflict became better known across the globe after a powerful Indian Ocean tidal wave, or tsunami, devastated Aceh on December 26, 2004, killing 168,000 people. This death toll was about ten times greater than the total killed during the entire thirty-year separatist conflict, which claimed between twelve and twenty thousand lives. The spotlight that shone on Aceh in the aftermath of the tsunami helped to advance a peace process that culminated in an agreement signed on August 15, 2005, outlining Acehnese autonomy.

In a 2005 report for the United Nations Development Program (UNDP), author Graham Brown attributed the separatist movement to "a distinct Acehnese local history greatly at odds with the broader history of Indonesia, with a long and—from their perspective—glorious history of resistance to various imperialist powers combined with a cultural identity more closely tied to Islamic orthodoxy than in much of the rest of the country." In his 2009 book on the conflict, Edward Aspinall, a professor at Australian National University in Canberra, singled out the Indonesian education system as a factor in fostering opposition to separatism. Indonesians are taught from an early age to value the ethnic diversity and multicultural nature of their country, which makes them less sympathetic to calls for Aceh independence. Aspinall cited a military officer who complained that "the ancestors of the Acehnese long ago swore oaths to Indonesian independence. Why now rebel? Betray: that's what you call it."

Acehnese anger over how the Indonesian government was exploiting Aceh's resources was the factor that tipped the scales from historic antagonism to full-scale conflict. In 1971 oil and gas were discovered in the region and quickly became a major source of wealth. However, it was not the Acehnese who profited most from it but foreign multinationals and the governing elite based in Indonesia's capital, Jakarta. Despite its newfound oil wealth, the poverty rate in Aceh actually grew during the conflict, although this was also a consequence of the damage that the conflict itself inflicted on the province. The situation has improved considerably since 2000. The 2005 agreement, for example, requires that 70 percent of the region's oil and gas revenue be returned to the provincial government in Aceh. The Acehnese authorities were also given control of the province's timber, minerals, and arable volcanic soils.

The Aceh independence movement has not received support from other countries, with the exception of Libya, where some Acehnese militants received training in the 1980s. In a February 2008 face-to-face interview, a U.S. government official who did not wish to be named commented on allegations of human rights abuses by the Indonesian forces in Aceh. Said the official, "We never made the conclusion that the human rights situation was intolerable." The United States and Europe instead backed efforts to broker peace between the Indonesian government and the Aceh rebels. Since that agreement was signed, they have strongly defended it. Former Finnish prime minister Martti Ahtisaari mediated those talks and was awarded the Nobel Peace Prize in 2008 in recognition of his peacemaking efforts. (Ahtissari was instrumental as well in Kosovo when it chose to secede from Serbia in February 2008.)

History

Settled about three thousand years ago by Malay immigrants, the Acehnese were Hindus before converting to Islam in the twelfth and thirteenth centuries. Aceh became a powerful, independent Islamic state, or sultanate, that by the seventeenth century exerted sovereignty over much of Sumatra and parts of modern-day southern Thailand. Aceh was an important trading center with direct ties to the Ottoman Empire. When the Netherlands began colonizing Indonesia in the 1600s, it left Aceh unmolested, as the latter had signed a friendship treaty with Great Britain that provided it with protection against Dutch aggression. However, in 1871 Britain reneged on this treaty and recognized Dutch sovereignty over Aceh. The Dutch subsequently declared war on the fiercely resistant Acehnese, who were not fully subjugated until the early 1900s. The Acehnese fought Japanese occupation as well from 1942–1945.

After World War II (1939–1945), many Acehnese joined the movement to win independence for Indonesia from the Dutch. Indonesian independence was first declared on August 17, 1945, and after four years of war and negotiation the Dutch accepted Indonesian independence on December 27, 1949. The Acehnese grew disillusioned with the newly independent government. Allying itself to a wider Islamist movement called Darul Islam, which opposed the secular Indonesian state, Aceh in 1953, led by Daud Beureueh, declared itself an independent state governed by Islamic law. According to Brown in his 2005 UNDP paper, the 1950s rebellion was more about changing the nature of the Indonesian state and less about secession. In 1959 the Indonesian government granted Aceh limited autonomy—notably over cultural and religious matters.

The highly centralized and authoritarian military leadership in Indonesia of General Suharto from 1966 to 1998 helped fuel separatist flames in Aceh. There was strong Acehnese resentment of the government's transmigration program, which encouraged large numbers of other Indonesians, notably from overpopulated areas in Java, to immigrate to Aceh. The Javanese settlers occupied a disproportionately high number of government, professional, and technical jobs in Aceh and bought up much of the land.

In 1976 a newly emerged separatist group, Gerakan Aceh Merdeka (GAM, or The Free Aceh Movement), declared independence for the province. The Indonesian government refused to accept this and managed to largely defeat GAM by 1982, forcing its leaders to flee to exile in Sweden. GAM's total membership at that time was no more than two hundred. GAM reemerged on the scene in 1989, launching new attacks that provoked massive retaliation from the government and prompted it to designate Aceh a Special Military Region. The third and final phase took place from 1998 to 2005 when, following the collapse of the Suharto regime, GAM took control of much of the Aceh countryside and the government stepped up its counterinsurgency efforts.

The post-Suharto Indonesian government made some concessions to the rebels—for example, withdrawing some troops from Aceh. However, it refused to consider granting independence, afraid such a move would inspire secessionist movements elsewhere in the country. Indonesia is very culturally diverse, consisting of five hundred linguistic groups living on 13,500 islands that stretch three thousand miles wide from mainland Asia to Australia. There are active separatist movements in the West Papua and South Moluccas regions, and in 1999 the eastern half of the island of Timor successfully seceded, securing independence as Timor Leste.

Just when the conflict seemed intractable, the landscape changed—literally and figuratively—on December 26, 2004, when a catastrophic tsunami devastated the region. The peace and autonomy agreement that followed led to elections for governor in December 2006 and for provincial and district legislative councils in March 2007. In each, former separatist rebels were victorious.

Leadership

GAM was the leading separatist group in Aceh during the thirty-year conflict. It had a political wing called the Aceh-Sumatra National Liberation Front (ASNLF) that was set up in 1989. When the two groups signed on to the 2005 peace accord, they were essentially casting aside their original goal of securing an independent state for Aceh. They agreed to stand in democratic elections and had decommissioned their weapons by the end of 2005. The two organizations have since morphed into a single democratic political party, the Aceh Party, which was established in May 2008. The Aceh Party was highly successful in the elections of April 9, 2009, winning 47 percent of the vote and securing 33 of the 69 seats in the Aceh Legislative Council, or parliament, on a turnout of 77 percent. The ruling party throughout Indonesia, the Democratic Party, also did well. The two parties' strong showing was widely seen as a sign that the Acehnese public approved the peace agreement that had been signed. Yusuf Irwandi, a former GAM spokesman, became governor of Aceh in February 2007. Other leading political figures in the province include Muzikir Manaf, chair of the Aceh Transitional Committee, a body set up to succeed

Hasan di Tiro (1925–2010)

AP Photo/Naofumi Takeuchi

HASAN DI TIRO was born in Pidie, Indonesia, on August 25, 1925. Di Tiro grew up in the Aceh region of Indonesia, an area where the people have their own language, Acehnese, and adhere to Islamic law in a stricter fashion than in many other parts of Indonesia. Moreover, his grandfather was Cik di Tiro, an Indonesian national hero who fought a war against Indonesia's Dutch colonial occupiers in the late nineteenth century and was also the last Sultan of Aceh. As a result of his grandfather's legacy, di Tiro and his family enjoyed an elevated status within the community.

In 1945 di Tiro received a law degree from the Islamic University of Indonesia, Yogyakarta. He then traveled to the United States and studied at both Columbia University and the University of Plano in Texas. Pursuant to the completion of his academic studies, di Tiro began working at Indonesia's United Nations mission in New York City. While at this position, di Tiro declared himself the foreign minister of the Darul Islam (House of Islam) movement, a group that was fighting to overthrow Indonesia's secular government and transform the nation into an Islamic state. Consequently, the Indonesian authorities stripped di Tiro of his citizenship; this resulted in his detention for several months as an illegal immigrant in the United States.

In 1974 di Tiro divorced his American wife, Dora, left their son Karim, and returned to Aceh, Indonesia. When he arrived, di Tiro petitioned the government to approve a contract that would give him a stake in Aceh's natural gas industry. His request was denied as the Indonesian government based in Jakarta acted to obtain full control of Aceh's natural resources. Witnessing the exclusion of the Acehnese people from the industry—and subsequent profits—di Tiro became determined to correct what he viewed as an injustice brought about by an illegitimate government. As a result, he founded Gerakan Aceh Merdeka (GAM), which means Free Aceh Movement.

Di Tiro's GAM was a militant group fighting the Indonesian government for the independence of the Aceh region; it began its violent campaign by attacking a Mobil liquefied natural gas refinery. In 1976, after the killing of foreign engineers, the Indonesian government began an extensive crackdown on GAM. Di Tiro was wounded in the fighting that ensued. To avoid being captured or killed, di Tiro fled to Malaysia for a short time and then moved on to Stockholm, Sweden, where he lived for the next three decades. While residing in Sweden, di Tiro was provided citizenship, lobbied the international community on behalf of the Free Aceh Movement, and also coordinated GAM's operations.

Fighting in Aceh between GAM and the Indonesian government continued until peace accords were signed in 2005, with di Tiro's approval; this marked the end to a conflict that had killed between fifteen and thirty thousand people over a thirty-year span. The peace agreement provided Aceh significant autonomy, yet fell short of granting the region full independence.

Di Tiro was permitted to move back to Indonesia after peace was established. When he arrived in 2008, he exclaimed in Acehnese, "Thank God, I've been able to come home." On June 3, 2010, Hasan di Tiro died of multiple organ failure in the capital of Aceh, Banda Aceh; he was granted Indonesian citizenship one day prior to his death.

GAM; the former GAM prime minister-in-exile, Malik Mahmud; Adnan Beuransah; and Tengku Yahya.

GAM was established in the 1970s shortly after oil and gas were discovered in Aceh. It was founded by Hasan di Tiro, a descendant of a legendary war hero who had fought the Dutch.

When GAM declared independence for Aceh in 1976, it justified this on the grounds that the oil and gas revenue had been "used totally for the benefit of Java and the Javanese." In the declaration, which spelled out the main grievances motivating the movement, GAM referred to "the foreign regime of Jakarta and the alien people of the island of Java," who "have stolen our properties: they have robbed us of our livelihood; they have abused the education of our children; they have exiled our leaders; they have put our people in chains of tyranny, poverty and neglect." One of GAM's top leaders, Abdullah Syafi'ie, was killed, alongside his wife and bodyguards, by Indonesian soldiers in 2002. An earlier Acehnese leader, Daud Beureueh, had supported the struggle by Indonesians to gain independence from the Netherlands, but after Aceh was integrated into the Indonesian state he rejected it for not being Islamic enough.

Current Status

The new autonomous Aceh administration is functioning relatively well. Hundreds of millions of dollars have flooded into its coffers—a mix of post-tsunami reconstruction aid and revenues from oil and gas activities. It is under pressure to distribute this windfall in an efficient and equitable way so that no group feels deprived of its fair share. According to a U.S. government official who worked in Indonesia, "the real challenge the ex-rebels face is to become good governors. This is not easy to do and they need help from the international community to develop these new skills." The Acehnese living in Aceh mostly support the current autonomy arrangement, although there are pockets of Acehnese living abroad—most notably in Malaysia, Scandinavia, and the United States—who tend to be more pro-independence.

While separatist violence has ceased, some ex-GAM fighters, resentful over not having benefited more from the large cash influx to Aceh, have become involved in organized crime, such as extortion rackets, kidnappings, and low-level bombings. In March 2008 a mob of a hundred people burned down an office of the Aceh Transitional Committee, killing six people. A March 2008 article in the *South China Morning Post*, a Hong Kong newspaper, reported that some Aceh highlanders

were annoyed that coastal areas hit by the tsunami received all the reconstruction aid and were now prospering, while other regions were worse off. Some in the central highlands, the region where non-Acehnese minorities such as the Gayo live, are seeking greater recognition of their distinct identity and needs. Iwan Gayo has emerged as a local leader there. Journalist Fabio Scarpello reported that the Indonesian government was considering splitting Aceh into several provinces. One GAM commander who strongly opposed this plan was quoted as saying, "we fought for one Aceh, not for several." The 2005 agreement prohibits changes to the boundaries of Aceh.

Aceh, generally viewed as the most consistently pious part of Indonesia, has grown more Islamic since gaining autonomy. On September 14, 2009, the Aceh parliament passed a law to punish adultery with stoning to death and homosexuality with whipping, journalist Lynn Lee from the Singapore newspaper *The Straits Times* reported. Rape, alcohol, and gambling were made punishable by four hundred lashes of the whip. Muslim-based political parties, such as the United Development Party, Prosperous Justice Party, and National Mandate Party, attract strong support in Aceh. According to Lee, "the separatist rebels who spent over two decades till 2005 fighting for Acehnese independence from Indonesia never lobbied hard for [the introduction of Islamic law]. It was always the pet project of the conservative Islamic parties which have dominated Aceh's legislature because they have more hardline interpretations of the Quran." She said that most Acehnese supported the new law even though most did not vote for Islamic parties in the April 2009 elections.

In October 2008, the former GAM leader, eighty-three-year-old Hasan di Tiro, returned from exile in Sweden. In his speech, which was read by former prime minister-in-exile Mahmud, di Tiro urged Acehnese to adhere to the peace agreement. "Guard the unity of Aceh and don't be goaded into criminal activities by subversive groups, in their attempts to sabotage the peace to make us fight amongst each other and break Aceh apart; if we are not careful, a bloody conflict will arise again . . . which will be to everyone's detriment." (Di Tiro died in June 2010.) The danger that lies ahead for the Acehnese is that a damaging political schism could open up due to antagonism between rival political factions—for example, between the followers of Mahmud and the followers of Yusuf Irwandi—that could shatter Aceh's newfound peace.

Further Reading

Allard, Tom. "No question over who wears the pants in West Aceh," *The Age* (Australia), May 27, 2010, www.theage.com.au/world/no-question-over-who-wears-the-pants-in-west-aceh-20100526-we1u.html.

Aspinall, Edward. *Islam and Nation: Separatist Rebellion in Aceh.* Stanford: Stanford University Press, 2009.

Brooks, Oakley. "Breakaway bids test Aceh's post-tsunami peace deal," *Christian Science Monitor,* March 13, 2008, www.csmonitor.com/2008/0313/p04s02-wogn.html.

Brown, Graham. "Horizontal inequalities, ethnic separatism and violent conflict: the case of Aceh," United Nations Development Program, 2005, http://hdr.undp.org/docs/publications/background_papers/2005/HDR2005_Brown_Graham_28.pdf.

Fitzpatrick, Stephen. "Hero returns to a fragile Aceh," *The Australian,* October 18, 2008, www.theaustralian.com.au/news/hero-returns-to-a-fragile-aceh/story-e6frg6t6-1111117782748.

Lee, Lynn. "Aceh conservatives leave their mark; Stoning law seen as last push to impose their agenda before leaving," *The Straits Times,* September 16, 2009, www.asianewsnet.net/news.php?id=7781&sec=1.

Reid, Anthony. *Verandah of Violence: The Background to the Aceh Problem.* Seattle: University of Washington Press, 2006.

BOUGAINVILLEANS
(Papua New Guinea)

People on the South Pacific island of Bougainville have, since 1975, fought for greater autonomy or independence from Papua New Guinea (PNG), an Asian country north of Australia. Roughly 150 miles long and 40 miles wide, Bougainville lies several hundred miles east of the PNG mainland and is closer geographically and culturally to the Solomon Islands, an independent country southeast of Bougainville. The population of Bougainville is 180,000, 95 percent of whom are Christian. They make up about 3 percent of the PNG population of six million. Bougainville, like the rest of PNG, is linguistically diverse, with twenty-six different languages, compared to PNG's eight hundred. A pidgin form of English, Tok Pisin, is the most widely understood language nationwide. Ethnically, Bougainvilleans are mostly Melanesians, whereas PNG is a mix of Melanesians, Papuans, Negrito, Micronesians, and Polynesians.

The islanders are a part of the British Commonwealth, and their official head of state is the British monarch, who is represented by a Governor General. Since 2001 the island has been an autonomous region within PNG. Bougainvilleans were granted an autonomous status that is unique among the country's twenty provinces after fighting an eight-year war with PNG in which one in ten Bougainvilleans died. The main cause of that conflict was Bougainvillean discontent over the Panguna copper mine in Bougainville. An Australian mining company called Bougainville Copper Limited (BCL), which is an affiliate of Rio Tinto, operated the mine from 1972 until 1989. It was one of the biggest in the world, extracting over three million tons of copper and nine million ounces of gold. The mine was a major source of revenue for the PNG government and accounted for about 40 percent of PNG's exports. However, it caused great damage to the environment as toxic waste was dumped on lands and waterways, mountainsides were bulldozed, and rainforests defoliated.

The war was one of the first environmentally driven conflicts of the post–cold war era. The PNG government's failure to protect the environment and distribute the mine's wealth equitably was the trigger for the independence movement. Several foreign countries and companies became embroiled in the conflict. The PNG prime minister, Julius Chan, admitted in February 1997 that he had entered into a contract with Sandline International, a private British military group, to supply mercenaries to fight the Bougainville rebels. The PNG military protested the use of these mercenaries, causing the government to fall and the Sandline troops to withdraw.

Bougainville's former colonial ruler, Australia, opposed the island's attempt to secede in the 1990s, although since 2000 it has been neutral on the issue. The government in the Solomon Islands was more sympathetic to the secessionists, providing them with aid and sanctuary. In response the PNG government in 1992 sent a search and destroy mission to the Solomon Islands to track down rebels. The United Nations (UN) deployed a small mission in 1998 to monitor a newly brokered cease-fire that helped disarm warring factions and facilitated the return of internally displaced refugees.

History

Populated by humans for thirty thousand years, the island got its name from French explorer Louis de Bougainville, who passed through in 1767. Bougainville first experienced European colonization in 1885 when Germany made it part of the German New Guinea protectorate. When World War I (1914–1918) broke out, Australia seized the lightly administered protectorate and in 1920 was authorized to administer it under a League of Nations mandate. During World War II (1939–1945), Bougainville was a battlefield for United States and Japanese troops, with the United States ultimately defeating Japan. Australia reassumed control in 1945 under a UN trusteeship that included the rest of modern-day PNG.

In the early 1970s, as PNG was preparing to gain independence from Australia, the Bougainvilleans began demanding some form of autonomous status. Just before PNG independence became official in September 1975, Bougainville declared independence, calling itself the Republic of the North Solomons. It failed to win recognition internationally, and in August 1976 secessionist leaders signed an agreement providing for regional autonomy within PNG.

Local resentment grew in the 1980s over the Panguna mine, given that three quarters of its three-thousand-strong workforce were non-Bougainvillean and most locals did not profit from it. Militants launched attacks on the mine in December 1988, causing it to shut down in May 1989. The militants, the Bougainville Resistance Army (BRA), escalated their assault, and PNG forces withdrew in March 1990. When the BRA subsequently declared Bougainville independent, the PNG responded by mounting a blockade that lasted until 1996 and led to the deaths of thousands of islanders, often due to lack of access to health care and medicine.

The discipline of the BRA eroded in the 1990s, and the group began to commit abuses on the local population, prompting some to join PNG forces and fight against the BRA. New Zealand and the Solomon Islands launched a series of peace-making initiatives. After several false starts a lasting cease-fire, the Lincoln Agreement, was signed on January 23, 1998. It was succeeded on August 30, 2001, by an agreement that gave greater autonomy to Bougainville, which opened a window to independence, with a consultative referendum to be held between 2015 and 2020.

Leadership

The BRA was the dominant militant group in Bougainville in the 1990s and the driving force in the conflict. It was disbanded under the 2001 peace agreement. The BRA was established by former mine employee, Francis Ona, who, on May 17, 1990, proclaimed himself president of Bougainville, which he called Meekamui, and set up a Bougainville Interim Government under the command of Sam Kauona. Ona never accepted the 2001 agreement, and along with about 15 percent of the ex-BRA formed a dissident faction, the Meekamui Defence Force (MDF). Ona died on July 24, 2005, and was succeeded by Noah Musingku. The MDF established a base for itself around the Panguna

Francis Ona (1953–2005)

FRANCIS ONA was born on February 15, 1953, the second eldest of twelve children, in Guava village on the island of Bougainville, Papua New Guinea (PNG).

In 1968 Ona attended St. Joseph's Rigu High School, and it was there that he first witnessed the tension between the people of Bougainville and the Australian government's administration of PNG. Notably, the government had granted both land and excavation rights to Bougainville's open-cast copper mine, the world's largest, to Cozinc Riotinto of Australia (CRA). Subsequently, as CRA began its exploration of the mine, located in Panguna, in the center of the island, disputes over landownership arose. To protest against the government and CRA, local landowners pulled all of their children out of school. Ona was among those taken out of the classroom; he returned to his studies shortly after the initial protest.

Ona graduated from the University of Technology with a degree in surveying in 1975 and began working for Bougainville Copper, owned by CRA. He trained as a bulldozer operator and truck driver on his days off. This helped him convince the company to allow him to build a road for the villagers connecting Guava village to the mine pit. Ona was increasingly troubled, however, as the mine appeared to be polluting the environment and the mine workers were being unfairly compensated.

In 1988, after sixteen years of strife between CRA and the Panguna Landowners Association, Ona and other landowners decided to take matters into their own hands. He and a band of like-minded associates, frustrated by the landowners' lack of results, formed the New Panguna Landowners Association to take the place of the original association. Moreover, Ona, inspired by the movie *Rambo: First Blood Part II*, starring Sylvester Stallone, amassed a group of warriors armed with bows and arrows, home-made shotguns, and World War II–era bombs and prepared to take action against CRA.

Ona and his followers proceeded to destroy power pylons to the mine, forcing its closure. The group's acts of sabotage catapulted it into full revolt. Ona justified the attacks by claiming that mining activities were polluting the Panguna River. The closing of the mine proved crippling to the PNG economy and spurred the government to deploy the National Defense Force. In response, the rebels, under Ona, consolidated into a secessionist Bougainville Revolutionary Army and proceeded to fight a civil war with the PNG government.

Ona proclaimed a unilateral declaration of independence for what he termed the "Republic of Bougainville" and appointed himself interim president in 1990. PNG retaliated with an economic blockade of the island. The Bougainville Interim Government lost many of its supporters through the years as Ona's movement split apart into numerous armed groups who fought one other for control. The conflict between Ona's rebels and PNG lasted ten years and resulted in the deaths of more than fifteen thousand people, mostly as a result of disease and starvation. Neighboring Australia opposed Ona and his rebels, although it did not support a full-scale invasion of the island. A cease-fire was declared in 1998, negotiated by the PNG prime minister, Bill Skate, and Ona's former vice president, Joseph Kabui.

Ona refused to be involved in negotiations and would not sign any peace agreements. A devoted group of rebels, including so-called cargo cultists—worshippers of the World War II–era cargo plane that had dropped in supplies during Japanese occupation—moved with him to a mountainous retreat in the jungle. They refused to allow the mine to reopen. Ona lived a secluded life in the jungle, only occasionally leaving to rally support. In 2004 he issued a claim that he was crowned king of the island.

In June 2005, an official Bougainville government was formed under a deal brokered by Australia and New Zealand and monitored by the United Nations. Elections were held; again, Ona refused to participate and instead staged opposition rallies. Joseph Kabui was elected president.

Ona died suddenly in July 2005, probably of malaria. He was survived by his wife and six children. The newly elected government is still determining how to negotiate with Bougainville Copper and the PNG government.

---

mine area and clashed with Bougainville government forces, although since 2007 it has taken steps to reconcile with the Bougainville autonomous administration.

The prominence of militant separatism has not stopped Bougainville from moving forward in developing a political framework for autonomy. In early 1995, the PNG parliament approved the creation of a Bougainville Transitional Government, including a thirty-two-seat parliament, with Theodor Miriung appointed as prime minister. Miriung was assassinated in October 1996. The autonomy deal of 2001 led to the adoption of a constitution in 2004 and elections in May and June 2005, won by former secessionist leader Joseph Kabui. Kabui became the president of Bougainville and head of the Bougainville People's Congress Party. Kabui died in June 2008. The president since June 2010, John Momis, favors reintegrating Bougainville with PNG.

Current Status

Hostilities have ceased and an autonomous government in Bougainville is functional. The PNG administration remains responsible for foreign affairs and defense policy. The Bougainville government is considering reopening the controversial Panguna mine as its revenues could be used to rebuild the island's infrastructure, which was severely damaged in the conflict. A 2009 study by BCL concluded that there was much more copper left in Panguna. If reopened, the Bougainville government would have the difficult task of reaching an agreement with PNG authorities on how to share the tax revenues among themselves.

Some Bougainvilleans are seeking compensation from the former mine operator, Rio Tinto, for alleged war crimes, crimes against humanity, and racial discrimination. A U.S. court ruled in August 2009 that their complaints could be heard in U.S. courts. This is embarrassing not just for Rio Tinto but also for the Australian government, which was strongly associated with the mine and which helped the PNG government to blockade Bougainville.

Now that the islanders have autonomy, they face a number of challenges. In particular, the Bougainvilleans must formulate a policy to combat the lucrative, but illicit, trade that has sprung up in ammunition left over from the conflict. Potentially even more detrimental to the island's future are the ill-effects of climate change. The sea level around Bougainville has risen 10 centimeters since 1990; because the island's highest point is just 1 meter tall, many plantations have been flooded, according to a June 2008 article in IRIN News, a UN news service. The PNG government has provided some financing for land purchases to help relocate several thousand people from endangered areas to less vulnerable spots.

In June 2010, the Bougainvilleans elected John Momis president. During the campaign Momis supported the island's remaining a part of PNG while his opponent (and the incumbent), James Tanis, campaigned for independence. However, according to an article in *The Economist*, "enthusiasm for secession is not waning. . . . But [independence] was not a big election issue, because of mounting confidence that PNG will honor the autonomy arrangements and hold the promised referendum [on independence]."

Further Reading

Connell, John. "Bougainville: the future of an island microstate," *The Journal of Pacific Studies* 28, no. 2 (2005): 192–217, www.usp.ac.fj/editorial/jpacs_new/vol28_2/vol28_JohnConnell.pdf.

Davies, Anne. "US class action against Rio Tinto clears hurdle," *The Age* (Melbourne, Australia), August 8, 2009, www.theage.com.au/business/us-class-action-against-rio-tinto-clears-hurdle-20090807-ecy8.html.

"Halfway to freedom; Bougainville's new president," *The Economist*, June 12, 2010, www.economist.com/node/16321684.

IRIN News (United Nations news agency). "Papua New Guinea: The world's first climate change 'refugees,'" June 3, 2008, www.irinnews.org/Report.aspx?ReportId=78630.

Regan, Anthony J., and Helga M.Griffin, eds. *Bougainville: Before the Conflict*. Canberra: Pandanus Books, 2005.

HMONG
(Laos)

The Hmong are a Southeast Asian ethnic minority living predominantly in Laos and Vietnam who have been in a precarious situation since 1975, due to some of them having fought against their governments. The Hmong are especially vulnerable in Laos, where the government is trying to hunt down a dwindling number of insurgents and has been accused of committing abuses against the civilian Hmong population. The government's distrust stems from the fact that many Hmong fought with the United States in the Vietnam War of the 1960s and early 1970s.

The Hmong make up 8 percent of the Lao population and number about 450,000 people. They are the third largest of forty-nine ethnic groups in Laos, the largest being the Lao (55 percent) and Khmou (11 percent). They live predominantly in the mountainous northern regions. There are up to a million Hmong in Vietnam, where they account for about 1 percent of the population. In international reporting, the Hmong are often grouped with the Montagnards, an ethnic minority in Vietnam, as both have been persecuted for having helped the United States in the Vietnam War. The Hmong have their own distinct culture, language, and religion, and are of Asian origin, whereas the Montagnards are Polynesian. The Hmong speak two languages that are not mutually intelligible and which derive from the Sino-Tibetan linguistic family. Many Hmong are Christian, having converted under French and American colonial rule or as a result of ongoing proselytizing efforts by Evangelical Protestant churches. Most are animist, an indigenous religion that professes belief in a spirit life for all living things, plants and animals.

Since 1975 Laos has operated a one-party system of communist government dominated by an authoritarian military, which is secretive and distrustful of outside influences. Access by independent observers to Laos' Hmong is restricted, making it difficult to obtain a clear picture of their situation or political aspirations. For example, journalists who tried to interview Hmong in 2003 and 2004 were arrested and their translators and guides jailed. Several journalists who did manage to meet with Hmong leaders confirmed there are at least a few hundred Hmong guerrillas eking out a perilous existence in hiding in the Lao jungle. These are the remnants of a much larger, Hmong-dominated "Secret Army" that fought on the side of the United States.

A March 2007 report from the human rights advocacy group Amnesty International concluded that the Lao army was continuing to launch attacks on the rebels, although "they no longer appear to pose a military threat to the Lao government." Journalists have reported them to be in a pitiful state. *Time* magazine's Andrew Perrin in April 2003 described them as "a ragtag army, with wailing families in tow, beseeching me to take news of their plight to the outside world," and wrote of "starving children, their tiny frames scarred by mortar shrapnel." The rebels have been reduced to foraging for food, often seeking and receiving sustenance from Hmong villagers who risk being severely punished by the Lao military for helping them. The Amnesty report said that Lao law-enforcement officers had separated Hmong women from their husbands and subjected them to slavery-like treatment, torture, and rape. Amnesty also noted that not all Hmong opposed the Lao government. There are some Hmong provincial governors, some sit in parliament, and at least one was appointed to the eleven-member Lao politburo, the government cabinet.

According to Susan Hammond from the War Legacies Project, a non-governmental group working in the region, in a January 2010 email exchange, "most Hmong are neither pro nor anti- Lao government, just neutral non-communist party members." Hammond said the rebels still hiding in the forest were a minority and that thousands of other ex-rebels had taken up amnesties offered by the Lao government and were now reintegrating into Lao society. In a January 2008 article for *The Nation*, a Thailand-based English-language newspaper, journalist Jim Pollard reported that these die-hards feared they would be killed by the authorities if they surrendered. However, Hammond said that "it has never been proven by any outside observers that the Lao government has conducted extermination campaigns amongst the Hmong insurgents."

Eight thousand Hmong have fled from Laos to Thailand since 2004. Most were placed in a refugee camp, Ban Huay Nam Khao, with several hundred others interned in the Nong Khai detention center.

According to an August 2009 opinion editorial in *The Nation*, the camp's residents were a mix of economic migrants, political refugees, and militants who fought with the United States in the 1970s. They were fleeing oppression from the Lao authorities, the article said. Their quest for asylum suffered a setback in 2006 when the Thai government concluded an agreement with the Lao authorities to send them back to Laos. Hmong advocates and human rights and refugee organizations strongly protested this move.

History

The Hmong traveled to Laos from China in the north in the late 1700s and early 1800s to escape massacres perpetrated by Imperial Chinese forces then expanding China's territory. They settled on large tracts of mountainous land granted to them by the Lao king. The Lao monarchy had been established in the fourteenth century by King Fa Ngum. In the late 1800s the Hmong came under colonial rule when France gradually conquered their homelands, forming the Indochina colony that included modern-day Cambodia, Laos, and Vietnam. Laos became a French protectorate in 1893 and the Lao-Thai border was fixed in 1907 in a treaty between France and Siam, the historical name of Thailand, a kingdom that succeeded in avoiding colonization. In the 1920s the Hmong mounted an unsuccessful revolt against French rule in which thousands were killed.

During World War II (1939–1945) the Hmong briefly came under Japanese rule. After the war, France tried to reclaim its Indochina colony but was defeated in 1954 by a communist army led by Ho Chin Minh, who became leader of the state of North Vietnam. The Pathet Lao, a communist movement in Laos allied to Ho's army, was meanwhile fighting to overthrow the constitutional monarchy that had been established in Laos after World War II. In the mid-1950s the United States, keen to stop communists taking power wherever they could, decided to intervene by providing economic and military support to the anti-communist state of South Vietnam.

By the early 1960s the North Vietnamese army, supported by the Soviet Union and China, was making incursions into Hmong homelands. This caused some of the Hmong to ally themselves with the United States, although others backed the communist Pathet Lao. The U.S. Central Intelligence Agency helped to create an anti-communist "Secret Army" led by Vang Pao and trained Hmong militants from bases in Thailand. The United States provided aerial support to the Hmong when the latter attacked North Vietnamese troops who were trying to reach South Vietnam by passing through Laos. The United States carried out 580,000 bombing missions in Laos during the Vietnam War.

The alliance with the United States ultimately proved catastrophic for the Hmong. About half of Vang's forty thousand–strong army was killed during the hostilities. The United States withdrew its forces in 1973, and the communist militants quickly won control, overrunning South Vietnam in April 1975 and Laos in May 1975. The Lao king and queen, whom many Hmong supported, disappeared, and a communist-dominated Lao People's Democratic Republic was declared. The Hmong faced ostracism, harassment, and retribution for having helped the United States. Tens of thousands of Hmong were killed, and 300,000 fled between 1975 and 1985. The United States resettled over 100,000, and France resettled several thousand in its overseas territory of French Guyana in South America. The remaining Hmong community became further diluted as Vietnamese immigrated into Hmong areas.

After communist governments in Eastern Europe collapsed in 1989, some Hmong held out hope that the communists in Laos and Vietnam would experience a similar fate, especially after Russia stopped backing Vietnam financially. However,

the regimes survived and gradually opened themselves up to foreign investment. In the 1990s U.S. president Bill Clinton normalized trade relations with Vietnam, and from 2001 Clinton's successor, George W. Bush, did so with Laos. Some U.S. politicians continued to highlight the plight of the Hmong, with the U.S. House of Representatives passing several resolutions. Some Hmong in Laos continued resisting communist rule. There were occasional attacks on the Lao army in the 1990s, and in 2003 the Lao authorities accused Hmong rebels of carrying out two attacks on public buses.

Leadership

Determining how much popular support for autonomy or independence there is in the Hmong community is extremely difficult because the Lao government does not permit the existence of any political parties other than the ruling communist party. According to Philip Smith, a Hmong advocate and director of the Center for Public Policy Analysis, a Washington, D.C.-based research organization, many Hmong separatist groups are "false flag" operations. Smith, in a June 2009 face-to-face interview, said these groups claimed to seek independence but are really outfits of the Lao military, which uses them as a pretext for catching and clamping down on civilian, political, and religious dissidents. "These are largely penetrated and set up as trust operations controlled by the Lao government and security forces. This has intensified in recent months and years," he said. He claimed that there were no groups calling for a Hmong homeland that were truly independent of the Lao government, adding "the vast majority of the Lao Hmong are not separatist or seeking independence but simply wish to live in peace and freedom."

The Hmong rebels hiding in the Lao jungle continue to resist integration into Lao society. They were believed to number seven thousand when the communists took over in 1975, but their ranks have dwindled since and may have fallen to just a few hundred by 2010. In January 2008, the Thai newspaper *The Nation* reported that the rebels were living in northern Laos, split into groups of about twenty people. The article cited a Hmong leader, Yang Lue, who complained that when the rebels tried to surrender, Lao government soldiers opened fire. In one such incident, Va Cher Her, the sister-in-law of a famous jungle leader Zong Zoua Her, was killed. The article said Hmong expatriates in the United States were telephoning Hmong leaders to advise them not to surrender.

The Hmong immigrant community in the United States is spread across a number of states, including California, Massachusetts, Minnesota, North Carolina, Rhode Island, and Wisconsin. They provide financial support and political leadership to the Lao Hmong and broadcast programs from radio stations in Thailand. Hmong ex-Secret Army chief Vang Pao settled in California, where he led the United Lao Liberation Front. In June 2007, Pao was charged in the United States with plotting to overthrow the Lao government, but the charges were dropped in September 2009.

Current Status

The Lao military continues to clamp down on militant Hmong resistance. *The Nation* reported in January 2008 that Hmong in the Lao army participated in at least one attack against Hmong rebels in the jungle. Laura Xiong, a U.S.-based Hmong advocate, said, "based on the information I received, the Lao troops no longer open fire at a larger group but are quietly shooting at them one at a time." Hmong militants are reluctant to surrender because the Lao government has previously broken promises to grant them amnesties. Citing U.S. photographer Roger Arnold, the article noted "when there are no international monitors, there is no evidence of who surrendered. How can they trust Lao leaders who make public

statements that there is no fighting in Laos when Hmong continue to flee to Thailand full of bullet wounds? And some Hmong Americans exploit their fears by telling them to stay in the jungle and that help is on the way. They get screwed by both sides and don't know who to trust."

The Lao government accuses the Hmong of causing unrest in the country through "bandit" activities such as carrying out ambushes on highways. The Hmong have also been accused of involvement in opium cultivation, an important source of revenue in the mountainous regions where they live. In the Khammoun province on the Vietnamese border, Hmong have been driven out of their homes for objecting to the use of their land for logging.

The refugee situation continues to be embarrassing for the Lao and Thai governments. On June 20, 2008, five thousand Hmong in the Huay Nam Khao camp broke down the camp fence and marched toward the Thai capital, Bangkok, to raise awareness of their situation. They were stopped within a few kilometers by the Thai authorities. The non-governmental organization Médecins Sans Frontières/Doctors Without Borders (MSF) said in a May 2009 briefing report that eight hundred were forcibly repatriated to Laos two days later. However, the Thai authorities, cited in a July 2008 article by IRIN News, a UN news agency, denied this. "These persons expressed the wish to return to Laos of their own accord after negotiations with the Thai officials proved that their demands could not be met," the Thai official said.

In a May 2009 briefing, MSF reported that the refugees were so desperate to avoid being sent back they were resorting to suicide attempts, hunger strikes, arson, and self-mutilation. About two hundred a month have been repatriated since December 2008. Some escaped back to Thailand and told MSF of beatings, rapes, and other abuses endured in Laos. The United Nations High Commission for Refugees has voiced concern over not being allowed into the camp to determine who might be eligible for political asylum.

Hmong advocate Smith said, "the Thai authorities have been appeasing the Lao government, which has been placing unreasonable demands on the Thai to hand over Hmong that Laos claims are enemies of the Lao state." The U.S. State Department in August 2009 sent a senior official to visit the camp, who pledged afterward to consider claims to resettle Hmong in the United States on a case-by-case basis. A group of nine U.S. senators wrote a letter in December 2009 voicing concern about forced repatriations of thousands of Hmong from Thailand to Laos. The refugee situation has attracted the attention of the European Parliament, which on November 26, 2009, passed a resolution calling for Hmong to be resettled in Thailand, the United States, Canada, the Netherlands, or Australia. The Parliament urged the Lao government to introduce multi-party elections and allow a peaceful political opposition. Until Laos moves in that direction, it is not possible to ascertain if most Hmong wish to remain part of a unitary Lao state or prefer autonomy.

Further Reading

Amnesty International. "Laos: Hiding in the Jungle—Hmong under Threat," March 23, 2007, www.amnesty.org/en/library/asset/ASA26/003/2007/en/cd2f2180-d3a7–11dd-a329–2f46302a8cc6/asa260032007en.pdf.

European Parliament resolution of November 26, 2009, on the situation in Laos and Vietnam, www.europarl.europa.eu/sides/getDoc.do?pubRef=-//EP//TEXT+TA+P7-TA-2009–0104+0+DOC+XML+V0//EN&language=EN.

Hamilton-Merritt, Jane. *Tragic Mountains: The Hmong, the Americans, and the Secret Wars for Laos, 1942–1992*. Bloomington: Indiana University Press, 1993.

Médecins Sans Frontières/Doctors Without Borders. "Hidden Behind Barbed Wire," May 20, 2009, www.dwb.org/press/release.cfm?id=3627&cat=press-release&ref=home-center-relatedlink.

"Old wars never die; The Hmong and Laos," *The Economist*, July 17, 2010. www.economist.com/node/16592276?story_id=16592276&fsrc=rss.

Perrin, Andrew. "Welcome to the Jungle," *Time*, April 28, 2003, www.time.com/time/magazine/article/0,9171,447253,00.html.

Pollard, Jim. "Hmong in Laos afraid to surrender," January 23, 2008, *The Nation* (Thailand), http://nationmultimedia.com/2008/01/23/opinion/opinion_30063121.php.

"Thailand: Refugee policy gets mixed reviews," IRIN News, July 14, 2008, www.irinnews.org/Report.aspx?ReportId=7922.

KAREN
(Myanmar/Union of Burma)

The Karen people in Myanmar/Union of Burma, who number about four million and account for 7 percent of the country's population, have mounted a military struggle since 1947 for self-government or independence. Their campaign has thus far not been successful, and the government of Myanmar has severely clamped down on them.

The Karen are concentrated in the south and east of the country, along a several-hundred-mile-long strip that borders Thailand, which lies to the east. They are one of many different ethnic groups in a country dominated by ethnic Burmese (68 percent). Other significant ethnic groups include the Shan (9 percent), Rakhines (4 percent), Chinese (3 percent), Indians (2 percent), and Mon (2 percent). The Karen speak twelve related languages that are not mutually intelligible and which form part of the Tibeto-Chinese linguistic family. At least two thirds of the Karen are Buddhist or animist, an indigenous religion that professes belief in a spirit life for all living things, plants and animals. A substantial minority is Christian, including the powerful S'ghaw subgroup.

Formerly known as the Union of Burma, since 1989 the country's ruling military junta has promoted the use of the name Myanmar, which is more closely associated with the ethnic Burmese majority; Karen opponents of the regime prefer to use the name Burma. The Myanmar government has also renamed the nation's capital, formerly known as Rangoon, "Yangon, " and attempted to rename the Karen people "Kayin," changes that many Karen similarly resent. Myanmar, despite its ethnic diversity, does not have a decentralized, federal system in which the Karen enjoy the right to govern their affairs—for example, to set culture or education policy. Instead, the Karen are part of the unitary state structure, formally divided into seven states and seven divisions, but in practice one where authority is heavily concentrated in Yangon.

The main group spearheading the separatist movement for the past six decades is the Karen National Union (KNU). It has been successively weakened since 1990 as the Myanmar military has escalated its counterinsurgency efforts. The Karen Human Rights Group, an independent association, said in a June 2009 report that the Myanmar military had succeeded in suppressing the rebellion by an effective strategy based on "the four cuts": cutting off the insurgents' access to food, finance, intelligence, and recruits. The military has also increased its numbers, from 180,000 in 1988 to 400,000 by the mid-1990s, said the group, which is a locally based organization set up in 1992 to document the human rights situation of the Karen. The KNU, by contrast, has only a few thousand soldiers, and its weapons are no match for the government.

The military has subjected most Karen civilians to its control, often by forcing them to relocate to sites near army bases where they are exploited for food, money, or labor, the report said. Villagers who flee to the forest to avoid such relocations are typically shot by government forces if spotted because they are viewed as legitimate targets. Free movement is further restricted by the liberal placement of landmines by the Myanmar government to protect it from rebel attacks.

The Karen separatist movement has been damaged by splits from within. According to Ashley South, an independent writer specializing in Myanmar and Southeast Asia who did fieldwork in Myanmar from 2001 to 2006, the KNU has since the 1960s "been dominated by a right-wing, Christian S'ghaw-speaking elite." This is a legacy of Christian missionaries, some of them American Baptists, who arrived in Burma in the early 1800s and converted many Karen.

South, writing for the *Contemporary Southeast Asia* academic journal in April 2007, said that most rank-and-file members of the KNU's military wing, the Karen National Liberation Army (KNLA), as well as most Karen villagers are Buddhist. In December 1994, some of these grassroots Karen rebelled against the Christian-dominated KNU leadership and set up the Democratic Karen Buddhist Army (DKBA). The DKBA allied itself with the Myanmar army and has been fighting against the KNU ever since. South criticized the Christian Karen elites for trying to impose a homogenous idea of "Karen-ness," arguing it has ultimately fuelled further ethnic conflict. But he also said that his fieldwork revealed "that very large numbers of people do subscribe to a distinct Karen identity."

The Karen inhabit a region that has been greatly affected by violent separatist conflict, including that of the Tibetans in China to their north, Malay Muslims in Thailand to the south, and Hmong in Laos to the east (see separate essays). Given the instability and destruction these conflicts have caused, the governments in this region tend to be strongly anti-separatist, and the Karen have received little support elsewhere in the region. However, its easterly neighbor, Thailand, has given sanctuary to some Karen militants, including Mae La, Mae Sot, and Noh Poe, who form part of the community of 130,000 Karen who have fled across Myanmar's border and established refugee camps in Thailand.

History

The Karen arrived in their current homeland some time between 1000 B.C.E. and 800 C.E. According to Karen authors, they originally came from Central Asia 2,500 years ago and migrated to modern-day Myanmar through Tibet and China. By the eighteenth century, the Karen were living in the hills of central and eastern Burma, mostly under the rule of Mon, Shan, or Burmese kingdoms. Some subgroups, such as the Red Karen, or Kayah, maintained their autonomy until the early nineteenth century.

From 1824 to 1886, the United Kingdom conquered the peoples of Burma. Under colonial rule, the Karen were viewed by the British as less of a threat than ethnic Burmese. Many Karen rose to high positions in the British civil service and military. The Karen joined the British army in substantial numbers, helping to suppress Burmese rebellions in 1886 and 1930–1932 and fighting alongside the British in the Anglo-Boer War of 1899–1902. In 1928 the Christian-educated jurist Dr. San C. Po published a book in which he advocated the creation of a Karen state.

Originally administered as part of the British colony of India, in 1937 Burma became a separate, self-governing colony. Ethnic Burmese nationalism began to grow, manifesting itself in the "Thakin" movement. When Japan invaded in World War II (1939–1945) and replaced the British as rulers, the ethnic Burmese allied themselves with the Japanese and helped to install a pro-Japanese government. An ethnic Burmese-rooted Burma Independence Army attacked the Karen and other ethnic minorities. Some Karen retreated to India with British forces and later helped Britain and its allies recapture Burma from Japan in 1945. However, by this time the Burmese had switched sides and were also fighting the Japanese.

In the late 1940s, as the British were preparing to depart Burma and recognize it as an independent country, the Karen voiced hope that they would be granted autonomy in some kind of federal structure. However, after Burma became independent in January 1948, no agreement could be reached on which territories to include in a potentially autonomous Karen state. Some Karen units in the Burmese army rebelled, marking the beginning of the separatist conflict. In the 1950s and 1960s other minority groups in Burma joined the Karen in armed opposition to the Burmese government, so by the 1970s almost a third of the country was controlled by a dozen rebel groups.

The Burmese government, initially a parliamentary democracy, was by the 1960s controlled by the military, which centralized and monopolized power under the leadership of General Ne Win. Massive popular protests in 1988 led to elections in 1990 that were won by the National League for Democracy (NLD), led by Aung San Suu Kyi. The KNU allied itself to the NLD because the NLD supported a federal, democratic state. But the military junta refused to give up power and instead placed Suu Kyi under house arrest, eventually releasing her in November 2010.

The government of Myanmar stepped up its military campaign against the Karen rebels in the 1990s. It inflicted severe blows in 1995 by capturing the KNU headquarters in the city of Manerplaw in January and seizing a KNU base in Kawmoora on the Thai border in March. By the late 1990s, thousands of Karen war refugees were fleeing to Thailand. Efforts by the KNU and Myanmar authorities to broker a cease-fire in 2004 failed, and in May 2006 the authorities renewed their offensive. In February 2007, a KNU splinter group, led by Htain Maung, made peace with the government.

Leadership

The KNU/KNLA is one of the oldest rebel groups still operating in Southeast Asia, having been founded in 1947. The KNU has sporadically entered into cease-fire talks with the government of Myanmar, but no peace agreement has ever been signed and the group retains its original "no-surrender" stance. According to the KNU's Web site, the group aims "to establish the Karen state with a just and fair territory and self-determination." The KNU has been increasingly on the defensive since the mid-1990s when the DKBA, which defected from the KNU, alleging it had a pro-Christian, anti-Buddhist bias, joined the Burmese military and attacked KNU-controlled Karen refugee camps.

The KNU's roots stretch back to the 1880s, when its precursor, the Karen National Association, was founded by Baptist Christian community leaders. The organization's strongman from the 1960s until his resignation in January 2000 was General Bo Mya. His successor, Padoh Mahn Sha, was shot dead at his home in Thailand on February 17, 2008. Another longtime leader, Saw Ba Thin Sein, died of natural causes in May 2008. The current leaders include a woman, Naw Zipporah Sein, who was elected General Secretary in October 2008, and David Takapaw, the Vice Chair.

A fringe faction of the KNU, calling itself God's Army, emerged in 1997. In January 2000, followers of this group took seven hundred people hostage at a hospital in Ratchaburi, a province in Thailand. The ten hostage-takers were killed in an assault by Thai forces a day later. God's Army, a cult-like organization led by twin boys, Johnny and Luther Htoo, born about 1988, was disbanded in October 2000. The brothers were given asylum in Thailand in January 2001.

The Karenni National Progressive Party (KNPP) is another long-standing separatist group, established in 1955. The KNPP abandoned armed struggle in March 1995 by unilaterally declaring a cease-fire, although by mid-1996 it had taken up arms again. Cease-fire talks with the government of Myanmar in 2007 failed to produce a settlement. The group's leaders are Khu Rimond Htoo, Khu Oo Reh, and General Aung Myat.

Non-violent, Karen civil society networks, such as the Karen Human Rights Group, have, under difficult circumstances, slowly been expanding activities since 2000, focusing on developing communities in areas controlled by the Myanmar government. Ashley South wrote in his April 2007 article in *Contemporary Asia* of the recent emergence of a more moderate "Union Karen" movement, which seeks greater autonomy for the Karen while remaining part of Myanmar/Union of Burma.

Current Status

The Karen have made little progress in their long campaign for self-government. The military struggle waged by their leadership has inadvertently inflicted severe hardship on their people as the government has systematically targeted Karen civilians in its crackdown. Government abuses committed against the Karen included forced labor, forced relocation, confiscation of lands, burning of villages, widespread rape, and the prohibition of schooling in their own language. The Burmese military has also used Karen villagers to clear landmines.

On May 3, 2008, Karen-populated areas of Myanmar were badly affected by Cyclone Nargis,

which devastated the country, killing over 100,000 people. In the ensuing rescue operation, government authorities were accused of aiding only ethnic Burmese. The government several years previously had been similarly accused of making it difficult for international aid organizations such as the Red Cross and Doctors Without Borders to provide humanitarian assistance to Karen areas. The government of Myanmar is often criticized internationally for its poor human rights record. Relations are especially strained with the European Union and the United States, although neither supports the Karen separatist movement.

The conflict has caused hundreds of thousands of Karen to flee their homes. Many live in one of ten Karen refugee camps set up in neighboring Thailand, and many Karen work in Thailand, often illegally. This influx of refugees has placed pressure on Thailand, although the Thai authorities have pledged not to repatriate Karen to unsafe areas. Thousands more Karen have fled to other countries in the region, notably Malaysia and Singapore. Some have ventured further and gained refugee status in industrialized countries such as Australia, Ireland, the Netherlands, and New Zealand.

A January 2008 article in *Newsweek* magazine reported that the United States, after the September 11, 2001, terrorist attacks, made it much harder for the Karen to be admitted. The author Anna Husarska, a policy advisor at the International Rescue Committee, a non-profit aid agency, wrote how the post–September 11 admission rules had "kept out people like Lincoln, a soft-spoken eighty-seven-year-old Karen. He had been labeled a terrorist for years by U.S. authorities, solely because he was a teacher in a school set up by a group of armed resisters in the Karen-controlled territory of Burma. Denied entry into the United States, his dream of joining his grandnephews in running a sushi bar in Florida went stale. He has asked that his refugee file be submitted to Australia." The United States enacted a law in December 2007 that made entry into the country easier for the Karen and groups in similar situations.

In June 2009, the government of Myanmar mounted a new offensive against the Karen, forcing the rebels to abandon more bases and triggering another exodus of several thousand refugees. The *Christian Science Monitor,* a U.S.-based newspaper, reported in June 2009 that "the attacks appear to underscore the determination of Burma's regime to snuff out what little armed opposition remains to its rule ahead of elections next year." The KNU is one of the few groups in Myanmar that has not signed a cease-fire agreement with the regime, journalist Simon Montlake reported. He cited Thai diplomats who claimed that Myanmar authorities had deliberately provoked the refugee influx to Thailand in retaliation for Thailand's having supported Burmese pro-democracy leader Suu Kyi. In March 2010, according to a report by the Thai-based Burmese online site Irrawaddy, six hundred of the refugees returned to Myanmar after being pressured to do so by the Thai authorities.

With a military junta still ruling over them with an iron fist, the outlook for the Karen remains somewhat bleak. As writer South noted in his April 2007 article in *Contemporary Asia,* well over a century since they forged a common identity, "the Karen remain the largest minority group in Southeast Asia without a state of their own in any meaningful sense."

Further Reading

Ardeth Maung Thawnghmung. "The Karen Revolution in Burma: Diverse Voices, Uncertain Ends," *East-West Center Policy Studies* 45 (South East Asia), April 21, 2008.

BBC Worldwide Monitoring. "Thai authorities said 'forcing' 600 refugees to return to Burma," April 1, 2010 (report in English by Thailand-based Burmese Irrawaddy Web site on March 31, 2010).

Husarska, Anna. "Kept in a State of Limbo," *Newsweek,* January 28, 2008, www.newsweek.com/id/96342.

Karen Human Rights Group, "Abuse, Poverty and Migration: Investigating migrants' motivations to leave home in Burma," June 2009, www.khrg.org/khrg2009/khrg0903.pdf.

Karen National Union Web site, www.karen.org/knu/KNU_His.htm.

Minority Rights Group. "World Directory of Minorities and Indigenous Peoples," www.minorityrights.org/4482/myanmarburma/karen.html (accessed November 2009).

Montlake, Simon. "Burma (Myanmar) presses rebels in bid to eliminate armed opposition," *Christian Science Monitor,* June 26, 2009, www.csmonitor.com/2009/0626/p06s09-wosc.html.

South, Ashley. *Ethnic Politics in Burma: States of Conflict.* New York: Routledge, 2008.

———. "Karen Nationalist Communities: The 'Problem' of Diversity," *Contemporary Southeast Asia* 33, no. 1 (April 2007), www.ashleysouth.co.uk/files/Contemporary_Southeast_Asia_April_2007.pdf.

MALAYS
(Thailand)

There are three million Muslims in southern Thailand who for over a century have fought the Thai authorities for greater autonomy or independence. They stand out from other Thai citizens both by virtue of their religion, Islam, and by their ethnicity, Malay. Thailand is an overwhelmingly Buddhist country, and most of its citizens are ethnic Thai. The Malay Muslims are geographically concentrated in the provinces of Pattani, Narathiwat, and Yala on the southern tip of Thailand bordering Malaysia. There they account for as much as 80 percent of the population. There are also some who live further north around the capital, Bangkok. Nationwide the Malay Muslims account for just 5 percent of the population.

Thailand is centralized politically; as a result the Malay Muslims do not enjoy any special autonomous status and are not well-represented in the country's political institutions. The Thai government has been widely accused by human rights groups of systematically repressing the ethnic identity and language of the Malay Muslims. The Thai state has been "bent on crafting an all-encompassing national Thai identity by assimilating the country's minorities," said Joseph Chinyong Liow, an assistant professor at the Institute of Defense and Strategic Studies at Nanyang Technological University in Singapore, in a 2006 paper for the *Asia Policy* academic journal. The Thai English-language newspaper *The Nation* said in an August 2007 article of the Malay-Thai relationship: "For the better part of the past hundred years, the Malays of Pattani were told that they must appreciate all that the Thai state has given them and that they must learn to embrace the values that define Thailand's nation-state. They have also been told that they need to learn to be obedient." The Malays are generally poorer than the Thai, partly a consequence of decades of neglect by the Bangkok authorities.

Separatist violence in the south has been a major problem for Thailand since an incident in January 2004 when militants raided an army battalion. About 4,300 people have been killed between that incident and January 2011. The violence has occurred predominantly in the three aforementioned majority-Muslim provinces. Most of the victims have been Muslim civilians. Freedom of movement has been restricted as the Thai authorities have tightened up border controls and occasionally closed its southern border with Malaysia. The Malaysian authorities are trying to steer a middle course in the conflict, voicing solidarity with their fellow Malays, while seeking to prevent an influx of extremist Malay militants onto their soil.

There is no single organization or leader directing the Malay Muslim insurgency. This has made it difficult to set in motion a peace process because it is not clear with which separatist faction the Thai government should be negotiating. According to a U.S. State Department report on terrorism in Thailand published in April 2009, the long-standing and ongoing conflict is Thailand's single biggest border security challenge. Thailand has meanwhile also been dealing with the fallout from two other separatist conflicts in neighboring countries: over a hundred thousand Karen and Hmong (see separate essays) have streamed into Thailand from, respectively, Myanmar to the west and Laos to the east.

According to Professor Liow from Nanyang University, there are strong parallels between the Malay Muslim insurgency in southern Thailand and the Moro Muslim insurgency in southern Philippines (see separate essay). Liow, who has analyzed the two conflicts in his academic papers, said both were primarily ethno-nationalist in motivation but had taken on a more explicit religious dimension over the past decade. Liow said that "Islam has come to be an increasingly potent avenue to comprehend, rally, articulate, and express resistance against the central state." The Malays became Muslim around the tenth century C.E. after Arab traders brought Islam to the region.

However, Liow warned against linking the Malay Muslim insurgency to the bloody campaigns of globally oriented Islamist groups such as al Qaeda, saying, "there is little evidence to suggest that the global jihad has taken root in Thailand." He has noted how the Malay militants—in contrast to the Arab-based al Qaeda or the Southeast Asian-based Islamist group Jemaah Islamiyah (JI)—have not targeted Westerners, nor have they employed these groups' hallmark instrument of the suicide bombing or claimed responsibility for their attacks.

A June 2009 report from the International Crisis Group (ICG), a non-governmental organization that produces research and analysis to help resolve world conflicts, concluded that international participation in the Malay separatist struggle was limited. "Although a few Malaysians have been arrested in southern Thailand for trying to join the struggle, there is no evidence of significant involvement of foreign jihadi groups," the ICG report said. Liow has pointed out, however, that there was evidence "pointing to Thailand's role as favored meeting place and transit point for Islamic terrorists."

History

The Malays of Thailand lived independently in various sultanates until the sixteenth century when the kingdom of Siam, the name by which Thailand was then known, began to exert influence over them. In 1902 Siam annexed them, dividing the region into three provinces. The new Thai rulers removed Malay Muslims from positions of authority and replaced them with Thai-speakers, which triggered a Malay resistance movement. Thailand was one of the few Asian countries not colonized by a European power or by the United States. The Malays living south of Thailand, in modern-day Malaysia, were colonized by the British. These local Malay leaders urged the British in 1945 to incorporate the southern Thai provinces into a nascent independent Malay state, but the British did not do this.

On April 28, 1948, a rebellion against Thai rule broke out in the village of Dusun Nyior in the province of Narathiwat. Malay peasants clashed with police, leading to the deaths of four hundred Malays and thirty police officers. More sustained Malay Muslim resistance began in the 1960s as armed separatist groups formed. The levels of violence peaked in the 1970s before subsiding in the 1980s and 1990s, a period when Thailand became more democratic. Policies were implemented to help the Malay-Muslim provinces develop, and the

Thai authorities showed greater sensitivity to Malay Muslim culture.

Despite this, separatist violence resumed in late 2001 and increased from 2004 when Malay Muslim militants raided an army camp in Narathiwat on January 4, leading the Thai government to declare martial law in the three majority-Muslim provinces. The militants, who previously were based in the countryside, increasingly began carrying out bombings and beheadings in urban centers and extending their attacks beyond Pattani, Yala, and Narathiwat to the Songkhla province to the north. On April 28, 2004, the militants attacked Thai forces, who responded with a counter-attack in which 108 militants and 5 police officers were killed. The dead included 32 militants killed by government forces in the historic Krisek mosque in Pattani, the mosque having been stormed after militants took refuge there. On October 25, 2004, 79 Malay Muslim men who had been arrested by Thai security forces died from suffocation while being transported in trucks, an episode known as the Tak Bai massacre.

The Thai government's counterinsurgency powers were enhanced by the Thai Parliament in August 2005, which passed a law allowing wiretapping, searches without warrants, censoring of news reports, and the banning of certain publications. The human rights organization Amnesty International accused the government of arbitrary detentions and use of excessive force and torture. The Thai authorities were criticized for adopting an exclusively military response to the conflict and for carrying out large-scale arrests without obtaining many convictions of detainees.

The government in March 2005 created a National Reconciliation Committee. In January 2006, the committee recommended political concessions. These included the adoption of Malay as a working language in the south, allowing Islamic law to apply in certain situations, and engaging in dialogue with the militants. When a new Thai government came to power in a coup d'état in October 2006, it adopted a more conciliatory approach, with the prime minister, Gen. Suraayud Chulanont, apologizing in November for some of his predecessor's heavy-handed policies and freeing some detainees. But the new government also sustained the fight against the Malay militants by reinforcing special armed units such as the Ranger Force, Volunteer Defense Corps, and Village Defense Volunteers. One such unit, the Village Protection Force, which Thailand's Queen Sirikit sponsored, was accused of extortion, beatings, and extrajudicial killings.

Leadership

The leadership of the Malay Muslim separatist movement is highly fragmented, with no single political party or military group representing them. A group called Barisan Revolusi Nasional–Coordinasi (BRN-C) is believed to be the dominant militant faction. The BRN-C has a military wing called the Runda Kumpulan Kecil (RKK) and a youth wing called Pemuda. The BRN-C's decentralized cell structure, consisting of autonomous local units, has made it difficult for the government to inflict a lethal blow on it. The BRN-C is a splinter group of the Barisan Revolusi Nasional (BRN), which was founded in 1963 in response to the forced registration of Islamic schools and the secularization of the school curriculum. The BRN split in the 1980s into the BRN-C, BRN-Ulama, and BRN-Congress, and the BRN-C emerged as the dominant faction.

The Pattani United Liberation Organization (PULO), established in 1968, is one of the older separatist groups. PULO's goal is the creation of an independent Islamic state carved out from the southern provinces where the Muslims form a majority. In past decades, PULO carried out attacks on Thai officials, school teachers, and Buddhist monks. However, more recently it has evolved into a political organization, most of whose leaders live in neighboring Malaysia. Other, more marginal insurgent groups include Bersatu, which is made up of former members of the BRN and PULO, the Pattani Islamic Mujahiddin Movement, the Pattani Islamic Liberation Front, and Pattani Freedom Fighters.

A manuscript called "Berjihad di Pattani," reputedly written in a town in Kelantan state in northern Malaysia, contains much of the core ideology embraced by the militant separatists. The manuscript calls for a holy war in which the former kingdom of Pattani will be liberated from the Thai colonialists and a Pattani Muslim state installed. Found on the bodies of some of the militants killed in the Krisek mosque in 2004, the Berjihad calls for acts of martyrdom and attacks on Muslims who collaborate with the occupiers. It is strongly Sunni Muslim in orthodoxy and therefore is critical of the veneration of saints espoused by Shia Muslims. According to Professor Liow, this creed can also be interpreted as a veiled attack on the official spiritual leader of Thai Muslims, the Chularajmontri, who is appointed by the authorities in Bangkok.

Current Status

Separatist violence continues intermittently in southern Thailand, and so too do government crackdowns against it. According to Liow, the government's counterinsurgency efforts have been hampered by "incessant politicking and a lack of coordination among the various agencies involved in information gathering and policy formulation." The local Malay Muslim population, despite often being the victims of the militants' attacks, does not trust the Thai authorities and so does not provide them with intelligence on militant activities, Liow said. The government scores occasional successes—for example, by seizing weapons caches—but it has been unable to make a serious dent in the insurgency.

The authorities introduced a new counterinsurgency tactic in May 2007 when the Thai army and police began to raid communities in the south and hunt down insurgents. Up to a hundred people were arrested per raid, including suspected militants

and their neighbors and friends, the Thai newspaper *The Nation* claimed in an August 2007 investigative report. Detainees were taken to a camp in the Pattani province, their names cross-checked with a government list of insurgents, and those with arrest warrants on them were locked up. The detainees deemed not "high risk" were sent to army camps for up to four months to be "re-educated" to become loyal Thai citizens—a program that included listening to a Muslim cleric urging them not to take up arms to liberate the Malay provinces.

The newspaper article accused the Thai authorities of having alienated locals to the point of provoking further militancy. A detainee from Narathiwat was quoted as saying, "Don't they know that if we were insurgents we wouldn't be sticking around to be taken in?" The detainee was highly critical of the government's re-education program: "They keep telling us that we must love the country in which we live. But what they are doing is actually pushing the people further away and possibly towards the insurgents." The article also claimed that the Malays were not necessarily opposed to remaining part of Thailand. "Although they detest the ethnocentric nature of Thailand's nation-state ideology, locals here said it doesn't necessary[ily] mean that they want to separate from the Kingdom," journalist Don Pathan said.

There have been sporadic international efforts to broker peace. On September 20–21, 2008, Indonesia's vice president, Jusuf Kalla, mediated talks in Bogor in Indonesia between the Thai government and the Pattani Malay Consultative Congress, an umbrella group claiming to represent the insurgents. Such efforts have been hard to sustain, however, in part because the Thai government has, since early 2008, been embroiled in a domestic power struggle resulting from the ousting of the former prime minister Thaksin Shinawatra in a 2006 coup. In late 2010, the Organization of The Islamic Conference, an intergovernmental association of 57 Muslim states, became involved in brokering peace talks between the Thai government and Malay separatists.

According to Liow, while the conflict is more colored by religion, it cannot be considered a major center for the pan-Islamic or global jihadi movement. Rather, it "remains rooted not only in the political ideology of Malay-Muslim nationalism and separatism but also in the state's misguided policies to deal with the violence." The ICG noted in its July 2009 report that the Malay Muslim movement is strongly religious, with militants often being recruited from Islamic schools, sometimes through "extracurricular indoctrination programs in mosques or disguised as football training." Recruits take an oath of allegiance and are given physical and military training before being assigned to different roles in village-level operations, the report said. It agreed with Liow's assessment that human rights violations committed by the Thai authorities have fuelled secessionism, as has the centralization of power in Bangkok. The ICG recommended that the government "respond to the insurgents' grievance in order to bring long-lasting peace to the region."

Further Reading

Human Rights Watch, " 'Targets of Both Sides': Violence against Students, Teachers, and Schools in Thailand's Southern Border Provinces," September 20, 2010, www.hrw.org/node/93085.

International Crisis Group. "Recruiting Militants in Southern Thailand," *Asia Report,* no. 170 (June 22, 2009), www.crisisgroup.org/library/documents/asia/south_east_asia/170_recruiting_militants_in_southern_thailand.pdf.

Khalik, Abdul, and Desy Nurhayati. "Thailand: Govt and Muslims agree to end southern conflict," *The Jakarta Post,* September 22, 2008, www.thejakartapost.com/news/2008/09/22/thai-govt-muslims-agree-end-conflict.html.

Liow, Joseph Chinyong. "International Jihad and Muslim Radicalism in Thailand? Towards an Alternative Interpretation," *Asia Policy,* no. 2 (July 2006): 89–108, www.nbr.org/publications/asia_policy/ap2/ap2_liow.pdf.

McCargo, Duncan. *Tearing Apart the Land: Islam and Legitimacy in Southern Thailand.* Ithaca: Cornell University Press, 2008.

"More substance needed in reaching out to Thai Muslims," *The Nation* (Thailand), January 2, 2011.

Pathan, Don. "Locals cling to hopes of a solution in South," *The Nation* (Thailand), August 23 and 24, 2007, www.nationmultimedia.com/specials/south2years/aug2307.php.

———. "OIC to take up issue of militancy in south," *The Nation* (Thailand), November 1, 2010.

Syukri, Ibrahim. *History of the Malay Kingdom of Patani.* Athens: Center for International Studies, Ohio University, 1985.

U.S. State Department. "Country Reports on Terrorism 2008" (Thailand), April 30, 2009, http://www.state.gov/s/ct/rls/crt/2008/index.htm.

MAORI
(New Zealand)

The Maori Aboriginal people living in New Zealand have, from the onset of British colonization two centuries ago, fought to preserve their identity. Despite having made advances since the 1970s in promoting their culture and language and in advancing claims to ancestral lands, many would like greater autonomy, albeit while remaining part of New Zealand. About 15 percent, or more than one in seven, New Zealanders claim Maori ancestry out of a population of 4.2 million. The overwhelming majority of New Zealanders, 70 percent, are of European ancestry, predominantly from the United Kingdom and Ireland. These descendents of white European settlers are called Pakeha by the Maori. The remaining 15 percent of the population is mostly of Asian, Pacific Island, or mixed race origin.

The country where the Maori have lived for two thousand years is in one of the most physically remote places in the world, situated 1,200 miles southeast of Australia in the southern Pacific Ocean and consisting of two large islands, North and South. About 80 percent of the Maori people live in cities. The urbanization process began in the 1940s when New Zealand became more industrialized and less reliant for trade on its former colonial master, the United Kingdom.

Most Maori have become Christian due to the influence of the immigrating British; however, culturally they remain quite distinct, with their own values, called *taha*. They have clearly recognizable physical features, a unique history, and a native language that is one of New Zealand's two spoken languages, the other being English. The Maori language declined dramatically as Maori increasingly moved to cities; additionally, legislation outlawed its use in schools. However, unlike the many other Aboriginal languages that are on the verge of extinction, since the 1980s Maori has experienced a remarkable revival. There has been a major rise in the number of Maori-language schools, as well as bilingual classes in primary and secondary schools. A government-funded Maori-language television station began broadcasting in 2004.

Many Maori do not accept the sovereignty of the Pakeha-dominated New Zealand government based in Wellington. That government has in practice been fully independent from the United Kingdom for about a century, although officially the head of state remains the British monarch, Queen Elizabeth II. The monarch is represented by an appointed

Governor General, currently Anand Satyanand, a New Zealand national of Indo-Fijian ancestry. One consequence of the British influence is that the Maori live in a country, which, like the United Kingdom, does not have a written constitution.

The right to practice their culture and peacefully campaign for greater autonomy exists for Maori. A political party was set up in 2004, the Maori Party, specifically to promote their interests. Maori relations with the New Zealand authorities are at times difficult. The single biggest cause of tension is the issue of restitution of ancestral lands that European settlers took from the Maori. While land tribunals were established as early as 1840 to prevent disputes, in practice Maori land rights were often ignored, especially in the early years of British settlement. The past forty years have seen considerable efforts on the part of the New Zealand authorities to make amends. Several land settlements have been made, although with less than 1 percent of the lands taken returned many Maori feel justice has not yet been done.

Militant Maori opposition to the New Zealand government has tended to take the form of occasional demonstrations rather than large-scale violent attacks. Such protests, which were especially frequent in the 1970s and 1980s, are still commonplace and often happen on the day New Zealanders commemorate the signing in 1840 of the Treaty of Waitangi, which forms the basis of the Maori-Pakeha legal relationship. The treaty, drafted in both English and Maori, has always been controversial, in part because there are differing interpretations of it. Maori autonomy campaigners insist that the treaty recognized Maori sovereignty over their lands and not merely the right to live on them. The demographic situation has changed dramatically since the signing. In 1840 there were only a couple thousand white settlers; by 2010 there were over three million New Zealanders of European ancestry.

The vast majority of Maori today are not advocating the creation of a separate Maori country. However, there are some more independent-minded Maori tribes, most notably the Tuhoe, who demand to be recognized as a separate nation that has the freedom to govern its affairs. Most Maori support efforts to promote their language and culture. Given their physical isolation on the world map, the Maori are remarkable for the strong links they have succeeded in forging with Aboriginal peoples elsewhere, especially in North America, where they have received considerable support. They have particularly close ties to Hawaiians, to whom they are ethnically related, both being Polynesian peoples.

History

According to tradition, the Maori came to New Zealand, known in Maori as Aotearoa, two thousand years ago and settled mostly in the North Island, subsisting by agriculture and fishing. A European presence was first registered in 1642 when the Dutch explorer Abel Tasman appeared. He was followed by the arrival of British explorer James Cook, who landed during his lengthy expedition (1768–1771). The British established permanent settlements from the early 1800s. There was occasional fighting between Maori tribes before colonization. The numbers killed in these battles—known as the "musket wars"—increased in the early 1800s after guns were introduced to Maori culture through contact with Europeans.

On February 6, 1840, Maori tribal leaders signed the Treaty of Waitangi with representatives of the British government. The treaty, which some Maori chiefs refused to sign, laid down the rights of the Maori to maintain ownership of the territories where they lived. The British viewed the treaty as having granted Britain sovereignty and consequently increased the rate of colonial settlement. As more British came, competition for land increased and a series of land wars took place between the 1840s and 1860s, resulting in British settlers confiscating millions of acres of Maori lands. The British introduced a policy of assimilation. At the same time, the Maori population declined dramatically from a million pre-colonization to as low as forty thousand by the late 1800s, mainly due to the introduction of disease against which the Maori had no immunity but also as a result of the adoption among the Maori of European guns. The Pakeha became increasingly independent of the United Kingdom, with New Zealand gaining dominion status in 1907 and becoming an independent member of the British Commonwealth in 1947.

Maori complaints about the illegal confiscation of their lands were vindicated by a royal commission in 1928, which found that treaties had been violated. This marked an important milestone in the ongoing process to "right the wrongs" of colonial history. In 1975 a Labor government established the Waitangi tribunal to investigate alleged violations of Maori land and fishing rights under the 1840 treaty. By 1985 some 70 percent of New Zealand's territory was subject to Maori land claims. There followed a slew of settlements. In December 1994, the government announced a "once and for all" settlement worth $728 million (NZ$1 billion) for four hundred separate Maori land claims, but many Maori leaders rejected the offer. In May 1995, the government signed an agreement with the Tainui confederation of tribes, returning 35,000 acres (2,000 hectares) of the 2.1 million acres (850,000 hectares) confiscated to settle grievances dating back to the 1860s. In the agreement, the government articulated its "regret and apologies." In November 1997, the authorities made a settlement for $124 million (NZ$170 million) to the Ngai Tahu tribe on New Zealand's South Island.

An important event that affected how non-Maori New Zealanders viewed the whole land claims process occurred in June 2003 when a court ruled that Maori tribes were entitled to also file claims of ownership of the seabed and foreshore. This caused major political waves as it raised the prospect that the Maori would have a say in how New Zealand's beaches were managed. The public grew more anxious as the media speculated this could cause ordinary New Zealanders to no longer be able to enjoy seaside holidays. The government responded by passing a law, the Foreshore and Seabed Act, to prevent this from happening. This in turn energized the Maori autonomy movement, leading to the creation of the Maori Party, which in 2008 entered government as a minority coalition partner to the National Party, which had ousted the Labor party.

Leadership

The Maori pride themselves on a lengthy history of organizing together to assert and negotiate their rights. In 1835, in response to rising Pakeha immigration, they set up a Confederation of Tribes to exercise Maori sovereignty, a body that still exists. In 1857 Maori elected a king, Te Wherowhero, to try to halt the ongoing sales of land to British settlers by placing the land under his jurisdiction. In 1892 Maori set up their own parliament, but the New Zealand parliament did not recognize it. Similarly unsuccessful attempts were made in 1992 and 2006 to establish representative bodies, called, respectively, the National Maori Congress and National Maori Leaders' Body.

The most influential political movement promoting Maori interests today is the Maori Party. Its co-leaders are Tariana Turia and Pita Sharples. Turia was formerly a Labor Party parliamentarian and Associate Minister for Maori Affairs, but she left the party in June 2004 in protest over the government's Foreshore and Seabed Bill, which she saw as a betrayal of Maori rights. She won a by-election on July 10, taking 90 percent of the vote. The party has attracted a sizeable share of the Maori vote, winning 2.2 percent of the nationwide vote in the 2008 general elections. The Maori Party has eclipsed many other Maori groups established from the 1970s, notably the Mana Maori Motuhake (Maori Self-Determination) set up in 1979 by Matiu Rata.

Seven seats in New Zealand's parliament are reserved for people of Maori ancestry. In practice this means that Maori voters can either vote for someone on the general list of candidates, or for someone on the Maori-only list. The main political parties each have several members of Maori descent. There have been parliamentarians of Maori descent who have served as ministers in government; the governor general from 1985–1990 was of partial Maori ancestry.

A key player in the Maori campaign for cultural rights was Nga Tamatoa, a group established in 1972 by Maori academics, which demanded that the Maori language be taught in schools. In 1975 it organized the Land March down the length of the North Island to the New Zealand parliament in Wellington to raise public awareness of Maori grievances. In 1982 the Kohanga Reo movement was established to promote Maori-language education. Initially focused on preschools, it has since expanded to all levels of education and receives some government support.

Current Status

Land claims are the single biggest unresolved issue for the Maori. They currently own about 5 percent of New Zealand's territory. Most of their claims are still awaiting judgment by the Waitangi land restitution tribunal. While the biggest political parties in New Zealand officially support the court process, some New Zealanders have grown wary of it, given the increasing scope of Maori claims. The former National Party leader, Don Brash, for example, has argued that the tribunals' process should be concluded as soon as possible as it promotes a culture of racial separatism.

The statistics show that Maori identity is strengthening. In the 2006 census, 565,329 New Zealanders identified themselves as Maori, up from 434,847 in 1991. But while the Maori people are asserting their distinctness, a push for a Maori state seems unlikely. Unlike some Aboriginal peoples who are geographically concentrated in a particular region, the Maori are dispersed throughout New Zealand and belong to various tribes that do not all share the same view on the autonomy issue.

Among both Maori and non-Maori, the issue of how the Maori should best be represented in elected government, such as in parliament or local councils, has become contentious. The Maori Party tried unsuccessfully in 2009 to have Maori-only seats designated on the Auckland super-city Council. The party has also been campaigning to have the seven Maori-only seats in the national parliament made a permanent fixture by the passage of legislation enshrining the principle, which could only be overturned by a 75 percent majority in parliament. Polls show that New Zealanders are evenly split on whether to keep or abolish the Maori-only seat system.

Maori protests against Pakeha racism are common, especially on Waitangi Day (February 6), the annual public holiday commemorating the 1840 treaty. In October 2007, police conducted raids on a small community of the Tuhoe tribe, arresting several Maori activists on suspicion of weapons and terrorism offenses. Charges were subsequently dropped for lack of evidence, and the police eventually apologized for the raids. Indeed, the operation was widely criticized for being too heavy-handed and for having damaged already-fragile relations between the Maori and New Zealand authorities. Maori autonomy campaigners scored a symbolic victory on February 6, 2010, when the New Zealand government permitted a Maori flag, the Tino Rangatiratanga, to be flown alongside the national flag from Auckland Harbor Bridge for Waitangi Day.

The Tuhoe nation is notable for having never signed the Treaty of Waitangi and for retaining a strong attachment to their Maori identity and sovereignty. Its leaders have called for the Tuhoe to be designated as a separate nation that would run a parallel legal system and govern its own affairs.

According to an August 2009 article in the New Zealand newspaper, *The Dominion Post*, "most New Zealanders subscribe to the 'live and let live' theory, at least publicly. Such tolerance, however, can be mistaken for indifference. It is unlikely that Kiwis would accept parallel 'justice' systems here, even if confined to personal and civil matters, be they for Maori or the religious." Having a parallel legal system would most likely create disputes over conflicting values and beliefs, for example, on an issue like family burial rights, the article noted.

The proportion of Maori who are unemployed remains above the nationwide average, while those Maori who are employed are disproportionately represented in the unskilled, low-wage sectors. Maori have below-average education levels and over half of all prison inmates in New Zealand are Maori. The Maori have higher suicide rates and their average life expectancy remains several years below the national average, although the gap is narrowing. Thus, while on political representation and autonomy the Maori have made more advances than many Aboriginal peoples, in their social development they suffer from the same problems that tend to afflict Aboriginals who have been colonized.

Further Reading

"Editorial: Flag shows progress is being made," *The New Zealand Herald*, February 6, 2010, www.nzherald .co.nz/flag-debate/news/article.cfm?c_id=1500876& objectid=10624452.

Higgins, Ean. "Maori set to rise in NZ poll," *The Australian*, November 7, 2008, www.theaustralian.news .com.au/story/0,25197,24612594–28737,00.html.

Mutu, Margaret. 2004. "The Humpty Dumpty Principle at Work: The Role of Mistranslation in the British Settlement of Aotearoa," in *For Better or Worse: Translation as a Tool for Change in the South Pacific*, ed. Sabine Fenton. Manchester, England: St. Jerome Publishing, 2004.

"Nose to Nose: A tense election with plenty at stake—especially for Maoris," *The Economist*, September 17, 2005, www.economist.com/world/ asia/displaystory.cfm?story_id=4408096.

Renwick, William, ed. *Sovereignty and Indigenous Rights: The Treaty of Waitangi in Indigenous Contexts*. Wellington: Victoria University Press, 1991.

"When law meets lore," *The Dominion Post*, August 31, 2009, www.stuff.co.nz/dominion-post/opinion/ editorials/2815860/Editorial-When-law-meets-lore.

MOROS
(Philippines)

The Moro Muslim minority in the Philippines has for centuries engaged in a persistent and violent struggle for autonomy and independence. Intermittent conflict between the Moros and Christian Filipinos since the early 1970s has killed 120,000 people and displaced millions from their homes. Most of the 4.5 million-strong Filipino Muslim population, which is ethnically Malay, lives on Mindanao, the largest island group in southern Philippines. The Moros are a minority in Mindanao, making up about 20 percent of the population, as they are nationwide, accounting for just 5 percent of all Filipinos. They are most numerically dominant in the smaller islands south of Mindanao next to Indonesia, which is a majority-Muslim country. The Moros, who are mostly Sunni Muslim in denomination, live in the only Asian country that has a majority-Catholic population. About 85 percent of Filipinos are Christian, and about 90 percent of these are Catholic. The religious divide is a dominant factor in the conflict, with widespread mutual mistrust between Christians and Muslims.

Within the Moro community, there are thirteen ethno-linguistic groups whose languages are mutually comprehensible, the dominant groups being Maguindanao, Marano, and Tausug. The Moro languages form part of the Malayo-Polynesian linguistic group, as does Tagalog, the most common ethnicity and widely spoken indigenous language in the Philippines. English is the most commonly used colonial language. The Moros are unified by their Islamic faith and a long-standing hostility toward the Filipino government, which is based in the nation's capital, Manila, situated on the northern Philippines island of Luzon. However, the Moros' campaign for autonomy has been hampered by internal divisions caused by ethno-linguistic differences and disputes over religious orthodoxy.

Much discontent springs from the fact that while Mindanao is the most fertile and mineral-rich part of the country—containing gold, copper, uranium, and timber—the Muslim-dominated areas of Mindanao are among the poorest in the country. This is partly due to decades of conflict, both between the Christians and Muslims and among Muslims themselves as various warlords fight to protect their fiefdoms. It is also because Christians control much of the minerals and land in Muslim areas, a legacy of large-scale immigration by Christian Filipinos, which diluted the Muslim population from 76 percent of Mindanao in 1903 to 20 percent by 1990. Despite this migration and the efforts made for five centuries to integrate the Moros into the non-Muslim population, first by the Spanish and then by the United States, Moro identity remains extremely strong.

Although an autonomous government—the Autonomous Region of Muslim Mindanao (ARMM)—has been operating in Muslim-dominated areas since 1990, it is widely acknowledged that it has not satisfied Moro aspirations for self-rule. In a November 2009 email interview, Eugene Martin, a peace worker in Mindanao from 2003–2007 for the United States Institute of Peace (USIP), a non-governmental organization, said "the ARMM has little real devolved power, as it depends on the central government in Manila to allocate budgetary resources for nearly every activity—education, infrastructure, health, etc." Islamic law, or *sharia*, is practiced in some areas controlled by dissident Moro militants where "there is lack of adequate and reliable justice," said Martin.

The Moro-Filipino conflict has attracted considerable international attention. The government in neighboring Malaysia has acted as a peace broker since the 1990s; however, the Filipino government has been wary of Malaysian involvement, as the Malaysian government at one time funded the leading Moro separatist group and gave sanctuary to its members. Malaysia's former pro-Moro stance came in retaliation for the demand by the Filipino government that Malaysia cede sovereignty of Sabah, a state in eastern Malaysia, to the Philippines. Arab countries have helped the Moros, with Libya and Egypt notably providing financial support to rival Moro factions in the 1970s. In the 1980s some Moro militants trained and fought with anti-Soviet *mujahideen* resistance fighters in Afghanistan. The Filipino government, in addition to fighting the Moros, has been trying to suppress a communist insurgency led by the New Peoples' Army, based in the northern island of Luzon.

The United States has remained a military ally of the Filipino government; however, with the end of the cold war the United States shut down the last of its military bases in the Philippines in 1992 and subsequently reduced development aid. The U.S. government was involved in peace-making efforts from 2003–2006, providing funding for the USIP. The USIP's Martin noted that "the Filipino government would exploit the ethnic divisions within the Moro autonomy movement, while we were working to try to get the Moros to unite." The USIP mission was terminated after the U.S. Congress cut its funding in 2006. The peace process was derailed in mid-2008 as a result of opposition to a new autonomy agreement. There are ongoing efforts to put it back together.

History

Filipino Muslims can trace their origins to the thirteenth century, when Islamic teachers arrived from Arabia and modern-day Malaysia and converted the local population to Islam. The Islamic communities established de facto states, or sultanates, that were similar to those in Indonesia and Malaysia, with the sultans acting as both secular and religious leaders. They became known as Moros from the early sixteenth century when the Spanish came and named them after the Muslim Moors, who had been expelled from Spain in 1492. The Spanish explorer Ferdinand Magellan claimed the islands for Spain in 1521, and the Spanish gradually converted most of the country to Christianity. But the Spanish never gained full control of the Moros and were often forced to defend their settlements against Moro attacks.

The United States replaced the Spanish as the colonial ruler in 1898, after it seized the Philippines during the Spanish-American war. The Moros resisted American rule, too, and twenty thousand people were killed in clashes from 1903 to 1935. With its superior firepower, the United States succeeded in taking control of Moro areas. It then chose to administer the Moro areas separately from the rest of the Philippines. After the United States made the Philippines a commonwealth in 1935, there was an increase in immigration by Christians from northern Philippines into Moro areas; in such cases, the arriving "homesteaders" were granted title to vast tracts of land. Japan occupied Moro lands from 1942–1945 along with the rest of the Philippines, as part of its campaign to take over much of Asia during World War II (1939–1945). The United States reassumed power after the Japanese were defeated but immediately began to prepare to hand over sovereignty to the Filipinos. The Moros urged the United States not to integrate them into the nascent independent Filipino republic that was formally established on July 4, 1946. The United States declined to grant them autonomy, however. The new Filipino government encouraged further migration of Christians to Mindanao, which exacerbated tensions and led to sporadic fighting between the Moros and the authorities.

Ferdinand Marcos, dictator of the Philippines from 1965 to 1986, suppressed Moro resistance. He declared martial law in 1972, used local vigilante groups to burn Moro villages, banned Moro languages in schools, and excluded Muslims from positions of political and economic power. In the 1970s he proposed creating an autonomous region in Mindanao, but this plan was rejected in a plebiscite. After Marcos was toppled in 1986, the new democratic government organized referenda on autonomy in thirteen provinces. Four provinces voted in favor, which led to the inauguration of the ARMM on November 6, 1990. The ARMM was expanded in 2001 to include Marawi City and the province of Basilan.

Despite advances made for self-government, sporadic violence continued, perpetrated by dissident groups dissatisfied with the autonomy arrangement. Indonesia took the lead in trying to broker peace in the 1990s, its efforts culminating in a new peace and autonomy agreement in 1996. A cease-fire was put in place in 1997 but broke down around 2000 as a result of growing tensions over the failure to properly implement the 1996 agreement. On November 19, 2001, forces loyal to Nur Misuari, the onetime governor of the ARMM who had recently been removed from his post, attacked a Filipino army base in Jolo, a volcanic island in southwest Philippines, killing a hundred people.

The United States renewed its ties to the Philippines after the September 11, 2001, terrorist attacks against the United States, perpetrated by the Islamist al Qaeda network. By stressing the Islamic fundamentalist dimension of the Moro conflict, Filipino president Gloria Arroyo succeeded in attracting more funds for counter-terrorist operations from the United States, with aid increased from $3.4 million in 2001 to $30 million in 2002.

Leadership

The Moro Islamic Liberation Front (MILF) is one of the main Moro separatist groups, with between ten and fifteen thousand armed combatants. The MILF's original goal was to establish an independent Moro state, but it now supports autonomy within the Philippines. It has engaged in intense militant activity for periods and been relatively peaceful at other times. Power was due to be handed over to the MILF under an autonomy agreement concluded with Filipino authorities in July 2008, but the Supreme Court in October 2008 ruled that agreement unconstitutional.

The MILF was set up in 1978 by Salamat Hashim, a hard-line militant trained in Egypt who lived in exile in Libya for twenty years until December 1997. In 2003 Hashim renounced terrorism and had begun to make peace with the Filipino authorities when he died suddenly on July 13. He was succeeded by Murad Ebrahim.

The MILF is a splinter organization of the Moro National Liberation Front (MNLF), which was founded by Nur Misuari in the early 1970s. The

MNLF concluded the 1996 peace agreement, and Misuari was elected governor of the autonomous region on September 9, 1996. His administration was criticized for infighting and corruption, however, and he eventually lost power. Other leading MNLF figures include Parouk Hussin and Muslimin Sema. The MNLF had a precursor, the Muslim Independence Movement, launched in 1968 by Muslims who wanted to create a *Bangsa Moro,* or Moro nation, and who conducted a full-scale revolt from 1969–1972.

Both the MILF and MNLF are nationally focused groups, but there is another, more globally focused Moro rebel group called Abu Sayyaf, meaning "Bearer of the Sword," which was established by dissident MNLF members in 1990–1991. Abu Sayyaf aims to first create an independent Islamic Moro state and build on that to help install a Muslim super-state across Southeast Asia. Led by Yasser Igasan, it is smaller than the MILF, with membership estimated at a few hundred guerrillas. It has been involved in kidnappings and is classified by the United States as a foreign terrorist organization. The MILF has denied accusations of having links to Abu Sayyaf, or to the Southeast Asian–based Islamist group, Jemaah Islamiyah (JI). Though the MILF does not share either group's vision of global jihad or holy war, it did allow JI members to train in the Abubakar camp in Mindanao beginning in 1990 until the Filipino authorities destroyed the camp in 2000.

Current Status

Militant Moro separatism remains a major threat to the security of the Philippines. The MILF killed thirteen Filipino soldiers and twenty-two police officers in 2008, according to the U.S. State Department's annual human rights report published in February 2009. There was a notable increase in the violence levels after the Supreme Court struck down the July 2008 autonomy agreement on the grounds that the Filipino government had exceeded its negotiating

authority. In the weeks that followed the ruling, over a hundred people—civilians, military and militants—were killed in a series of bombings, assassinations, and kidnappings, and 300,000 people were displaced. According to USIP's Martin in a November 2009 interview, the opposition to the autonomy agreement was spearheaded by Christian elites in Mindanao and Manila who were afraid of losing their lands under the accord's "ancestral domain" provisions. The accord would have increased the territory of the existing ARMM, allowed the Moro government to conduct international trade negotiations, and given them control over how their mineral resources could be exploited.

There was a surge in kidnappings in 2009, many of which were linked to Abu Sayyaf. A particularly high profile abduction was that of the Irish priest, Father Michael Sinnott, who was taken in October 2009 and held for thirty-two days by a group of Islamic fundamentalists, which had broken away from the MILF. The Filipino government initially blamed the MILF for the kidnapping but later retracted this accusation, which led the MILF to intervene to free the priest. Father Sinnott had worked in the Philippines since 1957 with a Columbian mission and had been operating a school for disabled children in Mindanao.

There remains major international involvement in the conflict, notably via the International Monitoring Team (IMT), which according to USIP's Martin, has helped "in preventing minor skirmishes from escalating into full scale conflict." The IMT suffered a setback on November 30, 2008, when Malaysia withdrew its participants. Peace-making efforts of regional inter-governmental organizations such as the European Union and the Organization of the Islamic Conference have borne some fruit, with a new cease-fire agreement between the Moro militants and Filipino authorities signed on July 28, 2009.

In June 2010, the Islamist separatist Abu Sayyaf organization abducted and beheaded three

Filipino civilians, the *New York Times* reported in an article by Carlos Conde. The attack came as newly elected president Benigno Aquino prepared to assume office. Aquino is unlikely to seek a compromise settlement with the Islamist separatists; however, he has indicated that he would continue the peace negotiations with the more secular MILF, which his predecessor, outgoing president Gloria Arroyo, had been conducting.

The root causes of the conflict have not gone away. The U.S. State Department reported in February 2009 that "many Muslims claimed that they continued to be underrepresented in senior civilian and military positions and cited the lack of proportional Muslim representation in national government institutions. Predominantly Muslim provinces in Mindanao lagged far behind the rest of the country in most aspects of socioeconomic development." Muslims remain marginalized, the State Department said, finding it difficult to get jobs or rent rooms if they use their real names or wear distinctive Muslim dress. The Moro languages are still not widely taught in schools, nor is fluency in them required for government jobs. In addition, the Moros have not been handed back any ancestral lands.

Peace worker Martin's prognosis for the future is somewhat pessimistic. "The longer the impasse continues, the more likely Moro radicals will gain influence." He warned that "while the MILF has been willing to forego independence and accept self-determination within the Philippine nation, succeeding generations of leaders may not."

Further Reading

Abinales, Patricio. "Sancho Panza in Buliok Complex: The Paradox of Muslim Separatism," in *Whither the Philippines in the 21st Century?* Institute of Southeast Asian Studies (2007): 277–312.

Conde, Carlos H. "Separatists Behead 3 Men in Philippines," *New York Times,* June 13, 2010, www.nytimes.com/2010/06/14/world/asia/14phils.html?scp=1&sq=abu%20sayyaf&st=cse.

Martin, Eugene G., and Astrid S. Tuminez. "Towards Peace in the Philippines," Special Report of the United States Institute of Peace, February 2008, www.usip.org/resources/toward-peace-southern-philippines-summary-and-assessment-usip-philippine-facilitation-proj.

McKenna, Thomas. *Muslim Rulers and Rebels.* Berkeley: University of California Press, 1998.

Quilop, Raymond Jose G., and Kathleen Mae M. Villamin. "Revisiting Mindanao: Taking Stock, Moving Through and Beyond," Armed Forces of the Philippines—Office of Strategic and Special Studies, 2009, http://philippines.academia.edu/RaymundQuilop/Books/100619/Revisiting-Mindanao—Taking-Stock—Thinking-Through-and-Moving-Beyond.

U.S. State Department. "2008 Country Reports on Human Rights Practices," February 25, 2009, www.state.gov/g/drl/rls/hrrpt/2008/index.htm.

TAIWANESE
(China)

The people of Taiwan, an island 100 miles southeast of China, have lived independently of China since 1949 and yet find themselves in the anomalous situation of not being recognized as an independent country. Relatively small in size—about 250 miles long and 90 miles wide—Taiwan is densely populated, with twenty-three million inhabitants, or 1.7 percent of the Chinese population of 1.3 billion. The people mostly speak Mandarin Chinese, although most also speak at least one native Taiwanese language: Minnan (also known as Hoklo, or Taiwanese), Hakka, or one of fourteen languages spoken by small indigenous tribes.

Taiwan is 93 percent Taoist or Buddhist and 4.5 percent Christian. Ethnically, it is 70 percent Hoklo, 14 percent Hakka, 14 percent Chinese, and 2 percent indigenous. The Hoklo and Hakka Taiwanese, who together account for 84 percent of the population, are descended from Chinese people who immigrated in the 1600s and 1800s. The Chinese arrived in the late 1940s as a consequence of the Chinese civil war, when the nationalist side was defeated by the communists and fled across the Taiwan Strait to establish a rival Chinese government in Taiwan.

Though China claims the island is part of China, most Taiwanese do not view themselves as solely Chinese. In a 2007 opinion poll conducted by Taiwan's Election Study Center at National Chengchi University in Taipei, 44 percent described themselves as "Taiwanese" compared to 5 percent as "Chinese." The proportion of self-describing Taiwanese rose by 27 percentage points between 1992 and 2007, while the proportion of self-describing Chinese fell by 21 percent during the same period. This is partly due to the fact that the Chinese immigrant generation that arrived on the island in 1949 is dying out. Almost half the respondents in the 1992 and 2007 polls saw themselves as both Chinese and Taiwanese.

On the independence question, the pendulum swings back and forth in Taiwanese public opinion. A poll in 2007 found that 55.6 percent supported the status quo (de facto but not de jure independence), with 21.3 percent favoring full independence and 11.6 percent supporting unification with China. Separatist, anti-Chinese sentiment has historically been strongest among the native Taiwanese; however, many offspring of the mainland Chinese who came in 1949, like native Taiwanese, feel a closer affinity to Taiwan than China.

The pro-independence movement was in the ascendant after Chen Shui-Bian was elected president of Taiwan in 2000. Chen refused to accept the "one China" principle so important to the Chinese government, according to which Taiwan is an integral part of China. Chen's predecessor, Lee Teng-Hui, had already begun to depart from the one China policy in the 1990s. The pendulum swung back in the opposite direction in 2008 toward favoring closer ties with China when the more pro-China Kuomintang (KMT) party won elections in Taiwan.

The Taiwanese government's official name is the Republic of China (ROC). This is another legacy of the civil war, specifically of the decision by the defeated nationalists to establish a rival government in Taiwan and to refuse to accept the legitimacy of the communist-led People's Republic of China (PRC) on the mainland. The Taiwanese people lived under military rule until the late 1980s, but today they live in a multi-party democracy. The Taiwanese government continues to try to gain recognition internationally, although it no longer claims to represent all of China. The United Nations has refused to allow Taiwan to join, although the World Trade Organization admitted Taiwan as a full member in 2002 under the name "Separate Customs Territory of Taiwan, Penghu, Kinmen, and Matsu."

China's growing economic and political clout makes states reluctant to give Taiwan official recognition. Nevertheless, many have major trade and investment links with Taiwan. China has floated the idea of granting Taiwan autonomy along the lines enjoyed by China's special administrative regions, Hong Kong and Macao, a formula known as "one country–two systems." But according to an August 2008 opinion poll by the Election Study Center, just 8.1 percent think this formula could be applied to Taiwan. Unlike Hong Kong and Macao, which were handed over to China by the United Kingdom and Portugal in 1997 and 1999, respectively, Taiwan has its own military and its own elected president.

China claims the right to use force to assert sovereignty over Taiwan. Since 1995 it has built up its military across the Taiwan Strait and aimed about 1,300 ballistic missiles at Taiwan. The United States, which has close ties to Taiwan, has been selling arms to the Taiwanese since 1979. The military buildup has not led to full-scale hostilities thus far, although there have been tense times, most notably in 1996 when China fired missiles over Taiwan. Since 2001 there has been a subtle shift in the U.S. position. As Washington has become more bogged down in fighting wars in Iraq and Afghanistan, its priority with Taiwan has been to avoid conflict.

History

The first people to settle in Taiwan arrived at least fifteen thousand years ago. Portuguese sailors passing the island in 1542 called it "Ilha Formosa," meaning beautiful island, and Formosa was the name commonly used to describe Taiwan by Westerners, although it has gradually fallen out of use. The Netherlands established a commercial base, the East India Company, in 1624 and developed sugarcane and rice plantations there. Many Chinese came to work on these plantations, marking the first significant wave of immigration from China. The Dutch were defeated in 1662 by a pirate warlord, Zheng Cheng-Gong. The Chinese defeated Zheng's successor in 1683 and made Taiwan part of the Chinese empire.

In 1895 China was forced to cede the island to Japan under the Treaty of Shimonoseki. The political elite in Taiwan established an independent Taiwan Republic in May 1895, but the Japanese crushed it within a few months and installed a Japanese administration. The Japanese had gained full control of the island by 1930, including the areas populated by indigenous peoples in the center and east, something neither the Dutch nor Chinese had ever achieved. The Japanese language was introduced and the Taiwanese economy modernized;

Taiwan subsequently became a significant exporter of industrial goods to Japan.

In China the monarchy was replaced in 1912 by a republic governed by the nationalist KMT. During World War II (1939–1945), as the KMT fought a civil war against the communists and Japan invaded parts of China, KMT leader Chiang Kai-shek in 1943 persuaded the United States, United Kingdom, and Soviet Union to allow Taiwan to be returned to China. After Japan was defeated in August 1945, the KMT took control of Taiwan. In the first years of KMT rule, the Taiwanese economy, infrastructure, and social system came close to collapse, triggering an uprising in Taiwan in 1947 that the Chinese military brutally repressed, killing between ten and twenty thousand people in the process.

In 1949 the KMT government retreated from its base in Nanjing on mainland China to Taiwan after being defeated by the communists, who had established the People's Republic of China (PRC) led by Mao Zedong. The KMT became the de facto government of Taiwan, although it claimed sovereignty over all of China. Japan formally renounced sovereignty over Taiwan in 1951 but did not in the process declare who had sovereignty over it. Martial law was applied by the KMT until 1987, first under Chiang Kai-shek (1949–1978) and then under his son, Chiang Ching-kuo (1978–1988). The island began to liberalize politically in 1986, the year the Democratic Peoples Party (DPP) was established as the first genuine opposition party. The ideological gap between Taiwan and China narrowed in the 1990s as China embraced a capitalist economic model.

On the global stage, the KMT lost a major battle in 1971 when the UN General Assembly accepted the PRC, the Beijing-based communist government, as the legitimate government of China and expelled the Taiwan-based ROC delegation. This crushing diplomatic defeat came about because the KMT had not controlled mainland China for over twenty years and because the United States had begun to normalize its relations with the PRC.

In 1994 the Taiwanese government renounced its claim to represent all of China, saying instead it represented just the Taiwanese people. The first direct presidential election in Taiwan took place in 1996 and was won by the KMT's Lee Teng-Hui, who had been president since 1988. The first transfer of power to another party took place in 2000 when the DPP's Chen won the presidential election. In 2005 the Chinese government passed an anti-secession law that authorized it to use military force to stop Taiwanese independence.

Leadership

The DPP is the leading political party in Taiwan that advocates independence. In 1999 the party declared that Taiwan was in effect already independent from China and that any change to this status could only occur if Taiwanese residents agreed to this in a referendum. The DPP's Chen held the presidency from 2000–2008; during his tenure greater emphasis was placed on the separate cultural identity of the Taiwanese people. The party won just 27 seats in the 113-seat parliament in the January 2008 elections, losing badly to the KMT. In the December 2009 local elections, the party rebounded somewhat, retaking control of key positions from the KMT. However, the DPP's gains likely had more to do with public anger with the KMT government over the severe economic recession that hit Taiwan from late 2008 than with a surge in support for independence.

The KMT has ruled Taiwan independently from the government on mainland China continuously since 1945, apart from the period from 2000–2008. The great paradox is that the KMT's official position is support for unification with China. The KMT's allies are called the Pan Blue coalition, in contrast to the DPP and its allies, who are called the Pan Green coalition. The KMT was established in 1912 by Sun Yat-Sen. Staunchly anti-communist, for most of the twentieth century it was led by Chiang Kai-shek. Its support base originally came from the mainland Chinese who fled to Taiwan in 1949. As Taiwan moved from military to democratic rule, the KMT expanded its base and pursued a more pro-Taiwan policy under President Lee (1988–2000), who was himself a native Taiwanese. The pro-China faction is currently in the ascendant within the KMT.

Despite the difficulties they have encountered in gaining membership on international bodies, the Taiwanese are very well organized internationally. Due to Chinese government opposition, they do not call their representation offices in other countries "embassies," using instead terms such as the Taipei Economic and Cultural Representative Office, which does not imply that Taiwan is an independent country. In 1991 Taiwan became a founding member of the Unrepresented Nations and Peoples Organization, an association based in The Hague that speaks out on behalf of autonomy movements. In 2003 the Taiwanese government established the Taiwan Foundation for Democracy to promote democracy at home and abroad. The foundation's president is Wen-cheng Lin and the chair is Wang Jin-Pyng.

Current Status

Relations between Taiwan and China have improved since the more pro-China KMT regained power in early 2008. In the presidential election on March 22, Ma Ying-Jeou won with 58.45 percent of the vote, compared to the DPP's 41.55 percent. Ma has a less confrontational style in his dealings with China than his predecessor, Chen. He has focused on strengthening links with the Chinese government. In July 2008, Ma began talks on extending trade and travel between China and Taiwan. A 1949 ban on direct flights between China and Taiwan had begun to be removed in the final years of the Chen presidency. Ma accelerated that process when he increased the number of fixed schedule flights and expanded the number of airports served, so by the end of 2009 there were over one hundred flights a week.

Chinese tourists are traveling to Taiwan in growing numbers, providing welcome income for the Taiwanese economy. About one million Taiwanese live in mainland China, mostly in Shanghai. But while the relations have improved, the KMT's plan to conclude a trade and investment agreement with China is unlikely to proceed without some pushback. Many Taiwanese are afraid that the island will be overrun by the Chinese economically—for example, through takeover by Chinese firms of Taiwan's telecommunications sector or financial institutions, or through the flooding of Taiwanese markets with cheap Chinese products. The islanders are keen to protect and preserve their distinct Taiwanese identity. Many would like to elevate the native Taiwanese languages to the same status as Mandarin in the education system, instead of teaching them as an extra subject, like a foreign language. Mandarin was made the language of instruction in schools by the KMT after it took power in 1945.

The risk of military conflict has diminished but has not disappeared. China continues to claim that it is legally permitted to use force to prevent Taiwanese independence. Taiwan continues to place orders with the United States for military hardware, including fighter jets, helicopters, and submarines. In January 2010, the U.S. government announced a weapons sale to Taiwan worth $6.4 billion. The Chinese government heavily criticized the move. Taiwan's defense budget for 2010 amounted to 16.6 percent of its gross domestic product. The U.S. government is attempting to steer a difficult middle course by not abandoning its old ally, Taiwan, and yet seeking to avoid a major confrontation with China, a country with which it is strengthening economic and political ties.

The Chinese government shows no signs of ending its campaign to prevent Taiwanese de facto independence from morphing into de jure independence. Beijing continues to fight Taiwanese efforts to gain membership on international inter-governmental bodies. It does show some flexibility: in May 2009, for example, it allowed Taiwan to attend the World Health Organization's assembly as an observer under the name "Chinese Tapei." The Taiwanese also use this name when competing in international sporting events such as the Olympic Games. In 2009 President Ma suspended the government's campaign, first launched in 1994, for Taiwan to join the United Nations after the latter in September 2008 had rejected yet again the island's membership bid.

While most countries do not formally recognize Taiwan as an independent country, many treat it in practice as a de facto independent country. For example, a large number recognize Taiwanese passports and have distinct visa and trade policies toward Taiwan that differ from their policies toward mainland China. About forty countries have representative offices in Taiwan—essentially, embassies in all but name. With Taiwan's unique situation, there is little precedent to indicate whether the island will slowly drift further into China's orbit or become a fully-fledged independent country.

Further Reading

Enav, Peter. "Opposition scores gains in Taiwan local elections," Associated Press, December 6, 2009.

International Crisis Group. "China and Taiwan: Uneasy détente," September 2005 Asia Briefing No. 42, www.crisisgroup.org/library/documents/asia/taiwan_strait/b042_china_and_taiwan_uneasy_detente.pdf.

Minnick, Wendell. "Taiwan Defense Budget Drops 6%," *Defense News*, September 28, 2009.

Republic of China Government Information Office, www.gio.gov.tw/mp.asp.

Rubinstein, Murray A., ed. *Taiwan: A New History.* Armonk, N.Y.: M. E. Sharpe, 2006.

Taiwan Documents Project (key documents on Taiwan's legal status and international relations), www.taiwandocuments.org.

Taiwan Foundation for Democracy, www.tfd.org.tw/english/index.php.

Tkacik, John J., Jr. *Reshaping the Taiwan Strait.* Westminster, Md.: Heritage Books, 2007.

Unrepresented Nations and Peoples Organization Web site, Taiwan member profile (accessed December 2009), www.unpo.org/content/view/7908/146/.

TIBETANS
(China)

The Tibetans of China have one of the most high-profile separatist movements in the world. Renowned for their Buddhist faith, with monks clad in billowing red and yellow garments, and their ongoing struggle to preserve their distinct way of life, they have long held the world's gaze. They are ethnically and culturally distinct from other Chinese citizens. They speak Tibetan, which is part of the Tibeto-Burman linguistic group. Their religion, which they have practiced since the seventh century, is a fusion of Buddhism and an older, indigenous religion called Bon. They live on the highest plateau in the world where the average elevation is nearly five thousand meters. They are bordered by India, Nepal, Bhutan, and Myanmar/Union of Burma to the south.

There are between five and six million Tibetans in China. They account for 0.5 percent of China's population; the region in which they live makes up 25 percent of China's territory. With 7.5 million Chinese now living in Tibet, Tibetans have become a minority in their homeland as a result of large-scale immigration by Han Chinese, China's main ethnic group. About half of China's Tibetan population lives in the Tibet Autonomous Region (T.A.R) in the province of U-Tsang, whose capital is Lhasa. Most of the remainder of the Tibetan population live in neighboring provinces to the east, historically called Amdo and Kham but which China has split up or incorporated into other provinces. Tibet's exiled leaders oppose this administrative division and demand that Chinese Tibetans be united in one autonomous entity with broad, clearly defined lawmaking powers. They reject China's assertion that Tibetans already have autonomy through the T.A.R. There are neighboring territories in northern India that are culturally Tibetan, notably Ladakh, Sikkim, and Tawang; Tibetan leaders are not, however, demanding that they be included in their proposed entity.

Tibetan and Chinese interpretations of their history diverge sharply. Tibetans insist that Tibet was never an integral part of China until China occupied Tibet in 1950. China insists it has had sovereignty over Tibet since the thirteenth century. With fifty-four other ethnic minorities in China, the government has a zero tolerance policy on separatism—or splittism, as it calls it—fearful that making concessions to one movement will embolden others and ultimately cause the country to break apart.

The United States has been a steadfast supporter of Tibetans because of its ideological opposition to communist, authoritarian China and because the Tibetan leader, the Dalai Lama, is a revered and popular figure in the United States. For example, President Barack Obama met with the Dalai Lama in February 2010 at the White House, despite the strong objections of China, a country with which the United States has a major trading relationship. Tibetans believe the Dalai Lama, whose birth name is Lhamo Dhondrub, is a reincarnation of the first Dalai Lama, who lived from 1391–1474. Traditionally, Tibetans, after the death of a Dalai Lama, recognize a young boy as his reincarnation. India, with its strong historical and cultural ties to Tibet, has been supportive, too. It allows its 100,000-strong Tibetan expatriate community to practice Tibetan culture and permits the Dalai Lama's government-in-exile to be based there. But India also maintains good relations with China and so does not formally recognize the Tibetan government—nor does any other country.

There are about 50,000 Tibetan expatriates, including 20,000 in Nepal, 10–15,000 in the United States, and 5,000 in Europe. They are well organized and have generated much sympathy for the Tibetan cause. In March 2008, when Tibetans inside China were clashing with the Chinese authorities and Han Chinese immigrants in Tibet, Tibetans in New Delhi, New York, and Sydney organized protests to show their solidarity.

Tibet's economy grew rapidly from 2000 after China implemented its Western Development Strategy, which involved subsidizing major infrastructure projects. Railways, highways, airports, oil and gas pipelines, petrochemical complexes, hydropower stations, and entire new cities were built. The first direct rail link connecting the T.A.R to China was completed in 2006. However, many Tibetans feel that they have not benefited from this growth. They resent that most of the jobs have gone to Han Chinese, who speak Mandarin Chinese, whereas 80 percent of rural Tibetans do not. Many feel the Tibetan language is under threat as Mandarin is increasingly the medium of instruction in Tibetan schools. They worry about the toll that the economic expansion has taken on their environment. For example, much of Tibet's forest has been cut down and native species such as the antelope brought to the brink of extinction. They want Tibetans to set their own environment, education, and language policies and to regulate migration of the Han to Tibet.

Chinese impressions of Tibetans are generally negative; intermarriage is rare. According to Lodi Gyari, the Tibetan government's envoy to the United States, "Tibetans feel neither trusted nor wanted in China. If you give a Tibetan name at a hotel, they will tell you it is booked out. Chinese immigration officials will question you because they view all Tibetans as suspect." Gyari, speaking at a seminar at the Heritage Foundation, a Washington, D.C., think tank, in March 2009, said Tibetans feel increasingly alienated from China.

History

Tibet emerged as an independent kingdom in the seventh century C.E. Relations with China were established during China's Tang dynasty (618–906). From the 1200s, Tibetans came under Mongol influence. In 1642 the Dalai Lama, already spiritual leader of Tibetans, became their political leader too. China helped Tibet to repel a Mongol invasion in 1717, after which it assumed a role as the dominant outside power, entering Tibetan territory in 1728, 1758, and 1792. During the 1800s, the neighboring state of Kashmir seized the region of Ladakh from Tibet. In 1890 the United Kingdom, which had been expanding its colony in India since the 1600s, seized the region of Sikkim from Tibet. In 1904, following a military expedition to Tibet led by Sir Francis Younghusband, the United Kingdom established trading posts at Yadong, Gyangze, and Gar. In 1907 the United Kingdom recognized China's sovereignty over Tibet.

The collapse of the Chinese monarchy in 1912 enabled Tibetans to assert their independence. They signed a treaty with Mongolia in 1913. However, apart from a British trade mission established in Lhasa in the 1930s, Tibetans did not have diplomatic relations with other countries, partly because its leaders thought that remaining secluded would help them to preserve the culture. During the 1930s and 1940s, China was preoccupied with a civil war between nationalists and communists and a Japanese invasion. In October 1949, the communist People's Liberation Army, which helped defeat the Japanese and won the civil war, invaded and occupied Tibet. Because Tibet had operated a feudal land ownership system, many Chinese historians depict this invasion as liberating the Tibetan peasants who until then were bound to their estate.

A peace deal, the 17 Point Agreement, was signed in 1951, with China pledging that Tibet's distinct religion and culture would be protected. In 1954 the Dalai Lama began talks with Chinese leaders on creating an autonomous region. However, in a March 2009 statement, the Dalai Lama said the situation rapidly deteriorated from 1956, with growing repression in U-Tsang and chaos and destruction in Kham and Amdo. Meanwhile, the U.S. Central Intelligence Agency was giving military assistance to a Tibetan resistance movement called "Four Rivers, Six Ranges." John Kenneth Knaus, author of a 1999 book on the mission, recounted how hundreds of men were airdropped and forty-nine killed. Knaus said he worked with the Dalai Lama's brother at the United Nations to get support for Tibetan independence; other countries were wary of helping, however, with France and the United Kingdom worried about the impact their support might have on their own colonies.

In March 1959, a Tibetan rebellion against Chinese rule erupted and was brutally crushed, with 80,000 Tibetans killed and 100,000 fleeing. In 1965 the Chinese government created the T.A.R. The period 1965–1976 was one of massive social upheaval for Tibetans, with Chinese authorities banning the practice of religion and destroying thousands of Tibetan monasteries and convents during the Cultural Revolution. U.S. military aid to Tibetan rebels ended when President Richard Nixon normalized relations with China in the early 1970s.

From 1974 the Dalai Lama's position began to evolve from pro-independence to pro-autonomy. In the late 1970s and early 1980s, the political atmosphere relaxed slightly in China; some of the destroyed temples were rebuilt. The Chinese leadership in 1979 began engaging with the Tibetan government-in-exile, and the Dalai Lama in 1987 formally adopted his "Middle Way" pro-autonomy stance. The China-Tibet dialogue was curtailed in 1993, just as China's economy began rapidly expanding and Han Chinese immigration to Tibet was increasing. Talks were relaunched in 2002, and while eight rounds were held no significant progress was made.

Leadership

The Dalai Lama is widely acknowledged as the spiritual and political leader of the Tibetan people. He was first recognized in this position in 1939 as a two-year-old boy when he became Tibet's fourteenth Dalai Lama. Although he consistently renounces the use of violence to achieve his goals, the Chinese authorities regularly accuse him of covertly supporting militant resistance and typically depict him as a demonic figure. His government has been based in Dharamsala in north India since 1960. It operates a legislative, executive, and judicial branch. Its leadership has been directly elected since 2001, the electorate consisting of exiled Tibetans. The Dalai Lama has delegated most day-to-day decisions to a cabinet chair, called a Kalon Tripa. The second most prominent Tibetan leader is the Panchen Lama, whose tenth incarnation died in Tibet in 1989. Since

The Dalai Lama (1935–   )

AP Photo/Scott Applewhite

THE DALAI LAMA was born on July 6, 1935, in a small town in northeast Tibet. His parents were farmers, his name at birth was Lhamo Dhondup, and he was the fifth of sixteen children. At two years old, after being recognized as the reincarnation of the previous Dalai Lama, Thubten Gyatso, Lhamo Dhondup was given the name Tenzin Gyatso. Soon after, at age six, the new Dalai Lama began his monastic education.

The position of Dalai Lama is both politically and culturally important in Tibet. "Dalai Lama" is translated to English as "Ocean Teacher," and he is the Buddhist leader of the Gelugpa ("Yellow Hat") sect of Tibetan Buddhism. Dalai Lamas are believed to be manifestations of Avalokiteshvara, or Chenrezig, the Bodhisattva of Compassion and patron saint of Tibet. Bodhisattvas are beings that have achieved enlightenment but choose to remain on earth to spread their wisdom.

When Tenzin Gyatso was fifteen, in 1949, Mao Zedong sent troops of the People's Liberation Army into Tibet. The Dalai Lama assumed full power as the political and spiritual leader of Tibet a month later. Moreover, he was officially enthroned as Tibet's head of state as the region entered a turbulent political time.

In May 1951, China developed its 17 Point Agreement, attempting to legitimize Tibet's incorporation into the People's Republic. As a result, the Tibetans lost virtually all of their autonomy with respect to diplomatic and military affairs.

The Dalai Lama, who was strongly pro-independence, travelled across China in 1954 to meet with then-leader Mao Zedong and other important Chinese officials, and to participate in the first National People's Congress. On September 11, 1954, Mao Zedong met with the Dalai Lama for the first time; later that year the Dalai Lama was elected vice chairman of the Standing Committee of the first National People's Congress.

In 1959, at age twenty-three, Tenzin Gyatso completed his monastic education, receiving a Geshe Lharampa Degree; this is essentially equivalent to a doctorate of Buddhist philosophy.

Later that year, in March 1959, Tibetans took to the streets, protesting Chinese rule. Chinese troops violently ended the attempted uprising, killing thousands of protesters and effectively forcing the Tibetan

then the Tibetans and Chinese have supported two different boys as his reincarnation.

With the Dalai Lama in exile since 1959, it is unclear how much support he has among Tibetans in Tibet. According to some Tibet scholars, the Chinese Tibetans have grown more radical due to the traumas they have endured under Chinese occupation. It is difficult to assess what most Chinese Tibetans want because they cannot form their own political party, as China is a one-party, communist state where the media is tightly controlled by the government. Some Tibetans have joined the Chinese communist party and risen up its ranks, although none have ever been on the nine-member Central Committee, or Politburo. There are non-governmental organizations (NGOs) in Tibet working on cultural issues, such as promoting the Tibetan language, but they tend to stay below the radar due to the difficult political climate. Tibetan monks remain a significant political voice, although they too are now strictly supervised by the Chinese authorities.

Several influential Tibetan NGOs are based in India. They include the Tibetan Youth Congress, the Tibetan Women's Association, and Guchusum, a pro-independence group of ex-prisoners. A prominent U.S.-based NGO is the International Campaign for Tibet in Washington, D.C., which supports self-determination for Tibetans. In New York, a more radical group that also includes non-Tibetans, called Students For A Free Tibet, has recently emerged, led by Tenzin Dorjee, resistance movement out of the country. In the ensuing chaos, the Dalai Lama fled to India on foot, settling in the northern area of Dharamasala. This location is now home to the Tibetan government-in-exile—the Central Tibetan Administration—and to many of the eighty thousand Tibetans who fled.

During his years in exile, the Dalai Lama has traveled the globe advocating for his people. The United Nations has adopted three resolutions in the General Assembly calling for the protection of Tibetans.

Though originally advocating for full independence, a status that Tibet has never officially held, in 1987 the Dalai Lama began to soften his stance on full autonomy. Instead, he developed the "middle way" philosophy, which calls for Tibetan autonomy under Chinese rule. As Tibetans protested against relocation of Han Chinese into their land, the Dalai Lama also introduced a five-point plan that advocated the designation of Tibet as a "zone of peace."

He was awarded the Nobel Peace Prize in 1989 for opposition to the use of violence while working toward Tibetan self-rule in the face of the brutal oppression of which the Chinese government has been accused, including rape, murder, and silencing.

In 1991 the Dalai Lama published an autobiography entitled *Freedom in Exile*. He detailed atrocities committed against his people in addition to describing his own life. In 1993 talks between the Tibetan government-in-exile and Beijing broke down. As a result, the Dalai Lama's ability to interact with the Chinese government waned; communication was tentatively reestablished in 2002.

The year 2008 was extremely tense for the Chinese and the Dalai Lama–led Tibetan government-in-exile. Protests sparked by commemoration of the anniversary of the 1959 uprising turned into riots and cooled the progress that had been made as the Chinese government denounced the Dalai Lama's "middle way" compromise. This increase in violence has led to some dissatisfaction with the Dalai Lama's commitment to peaceful resistance. Even so, younger Tibetan activists generally revere the Dalai Lama and approve his leadership tactics.

The Dalai Lama continues to travel the world, speaking to audiences and world leaders about his philosophy of peace and advocating for Tibetan autonomy under Chinese rule.

a Tibetan exile. Speaking at a Heritage Foundation discussion in October 2009, Dorjee said that "no empire has lasted and the Chinese empire will not last either because it is rotten to the core."

Current Status

The most serious outbreak of violence in Tibet in decades occurred in March 2008. It began with a march led by Tibetan monks in Lhasa to commemorate the anniversary of the failed 1959 rebellion, and escalated into violent clashes across Tibet in which scores were killed. The Associated Press (AP) reported that "much of the violence appears to have been committed by Tibetans attacking ethnic Han Chinese." AP's Tini Tran wrote that crowds hurled rocks at security forces, hotels, and restaurants and characterized it as Tibetans venting their pent-up anger over the Han Chinese reaping the benefits from Tibet's economic growth.

An eyewitness account in *The Economist* magazine in March 2008 said "shops owned by Tibetans were marked as such with traditional white scarves tied through shutter-handles. They were spared destruction. Almost every other one was wrecked." The Han Chinese "were baffled and enraged by the slow reaction of the security forces." Initially, there were calls for countries to boycott the August 2008 Olympic Games in Beijing, but ultimately there was no boycott. China subsequently tightened controls—for example, not allowing monks to leave their monasteries.

In March 2009, South Africa got dragged into a China-Tibet controversy when it rejected a visa application from the Dalai Lama, who had planned to attend a peace conference in Cape Town. China, which has strong commercial ties to South Africa and buys much of its natural resources, had asked the South African government not to grant the visa. The visa refusal caused a bitter split within the South African government. Two other revered figures in South African politics, Bishop Desmond Tutu and former president Frederik de Klerk, boycotted the conference in protest.

The influx of Han Chinese has altered Tibet dramatically. In a March 2008 article in *Time* magazine, Pico Iyer, author of a biography of the Dalai Lama, noted that Lhasa has been turned from a small traditional settlement into "an Eastern Las Vegas" due to Chinese immigration. There were now 238 dance halls and karaoke parlors and 658 brothels. One Tibet academic suggested that Tibet's high altitude, situated in a plateau in the Himalayan Mountains, might deter Chinese from permanently settling there. Robert Thurman, a professor of Indo-Tibetan Buddhist studies at Columbia University in New York, said at a Heritage Foundation talk in March 2008 that the Tibetans have had centuries to adapt to this but the Chinese have not and suffer from chronic mountain sickness. Chinese women in Tibet have higher than average miscarriage rates, he noted.

Talks between Chinese and Tibetan leaders have stalled. China insists it will only negotiate if the Tibetans accept that independence can never be an option and that Tibet has been part of China since ancient times. The Dalai Lama has called this demand "unreasonable and inaccurate," adding "distorting history for political purposes is incorrect." Some observers believe the Chinese are waiting for the popular and charismatic Dalai Lama to die, which, it is contended, will leave Chinese authorities in a stronger negotiating position. It is possible the

Tibetans, presently unified behind the Dalai Lama, could fragment into rival factions when he dies, especially if there is no clear successor. Just as likely, China could come to regret its uncompromising stance if the death of the Dalai Lama radicalizes Tibetans and leads them to push for nothing short of independence. As the Dalai Lama remarked in March 2009, the status quo will not last indefinitely: "There is no country in the world today, including China, whose territorial status has remained forever unchanged, nor can it remain unchanged."

Further Reading

Baldauf, Scott. "South Africa turns away Dalai Lama, political firestorm follows," *Christian Science Monitor,* March 26, 2009, www.csmonitor.com/World/Africa/2009/0326/p04s01-woaf.html.

Bass, Caitriona. *Education in Tibet: Policy and Practice Since 1950.* London: Zed Books, 1999.

"The Future of Tibet: Dialogue Between a Tibetan and a Chinese," video recording of seminar at The Heritage Foundation's Lehrman Auditorium, March 25, 2009, www.heritage.org/Events/2009/03/The-Future-of-Tibet-Dialogue-Between-a-Tibetan-and-a-Chinese.

Iyer, Pico. "A Monk's Struggle," *Time,* March 31, 2008, www.time.com/time/world/article/0,8599,1723922,00.html.

———. *The Open Road: The Global Journey of the Fourteenth Dalai Lama.* New York: Vintage Books, 2009.

Knaus, John Kenneth. *Orphans of the Cold War: America and the Tibetan Struggle for Survival.* New York: Public Affairs Books, 1999.

Lazar, Edward. *Tibet: The Issue Is Independence.* Berkeley: Parallax Press, 1994.

Rabgey, Tashi, and Tseten Wangchuk Sharlho. "Sino-Tibetan Dialogue in the Post-Mao Era: Lessons and Prospects," *East West Center Policy Studies* 12 (2004), http://www.eastwestcenter.org/fileadmin/stored/pdfs/PS012.pdf.

Tibetan government-in-exile Web site, www.tibet.net.

"Tibet's Future: Does It Have One?" video recording of seminar at The Heritage Foundation's Lehrman Auditorium, March 11, 2008, www.heritage.org/Events/2008/03/Tibets-Future-Does-It-Have-One.

Tran, Tini. "Tibetan protests escalate into violence," Associated Press, March 14, 2008, www.foxnews.com/wires/2008Mar14/0,4670,ChinaTibet,00.html.

"A Week in Tibet," *The Economist,* March 19, 2008, www.economist.com/displayStory.cfm?story_ID=10875823.

UYGHURS
(China)

The Uyghur people in the province of Xinjiang in northwestern China face growing repression by the Chinese government, due to efforts by some of their leaders to gain greater autonomy or independence. The situation is especially tense because China has a militantly anti-separatist government that is unwilling to negotiate with Uyghur leaders. The Uyghur culture has been adversely affected by large-scale immigration by non-Uyghur Chinese to Xinjiang.

The Uyghurs represent between 1 and 2 percent of China's population; Xinjiang accounts for about a sixth of the area of China. Xinjiang's Uyghur population is officially put at nine million, but some Uyghurs say the government is undercounting them and that the actual Uyghur population is about sixteen million. What is not disputed is that a growing number of Xinjiang residents, possibly even a majority, are ethnic Chinese, known as Han Chinese. The steady stream of Han to Xinjiang has dramatically changed the province's demographics. The Uyghurs made up 75 percent of the population in 1955. Two other ethnic minorities, Kazakhs and Hui, are found in significant numbers in Xinjiang.

The Uyghurs are a Turkic people, ethnically related to Kazakhs, Kirghiz, and Tajiks. They speak their own language but are increasingly obliged to learn Chinese, too. They are predominantly Muslim and use an Arabic script. The province's official title is the Xinjiang Uyghur Autonomous Region (XUAR). Many Uyghurs prefer to call it East Turkestan, both because they dislike the Chinese "Xinjiang" and resent the implication that the Uyghurs already enjoy autonomy. There are sizable Uyghur communities in neighboring countries, notably Afghanistan, Kazakhstan, Kyrgyzstan, Russia, Tajikistan, Turkmenistan, Uzbekistan, and Mongolia.

According to James Millward, an associate professor of history at Georgetown University in Washington, D.C., and author of the 2007 book *A History of Xinjiang,* the Chinese government maintains that all Chinese are descended from the same ethnic group. Millward, at a talk given in January 2008, said that China has inadvertently caused a sharpening of ethnic identity by categorizing the different ethnic groups and then channeling resources on this basis.

According to a July 2007 report by the Uyghur American Association (UAA), a leading Uyghur advocacy group, China from the mid-1980s adopted education policies detrimental to Uyghur culture. Since 2002 all Uyghur children have been required to conduct studies in Chinese as well as Uyghur. China says this policy is necessary to promote bilingualism, but opponents say its real intention is to marginalize the Uyghur language. The number of students in bilingual schools has risen from 2,629 in 1999 to 145,000 in 2005.

The Uyghur population has been greatly diluted since the 1990s in the face of an influx of hundreds of thousands of Han Chinese—a migration pattern that has been strongly encouraged by the Chinese government. The Uyghurs are no longer a majority in Xinjiang, which makes it harder for them to demand greater autonomy or an independent homeland. Their situation is not unlike that of the Tibetans in China (see separate essay), who have also seen the in-migration of large numbers of Han Chinese and who also reject China's assertion that Tibet already enjoys autonomy. Georgetown's Millward said he had observed a rise in tensions between Han Chinese and Uyghurs since 1990. He said intermarriages were increasingly rare, although the religious and linguistic divide was partly responsible for this. The tensions have been exacerbated by a widespread perception among Uyghurs that the Han have benefited most from the strong economic growth the province has experienced since the 1980s.

Rebiya Kadeer, the unofficial leader-in-exile of the Uyghurs, has accused the Chinese government of committing "cultural genocide against the Uyghur people." Speaking in October 2009 at the Heritage Foundation, a Washington, D.C., think tank, Kadeer claimed the Chinese government had transferred 300,000 Uyghur girls aged between fourteen and twenty-eight years to other regions of China since June 2006. She said this was ostensibly done to give the girls jobs, but in practice they were not paid the salaries promised and were systematically sexually harassed in factories. Some fled these conditions and ended up in the hands of human-traffickers, while others escaped by marrying Chinese men.

On the international stage, there is growing awareness of the Uyghurs. This is partly due to the violent clashes between Uyghurs and Han Chinese and Chinese security forces in July 2009. Scores were killed, and the Chinese mounted a major crackdown afterward. In addition, the United States drew attention to Uyghurs in its protracted efforts to find countries willing to resettle twenty-two Uyghurs the United States had detained at its terrorist prison in Guantanamo Bay, Cuba, following the September 11, 2001, attacks. The detainees were alleged to have received weapons training in al Qaeda terrorist camps in Afghanistan.

History

Descended from nomadic herders, the Uyghurs have lived in Xinjiang for several thousand years. Their region was historically a major commercial crossroads, forming part of the so-called Silk Road that linked China, India, Central Asia, and Europe. Buddhism, Christianity, and Islam each had a strong influence over them, although today they are predominantly Sunni Muslim. In 1759 the Qing dynasty of the Chinese empire annexed the Uyghur territories and renamed the region Xinjiang, which means "New Territory" in Chinese. In the 1800s the Chinese began encouraging non-Uyghurs to immigrate to Xinjiang.

In 1864 Uyghur and other Muslim groups, led by Yakub Beg and aided by the Ottoman Empire in Turkey, rebelled against the Chinese government and established a state around the city of Kashgar. The new state signed treaties with Russia in 1872 and with the United Kingdom in 1874. But the Chinese had regained control of the region by the end of the 1870s, and in 1884 they made Xinjiang a province of China. The Uyghurs' next attempt at creating an independent state came in November 1933 when a Republic of East Turkestan was proclaimed.

It was crushed in 1934 by forces led by the Chinese warlord Sheng Shicai, who received military assistance from the Soviet Union, which feared that an independent Uyghur state would fuel separatism in the Soviet Union's Central Asian Republics. China was meanwhile embroiled in a civil war between the nationalists and communists and was also fighting Japan, which in 1931 had invaded Manchuria in northeastern China. In late 1944, a Soviet-dominated second East Turkestan Republic was declared, lasting until October 1949 when the warring communists finally defeated the nationalists and seized control of Xinjiang.

Under communist rule, Uyghur nationalists were purged from the government; some were forcibly resettled in other parts of China. They experienced great economic change and social upheaval when the government implemented its Great Leap Forward modernization policy (1958–1961), followed by the Cultural Revolution (1966–1976). The Uyghurs' sense of national identity strengthened in the 1980s as the political atmosphere in China relaxed somewhat, and Xinjiang was visited by growing numbers of tourists, businesspeople, and journalists. However, after the Soviet Union collapsed in 1991 and independent nation-states such as Kazakhstan and Tajikistan were established on China's border, the authorities grew more fearful of Uyghur separatism. In April 1990, an armed uprising took place in the town of Baren in Xinjiang where organizers used mosques to disseminate a call to arms. In 1992–1993 explosions and bombings occurred. There was a further spike in violence in 1996–1998, which China responded to by rounding up suspected terrorists.

Xinjiang underwent a major economic transformation in the 1990s under the government's Great Western Development campaign, which involved expanding the province's infrastructure and exploiting its natural resources. As China rapidly industrialized, the demand for Xinjiang's energy supplies soared. The province contains 38 percent of China's coal and 25 percent of its oil and gas. Many Uyghurs felt excluded from the newly created wealth, which they viewed as primarily benefiting the recently arrived Han Chinese immigrants. There was also resentment that the natural resources extracted were sent mainly to eastern China where most of the industrialization was occurring.

The September 11, 2001, terrorist attacks on the United States had negative consequences for the Uyghurs. Although they were not connected to the attack, the Chinese government henceforth labeled Uyghur dissidents terrorists, linked them to Islamist terrorist groups such as al Qaeda, and likened their clampdown on Uyghur opponents to U.S. president George W. Bush's "war on terror." In 2004 Chinese authorities launched a campaign against "the three evils of separatism, extremism, and terrorism."

Leadership

As the Chinese communist government does not allow the establishment of alternate political parties, pro-autonomy or independence Uyghurs do not have legal channels to further their political goals. They are reluctant to push for reform within the ranks of the ruling communist party because joining requires them to renounce their religion (the party is officially atheist) and most are unwilling to do this. Some Uyghurs have turned to militancy and forged links with Islamic groups. In August 2002, the United States, under pressure from China, agreed to designate the East Turkestan Islamic Movement a terrorist organization.

Advocating autonomy or independence by peaceful means is difficult because the Chinese government is so virulently opposed to separatism. Amy Reger, a researcher at the UAA, described in a December 2009 article on the Huffington Post news Web site how a Uyghur economist, Ilham Tohti, was arrested and detained for creating a Web site to promote Uyghur-Chinese dialogue. Given this

Rebiya Kadeer (1947–   )

REBIYA KADEER was born to a poor family in Altay, Xinjiang, China, on January 21, 1947. She became a twice-married mother of eleven, a businesswoman christened "the millionairess," and a polarizing political figure in China.

Kadeer is the leader of the Uyghur people, a Turkic ethnic group that lives primarily in the Xinjiang Uyghur Autonomous Region in the People's Republic of China. The Uyghurs are predominantly Muslim.

She first married in 1965 and moved away from her home city. In Aksu, Xinjiang, she ran a clothing business with her husband but was labeled a "class enemy" during the Cultural Revolution. These complications ended her marriage.

In 1976 she opened a laundromat, which then became a department store specializing in Uyghur clothing. Kadeer married Sidik Rouzi, an associate professor, in 1981. They moved to Urumqi, where she continued building her business empire. She developed a huge cross-border trade center, and by the mid-1990s she was the richest woman in China. Her businesses garnered her the moniker, "the millionairess."

Kadeer used her status to lift other Uyghur women out of poverty, helping them start businesses, and to advocate for their causes. She started the foundation 1,000 Families Mothers' Project.

Her business acumen and philanthropy work earned her praise and political clout in China. In 1993 she was appointed to China's national advisory group, the Chinese People's Political Consultative Conference (CPPCC). In 1995 she served as a delegate to the United Nations World Conference on Women.

In 1996 her husband, a Uyghur partisan, fled China for the United States. He was a former political prisoner and had been incarcerated for campaigning publically against the government's treatment of the Uyghur population. After he left China, Kadeer's passport was seized and she was barred from reappointment to the CPPCC in 1998.

In August 1999, on her way to a meeting with a visiting delegation from the U.S. Congressional Research Service, with whom she was slated to discuss political prisoners in Xinjiang, she was arrested. The following month Kadeer was charged with "providing secret information to foreigners" by the Chinese government and for sending publically available newspapers to her husband in the United States. She was tried secretly and sentenced in March 2000 to eight years in prison, although her sentence was reduced by one year in 2004.

While in prison, she won the Rafto Prize for human rights for her work with Uyghurs in the autonomous region of Xinjiang, including her "Thousand Mothers Project." She had also established schools for Uyghurs who did not have the opportunity to attend day schools.

Upon her release in 2005, she was exiled to the United States. She was then elected president of the World Uyghur Congress.

Three of her sons have been imprisoned, prompting Amnesty International to petition for their release.

July 2009 saw a rash of riots in Uyghur cities, which the Chinese government claimed were organized by Kadeer, going so far as to produce letters allegedly written by some of her family blaming her and asking her to stop interfering. Kadeer denies any involvement.

From her base in the United States she has become the head of several Uyghur organizations, including the World Uyghur Congress and the Uyghur American Association, and she continues to speak out against the Chinese government's treatment of the Uyghur people. She was featured in a documentary short by Jeff Daniels, titled *The 10 Conditions of Love*. The documentary, which was scheduled to premiere at the 2009 Melbourne International Film Festival, saw its Web site shut down and replaced with anti-Kadeer slogans, and several Chinese directors pulled out of the event after festival organizers refused to rescind their invitation to Kadeer.

Kadeer and her husband currently live in the United States in the Washington, D.C., area.

---

political climate, it is difficult to ascertain what proportion of Uyghurs support greater autonomy or independence.

Much of the autonomy movement is led by expatriates residing in Australia, Canada, Germany, Turkey, and the United States. Rebiya Kadeer has become a pivotal figure, especially since the Chinese government accused her of orchestrating the riots that broke out in July 2009. Kadeer is president of the UAA and heads the International Uyghur

Human Rights and Democracy Forum from her base in Washington, D.C. The UAA has a research arm, the Uyghur Human Rights Project, which produces reports highlighting issues of concern such as the state of the Uyghur language. The Project receives financial assistance from the National Endowment for Democracy, a nonprofit organization funded by the U.S. Congress that promotes democracy around the world.

Kadeer is not calling for an independent Uyghur state or armed resistance to the Chinese government. Speaking at the Heritage Foundation on October 8, 2009, at a seminar on religious persecution in China (see reference in Tibetans' essay), she said political reform would come from "peaceful negotiation" and "not the barrel of the gun." Kadeer is also president of the World Uyghur Congress, an umbrella organization representing various Uyghur groups, which is headquartered in Munich, Germany.

China claims that the Uyghurs already have autonomy through the provincial government established in 1955 and based in Urumqi. Article 4 of the Chinese constitution recognizes the right of ethnic minorities to regional autonomy and to develop and preserve their language and customs, but Uyghur autonomy advocates claim these rights exist on paper only.

Current Status

The year 2009 proved the most turbulent in Uyghur-Chinese relations in recent history. On July 5 there were violent clashes in Urumqi in which 197 people were killed. The Chinese dispatched 130,000 troops from other regions to restore order. Addressing the European Parliament's human rights subcommittee on September 11, 2009, Kadeer warned, "Through its demonization of Uyghur protesters in the official media, [the government] is attempting to justify the impending mass executions of Uyghurs." She claimed the unrest had originated with the killing of thirty Uyghurs by Han Chinese at a toy factory in Guangdong province in southeastern China. Uyghurs had responded with a peaceful protest on July 5 but were met by force, with Chinese security forces using live ammunition and shooting dead fifty protesters. Kadeer acknowledged that some Uyghurs had killed and injured Han Chinese, but followed by noting that between three and four thousand Han Chinese took to the streets on July 6–7 and killed 150–200 Uyghurs.

In November 2009, the Uyghur community in Germany, which numbers five hundred, came under the spotlight after German police raided the homes of four Chinese nationals suspected of spying on the Uyghurs on behalf of the Chinese government. Similar accusations were leveled against a Chinese diplomat in 2007. The raids took place in Munich, the city where the World Uyghur Congress is based. In December 2009, attention shifted to Cambodia after the Cambodian government repatriated twenty Uyghur asylum-seekers to China. Kadeer criticized the move in an article in the *Wall Street Journal*, saying that "China's track record of mistreating repatriated Uyghur refugees leads us to fear that they can expect even worse on Chinese soil." She suggested that China wanted them because it was afraid they would make embarrassing revelations about the July 2009 riots.

Reporting from the Xinjiang capital, Urumqi, in June 2010, the *Washington Post*'s Lauren Keane found that "last summer's chaos has been replaced with a level of fear that is striking, even for one of China's most repressed regions." She said residents were terrified of talking, not just to journalists, but even to one another about the riots. Keane noted that the Chinese government had announced a $1.5 billion development plan for Xinjiang in May and had begun restoring Internet and cell phone text messaging access, after limiting or blocking it for ten months.

As for the Uyghurs held at Guantanamo Bay, the Chinese government would like to prosecute them for plotting against the state, but the U.S. administration has refused to hand them over to China as it believes they could be tortured or worse. Instead, it has transferred some to Albania, Bermuda, Switzerland, and Palau, and continues to ask other governments to resettle the remainder. However, governments are reluctant to take them given China's strong opposition to the detainees being sent anywhere other than back to China.

The Uyghurs increasingly accuse China of trying to destroy their cultural heritage by repressing the Uyghur language and restricting the practice of their religion, Islam. For example, the Uyghurs are no longer permitted to travel to Mecca in Saudi Arabia for the Hajj, the pilgrimage to the birthplace of the prophet Mohamed that all Muslims are supposed to make. On the economic front, there is evidence that the wealth flowing into Xinjiang due to China's rapid economic growth is benefiting the Han Chinese immigrants more than the Uyghurs. The gross domestic product per capita in Urumqi, which is 73 percent Han Chinese, is nine times greater than in the city of Hotan, which is 97 percent Uyghur, according to a September 2009 report from the UAA.

The report claimed that "ethnic relations between Han Chinese and Uyghurs are at their lowest point in decades." This was due primarily to the Chinese government's "complete lack of introspection into the failures of its own policies, combined with its reliance on brute force to maintain order." With neither side showing an inclination to compromise or even engage in dialogue, the probability of continued conflict seems high.

Further Reading

Ching, Frank. "Thorny problem of the Guantanamo Uighurs," *New Straits Times*, December 23, 2010, www.nst.com.my/nst/articles/21nk/Article.

Isenson, Nancy, ed. "German police raid homes of suspected Chinese spies," *Deutsche Welle*, November 25, 2009, www.dw-world.de/dw/article/0,,4923095,00.html.

Kadeer, Rebiya. *Dragon Fighter*. Carlsbad, Calif.: Kales Press, 2009.

———. "The Long Arm of China," *Wall Street Journal*, December 21, 2009, http://online.wsj.com/article/SB100014240527487043767045746070015043035 82.html.

Keane, Lauren. "One year later, China's crackdown after Uighur riots haunts a homeland," *Washington Post*, June 15, 2010, www.washingtonpost.com/wp-dyn/content/article/2010/06/14/AR2010061405054.html.

Millward, James. "Violent Separatism in Xinjiang: A Critical Assessment," *East-West Center Policy Studies* 6 (2004), www.eastwestcenter.org/fileadmin/stored/pdfs/PS006.pdf.

Reger. Amy. "China's Media 'Openness' in East Turkestan," The Huffington Post, December 16, 2009, www.huffingtonpost.com/amy-reger/chinas-media-openness-in_b_394538.html.

Teague, Matthew. "The Other Tibet," *National Geographic*, December 2009, http://ngm.nationalgeographic.com/2009/12/uygurs/teague-text.

Tyler, Christian. *Wild West China: The Taming of Xinjiang*. New Brunswick: Rutgers University Press, 2004.

Uyghur Human Rights Project, "Separate but Unequal: The Status of Development in East Turkestan," September 28, 2009, http://uyghuramerican.org/docs/Sept-28-Separate-and-unequal.pdf.

South and West Asia

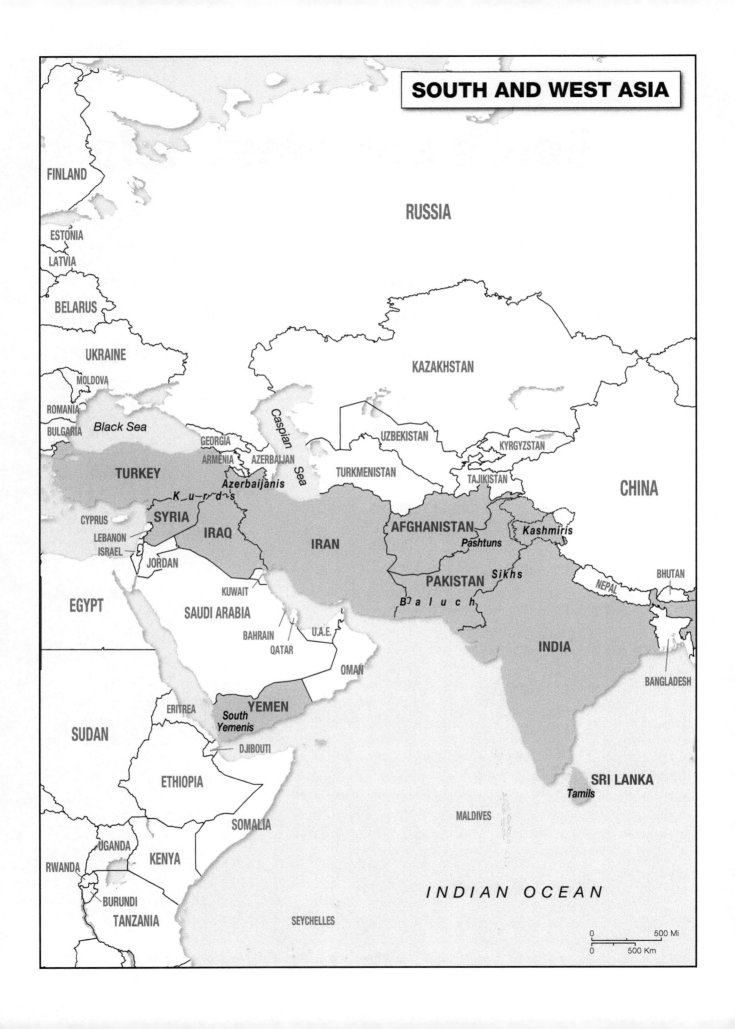

SOUTH AND WEST ASIA

FINLAND

ESTONIA

LATVIA

BELARUS

UKRAINE

MOLDOVA

ROMANIA

BULGARIA

Black Sea

RUSSIA

KAZAKHSTAN

GEORGIA

ARMENIA AZERBAIJAN

Caspian Sea

UZBEKISTAN

KYRGYZSTAN

TURKMENISTAN

TAJIKISTAN

CHINA

TURKEY

Azerbaijanis

K u r d s

CYPRUS

SYRIA

LEBANON

ISRAEL

IRAQ

JORDAN

IRAN

AFGHANISTAN

Kashmiris

Pashtuns

PAKISTAN

Sikhs

NEPAL

BHUTAN

B a l u c h

KUWAIT

EGYPT

SAUDI ARABIA

BAHRAIN

QATAR

U.A.E.

INDIA

OMAN

BANGLADESH

ERITREA

YEMEN

South Yemenis

DJIBOUTI

SUDAN

ETHIOPIA

SRI LANKA

Tamils

MALDIVES

SOMALIA

UGANDA

RWANDA

KENYA

INDIAN OCEAN

BURUNDI

TANZANIA

SEYCHELLES

0   500 Mi

0   500 Km

AZERBAIJANIS
(Iran)

In northwestern Iran there is a large population of ethnic Azerbaijanis, also known as Azerbaijani Turks, who since the 1990s have increasingly been asserting their distinct identity. The establishment of an independent or autonomous government is not a realistic prospect, given staunch opposition from the Iranian government. Efforts instead are focused on bolstering the Azerbaijani language.

There are between sixteen and twenty-four million Azerbaijanis in Iran, accounting for between 25 and 40 percent of the population and forming the second largest ethnic group after Persians, who account for 50 percent of the population. Cities with majority Azerbaijani populations include Tabriz, Urmia, Ardabil, and Zanjan. Millions have also migrated to the Iranian capital, Tehran, where they account for at least a third of the residents. Their mother tongue is Azerbaijani, a Turkic language. They are predominantly Shia Muslim, with some Sunni Muslims.

A sense of common identity among Iran's Azerbaijanis has been growing since 1991 when Azerbaijanis living just north of Iran stepped out from the crumbling Soviet Union to establish an independent country. There are two to three times as many Azerbaijanis living in Iran as there are in Azerbaijan, where they number seven million. Apart from the Azerbaijani separatists, there are also Azerbaijani irredentists—those who would like to unite all Azerbaijanis in a single state. For example, the slogan "one Azerbaijan, capital Tabriz" is often chanted at soccer matches in Tabriz, where soccer games have become a rallying point for Azerbaijani nationalists. Iran's Persian-dominated ruling elite is wary of separatist and irredentist sentiment, aware that the country is made up of many minorities, such as Ahwazi Arabs, Baluch, and Kurds (see separate essays).

Compared to the other minorities in Iran, such as the Baluch and Kurds, Azerbaijanis are generally viewed as having a favorable status. This may be because they are mainly Shia Muslim, like most Iranians, whereas Kurds and Baluch are mostly Sunni Muslim. Intermarriage between Azerbaijanis and non-Azerbaijanis is not unusual, and many Azerbaijanis have been assimilated into Iran's ruling elite, including its clergy, political class, and military. Iran's Supreme Leader, Ayatollah Khamenei, had an Azerbaijani mother, while Iranian opposition leader Mir-Hossein Mousavi also has Azerbaijani roots. According to author and regional expert

Selig Harrison, writing in the *New York Times* in December 2009, Khamenei's "selection as the Supreme Leader was in part a gesture to the Azeris designed to cement their allegiance to Iran and to blunt a covert campaign by ethnic kinsmen in neighboring Azerbaijan to annex them."

Despite such gestures, many Azerbaijanis feel alienated from the Iranian government, viewing it as Persian-dominated and hostile to the Azerbaijani language and culture. One of their biggest complaints is that the Azerbaijani language is not taught in schools. Many activists seeking to change this situation, notably university students who have organized extracurricular Azerbaijani language classes, have been arrested. The Azerbaijani autonomy movement has received little from foreign governments, although the United States is sometimes accused of doing so covertly through its support of democracy movements in Iran.

History

Thought to be living in their present homeland for seven thousand years, Azerbaijanis came under Turkic influence from the fifth to eleventh centuries, resulting in the emergence of their distinct language. In the 1500s, the Persians and Ottomans competed for control of Azerbaijani territories, the Persians edging out the Ottomans in 1603. Northern Azerbaijanis came under the control of Russia from the 1800s, while Persians continued governing the south. Separatist sentiment tended to be stronger among Azerbaijanis in Russia as the religious, historical, and cultural ties were not as strong there as they were in Persia.

According to Alireza Asgharzadeh, a sociology professor at York University, Toronto, and author of a book on racism in Iran, Azerbaijanis grew more alienated from the state from the 1920s as Persian nationalism increased. Asgharzadeh, in an August 2009 email interview with U.S.-based

Iranian Azerbaijani cultural rights activist Farzin Farzad, said Persian leader Reza Shah in 1934 changed the country's name to Iran, meaning "land of Aryans." He also banned non-Persian languages from schools and government.

At the close of World War II (1939–1945), a Soviet-backed separatist Azerbaijani region formed in Iran but crumbled in 1946 in the face of opposition from the United States and United Nations. Soviet-controlled Azerbaijan's emergence as an independent state in 1991 had a huge impact on Iran's Azerbaijanis, spurring them toward greater activism, activist Farzad said in a February 2010 face-to-face interview. In 1995 Mahmudali Chehregani set up the Southern (that is, Iranian) Azerbaijan National Awakening Movement (SANAM, or GAMOH).

Farzad, a member of the Canadian-based Association for the Defense of Azerbaijani Political Prisoners (ADAPP), said another watershed was the May 2006 publication by an Iranian government newspaper of a cartoon depicting a cockroach speaking Azerbaijani.

The cartoon triggered protests that were attended by over a million people, provoking a clampdown on the part of the authorities in which thousands were arrested and dozens killed. The cartoon reinforced the impression already held by many Azerbaijanis that they were discriminated against by the Persian majority. Later in 2006 it was reported that there were large demonstrations for linguistic rights by Azerbaijanis in Iran and in Azerbaijan.

Leadership

Iranian Azerbaijanis do not have a regional or autonomous government. There is no single, unified political party representing the autonomy movement but rather many different groups. For example, Chehregani set up GAMOH in the mid-1990s to call for the use of the Azerbaijani language in schools in majority-Azerbaijani areas. His party grew until 2002 but has declined since 2004. Another group is the South Azerbaijan Independence Party (Guney Azerbaycan Istiqlal Partisi, or GAIP), whose leader is Saleh Ildirim. There is also the Canadian-based ADAPP led by Fakteh Zamani, the Federal Democrat Party, and the Dunya Azerbaijan Congress (World Azerbaijan Congress).

Earlier separatist leaders include Sattar Khan (1908–1909), Hiya Bani (1920), Pishevari (1945–1946), and Shariat-Madari (1979–1980).

The large number of Azerbaijanis who have been assimilated into the Iranian government are known by separatist Azerbaijanis as "manqurts," meaning they have forsaken their roots and embraced Persian domination, including the suppression of the Azerbaijani language. Up to 60 percent of the Iranian army is Azerbaijani; they are likewise well-represented in the Iranian Revolutionary Guard Corps, the more ideologically driven militia.

Given the repressive political climate in Iran, much of the pro-autonomy, independence, and irredentist movement is directed from neighboring Azerbaijan. A political party that advocates annexing the Azerbaijani-populated regions of Iran was launched in 1989. Called the Azerbaijan Popular Front Party, it was created by Abulfaz Ali Elchibey. Such irredentist sentiment has encouraged the Iranian government to clamp down on separatists, who they view as a threat to the state.

Current Status

While the Western media focuses mainly on the pro-democracy movement in Iran, less attention has been paid to the growing campaign of Azerbaijanis to assert their linguistic and cultural rights. In March 2008, the radio station Radio Free Europe, which is funded by the U.S. Congress, announced plans to start Azerbaijani-language broadcasts in Iran. However, according to activist Farzad, as of June 2010 there was no Azerbaijani-language media in Iran reporting on the campaigns of Iranian Azerbaijanis. There is a Chicago-based television channel, Gunaz TV, started by Ahmad Obali, broadcasting by satellite into parts of Iran. Irredentism remains a significant force. In a March 2008 article in *Zerkalo*, a newspaper in Azerbaijan, politician Araz Alizada was cited asserting: "Iran is a state of Azerbaijanis. All key posts are occupied by Azerbaijanis. . . . Some 80 per cent of professors and teachers are Azerbaijani. There are 170 generals in the army and 112 of them are Azerbaijanis."

University-led protests calling for the Azerbaijani language to be allowed in schools and government continue. Amnesty International, in a report published in 2009, noted that student Asgar Akbarzadeh was sentenced to five years in prison in December 2008 for forming an illegal political party, preparing "pan-Turkist" documentation, taking part in Azeri folk dance gatherings, and sending information to human rights Web sites. Babak Castle, where the local leader Babak Khorramdin fought off Arab invaders in the eighth century, has become a rallying point for the pro-autonomy campaign. According to Farzad, large groups began congregating there after 2000—one million people in 2001—although since 2004 the government has tried to prevent such gatherings.

The pro-democracy movement in Iran, which gathered momentum in summer 2009 following protests over disputed presidential elections, is not allied to the Azerbaijani autonomy movement. According to Selig Harrison, the democracy movement, "like most of the clerical, military, and business establishment, is dominated by an entrenched Persian elite and has so far refused to support minority demands." While an independent Azerbaijani state or autonomous region in Iran looks unlikely in the next ten years, the pro-autonomy movement is likely to further develop as Azerbaijanis in Iran grow more confident about asserting their ethnic heritage.

Further Reading

Harrison, Selig S. "Tehran's biggest fear." *New York Times,* December 27, 2009, http://www.nytimes.com/2009/12/28/opinion/28iht-edharrison.html.

Mirqadirov, R., and R. Rustamov. "Americans are not going to incite Azerbaijani separatism but political analysts and politicians do not believe them," *Zerkalo,* (Azerbaijani newspaper), March 13, 2008, as translated by BBC Worldwide Monitoring, March 14, 2008.

Nassibli, Nasib. "The Azerbaijan Question in Iran: A Crucial Issue For Iran's Future," *South Azerbaijan* (Iranian Azerbaijani Web site accessed January 2010), http://southaz.blogspot.com/2009/07/azerbaijan-question-in-iran-crucial.html.

Shaffer, Brenda. *Borders and Brethren: Iran and the Challenge of Azerbaijani Identity.* Cambridge: Harvard University, 2002.

BALUCH
(Afghanistan, Iran, Pakistan)

The Baluch people of Afghanistan, Iran, and Pakistan have been fighting for greater autonomy or independence since 1948. An increasingly unstable Pakistan and an extremely repressive political climate in Iran have bolstered their aspirations for independence and fuelled anti-government militancy.

The Baluch population is officially ten million, but many Baluch say government census figures undercount them and that their true total is between fifteen and twenty million. There are six million in Pakistan, most of whom live in Baluchistan, one of Pakistan's four provinces, which accounts for 40 percent of the country's territory but just 4 percent of the population. There are 1.5 million in Iran, where they constitute 2 percent of the population and are concentrated in the southeastern provinces of Sistan and Baluchistan. In Afghanistan, they make up 2 percent, number under a million, and live in the south and southwest. More than a million Baluch have immigrated to Arab states, especially to Oman, but also to Bahrain and the United Arab Emirates (UAE). Smaller numbers live in Australia, Canada, Norway, Sweden, the United Kingdom, and the United States.

The Baluch have two native languages, Baluchi and Brahui. Although widely spoken, these are not used as a medium of instruction in the schools they attend. They are predominantly Sunni Muslim, with small minorities of Shia and Zikri Muslim and some Hindus. In a face-to-face interview in January 2010, Ahmar Mustikhan, a Baluch pro-independence activist living in Washington, D.C., said that Baluch are "very proud of [their] secularism." Mustikhan said this distinguished them from Pashtuns (see separate essay) and Punjabis, the two largest ethnic groups in Pakistan, who are more overtly religious. Many Pashtuns, for example, support the Islamist Taliban movement, which seeks to enforce an ultra-conservative interpretation of Islam in the areas it controls.

Since its founding in 1947, Pakistan has been ruled predominantly by Punjabis, who have dominated both the administration and the military. Baluchistan has large reserves of gas, concentrated in the Sui area, which supplies factories, businesses, and homes across Pakistan. Many Baluch feel they do not receive a fair share of revenues from these gas fields and worry that their land will be taken over by outsiders. According to Mustikhan, "we get the equivalent of 11 days worth of revenues out of 365.

Meanwhile, our locals have to cook with wood for fuel because there is no gas pipeline to their community." Violent local opposition to the unfair exploitation of Baluchistan's resources has made it harder for the government to further expand the province's petroleum industry. Baluch also resent the strong and growing presence of Pakistani military bases, or "cantonments," in Baluchistan, including in Kohlu, Sui, Gwadar, Dera Bugti, and Quetta.

In Iran, political repression of Baluch is severe. Iranian Baluch enjoy little political or cultural autonomy, are not strongly organized politically, and have little representation in the administration. The Iranian authorities have executed Baluch militants for alleged covert collaboration with the United States. Iranian policy is predicated on the Persian-dominated government's fear that recognition of the country's large number of national minorities, such as Baluch, Kurds and Azerbaijanis (see separate essays), will threaten the state's existence. Iranian Baluch have pursued a low-level rebellion since 1979, but this rebellion has escalated since 2006. The Iranians accuse the separatists of plotting to create a Greater Baluchistan made up of the Baluch regions in Afghanistan, Iran, and Pakistan.

Political repression has exacerbated Baluch militancy in Pakistan, too. An October 2007 report from the International Crisis Group (ICG), a non-governmental organization, reported that thousands had disappeared in the conflict, including political activists, students, doctors, lawyers, journalists, and shopkeepers. The ICG claimed that the Pakistani military was supporting Islamist groups to counter the Baluch and had rigged elections in 2002 to marginalize secular Baluch nationalist parties. "With the nationalist parties under siege, many young activists are losing faith in the political process and now see armed resistance as the only viable way to secure their rights," the report found. According to Mustikhan, "had we got autonomy in a federal system, we would have been loyal to the state. But you need more than cricket [a popular sport in Pakistan] to keep a country together." Mustikhan called for the region's borders to be redrawn along ethnic lines, arguing that "nation states are better because people are more accountable for what they do."

The Pakistani government accuses neighboring India of supporting the Baluch insurgency, but Baluch separatists deny India's involvement. Some Baluch insurgents have found a safe haven in the Afghan province of Kandahar. Western governments have generally shown little sympathy for the Baluch separatists. The U.S. government has supplied the Pakistani government with helicopter gunships and F-16 fighter jets, which Pakistan has used to suppress the insurgency, while the United Kingdom has outlawed the main Baluch separatist organizations as terrorist groups.

History

The Baluch originated in Aleppo, a city in Syria, with a civilization dating back to 4000 B.C.E. They migrated eastward from the ninth century C.E. along the Caspian Sea region and had settled in their present homeland by the fourteenth century. They managed to resist efforts by Afghans, Persians, and Sikhs to gain control over them, while sporadically absorbing diverse immigrant tribes from Central Asia fleeing Turkish and Mongol invasions.

Despite persistent feuding among Baluch tribal leaders, the Baluch's regional influence rose from the 1400s. In the 1700s they succeeded in maintaining the unified independent state of Kalat in Baluchistan, ruled by a prince, or khan. In the 1800s the British gained a foothold, occupying Kalat in 1839 and later giving some Baluch territory to Afghanistan. The Persian army defeated Baluch forces in the Kerman province in 1849 and suppressed several Baluch revolts in the late 1800s. The Baluch repelled the Iranians in the early 1900s under the leaderships of Bahram Khan and his nephew, Mir Dost Muhammed. In 1928 Reza Khan, a Persian, rose to power in Iran and began annexing Baluch areas. Since then Iran has suppressed Baluch separatists, forcing them to go underground or emigrate; meanwhile, immigration by non-Baluch into Baluch areas has made the Baluch a minority in their homeland and heightened fears of loss of identity.

The first Baluch leader to publish a map of a Greater Baluchistan was Mir Abdul Aziz Kurd in 1933. In the 1940s, when the British were preparing to hand over authority of their Indian colony, both the Muslim League—the group that supported the creation of Pakistan—and the departing British promised the Baluch an autonomous or quasi-independent status. However, once established the Pakistani military reneged on this commitment and seized control of Kalat in March 1948, forcing the Khan to cede sovereignty. Power in Pakistan became centralized. In 1973 the Baluch launched a rebellion, which lasted until 1977 and resulted in the deaths of five thousand insurgents and three thousand government troops; many Baluch fled to Afghanistan.

Baluch anti-government sentiment in Pakistan spiked again following the government's decision to conduct nuclear tests in the Chagai Hills of Baluchistan in May 1998. No environmental impact assessment was done in advance, and afterward there were reports of livestock dying and unusual skin diseases. In October 1999, the powerful Bugti and Marri tribes launched an armed insurrection. The conflict escalated in January 2005 after Baluch were incensed by the government's mishandling of the rape case of medical doctor and women's rights advocate Shazia Khalid. Violence erupted and the government responded with extra-judicial killings, torture, and arbitrary arrests. Up to 200,000 people were displaced by the fighting, fleeing to camps elsewhere in Pakistan. The Pakistani government was criticized for denying access to the refugee camps to the media and to United Nations aid workers.

A committee of the Baluch provincial parliament made proposals in 2005 for increased Baluch autonomy, troop withdrawals, and a larger share of gas revenues for Baluch. But the government ignored the committee recommendations and persisted with a military response. The authorities claimed that the Baluch were harboring terrorists from the Islamist al Qaeda network, which Baluch tribal leaders denied. In August 2006, an elderly Baluch leader Nawab Akbar Khan Bugti, who opposed the government's efforts to exploit the gas reserves in Sui, was assassinated by Pakistani forces. In November 2006, another leader, Sardar Akhtar Jan Mengal, was imprisoned as part of a round-up of thousands of Baluch nationalists. These events caused many Baluch to lose hope that their goals could be achieved through peaceful, political means.

Leadership

The Baluch separatist movement has historically been hampered by a fragmented political leadership; however, since 2005 it has become more unified and better organized. The movement has also obtained increased funding, notably from expatriates living in the Persian Gulf and from Arabs sympathetic to its cause. The dominant militant group is the outlawed Baluchistan Liberation Army (BLA), which is believed to be led by the Bugti and Marri clans that are based in Pakistan. One of the earliest separatist leaders was Baluch nationalist Magassi, who in 1934 called for an independent state.

Baluch parties are permitted in Pakistan. The Baluchistan National Party (BNP) was established in 1996 by Sardar Attaullah Mengal and is led by his son, Sardar Akhtar Jan Mengal. The Jamhoori Watan Party (JWP) was established in 1990 by Nawab Bugti, who was assassinated in 2006. Since Bugti's death, various members of his family have been competing for the leadership. There is the Baluch Haq Talwar party, founded by Balaach Khair Bakhsh Marri, a veteran of the 1970s Baluch insurgency. And there is the Baluch National Party, which was established in 2003 and is led by Dr. Abdul Hayee. These four groups have formed an alliance called Baluch

Ittehad (Baluch Unity). The 35th Khan of Kalat, Mir Suleman Daud, remains politically active. Exiled since 2006 to the United Kingdom, he has pledged to work toward an independent Baluchistan.

There is a provincial government in Baluchistan in Pakistan, but Baluch nationalists say that its authority has consistently been undermined by the central Pakistani government, which is based in Islamabad. According to one Baluch political analyst, cited in the 2007 ICG report, the provincial government is "corrupt to its core. Eighty percent of the development funds are pocketed by politicians and officials."

In Iran, Baluch political parties are not allowed. An increasingly violent separatist insurgency has been mounted by one group, Jundallah. Iran claims this group is secretly being supported by the United States, which has had poor relations with Iran since the 1979 Islamic revolution. Jundallah is led by Abdolmalek Rigi and is more religiously oriented than its Baluch separatist equivalents in Pakistan. Exiled Iranian Baluch political dissidents established the Baluchistan People's Party (BPP) in September 2003. The BPP has become a member of the Hague-based Unrepresented Nations and Peoples Organization. It presented its case to the Danish and Swedish parliaments in 2004.

Current Status

In socioeconomic terms, Iranian and Pakistani Baluch are generally worse off than their compatriots, with below-average literacy rates, fewer available educational institutions, lower life expectancy, and higher poverty levels. On the political front, the Baluch of Pakistan have grown more militant in response to government suppression. As the ICG report noted, "by targeting the Baluch leadership, marginalizing secular nationalist parties, sidelining the provincial legislature, forging ahead with contentious development plans, and using military force to subdue dissent, the government has shown

a disregard for the political process that is now widely mirrored in Baluchistan. Many young Baluch have lost faith in politics and picked up the gun." In a March 2009 interview for the British newspaper *The Independent*, the Khan of Kalat warned that "continued repression of the Baluch, coupled with the de facto silencing of their tribal leaders, is forcing many secular separatists into the arms of the Taliban instead."

The replacement of Gen. Pervez Musharraf, Pakistan's president from 2001–2008, with a civilian, popularly elected government in spring 2008 opened a window of opportunity for political dialogue. However, this change in leadership has not yet led to major progress toward a political settlement. In late 2009, Baluch tribal leaders rejected concessions offered by the Pakistani government because they did not give Baluch the right to own the natural resources located in their region. In a January 2010 report, Human Rights Watch accused the army of sabotaging the government's reconciliation efforts by refusing to help locate the many Baluch who disappeared under the Musharraf regime. Baluch anti-government resentment bubbled up again in August 2010 when Pakistan was ravaged by major flooding. The Baluch political leadership alleged that the Pakistani authorities were neglecting Baluchistan in the flood relief effort to which large amounts of international aid had been donated.

There is much tension surrounding the construction of a new port in the city of Gwadar in Baluchistan. Built mainly by Chinese companies and operational since 2008, the government intends Gwadar to become a major world port, but Baluch are worried that development will trigger an influx of millions of non-Baluch immigrants. Activist Mustikhan said that "ethnic flooding" has not occurred thus far only because immigrants have been deterred by Baluch militant attacks on installations and officials in Gwadar. Baluch also resent that thousands of acres of land has been handed over to

Pakistani civilian and military officials and retired judges.

Iranian Baluch militancy has intensified since 2007. Jundallah has carried out attacks in the cities of Pishin and Zehadan and killed members of the Iranian Revolutionary Guard. The UAE-based newspaper, *Gulf News,* reported in May 2008 that the violence "has managed to render vast chunks of southeastern Iran unsafe for travel." Journalist Amir Taheri said that the Baluch's main grievances were suppression of their Sunni mosques; Iranian government–funded efforts to convert Baluch to Shia Islam; restrictions on the Baluch's ability to go on the Hajj pilgrimage to Mecca; the exclusion of Baluch from positions in central government; and the encouragement of non-Baluch immigration into Baluch cities. In June 2009, the Iranian television channel Press TV aired detailed allegations of U.S. links to Jundallah. Citing an interview with Abdolhamid Rigi, the brother of Jundallah's leader, Abdolmalek Rigi, the news channel reported that CIA and FBI agents had held several confidential meetings with the Jundallah leader from 2005 in the Pakistani cities of Karachi and Islamabad. The United States had offered weapons, safe havens in Afghanistan, and professional trainers. It had also inquired how many people the group could gather for military training.

In December 2010, the U.K. newspaper *The Guardian* published a U.S. State Department memo which revealed international talks in late 2009 and early 2010 to give Baluch separatist leader Brahmdagh Bugti political asylum in Ireland. These talks, being brokered by the UN High Commission for Refugees, collapsed after the U.S. government recommended against it after consulting the Pakistani intelligence authorities, who opposed the asylum plan, the memo showed. Bugti has meanwhile been living in neighboring Afghanistan.

In a December 2010 face-to-face interview, Baluch independence activist Ahmar Mustikhan said at least sixty Baluch had gone missing since July 2010—victims of the Pakistani military's "enforced disappearance" tactics. Since 2005, there were 1,100 cases of enforced disappearances, he added. "The conflict is very under-reported. It is a very remote area and the Pakistani government restricts journalists' access to it," he said.

The Baluch independence movement may have attracted little attention in the West, but activist Mustikhan was confident the tide of history was turning in the Baluch's favor: "We hope the U.S. and other western nations will get so frustrated with the Pakistani government that they will support us. We are the west's natural allies against the Islamists who preach hatred of the west every day."

Further Reading

Brulliard, Karin. "Pakistani flooding inflames divisions," *The Washington Post,* September 11, 2010, www .washingtonpost.com/wp-dyn/content/article/2010/ 09/10/AR2010091006723.html?wprss=rss_print/ asection.

Harrison, Selig S. *In Afghanistan's Shadow: Baluch Nationalism and Soviet Temptations.* New York: Carnegie Endowment, 1981.

———. "Pakistan: The State of the Union," Center for International Policy special report, April 2009, www .ciponline.org/asia/reports/pakistan_the_state_of_ the_union.pdf.

Human Rights Watch. "Pakistan: Military Undermines Government on Human Rights," January 20, 2010, www.hrw.org/en/news/2010/01/20/pakistan-military-undermines-government-human-rights.

International Crisis Group. "Pakistan: The Forgotten Conflict in Balochistan," *Asia Briefing* 69, October 22, 2007, www.crisisgroup.org/home/index. cfm?id=5131&l=1.

Pirsing, Robert G. "Baloch Nationalism and The Geopolitics of Energy Resources: The Changing Context of Separatism in Pakistan," Asia-Pacific Center for Security Studies, April 2008, www.strategicstudies institute.army.mil/pdffiles/PUB853.pdf.

Taheri, Amir. "Iran's wild east is on the boil," *Gulf News,* May 7, 2008, http://gulfnews.com/opinions/colum nists/iran-s-wild-east-is-on-the-boil-1.103916.

Taylor, Jerome. "From Pakistan to Cardiff: The King of Kalat," *The Independent,* March 16, 2009, www .independent.co.uk/news/uk/this-britain/from-pakistan-to-cardiff-the-king-of-kalat-1645740.html.

KASHMIRIS
(India, Pakistan)

The fifteen million people who live in Kashmir, a northwestern region on the Indian subcontinent, have since 1947 been divided between countries, with no consensus over who should govern them. India claims all of Kashmir and occupies about half of it; Pakistan and China occupy the remainder. Some Kashmiris would prefer for Kashmir to become an independent country, or at the very least be given much greater autonomy than it presently enjoys.

Kashmiris make up 2 percent of the Pakistani population and 1 percent of the Indian population; Chinese-occupied Kashmir is uninhabited. Most Kashmiris are Muslim, although there are Kashmiri Hindus, Buddhists, Sikhs, and Christians as well. Their language, Kashmiri, is spoken predominantly in the Kashmir valley region.

Once a unitary state governed by a prince, called a maharaja, Kashmir has been split between China, India, and Pakistan since British colonial rule ended in 1947. The Indian-governed portion, Jammu and Kashmir, is one of India's twenty-eight states. The Pakistani-governed section consists of a narrow strip of land Pakistan calls Azad Kashmir, meaning Free Kashmir, and a larger chunk called Gilgit-Baltistan, or the Northern Areas. China controls two noncontiguous portions of Kashmir. Indian-controlled Kashmir has a population of eleven million and a capital city, Srinagar. The Indian-controlled Kashmir valley, historically renowned for its cashmere wool industry, is 95 percent Muslim. Pakistan-controlled Kashmir has a population of four million, is overwhelmingly Muslim, and has as its capital Muzaffarabad.

A separatist insurgency in Indian-controlled Kashmir broke out in 1989. The level of violence declined from 2004 until 2010 when there was a renewed spike in violence. An estimated fifty thousand people have been killed in the insurgency. Several hundred thousand Kashmiri Hindus have fled to other parts of India, while thirty thousand Kashmiri Muslims have taken refuge in Pakistan. The non-governmental organization Human Rights Watch (HRW) concluded in a September 2006 report that both the militant separatists and the Indian army and police had committed grave human rights abuses. Eight thousand Kashmiris, supposedly taken into Indian custody, remained unaccounted for. Kashmiri secessionists murdered nearly six hundred politicians and attacked ethnic minorities such as the Gujjars and Bakarwals, HRW reported.

Pakistan has played a major role in the insurgency. Pakistani intelligence agents helped to train Kashmiri rebels in the 1990s. Pakistani support gradually diminished in the 2000s, however, largely due to pressure from Western governments, notably the United States. Pakistan's encouragement of Kashmiri separatism has created serious friction between it and India, pushing the two nations to the brink of full-scale war on several occasions. The international community has worked to defuse these tensions, aware of the threat such a conflict poses to the world given that both Pakistan and India possess nuclear weapons.

In the eyes of the international community, as expressed through various United Nations resolutions adopted since 1949, Kashmir is a disputed territory that belongs neither to India nor Pakistan. The de facto borders separating the Indian, Pakistani, and Chinese-controlled parts of Kashmir are referred to as, in the case of the India-Pakistan border, the Line of Control, and in the case of the India-China border, the Line of Actual Control. These have remained mostly unchanged since 1949, when the first war between India and Pakistan over Kashmir ended. The UN since 1949 has deployed a small mission of peacekeepers to Kashmir.

The Kashmiri people have never been asked in a referendum whether they prefer to be ruled by India, by Pakistan, or by themselves. The UN Security Council in 1948 called for a "free and impartial plebiscite" to determine Kashmir's status, but independence was never included as an option. Kashmiris could only pick between Indian or Pakistani rule. India argues that a referendum is not necessary because the Kashmiri parliament in 1952 voted to confirm Kashmir as an integral part of India. India has been unable to convince the UN to support this position, however. Its political leverage is weakened somewhat by the fact that it does not have a permanent seat on the UN Security Council, despite being the world's second most populous nation.

An opinion poll commissioned by Indian and Pakistani media outlets and published in August 2007 by the online news service Kashmir Newz found that 87 percent of respondents from the Muslim-dominated Kashmir valley region favored Kashmiri independence. However, any attempt to change the status quo in Kashmir—for example, to install a unified and independent state—would need the backing of both the Indian and Pakistani governments, and possibly China's as well. Given that India considers all of Kashmir to be part of India, and that Pakistani support for Kashmiri separatism is widely seen as part of a long-term goal to make Kashmir part of Pakistan, an independent Kashmiri state seems unlikely.

History

Kashmiris have over the past two millennia come under the influence of many foreign populations, including Hindus from India; Buddhists from Central Asia; Muslims from Arabia, Turkey, and Afghanistan; Sikhs from Pakistan; and Christians from Europe. By the 1850s the British ruled Kashmir indirectly through the local maharaja. The maharaja was a member of the Singh dynasty. The state of Jammu and Kashmir formed part of the Britain's larger colony, India. Kashmir's push for independence began in 1931 with the establishment of the All Jammu and Kashmir Muslim Conference (MC) by Sheikh Abdullah. The maharaja, Hari Singh, jailed Abdullah in 1946 for dissent.

Britain brought its colonial rule in India to an end on August 15, 1947. Individual states within British India mostly chose to join either newly independent India, which was majority Hindu, or newly independent Pakistan, which was majority Muslim. Maharaja Singh, a Hindu ruling over a majority-Muslim state, initially did not decide to join with either. When Pakistani armies subsequently invaded, the maharaja asked for India's help. India sent soldiers, and a war between India and Pakistan ensued in which India won control of most of Kashmir. The maharaja had meanwhile, on October 26, 1947, signed an instrument of accession to join India. India promised autonomy for Kashmir, but this did not materialize and pro-autonomy and pro-referendum politicians in Kashmir were jailed in the 1950s and 1960s. Indian prime ministers Indira Gandhi and Rajiv Gandhi, her son and successor, entered into alliances with Kashmiri leaders in the 1970s and 1980s, including with Sheikh Abdullah and his son Farooq; this did not result in any new autonomy framework, however. The 1987 Kashmir parliamentary elections were marred by allegations from separatist candidates that the ruling parties had rigged the vote. The 1989 Indian parliamentary elections were boycotted by the separatists.

When the insurgency began in 1989, many Kashmiris initially backed the rebels. A September 2006 Human Rights Watch report cited separatist leader Abdul Ghani Bhat, saying, "We were fools. We thought freedom was round the corner. All we had to do was come out on the streets in protest. Pakistan would send its army to support us, the world would see that every Kashmiri wanted freedom, and India would be forced to agree. Instead, we ended up with all this violence." India clamped down hard by passing the Disturbed Areas Act in 1990, which boosted the army and police's counter-insurgency powers and led to wide-scale arrests, detentions, and extra-judicial killings. By the mid-1990s Indian forces had gained the upper hand on the rebels.

In the late 1990s, the insurgency changed from being a mainly homegrown movement to one run mostly from Pakistan by Islamic militants backed by Pakistani intelligence officials. After the September 11, 2001, terrorist attacks on the United States, the Pakistani government's support for the insurgency dropped off in response to pressure from the United States, its close military ally and an important weapons supplier. U.S. opposition to the Kashmiri insurgency stemmed directly from the 9/11 attacks, which had been carried out by al Qaeda, a terrorist group given sanctuary in neighboring Afghanistan by the Islamist Taliban government. Pakistan had supported the Taliban prior to 9/11.

Militant attacks continued to kill hundreds in the first decade of the twenty-first century in Kashmir. Some attacks were perpetrated by Kashmiri-focused groups, such as JKLF-A, others by more globally oriented Islamist groups, such as Lashkar-e-Toiba and al Qaeda. Meanwhile, a peace process, helped by growing war weariness among Kashmiris, was gathering steam. In November 2003, India and Pakistan announced a cease-fire. From 2004 the Indian government became more willing to engage in dialogue with Kashmiri separatists. Tensions were further defused in October 2005 following an earthquake in the region that helped to generate political goodwill.

Leadership

Kashmiri political leadership is highly fragmented. This is due in no small part to the fact that Kashmir is split between different countries. But the ethnic, cultural, and religious diversity of Kashmiris plays a role as well. In India, a democratic, secular state, there are pro-independence Kashmiri political parties that can compete in elections as long as they do not advocate violence. Twenty-six such Kashmiri groups came together in 1993 and established the All Parties Hurriyat Conference (APHC) with the goal of reuniting the "occupied territories" through peaceful means. The APHC has offices in both India and Pakistan. It boycotted elections in India in 2002 and 2004. The party's leading figures are Mirwaiz Umar Farooq and Syed Ali Geelani. Key individual Indian-based Kashmiri political parties include the Jammu Kashmir Democratic Freedom Party, founded in 1998, and the Jamaat-e-Islami Jammu Kashmir, the Indian branch of a Pakistan-based party established in 1941.

The first Kashmiri pro-independence party, the Jammu Kashmir Liberation Front (JKLF), was established in 1964. The JKLF split in 1995 into the militant JKLF-A, which was led by the party's founder, Amanullah Khan, and was based in Pakistan, and the JKLF-Y faction led by Muhammad Yasin Malik, which opposed violence and based itself in India. Another group, the United Jihad Council (UJC), was established in 1994 and consists of fifteen organizations committed to separating Jammu and Kashmir from India. Some of the groups in the UJC coalition support an independent Kashmir; others would like to see Kashmir made a part of Pakistan. The UJC's chairman is Syed Salahuddin. He is also the dominant figure in Hizbul Mujahideen (HuM), a militant group established in 1989 that aims to make Jammu and Kashmir a separate Islamic country.

Pakistani-controlled Azad Kashmir has its own regional government, including a forty-nine-member parliament and a governing council whose membership includes the president and prime minister of Azad Kashmir and the president of Pakistan. According to HRW's September 2006 report, the Pakistani military and intelligence services dominate the government, and freedom of expression is curtailed in the region. HRW said those who openly advocate Kashmiri independence face persecution and cannot stand for office. There are numerous Pakistan-based militant groups whose goal is to separate Jammu and Kashmir from India. One of the better known groups is Lashkar-e-Toiba (LeT), which means "Army of the Pure." Established in 1993, LeT has carried out many bombings and suicide missions, including the November 2008 attacks in Mumbai, India, which killed 173 people.

Current Status

Following a gradual decline in separatist violence in Kashmir from 2004, dialogue between the Indian government and Kashmiri separatist leaders began to develop. Their discussions centered on the granting of greater autonomy to Kashmiris rather than on options for independence. The Pakistani government is opposed to an autonomy arrangement. Demilitarization is a key demand of the separatists. There is widespread local resentment over the presence of 600,000 troops in Indian-controlled Kashmir. According to HRW's 2006 report, "there have been some proposals towards a possible solution, including the demilitarization of Kashmir and eventual self-rule for Kashmiris." However, the report added that "most analysts believe this to be premature because neither country will want to relinquish its military presence in the areas under their control."

The drop in violence from 2004–2010 provided a much-needed boon to the Kashmiri economy. The tourism industry, which slumped to just a few thousand visitors a year during the 1990s, had risen to 850,000 visitors by 2008. Commerce between the Indian- and Pakistan-controlled parts of Kashmir increased. On October 21, 2008, India and Pakistan reopened trade routes, allowing trucks carrying locally produced food to cross the border in both directions. Journalist Jeremy Page, reporting for the British newspaper *The Times*, said that schoolchildren on the Pakistani side waved banners proclaiming "Kashmir will become Pakistan" and "Long Live Kashmir freedom movement." He said India hoped that the normalizing of trade in Kashmir would help to quell separatist sentiment. Page reported that so-called peace buses between Srinagar, India, and Muzaffarabad, Pakistan, had been operating since 2005. However, he noted that only nine thousand passengers had used the buses thus far due to the lengthy security checks. There are still no telephone links between the two sides. Investors are still reluctant to come to Kashmir given the fragile political situation, although in 2010 the Indian government began to implement a significant aid package aimed at developing Kashmir's economy.

Muslims form a majority in Kashmir, but the Indian government has been accused of trying to encourage Hindus to move to Muslim areas. In late June 2008, Muslim secessionists protested against the government's decision to transfer 100 acres (40 hectares) of forest to Hindus so that they could create shelters for the annual pilgrimage to Shri Amarnath, a Hindu shrine. But according to Kashmir experts Sumit Ganguly and Kanti Bajpai, writing in *Newsweek* magazine in September 2008, allegations that the Indian authorities have plans to carry out so-called ethnic flooding are baseless. "Despite demands from Hindu zealots, New Delhi has refused to dismantle constitutional provisions that prohibit non-Kashmiris from acquiring land in the state, and at no time has the government encouraged migration to Kashmir." They argued that Indian Kashmiris do not have sufficient grounds for seceding because while Indian forces had committed human rights abuses since 1989 in their counter-insurgency campaign, the Kashmiri people have not been systematically persecuted. In addition, they can compete in free and fair elections and the media is allowed to report on human rights abuses.

Given Kashmir's proximity to Afghanistan, a major war zone where dozens of countries have deployed troops in a bid to suppress Islamist militancy and bolster the Afghan government, the international community is very aware of the Kashmir conflict. The U.S. president Barack Obama has been encouraging peace talks through a policy of "quiet diplomacy," reported Emily Wax in the *Washington Post* in December 2009. His new low-key approach has not been universally welcomed. Mirwaiz Umar Farooq, chair of the APHC, cited in a May 2010 article published by the Indian newspaper, *The Hindu*, dismissed quiet diplomacy as a tactic aimed at creating confusion among Kashmiris.

In June 2010, after almost a decade of decreasing levels of violence, the conflict flared up once more.

Over a hundred civilians were killed by the end of the year, mostly stone-throwing youths. In September 2010, Kashmiri separatist leaders rejected the Indian government's offer to release hundreds of young detainees and to review their security presence in the area. At an October 2010 talk at the Heritage Foundation think tank in Washington D.C., Dr. Walter Anderson, an expert on the conflict from Johns Hopkins University, said the upsurge was caused by a growing feeling of discontentment and pessimism among the urban Muslim population in Kashmir valley. "With their indigenous industries like carpet-making on the decline for decades and the presence of 400,000 security forces around the valley, their futures seem bleak," Anderson said. The spike in violence has been a setback to efforts to find a long-term political settlement on Kashmir's status.

Further Reading

Ganguly, Sumit, and Kanti Bajpai. "Secession Dreams: With an eye on Georgia, Kashmiris once again entertain the prospect of independence. It's not a good idea," *Newsweek,* September 15, 2008, www.newsweek.com/id/156935.

Human Rights Watch. "Everyone Lives in Fear," September 11, 2006, www.hrw.org/en/reports/2006/09/11/everyone-lives-fear.

Lamb, Alistair. *Kashmir: A Disputed Legacy, 1846—1990.* Hertingfordbury: Roxford Books, 1991.

"Majority for independence in Kashmir: Indo-Pak Poll," Kashmir Newz, August 13, 2007, www.kashmirnewz.com/n000206.html.

"Manmohan must hold meaningful talks with Kashmiri people: Mirwaiz," *The Hindu* (Indian newspaper), May 22, 2010, www.thehindu.com/2010/05/22/stories/2010052264311100.htm.

Page, Jeremy. "Trucks bear the fruits of peace as trade route reopens after 61 years," *The Times* (London), October 22, 2008, www.timesonline.co.uk/tol/news/world/asia/article4988311.ece.

Quraishi, Humar. *Kashmir: The Untold Story.* New Delhi: Penguin Books India, 2004.

Wax, Emily. "Obama's apparent low-key approach to Kashmir disappoints some in disputed region," *The Washington Post,* December 30, 2009, www.washingtonpost.com/wp-dyn/content/article/2009/12/29/AR2009122902930.html.

KURDS
(Iran, Iraq, Syria, Turkey)

The Kurds are one of the most populous nations in the world not to have their own state. Often overlooked by historians for much of their existence, the Kurds endured severe repression in the twentieth century in the four countries where they mostly live: Iraq, Iran (formerly Persia), Syria, and Turkey. Since the 1990s they have made some advances in enhancing their cultural rights and, in the case of Iraq, in securing regional autonomy. Kurdish efforts at gaining independence have been bloody, especially in Turkey where tens of thousands have been killed in clashes since 1984.

The Kurds number twenty-five million in their homeland in the Middle East. There are twelve million in Turkey, where they make up 18 percent of the population; five million in Iraq, where they account for between 15 and 20 percent of the population; five million in Iran, where they make up 7 percent of the population; and between one and two million in Syria, where they account for 5 to 10 percent of the population. There are also several million Kurds who have left the region; most of these are in Europe. Many Syrian Kurds moved to Germany, many Iranian Kurds moved to Austria, and many Iraqi Kurds moved to Denmark, Finland, Norway, and Sweden. There are

a further 1 to 1.5 million in the former republics of the Soviet Union, such as Armenia and Azerbaijan.

The Kurds have their own language, Kurdish, which is Indo-European. Kurdish has two main dialects, Kurmanji, spoken by Turkish and Syrian Kurds, and Sorani, spoken by Iraqi and Iranian Kurds. There are many restrictions on the use of Kurdish in schools and publications and in public life generally, although the situation varies considerably depending on the country. Repression of Kurdish is probably most severe in Syria. In religion, Kurds are predominantly Sunni Muslim, but there are also Kurdish Christians, Jews, and Zoroastrians (a religion founded in Iran over 2,500 years ago). In comparison to many of their Arab neighbors, Kurds tend to be less religiously conservative. Kurdish women, for example, are rarely veiled and can mix with men more easily than Arab women. The Iraqi Kurdish city of Sulaymaniyah had a unit for women soldiers in the 1990s, noted Quil Lawrence in his 2008 book on the Iraqi Kurdish independence movement. Kurds also tend to have a more tolerant attitude toward alcohol consumption.

Because Kurds have since the early 1920s been divided between four countries whose borders have remained more or less fixed, their autonomy movement is quite fragmented and relations between Kurds in different counties have at times been strained. There are a few Kurds who are calling for a greater Kurdistan that would unite all majority-Kurdish regions into a single state, but given how difficult it would be politically to achieve this, most focus their energy on enhancing cultural rights and securing autonomy within their existing states.

In Iraq, Kurds live mainly in three provinces: Duhok, Erbil, and Sulaymaniyah. Since 1991 they have enjoyed autonomy under the Kurdistan Regional Government (KRG). Iraqi Kurds are in the strongest position both politically and economically. This stems largely from the first Gulf War in 1991, when the United States and its allies mounted a military offensive against Iraq after Iraqi leader Saddam Hussein sent his troops into Kuwait in August 1990 to occupy and annex it. After ending Saddam's occupation of Kuwait, the Western alliance established a "no fly" zone in northern Iraq to protect the Kurds. Prior to this, Saddam had systematically persecuted the Kurds. In 1988, for example, a gas attack on the village of Halabja killed thousands. Kurdish autonomy was further bolstered by the second Gulf War in 2003 when a U.S.-led alliance invaded Iraq, ousted Saddam, and has attempted to install a federal, democratic Iraqi government. U.S. military involvement has proved helpful in advancing Kurdish autonomy in Iraq, even though this was never the primary purpose of the U.S. missions.

There is evidence that Iraq's Kurds are more secular than other Iraqis. Haje Keli, of the independent publication *Kurdish Herald,* reported in February 2010 that the KRG passed a law in 2008 to restrict the practice of polygamy. Whereas in the rest of Iraq a man may take up to four wives, in accordance with Islamic law, in Kurdish Iraq a man may take up to two wives; moreover, he may only take a second wife if his first cannot have children or suffers from a disease. The law was the culmination of a campaign launched by a women's rights group.

In Turkey, the Kurds have benefited from pressure the European Union (EU) exerted on the Turkish government to grant Kurds greater cultural rights as a precondition to entrance into the EU. This pressure has led to tangible improvements, such as the establishment of printing houses for Kurdish-language books and the appearance of street signs in Kurdish. Turkey is also the country where the Kurdish independence campaign has been most violent. An outlawed separatist militant group, the Kurdistan Workers Party (PKK), has conducted an insurgency since 1984 in which forty thousand people, both Turks and Kurds, have been killed. The violence peaked in the 1990s but remained problematic throughout the 2000s.

As Turkey's EU membership bid has lost steam since 2006 due to opposition from some EU countries, the EU's influence over Turkey has decreased. The Turkish government has instead grown more sensitive to accusations by Turkish nationalists that it is "too soft" on the Kurds. "Fearful of a nationalist backlash, the government seems unable to press ahead with substantive reforms until the PKK halts its attacks. The PKK says it reserves the right to pursue its armed attacks until its own conditions are met," wrote Amberin Zaman, Turkish correspondent for *The Economist* magazine in a February 2010 policy brief for the German Marshall Fund of the United States. The PKK is demanding that Kurdish politicians detained by Turkey since April 2009 be released and wants to begin negotiations with the government. One strong opponent of launching talks is PKK leader Abdullah Ocalan, who is widely reviled by the Turks as a terrorist and who has been imprisoned in Turkey since 1999. The civilian government's efforts to talk to Kurdish leaders are often opposed as well by the Turkish military and Turkish constitutional court, which tend to be more hardline on the Kurdish question.

In Iran, Kurds have limited freedom to express their culture. It is permissible to both speak and write in Sorani, and the Kurdish language is taught as a subject in private schools. There is also a distinct Kurdish province, although not all Iranian Kurds reside inside its area and it does not entitle Kurds to a level of autonomy comparable to what Iraqi Kurds enjoy. Iran's Kurds have grown more assertive in demanding their rights. This is provoking a backlash from the Iranian government, which is also fending off separatist sentiment from other ethnic minorities, including the Baluch and Azerbaijanis (see separate essays).

In November 2009, the head of Iran's police force, Gen. Esmail Ahmadi-Moghaddam, accused Western powers of trying to split up Iran by supporting ethnic minorities. In a speech given at Orumiyeh University and reported by BBC Monitoring Service, the general said the same forces that targeted the Soviet Union and Eastern Europe during the cold war, ultimately triggering the collapse of those regimes, were now targeting Iran. He denied that the Kurds were a separate people, insisting they were a branch of a single Iranian nation. He accused the United Kingdom of having deliberately placed many ethnic groups inside Iran when it drew up Iran's borders in order to incite separatism. He maintained that Iranian Kurds would not demand their own state and claimed that "every Iranian Kurd who travels to Iraqi Kurdistan and returns to Iran kisses the ground of our country as soon as he or she passes our borders."

In Syria, the Kurds are concentrated in the north and east, in towns such as 'Ain Arab, Aleppo, Amuda, Derik, Qamishli, and Ras-al-Ain. They are not free to express their culture; the Kurdish language is banned from schools and public life. Article 267 of the Syrian constitution forbids people from advocating secession for the purpose of uniting with another country, even by peaceful means. The Syrian government revoked the citizenship of 120,000 Kurds in 1962, and these stateless people have since swelled to 300,000 due to natural growth. A November 2009 report by Human Rights Watch said that the Syrian Kurds "have traditionally been a divided and relatively quiescent group, especially compared to Kurds in Iraq and Turkey." However, they have grown more vocal in asserting their identity since 2004. The government has responded by clamping down harder than before; Syria is known for its extremely repressive political environment.

According to Sirwan Kajjo, a Syrian Kurdish activist granted political asylum in the United States in 2007 after fleeing persecution by the Syrian authorities, the real number of Syrian Kurds is three million, or 15 percent of the population. However, the government does not wish to acknowledge Kurds' separate identity and so does not count this total in its census, Kajjo said in a February 2010 face-to-face interview. Kajjo, who since 2008 has been teaching Kurdish to U.S. government officials in Washington, D.C., said that while Kurds speak Kurdish at home, the language is actively discouraged by the authorities. He said Syrian Kurds by inclination were secular but that the Syrian government had pushed them to become more religious and to adopt Shia Islam, the faith of the ruling religious group of Syria, the Alawis. Kajjo noted that only a small number of Syrian Kurds work within the administration or the military, as Kurdish society frowns upon such participation.

History

The Kurds are thought to have lived in their current homeland for at least two thousand years. The areas where they lived became occupied from the twelfth century by Arabs. During the Arab conquests, many Kurds were forcibly converted from their Zoroastrian faith to Islam. One of the great leaders of this era, Saladin, was himself Kurdish. However, Kurds today have mixed feelings about Saladin, who saw himself primarily as a Muslim crusader and not as a leader of the Kurds. In the late 1100s Saladin's political and military prowess enabled him to unify Muslim kingdoms in the Kurdish region and beyond. In 1187, at the battle of Hattin, Saladin's forces inflicted

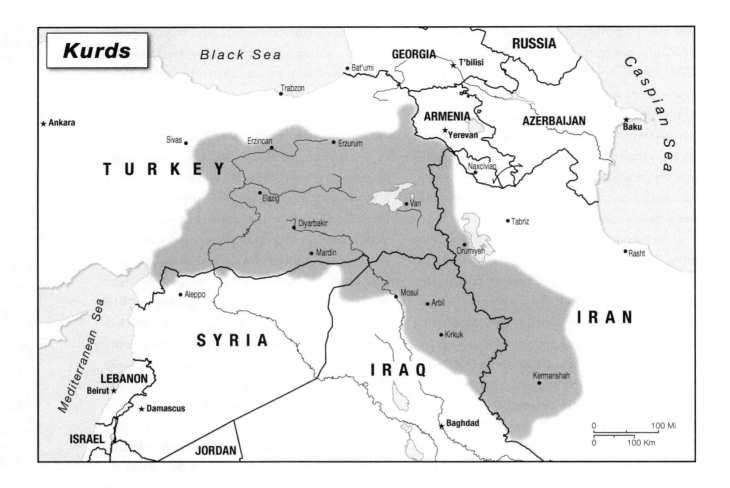

a historic defeat on Christian crusaders who had arrived in the Middle East from Europe in the late 1000s. The Kurds were administered by various emirates until the early 1500s, after which they were divided between the two great empires of the Middle East, those of the Ottoman Turks and the Persians.

A third empire, Russia to the north, began expanding toward Kurdish territories from the 1800s. The Kurds by 1900 were caught in the crossfire between the Ottomans and Russians; they were also being decimated by famines. During World War I (1914–1918), some Kurds participated in attacks orchestrated by the Turkish government on the Armenian community, in which up to a million Armenians were killed. After the war the Ottoman Empire, which had administered most of the Kurdish areas, was dissolved. Kurds' hopes for statehood were raised when the U.S. president, Woodrow Wilson, at the 1919 Versailles peace conference, advanced the concept of self-determination for nations.

The 1920 Treaty of Sevres recognized the Kurds as a separate people and supported their right to form their own country. But a Kurdish state never materialized because the new leader of Turkey, Mustafa Kemal, fought to prevent it, aware that a Kurdistan could threaten Turkey's existence given its large Kurdish population. The 1923 Treaty of Lausanne, in which the nascent Turkish state's borders were internationally recognized, was the final nail in the coffin for Kurdish hopes for statehood, leaving the Kurds divided and unrecognized. The following eight decades would see sporadic Kurdish attempts at securing autonomy or independence in various places, most of which failed.

Apart from Turkey, the newly created states in which the Kurds found themselves were Iraq, which the United Kingdom administered as a protectorate;

Syria, a French-administered protectorate; and Persia, which in 1935 renamed itself Iran. The Kurds' first attempt to assert their separate identity came in 1919 in Iraq, when Kurdish leader Sheikh Mahmoud declared himself the King of Kurdistan. The colonial rulers, the British, quickly suppressed the uprising, using mustard gas against Mahmoud's followers in its counter-insurgency efforts. Iraq gained its independence from the United Kingdom in 1932. In Turkey, the Kurds rebelled in 1924, 1932, and 1937. In each case the uprising was repressed by the Turkish authorities, led by Kemal, who was given the title Ataturk, or "father of Turks," because he was so instrumental in shaping Turkey as a unitary, pro-Western, secular state. Meanwhile, in French-run Syria, from the 1920s until 1945, the Kurds were treated similarly to other ethnic groups, such as Arabs, Aramaic-speaking people, Armenians, Assyrians, and Turkmen. In December 1945, a Kurdish Republic of Mahabad was declared in Iran, comprising a small sliver of Iranian territory in the northeast. The secessionist republic lasted for a year before Iran's leader, the Shah, supported by Western governments, suppressed it. The Russians initially helped the Kurdish separatists but later withdrew their support.

The rise of Arab nationalism in the 1950s proved detrimental to the Kurdish autonomy movement, especially in Iraq and Syria, both of which have majority Arab populations. From 1963 the plight of the Kurds in Syria worsened after the Baath Party seized power. Kurdish towns were given Arabic names and the government, in a bid to prevent the immigration of Turkish Kurds to Syria, revoked the citizenship of 120,000 Kurds. In the 1970s the government forcibly removed Kurds from their homeland and resettled them in other parts of Syria. In parallel, Syria resettled Arab families in Kurdish regions, often displacing Kurds in the process.

Iraqi Kurds mounted an insurgency against the Iraqi government from 1968–1970 that led to concessions, including limited regional autonomy,

recognition of their language, and a fixed number of seats in the national parliament. However, in the 1970s and 1980s Iraqi leader Saddam Hussein forcibly removed thousands of Kurds from the oil-rich city of Kirkuk and dispersed them throughout Iraq, in particular around the Iraqi capital, Baghdad, and the city of Basra in the south. Saddam also resettled Iraqi Arabs, mostly Shia Muslims from the south, in Kirkuk to dilute the Kurdish population. Saddam's increasingly brutal repression of the Kurds from the 1980s became more widely known—and internationally condemned—after he ordered the use of poison gas against Kurdish civilians in the town of Halabja in March 1988. Although Iraqi Kurdish autonomy was consolidated in the wake of the U.S.-led invasion of Iraq in 2003, the conflict also destabilized the region. There were frequent terrorist attacks during the 2004–2006 civil war fought mainly between Sunni and Shia Arabs, who were competing for control of the federal Iraqi government.

In Syria, President Hafez al-Assad began to build political alliances with the Kurds from the mid-1970s, placing some in the army and allowing them greater cultural freedom. In an effort to destabilize rival governments in neighboring Iraq and Turkey, Assad supported Kurdish rights activists in those countries. For example, Jalal Talabani, leader of the Iraqi Patriotic Union of Kurdistan (PUK) party, used Syria as a safe haven in the 1970s, while the Turkish Kurds' PKK based itself in Syria in the 1980s and early 1990s. When President Assad died in 2000 and was succeeded by his son, Bashar, Kurds initially held out hopes for a more relaxed political climate in which their concerns about cultural freedoms might be addressed. But Bashar's early promises of reform were not followed up by concrete actions. In 2002 he ordered the arrest of people attending a forum he had set up precisely to discuss issues such as political liberalization. Syria's hostilities with its neighbor and enemy, Israel, which have been more or less constant since Israel declared its independence in 1948, have not helped the Kurdish cause. The hostilities have set up a war-like atmosphere that gives the Syrian government a pretext for maintaining severe restrictions on political freedoms.

On March 12, 2004, Kurds in the northeastern Syrian town of Qamishli clashed with government forces, leading to the deaths of at least thirty-six people and the arrests of several thousand. The conflict began at a soccer match between a Kurdish team and an Arab team. Tensions between rival supporters spilled over into violence, resulting in the deaths of three children. The violence escalated at the funerals of the victims. Following the Qamishli incident, relations between the Syrian government and the Kurds have further deteriorated. Since 2005 the authorities have repressed at least fourteen political and cultural gatherings, including the Kurds' celebration of their new year, Newroz (or Nowruz).

Leadership

There is no single leader or party representing all of the Kurds. Rather, Kurdish leadership is organized mainly along national lines, based in the four Middle Eastern countries where they predominantly live. In the autonomous Kurdish region of Iraq, the strongman since 1979 has been Masoud Barzani, who became the president of the KRG in 2005. Barzani by 2011 was the single most powerful Kurdish political leader by virtue of the large degree of autonomy the KRG enjoys. His government has representative offices (they are not embassies, as the KRG does not claim independence) to the EU, United States, and United Nations. Barzani was born on August 16, 1946—the same day the party he leads, the Kurdistan Democratic Party (KDP), was founded. His father was the leader of the short-lived Kurdish Republic of Mahabad declared in Iranian Kurdistan. After that regime fell, the Barzani family fled to the Soviet Union, returning to Iraq a decade later. The KDP began an armed struggle in 1961. The current president of Iraq, Jalal Talabani,

is also Kurdish. Talabani's PUK party is the main rival to Barzani's KDP. Both parties officially support self-determination and the right of the Kurds to determine who should govern them.

In Turkey, the most powerful militant Kurdish pro-independence organization is the PKK, which was established in 1978. The Turkish government sentenced the PKK leader, Abdullah Ocalan, to death in 1999, but in response to pressure from the EU it did not carry out the sentence. In 2002 Turkey abolished the death penalty. Prior to his arrest, Ocalan had established one military base in the Syrian city of Latakia and another in the Syrian-controlled Lebanese capital, Beirut, under a deal he struck with the Syrian government in 1993. According to activist Sirwan Kajjo, the Iranian government in the 1990s helped Ocalan fight the Turkish government in return for Ocalan's distancing himself from Syrian Kurds to the extent of denying they were a distinct ethnic group like the Turkish Kurds. Kajjo claimed that Ocalan had ordered the killings of Kurdish politicians in Syria and had forced Syrian Kurds, mostly college students, to go to Turkey to fight from 1993–1998. The Turkish government responded to Syria's support for the PKK by sending troops to the Syrian border. Kajjo said Ocalan, whom he considered a terrorist, had also fought against Iraqi Kurdish leader Barzani from 1995–1998 after Ocalan received support from Barzani's arch-enemy, Saddam Hussein. Responding to pressure from Turkey, Syria eventually abandoned its support of Ocalan, expelling him from Syria in 1998 and closing the PKK camps. While there are Kurdish political parties in Turkey, they are in constant danger of being banned. The newest group, founded in 2008, is the Peace and Democracy Party (BDP), which advocates Kurdish autonomy in a confederated Turkish state.

The Iranian government is similarly hostile to the Kurdish autonomy movement, although Kurdish political parties are permitted. Barzani's KDP has an Iranian branch, the PDK, which favors autonomy.

Abdullah Ocalan (1948–)

ABDULLAH OCALAN was born in the village of Omerli, located in southeastern Turkey near the Syrian border. Although his family was poor, he was able to enter Ankara University to study political science.

Turkey's political climate was growing turbulent in the 1970s, as left- and right-wing groups emerged as political contenders. While attending university, Ocalan tried his hand at political organizing, founding in 1973 an on-campus Maoist group with the goal of socialist revolution. He dropped out of university before 1978, the year he founded the Kurdistan Worker's Party (PKK).

The PKK was an extreme left nationalist group, founded with the intention to create an independent Marxist Kurdish state. While the PKK from its inception was intent on pursuing armed conflict, it took years to become the guerrilla army that it is known as now.

Ocalan fled Turkey before the 1980 military coup, settling in Syria and conducting PKK business from Damascus. From its bases in Syria, the PKK began its military onslaught against Turkey. The PKK declared a Kurdish uprising in 1984, launching a long-armed struggle to create an independent Kurdish state. Known as "Apo," or uncle, Ocalan ran the military campaign from Syria but never fought on the front lines. The PKK focused initially on rural insurgency but shifted its tactics to include urban terrorism as the fighting progressed. While Ocalan is viewed as a hero to the many Kurds who wish for independence, the Turkish government as well as the Turkish media use a different epithet: "murderer."

The PKK war officially lasted for sixteen years, ending with Ocalan's capture in 1999. At its inception, there were tens of thousands of PKK guerrilla troops fighting against NATO's second largest army.

Turkey holds Ocalan personally responsible for the deaths of an estimated forty thousand people, since the militarization of the PKK in 1984. After the PKK began suffering heavy losses, Ocalan sought a negotiated solution. The Turkish government refused, however. Turkey's position is that Kurdish autonomy is a threat to the state; at the time of Ocalan's arrest, broadcasts in the Kurdish language were illegal.

In 1998 Turkey increased pressure on Syria, even threatening military action. Ocalan fled the country, aided by Greek diplomats in his quest to find a country willing to grant him asylum. Ocalan was captured in the Greek embassy in Nairobi, Kenya, in 1999 by Turkish Special Forces.

Ocalan's arrest spurred violent protests in Turkey and other countries with large Kurdish populations. There were instances of self-immolation to protest his capture, and in some cases hostages were taken. PKK guerrillas staged several deadly attacks in Turkey, which left over a dozen people dead. Many expressed outrage when Ocalan, upon his return to Turkey, was walked to prison with a Turkish flag held before him—an event that was broadcast on television. Ocalan's capture did spur a cease-fire, however, as the PKK had been effectively defeated by the Turkish military.

During his trial for treason, which got under way in May 1999, Ocalan apologized to the mothers of Turkish soldiers. For his own protection he was placed inside a bullet-proof glass box when testifying and was the only prisoner on the Imrali prison island. Ocalan was found guilty and sentenced to death. However, in 2002 Turkey's parliament abolished capital punishment in its effort to gain entry into the European Union. On October 4, 2002, Turkey formally commuted Ocalan's death sentence to life in prison. There have been no formal executions in Turkey since 1984.

Since his arrest, there have been annual protests over his captivity. In 2003 thousands of Kurds in France, Greece, and Turkey, concerned over the conditions of Ocalan's detainment, attended rallies to demand his release. Ten thousand people gathered in Strasbourg, France, on the fourth anniversary of his capture.

The PKK resumed its armed conflict with Turkey in 2004, though many PKK commanders were reluctant given the relative weakness of their guerrilla army.

In 2005 the European Human Rights Court ruled that the 1999 trial had been unfair and called for the reopening of Ocalan's case. But Turkey's president refused, citing legal obstacles that he said would need to be dealt with by parliament before this could occur. In 2007 the Council of Europe's committee of ministers dropped its request that Turkey reopen the case.

Ocalan appears to retain a loose hold on the PKK and in 2006 through his lawyer called on its leaders to begin an unconditional cease-fire. The degree of influence he now wields in the organization remains unclear. In November 2007, Ocalan abandoned his support of and insistence on an independent Kurdish state, saying instead that he was open to a democratic solution and willing to settle for Kurdish autonomy inside the Turkish state.

Ocalan published a book, *Prison Writings: The Roots of Civilization*, in 2007, which is based on a study of Kurdish history he undertook while in prison.

There is also a party called Komala, which means "society" in Kurdish. According to activist Kajjo, Iraq's Kurdish leaders, Barzani and Talabani, previously worked against the Iranian Kurdish parties to gain support from the Iranian government in their struggle against Saddam in Iraq. Abdul Rahman Qasimlo, the head of the PDK, was assassinated in Vienna in 1989. The president of Iran, Mahmoud Ahmadinejad, was reputedly involved in the assassination. As for militant groups, the PKK has an Iranian branch called Party for a Free Life in Kurdistan (PJAK), which has mounted an insurgency against the Iranian military since 2003. In February 2010, PJAK assassinated Iranian prosecutor Vali Haj Gholizadeh in retaliation for the tough line he took against Kurdish political prisoners.

In Syria, where the ruling Baath Party is the only party officially permitted, the Kurdish leadership is weak and fragmented. In the 1980s and 1990s the government tolerated unlicensed Kurdish parties that did not demand autonomy or independence; however, since 2000 it has become increasingly difficult for Kurdish parties to operate. Active groups include Yekiti (meaning "union"), led by Ismael Hame; Azadi (meaning "freedom"), led by Khayredine Mourad; Pesharoj (meaning "future"), led by Meshal Tammo; the Kurdish Left Party, led by Mohamed Mousa; and KDP-S, led by Abdulhakim Bashar.

Kajjo said he joined Yekiti at age sixteen and not long after fled to Beirut, Lebanon, to escape arrest. In Beirut he worked as a journalist for a Kurdish television channel. He said the PKK had a Syrian branch called the PYD, but claimed it was not active, nor was there any other militant separatist Kurdish group based in Syria. An earlier Syrian pro-Kurdish party, the Kurdish Democratic Party of Syria, was established by intellectuals in 1957 and still exists as an underground party. A few Syrian Kurds have advanced within the Syrian administration, such as Mahmud Ayobi, who was prime minister from 1972–1976.

Current Status

Although the Kurds have made advances over the past decade in obtaining cultural freedom and increased autonomy, their overall position in each of the four states where they predominantly live remains somewhat precarious. Kurdish separatism in Turkey has continued to destabilize the country. In February 2008, several thousand Turkish soldiers crossed several miles over the Turkey-Iraq border in a bid to crush PKK militants, who were using Iraq as a staging point for launching attacks in Turkey. The Turkish government said the incursion was justified because the U.S. troops stationed in Iraq were not doing enough to curb PKK activities. Hopes that a peace agreement could be reached between the PKK and Turkish government were raised in 2009 after the government started to adopt a more conciliatory stance. It eased restrictions on Kurdish language broadcasting, and in August 2009 Turkish prime minister Tayyip Erdogan made a ground-breaking speech in which he acknowledged the common pain felt by Turkish and Kurdish mothers from the twenty-five year conflict. In October 2009, the government allowed a group of PKK militants to return to Turkey from their base in northern Iraq.

The rapprochement suffered a setback when the returnees gave what were perceived by some as victory speeches while addressing their supporters in southeastern Turkey. Further momentum was lost in December 2009 after the PKK killed seven Turkish soldiers in the northern Turkish province of Tokat. That same month, the Turkish constitutional court banned the largest pro-Kurdish party, the Democratic Society Party (DTP), for its supposed links to the PKK. The DTP immediately reconstituted itself as the Peace and Democracy Party (BDP).

Throughout 2009 Turkish authorities arrested and imprisoned hundreds of Kurdish activists and protesters, including five elected mayors whom it charged with supporting the PKK. In January 2010, two Turkish police officers gunned down a twenty-nine-year-old man, Emrah Gezer, for singing a Kurdish song. On February 15, 2010, demonstrations to mark the eleventh anniversary of the capture of PKK leader Ocalan escalated into violence and mass arrests. With parliamentary elections pending in 2011, the government is reluctant to make concessions.

The situation for the Kurds in Iraq is better. The security situation throughout the country has slowly improved, although in 2010 there were still on average ten explosions a year in Kurdistan. Iraqi Kurds are anxious, however, about the phased withdrawal of eighty-five thousand U.S. troops, due to be completed by the end of 2011. The ongoing departure is encouraging the KRG to improve the strained relations it has had with neighboring Turkey, aware that it may need Turkey's support should its autonomy come under threat. The Turkish government is likely to make any support conditional upon the KRG's clamping down on the PKK in northern Iraq and repatriating PKK activists to Turkey under a proposed amnesty, an August 2009 *Economist* magazine article reported.

Despite being generally content with their autonomous status, it is not implausible that Iraq's Kurds will go further and declare independence, especially given that there is an article on self-determination in the Iraqi constitution. When the KRG held a consultative referendum on this issue, 98 percent voted for independence. The Iraqi central government is unlikely to allow it to secede, however, in part because much of Iraq's oil is located in Kurdish areas. The city of Kirkuk is a major bone of contention. Originally predominantly Kurdish, Saddam's ethnic cleansing and flooding policies reduced Kurds to a minority there. Since Saddam's demise, many Kurds have exercised their constitutional right to return. They now make up 60 percent of Kirkuk's population, with the remaining 40 percent a mix of Arabs and Turkmen. The Iraqi government is trying to stem the influx of Kurds to Kirkuk, alleging

that many of the new arrivals are not originally from Kirkuk—or even Iraq—but are Turkish and Syrian Kurds. Administratively, Kirkuk is not part of Iraqi Kurdistan; it has its own autonomous government, or governorate. Although local leaders would like it to become integrated into the KRG, the Iraqi government objects to this, given the city's economic importance on account of its rich oil supplies.

President Barzani of the KRG, in a question-and-answer session at the Brookings Institution in Washington, D.C., in January 2010, said, "the historical, demographic, and geographic facts prove that Kirkuk has been part of the Kurdish identity." Barzani also gave his views on a related issue: how to divide up Iraq's oil and gas revenues, which are controlled by the federal government. Iraqi Kurds receive 17 percent of the revenue, but Barzani argued they should get more. Additionally, he complained that the Kurds were not sufficiently well represented in the Iraqi military, accounting for just 8 percent of it. Despite his grievances, Barzani said he wanted to "remain part of a federal, democratic Iraq," while adding, "if Iraq goes back to dictatorship, we will not be able to live under this." Barzani saw the KRG's existence as a boon to all Kurds, noting, "we can be a bridge to Kurds in Turkey and Europe and can be a gateway for business elsewhere because we are secure."

In Syria, the political climate has grown more hostile. Throughout 2008 and 2009, the top Syrian Kurdish leaders were sporadically detained or jailed. In March 2008, Syrian police stopped a musical event organized by the KDP-S party; in April the government banned the raising of the Kurdish flag; and in May the government opened fire on a crowd in the Kurdish city of 'Ain Arab. The government passed a law on September 10, 2008, that restricts the right of Syrian Kurds to buy or sell property, which triggered protests in November 2008. Known as Decree 49, the government justified the law on the basis of the Kurds' proximity to the strategically sensitive border regions; activist Kajjo said the law's real purpose was to pressure Kurds to move away from their homelands and into Arab cities in search of employment to dilute the Kurdish population. On March 21, 2010, Syrian security forces opened fire on a group of Syrian Kurds celebrating their new year, the Newroz, killing one man.

In Iran, government repression of Kurdish separatism has intensified. Sayeh Hassan, a Toronto-based democracy activist writing for the Iraq-based independent publication the *Kurdish Herald*, reported in February 2010 that two activists had recently been executed: Ehsan Fatahiyan on November 11, 2009, and Fasih Yasamani on January 6, 2010. Hassan, a criminal defense lawyer, said that eighteen Iranian Kurdish activists were on death row, including two women. "All of these individuals were subjected to torture and 'tried' behind closed doors in sham trials," she said. Yasamani had been convicted for belonging to the outlawed rebel group PJAK. Hassan warned that the clashes between Iranian Kurds and the Iranian authorities could increase to "much higher levels as a result of the executions of peaceful Kurdish activists."

Of the four countries where Kurds mostly live, Iraq appears to be the place where Kurds stand the greatest chance of establishing an independent state. But most analysts think it unlikely they will push for this in the next five years. The Iraqi government would probably resist such a move, as would Iraq's neighbors—Iran, Syria, and Turkey—worried that it would incite their own Kurdish communities to demand independence. The Iraqi Kurdish leadership is aware of how fragile its newly attained and much-treasured autonomous status is. It has proceeded with caution, neither threatening secession from Iraq nor providing material support to Kurdish secessionists or autonomy rights campaigners in neighboring countries.

Further Reading

Dogan, Yonca Poyraz, and Ercan Yavuz. "Erdoğan makes emotional appeal for unity on Kurdish initiative," *Today's Zaman,* August 12, 2009, www.todayszaman .com/tz-web/news-183728-erdogan-makes-emotional appeal-for-unity-on-kurdish-initiative.html.

Free Life Party of Kurdistan, or PJAK (Iranian-based Kurdish political party) Web site, www.pjak.org.

Hassan, Sayeh. "Rising Conflict in Iranian Kurdistan," *Kurdish Herald,* February 2010, www.kurdishherald .com/issue/v002/001/article06.php.

Human Rights Watch. "Group Denial: Repression of Kurdish Political and Cultural Rights in Syria," HRW report, November 26, 2009, www.hrw.org/sites/ default/files/reports/syria1109web_0.pdf.

Keli, Haje. "Polygamy in the Muslim world and new restrictions in Iraqi Kurdistan," *Kurdish Herald,* February 2010, www.kurdishherald.com/issue/v002/001/ article08.php.

Kurdistan Regional Government of Iraq's Mission to the European Union Web site, www.krgeu.com.

"Kurd's death at Nowrouz celebration highlights growing tide of cultural and political repression," *Los Angeles Times,* March 29, 2010, http://latimesblogs.latimes. com/babylonbeyond/2010/03/syria-one-dead-in-crackdown-on-kurdish-cultural-celebrations.html.

Lawrence, Quil. *Invisible Nation: How the Kurds Quest for Statehood Is Shaping Iraq and the Middle East.* New York: Walker Publishing Company, 2008.

Patriotic Union of Kurdistan (Iraqi-based Kurdish political party) Web site, www.puk.org.

"Peace time," *The Economist,* August 27, 2009, www.eco nomist.com/world/europe/displayStory.cfm?story_ id=14313719.

Rudaw (Iraqi-based Kurdish weekly newspaper) Web site, www.rudaw.net.

Unrepresented Nations and Peoples Organization. "Presidential and Parliamentary Elections Kurdistan Regional of Iraq," Election Observation Report, July 25, 2009.

Washington Kurdish Institute (non-governmental organization whose mission is to raise awareness of Kurdish issues and to develop Kurdish civil society) Web site, www.kurd.org.

Yekiti (Syrian-based Kurdish political party) Web site, www.yekiti-party.org/en/index.php.

Zaman, Amberin. "Turkey's Kurdish Opening: Shifting Into Reverse Gear?" German Marshall Fund of the United States, *On Turkey* series, February 19, 2010, www.gmfus.org/publications/article.cfm?id=814& parent_type=P.

PASHTUNS
(Afghanistan, Pakistan)

The Pashtun people of Afghanistan and Pakistan have for centuries been resisting control by foreign and regional governments. A fragmented leadership structure and lack of consistency in their political goals, however, has prevented them from forging an independent Pashtun state. International attention increased markedly after Pashtuns were linked to the September 11, 2001, terrorist attacks on the United States. This was due to a Pashtun-dominated Islamist group, the Taliban, having given sanctuary to al Qaeda, the Islamist group responsible for the 9/11 attacks.

The Pashtun population is forty-one million, of which 40 percent live in Afghanistan and 60 percent in Pakistan; upward of a million Pashtun live in the Arab Gulf states. Concentrated in the south and east, Pashtuns are the largest ethnic group in Afghanistan, numbering fifteen million and accounting for 40 percent of the population. They have dominated the Afghani government since the country was created in 1747. In Pakistan, where they are also called Pathans, they number twenty-five million, are the second largest ethnic group after Punjabis, and live mainly in the North West Frontier Province, which in April 2010 was renamed Khyber Pakhtunkhwa. They have their own semi-autonomous region, the

Federally Administered Tribal Areas (FATA), in northwestern Pakistan on the Afghan border. The FATA is governed both by customary law, known as *Pakthunwali,* and by the central Pakistani government under the Frontier Crimes Regulations. These regulations date from 1848. Three million Pashtuns have migrated out of the tribal areas in recent decades and live in large cities such as Karachi in the south.

The Pashtuns are overwhelmingly Muslim, their conversion occurring in the eighth century C.E. as they came into contact with Arabs. They speak Pakhto, or Pashtu, an Indo-European language. The Pashtuns use tribal councils called *Jirga* to resolve local disputes. Although divided along tribal lines, they have tended to unite together to combat outside interference. Many apply a conservative social code in which women are excluded from affairs outside the home and are required to wear the *burqa,* a full-length garment that conceals the entire body from public view. For years, the Pashtuns subsisted on wheat growing and animal rearing, but in recent decades some have turned to opium cultivation and drug-trafficking.

The Pashtun community has been divided between Afghanistan and Pakistan since 1893 when the United Kingdom, the dominant colonial power in the region, drew up the Durand Line that roughly corresponds to the current Afghan-Pakistan border. Most Pashtuns consider the Durand Line an arbitrary divide and feel under no obligation to respect it. Afghan governments have consistently opposed the border, although views on who should govern the Pashtuns have varied. The three main alternatives to the status quo are to (1) transfer the majority-Pashtun parts of Pakistan to Afghanistan; (2) create a truly autonomous Pashtun region within Pakistan; or (3) allow Pashtuns to form their own state. Separatist sentiment was most pronounced around 1946, just prior to Pakistani and Indian independence, when the Pashtuns were asked to choose to live in one or the other but were denied the option of independence. The referendum on their status was consequently boycotted by pro-independence Pashtuns. Ninety-nine percent of those who did vote opted to join Pakistan, although there were widespread claims of electoral fraud.

Pashtun militancy since the 1980s has mostly manifested itself in religious, Islamist form; however, regional experts are beginning to stress the ethnic dimension of the fighting. Author Selig Harrison, a scholar at the Washington, D.C.-based Center for International Policy, wrote in May 2009: "To western eyes the struggle raging in Pakistan with the Taliban is about religious fanaticism. But in Pakistan it is about an explosive fusion of Islamist zeal and simmering ethnic tensions that have been exacerbated by U.S. pressures for military action against the Taliban and its al-Qaeda allies." The Taliban, named after the Pashto word meaning "students" or "seekers," has controlled parts of Afghanistan and Pakistan since the mid-1990s.

Western countries have had a major military and civilian presence in Pashtun areas of Afghanistan since the September 11, 2001, terrorist attacks. The United States and NATO hope to suppress Pashtun militancy, build a strong and democratic government, and create better economic opportunities to stabilize the region long term. Above all,

they want Pashtuns to stop providing a safe haven to Islamist terrorist groups like al Qaeda, whose goal is to destroy secular Western governments. International interest in the region is also fuelled by the knowledge that Pakistan possesses close to seventy nuclear weapons and that these weapons could fall into the hands of al Qaeda should the government collapse. While Pakistan is a strong military power, it has not been able to bring the Pashtun tribal areas under its control. Indeed, there are widespread allegations that elements within the Pakistani government are covertly sponsoring the Taliban, as part of a strategy to eliminate secular, ethnic-based separatist movements such as those advocating an independent Pashtun country.

History

Living for many centuries at the crossroads of Central Asia, the Indian subcontinent, and the Middle East, the Pashtuns have witnessed continual invasions, including by the Persians, Greeks, Scythians, Arabs, Mughals, Turks, and Uzbeks. By the 1800s, Russia and the United Kingdom were the dominant colonial powers. The British successfully used the area as a buffer against Russian influence and gained some control over the Afghan government from 1880, although the latter became fully independent in 1919. The Afghan authorities continually sought to extend their influence beyond the capital, Kabul, into Pashtun areas but met with only limited success due to the inhospitable terrain and to resistance from Pashtun tribes.

In Great Britain's neighboring colony of India, Viceroy Lord Curzon in 1899 created the North West Frontier Province and built up a military presence there, but Britain never succeeded in fully controlling the Pashtuns. When the British transformed India into two independent countries, Pakistan and India, they did not offer the Pashtuns the choice of forming their own state. The Afghan government supported the creation of such a state in

Pakistan, which helped to poison Afghan-Pakistan relations and led to sporadic closures of the countries' mutual border. During the cold war between the United States and the Soviet Union (1945–1980), the Pashtuns were caught between the two superpowers. The Afghan government remained closer to the Soviets, whereas the Pakistani government was a staunch U.S. ally.

In 1978 Pashtun dominance of the Afghan government ended when the Soviets invaded and installed a new regime led by Tajiks, the second largest ethnic group in Afghanistan. Three million Pashtuns fled to Pakistan. The United States, Pakistan, and Saudi Arabia provided funding to a Pashtun-based, anti-Soviet resistance movement. The Pashtun political leadership grew more religious as Pashtun tribal clerics, previously confined to the religious sphere, flexed their political muscle. The resistance fighters, called *mujahedin,* meaning "soldiers of God," inflicted serious losses on the Soviets, killing thirty thousand troops and leading Soviet leader Mikhail Gorbachev in 1988 to order a troop withdrawal. The Soviet pull-out precipitated the collapse of the Afghan government, at which point U.S. interest in the region declined.

By the mid-1990s, the Taliban had gained control of much of Afghanistan, including non-Pashtun areas. The Taliban was condemned in the West for its human rights record, especially for forcing women to entirely retreat from public life. Western nations also opposed the Taliban because it provided a safe haven for Osama bin Laden, the Saudi national who in the 1990s based his violently anti-Western Islamist group al Qaeda in Afghanistan. Bin Laden's anti-U.S. stance was motivated in part by the presence of the U.S. military in his native Saudi Arabia during the first Gulf War in 1991. The United States responded to al Qaeda's September 11, 2001, terrorist attacks by invading Afghanistan, overthrowing the Taliban, and replacing it with a government dominated by Uzbeks and Tajiks from northern Afghanistan. This caused resentment among Pashtuns, many of whom continued to support the Taliban.

In Pakistan, the central government failed to live up to its promise, enshrined in the 1973 constitution, of granting greater autonomy to the Pashtuns. Instead, Pakistan continually sought to extend its control over the tribal areas. It had multiple and changing motivations for adopting this strategy: fear of rising Soviet influence in neighboring Afghanistan, a mass influx of Pashtun refugees, the growth of opium cultivation and heroin-trafficking, and a rise in militancy and weapons smuggling. The Pakistani government was pro-Taliban in the 1990s but officially turned against it after the September 11, 2001, attacks, in response to pressure from the United States, which was funding Pakistan's counter-insurgency efforts.

Leadership

The tribal nature of Pashtun society has hindered the growth of Pashtun political parties. In a January 2010 email interview, author Nick Howenstein, a PhD student at Indiana University studying the tribal Pashtun insurgency, said, "[Pashtuns] have no pan-tribal authority, but in the face of an external threat the tribes draw together to defend themselves." In Afghanistan the Pashtuns have been out of power since 2001. In Pakistan they enjoy a degree of autonomy in the North West Frontier Province/Khyber Pakhtunkhwa and in the FATA. Since 2000 the Pakistani military, assisted sometimes by unmanned U.S. aircraft, has tried to extend its control over these areas in response to rising militancy.

The main Pashtun-dominated, secular political party in Pakistan is the Awami National Party, led by Asfandyar Wali Khan and founded in 1986. The party favors greater autonomy for Pashtuns and Pashtun control over their natural resources. The party had long campaigned for the renaming of the North West Frontier Province to Pashtunkhwa, its pre-colonial name. The other pro-autonomy party

Khan Abdul Ghaffar Khan (1890–1988)

KHAN ABDUL GHAFFAR KHAN was born in 1890 in Charsadda, a town in the Peshawar valley area of modern-day Pakistan. At the time of his birth, Pakistan was part of the British-ruled colony of India. Khan came from a traditional Pashtun family; his father, Behram Khan, was a farmer, landlord, and head of the Mohammedzais (Sons of Mohamed) tribe.

Khan attended a school set up in the area by British missionaries and excelled in his studies. After completing his high school education, Khan was offered a position in a unit comprised of Pashtun and Sikh soldiers in the British Indian military, but turned it down. Next, Khan was presented with the opportunity to study at a university in London, but because his mother disapproved he rejected this offer as well.

Khan spent a few years working as a farmer for his father; then, in 1910, he decided to dedicate himself to bringing education and knowledge to Pashtun children. Subsequently, Khan founded a school in the town of Utmanzai and gained a great deal of respect with its success.

Starting in 1915, Khan spent three years traveling around the varied districts of the Pashtun tribal area in an effort to offer opportunities to more Pashtun children. As a result of these travels, he earned the name Badshah Khan, or "King of Chiefs."

In 1919 Khan became involved in the fight for reform and the end to oppression by the British Indian government. At this point he began to communicate with another pro-reform activist, Mahatma Gandhi. Both were specifically targeting the Rowlatt Act. This was a piece of legislation that granted the British Indian government the power to incarcerate, without trial, anyone deemed to be a threat to the government. The year 1919 also marked the first of many times that Khan would be arrested throughout his life.

Utilizing his influence in the Pashtun tribal areas, Khan formed a series of groups throughout the 1920s aimed at improving the status of Pashtuns within British India. These included Anjumen-e Islah ul Afghena, Anjuman-e Zamidaran, and Pustun Jirhah. In 1929 the most significant of Khan's organizations was created, Khudai Khidmatgar (God's Servants). This group was conceived as a professional and disciplined army for peace. Distinguished by their red shirts, members of Khudai Khidmatgar swore that they would fight the problems of society, such as poverty and the lack of basic rights and education, and would do so only through peaceful means. By 1930, one year after its founding, Khan's Khudai Khidmatgar numbered over 300,000 members. Furthermore, the organization expanded significantly in 1932 when it began to accept women.

In addition to leading the Khudai Khidmatgar, Khan worked closely with the Indian National Congress, a political party advocating independence for India, until 1947, when India became an independent nation. Additionally, Khan was a member of the Congress Working Committee, the executive body of authority within the Indian National Congress. In 1931 the Indian National Congress asked Khan to serve as the organization's president; Khan refused the offer, however, to avoid making himself appear as more than a common fighter for his cause. Furthermore, in 1939 Khan briefly resigned from the Congress Working Committee when its members considered a shift away from a non-violent philosophy; he rejoined after they backed down.

Khan continued the fight for reform and additional rights for the Pashtun people after the partition of India. The British did not grant the Pashtun a country of their own but split them between Afghanistan and Pakistan. Khan was imprisoned often as a result of his activism. The majority of Khan's fifty-two years in prison was spent in Pakistan. The Pakistani authorities disapproved of Khan, viewing him as a friend of India because of his past ties with Indian pro-independence factions. Following the independence of India and Pakistan in 1947, the Pakistani government launched a harsh crackdown on Khan's Khudai Khidmatgar.

In 1985 Khan received a nomination for the Nobel Peace Prize. He was granted the Bharat Ratna in 1987; this is the most prestigious honor that the Indian government can confer upon a civilian. Khan was the first non-citizen to receive this award.

Khan died on January 20, 1988. His funeral in Jalalabad prompted a brief cease-fire between the *mujahedin* Afghani militants and Soviet forces fighting in Afghanistan, as well as the first visit of an Indian head of state to Pakistan in over thirty years. He is remembered as a unique leader of the Pashtuns, able to take a traditionally aggressive people down a non-violent path. Khan's unwavering dedication to the pacifist philosophy and Pashtun cause is exemplified by his nickname, Frontier Gandhi.

in Pakistan is the Pashtun Milli Awami Party, led by Mahmood Khan Achakzai. Neither party is calling for an independent Pashtun state.

Earlier Pashtun tribal leaders include Qais Abdur Rashid (571–661 C.E.) and Ahmad Shah Durrani (1722–1773), who founded Afghanistan in 1747 by uniting Pashtun tribes. Amir Abdul Rahman Khan (1840–1901) made an agreement with the British in 1893 that demarcated the border between Afghanistan and what would later become Pakistan. In the early 1900s, Khan Abdul Ghaffar Khan (1890–1988) became the first Pashtun leader to demand an independent homeland for Pashtuns. In the 1980s, Pashtun resistance to the Tajik-led, Soviet-sponsored government in Afghanistan was spearheaded by Gulbuddin Hekmatyar.

The Taliban, which ruled most of Afghanistan from 1996–2001 and is now fighting the Afghan and Pakistani governments, as well as the U.S.-led coalition forces, is not a classic separatist group. Its main goal is to install Islamic government in areas it controls rather than to create a Pashtunistan. According to a January 2009 report from the Washington, D.C.-based Center for Strategic and International Studies, the Taliban "has replaced Pashtun nationalism [with] religious nationalism which has taken the form of political Islam." The Afghan Taliban leader is Mohammad Mullah Omar. In Pakistan, the Taliban is called Tehrik-e-Taliban (TTP) and is headquartered in the South Waziristan region in the FATA in its Swat valley stronghold. The leadership is fragmented; key figures include Hakimullah Mehsud, Waliur Rehman, and Maulvi Omar. Banned in Pakistan since 2008, TTP is allied with al Qaeda and has been resisting a U.S.-led military offensive since 2001.

Current Status

The secular Pashtun autonomy movement has been largely overshadowed by the rise of the Taliban, which has imposed Islamic law, or *sharia,* in many Pashtun areas. The United States has increased pressure on Pakistan to seize control of Pashtun tribal areas, mainly to give U.S. and other NATO troops in Afghanistan relief from persistent attacks from Pakistan-based militants. The Pakistani army was initially reluctant to mount a full-scale offensive, believing that to do so would add fuel to existing militancy and might in fact lead to defeat. Author Selig Harrison wrote in May 2009 that the authorities feared "strengthening Pashtun sentiment for an independent 'Pashtunistan' embracing 41 million people in big chunks of Pakistan and Afghanistan." In October 2009, Pakistan finally launched a major offensive, deploying thirty thousand troops. According to Syed Saleem Shahzad, writing in the *Asia Times* newspaper in October 2009, "the chances of a decisive military victory remain remote . . . given the nature of the opposition and the tough territory." Pashtun-led violence continues in Afghanistan, too. On January 18, 2010, Taliban suicide bombers and gunmen attacked shopping centers, a cinema, and a hotel in the capital of Kabul, killing at least twelve people. In April 2010, Pashtun nationalists celebrated when, in a package of constitutional changes adopted in Pakistan, the North West Frontier Province was renamed Khyber Pakhtunkhwa.

There is heavy international involvement in Pashtun concerns. Military and civilian missions from forty countries in America, Asia, and Europe are deployed in Pashtun regions of Afghanistan, tasked with bringing peace and stability. The United States supplies the lion's share of these troops and officials. Daniel Feldman, U.S. Deputy Special Representative in Afghanistan and Pakistan, claimed in a press conference in January 2010 that progress was being made, citing agriculture, health, and education programs, and anti-corruption training for government officials. The United States is providing extensive military aid to the Pakistan government, with $2 billion earmarked from 2010–2014.

The U.S.-led military campaign against Pashtun-based Islamist militancy has come under growing criticism. Selig Harrison argued in May 2009 that the United States should stop its air strikes in Pashtun areas because it makes the people feel further victimized and boosts the militants. "Politically, U.S. policy should be revised to demonstrate that America supports the Pashtun desire for a stronger position in relation to the Punjabi-dominated government in Islamabad." He suggested Pashtuns could be pacified by giving them greater representation in the Pakistani government and army, which is dominated by Punjabis, and by creating a unified, genuinely autonomous Pashtun province within Pakistan.

Militants continue back and forth across the porous Afghan-Pakistan border. Pakistan has proposed the construction of a fence and the laying of mines to stop this illegal flow, but the Afghan government is opposed to such measures. Malou Innocent, foreign policy analyst at the CATO Institute, a libertarian think tank in Washington, D.C., warned at a conference in June 2009 that peace remains a distant prospect. "The Pashtuns have a code of honor that requires them to avenge all attacks. All the men carry arms and they carry out vendettas for decades," she said. In a similar vein, scholar Nassim Jawad noted in a 1992 report for Minority Rights Group International, a London-based organization, that "the fierce independence of Pashtuns has never allowed prolonged rule by outsiders." He added, "as long as foreign intervention continues both inside and outside Afghanistan, there is little chance for national reconciliation and resolution of the crisis within the country."

According to Manzur Ejaz, writing in an August 2009 article for the Pakistan newspaper the *Daily Times*, "a small section of intelligentsia still carries the nationalist aspiration and sees an opening for redrawing the boundaries on the basis of ethnicity." The political reality, however, is that an independent Pashtunistan does not seem a viable option in the next ten years, nor does full integration of Pashtun areas into the administrative structures of either Afghanistan or Pakistan.

Further Reading

Brulliard, Karin. "Name change fuels ethnic tensions; Protests over renaming of restive Pakistani province overshadow government reforms," *The Washington Post,* April 18, 2010, www.washingtonpost.com/wp-dyn/content/article/2010/04/16/AR2010041602398.html.

Ejaz, Manzur. "Washington Diary: Pashtun nationalism," *Daily Times,* August 19, 2009, www.dailytimes.com.pk/default.asp?page=2009\08\19\story_19–8-2009_pg3_5.

Harrison, Selig. "Understanding ethnic dimension key to problem," *The Irish Times,* May 13, 2009, www.irishtimes.com/newspaper/world/2009/0513/1224246387970.html.

International Crisis Group. "Pakistan: The Militant Jihadi Challenge," *Asia Report* no. 164, March 13, 2009, www.crisisgroup.org/home/index.cfm?id=6010.

Jawad, Nassim. "Afghanistan: A Nation of Minorities," Minority Rights Group International report, 1992, www.minorityrights.org/4049/reports/afghanistan-a-nation-of-minorities.html.

Khan, Abdul Ghaffar. *My Life and Struggle* (an autobiography). New Delhi: Hind Pocket Books, 1969.

Nawaz, Shuja. "FATA—A Most Dangerous Place: Meeting the Challenge of Militancy and Terror in the Federally Administered Tribal Areas of Pakistan," Center for Strategic and International Studies report, January 2009, http://csis.org/files/media/csis/pubs/081218_nawaz_fata_web.pdf.

"Pakistan and the Future of U.S. Policy," Cato Institute policy forum, June 23, 2009, www.cato.org/event.php?eventid=6215.

Shahzad, Syed Saleem. "A New Battle Begins in Pakistan," *Asia Times,* October 19, 2009, www.atimes.com/atimes/South_Asia/KJ20Df05.html.

SIKHS
(India)

The Sikhs, a religious community living mostly in India, have a centuries-old tradition of separatism based on their distinct faith. In the 1980s and 1990s, secessionist sentiment led to violent conflict with the Indian government. While the violence has mostly subsided, many Sikhs, inside and outside India, still aspire to an independent Sikh country, which would be called Khalistan.

In India, the Sikhs number twenty-two million and form 2 percent of the total Indian population. Sixteen million make up the majority in the state of Punjab, which borders Pakistan in the northwest. Four million live in Indian states neighboring Punjab and in the Indian capital, New Delhi. Another four million live outside India, mainly in English-speaking countries such as Australia, Canada, and the United Kingdom. Sikhism is the fourth largest religion in India after Hinduism (83 percent), Islam (11 percent), and Christianity (2.3 percent). The Sikhs speak Punjabi, an official language of India spoken by 3 percent of the population.

Sikhism is one of the world's newer faiths. Founded in the late 1400s by Guru Nanak (1469–1539), Sikhism was conceived as an egalitarian philosophy opposed to India's rigid social hierarchy, its caste system, and to oppression by the Muslim Moghul Empire. Nanak's followers were known as *sikhs*, which means "disciples." The zenith of the Sikhs' political fortunes came in the early 1800s when their leader, Ranjit Singh, consolidated numerous warring Sikh kingdoms into a single entity that spanned much of the northwestern Indian subcontinent. Sikhs are recognizable by their traditional dress and the distinctive appearance of the males, who wear beards, grow their hair long under turbans, and carry the Kirpan, a ceremonial sword. Male Sikhs use the surname "Singh," meaning lion, while females use "Kaur," meaning princess. The Sikh holy book, the Guru Granth Sahib, was compiled in 1604, and Sikhs worship at temples called Gurdwaras.

Many Sikhs are deeply attached to their religion; some believe an independent Sikh country would be the best way of preserving Sikh values and customs. Sikh separatism is also rooted in resentment over the manner in which the Indian government has managed Punjab's water resources. And Sikhs retain a deep and longstanding grievance with the Indian government over its decision, in June 1984, to send in troops to storm the Golden

Temple, the Sikhs' holiest shrine in the city of Amritsar in Punjab, which militant separatists were occupying. About five thousands Sikhs, both militants garrisoned there and visiting Sikh pilgrims caught in the crossfire, were killed during the military's Operation Blue Star. Countless historic Sikh artifacts and documents were destroyed. Many Sikhs believe the operation was a deliberate attack on their faith and identity and would like the Indian government to apologize and make amends. Some demand that compensation be paid to the victims of Operation Blue Star, to the victims of anti-Sikh violence instigated by Indian authorities, and to the victims of human rights abuses committed by government forces when repressing the Sikh separatist insurgency.

Their grievances notwithstanding, many analysts would be reluctant to describe India's Sikhs as marginalized or underprivileged. Indeed, there is a common perception of them as one of the more politically and economically advantaged groups in Indian society. For example, despite their small numbers, it was a Sikh economist and politician, Manmohan Singh, who, on May 13, 2004, became the first non-Hindu prime minister of India since the country was founded in 1947. The Sikhs have their own political party, Shiromani Akali Dal (The Eternal Party), which has periodically governed Punjab, often in coalition with the main Hindu nationalist party, the Bharatiya Janata Party (BJP). In keeping with tradition, Sikhs are well represented in the Indian army. A Sikh general, Joginder Jaswant Singh, served as Chief of Army Staff from 2005–2007. There are, however, many Sikhs in Punjab who are poor peasants, and a number of these have committed suicide since 1990 in the face of indebtedness and economic hardship.

The Indian government has rejected the separatists' demands for an independent Sikh country, and since 2008 advocates of separatism have been prohibited from traveling abroad. Most foreign governments have clamped down on Sikh militancy within their own countries, notably in the Western countries where many Sikhs live. However, the intelligence services of India's neighbor and geopolitical rival, Pakistan, have been accused of providing sanctuary, weapons, and explosives training—and even heroin—to Sikh guerrillas to support their campaign. The Sikh expatriate community has been another important source of support and funding for the militants since the 1980s. For example, Talwinder Singh Parmar, one of the leaders of the militant secessionist Babbar Khalsa organization founded in 1978, was based in the Canadian city of Vancouver. He masterminded the single most deadly Sikh separatist terrorist attack to date: the June 23, 1985, bombing of an Air India flight, which exploded off the Irish coast en route from Toronto to Mumbai (then called Bombay), killing all 329 on board.

History

Established in the late 1400s, Sikhism expanded throughout the 1500s, prompting concern on the part of regional powers. In 1606 the Muslim Mughal emperor, Jahangir, executed for alleged rebellion the fifth Sikh guru, Arjan Dev, who had compiled the Guru Granth Sahib and constructed the Golden Temple. In 1699 the tenth and last Sikh guru, Gobind Singh, instituted a ceremony in which Sikhs were initiated into a military order called the Khalsa, or "army of the pure." Its members wore uncut hair, a long knife, comb, steel bangle, and distinctive above-the-knee breeches. Gobind's rule marked a growing militarization, a trend that helped Sikhs to avoid subjugation by regional powers and, eventually, to establish their own kingdom under Ranjit Singh. When Ranjit died in 1839, however, Sikhs fought one another over who should succeed him. The British, who had already established a colony in India, exploited the division, annexing the Sikh kingdom in 1849 and disbanding the Sikh army. Many Sikhs were absorbed into the

British military; others migrated to distant parts of the British Empire.

By the late 1800s, fundamentalist Sikhs had begun purging their religion of Hindu birth, marriage, and death ceremonies, attaching more importance to the Guru Granth Sahib. In the 1920s, the British agreed to let the Sikhs run their own religious institutions, or Gurdwaras. The plight of the Sikhs became precarious in the late 1940s when the British were preparing to transform their Indian colony into a Muslim country, Pakistan, and a Hindu-dominated but secular one, India. On August 15, 1947, the Sikh community was split in two by the new India-Pakistan border. Reluctant to form part of an explicitly Muslim country and unable to form a Sikh-majority country, the Sikh leadership opted to join India. Millions of Sikhs crossed into Indian Punjab, and many were killed in the mass violence that accompanied partition.

In 1966 India subdivided Punjab into three new states. One of the states, also called Punjab, had a Sikh majority. By the late 1970s, Indian prime minister Indira Gandhi's tendency to centralize authority had triggered mounting tensions, with violence breaking out in 1978. A Sikh religious revival developed in parallel, a reaction against the consumerist trend that resulted from the dramatic modernization of Punjab's agricultural economy from 1967–1978. In 1981 Sikh extremists hijacked a plane, and the All India Sikh Students Federation demanded an independent Khalistan. In October 1982, several thousand Sikh autonomy advocates stormed the Indian parliament. Secessionists garrisoned in the Golden Temple were meanwhile directing an insurgency in which hundreds were killed. The bloodbath and rioting that followed the June 1984 storming of the Golden Temple bolstered the militants. On October 31, 1984, Indira Gandhi was murdered by two of her bodyguards, both Sikhs who were angry at her for having ordered the storming of the temple. Gandhi's murder led to anti-Sikh riots in which more than three thousand people, mostly Sikhs, were killed.

Gandhi's son and successor, Rajiv Gandhi, launched peace talks, and in July 1985 he signed the Punjab Accord with Harchand Singh Longowal, leader of the Akali Dal. The accord designated the city of Chandigargh the exclusive capital of Punjab, no longer to be shared with the neighboring state of Haryana. Although the agreement gave Sikhs more control over their affairs, some Sikhs felt it did not go far enough, and Longowal was assassinated by extremists in August 1985. Sikh militancy continued throughout the 1980s and early 1990s, but by 1993 government forces had succeeded in crushing the insurgency. Secessionist militancy declined thereafter; however, sporadic attacks against Sikhs, such as the March 2000 killing of forty Sikhs in the neighboring Indian state of Jammu and Kashmir, continued.

Leadership

The main Sikh political party, the Akali Dal, established itself as an independence movement in the 1920s when the British still ruled the Indian subcontinent. Since India's independence, the party has concentrated its efforts on gaining and keeping control of the Punjab government, increasing the Punjab government's powers, and preserving the Sikh faith. The party competes in national elections, securing 4 of the 552 seats in the Indian Parliament in the 2009 ballot.

The party's leading figures are Parkash Singh Badal, Sukhbir Singh Badal, and Sukhdev Singh Dhindsa. Dissidents have split from the party periodically; Sardar Simranjit Singh Mann set up a party in the mid-1990s that competes in elections. Called Shiromani Akali Dal (Amritsar), it has not won a seat in parliament since 1999. In November 2006, Mann was acquitted by a court of sedition charges for allegedly calling for the creation of an independent Khalistan. In 1999 Gurcharan Singh Tohra launched the All India Shiromani Akali Dal. When he died in 2004, Jaswant Singh Mann created a party under the same name.

Jarnail Singh Bhindranwale (1947–1984)

AP Photo

JARNAIL SINGH BHINDRANWALE, the renowned Sikh militant leader, was born in Rode, a village in the Faridkot District of Punjab, in 1947. Bhindranwale was the youngest of seven brothers in a family of peasant farmers. Bhindranwale worked as a farmer until 1965. At this point he became a student at the Damdami Taksal, a renowned Sikh educational institute in Bhinder Kalan village. There he studied Sikh religion and history and was inspired to add "Bhindranwale" to his birth name, which was Jarnail Singh.

In 1966 Bhindranwale returned to his family and lived as a farmer once again. That same year he married Bibi Pritam Kaur; they had two sons, Ishar Singh, born in 1971, and Inderjit Singh, born in 1975.

In August 1977, the head of the Damdami Taksal, Sant Kartar Singh Khalsa, was killed in a car accident. Before he died, it was reported that he had indicated that Jarnail Singh Bhindranwale should be his successor. When offered the position, Bhindranwale accepted and formally became the head of the institute that same month.

Bhindranwale's influence as head of the training institute enabled him to promote so-called pure Sikhism. Followers of this ideology shun intoxicants and disapprove of the trimming of the beard. Bhindranwale gained notoriety for his aggressive enforcement of this philosophy. Bhindranwale's pursuit of purity led him to regard those who did not live up to his standards as impure or untrue Sikhs. The Nirankaris were a group of Sikhs that Bhindranwale regarded as impure. On April 13, 1978, Bhindranwale led a protest at a Nirankari convention; the melee that ensued resulted in the deaths of thirteen individuals. Bhindranwale blamed the Nirankaris for the incident, yet all those involved were acquitted of any wrongdoing, on January 4, 1980.

Shortly after the April 13 events, Bhindranwale became involved in politics. In 1979 he put forward candidates to run in the elections for the Shiromani Gurdwara Prabandhak Committee, also known as the Parliament of Sikhs. Bhindranwale's candidates were defeated by the established Shiromani Akali Dal party.

On September 9, 1981, Lala Jagat Narain, a prominent newspaper owner and critic of Bhindranwale, was murdered. Bhindranwale was suspected of involvement in the crime, and an order for his arrest was issued. Bhindranwale was allowed to choose the time and place to turn himself in. On September 21, 1981, following a shootout with police forces, Bhindranwale was taken into custody. However, less than a month later, on October 14, 1981, Bhindranwale was released when the police acknowledged that there was not enough evidence to connect him to Narain's murder.

Bhindranwale promoted the Narain episode as evidence of a larger conspiracy against the Sikhs, gaining the support of several moderate Sikhs in the process. In 1982 the Indian authorities sought to arrest Bhindranwale again, but he was able to elude them. Several of his allies were taken into custody, and Bhindranwale then endeavored to have them released.

In an effort to avoid arrest, Bhindranwale moved his base of operations from the town of Mehta Chowk to the Darbar Sahib compound in the Indian city of Amritsar. One of Sikhism's holiest sites, the Harmandir Sahib (Golden Temple) is located in the compound. From his new base, Bhindranwale led a violent campaign against Hindus in the Indian state of Punjab.

In response to the numerous murders carried out by Bhindranwale's followers, the Indian government prepared to crack down on the militant movement's operations. The Indian military moved into the region and declared martial law. With the help of noted Indian military general Shabeg Singh, Bhindranwale proceeded to fortify the Golden Temple and stockpile weapons and ammunition.

On June 5, 1984, the Indian military, under orders from Prime Minister Indira Gandhi, undertook Operation Blue Star, an attempt to enter the temple complex and defeat the militants. Heavy fighting resulted in the deaths of several thousand individuals and the damage and destruction of numerous sacred Sikh artifacts. In the end, all of the Sikh militants were either killed or captured; Bhindranwale's body was identified on June 7. In the days following the conclusion of Operation Blue Star, false rumors spread throughout the country that Bhindranwale had actually escaped.

While Bhindranwale never explicitly stated that he was taking action with the aim of establishing an independent Sikh country, or Khalistan, Bhindranwale's followers did make that claim. Today, the Sikh community and its highest authority, the Akal Takht, regard Bhindranwale as a martyr. Many of India's Hindu population, however, remember him as a terrorist.

The most well-known Sikh militant organization is Babbar Khalsa International (BKI), established in 1978. Led by Wadhwa Singh, it supports a Khalistan consisting of Indian Punjab combined with Sikh-populated areas of adjoining states. BKI is active in Europe, India, and North America, and is banned in many countries. Other militant groups include the Khalistan Commando Force and Khalistan Zindabad Force. A group called Dal Khalsa campaigns for a Khalistan through peaceful means. Established in 1978, this group is led by Harcharanjit Singh Dhami. There are many global Sikh separatist organizations, most notably the International Sikh Youth Federation, which Canada, India, the United Kingdom, and the United States have designated a terrorist group.

Sikh religious leadership is provided by an elected assembly, the Central Gurdwara Management Committee. Established in 1925, the committee manages Sikh shrines; its substantial budget is derived from donations collected at shrines. Theological differences exist among Sikhs. The conflict between orthodox Sikhs and Nirankaris, a "heterodox" offshoot that developed in the 1800s, has been at the root of troubles in Punjab since 1978. Sikh training institutes are maintained as well. Jarnail Singh Bhindranwale, who led the takeover of the Golden Temple in 1982, headed one such institute, the Damdami Taksal. Its focus is on personal morality. Members are encouraged to abstain from perceived vices such as alcohol consumption, tobacco use, and movie watching. Bhindranwale was killed in Operation Blue Star in June 1984.

Current Status

While there is little indication of an imminent return to the violent secessionism of the 1980s, several Sikh militant groups remain active. The militants killed in the Golden Temple assault are viewed by some as martyrs who laid the foundation of an independent Sikh country. Some Sikhs arrested during Operation Blue Star are still in jail; this remains a source of resentment. The Indian newspaper *The Tribune*, which is based in the Punjab capital Chandigargh, reported in June 2009 that separatist leaders, including Simranjit Singh Mann, "virtually hijacked" a ceremony held to commemorate the twenty-fifth anniversary of Operation Blue Star, shouting out pro-Khalistan slogans.

While most Sikhs are not pushing for a Khalistan, many would like to see greater devolution of powers to Punjab. For example, the 1973 Anandpur Sahib Resolution adopted by the Akali Dal, which calls for Punjabi autonomy in all policy areas apart from foreign policy, defense, currency, and communications, has not been implemented. Nor has the 1985 Punjab Accord.

The Sikh religious community meanwhile must contend with infighting. In May 2009, fundamentalists murdered a guru, Sant Rama Nand, who was visiting a temple in Vienna, Austria. Nand was the leader of a Sikh sect called the Dera Sach Khand, whose beliefs some Sikhs consider blasphemous. The Sikhs have also come under attack in a neighboring region in India, Kashmir, which has its own separatist movement (see separate essay); Sikhs make up 5 percent of the Kashmiri population. The attacks have prompted some to abandon their lands in rural areas and move to Srinagar, the state capital of Jammu and Kashmir. *The Tribune* reported in May 2009 that the Taliban, an Islamist militant group, had committed atrocities against the Sikh minority living in neighboring Pakistan.

The Sikh expatriate community in Europe and North America has seen a decline in support for an independent Khalistan; however, some among the younger generation are embracing the idea. Journalist James Keller, in an April 2008 article for *The Globe and Mail*, a Canadian newspaper, reported that a group of teenagers in British Columbia sparked controversy by wearing t-shirts emblazoned with the word "Khalistan" on the front and a quote from Bhindranwale, leader of the Golden Temple rebellion, on the back. He cited a Canadian Sikh teenager's complaining that people "tend to misunderstand the whole concept of Khalistan. Right when they hear the word, they get scared. They think that this is a violent movement or there's going to be people killed."

Journalist Robert Matas, in a June 2009 article for the same newspaper, wrote that young Canadian Sikhs were "more educated, articulate and informed than their parents. Confident of their place in Canada, they engage in the fight for justice and human rights in Punjab as they would for victims in Rwanda, Palestine, or Tibet. They shrug off those who see them as defending extremists, terrorists, and Sikh separatists." He cited the assertion of Canadian Sikh Perpinder Singh Patrola, a thirty-one-year-old lawyer, that "[Sikhs] have resources that did not exist fifteen, twenty years ago. We may feel emotions, but we can move beyond raw emotion and look at actual facts and figures." Matas reported that in the 2009 elections for the Guru Nanak Sikh Gurdwara in Surrey, a Vancouver suburb, younger candidates who favored reintroducing traditional Sikh customs performed well. Because they are free from threats posed by the Indian state and more attuned to separatist movements around the world, Sikhs abroad are likely to continue to be a driving force behind the Punjab-based separatist movement.

Further Reading

Center for International Development and Conflict Management. "Minorities At Risk Project" database, University of Maryland, www.cidcm.umd.edu/mar/data.asp.

Keller, James. "Teens spark debate about Sikh politics," *The Globe and Mail,* April 28, 2008.

Library of Congress, "India—Sikhism," http://country studies.us/india/56.htm.

Matas, Robert. "Fighting For The Truth," *The Globe and Mail,* June 6, 2009.

Singh, Gurharpal. *Ethnic Conflict in India: A Case Study of Punjab.* Basingstoke: Palgrave Macmillan, 2000.

Singh, Pritam. *Federalism, Nationalism, and Development: India and the Punjab Economy.* London: Routledge, 2008.

———. "The Political Economy of the Cycles of Violence and Non-Violence in the Sikh Struggle for Identity and Political Power: Implications for Indian Federalism," *Third World Quarterly* 28, no. 3 (2007): 555–570.

Walia, Varinder. "Separatists try to outsmart jathedars at Akal Takht," *The Tribune* (India), June 6, 2009, www.tribuneindia.com/2009/20090607/punjab.htm#3.

SOUTH YEMENIS
(Yemen)

In 2009 a secessionist movement in southern Yemen that had lain relatively dormant for over a decade was resurrected. A coalition of religious and secular activists was forged, and its aim was to regain independence for South Yemen.

South Yemenis number five million and account for 20 percent of the Yemeni population. The region they inhabit makes up 60 percent of Yemen's total territory. The South Yemenis are situated in a geopolitical hotspot, with the world's largest oil producer, Saudi Arabia, to their north and two major shipping channels, the Gulf of Aden and the Red Sea, to their south and west, respectively. Like northern Yemenis, the southerners are Arabs who speak Arabic. However, in religious matters they differ from their northern countrymen: most southerners are Shafi'i, a branch of Sunni Islam, while most northerners are Zaidi, a branch of Shia Islam.

The south had a state of its own—South Yemen—from 1967 until May 22, 1990, when it united with North Yemen by mutual consent. A group of southerners, bitter at how the new administration became dominated by northerners, tried to secede in 1994, but their armed revolt was quickly crushed. The rise in secessionist sentiment in 2009 has attracted a broader support base than the 1994 movement, and the powerful Islamist tribal leader Tariq al-Fadhli has thrown his weight behind it. Al-Fadhli helped the government to suppress the 1994 revolt. He ended his fifteen-year alliance with it in April 2009 and joined the secessionists. Al-Fadhli has a militant background, having fought as a jihadist against the Soviet-sponsored communist government of Afghanistan in the 1980s alongside Saudi national Osama bin Laden and other Arab jihadists. His hostility toward the earlier separatist movement was motivated by the experience of having seen his father's land seized by the Marxist South Yemen government in 1967, after which the family moved to Saudi Arabia. Al-Fadhli's support for the Yemeni government from 1994–2009 enabled him to reclaim his father's lands.

The secessionists' adversary is Yemen's long-standing president, Ali Abdullah Saleh, a northerner who led North Yemen from 1978–1990 and who has ruled the unified Yemen since 1990. His party, the General People's Congress (GPC), is dominated by northerners. However, his grip on the country has been weakening and his popularity fading, mainly as a result of his inability to develop the country's economy. Despite possessing natural gas and oil reserves, in 2009 Yemen ranked 140 out of 182 countries in the United Nations Human Development Index. Saleh's administration has failed to reliably provide essential services to its citizens such as healthcare and electricity. Given the weak central government, Yemenis rely heavily on traditional tribal structures, especially outside urban areas.

Yemen is a heavily armed country, with an estimated sixty million guns, or almost three per person on average. Despite this, the recent upsurge in separatism so far has not resulted in a full-scale militant insurgency. Instead there have been loosely organized public protests that often lead to violent clashes with Yemeni security forces. The security forces have arrested many separatists; advocating secession—even by peaceful means—has been illegal since 2003.

The southerners' major economic grievance is the government's management of the country's gas and oil facilities, which provide 75 percent of the state's revenue. Southerners resent that despite their being situated in the south, President Saleh's northern-dominated government retains complete control over the country's gas and oil facilities. There is also residual bad feeling over the fact that the government forced the retirement of 100,000 southerners who were serving in the Yemeni army and civil service in 1994 when they took the part of the secessionists.

A more deep-rooted cause of southern separatism is the cultural chasm between the north and south. According to Barak Barfi, an independent analyst and journalist who presented a report on Yemen at the New America Foundation think tank in Washington, D.C., in January 2010, "the southerners see themselves as intellectually and culturally superior because they were exposed more to Europe in colonial times." Barfi added that *qat*, the mildly narcotic leaf widely consumed in Yemen, was much less socially acceptable in the south than in the north, where it has severely depleted the industriousness of the society. Given their recent experience living under a Marxist government, southerners tend to be less religiously conservative, especially around Aden, the largest city in the south. That said, southern tribal areas tend more toward the traditional, and southern Yemen in general has grown more Islamic since unification.

The secessionists have received some support from Saudi Arabia, partly because many Saudis sympathize with the separatists' portrayal of the south as being oppressed by a colonizing north, but also because some Saudis view it as a means of keeping Yemen weak. President Saleh's support for Iraqi president Saddam Hussein during the invasion of Kuwait in 1990 prompted Saudi Arabia and Kuwait to support the south in the 1994 revolt. The United States, European Union, and Arab League supported unification and are generally opposed to southern secession.

History

The southerners have a history of settlement stretching back thousands of years. They are referenced in the Bible as the Kingdom of Sheba, but many Yemeni kingdoms and principalities have existed throughout the centuries under different names. By the 1500s, the north was ruled by the Ottoman Turks. From 1839, the British began colonizing the south, establishing a protectorate around the port of Aden and gradually extending control by entering into treaties with local rulers. Originally governed as part of British India, Aden became a separate British colony in 1937. Meanwhile, the northern Yemenis had become independent from the Turks in 1918. They initially created a theocratic state ruled by an imam, but in 1962 the army overthrew the imamate and established the Yemen Arab Republic, also known as North Yemen.

The British ended their rule in the south in 1967, and an independent state, the People's Democratic Republic of Yemen, was founded on November 30. Politically left-leaning from the outset, South

Yemen became overtly Marxist in 1970. Hundreds of thousands of South Yemenis emigrated to North Yemen in the 1970s and 1980s, provoking tensions between the two Yemeni states. A unification movement was launched in 1972 and slowly gathered momentum, with North and South Yemeni leaders agreeing on March 30, 1979, to accelerate the process. A Yemen Council was established on December 2, 1981, to promote political, economic, and social integration.

The unification drive picked up speed after 1985 when Mikhail Gorbachev became leader of South Yemen's closest ally, the Soviet Union. Reformist-minded Gorbachev withdrew Soviet troops and advisors from South Yemen, ceased subsidizing it, and pushed the South Yemenis to liberalize their economy. Meanwhile, North Yemenis grew more enthusiastic about unification, which would merge South Yemen's oil and gas reserves with their own faltering economy. In 1990 the old North Yemen capital, Sana, became the political capital of unified Yemen, while the former South Yemen capital, Aden, was declared Yemen's economic capital. A northerner, Ali Abdullah Saleh, became president, and a southerner, Ali Salim al-Beidh, vice president. The south grew more Islamic, with polygamy becoming legal and Islamic dress codes adopted by many southern women.

By late 1993, relations between Saleh and al-Beidh had deteriorated. Al-Beidh demanded greater decentralization of authority and called for investigations into a spate of assassinations of his fellow party members. In April 1994, hostilities ignited between the northern and southern military units, which had never been merged, and on May 21 al-Beidh announced the south's secession. The Yemeni military quickly defeated the secessionists, taking Aden in July 1994. Al-Beidh was dismissed and went into exile, and many southerners were purged from the government.

The secessionist movement was largely eclipsed in the late 1990s and early 2000s by the attacks against the Yemeni government carried out by the Islamist terrorist network al Qaeda. Some al Qaeda operatives had formerly fought with al Qaeda leader Osama bin Laden in Afghanistan. Meanwhile, in northern Yemen, a popular Zaidi cleric Hussein al-Houthi launched a rebellion in 2004 in response to a perceived lack of religious freedom. Al-Houthi was killed in September 2004, but his brothers continued the rebellion.

Attempting to simultaneously suppress three separate anti-government insurgencies put an increasing strain on the Yemeni government. By 2005 President Saleh was trying to reintegrate southerners into his administration, pardoning some of the former secessionists and reconciling with al-Beidh. But his efforts were undermined by southern resentment over the large—and since 1994, continuous—presence of Yemeni troops in Aden. The Saleh government's failure to reinstate, or pay pensions to, approximately 100,000 southern military and civilian officials forcibly retired in 1994 remained a further bone of contention.

Leadership

The current wave of separatism in the south is led by a diverse and loosely structured coalition that in June 2009 established the Southern Movement and appointed a Council for the Leadership of the Peaceful Revolution of the South. The movement includes top figures from the Yemeni Socialist Party (YSP), the main southern political party; tribal sheikhs such as al-Fadhli; forcibly retired civil servants and military; and lawyers, academics, students, and journalists angry over the government's anti-separatist crackdown. The movement, while still extremely fragile, has succeeded in bringing together secular and Islamist forces that were formerly bitterly divided.

The YSP was the ruling party of South Yemen from its establishment in 1978 until unification in 1990. It served in a coalition government with the northern-based GPC party in the early 1990s. By

Tariq al-Fadhli (1967–   )

Yemen Tribune

TARIQ AL-FADHLI, credited with founding Yemen's jihadist movement, was born in South Yemen (then an independent country, distinct from North Yemen) in 1967. That same year, the British, who had been in control of South Yemen since 1839, left the area, and the Marxist Yemen Socialist Party (Al Hizb al-Ishtiraki al-Yamani, or YSP) took control. Subsequently, much of the land and power held by al-Fadhli's family was diminished or taken away. As a result, the family fled to Lebanon for a short period before moving on to Saudi Arabia, where al-Fadhli grew up.

In 1987, at age nineteen, al-Fadhli brought his formal education to a halt and left Saudi Arabia to fight against the Soviets in Afghanistan. Al-Fadhli's motive in taking up this fight was revenge on the Communists for driving his family from South Yemen. From 1987–1990, al-Fadhli participated in attacks against the Soviets and was wounded in the final battle for Jalalabad. It was during his time in Afghanistan that al-Fadhli met and fought alongside Osama bin Laden.

After hostilities ceased in Afghanistan, al-Fadhli returned to Saudi Arabia and then traveled to Yemen, which had just become a unified country by the mutual agreement of North and South. In joining together, a coalition government was created that granted significant power to al-Fadhli's longtime enemy, the YSP. Employing its new power, the YSP had al-Fadhli arrested for the assassination of a YSP party leader and also accused him of involvement in attacks on two hotels in Aden, the largest city in southern Yemen and its former capital. Al-Fadhli denied all charges yet was imprisoned for the next three years.

In 1994 tensions between the northern and southern factions of the Yemeni government had reached a boiling point, and civil war broke out. Yemeni president Ali Abdullah Saleh met with al-Fadhli and offered to release him from prison on the condition that he gather his fellow jihadists and fight against South Yemen. Al-Fadhli accepted and subsequently played a key role in leading the North to victory. As a result, President Saleh brought al-Fadhli into his senior leadership and returned to al-Fadhli much of the land that his family had lost to the YSP in the late 1960s. Moreover, after the civil war was over al-Fadhli flew to Sudan to thank Osama bin Laden for the material support that he provided to North Yemen; this included weapons, ammunition, and foreign fighters. According to al-Fadhli, this was his last meeting with bin Laden.

For the next fifteen years al-Fadhli lived in Yemen and supported President Saleh's government. In April 2009, however, al-Fadhli broke this alliance and defected to southern Yemen's secessionist movement, the Southern Movement (SM). Al-Fadhli decided that he would no longer tolerate President Saleh's administration, which he believe had treated the people of southern Yemen unfairly by denying them proper rights, discriminating against them, and seizing the profits from the south's gas and oil reserves.

Since switching sides, al-Fadhli has lived in Zinjibar, the center of the region that his family once controlled. He rarely leaves his heavily guarded compound, wary of capture or assassination by Yemeni security forces. President Saleh's government has since labeled al-Fadhli a terrorist and grouped him with al Qaeda's leadership, which supports the SM. Al-Fadhli has dismissed Saleh's claims, maintaining that he despises al Qaeda and its terrorist attacks on civilians and reminds critics that he was a close ally of President Saleh for over fifteen years. In fact, al-Fadhli's clear support of the United States has made it difficult for the terrorist label to stick; he has offered to assist the United States in combating terrorism. In a recent video, al-Fadhli can be seen raising the American flag in his compound and singing "The Star Spangled Banner," the U.S. national anthem.

Currently, al-Fadhli has sixteen children and spends his time promoting the SM. He is careful to present himself as a patriot in his effort to avoid being labeled as a hard-line Islamist. Further, he endeavors to gain the trust of those in the SM who are unconvinced of his loyalty in light of his long alliance with President Saleh. Overall, al-Fadhli brings years of combat experience to the SM. His reputation and standing within the region have the potential to enhance the movement's legitimacy and support.

the mid-1990s, however, the parties were squabbling bitterly over the speed at which northern and southern military units should be integrated, as well as over anti-corruption and terrorism policies. Since 2005 the two sides have engaged in talks aimed at bridging the gap between them. The YSP continues to compete in Yemeni elections, although it has occasionally boycotted sessions of the Yemeni Parliament. The dominant figure in the YSP for the past two decades has been exiled Yemeni vice president al-Beidh. Other top figures include Yassin Said Numan, Ali al-Sarari, Ali Saleh Muqbil, Hasan Ba'um, and Salah Shanfara. Several YSP leaders were put on trial in July 2008 for encouraging secession. Other leaders are hiding in the mountains.

The YSP was established as an amalgamation of various parties, including the National Liberation Front (NLF), the left-leaning party that won control of South Yemen after independence in 1967. The NLF had achieved dominance by defeating a rival party, the Front for the Liberation of the Occupied South. The NLF was originally led by Qahtan al-Shaabi; al-Shaabi was ousted in June 1969 by more leftist factions led by Salim Rubayi Ali, who was pro-Chinese, and Abd al-Fattah Ismail, who was pro–Soviet Union.

Another separatist group is the Sons of Yemen League, set up in 1990 to represent the interests of tribal leaders in the south. Its leader is Abd al-Rahman al-Jifri, who was vice president of the short-lived 1994 South Yemen republic and who fled to London, England, when the secessionist government fell. In 2004 the Southern Democratic Assembly was established in the United Kingdom. Led by Ali Nasser Mohammed, a former Yemeni president, its goal is self-determination or federalism.

Current Status

There was a marked rise in separatist protests in southern Yemen in 2009. In April and May, Yemeni security forces and separatists clashed in the town of Al Habilayn and in July in Zinjibar, leading to several deaths and injuries. In September there were further protests in Al Habilayn, with demonstrators attacking government buildings, removing Yemeni flags, and displaying South Yemen flags, reported Mohammed Al-Mukhashaf of Reuters news agency. Longtime southern leader al-Beidh, exiled in Germany, was cited in the article, asserting that "the government's behavior has pushed people over the barrier of fear to protest on the streets." He called on Iran, a major regional power, to support the movement.

The Yemeni government has grown more hard-line in responding to separatist sentiment. A December 2009 report from Human Rights Watch (HRW) accused Yemeni security forces of carrying out unlawful killings, arbitrary detentions, and beatings, and of restricting freedom of assembly and speech. HRW said the government had prosecuted people who advocated peaceful secession, including Qasim Al-Askar Jubran, a former Yemeni ambassador to Mauritania. The authorities had barred publication of eight newspapers because of their coverage of the south, created a new court in which to try journalists, and arrested academics and bloggers, according to HRW.

The report cited emerging secessionist leader al-Fadhli telling HRW, "I am in favor of [armed] resistance and instituting a military movement," while adding that his secessionist allies were "unanimously in favor of [limited] self-defense and the peaceful option." Al-Fadhli denied he wanted to install an Islamist regime in the south. A November 2009 article by Rafid Fadhil Ali, published by the Jamestown Foundation, a Washington, D.C., think tank, said al-Fadhli had transformed himself from a global jihadist to a South Yemen nationalist. "We have been invaded fifteen years ago and we are under a vicious occupation. So we are busy with our cause and we do not look at any other cause in the world," al-Fadhli told the Arab daily newspaper, *Al-Sharq Al-Awsat*, in May 2009.

As the southern movement gathered steam, hostilities between the Yemeni army and the Houthi tribe in northern Yemen, which first broke out in 2004, escalated in August 2009. Al Qaeda stepped up activities, too, killing four South Korean tourists in March 2009 as retribution for South Korea's support of the United States in the war against al Qaeda. In May 2009, the leader of al Qaeda in Yemen, Nasir al-Wahayshi, declared his support for the secessionists. According to independent analyst Barak Barfi, there is little evidence that al Qaeda provides material support to the secessionists; rather, al-Wahayshi's show of solidarity was intended to undermine the Yemeni government and precipitate its collapse. The United States and Europe, which had distanced themselves from the Yemeni government somewhat in light of the latter's poor human rights record, began renewing ties in early 2010. The shift came as al Qaeda's growing presence in Yemen became apparent after a Nigerian man trained in Yemen tried unsuccessfully to blow up a U.S. passenger plane flying from Amsterdam to Detroit on December 25, 2009.

In June 2010, the YSP's central committee published a report in which it suggested Yemen could only be kept together if there were a radical overhaul of its constitutional structure. An article in the English-language Yemeni newspaper, *Yemen Observer*, reported that the YSP was advocating "adopting a complex state instead of [a] simple state in a federal system that ensures a wide popular participation of power and wealth." Widespread poverty, a faltering economy, and high unemployment and inflation continue to further weaken the Yemeni government. Most analysts think it unlikely the secessionists will prevail within the next couple of years, given the fragility of their coalition coupled with the Yemen government's wielding of a functioning military. Nevertheless, in the long term the unity of the country appears to be under threat.

Further Reading

Ali, Rafid Fadhil. "The Jihadis and the Cause of South Yemen: A Profile of Tariq al Fadhli," *Terrorism Monitor* 7, no. 35 (November 19, 2009), www .jamestown.org/single/?no_cache=1&tx_ttnews[tt_ news]=35757&tx_ttnews[backPid]=61&cHash= 5ff5374579.

Barfi, Barak. "Yemen on the Brink? The Resurgence of al Qaeda in Yemen," New America Foundation, January 25, 2010, www.newamerica.net/sites/newamerica .net/files/policydocs/Barfi.pdf.

Dresch, Paul. *A History of Modern Yemen*. Cambridge: Cambridge University Press, 2000.

Haidarah, Fattah, A. "Socialist Party proposes unity resolution," *Yemen Observer*, June 23, 2010, www .yobserver.com/front-page/10018995.html.

Hammond, Andrew, and al-Mukhashaf, Mohammed. "Clashes in south Yemen as separatists protest," Reuters, September 30, 2009, www.reuters.com/ article/idUSLS286712.

Human Rights Watch. "In the Name of Unity: The Yemeni Government's Brutal Response to Southern Movement Protests," HRW report, December 2009, www.hrw.org/sites/default/files/reports/south yemen1209web.pdf.

Worth, Robert F. "In Yemen's South, Protests Could Cause More Instability," *New York Times*, February 27, 2010, www.nytimes.com/2010/02/28/world/ middleeast/28yemen.html?pagewanted=2.

TAMILS
(Sri Lanka)

The Tamils of Sri Lanka, who number about 3.7 million and account for 18 percent of the population, beginning in 1983 waged one of the bloodiest and longest separatist conflicts of the last century. Although they suffered a crushing military defeat in 2009, many Tamils continue to desire an independent homeland—a "Tamil eelam"—where they will feel neither discriminated against nor under threat as an ethnic minority in a unitary state. However, the only change the Sri Lankan government is willing to consider is greater devolution of power to local and regional authorities.

Eighty-five percent of Tamils are Hindu; the remaining 15 percent are mostly Christian. A majority of Tamils are known as Ceylon Tamil ("Ceylon" is the former name of Sri Lanka), meaning their ancestors may have lived on the island for at least fifteen centuries. Ceylon Tamil are concentrated in Sri Lanka's Northern Province, where they form an overwhelming majority, and in the Eastern Province, which is more ethnically mixed. A million Tamils are known as Up Country, or "estate," Tamil; these people arrived in the 1800s from India, Sri Lanka's northerly neighbor, to work on British-run tea plantations. The Up Country Tamil live mostly in the central highlands and are typically less separatist-minded than the Ceylon Tamil. The Up Country Tamil have struggled to secure Sri Lankan citizenship, which was revoked in 1948 when the island became independent. Many returned to India under a 1965 India–Sri Lanka agreement, while some moved to the Ceylon Tamil north during the separatist conflict to escape persecution.

The Tamils' dispute is with the Sinhalese, who are predominantly Buddhist (Buddhism is the state religion) and who make up 74 percent of the country's population. A further 7 percent of Sri Lankans are Tamil-speaking Muslims. The Tamils' language is very different from the Sinhalese language. There is strong resentment among Tamils over the dominance of the Sinhalese language, the use of which has grown since the 1950s in both government and business. Another source of tension is the ongoing migration of Sinhalese into Tamil areas, which began in the 1800s under British rule but increased sharply in the 1970s, as the government implemented programs to develop sparsely populated regions. Many Tamils believe the government is deliberately trying to change the country's demographics to make an independent Tamil homeland unviable. Neither Tamils nor Sinhalese have ever been consulted in a referendum on what type of state they would like to live in, although Tamils in a 1977 election voted overwhelmingly for a pro-independence political party. It is illegal for Tamils to campaign for independence, even through peaceful means.

A hundred thousand people died and one million people were displaced in the separatist conflict that raged from 1983–2009. The insurgency was led by the Tamil Tigers, whose official name is the Liberation Tigers of Tamil Eelam (LTTE) and who are renowned for pioneering the use of the suicide bomber as a core weapon. At least 270 Tigers were killed on suicide missions. Researcher Muttukrishna Sarvananthan from the Sri Lankan–based Point Pedro Institute of Development described in a 2007 paper for the EastWest Institute the damage the Tigers have caused their own people. Through violence, overtaxation, and trade monopolies, they have triggered a mass exodus of human and financial capital from the northerly city of Jaffna, the LTTE's one-time stronghold, to the Sri Lankan capital, Colombo, in the south. "The LTTE has never articulated any clear economic or development policy framework, because for them development is possible only after the liberation of the 'homeland,'" Sarvananthan said. The conflict has caused the infrastructure to decay, tourism to decline, and universities to close in Tiger-controlled areas.

The key foreign player in the conflict has been India, where fifty million ethnic Tamils live, including many Ceylon Tamil war refugees. India's Tamils live mostly in the Indian state of Tamil Nadu, located in the southeastern tip of the country, across the Indian Ocean from Sri Lanka's Tamils. They are not seeking to secede from India. India's position in the Sri Lankan Tamil conflict has fluctuated. Indira Gandhi, prime minister from 1966–1977 and 1980–1984, openly backed the Tamils' campaign for autonomy, backed federalism in the late 1970s, and provided weapons and training to separatist militants in the early 1980s. However, her son and successor, Rajiv Gandhi, alienated many Tamils by sending a large peace-keeping force in 1987 that clashed with the Tigers.

Since 2000 the Sri Lankan government has received strong support from India, China, and Muslim countries in its counter-insurgency efforts. These states have also strengthened trade ties with Sri Lanka. By contrast, the United States, Europe, Canada, South Africa, Australia, and New Zealand have criticized the government for causing the suffering of Tamil civilians. The United States, EU, Japan, and Norway formed the Tokyo Group, which has tried to broker a long-term political solution between Tamils and Sinhalese. The United Nations has tried to alleviate the humanitarian crises that stemmed from the conflict, with the UN High Commission for Refugees deploying a large staff. While no foreign government supports the Tamil separatists, the Tigers have been able to turn to the large Tamil expatriate community dispersed across the world for support and funding.

History

The first Tamil kingdoms in Sri Lanka were established as early as 500 C.E., with the Tamils gradually becoming firmly established in the north. From 1505 they came under Portuguese influence, and some Tamils converted to Catholicism. From 1658 the Dutch superseded the Portuguese. The Portuguese and Dutch administered the Tamil and Sinhalese parts of the island separately. In 1796 the Dutch ceded the island to Britain, and the British introduced the first island-wide administration. U.S. Protestant missionaries set up schools around Jaffna under British rule. Living in a dry region with limited agricultural opportunities, many Tamils pursued non-agricultural professions or pursued a university education; as a result, Tamils became disproportionately well-represented in the civil service.

When the British ended their rule on February 4, 1948, the Tamils did not demand a separate country but rather a fifty-fifty power-sharing arrangement with the Sinhalese. However, the Sinhalese majority refused this. Over the next forty years, a series of pro-Sinhalese policies had the effect of radicalizing the Tamils. In 1956 Sinhalese became the sole official language; English was dropped, making it harder for Tamils to obtain government jobs. This and similar pro-Sinhalese policies caused the proportion of Tamils in the civil service to fall from a high of 40 percent at the time of independence in 1948 to 10 percent by the 1970s. In 1971 a new education law was enacted forcing Tamil students competing for places in universities to obtain higher grades than their Sinhalese counterparts to qualify for admission, and 1972 saw the removal of a special constitutional protection enjoyed by Tamils as an ethnic minority.

Susan Hayward, Sri Lanka expert at the Washington, D.C.-based United States Institute of Peace, said in a February 2008 telephone interview: "There is no doubt the Tamil separatist movement resulted from a reduction in Tamil political, economic, and social self-determination, real and perceived." She said Tamils were favored under British rule and so felt disenfranchised after independence as access to jobs, education, and political power diminished.

Frustrated by a lack of progress in obtaining their goals through parliamentary means, armed groups took shape. Skirmishes escalated into full-scale hostilities in July 1983 after thirteen soldiers were killed in the city of Jaffna, triggering riots in which four hundred people, mostly Tamils, were killed. The balance of power shifted from Tamils advocating independence through peaceful means to militant pro-independence activists. In 1987, as Sri Lankan forces were trying to recapture Jaffna, India airdropped food parcels, provoking Sri Lankan government protests. India and Sri Lanka signed an agreement that was supposed to grant the Tamils more autonomy, but the ongoing violence prevented its implementation. An Indian peace-keeping force was established on the island; by 1988, it had swelled to eighty thousand. The force was brought home to India in 1990 at the request of the Sri Lankan government after it engaged in bloody clashes with the Tigers.

In May 1991, a Tamil suicide bomber assassinated Indian prime minister Rajiv Gandhi, and in May 1993 the LTTE assassinated Sri Lankan president Ranasinghe Premadasa. Fighting between government and LTTE troops intensified in 1995. Meanwhile, ultra-nationalist Sinhalese in the south were assassinating politicians they accused of conceding too much to the Tamils. Sinhalese Buddhist monks played an important role in bolstering Sinhalese nationalism. From the 1990s until 2009, Norway acted as mediator between the warring sides; many Sinhalese accused the Norwegians of being pro-Tamil.

In July 2001, the Tigers destroyed a dozen fighter aircraft and six passenger airplanes at Colombo airport. When the Indian Ocean tsunami hit Sri Lanka in December 2004, killing thirty-five thousand people in predominantly Tamil areas, the Sri Lankan government began working with the LTTE on reconstruction. But this embryonic rapprochement was stopped in its tracks in 2006 when the Supreme Court, petitioned by nationalist Sinhalese groups, ruled such cooperation illegal.

Leadership

The most renowned Tamil separatist group, the LTTE, was established in 1972 by Velupillai Prabhakaran. The LTTE is notable for having a disproportionately high number of Christians among its leadership. At the height of their power in the 1980s and 1990s, the Tigers had their own broadcasting authority, judiciary, police, navy, air force, banking system, and customs authority. They were technologically innovative, once hijacking a satellite to enable them to disseminate broadcasts across the Indian subcontinent. They bought much of their weapons and light aircraft from foreign governments using illicit channels, with the Tamil diaspora providing funding. Their leader since July 2009, Selvarasa Pathmanathan, a former spokesman, was arrested by the Sri Lankan authorities in August 2009.

The LTTE has been accused of committing grave human rights abuses, including expelling Muslims in LTTE-controlled areas for collaborating with the Sri Lankan government. It has been criticized for illegally collecting taxes, imposing restrictions on fishing, placing landmines on agricultural lands, and forcing opponents into exile. The United States classified the Tigers as a terrorist group from 1997. The EU followed suit in 2006, and the two have shared intelligence to try to clamp down on the Tigers' activities.

The first demand for a Tamil state was made by the All Ceylon Tamil Congress, established in 1944. The Tamil Federal Party was created in 1949 with the goal of making Sri Lanka (then called Ceylon) a federal state where Tamils had the right to self-determination. The rise of Sinhalese Buddhist nationalism in the 1950s hurt the party and bolstered more radical Tamil voices. In 1976 a political party calling for an independent Tamil state, the Tamil United Liberation Front, was established. It became the largest party in the Tamil areas, achieving considerable success in the July 1977 parliamentary elections; in 1983, however, the party lost parliamentary representation when it failed to renounce separatism.

A high-profile advocate of the Tamils has been Grammy Award–winning and Oscar-nominated rapper M.I.A., whose birth name is Mathangi Arulpragasam. Raised in Sri Lanka, India, and the United Kingdom, she has attracted controversy for her political views. M.I.A. has accused the Sri Lankan government of genocide. The United States denied her a visa in 2006 for her alleged support of the Tigers.

In contrast to many Ceylon Tamil, the Up Country Tamil have tended to support nonseparatist Tamil parties that focus on economic rights. These include the Ceylon Workers Congress, which was established as a labor movement in 1939.

Current Status

In 2008 the separatist conflict escalated and there were ground assaults, sea battles, air strikes, and suicide bombings, as the tide began to turn decisively against the LTTE. In January 2009, government forces captured LTTE headquarters in the city of Kilinochchi. A final government push, launched in April, completely crushed the Tigers in May 2009. LTTE leader Prabhakaran, along with his son and heir, Charles Anthony, and eight thousand Tamil civilians were killed. Allegations of war crimes against the Sri Lankan authorities were made when British television aired video showing soldiers killing unarmed, naked, and blindfolded Tamils. The Sri Lankan government maintains that the video was doctored. The government subsequently prohibited journalists and other independent observers access to Tamil areas, which made it difficult to verify allegations of abuse.

The government also imposed a trade embargo, which triggered a humanitarian crisis because aid agencies were prevented from providing relief to war-ravaged Tamil areas. Three hundred thousand Tamils fled their homes and sought safety in refugee camps. In September 2008, the Sri Lankan government ordered humanitarian organizations in the Tiger-controlled Vanni region to leave due to security concerns; severe malnutrition in the camps ensued. The Sri Lankan forces were accused of indiscriminate shelling of buildings, including hospitals. The government in turn accused the Tigers of forcibly recruiting locals and of using the camp refugees as human shields.

The conflict has taken a severe toll on the Tamils, whose region is now the poorest in the country. About a quarter of Jaffna's residents left during the conflict. The government in late 2009 began resettling the Tamil refugees, after carefully screening them to ensure there were no LTTE militants hiding among them. A September 2009 article by Mian Ridge in the *Christian Science Monitor* cited Suhas Chakma of the Indian-based Asian Center for Human Rights criticizing the government's screening process. "It seems absolutely racist to treat every Tamil as if he was a potential member of the Tamil Tigers," Chakma said.

However, author and world affairs commentator, Gwynne Dyer, writing in January 2010 in the *Canberra Times*, an Australian newspaper, defended the Sri Lankan government's actions. Dyer wrote that the "well-meaning foreign pleas last May for a ceasefire to protect the Tamil civilians trapped with the Tigers were quite rightly ignored by the Sri Lankan forces. The Tigers always made sure they had lots of innocent civilians around when they fought." Dyer also wrote that "the problem lies not in the past, but in the future. The Tamils are always going to be there, and the prospect of a peaceful future for Sri Lanka depends on reconciling them to coexistence with the Sinhalese in a state that treats both communities fairly."

The international community has begun to investigate allegations of war crimes committed during the conflict by both the LTTE and the Sri Lankan government. In April 2010, Norway's foreign minister, Jonas Gahr Store, announced that his country, formerly a mediator in the conflict, "has currently no special role in the country" given the military defeat of the Tigers. Norway had tried and failed to broker a peace agreement between the Tigers and the Sri Lankan government. The Tamil diaspora has moved to fill the power vacuum left by the Tigers' demise by establishing the Transnational Government of Tamil Eelam. They held elections in May 2010—deemed illegal by the Sri Lankan government—in which Tamil communities from many Western countries elected 135 "government" members.

In Sri Lanka, the government's popularity has been buoyed as a result of its defeat of the Tigers.

President Mahinda Rajapaksa was reelected in January 2010, winning 57.8 percent of the vote to defeat Gen. Sarath Fonseka, who led the final anti-Tiger offensive. Rajapaksa has voiced support in principle for devolving powers to regional governments and for creating an upper house of parliament that would give Tamils greater influence in government. However, autonomy for the Tamils is not a priority for him. "Sri Lankans are not worried about these things, they [the worries] are only from outsiders and NGOs with nothing better to think about," he said during the elections.

Further Reading

Cheran, R. *Pathways of Dissent: Tamil Nationalism in Sri Lanka.* New Delhi: Sage, 2009.

Daly, John C.K. "LTTE: Technologically innovative rebels," Swiss Federal Institute of Technology, June 5, 2007, www.isn.ethz.ch/isn/Current-Affairs/Security-Watch/Detail/?ots591=4888CAA0-B3DB-1461–98B9-E20E7B9C13D4&lng=en&id=53217.

Dyer, Gwynne. "Sri Lanka's Tamils face an uncertain future," *Canberra Times,* January 8, 2010.

Nissan, Elizabeth. "Sri Lanka: Historical Context," Conciliation Resources (non-governmental organization), 1998, www.c-r.org/our-work/accord/srilanka/historical-context.php.

Rajasingham, K. T. "Norway-Sri Lanka relations normalized: Erik Solheim sidelined," *Asian Tribune,* April 17, 2010, www.asiantribune.com/news/2010/04/17/norway-sri-lanka-relations-normalized-erik-solheim-sidelined.

Reinhart, Anthony. "Thousands of Tamil Canadians vote for 'government,'" *The Globe and Mail* (Canada), May 3, 2010, www.theglobeandmail.com/news/national/toronto/thousands-of-tamil-canadians-vote-for-government/article1554320.

Ridge, Mian. "Sri Lanka under fire for lack of Tamil reconciliation," *Christian Science Monitor,* September 21, 2009, www.csmonitor.com/World/Asia-South-Central/2009/0921/p06s06-wosc.html.

Sarvananthan, Muttukrishna. "Economy of the Conflict Region in Sri Lanka: From Embargo to Repression," *East-West Center Policy Studies* 44 (2007), www.east-westcenter.org/fileadmin/stored/pdfs/ps044.pdf.

"Sri Lanka's election: Victory for the Tiger-slayer," *The Economist,* January 28, 2010, www.economist.com/world/asia/displaystory.cfm?story_id=15393468&fsrc=rss.

East Europe

EAST EUROPE

Barents Sea

NORWAY

SWEDEN

FINLAND

ESTONIA

LATVIA

LITHUANIA

RUSSIA

RUSSIA

BELARUS

POLAND

GERMANY

CZECH REP.

SLOVAKIA
Hungarians

UKRAINE

MOLDOVA
Transnistrians

AUSTRIA

HUNGARY

SLOVENIA
CROATIA

ROMANIA

Hungarians

Crimeans

BOSNIA &
HERZEGOVINA

SERBIA

Serbs

North
Caucasians

ITALY

MONTENEGRO

KOSOVO

BULGARIA

Black Sea

GEORGIA

Abkhazians

South Ossetians

Caspian Sea

MAC.

ALBANIA

ARMENIA

AZERBAIJAN

Karabakh Armenians

TURKMENISTAN

GREECE

TURKEY

KAZAKHSTAN

Mediterranean Sea

CYPRUS

Turkish
Cypriots

SYRIA

IRAQ

IRAN

LEBANON

ISRAEL

JORDAN

LIBYA

EGYPT

SAUDI
ARABIA

KUWAIT

0   500 Mi

0   500 Km

ABKHAZIANS
(Georgia)

In the southern Caucasus state of Georgia, Abkhazia, a separatist enclave bordering the Black Sea, has governed itself independently since 1992 despite being considered by most countries an autonomous republic within Georgia. Abkhazia's de facto statehood, although precarious, found more solid footing in August 2008 when its northerly neighbor, Russia, recognized it following a brief war in the nearby separatist enclave of South Ossetia (see separate essay).

Abkhazia hugs the Black Sea coastline, stretching about 100 miles north-south and 125 miles east-west. There are between 50,000 and 100,000 Abkhazians living there, accounting for between 1 and 2 percent of the population of Georgia. According to the Minority Rights Group International's "World Directory of Minorities and Indigenous Peoples" (accessed December 2010), 35 percent of Abkhazia's residents are ethnic Abkhazian. Georgians used to outnumber Abkhazians, but as many as 260,000 fled during a war that Georgians and Abkhazians fought in 1992–1993. Abkhazians have thus become the single largest ethnic group in Abkhazia, although there remain sizable minorities of Armenians, Georgians, Greeks, Russians, and Ukrainians. Five hundred thousand ethnic Abkhazians live in Turkey, the descendants of political refugees who fled Russian domination in the 1800s.

The Abkhazians have their own language, which is a Caucasian language related to Circassian. Russian is the most widely used language among Abkhazians, however; Georgian is rarely spoken. Abkhazians strongly opposed a law that Georgia adopted in 1990, when still part of the Soviet Union, that made it obligatory to teach Georgian in all schools in Abkhazia. In religion, Abkhazians are a mix of Orthodox Christians and Muslims, with pagan influences as well. The number of Christians has increased sharply since the early 1990s. Abkhazians distanced themselves from Georgians, who are also Eastern Orthodox, by establishing a separate diocese in 1993. Under the leadership of an Abkhazian priest, Father Vissarion, Abkhazian Christians have tried—thus far unsuccessfully—to be included within the Russian Orthodox Church.

The enclave is viewed with warmth and nostalgia by many Russians, as the area in Soviet times was a popular destination for seaside vacationers. The tourism trade declined in the 1990s and 2000s. According to a July 2008 article in *The Economist* magazine, the population of the Black Sea resort of Ochamchira fell from twenty-five thousand in

1993 to just three thousand in 2008. "A derelict cement tower and rusty fairground wheel are the backdrop to an empty stretch of Black Sea coast that was once the Soviet Riviera," the article said. The Abkhaz authorities claim that tourism is on the rise once more.

Russia is the most ardent defender of Abkhazian independence. This was not always the case: until August 2008, Russia officially considered Abkhazia part of Georgia, despite providing support to the Abkhazian authorities. Russia has several thousand soldiers stationed in Abkhazia and is one of the few countries willing to trade with it, purchasing agricultural commodities including nuts, citrus fruits, grapes, and tobacco. Russia has issued Russian passports to many Abkhazians. Since 2008 the Abkhazians have conducted diplomatic relations with Ecuador, Nauru, Nicaragua, Transnistria (itself a separatist state; see separate essay), and Venezuela. These are governments that either have poor relations with, or are not very dependent on, the United States and European Union, both of which firmly oppose Abkhazian independence. The EU, despite not recognizing Abkhazia, provided $34 million (€25M) in funding between 1997 and 2006 in a bid to make it less dependent on Russia. The EU has also promoted dialogue between Abkhazian and Georgian leaders to try to resolve the conflict. Abkhazia has been a member of the Unrepresented Nations and Peoples Organization, an advocacy group for autonomy and separatist movements based in The Hague, since 1991.

In December 1993, a cease-fire that is monitored by a United Nations mission based in Georgia was signed. Full-scale war has not resumed since; however, there have been intermittent outbreaks of violence. Economically, Abkhazia has been badly affected by the conflict and by its political isolation, according to regional expert Gerard Toal, a professor of Government and International Affairs at Virginia Tech University. Speaking at George Washington University in Washington, D.C., in February 2010, Toal, who visited the region in September 2009, described the former thriving seaside resort as a devastated, desolate place, full of abandoned beachfront properties. The border separating Abkhazia from Georgia proper had been tightened up, he added, and Abkhazians were finding it difficult to travel as Abkhazian passports are not widely recognized.

Georgia remains firmly opposed to Abkhazian independence. It believes that recognizing Abkhazia could cause Georgia to break up entirely, given the threat of secession it faces from both South Ossetia and Ajara. Ajara is a former separatist enclave that the Georgian government managed to reintegrate through negotiation in 2004. Georgia has economic motivations too: Abkhazia forms a sizable chunk of its territory and has, because of its Black Sea location, the potential to generate large tourist revenues from resorts like Gagra, Pitsunda, and Sukhum.

History

While linguistic evidence indicates Abkhazians have lived close to Georgians for upward of two thousand years, some Georgian nationalists argue that Abkhazians arrived in their current homeland as late as the 1600s. Abkhazia scholar George Hewitt, in a 1993 article in *Central Asian Survey*, said Abkhazians were united inside a single kingdom by Leon II about 780 C.E. This lasted until 975 C.E., when Bagrat III became the first king of a unified Georgia. In 1810 Abkhazia became a Russian protectorate, and in 1864 Russia annexed Abkhazia. At the end of World War I (1914–1918), as the Russian Empire disintegrated, Abkhazians became part of newly independent Georgia. By 1921 Georgia and Abkhazia had fallen under Russian control again, and Abkhazia was made a republic in the newly constituted Soviet Union. In February 1931, Abkhazia was transformed into an autonomous republic of Georgia.

Many Georgians and Russians immigrated to Abkhazia from the 1930s, an influx promoted by

Lavrentiy Beria, head of the Soviet Union's secret police. Beria was an Abkhazian-born Mingrelian. The Mingrelians are an ethno-linguistic group closely related to the Georgians; Abkhazians see Mingrelians as a distinct people, but Georgians do not. Abkhazian culture was repressed, with Abkhaz-language schools and publishing houses closed and Abkhazians forced to adopt Georgian script. The political climate changed after 1985 when the Soviet Union elected a reformist-minded president, Mikhail Gorbachev, who instituted greater political freedoms through his *glasnost* policy of greater openness and freedom of information. This triggered a surge of nationalism among Georgians, which in turn antagonized Abkhazians.

In 1989 Abkhazians were just 17 percent of the population of Abkhazia, while Georgians made up 44 percent. Many of these were Mingrelians who tended to steer a neutral course in the Abkhaz-Georgian conflict. In March 1991, 98 percent of voters in Abkhazia supported President Gorbachev's proposal for a more loosely confederated Soviet Union, a plan that would have given Abkhazia greater autonomy. That plan was never implemented, however, because a failed coup against Gorbachev in August 1991 precipitated the complete dissolution of the Soviet Union. When the United Nations recognized Georgia's independence on December 21, 1991, Abkhazia was considered part of Georgia.

On July 23, 1992, Abkhazia's parliament declared independence. Georgia, still struggling to establish its statehood, dispatched paramilitary forces to take control of Abkhazia. However, by late 1993 Abkhazian militias, assisted by militias in the neighboring northern Caucasus, had repelled the Georgians. Russia initially supported Georgia but then switched sides and provided troops for the Abkhazians. Massacres were committed, and there was a mass exodus of refugees, mostly of Georgians and Mingrelians. Abkhazia's population plummeted from 550,000 to 220,000. Beginning in January 1994, Russian troops were deployed in the region to act as a buffer between Georgian and Abkhazian forces.

Violence in the zone dividing Abkhazia from the remainder of Georgia flared up in May 1998, causing the departures of a further thirty-five thousand Georgians from Abkhazia, some of whom had only recently returned home. In an October 1999 referendum, 97 percent of voters in Abkhazia backed independence. Georgia rejected the results of the referendum, however, and pointed out that Georgian refugees had not been allowed to vote. By the early 2000s the Abkhazia-Georgia conflict was dubbed one of the four "frozen conflicts" of the ex-Soviet Union, alongside Nagorno Karabakh, South Ossetia, and Transnistria (see separate essays). Dov Lynch, in his 2004 book on these conflicts titled *Engaging Eurasia's Separatist States,* described "an impasse of volatile stability . . . nobody is happy but nobody is terribly unhappy either, and life goes on." The conflict began to thaw in 2004 with the election of the passionately anti-separatist Mikheil Saakashvili to the presidency of Georgia. In July 2006, Saakashvili's troops seized control of part of Abkhazia, the Kodori Gorge, and a government-in-exile was established there.

Leadership

The Abkhazians have a functioning government based in the city of Sukhumi. Abkhazians sought to separate themselves from Georgians as early as June 1988 when sixty leading Abkhazians sent a letter to Soviet leader Gorbachev urging him to address their concerns over the "Georgianization" of Abkhazia. The dominant figure in Abkhazian politics in the 1990s and early 2000s was Vladislav Ardzinba (1945–2010). An academic by training, Ardzinba became a leading figure in 1992 after helping to recruit Chechen militants to repel Georgian paramilitaries from Abkhazia. He was elected president in 1994 and held that position until 2005. Ardzinba signed a non-aggression pact with Georgian president Eduard Shevardnadze on August 15, 1997, but the two men could not agree on a long-term settlement. He was reelected president in October 1999 with 99 percent of the vote, but did not stand for a third term due to ill health.

The October 2004 Abkhaz presidential election was hotly disputed. A candidate supported by the Russian government, Raul Khajimba, competed against a former prime minister, Sergey Bagapsh. Both candidates claimed victory. After weeks of negotiations, a "unity" ticket was put together, with Bagapsh as president and Khajimba as vice president, which 90 percent of voters backed in January 2005. That Abkhazians chose not to elect Moscow's preferred candidate was viewed as evidence that Russian dominance over Abkhazia had its limits. President Bagapsh, whose wife is Mingrelian, received strong support from the Mingrelian community in Abkhazia.

The March 2007 Abkhazian parliamentary elections were won by the United Abkhazia party, which supported President Bagapsh. Twenty-six of the elected representatives were Abkhazian, three were Russian, three Armenian, two Georgian, and one Turkish. United Abkhazia, initially an informal vehicle for promoting Bagapsh, formally constituted itself as a party in early 2009. Bagapsh was reelected president in December 2009. Other prominent Abkhazian politicians include Prime Minister Sergei Shamba; Vice President Aleksandr Ankvab; wealthy businessman and leader of the opposition Economic Development Party Beslan Butba; and leader of the People's Party of Abkhazia, Yakub Lakoba.

A more regionally focused separatist movement, the Confederation of Mountain Peoples of the Caucasus, established itself in Abkhazia in 1991. Led by a North Caucasian academic, Yuri Shanibov, the Confederation helped the Abkhazians in their war of independence with Georgia from 1992–1994. The Confederation has also advocated independence for other North Caucasian peoples (see separate essay).

Current Status

Tensions between Abkhazia, Georgia, and Russia increased sharply in 2008, manifested in belligerent political rhetoric coupled with sporadic outbreaks of violence. A return to full-scale hostilities was avoided in part due to mediation efforts by the United States and the EU. However, a five-day war did take place in South Ossetia in August 2008. Russian troops seized the opportunity presented by the conflict to tighten their control over Abkhazia. On August 28, Russia formally recognized Abkhazia's independence and pledged to keep its 3,500 troops there. The Russians opened military bases, in contrast to the EU, which was unable to even deploy officials to Abkhazia to monitor the August 2008 cease-fire that French president Nicolas Sarkozy brokered.

The Abkhazian authorities are trying to promote the Abkhazian language; however, Russian culture continues to dominate, making this difficult. According to a 2008 article in *The Economist*, 90 percent of Abkhazians have Russian citizenship and are "watching Russian television, using Russian money, and receiving Russian pensions." The article noted that "even if integration with Russia seems unappealing, to many the idea of being part of Georgia is worse." The Georgian government, which initially under President Saakashvili adopted a tougher stance toward Abkhazia, seems somewhat more conciliatory following the August 2008 conflict in South Ossetia. Under pressure from the EU, with which Georgia is trying to forge closer ties, the Georgian government adopted a new strategy in January 2010 that ruled out a military option for Abkhazia.

Abkhazian opposition leader Beslan Boutba is advocating a diminution of Russian influence through greater investment from non-Russian sources, reported Paul Rimple in an October 2008 article for the *Christian Science Monitor*. However, Georgia fiercely opposes efforts by Abkhazians to forge trade links with other countries. For example, in August 2009 a Georgian court sentenced a Turkish ship's captain to twenty-four years in prison for attempting to transport petrol and diesel to Abkhazia, reported journalist Daniel McLaughlin in a September 2009 *Irish Times* newspaper article. Turkey would be a prime candidate for establishing closer trade ties given its geographic proximity, lying just across the Black Sea, coupled with shared cultural links. Half a million ethnic Abkhazians live in Turkey. The July 2010 opinion of the International Court of Justice, which found that Kosovo's 2008 declaration of independence from Serbia did not violate international law, was seized upon by the Abkhaz leadership as justification for its existence. Abkhaz President Sergey Bagapsh was quoted by the Russian news agency Interfax on 22 July as proclaiming the court had "reaffirmed Abkhazia's and South Ossetia's rights to self-determination." He added that these two secessionist enclaves had "far more historical and legal grounds for independence than Kosovo does."

Abkhazian resentment of Russians is mounting, especially in the tourism and property sector, as many Russians have bought up real estate on the Abkhazian coast that had been abandoned by the Georgians who fled in the 1990s. This hostility cuts both ways: in a February 2010 posting on the Russian political commentary Web site politikum.ru, Andrey Yepifantsev accused Abkhazian officials of exploiting legal loopholes to steal thousands of properties from Russians, Greeks, and Armenians. In an article translated by BBC Worldwide Monitoring, Yepifantsev noted bitterly that over a hundred Russian peacekeepers had been killed defending Abkhazia and that Russia had given $122 million (3.6 billion Russian rubles) to Abkhazia in 2009.

The Georgian refugees who fled in 1992 continue mostly to stay away, a fact that promises to be a make-or-break issue in talks on a long-term settlement. The Abkhazians are unlikely to allow the Georgian refugees to come home unless Georgia in return agrees to recognize Abkhazia's independence. According to Professor Toal, Abkhazians make a distinction between the refugees: Mingrelians, they say, can return because Mingrelians are native to the region and can be reintegrated, but Georgians, who settled in Abkhazia as recently as the 1930s, cannot. According to Toal, "Abkhazia is not likely to ever reintegrate into Georgia in our lifetime. The Abkhazians see themselves as an independent state. They have crossed that threshold." Abkhazia, with its own defense capabilities coupled with solid military backing from Russia, is well positioned to prevent Georgia from regaining a foothold within the next decade.

Further Reading

BBC Monitoring Trans Caucasus Unit, "Georgia: Abkhaz leader upbeat on Hague court's decision on Kosovo," July 22, 2010 (original source: Russian news agency Interfax).

Hewitt, G. B. "Abkhazia: A problem of identity and ownership," *Central Asian Survey* 12, no. 1 (January 1993).

Hewitt, George. "Vladislav Ardzinba; Historian who became the first President of Abkhazia," *The Independent,* April 19, 2010, www.independent.co.uk/news/obituaries/vladislav-ardzinba-historian-who-became-the-first-president-of-abkhazia-1948231.html

Lynch, Dov. *Engaging Eurasia's Separatist States.* Washington, D.C.: United States Institute of Peace, 2004.

Matsuzato, Kimitaka. "Inter-orthodox Relations and Transborder nationalities in and around Abkhazia and Transnistria," *Religion, State, and Society* 37, no. 3 (2009).

McLaughlin, Daniel. "Georgia to meet Russians over Abkhazia sea blockade," *The Irish Times,* September 8, 2009.

Rimple, Paul. "After summer war, identity crisis grips Abkhazia," *Christian Science Monitor,* October 20, 2008.

"Tales from the Black Sea; Georgia, Abkhazia and Russia," *The Economist,* July 5, 2008.

Yepifantsev, Andrey. "An inauguration against the backdrop of a scandal," Politkom.ru, February 12, 2010, translated by BBC Worldwide Monitoring. "Russian Web site sees Abkhaz president's second term starting amid scandal," February 24, 2010.

CRIMEANS
(Ukraine)

Ukraine's only autonomous republic, Crimea, has a population of 2.7 million and accounts for 4 percent of Ukrainian territory and 5 percent of its population. Sixty-two percent of Crimeans, or 1.7 million, are Russian; 23 percent, or 620,000, are Ukrainian; and 13 percent, or 350,000, are Tatar. The ethnic Russian and Tatar peoples in Crimea have had increasingly strained relations with the Ukrainian government and with each other since Ukraine became an independent country in 1991. Situated along the Black Sea, Crimea is a peninsula that is attached to the rest of Ukraine by a narrow strip of land. It is separated from Russia by a similarly narrow stretch of sea.

The Tatars are a Turkic people who speak a Turkic language and are Sunni Muslim; the Russians are a Slavic people who speak Russian and are Orthodox Christian. The Crimean Tatars are distinct from the Tatars of Tatarstan, who make up about 50 percent of the population of that autonomous south-central Russian republic. A third group of Tatars lives in Uzbekistan; this group was deported there from Crimea in 1944 by Soviet leader Joseph Stalin. Stalin's deportations represented the low point of the Crimean Tatars' fortunes. Tatars had made up

90 percent of the Crimean peninsula's population as late as the 1700s.

Much of Crimea's Russian population arrived in the 1940s, encouraged to settle there in place of the Tatars, who had been banished to Central Asia as punishment for alleged collaboration with Nazi Germany. The Crimean Russians were content with their status when both Ukraine and Russia were part of the Soviet Union. However, after the Soviet Union was dissolved in 1991 they grew more anxious about their position in an independent Ukraine, even though their numerical majority in Crimea allowed them to continue dominating the autonomous government there. The Crimean Russians feel little affiliation to Ukraine and would prefer to build stronger links with Russia. They would like Russian, which is the dominant language of Crimea, to be recognized as an official language of Ukraine. Some, more radical voices would like Russia to re-annex Crimea, although Russia has shown little indication it intends to do so. Crimean Russians tend to identify most strongly with the Soviet era, when many served in the military.

Crimean Tatars are demanding guaranteed minimum representation in the Crimean and Ukrainian parliaments; they are also working to have the

Tatar language established as an official language of Crimea, eager to revive it after its Soviet-era repression. Some Crimean Tatars would also like greater self-government. On the economic front, Tatar leaders demand either a restitution of properties they lost following the 1944 deportations or an increase in aid from the Ukrainian government to help Tatars resettle in Crimea. The Crimean Russians tend to oppose these demands. The Tatars generally have better relations with the Ukrainians than with the Russians. Some Crimean Russian nationalists have even accused the Crimean Tatars of being proxies of the Ukrainian government. The Ukrainian government gave $7 million to help Tatar returnees in 2009 resettle and reintegrate into their former homeland, although Tatars complain this was insufficient.

The Crimean Russians' position has been strengthened by the presence of a Russian naval base in the Crimean port of Sevastopol, a remnant of a bygone era when the Soviet Union's Black Sea fleet was stationed there. This base was to have been vacated by the Russians when their lease expired in 2017, but in April 2010 Russia and Ukraine extended the lease until 2042. The Russian military is keen to stay on given the strategic advantages the base affords them. Some 200,000 Crimean Russians are thought to have Russian passports; if Russia did wish to intervene in the region's affairs, it would probably justify its intrusion under the guise of protecting Russian citizens. This could happen, for example, if there were an escalation in the frequency and intensity of clashes between Crimean Russians and Crimean Tatars or Ukrainian authorities. There are allegations that some of the Russian naval officers in Sevastopol are covert agents of the Russian secret service who are spying in Crimea and meddling in Crimean politics.

The Ukrainian government's policy toward Crimea is largely contingent upon whether the president is pro-Russian or pro-Western. The incumbent president, Viktor Yanukovych, elected in December 2009, is pro-Russian and is favored heavily by the Crimean Russians. The Tatars, by contrast, were strong supporters of Yanukovych's main challenger in the elections, Yulia Tymoschenko, who is more pro-Western and favors Ukraine's entry into the European Union. Tatars were upset by Yanukovych's appointment in March 2010 of Anatoly Mogilev as Ukrainian Interior Minister. Mogilev is a former chief of police of Crimea, who has spoken out in defense of the 1944 deportation of Crimean Tatars. They were similarly irked when Yanukovych, on April 21, 2010, signed an agreement with Russian president Dmitry Medvedev extending the lease of Russia's Black Sea fleet in Crimea in return for Russian discounts on its gas exports to Ukraine.

History

The Tatars began settling Crimea around the 1200s. They established a state, or khanate, in 1441 under the leadership of Haci Giray Khan. The Ottomans, another Turkic people, conquered Crimea in the 1470s but allowed the Tatars to govern autonomously. By the late 1600s Russia was beginning to challenge Ottoman supremacy in the region. Russian armies invaded the peninsula in 1736, and Russian empress Catherine the Great annexed it in 1783. Russians and other Slavic peoples began immigrating in relatively small numbers; Tatars started to emigrate. During the Crimean War (1853–1856), fought between various European powers to gain control and influence over the region, Russia encouraged Tatars to leave, accusing them of collaborating with the British and French. This triggered an exodus of up to 150,000 Tatars.

During World War I (1914–1918) Tatars tried unsuccessfully to create an independent Crimean Tatar Republic. Crimea was made an autonomous Soviet Socialist Republic in 1921. At the end of World War II (1939–1945), Stalin deported the Crimean Tatars eastward to other Soviet republics, mainly to Uzbekistan, but also to Kazakhstan, Tajikistan, and Turkmenistan. Crimea was annexed to Russia, and more Russians immigrated there. In 1954 Stalin's successor, Nikita Khrushchev, gave Crimea to Ukraine as a gift. This decision was not as consequential then as it would later become as both Russia and Ukraine were then a part of the Soviet Union. Tatars began returning to Crimea in small numbers beginning in 1967. However, it was not until the election of the reformist-minded Mikhail Gorbachev in 1985 that Tatars began to return in larger numbers, having received official permission to do so in 1988.

In 1991, when Ukraine became an independent country after the peaceful dissolution of the Soviet Union, Crimea became an autonomous republic of Ukraine. In February 1992, the parliament of Russia voted to reassert Russia's sovereignty over Crimea, but the Ukrainian government opposed the move and insisted that Crimea's status as an integral part of Ukraine was not a matter for negotiation. In June 1992, the Ukrainian and Russian presidents signed an agreement to divide up the Soviet Black Sea fleet, consisting of eight hundred ships, between them equally. In June 1995, Russia purchased some of Ukraine's fleet, which gave Russia 81 percent of the ex-Soviet fleet. In 1997 Russia signed a twenty-year lease to keep its fleet in Sevastopol and at the same time officially recognized that Crimea was a part of Ukraine.

The Ukrainian government in March 1995 revoked much of the autonomy that Crimea had enjoyed and imposed direct rule in reaction to a series of separatist steps that the Russian-dominated Crimean Parliament had taken in 1994. Crimean autonomy was partly restored in August 1995 on the condition that the Ukrainian president would have the right of approval over candidates for the Crimean premiership. In January 1999, Crimea adopted a new constitution that granted the Crimean government greater budgetary powers.

Meanwhile, large-scale immigration by Tatars to Crimea continued. By the end of the 1990s the Crimean Tatar population had rebounded to 250,000. The Tatars were helped by changes to the Ukrainian law, such as the softening in 1997 of language, citizenship, and residency requirements. The returning Tatars began to demand restoration of the properties that had been seized from them by Stalin. These actions led to an increase in tensions between the Tatars and resident Russians. There were sporadic violent clashes between the communities, resulting in hundreds of injuries and the occasional fatality. The conflicts stemmed primarily from a competition for resources, itself a consequence of the stream of returning Tatars. The Crimean Russians felt threatened by the growth of the Tatar population. Russian-dominated Crimean municipalities tried to limit Tatars' access to housing, land, and employment.

Leadership

The Crimean Russian and Tatar communities have separate political leaderships with very different goals. The autonomous government of Crimea, based in Simferopol, is dominated by ethnic Russians. The Tatars are underrepresented in the Crimean parliament, holding just seven out of a hundred seats in 2008. Ukraine's President Yanukovych in March 2010 appointed Vasyl Dzharty Crimea's prime minister. Crimea has had about twenty different prime ministers since 1991, including Viktor Plakyda, Anatoly Burdyuhov, Anatoly Matviyenko, Valery Kunitsyn, Valery Horbatov, Serhiy Kunitsyn, Anatoly Franchuk, and Arkady Demydenko. The Crimean Parliament elected an ethnic Russian separatist, Yuri Meshkov, president in January 1994. In May 1994, the Crimean Parliament voted to restore the peninsula's pro-independence constitution of May 1992.

There are several ethnic Russian political parties. These include the Russian Party of the Crimea, established in September 1993 by Sergei Shuvainikov; the Party for the Economic Revival of

Mustafa Djemilev (1943–   )

MUSTAFA DJEMILEV was born on November 13, 1943, and is widely acknowledged for his role as leader of the Crimean Tatar National Movement. Six months after his birth, the Crimean Tatar people were expelled from their native Crimea by Soviet leader Joseph Stalin and his Soviet forces. Djemilev's family relocated to Andijan, a region of Uzbekistan. In 1961, at age eighteen, Djemilev began his long career of advocacy for the Crimean Tatars. Djemilev's first endeavor was a pivotal role in the founding of the Union of Young Crimean Tatars; this group was composed of Djemilev and several of his Crimean Tatar friends who longed for the restoration of Crimean Tatar rights. The group sought to secure the opportunity for the Tatar people to return to their homeland of Crimea on the northern coast of the Black Sea.

Over the next thirty years Djemilev would almost continually be accused of anti-Soviet activities. Djemilev endured several arrests, six extensive prison terms, and forced hard labor. On one occasion, Djemilev sought to protest accusations against him by undertaking a hunger strike; Djemilev persisted for 303 days, surviving the ordeal only as a result of the Soviet prison authorities' force feeding. The year 1986 finally marked the end of Djemilev's life in prison; he was released from Soviet custody following negotiations between U.S. president Ronald Reagan and Soviet president Mikahil Gorbachev. After being set free, Djemilev became involved in formal organizations that enabled him to further the Tatars' cause. Most notably, in 1989 Djemilev was elected head of the Crimean Tatar National Movement. Shortly after, with the weakening and ultimate dissolution of the Soviet Union, Djemilev and his family returned to Crimea and settled down in the town of Bakhchisaray.

Throughout the 1990s, Djemilev used his position to provide support to Crimean Tatars; Djemilev was instrumental in aiding Tatars who wished to return to their homeland. By the end of the 1990s, over 250,000 Crimean Tatars had returned from exile and resettled in Crimea. Djemilev's advocacy did not end with the return of Crimean Tatars to their homeland, however. Djemilev went on to pursue equal rights, fair representation, and economic opportunity for Tatars in their homeland. Moreover, Djemilev has endeavored to gain representation for the Crimean Tatars in the Crimean and Ukrainian governments.

In October 1998, Djemilev was awarded the prestigious Nansen Medal from the United Nations High Commissioner for Refugees for his role in advancing the return of the Crimean Tatars to Crimea and improving their status. The Nansen Medal is given out each year to recognize acts that better the standing of refugees. Djemilev has also been recognized by the Turkish people, who share a degree of ancestry with the Crimean Tatars. The Turks have made Djemilev an honorary citizen and have named a street and a park for him in the Turkish capital, Ankara.

Djemilev continues to advocate peacefully for the rights of the Crimean Tatar people and strives to assist as many of them as possible in returning to their homeland. He currently serves as chairman of the Majlis (Parliament) of the Crimean Tartar people and as a member of the Verkhovna Rada (Ukrainian Parliament).

Crimea, led by Vladimir Sheviov and established in autumn 1992; and the Republican Movement of Crimea, which the secessionist president Meshkov set up in January 1994. Crimean Tatar leaders claim that the Russian-dominated autonomous government in Crimea is covertly helping to create Russian "Cossack" units comprised of up to five thousand militias.

The establishment of a newer movement, the Russia Unity Movement, was reported by the Kiev-based news agency UNIAN in December 2009. The news organization said that the movement had organized a rally on December 19, 2009, of 2,500 activists during which the flags of Russia, the Russia Unity Movement, the Russian Community of Crimea, and the Civic Activists of Crimea were unfurled, and prayers were said for St. Nicholas Day. One of the leaders, Serhiy Aksyonov, was reported to have proclaimed: "The majority of Crimean residents are Russian. We speak Russian and we think Russian. It is high time we installed the rule of majority in Crimea."

Crimean Tatars have their own one-hundred-seat parliament called the Mejlis, which is elected every five years but is not recognized by the Ukrainian authorities. Mustafa Djemilev has been its leader since 1995. The main Crimean Tatar political party is the Organization of the Crimean Tatar National Movement. A more radical group, the National Party, was formed in 1993 and named after a party that had tried to establish an independent Crimean Tatar republic in 1917–1918. The National Movement of the Crimean Tatars, led by Vashtiy Abdurayimov, formally constituted in 1987 but having roots stretching back to the 1960s, is an older Crimean Tatar group.

Current Status

The August 2008 war in South Ossetia, in which Russian support for Georgia's separatist enclaves of Abkhazia and South Ossetia (see separate essays) consolidated the enclaves' de facto independence from Georgia, was viewed with great interest in Crimea. After Russia recognized Abkhazian and South Ossetian independence, some expected Moscow to begin inciting the ethnic Russians of Crimea to secede from Ukraine, but this did not happen. However, the Russian-dominated Crimean Parliament in September 2008 endorsed Russia's recognition of Abkhazia and South Ossetia.

In a September 2008 interview for the Ukrainian newspaper *Kontrakty*, Crimean Tatar leader Djemilev said, "about 70 percent of Russian-speaking citizens [in Crimea] see their fate with Russia." He added that "the problem is that they are not ready to take their belongings and move there, they want to take our historical homeland to Russia with them." He claimed Crimean Russians had been brainwashed by propaganda spread to justify the 1944 deportations that depicted Tatars

as barbarians and parasites who have always betrayed Russians. He supported the right of self-determination but said this "does not automatically mean setting up a new, independent country." Tatars would be content with "national-territorial autonomy as part of the Ukrainian state," he said.

While returning Crimean Tatars have mostly obtained Ukrainian citizenship, they continue to compete with Crimean Russians for access to land and housing, which has become very expensive given the rapid rise in population. The construction of religious buildings is an especially contentious issue. There has been a bitter dispute over a proposed mosque in Simferopol. The Crimean authorities in 2004 approved its construction, but in 2008 the ethnic Russian-controlled Simferopol City Council halted the project, citing environmental concerns. Tatars protested the decision by depositing symbolic pieces of limestone at the site, an October 2009 *New York Times* article by Clifford J. Levy reported. Levy wrote that "the three sides [Tatars, Russians, and Ukrainians] jockey for power on the peninsula, and the mosque has been one focal point." He cited Larisa Tsybulskaya, a forty-five-year-old Russian living near the site, complaining that "they are squatting on our land. Why do they have to cut all this land off and give it to one nationality for a mosque?"

On February 15, 2010, Crimean Tatar language experts meeting in Simferopol approved a proposal to stop the use of the Cyrillic alphabet (traditionally used for writing the Russian language) and replace it with the Latin alphabet; they further agreed on a set of grammar and spelling rules. In a report of the meeting posted on Radio Free Europe's Web site, one of the leaders, Eden Mamut, said it was "an important step in helping unite some 1.4 million Crimean Tatars who live in several countries, the majority in Turkey." The Tatars used the Arabic alphabet before the Soviets seized power in 1917. The Soviets forced them to use the Latin alphabet initially, along with other Muslim minorities of the Soviet Union, and Cyrillic script from the 1940s. Most Tatars who live outside post-Soviet countries use either the Arabic or Latin alphabet.

Internationally, the Crimean Tatars have a sympathetic ear in the European Parliament, which in March 2010 hosted a hearing for them. The conference was organized by the Unrepresented Nations and Peoples Organization, an advocacy group for autonomy and separatist movements based in The Hague, which the Tatars joined in 1991. The EU has some sway over Ukraine, given Kiev's interest in joining the EU. The EU is also a potential source of considerable funding should it decide to promote Crimean Tatar culture and society. The long-term challenge for the Russians and Tatars is to agree on a system of government for Crimea that enables each to achieve its political aspirations: cultural autonomy for Tatars and territorial autonomy or independence for Russians.

Further Reading

"Background Documents," European Parliament, hearings, Brussels, March 17, 2010, www.unpo.org/content/view/10843/81.

"Eggs hurled as Ukraine extends Russian naval base lease," *The New Zealand Herald,* April 28, 2010, www.nzherald.co.nz/world/news/article.cfm?c_id=2&objectid=10641314.

Korostelina, Karina. "The impact of national identity on conflict behavior: Comparative analysis of two ethnic minorities in Crimea," *International Journal of Comparative Sociology,* nos. 3–4 (2004): 213–230.

Levy, Clifford J. "Crimean Mosque Project Stirs Debate and Trauma," *New York Times,* October 29, 2009, www.nytimes.com/2009/10/30/world/europe/30crimea.html?_r=1.

"Linguists Urge Crimean Tatars To Switch To Latin Alphabet," Radio Free Europe–Radio Liberty, February 17, 2010, www.rferl.org/content/Linguists_Urge_Crimean_Tatars_To_Switch_To_Latin_Alphabet/1960330.html.

"Pro-Russian activists rally in Ukraine's Crimea," BBC Worldwide Monitoring, December 19, 2009, translation of report from Ukrainian news agency UNIAN, December 19, 2009.

HUNGARIANS
(Romania, Serbia, Slovakia)

Between 2.5 and 3 million ethnic Hungarians, or about a quarter of the total ethnic Hungarian population, live outside Hungary in the countries that border it: Austria, Croatia, Romania, Serbia, Slovakia, and Ukraine. Since 1990 they have increasingly been asserting their identity in a largely peaceful campaign in the countries where their population is greatest. They are focused mainly on cultural autonomy, especially on bolstering their language rights.

Apart from Hungary, which has a population of ten million, the country with the largest number of ethnic Hungarians is Romania, with 1.5 million, or 7 percent of the population. The country where Hungarians constitute the highest proportion of the population is Slovakia, where they make up 10 percent of the population and number 550,000. In Serbia, Hungarians number 300,000, or 4 percent of the population. There are also 160,000 Hungarians in Ukraine, 17,000 in Croatia, 9,000 in Slovenia, and 6,000 in Austria. In Romania, they live mainly in Transylvania, a northwestern region; in Serbia they live predominantly in Vojvodina, a province in the north; and in Slovakia they live mostly in the south.

Hungarians speak Hungarian, which comes from the Finno-Ugric linguistic family that includes Finnish and Estonian. Many ethnic Hungarians also speak the language of the country where they live. Ethnic Hungarians are predominantly Christian, as are most Romanians, Serbs, and Slovaks. They are mainly Catholic in denomination, as are Slovaks; Romanians and Serbs are mostly Orthodox Christian.

The Hungarian community fragmented when Hungary lost two-thirds of the territory it governed and one third of its population at the end of World War I (1914–1918) after supporting the losing axis of Austria, Germany, and Turkey. According to Tibor Szendrei, a Hungarian journalist for the EU affairs newspaper *Europolitics,* "the 1920 Trianon Treaty, which reduced Hungary's territory, was very painful. Quite a few Hungarians still see it as unjust." Szendrei, in an April 2010 telephone interview, said the resulting ethnic tensions had occasionally spilled over into violent clashes, although there has been nothing akin to a separatist insurgency.

The Hungarian minorities do not have autonomous governments in Romania, Serbia, or Slovakia. While desired by some, autonomy would be difficult to obtain because the Hungarian populations do not live in ethnically homogenous, geographically contiguous regions but are instead mixed in with other ethnic groups. Under communist rule from the late 1940s until 1990, the importance of ethnic identity was downplayed. The fall of communism in Eastern Europe triggered a resurgence of nationalism. In this new climate the status of Hungarians outside Hungary has become a contentious issue.

In Romania, support for autonomy or reunification with Hungary is low. Hungarians are officially the largest ethnic minority in Romania, although in fact they are likely outnumbered by Roma (also known as Gypsies) who have historically been undercounted in the census, in part because many Roma do not have a fixed abode. Many Hungarians would like greater control over their education system and an enhanced role for the Hungarian language in public life. Dissatisfaction persists, for example, over the structure of the University of Babes-Bolyai in the city of Cluj-Napoca. Formerly two distinct universities—Babes for Romanian-speakers and Bolyai for Hungarian-speakers—the two were merged in 1959; since then many Hungarians have sought to re-separate the two, thus far unsuccessfully. Hungarian-language schools operate at the primary and secondary levels, and Hungarian-language newspapers and television channels are represented in the media.

In the Serbian province of Vojvodina, Hungarians make up only 14 percent of the population; the remainder is comprised largely of Serbs (65 percent), with some twenty-four other ethnic groups, including Croats, Montenegrins, Roma, Romanians, and Slovaks, forming the balance. While Vojvodina has for part of its history enjoyed autonomy, this status cannot be said to have conferred autonomy on ethnic Hungarians, given Vojvodina's majority-Serbian population.

In Slovakia, there exists a legacy of ill will between Slovaks and Hungarians that stems from a history of Hungarian rule over Slovaks (1000 C.E.–1918). Since Slovaks established their own country in January 1993, they have been promoting Slovak identity—to the detriment, some feel, of Hungarian identity. Some Hungarians in Slovakia are demanding self-government. Given that the Hungarian population is not concentrated in a specific area, it would be difficult to demarcate an autonomous region.

The other major expatriate Hungarian community, in Ukraine, does not have a strong autonomy movement. Poorer than the Hungarians of Romania, Serbia, and Slovakia, their ethnic identity was repressed under Soviet rule from 1945–1991. Since Ukraine became independent in 1991, the Hungarians there have enjoyed increased freedom to campaign for cultural autonomy.

Hungarian governments have generally supported the demands of ethnic Hungarians for greater autonomy and enhanced community rights but have not favored a redrawing of Hungary's borders. Recent years have seen a marked rise in influence of the European Union, which Hungary and Slovakia joined in May 2004, Romania in January 2007, and which Serbia hopes to join by 2014. EU membership has helped to raise the living standards of many Hungarians residing outside of Hungary, especially in Romania and Slovakia, to levels comparable to those inside Hungary, thus muting the economic incentive to immigrate to Hungary.

History

Hungarians were originally from eastern Russia and migrated to their homeland in Central and Eastern Europe in the late ninth century C.E. The founding father of Hungary, King Stephen (he became Saint Stephen posthumously when canonized in 1083), was installed as the first ruler of Hungary in 1000 C.E. Stephen forged a pact with the Roman Catholic Church under which he agreed to convert Hungarians from paganism to Christianity in return for receiving the Pope's approval to rule over the domains that he had conquered. From the early 1500s the Ottoman Turkish Empire increasingly encroached on Hungary, making Transylvania an autonomous Ottoman principality in 1571. Although the Ottomans were Muslim, they did not force the Hungarians to convert to Islam. From the 1600s the Hapsburgs, the Catholic monarchs of Austria, began to eclipse the Ottomans as the dominant power in the region. The Hapsburgs gradually extended their influence over Hungarian domains.

In 1867 Austrian and Hungarian leaders signed The Compromise, an agreement by which the Hungarian and Austrian domains formed their own parliaments and governments. The Hapsburg monarch continued to be the common ruler. This period of dual government, which some Hungarians view as a golden age, ended when Europe's borders were drastically altered at the end of World War I (1914–1918). After 1918 a third of Hungarians found themselves part of the newly constituted states of Czechoslovakia, Romania, and Yugoslavia, while two-thirds remained in a dramatically truncated Hungary.

During World War II (1939–1945) Hungary's alliance with Nazi Germany enabled it to temporarily regain its lost territories, only to lose them again when the Nazis were defeated in 1945. After the war, ninety thousand Hungarians who had been living in Czechoslovakia were expelled and moved to Hungary under the Benes Decrees adopted by the Czechoslovak government-in-exile. From the late 1940s until 1989, ethnic Hungarians lived under communist rule in Czechoslovakia, Hungary, Romania, the Soviet Union, and Yugoslavia. According to journalist Szendrei, "Hungarians outside Hungary could not express their political aspirations in communist times because once they started to speak about autonomy their governments viewed them as separatists." In Romania, Hungarians were forcibly assimilated and moved to other regions under the rule of Nicolae Ceaucescu from 1967–1989. In Czechoslovakia, Hungarians were nominally granted the right to Hungarian-language education in 1968, although in practice this right was not respected.

The collapse of one-party communist rule in Central and Eastern Europe in 1989 and the subsequent emergence of multi-party democracies allowed ethnic Hungarians to organize themselves politically in Romania, Slovakia, and Yugoslavia. The rise of nationalism in these countries brought new problems as Hungarians remained the minority communities. In Yugoslavia in 1990, the government of Serbia—then still a constituent republic of Yugoslavia—revoked the autonomous status granted to Vojvodina in 1974. Yugoslavia began to disintegrate in the early 1990s, finally ceasing to exist in 2006 when Serbia and Montenegro split. Czechoslovakia split itself into the Czech Republic and Slovakia in 1993. The prime minister of Slovakia until 1998, Vladimir Meciar, was a Slovak autocrat who adopted anti-Hungarian language policies, such as prohibiting bilingual signposts.

From 1998, prodded by the EU, Slovakia took steps to extend Hungarian language rights by creating a Hungarian-language university in the city of Komarno that opened in January 2004. Meanwhile in Hungary, voters in December 2004 rejected a proposal to grant ethnic Hungarians living outside Hungary the right to obtain a Hungarian passport. The referendum failed to pass—even though 51 percent of those who voted backed it—because the turnout was too low, just 38 percent of eligible voters. In Slovakia, tensions between Hungarians and Slovaks increased from 2006 following the election of a more nationalistic Slovak government led by Robert Fico. A notable flashpoint was the 2006/2007 controversy surrounding a police investigation into a complaint filed by an ethnic Hungarian student. The alleged victim, Hedviga Malinova, claimed she had been beaten by youths on the street who overheard her speaking Hungarian, but police concluded she fabricated the story.

Leadership

Hungarians have their own political parties in Romania, Serbia, and Slovakia, which tend to campaign for autonomy and language rights rather than for secession or unification with Hungary.

In Romania, the main group is the Democratic Union of Hungarians (UMDR), also known as the Democratic Alliance of Hungarians in Romania. Established in 1989 and led since 1993 by Bela Marko, the UMDR was the junior coalition partner in the Romanian government from 1996–2008. It won 6 percent of the vote in Romania's November 2008 elections, taking 9 seats out of 137 in the Senate and 22 out of 334 in the national assembly. The UMDR was the only Hungarian party in Romania to reach the 5 percent threshold required for parliamentary representation. Other prominent UMDR figures include Executive President Hunor Kelemen and parliamentarian Laszlo Borbely. While the UMDR is moderate, more radical factions have emerged from it. These include the Self-Administration of the Hungarian Community from Transylvania (ACMT), led by Protestant Bishop Laszlo Tokes, and the Hungarian Civic Union (UCM), led by Tibor T. Toro.

In Serbia, many Hungarian political parties have been established since the 1990s. These include the League of Vojvodina Hungarians, led by Istvan Pastor; the Democratic Party of Vojvodina Hungarians (DSVM), established in 1997 and led by Andras Agoston; the Alliance of Vojvodina Hungarians (SVM), established in 1994 and led by Jozsef Kasza; and the Democratic Community of Vojvodina Hungarians (DZVM), established in 1990 and led by Sandor Pal. A coalition of Hungarian parties won 4 seats out of 250 in the May 2008 Serbian parliamentary elections.

In Slovakia, there is the Magyar Koalicio Partja (MKP), or Party of Hungarian Coalition, established in June 1998, whose leaders include Pal Csaky and Jozsef Berenyi. The MKP has called for a self-governing Hungarian region to be established in southern Slovakia. The party won 4 percent of the vote in the June 2010 Slovak elections, failing to win a seat in parliament for the first time since its creation. The MKP served as a junior coalition partner in the Slovak government from 1992–1998 and returned to government again in June 2006. Some MKP members defected from the party in June 2009 to form a more moderate group, Most-Hid, which means "bridge" in Slovak. Most-Hid won 8 percent of the vote in the 2010 elections and entered the Slovak government as a minority coalition partner

In Hungary, the far-right Jobbik party supports the Hungarian autonomy movements outside Hungary and wants to renegotiate the 1920 Trianon Treaty. Hungarians living outside Hungary have begun to represent themselves internationally. In September 2009, the Office for the European Representation of Hungarian National Minorities opened in Brussels, the seat of the EU.

Current Status

In Slovakia, language rights remain an extremely contentious issue. In July 2009, the Slovak government pushed through a law to promote the Slovak language; the law allows the imposition of fines of $6,570 (€5000) on public institutions that fail to use the state language, Slovak. The law applies to districts where minorities form less than 20 percent of the population. Asked about this move at a March 2010 seminar at Johns Hopkins University's School for Advanced International Studies in Washington, D.C., Knut Vollebaek, the Organization for Security and Co-operation in Europe's High Commissioner for National Minorities, said "the law is not necessarily good but it does not breach international standards." Vollebaek added that "the wording was vague. The Slovak and Hungarian governments came to us and we helped the Slovak government develop guidelines, which are now in place."

Hungarian journalist Szendrei in the April 2010 interview described the law as "madness," noting "a Hungarian patient going to see his Hungarian doctor would normally speak Hungarian. Now they are expected to speak Slovak together." Szendrei claimed that "Slovakia is a newly-created entity so its government needs laws like this to keep it unified." The Hungarian autonomy movements continue to campaign for greater linguistic rights, but it is an uphill battle. According to Szendrei, "it is hard to say anymore how many actually speak Hungarian. I know families in Slovakia and Romania where the older generation speaks mostly Hungarian, while the younger generation speaks mainly Romanian and Slovakian because they need to know the host country's language to get a job."

In August 2009, another controversy erupted in Slovakia when Hungarian president Laszlo Solyom was stopped by Slovak authorities while crossing the border into Slovakia. Solyom had been planning to unveil a statue of Hungary's founding father, Saint Stephen, in the predominantly ethnic Hungarian city of Komarno in Slovakia. But the Slovak government decided that Solyom's visit would incite Hungarian separatist fervor and denied him entry. The Slovaks criticized Solyom's timing, noting that the visit coincided with anniversary ceremonies for the 1968 invasion of Czechoslovakia by five armies, including the Hungarian army. The incident put a serious dent in Slovak-Hungarian relations. Even before this spat, inter-ethnic tensions had led to violence at a soccer game in the town of Dunajska Streda in Slovakia, in November 2008. Slovak police beat up Hungarians after rival supporters displayed insulting banners and shouted slogans at one another.

In December 2009, the Serbian Parliament voted to restore the autonomy that had been taken away from Vojvodina in 1989. Hard-line Serbian nationalists criticized Serbia's moderate prime minister, Boris Tadic, for supporting the restoration. According to a December 2009 article on Radio Free Europe's Web site, the Serbian Parliament had "a long and heated debate that included a nationalist deputy throwing his shoe at the parliament's speaker in protest."

In the April 2010 parliamentary elections in Hungary, the far-right Jobbik party, which favors reintegrating all Hungarian-speaking regions into Hungary, won a historically high share of the vote, 16 percent. In June 2010, the Hungarian government passed a law that makes it easier for Hungarians living outside the country to obtain Hungarian citizenship. The law was heavily criticized by the Slovak government, which retaliated by immediately passing a law enabling it to strip Hungarians in Slovakia of their Slovak citizenship should they apply for Hungarian citizenship. Romania, whose ethnic Hungarian community is much larger than Slovakia's, did not raise objections. Romania itself issues Romanian passports to citizens of its neighbor Moldova, which is made up predominantly of ethnic Romanians.

While some Slovaks retain concerns about the irredentist aspirations of Hungarians intent on reuniting all ethnic Hungarians in a single country, for many this issue no longer seems relevant. Hungarians are already reuniting—as citizens of the EU, a border-free trading zone with an ever-strengthening political identity. The changes in the political and economic landscape that EU membership is bringing reduce the likelihood that Hungarians outside of Hungary will pursue secession.

Further Reading

Beary, Brian. "Ethnicity Still Matters in EU-10: Some minorities want greater autonomy," short feature in "The New Europe," *CQ Global Researcher*, August 2007.

Democratic Alliance of Hungarians in Romania Web site, www.rmdsz.ro.

"Frost bite," *The Economist,* August 29, 2009, www.econ omist.com/world/europe/displaystory.cfm?story_id=14313687.

LeBor, Adam. "Hungary's passport law is a diversion," *The Guardian,* June 8, 2010, www.guardian.co.uk/commentisfree/2010/jun/08/hungary-passport-law.

Office for the European Representation of Hungarian National Minorities (HUNINEU) Web site, www .hunineu.eu/index.php?mdl=home.

Party of the Hungarian Coalition in Slovakia Web site, www.mkp.sk/eng.

"Serbia's Vojvodina Regains Autonomy," Radio Free Europe/Radio Liberty, December 15, 2009, www.rferl .org/content/Serbias_Vojvodina_Regains_Autonomy/1904999.html.

"Slovaks defiant over language law," BBC News, July 22, 2009, http://news.bbc.co.uk/2/hi/europe/8162643 .stm.

KARABAKH ARMENIANS
(Azerbaijan)

Since 1994 ethnic Armenians living in Nagorno Karabakh (NK), a small mountainous region of Azerbaijan, a country in the south Caucasus, have enjoyed de facto independence. They secured their separation from Azerbaijan in a war with the Azerbaijani military fought from 1992–1994. But NK's independence has never been recognized by any country, and it remains a separatist enclave. The conflict in NK is sometimes referred to as a "frozen conflict," meaning that while hostilities have mostly ceased, its status is undetermined.

The NK population is 138,000, or 1.5 percent of the Azerbaijan population. A further 18,000 Armenians live in other parts of Azerbaijan. NK residents are 95 percent ethnic Armenian, which sets them apart from the rest of Azerbaijan, which is made up of 91 percent Azeris, an ethnically Turkic people. Karabakh Armenians speak Armenian and are Christian, in contrast to Azeris, who speak Azerbaijani and are mostly Sunni Muslim. To the west of NK lies the state of Armenia, a country with three million Armenians.

NK is technically landlocked inside Azerbaijan, having no border with Armenia or any other country. In practice, however, it has been connected to Armenia via the so-called Lachin corridor, an area comprised of seven districts surrounding Karabakh that ethnic Armenian forces from both NK and Armenia seized control of in 1992. Consequently, 22 percent of Azerbaijan's territory is now under Armenian control. NK proper accounts for one third of the Azerbaijani territory that is under Armenian occupation, with the surrounding districts making up two thirds of the area. Once predominantly populated by Azeris, the Lachin corridor has since the war been transformed into an Armenian enclave, with new houses being built and old ones redistributed. Lachin, for example, has gone from a town of 47,000 Azeris and Kurds to one of 10,000 Armenians.

Karabakh Armenians claim that their region has historically been populated by Armenians and as such should not be governed by Azerbaijan. The grievances they had while still under Azerbaijan's control (pre-1992) included an alleged lack of educational and cultural rights and neglect of Armenian monuments. Both NK and Azerbaijan are generally poorer than Armenia. Karabakh Armenians claimed they were worse off than Azeris, too, although the Azeri authorities disputed this. Since the war, NK has severed links with Azerbaijan, dismantling for example a railroad linking NK to the Azeri capital Baku. At the same time NK has strengthened its links with Armenia by constructing power lines and roads to Armenia. Author and state-building expert Seth Kaplan wrote in his 2008 book, *Fixing Fragile States,* that "commercial and social contact between the two peoples [Armenians and Azeris], who had lived as neighbors for centuries and who continue to work alongside one another in markets, retail stores, and restaurants in Georgia and Russia, are almost non-existent across their common border." The Armenian government issues passports to NK residents wishing to travel abroad.

There has been considerable international attention paid to the NK dispute. The main multilateral body trying to keep the peace and broker a long-term settlement is the Organization for Security and Co-operation in Europe (OSCE). It has set up the Minsk Group, a mechanism to facilitate negotiations that is co-chaired by France, Russia, and the United States. No agreement has been reached thus far on deploying an international peace-keeping force to NK, which means the 1994 cease-fire has been largely self-regulated. The OSCE has been criticized for being too focused on promoting contacts between top officials in the central Armenian and Azeri governments instead of giving the Karabakhs, both Armenian and Azeri, greater prominence. However, neither the Armenian nor Azeri governments have been keen to enhance the Karabakhs' role in the talks.

Russia, which lies on the northern Azerbaijan border but is not connected to NK directly, has not supported NK's secession effort, even though Moscow is one of Armenia's closest allies. Russia has military bases in Azerbaijan that it rents out from the Azeri government. The European Union and the United States have devoted some resources to resolving the NK dispute, motivated in part by Azerbaijan's geostrategic significance as a major source and transit country for oil and gas.

The United States has advanced the idea of NK remaining part of Azerbaijan but retaining a large degree of autonomy, including having its own currency and army. Turkey, which has close relations with its fellow-Turkic nation Azerbaijan and has historically had difficult relations with Armenians, has supported Azeri efforts to keep NK. In a show of solidarity, the Turks closed their border with Armenia in 1993 during the conflict, only reopening it in October 2009.

Essentially, NK has four options: (1) continue as a de facto yet unrecognized independent state; (2) have its independence legitimized internationally; (3) reintegrate itself into Azerbaijan in some form; or (4) annex itself to Armenia. If NK is reintegrated into Azerbaijan, it is likely to acquire special autonomous status and be allowed to retain a channel by which it connects to Armenia.

History

NK has been self-governing for much of its history, although regional powers have constantly competed with one another to gain sovereignty over it. The region came under Persian control in 1603 after the Persians edged out their main geopolitical rival, the Ottoman Turks. In the early 1800s the region came under Russian control. In the meantime, successive waves of Azeri immigration to the region effectively separated NK's Armenian population from co-ethnics in Armenia. In February 1918, toward the end of World War I (1914–1918), NK was integrated into a newly created Trans-Caucasian Federation of Armenia, Azerbaijan, and Georgia. When this federation collapsed in May 1918, NK became part of Azerbaijan after the latter declared independence from Russia.

Russia regained regional control of the Caucasus in 1920 and made NK part of a newly constituted Soviet Republic of Armenia. In 1923 the emerging leader of the Soviet Union, Joseph Stalin, who was Commissar for Nationalities at the time, transferred

NK to the Azerbaijani Soviet Republic and designated it an autonomous *oblast* (region). NK's status remained unchanged until 1988 when Armenia and Azerbaijan—both still part of the Soviet Union—began arguing over who should administer it. In February 1988, the NK autonomous government, encouraged by the greater political freedoms that Soviet leader Mikhail Gorbachev had introduced, asked for the transfer of NK to Armenia. The Soviet authorities briefly attempted to rule NK directly from Moscow before returning it to Azerbaijani control in November 1989. On August 30, 1991, Azerbaijan declared independence from the Soviet Union, taking NK with it; Armenia declared independence on September 23, 1991.

The NK authorities organized a referendum on independence in December 1991, which passed, although the Karabakh Azeri minority boycotted the vote. The NK Parliament declared independence on January 6, 1992; this action added fire to the ethnic violence that had been on the rise since 1988, and thereafter a full-scale war broke out between Armenians and Azeris. By May 1994, when a cease-fire was signed, Armenian troops had secured control of over 90 percent of NK as well as the surrounding Azeri districts. Thirty thousand people were killed in the war, and human rights violations such as hostage-taking, indiscriminate shelling, and summary executions were committed by both sides. The conflict changed NK's demographics dramatically as the Karabakh Azeri minority fled, their numbers dwindling from 22 percent of NK in 1989 to less than 5 percent by 2010; the Armenian share of the population rose from 75 to 95 percent. In addition, 724,000 Azeris and Kurds fled Armenia and NK to resettle in Azerbaijan, and 413,000 Armenians fled from Azerbaijan to resettle in Armenia and NK.

By 2007 the cease-fire was barely holding; some three thousand people had been killed in intermittent violence since 1994. At the same time, the region's geostrategic importance was growing as a result of its oil and gas reserves. When a major oil pipeline (BTC) was constructed running from the Azeri capital, Baku, to Ceyhun in Turkey, it bypassed Armenia and took a more circuitous route through Georgia in order to avoid the Armenian-Azeri dispute over NK. According to author Kaplan, the BTC pipeline "signaled the rise of Azerbaijan from a backwater state to a significant energy supplier to the west and a strategic partner of the U.S." It gave the Azeris a generous source of income that was used to strengthen its military, which had been comprehensively defeated by the Armenians in the war. The OSCE's Minsk Group meanwhile continued mediating talks, but failed to score a major breakthrough. In December 2006, NK held another referendum in which 99 percent voted for independence. The result was not recognized internationally.

Leadership

Karabakh Armenians have since 1992 operated a de facto independent state that has its own legislature, executive, and military, and is based in the city of Stepanakert. The legislature consists of a single-chamber, thirty-three-seat parliament whose most recent elections were held in May 2010. The main political parties are the Democratic Artsakh Party, the Free Homeland Party, the Armenian Revolution Federation-Dashnaktsutyun, and Movement 88. NK is subdivided into regions and communities and has elected local self-governing bodies, with elected heads in the larger towns. On the military side, according to an International Crisis Group (ICG) report on NK from September 2005, it "may be the world's most militarized society." NK has 18,500 soldiers, 10,000 from Armenia and 8,500 from NK, plus 20–30,000 reserves, which means that 6 percent of the NK population serves in the army. The Armenian government supplies the NK army with weapons; the army units themselves are officially NK-controlled.

The Azeri government has characterized the NK leaders as warlords. In contrast, the NK authorities have tried to legitimize themselves on the international stage by pointing out that they have a democratically elected president and an army under civilian control. In 2000 NK president Arkady Ghukasian sacked and jailed the commander-in-chief of the NK army, Samvel Babayan. Babayan was convicted of attempting to assassinate the president. After this incident the army's political influence declined. The political leadership in NK tends to be more hard-line than in Armenia on the question of NK's status.

The first president of the breakaway NK republic was Robert Kocharian, elected by the NK Parliament in 1994 and by popular vote in November 1996. In a sign of how close Karabakh Armenians have grown to Armenia, Kocharian went on to become prime minister of Armenia on March 20, 1997. Other leading NK politicians include former president Ghukasian, who served from 1997–2007; Bako Sahakian, president since 2007; Georgi Petrosian, foreign minister since 2005; and Anushavan Danielian, prime minister from 1999–2007.

The internally displaced NK Azeri minority has recently grown more organized, holding its first officially sponsored Congress on June 5, 2009. The Karabakh Armenians have thus far refused to negotiate directly with Karabakh Azeris or allow them a say in determining NK's final status. "Policies of mutual exclusion have long impeded dialogue," the ICG concluded in an October 2009 report. In neighboring Armenia, some parties, including the Armenian Pan-National Movement, which was established in 1989 by Levon Ter-Petrossian, would like NK to formally secede from Azerbaijan as a prelude to its being annexed by Armenia.

Current Status

By early 2008, NK and Armenian leaders were insisting that NK's independence was irreversible. Years of propaganda had hardened public opinion, leaving politicians little reason to make compromises. Maps were being sold in Armenia that showed not just NK as part of Armenia, but also the seven surrounding districts Armenians have occupied since 1992 as part of Armenia. Towns in these occupied districts have been given Armenian names, and Azeri buildings and infrastructure has been destroyed. The military standoff continues, with Armenian and Azeri troops separated by as little as forty meters. Small-scale armed skirmishes increased from early 2008, with greater use of mortars being reported as both the Azeri and Armenian governments boosted military spending. The drift toward maintenance of the status quo occurred in part, argued state-building expert Kaplan, because Western powers like the EU and the United States have been overly passive in their mediation efforts. Kaplan added that the continuation of international aid and investment to both Armenia and Azerbaijan was providing little incentive for compromise.

The dynamics changed, however, after the August 2008 war between neighboring Georgia and its secessionist republic, South Ossetia (see separate essay). Russia helped South Ossetia consolidate its independence from Georgia but notably did not adopt this policy towards NK, much to the disappointment of Armenia. Indeed, the Georgia–South Ossetia conflict tended to focus minds on resolving the NK conflict. By late 2008, the presidents of Armenia and Azerbaijan were making conciliatory statements. A thawing of relations between pro-Azerbaijan Turkey and Armenia in 2009 helped to advance the negotiations for a final settlement. So, too, did Russian president Dmitry Medvedev's attempts to assume a role of honest broker in a bid to curry respect and influence in the region. The political landscape shifted in the opposite direction, however, in July 2010 when the International Court of Justice ruled that Kosovo's February 2008 declaration of independence from Serbia did not violate international law. Drawing strength from the ruling, the secessionist Nagorno Karabakh foreign ministry said it had "an extremely important legal, political, and moral significance and sets a precedent that cannot be confined to Kosovo."

The most difficult issue to be resolved remains NK's final legal status. It is plausible that a comprehensive agreement will lead to a referendum on independence. If that happens, the key players will need to agree on whether the thousands of Azeris who fled NK in the early 1990s can vote. If the NK Azeris are allowed to vote, an independence referendum would probably still pass given that Armenians remain a solid majority. Another unresolved issue is whether to allow over a million Armenian and Azeri refugees displaced by the 1992–1994 conflict to return home. A settlement will also have to stipulate whether Armenians would be permitted to continue occupying the Azeri districts that connect NK to Armenia. The Azeri government is adamant that the Armenians must withdraw from these territories; Karabakh Armenians, for their part, are just as determined to retain control over them for the sake of security. On June 26, 2010, the leaders of France, Russia, and the United States issued a joint statement on NK urging Armenia and Azerbaijan to continue moving forward toward a peace settlement. The statement called for the status of NK "to be determined in the future by a legally-binding expression of will, the right of all internally-displaced persons and refugees to return, and international security guarantees, including a peacekeeping operation."

Any long-term peace deal is likely to also involve the deployment of an international peacekeeping force. By the end of 2009, there were just six OSCE officials monitoring the 1994 cease-fire, equipped with a weak mandate to investigate cease-fire violations. If a bigger force is deployed and given greater powers, the question of which countries' forces should be represented will be a sensitive one. Iran, Azerbaijan's southerly neighbor, is reportedly uneasy about the prospect of an international force stationed on its borders that would include troops from its longtime political foe, the United States. The policy that Russia adopts will be crucial in determining what happens to the Karabakh Armenians. If Moscow backs NK secession, as it has done in Abkhazia and South Ossetia, it will be much more difficult for Azerbaijan to reintegrate the region. And if NK does split from Azerbaijan, residents' immediate dilemma will be whether to remain independent or unify with Armenia.

Further Reading

Baghdasarian, Gegham. "A Karabakh Armenian perspective," *Conciliation Resources*, 2005, www.c-r.org/our-work/accord/nagorny-karabakh/karabakh-armenian-perspective.php.

De Waal, Thomas. *Black Garden: Armenia and Azerbaijan through Peace and War.* New York: New York University, 2003.

Huseynov, Tabib. "A Karabakh Azeri perspective," *Conciliation Resources*, 2005, www.c-r.org/our-work/accord/nagorny-karabakh/karabakh-azeri-perspective.php.

International Crisis Group. "Nagorno-Karabakh: Getting to a Breakthrough," *Europe Briefing*, no. 55 (October 7, 2009), www.crisisgroup.org/home/index.cfm?id=6338&CFID=31946915&CFTOKEN=22157002.

———. "Nagorno-Karabakh: Viewing the Conflict from the Ground," *Europe Report*, no. 166 (September 14, 2005), www.crisisgroup.org/library/documents/europe/caucasus/166_nagorno_karabakh_viewing_the_conflict_from_the_ground.pdf.

Kaplan, Seth. *Fixing Fragile States: A New Paradigm for Development.* Westport, Conn: Praeger Security International, 2008.

"Karabakh Armenians Buoyed By Kosovo 'Precedent,'" *Radio Free Europe*, July 27, 2010.

NORTH CAUCASIANS
(Russia)

Since the early 1990s, the North Caucasus region in southern Russia has been severely affected by violence, much of it separatist-inspired. This has been most evident in the autonomous republic of Chechnya, which has fought two wars for independence with Russia since 1994. But there are dozens of other ethnic groups, including Cherkess, Ingush, and Ossetian, that are also seeking greater autonomy or independence. The diffuse and diverse nature of the ethnic strife has made the North Caucasus one of the most unstable regions in the world.

The conflict zone is primarily concentrated in six nominally autonomous Russian republics: Chechnya, Dagestan, Ingushetia, Kabardino-Balkaria, Karachay-Cherkessia, and North Ossetia. This region is ethnically heterogeneous, a legacy of the Soviet era when authorities deliberately constructed multi-ethnic administrative units to weaken ethnic identity. When the Soviet Union was dissolved in 1991, some of these ethnic groups began to fight for greater independence from Moscow.

North Caucasians number about six million, or 4 percent, of Russia's total population of 140 million. Five of the six North Caucasian republics occupy a relatively small area stretching about 250 miles from east-west and 100 miles north-south. The sixth republic, Dagestan, is larger, stretching some 300 miles north-south and 150 miles east-west. The North Caucasus region is bordered to the south by Azerbaijan and Georgia, both of which are contending with their own separatist enclaves: Nagorno-Karabakh in Azerbaijan and Abkhazia and South Ossetia in Georgia (see separate essays). There are dozens of different but related languages spoken in the region; many of its inhabitants also speak Russian, and there are significant minorities of ethnic Russians living among them. Islam is the dominant religion, although there are some Christians, too; the Ossetians, for example, are mainly Eastern Orthodox.

The latest Russian census figures, which date from 2002, give the following population estimates per ethnic group: 80,000 Balkars, 1.36 million Chechens, 50,000 Cherkess, 413,000 Ingush, 393,000 Kabards, 165,000 Karachay, and 514,000 Ossetians. Hidden within these figures are the Circassians, a people whom Soviet—and later Russian—authorities divided up into three subgroups based on where they lived. Some Circassians would like to see these groups—the Adygei (population 100,000), Cherkess, and Kabard—united in a single Circassian territory.

Dagestan stands out from the other republics in being extremely heterogenous. With a population of 2.6 million, most of whom are Muslim, Dagestan has fourteen official ethnic minorities. The largest group is the Avars (814,000, or 29 percent of Dagestan's population), who have historically had tense relations with the Kumyks (422,000, or 14 percent), a Turkic-speaking people from the lowlands. Dagestan also contains Lezgins (412,000, or 13 percent), an ethnic group territorially divided between Russia and Azerbaijan. Another influential minority in Dagestan is the Dargins (16 percent), who converted to Islam in the eighth century C.E. and who compete with the Avars for control of the political leadership of Dagestan. The Dargins held the presidency of Dagestan from 1983 until 2006, when an Avar, Mukhu Aliyev, became president. The Avars and Kumyks had their own principalities before Russia colonized the region in the 1800s.

The region has been a zone of conflict since the early nineteenth century and remains one of the most militarized places in the world. There are well over a dozen militant groups based there. These groups pursue varying goals. In some instances, the aim is to subjugate a rival insurgent group; in others, to achieve greater autonomy for their republic. And in still other cases a group is seeking self-determination or independence for their people. The insurgents have tended to target the Russian military, local police, and government officials. The total numbers killed throughout the North Caucasus from 1994–2009 is estimated at 75,000–100,000, according to academics and regional experts Kristin Bakke, John O'Loughlin, and Michael Ward. In a November 2009 article in *Annals of the Association of American Geographers*, they acknowledged that the focus of their paper—reconciliation—was somewhat premature in that "we are not yet in a post-war situation so little reconciliation has been possible."

The republic that has seen the highest levels of violence since 1990 has been Chechnya. The Chechens fought wars with the Russian authorities from 1994–1996 and from 1999–2007. The Russian government admits to having had four thousand soldiers killed since 1990 as a result of the Chechen conflict, although the true figure is thought to be much higher as attacks in the region are relatively underreported. The Chechen conflict caused tens of thousands of people to flee their homes. Some of these have returned home, either because the security situation has improved or because local officials pressured them into doing so. Between 2004 and 2009, forty-six thousand Internally Displaced Persons returned home from Dagestan and Ingushetia, with most ending up in Chechnya.

Russia, an independent country again since 1991, has never been tolerant of separatism. However, its policy became particularly hard-line under the leadership of Vladimir Putin, Russia's prime minister from 1999–2000, president from 2000–2008, and prime minister again since 2008. Putin was not slow to order the Russian military to use often brutal force to restore order and central authority in the North Caucasus. Putin's willingness to deploy tough tactics after he was made prime minister in August 1999 made him popular with many Russians and helped him to become president in May 2000. Putin used the terrorist attacks of September 11, 2001, on the United States, which were masterminded by the Islamist al Qaeda group, as a further pretext for clamping down hard on separatist dissent in the predominantly Muslim North Caucasus. Putin's justifications gained more traction as the separatists did become increasingly Islamist-oriented from 2000 and developed links with Islamist militants in Afghanistan, Egypt, Jordan, and Pakistan. Although human rights groups have constantly highlighted human rights abuses carried out by the Russian authorities in the North Caucasus, Western governments' condemnation of Russia has been more muted since the September 11 attacks.

A distinguishing characteristic in the tensions between the North Caucasus peoples and the

Russian government is the religious dimension. Most North Caucasians are Muslim, while most Russians are Christian (generally of Russian Orthodox denomination), atheist, or agnostic. There has been a growing tendency among North Caucasians to reintroduce Islamic traditions and laws, a trend that the predominantly secular Russian government has eyed with suspicion. According to Gregory Shvedov, a Caucasus-based journalist and editor with the Caucasian Knot, an Internet-based news agency, the rise in the popularity of Islamic courts is understandable given the prevailing lawlessness. "The regular courts do not work and the governments are corrupt. Many in the region who are not Islamist insurgents support adopting Sharia or Islamic law because it gives them some recourse to justice," he said at a February 2010 seminar at the Center for Strategic and International Studies (CSIS) in Washington, D.C. In Chechnya, a decree adopted in 2006 requiring women entering government institutions to wear headscarves was still being enforced at the end of 2009, the U.S. State Department noted in its annual human rights report on Russia released in March 2010. The State Department said that while polygamy remained illegal in Chechnya, local authorities were encouraging Chechen men to take more than one wife.

While conflict has been persistent in the North Caucasus since 1990, the motivations behind the fighting vary considerably from republic to republic. The Chechens have tended to be the most pro-independence group. The priority for the Ingush, by contrast, has been to retake Prigorodony, a region it ceded to neighboring North Ossetia in 1957. Ingush militias clashed with the North Ossetian military over Prigorodony in 1992, although there has been no large-scale fighting since then. Whereas Chechens have a centuries-old attachment to the Islamic faith, the Ingush converted to Islam relatively late, in the 1860s. The leadership of North Ossetia has tended to be more loyal to Moscow than has the leadership in

Chechnya. There was, however, an anti-government insurgency in North Ossetia in 2005–2006.

Dagestan, despite its multi-ethnic makeup in which various groups compete for political power in the regional government, has also seen the growth of a pro-independence movement. The movement is believed to have close links with separatists in neighboring Chechnya. But according to a June 2008 report from the International Crisis Group (ICG), "Dagestan is not a second Chechnya. Secession has no public support, but the porous border between the two republics has contributed to the problems." An Islamist group called Shariat Jamaat has carried out much of the violence, killing hundreds of security forces, politicians, administrators, and journalists since 2003, the report noted. The ICG found that while in the early 1990s some Dagestanis wanted their republic to be carved up along ethnic lines, these calls "have faded and been replaced by greater commitment to Dagestani unity."

In the western part of the North Caucasus, the largest group seeking more autonomy are the Circassians. One of their grievances is the failure of Russia to acknowledge a genocide some Circassians claim Russia conducted in the 1800s in which 1.5 million Circassians were massacred or deported from their homeland. The several-million-strong Circassian community is concentrated in Russia, Turkey, Jordan, and Syria. According to Fatima Tlisova, a U.S.-based Circassian journalist writing in January 2010 in the *Eurasia Daily Monitor*, a publication of the Washington, D.C.-based think tank The Jamestown Foundation, "today only less than one million Circassians remain in their homeland. The majority of them live in three North Caucasus republics separated by artificial boundaries, officially identified as Kabardins, Cherkess, Adygs, Shapsugs—that is, not by their ethnic names but by their geographic locations." Tlisova said that "by cutting Circassian territory into separate pieces and giving them different names, Russia effectively achieved the aim of eradicating the national identity of Circassians, as well as visually erasing Circassia from the geopolitical map of the region."

History

The North Caucasus peoples have come under various outside influences over the past two thousand years, including that of the Byzantines, Persians, Arabs, Mongols, and Ottomans. However, the dominant power from the 1700s has been Russia. The North Caucasians came under Russian control at different periods, with the Ossetians, for example, subjugated as early as 1774. Most of the others became integrated into the Russian Empire during the Russian-Caucasian wars that were fought from 1817–1864. The Chechens and the peoples of Dagestan were among those who resisted the Russians most fiercely, with the Chechens finally surrendering to the Russians in 1864.

When the Russian Empire collapsed at the end of World War I (1914–1918) and was replaced by the Soviet Union, the territorial boundaries were redrawn and the peoples were accorded various and changing forms of self-government. Chechens were given autonomy in 1922, but in 1934 they were merged with Ingushetia to form an autonomous region called the Chechen-Ingush republic. In 1934 North Ossetians formed their own autonomous republic. The Soviets created the autonomous region of Kabardino-Balkaria in 1922 and made it an autonomous republic in 1936. Dagestan was another autonomous republic, one where the central authorities in Moscow succeeded in keeping tight control by exploiting divisions between Dagestan's many ethnic groups.

Many ethnic Russians immigrated to the North Caucasus from the 1920s. During World War II (1939–1945), Soviet leader Joseph Stalin deported hundreds of thousands of North Caucasians to Central Asia to punish them for alleged collaboration with Nazi Germany, whose troops had invaded the Soviet Union in June 1941. Many of those deported died either during the train journey or within their first year of arriving in their new home. The episode inflicted a deep and lasting wound on Russian-Caucasian relations. Most of the deportees were allowed to return home from the mid-1950s by Stalin's successor, Nikita Khrushchev, who rolled back some of Stalin's harsher policies. In 1957 Khrushchev reestablished the Chechen-Ingush republic, which had been broken up into various administrative units in 1944. He also ordered that part of Ingushetia—Prigorodny—be handed over to North Ossetia. Many Ossetians had migrated to Prigorodny in the 1940s after the Ingush, who had been living there, were deported. The Balkars of Kabardino-Balkaria were allowed to return from exile in 1956 but were not given back the lands they had lost.

As the political climate became somewhat more relaxed in the 1970s, nationalism began to grow in the North Caucasus. The Soviets adopted a new constitution in 1977 that in theory permitted individual republics to withdraw from the union, although in practice no republic attempted to secede. When the Soviet Union was dissolved in December 1991, the North Caucasian republics became part of the Russian federation. Russia, in adopting a new constitution in 1993, did not adopt a provision permitting its constituent republics to secede.

Chechnya first declared its independence in November 1991. It was not until December 1994, however, that Russia launched a full-scale military invasion of Chechnya. The Chechens resisted fiercely, but in February 1995 the Russians captured the Chechen capital Grozny. Ten thousand Russians and twenty-five thousand Chechens were killed in the fighting. Chechen gunmen in June 1995 seized a hospital in the southern Russian town of Budennovsk, holding a thousand people hostage until the hostage-takers were given safe passage to Chechnya. This confrontation with Russian forces led to the deaths of 120 people and was viewed as a humiliation for Russia. Meanwhile, there were sporadic

skirmishes between Chechen and Russian forces, and Chechen militia groups carried out many kidnappings and killings. A peace settlement between the Russian and Chechen authorities was signed in August 1996 in Khasavyurt, Dagestan.

Under the leadership of Vladimir Putin from 1999–2008 Russia became more hard-line in repressing separatism, all the while enduring thousands of attacks, although it was not always clear which of these attacks were separatist-motivated. From 1999 the Chechen conflict began to spill over into the surrounding republics and even into the heart of Russia. In October 2002, for example, forty-one Chechen separatists took eight hundred people hostage in a Moscow theater. A siege ensued; when Russian forces ultimately stormed the theater all of the rebels and 130 hostages were killed. The deadliest—and a particularly heinous—incident arising from the

Chechen conflict occurred in October 2004 when a pro-Chechen militia took over and occupied a school filled with youngsters in Beslan, North Ossetia. When Russian troops stormed the school 30 rebels and 340 hostages, many of them children, were killed. A key political development came about in March 2003 when 96 percent of Chechen voters backed a constitution making Chechnya a self-governing republic with an elected parliament and president.

Ingushetia separated itself from the Chechnya-Ingush republic in 1991 and declared itself an autonomous republic within Russia in June 1992. Russian authorities backed the Ingush, believing this would weaken Chechnya's bid for independence. Tensions between the Ingush and the North Ossetians over Prigorodny had been on the rise since September 1990 when the North Ossetian government suspended the citizenship rights of its Ingush minority. Russia's president, Boris Yeltsin, deployed troops in 1992 to calm the fighting between Ingush and Ossetians. Meanwhile, the North Ossetians were providing assistance to the South Ossetians in neighboring Georgia, where in 1991 the separatist enclave of South Ossetia had been established (see separate essay). Some Ossetians called for North and South Ossetia to be merged into a single autonomous region. North Ossetian militants targeted the Russian military from 2000 and carried out attacks on passenger trains. Ingush-Ossetian tensions flared again after the 2004 Beslan attacks, for which the North Ossetians blamed Ingushetia. In June 2006, the Ingush Parliament demanded that North Ossetia return Prigorodny.

Thousands of refugees from the Chechen conflict of 1994–1996 fled eastward into neighboring Dagestan. Relations between Dagestan and Chechnya deteriorated in the late 1990s due to the efforts by some Chechens to incorporate part of Dagestan—the city of Khasavyurt—into Chechnya. In August 1999, Islamist warlords Ibn Al-Khattab, a Jordanian by birth, and Shamil Basayev, a Chechen, who were increasingly expanding their network into other republics, declared a Chechen-Dagestani Islamic state; thereafter their followers invaded Dagestan. This triggered a deployment of Russian troops, who repelled the rebels within a couple of weeks. The ICG's June 2008 report noted that "the violence in Dagestan is mainly caused by jihadi fighters, not inter-ethnic tensions."

In Karachay-Cherkessia, the regional parliament declared a republic in November 1990. However, this move masked deep divisions between the Karachays, who wanted their own state, and the Cherkess, who wanted to unite with other Circassian peoples in the region. Kabardino-Balkaria declared its sovereignty in November 1991, while the Balkars' own parliament in December 1991 voted to create a separate Balkar republic within Russia, reconfirming this demand in November 1996. The Kabard-dominated regional government arrested Balkar

activists in response and banned Balkar political parties. In May 2005, Balkars protested against a planned revision of Kabardino-Balkaria's administrative subdivisions. The Kabardino-Balkarian government responded by banning Balkars from holding a referendum on the issue.

By late 2007, the violence had died down somewhat in Chechnya but was increasing in other republics, especially in Dagestan and Ingushetia. In July 2007, the Russian government deployed an extra 2,500 troops to Ingushetia in response to a growing number of attacks on pro-Russian targets.

Leadership

While the North Caucasian Russian republics have various degrees of autonomy, the past decade has seen a concerted effort by the Russian government to reassert control over the region. In January 2010, for example, Russian president Dmitry Medvedev created a new North Caucasian Federal District and appointed a high-profile businessman and politician, Alexander Khloponin, as special envoy to the region.

The dominant political figure in Chechnya is President Ramzan Kadyrov. A former separatist rebel and warlord, Kadyrov has since reconciled with the Russian authorities and is no longer demanding independence for Chechnya. He has gradually strengthened his grip on power in Chechnya, becoming prime minister in March 2006 and president in February 2007. Kadyrov has achieved some popularity among Chechens for having rebuilt the republic after the war and for establishing relative stability. However, he has also accrued a growing list of critics because of his persistent human rights violations. The Chechen president from 1991 until he was killed in a rocket attack in April 1996 was Dzhokhar Dudayev. He was succeeded by Zelimkhan Yandaribev, who entered into a cease-fire agreement with Russian president Yeltsin. Yandaribev was defeated in the February 1997 presidential elections by Aslan Maskhadov. In February 1999, Maskhadov issued a decree ordering the imposition of Islamic law in Chechnya. That same month Chechen military leaders established an Islamic Council and elected Shamil Basayev its leader. In October 2003, Akhmad Kadyrov (father of future president Ramzan Kadyrov) was elected president, winning 80 percent of the vote. Kadyrov, who was pro-Moscow, was assassinated in May 2004. His successor was Alu Alkhanov, elected president in August 2004 with 74 percent of the vote.

In Ingushetia, the local leadership is perceived as being particularly close to Moscow. The Ingush president from 2002 was Murad Zyazikov, who was replaced in October 2008 by Yunus-bek Yevkurov. In North Ossetia, the president from 1998 was Aleksandr Dzasokhov, who was succeeded by Taymuraz Mamsurov in May 2005.

In Dagestan, the president is not as powerful a figure. Rather, power is wielded by a dozen influential oligarchs. The Islamic religious leaders, or imams, exert strong influence through their control of the Hajj, the pilgrimage Muslims are supposed to make to Mecca at least once in their lifetime. The Dagestani president since 2006 has been an Avar, Mukhu Aliyev. From 1983–2006 Dagestan was led by an ethnic Dargin, Magomedali Magomedov. A Dagestani-based Islamist group, Shariat Jamaat, was established in 1999 by Rasul Makasharipov. The group pledged allegiance in 2007 to Doku Umarov, a Chechen warlord, and adopted as its goal the creation of a North Caucasian emirate. Another group, the United North Caucasian Front, joined with Shariat Jamaat in 2005.

There is also a separatist movement among the Lezgin people. In 1990 the Lezgin Democrat Movement Sadval (Unity) was established, and in December 1991 a Lezgin National Council was created with the goal of unifying all Lezgins in a single territory. There are 412,000 Lezgins in Dagestan and a further 178,000 living in the neighboring country of Azerbaijan. In 1995 the Aplan party was set up, which called for a new state, Lezgistan, made up of Lezgin-populated regions in Russia and Azerbaijan. The Lezgin separatist movement was weakened by a split in 1998 between a radical pro-independence faction and a moderate pro-autonomy faction. In March 1999, the Federal Lezgin National Cultural Autonomy Organization was established to push for greater cultural freedom.

In Kabardino-Balkaria, the minority Balkar people set up a party, Tere, to protest the Kabards' domination of the government. The president of Kabardino-Balkaria since September 2005 has been Arsen Kanokov, a Kabard. The leadership of Kabardino-Balkaria sought to assert greater independence in the 1990s, although from 2000 it faced pressure from Moscow authorities to suppress separatism. North Caucasus journalist Tlisova reported in a November 2009 article for The Jamestown Foundation that the Kabardino-Balkaria parliament had, in a 39–37 vote, amended the republic's 1996 constitution. The lawmakers erased a clause that proclaimed that the people of Kabardino-Balkaria were "the highest authority," in response to a ruling from the Russian constitutional court that insisted the "people of the Russian federation" were the highest authority. The parliament also erased a clause that put the Circassian language on an equal footing with Russian. The parliament of Adygea, a Russian republic 100 miles west of Kabardino-Balkaria where 100,000 Circassians live, deleted this clause, too. Given that most Circassians actually live outside Russia, international groups, such as the World Circassian Association based in Kabardino-Balkaria, have been established to advance their interests.

In Karachay-Cherkessia the unelected leader from 1979–1999 was Vladimir Khubiev, a Karachay. He was succeeded in May 1999 in the republic's first free presidential election by Vladimir Semyonov, who is half-Karachay, half-Russian. Semyonov was succeeded in 2003 by another Karachay, Mustafa Batdyev. Batdyev was succeeded in 2008 by Boris Ebzeyev.

Ramzan Kadyrov (1976–   ) and Akhmad Kadyrov (1951–2004)

AP Photo/Musa Sadulayer

RAMZAN KADYROV was born in the Chechen town of Tsentoroi, the son of **Akhmad Kadyrov**, a Chechen separatist born to a dissident Chechen family who had been expelled to the Kazakh Soviet republic. Both Akhmad and Ramzan fought in the first Chechen war as militia leaders, and in 1995 Akhmad was named the Chief Mufti of the secessionist Chechen Republic. As Chief Mufti, Akhmad declared the war against Russia a *jihad*, or holy war.

Akhmad was a moderate Muslim often at odds with those who followed more strict and conservative versions of Islam. One such version, Wahabism, an ultra-conservative interpretation of Islam, took hold of many of the Chechen armies that remained after the de facto independence of the region. Moreover, several Islamic boarding schools had been built specifically to support militant Wahabi groups. The theological split between radical Wahabis and moderate secularists spurred numerous arguments between the two factions. For example, many Wahabis wished to see the moderate president, Aslan Maskhadov (elected in 1997) overthrown.

Akhmad viewed the extremists as outsiders who were threatening the more moderate Chechen Sufi traditions and state. He disapproved when Wahabi Chechen warlords, part of the Islamic International Peacekeeping Brigade, invaded the neighboring Russian republic of Dagestan in August 1999 to support a group of militant Islamists. The boiling religious rivalry eventually pushed Akhmad to leave the Chechen secessionist insurgency and support the Russian forces during the Second Chechen War. He was subsequently stripped of his position as Chief Mufti, after which both father and son led militias with Russian support.

In June 2000, Russian president Vladimir V. Putin appointed Akhmad interim head of the Chechen government in recognition of his newly adopted, pro-Russia stance and his moderate religious views. Rebels continued bombing, but nevertheless Akhmad proved popular, winning the presidency of Chechnya in October 2003. Akhmad worked to secure amnesty for former rebel fighters and allowed them to join the Chechen police forces or Chechen militias if they surrendered.

Akhmad Kadyrov was assassinated on May 9, 2004, killed by a bomb in the Dinamo soccer stadium in Grozny during a Soviet Victory Day military parade. After his father's assassination, Ramzan Kadyrov was appointed deputy prime minister, moving up from his previous position as head of the Chechen Presidential Security Service (also known as the Kadyrovites).

Current Status

By the time Vladimir Putin handed over the Russian presidency to Dmitry Medvedev in May 2008, Russian control of the North Caucasus had become much stronger than it was in the 1990s. However, the region had been badly hurt by two decades of conflict. Since 2000 Russian laws have been amended to make it more difficult to criticize the Russian government; this has had the effect of severely limiting debate on possible solutions to the separatist conflicts with which it is faced. By late 2008, with all television broadcasting and most newspapers under state control and the government suppressing Web sites that voiced opposition, even reporting on the political situation in the North Caucasus had become dangerous.

Political violence across the North Caucasus region remains a serious problem. In 2008 there were 795 incidents of violence, and in 2009 there were 1,001, according to statistics presented by North Caucasus expert Sarah Mendelson, a director at the CSIS think tank. Speaking at a seminar in February 2010, Mendelson said that the highest incidence levels of violence for 2009 were recorded in Ingushetia (420), followed by Dagestan (330), Chechnya (280), Kabardino-Balkaria (50), and North Ossetia (20). Those killed were mostly

At the beginning of 2005, Ramzan's sister, Zulai Kadyrova, was detained by Dagestani police. This situation ignited a violent confrontation in which Ramzan led 150 armed men into the police station where his sister was being held and freed her, assaulting police officers in the process. Ramzan built a reputation for ruthlessness and was known to be unafraid to use violence. He also tended to publically stated, lofty goals: to rebuild the bombed out city of Grozny, to build an enormous mosque, and to stabilize the region.

When Chechen prime minister Sergei Abramov was injured in a car crash in November 2005, Ramzan took his place, becoming the "caretaker" prime minister and the de facto ruler of the region. As prime minister, he began to implement elements of Islamic law, or *sharia*, for example, banning gambling and in-country alcohol production. He also spoke out in favor of polygamy. He remained staunchly pro-Putin in his politics.

Abramov resigned from his post in March 2006 on the condition that Ramzan take his place. Ramzan became prime minister shortly afterward. Some of his first actions were to decree that women in Chechnya wear headscarves and to ask for more money to rebuild the region. Kadyrov also promised to prosecute military commanders who had been deemed responsible for the deaths or disappearances of Chechen civilians. Overall, 3,500–5,000 Chechens are considered missing, but there is no count of how many disappeared during the war and how many disappeared afterward. Ramzan himself has been accused of permitting extreme methods to root out "spies."

In 2007 Russian president Putin signed a decree removing the Chechen president, putting Ramzan into the position of acting president. He formally took office later in the year, having just become old enough to legally hold the job.

The year 2010 finds Grozny a much-changed city from that which Ramzan's father had controlled. It is now prosperous, with civilians able to go shopping and eat in cafes after dark. It is also home to Europe's largest mosque. However, some civilians remain uneasy, concerned over the president's personal power; in fact, Ramzan's face appears prominently on posters pasted throughout the city.

Ramzan is married and has five children. He built an enormous presidential estate in the region, which includes a private zoo that houses lions, leopards, pumas, and a tiger. He enjoys boxing and has personally met Mike Tyson.

The Kadyrovs are an example of secessionist leaders who ultimately reconciled with their government—Russia. In the Kadyrovs' case, reconciliation came about as a result of a split stemming from religious differences within the separatist movement they originally championed. The Kadyrovs aligned themselves with the moderate Muslims and opposed the extremist faction in the movement. Since coming to power, however, Ramzan has embraced Islamic law, or *sharia*.

Russian military, Caucasian militants, and human rights advocates and journalists. In August 2008, a well-known Ingush journalist, Magomed Yevloyev, was shot in the head while in police custody. This triggered protests in Ingushetia and militant attacks in Chechnya, Dagestan, and Kabardino-Balkaria. In September 2008, the Moscow Helsinki Group, a human rights advocacy organization, warned that Ingushetia was on the brink of war and that Russia had been overzealous in pursuing Islamist militants.

At the CSIS seminar on conflict in the North Caucasus, Caucasian journalist Shvedov said of Chechnya: "It paints an image of success but in practice there is a lack of control. The number of rebels is growing." Shvedov said that from July to December 2009 Russian president Medvedev had instituted a softer approach toward the region, no longer focusing solely on a military solution as Putin tended to do. "Issues that could not be discussed under Putin, such as whether to allow Dagestan [to] adopt Sharia where there is strong support for it, can be openly discussed. There is room to listen and receive recommendations," Shvedov said. Meanwhile, the United States seems to be toughening its stance toward North Caucasian separatists. In June 2010, the U.S. State Department declared that Doku

Umarov, who aims to create an independent North Caucasus country based on Islamic law, was a terrorist. Umarov had claimed responsibility for directing the March 29, 2010, bombings of the Moscow subway, an article by Ellen Barry in the *New York Times* reported. The article cited the Russian tabloid newspaper *Komsomolskaya Pravda* welcoming the U.S. move, saying "American leadership has finally acknowledged that Caucasian terrorist and the notorious Al Qaeda are links in the same chain."

Two researchers on the North Caucasus from Georgetown University in Washington, D.C., who examined data from the period October 21, 2009, to January 31, 2010, found disturbing levels of violence. According to Kevin Jones and Gregory Zalaski, who presented their data in March 2010 at a seminar at George Washington University in Washington, D.C., the situation varies from republic to republic. Most of the attacks in Chechnya were carried out by the Chechen authorities and tended to cause fatalities. In Dagestan and Ingushetia, there were more attacks overall but they caused fewer fatalities, and there was greater uncertainty over who carried out those attacks. The ICG, in its 2008 report, forecast that while a full-scale war was unlikely to develop in Dagestan, sporadic violence, much of it Islamist-inspired, would probably continue.

Russia's decision in August 2008 to recognize the independence of neighboring Georgia's two secessionist enclaves, Abkhazia and South Ossetia (see separate essays), has triggered "a new separatism" in the North Caucasus, claimed journalist Shvedov. The new movement, which is supported by the diaspora communities, was notably much less Islamist-centered than the separatist violence of the 1990s and early 2000s, he said. Shvedov noted that a movement was gathering momentum to unify the highly fragmented North Caucasus region and that the idea of organizing a Pan-Caucasus Olympic Games had taken root.

In March 2010, the U.S. State Department, in its annual report on human rights in Russia, warned that the North Caucasus "remained an area of particular concern. The government's poor human rights record . . . worsened, as the government fought insurgents, Islamist militants, and criminal forces." The U.S. government report added that both the local authorities and the insurgents were responsible for killings, torture, abuse, violence, and abductions. The number of extra-judicial killings and disappearances in Chechnya, Dagestan, and Ingushetia had increased markedly. Chechen president Kadyrov was operating a private militia that targeted families of suspected insurgents. The number of federal Russian forces was, meanwhile, on the decline, with the government announcing plans in April 2009 to cut troop levels from fifty to twenty-five thousand.

In Ingushetia, a failed assassination attempt on President Yevkurov in June 2009 triggered a counter-terrorism clampdown, the State Department said. The authorities in Kabardino-Balkaria had also mounted a counter-terrorism clampdown, and the insurgency in Dagestan was widening. The report criticized the Russian government for failing to investigate allegations of human rights abuse in Chechnya. In January 2009, President Kadyrov's former bodyguard-turned-critic, who claimed to have witnessed Kadyrov torturing prisoners, was assassinated in Vienna, Austria. Another Kadyrov ally-turned-critic, Sulim Yamadeyev, was shot in Dubai in March 2009. Human rights activist and journalist Natalia Estemirova was killed in Grozny in July 2009. And a couple who ran a charity to help Chechen children with disabilities caused by the conflict, Zarema Sadulayeva and Alik Dzhabrailov, were killed in August 2009. Their murders caused some other non-governmental organizations to leave Chechnya because of safety fears.

A "week in review" summary of November 2009 from the Caucasian Knot news Web site highlights just how diffuse the violence is. In one day, the administrative head of a municipal district in Ingushetia was shot dead, while the decapitated bodies of a court officer and police inspector in Kabardino-Balkaria were found, reportedly killed by an underground extremist group Shura. In March 2010, the violence spilled over into the Russian heartland once more when two female suicide bombers, allegedly Caucasian militants, conducted twin attacks in the Moscow subway that killed thirty-eight people and wounded sixty.

Some Circassian exiles, notably in Jordan and Turkey, are trying to return to Russia. Journalist Fatima Tlisova, in a January 2010 article for The Jamestown Foundation, accused Russia of creating bureaucratic hurdles to prevent their return. She said that many who do return are subsequently deported by Russia for not complying with procedural requirements. A campaign was under way, she reported, for the Circassian peoples to identify themselves as Circassians in the 2010 Russian census. She said this "may become the starting point for the Circassians to reach their frequently-announced demand—the reunification of three republics into one Circassian republic."

There remains a refugee problem in the North Caucasus. Chechen refugees in camps in Ingushetia were confronted in early 2009 by Chechen security forces urging refugees to return home. According to the U.S. State Department, as of December 31, 2009, the refugee count for the region was as follows: 8,900 Chechens in Ingushetia; 2,800 Prigorodny residents in Ingushetia; 3,600 Chechens in Dagestan; 4,200 Chechens internally displaced in Chechnya; and 10,000 South Ossetians in North Ossetia. Chechen authorities, meanwhile, were refusing access to prisons to the International Committee of the Red Cross.

Looking forward, Russian authorities are worried about North Caucasus separatists trying to exploit the 2014 Winter Olympic Games in Sochi, a Black Sea resort fifty miles west of Karachay-Cherkessia, to draw attention to their cause. Russia is highly unlikely to allow any of the republics to secede, although a more conciliatory approach from President Medvedev may result in some political power being devolved from Moscow to the republics.

Further Reading

Bakke, Kristin M., John O'Loughlin, and Michael Ward, "Reconciliation in Conflict-Affected Societies: Multi-level Modeling of Individual and Contextual Factors in the North Caucasus of Russia," *Annals of the Association of American Geographers* 98, no. 1 (November 2009).

Barry, Ellen. "U.S. Names Chechen Militant a Terrorist," *New York Times,* June 24, 2010, www.nytimes.com/2010/06/25/world/europe/25moscow.html?hp.

Dunlop, John. *Russian Confronts Chechnya: Roots of a Separatist Conflict.* Cambridge: Cambridge University Press, 1998.

Goldfarb, Alex, with Marina Litvinenko. *The Making of a Dissident: The Poisoning of Alexander Litvinenko and the Return of the KGB.* London: Simon and Schuster, 2007.

International Crisis Group. "Russia's Dagestan: Conflict Causes," *Europe Report,* no. 192 (June 3, 2008), www.crisisgroup.org/home/index.cfm?id=5466&CFID=31946915&CFTOKEN=22157002.

Minority Rights Group International, "World Directory of Minorities and Indigenous Peoples," www.minorityrights.org/directory (accessed March 2010).

Moscow Helsinki Group. "Chechnya 2003: Political Process Through the Looking Glass," 2004, www.mhg.ru/english/34AFA9F.

Tlisova, Fatima. "Moscow Excises 'Separatist' Articles from Constitutions of Circassian Republics," *Eurasia Daily Monitor* 6, no. 213 (November 18, 2009), www.jamestown.org/programs/ncw/single/?tx_ttnews%5Btt_news%5D=35743&tx_ttnews%5BbackPid%5D=187&no_cache=1.

———. "Moscow Uses Commission on 'Historical Falsification' to Deny Circassian Rights," *Eurasia Daily Monitor* 7, no. 14 (January 21, 2010), www.jamestown.org/programs/edm/single/?tx_ttnews%5Btt_news%5D=35942&tx_ttnews%5BbackPid%5D=27&cHash=f817b1aeb7.

U.S. Department of State. "2009 Human Rights Report: Russia," March 11, 2010, www.state.gov/g/drl/rls/hrrpt/2009/index.htm.

"Week in the Caucasus: Review of main events of November 23–29," Caucasian Knot, December 2, 2009, www.eng.kavkaz-uzel.ru/articles/11888/?print=true.

SERBS
(Bosnia, Kosovo)

Ethnic Serb minorities in the Western Balkan countries of Bosnia and Herzegovina and Kosovo have, since these states were founded in 1992 and 2008, respectively, pushed for greater autonomy. Bitter conflicts over the past two decades have heightened separatist sentiment. In the case of Bosnia, it may lead to the secession of Serbs within the next five years in response to severe political tensions between the Bosnian Serb and Bosnian governments.

The 1.7 million Serbs in Bosnia make up 31 percent of the country's population. They live mainly in the north and east. The Serbs are less numerous than the Bosnian Muslims, or Bosniaks, who make up 48 percent of the population. Croatians account for 14 percent of Bosnians. In Kosovo, which is 88 percent ethnic Albanian, the Serbs number 130,000, or 7 percent of the population. About half of Kosovo's Serbs live in a contiguous area in northern Kosovo where they form a majority. The other half is dispersed in pockets in southern Kosovo where they form a minority. Serbia, home to 6.3 million Serbs, borders both Bosnia and Kosovo. There are also Serb minorities in Croatia (200,000), Montenegro (200,000), and

Slovenia (40,000), although separatism is not as acute an issue in these countries.

The Serbs are mostly Orthodox Christian; in contrast, Bosniaks and Kosovar Albanians are Muslim. Serbs are a Slavic people whose language, Serbian, is very similar to Bosnian, which Bosniaks speak. The Bosniaks are ethnically Slavic as well, but converted to Islam in the 1500s when the Balkans were ruled by Ottoman Turks. Kosovar Albanians are a distinct ethnic group with their own language, Albanian.

The Bosnian Serbs created an autonomous administrative entity, called Republica Srpska, in 1992 while Bosnia was in the process of seceding from Yugoslavia. Republica Srpska shares a common currency, judiciary, and tax and customs system with the rest of Bosnia, but otherwise operates fairly independently. Since February 2008, when Kosovo declared independence from Serbia, the Bosnian Serb leadership has frequently hinted it may secede from Bosnia. Virtually all foreign governments, including Serbia, are opposed to independence for Republica Srpska. The Bosniaks, the dominant group in the Bosnian central government, fiercely oppose secession. They fear it will encourage secessionism among Bosnia's Croats, a Catholic minority, turning Bosnia into a greatly reduced country in size and one that is almost exclusively Muslim.

In Kosovo, the ethnic Albanian-dominated central government has limited control over the majority-Serb municipalities in the north. The government of Serbia has strong influence over the northern Kosovo Serbs and helps to pay the locals' pensions and police salaries. Northern Kosovo is where most of Kosovo's mineral resources, including lead, cadmium, silver, and iron, are found. In the south, there are self-governing Serb municipalities, but the Serbian government does not have as much influence over them. The European Union and the United States, both of whom exert influence in the region, are strongly opposed to the creation of an independent Serbian Kosovar country. Such an entity would be difficult to operate in practice because the Serb minority is so dispersed across Kosovo. Further fragmentation of an already fragmented region is not welcome internationally. Kosovo's southerly neighbor, Macedonia, would probably oppose secession, too, for fear it might encourage Macedonia's ethnic Albanian minority to seek greater autonomy or independence.

International mediators and administrators have urged the Kosovars to stay united and focus on the common goal of EU membership. These pro-unity voices argue that once Kosovo and Serbia are inside the EU, any national borders dividing them will be less relevant as free movement of people, goods, capital, and services across borders is the EU norm. Kosovo's path to EU membership faces one major obstacle: five EU countries—Cyprus, Greece, Romania, Slovakia, and Spain—do not recognize Kosovo's independence. They consider it still part of Serbia. They have opposed Kosovo's secession mainly because they have separatist movements on their own territory (see separate essays) and are worried that recognizing Kosovo will set a destabilizing precedent. By September 2010, seventy countries, including the United States and most European states, had recognized Kosovo. However, 122, including China, Russia, and Serbia, had not.

There remains a large contingent of international peace-keepers in Bosnia since 1995 and in Kosovo since 1999, aimed at preventing further conflict between the Serbs, Albanians, Bosniaks, and Croats. A NATO-led military force of ten thousand, which has a United Nations mandate, keeps the peace in Kosovo, assisted by an EU force that provides support and training to local police and judiciary and customs authorities. In Bosnia, the EU has deployed a two-thousand-strong military and police mission aimed at bolstering the fragile country.

In general, the specter of separatist movements triggering the emergence of a myriad of microstates in the Balkans—each one with its own currency, army, and government—is distinctly unappealing to the international community. The recent history of Balkan states, which includes several extremely destructive wars, has led to the coining of the term "Balkanization," which means to break up into smaller and often mutually hostile units.

History

Serbs first settled in Bosnia in the seventh century C.E. and in Kosovo in the eleventh century. Kosovo is an important place in terms of Serb heritage; many of their most revered religious sites were built there. The Ottoman Turks gained control of Bosnia and Kosovo in the fourteenth and fifteenth centuries after inflicting a legendary defeat on the Serbs at the Battle of Kosovo in 1389. Many Albanians and Turks moved to Kosovo, which diluted the Serb population. In Bosnia, some locals converted to Islam while others remained Orthodox Christian; this served to make religion an increasingly important aspect of identity.

The Serbs broke free from Ottoman rule and founded their own state in 1835, although its independence was not formally recognized until 1878.

Despite the Serbs being on the winning side in the Russo-Turkish War (1877–1878), in the peace settlement that followed Bosnia was given to the Hapsburg Empire. In 1912, Serbia regained control of most of Kosovo. At the end of World War I (1914–1918), Serbs across the Balkan region became part of a new country of mostly south Slavic peoples called the Kingdom of Serbs, Croats and Slovenes. This country was renamed Yugoslavia in 1929.

The ethnic Albanians in Kosovo gained greater autonomy when the Yugoslav constitution was revised in 1974. Serbs in Kosovo resented this; in particular, they objected to the imposition of the Albanian language in government administration and in many of Kosovo's schools. A watershed moment came in April 1987 when emerging Serbian leader Slobodan Milosevic attended a rally of Serbs in Kosovo and pledged solidarity. In 1989 Kosovo saw its autonomy revoked. In 1991 Yugoslavia began to break up. In March 1992, a majority of voters in a referendum in Bosnia voted to secede. The Bosnian Serbs boycotted the vote; their leaders partitioned Bosnia and forced non-Serbs in their Serb-designated zone to leave. Serbs living in Bosniak and Croat areas faced similar persecution as a full-scale war broke out.

In July 1995, the Bosnian Serb army and police murdered eight thousand Bosniak men and boys in the town of Srebrenica, a massacre the International Court of Justice in 2007 judged was genocide. The war ended with the signing of an agreement in Dayton, Ohio, in November 1995. The terms of the agreement provided Bosnian Serbs their own autonomous entity, Republica Srpska, as part of an independent Bosnia. A NATO-led force of sixty thousand peacekeepers was deployed to enforce the agreement, and the international community secured the return of many Bosniak refugees to Bosnian Serb areas.

In Kosovo, relations between Serbs and Albanians deteriorated throughout the 1990s. The Albanians launched an insurgency in 1998. Serbia responded with a counterinsurgency that led hundreds of thousands of Albanians to flee. In March 1999, NATO intervened to defend Kosovar Albanians, bombing Serb targets until Serbia withdrew its forces from all of Kosovo in June. Sixteen thousand NATO troops, including troops from the United States, Ireland, Turkey, Germany, Italy, and France, were deployed to enforce the cease-fire.

From 2000 the political leadership of Serbia see-sawed between pushing to reintegrate some of Kosovo's majority-Serb municipalities and returning all of Kosovo to Serb rule. Neither objective was achieved because the Albanian majority in Kosovo, backed by NATO, opposed any move that gave Serbia a say in the governance of Kosovo. In March 2004, attacks on Kosovar Serbs prompted 3,600 Serbs to flee their homes, and many Serb churches and houses were destroyed. Talks on Kosovo's final status were launched in the UN in 2005, but no agreement was reached. Former Finnish prime minister Martti Ahtisaari in late 2007 presented a plan for EU-supervised independence for all of Kosovo.

Leadership

In Bosnia, the Serb leadership operates at two levels: that of the central Bosnian government in Sarajevo and that of the Republica Srpska administration in Banja Luka. Nebojsa Radmanovic was popularly elected in October 2006 as the Serb representative on the three-person Bosnian presidency, which rotates every eight months among Serbs, Croats, and Bosniaks. In October 2010, he was re-elected to another term. Bosnian Serbs can veto significant changes to Bosnia's constitutional order, which is a source of tension with Bosniaks who accuse the Serbs of using their veto to paralyze the central government.

Republica Srpska has a president, prime minister, and eighty-three seat parliament. By early 2011 the dominant political figure in Republica Srpska was Milorad Dodik, president and leader of the Alliance of Independent Social Democrats.

Radovan Karadzic (1945–   )

RADOVAN KARADZIC was born in a stable in Savnik, Montenegro, in June 1945. Vuko Karadzic, his father, was a member of the Chetniks, what remained of the ultra-nationalist Serb military that was active during World War II (1939–1945). Vuko spent much of his son's youth in prison.

© Shone Vlastimir Nesic/Sygma/Corbis

Karadzic attended the Sarajevo University of Medicine in 1960; he then came to America to study at Columbia University in 1974. He has a PhD in psychiatry.

He met his wife, Ljiljana, in Sarajevo. Karadzic began writing poetry in the early 1970s. He also met and was heavily influenced by Serb writer Dobrica Cosic, a leader in the Serbian national revival movement. Cosic encouraged Karadzic's nationalistic tendencies and urged him to become a politician.

In 1985 Karadzic was imprisoned for embezzlement and fraud. After serving a shortened sentence, he continued his career as a psychiatrist before turning to politics.

He was a member of the Green Party but became a founding member of the Serb Democratic Party (SDS) in 1990. The SDS was founded in part to regain power over the ethnic Croat parties in Bosnia. Karadzic held the position of president of the SDS for six years, from 1990–1996.

Beginning as early as July 1991, Karadzic and other Bosnian-Serb leaders looked to control regions in Bosnia that they considered integral parts of the Serb Republic.

Bosnia-Herzegovina was recognized by the United Nations as an independent state in 1992, and Yugoslavia was split up. Karadzic, with SDS support, claimed he was president of the new Serbian Republic of Bosnia and Herzegovina (Srpska Republica).

As the commander of his self-styled republic, Karadzic worked to eradicate the Muslim population. Karadzic claimed he was trying to "protect" Christian Serbs from Bosnian Muslims. He planned and carried out a campaign to "ethnically cleanse" Bosnia of Muslims. During his forty-three-month siege on Sarajevo, Karadzic pursued a systematic approach to killing or driving out the tens of thousands of non-Serbs who lived in Serbian towns and villages. He set up detention camps, including the Omarska camp, which Human Rights Watch classified as a concentration camp, and effected a death toll that ultimately reached between 150,000 to 200,000, with as many as 20,000 rapes. At the same time, other ethnic cleansing campaigns were being carried out by Bosnian Croats, and there were cases of Bosniaks committing war crimes.

The most notorious incident was the Srebrenica massacre of July 1995. Ruled genocide by the International Criminal Tribunal for the former Yugoslavia, the Srebrenica massacre ranks as the largest mass murder in Europe since World War II. Srebrenica was declared a protected area by the UN, which had stationed UN Protection Forces there to protect the forty thousand Bosnian Muslims who lived in the area. Despite this, over eight thousand Muslim men and boys were killed systematically, and thousands of others were killed by units of the Army of Republica Srpska. Karadzic and the commander of the Bosnian Serb Army, Ratko Mladic, were indicted by the International Criminal Trial for the Former Yugoslavia because of their responsibility for this atrocity.

Karadzic was forced out of power and into hiding in 1996, as U.S. president Bill Clinton brokered a peace accord that brought a cessation to the fighting in Bosnia. Karadzic maintained a group of eighty armed guards to protect him as he evaded capture on Vucevo Mountain.

Karadzic spend over a decade hiding from authorities on charges of war crimes. While in hiding, he was helped by a network of Serbian nationalists and was even able to visit his wife multiple times. He published an illustrated children's book, a book of poetry, a play, and a novel while in hiding. The novel, *The Miraculous Chronicle of the Night*, which was published in October 2005, is set in Sarajevo in the 1980s. Met with both criticism and acclaim, it was short-listed for Serbia's top literary award, the Golden Sunflower.

He was found and arrested on July 21, 2008, and was sent to the International Criminal Tribunal for the Former Yugoslavia in The Hague. Karadzic's boycott of his trial in the fall of 2009 forced a six-month delay, but it resumed proceedings on March 1, 2010. Karadzic is representing himself and currently denies any responsibility for genocide in Bosnia.

There is also a Serb Democratic Party (SDS), led by Mladen Bosic; two groups each called the Serb Radical Party, one led by Milanko Mihajlica and the other led by Mirko Blagojevic; and the Socialist Party of Republika Srpska, led by Petar Djokic. Bosnian Serbs have their own police force, which is a further source of tension with Bosniaks who allege that some of these officers participated in the Srebrenica genocide. The Bosnian Serb leaders during the 1992–1995 war were Radovan Karadzic on the civilian side and Ratko Mladic on the military side. Both have been indicted for war crimes. As of January 2011, Karadzic was being tried by the International Criminal Tribunal for the Former Yugoslavia in The Hague; Mladic remained a fugitive.

In northern Kosovo, the majority-Serb municipalities have autonomy and can maintain direct links with the Serbian government. The Kosovo central government is based in the city of Pristina. Kosovo's Serbs are guaranteed 10 seats in the 120-seat parliament. Serbs tend to be underrepresented in administrative positions in the Kosovo government; this contrasts with the pre-1999 situation when they were overrepresented. The main Kosovar Serb political parties and leaders are the Serb National Party (SNS), led by Mihailo Scepanovic; the Serbian Kosovo and Metohija Party (SKMS), led by Dragisa Miric; the Serbian Democratic Party of Kosovo and Metohija (SDSKIM), led by Slavisa Petkovic; and the Serbian National Council of Northern Kosovo and Metohija, or SNV, led by Milan Ivanovic.

Serbs in Bosnia and Kosovo look to the government of Serbia for support. Belgrade backs the calls of Bosnian Serbs for greater autonomy and considers all of Kosovo part of Serbia. The EU and NATO wield considerable power in Bosnia and Kosovo as a result of their large military and police missions. They are viewed with suspicion by Serbs, given strong European and American support for an independent Bosnia and Kosovo.

Current Status

The Kosovo Serb population, 300,000 in 1999, had dwindled to 125,000 by 2010 due to the adverse political and economic climate. Unemployment in Kosovo hovered around 50 percent. Because all of Kosovo remains in limbo, with some states recognizing it but others not, the future for Kosovo's Serbs is unclear. In a February 2008 telephone interview, French journalist Nicolas Gros-Verheyde, reporting from northern Kosovo, said that Serbs there had closer links to Serbia than to Kosovo. Their electricity came from Serbia, they carried different license plates on their cars from Kosovar Albanians, and they used Serbia's mobile telephone networks. "There is very little contact between the communities. Our Serb translator would not get out of the car when we drove through the Albanian areas," said Gros-Verheyde, correspondent for the Brussels-based EU affairs newspaper *Europolitics*. "When I was visiting in 1990 people mixed more but two decades of wars has bred greater mistrust," he said. Asked about the possibility of Kosovo's Serbs seceding, he said, "if you split Kosovo in two it will only cause more problems. It will encourage Republica Srpska to secede too, even though neither historically has been a distinct administrative unit."

The international peace-keeping and state-building missions in Kosovo are likely to remain deployed for several years, given the precarious political climate. The international presence has prevented a resumption of full-scale hostilities between Serbs and Albanians. However, by 2010 the simultaneous existence of a NATO and an EU mission was causing its own tensions. The NATO force was supposed to have been phased out in 2008, but because the world's main powers failed to agree on Kosovo's status it remained in place. The UN Security Council is split, with China and Russia opposing Kosovo's independence, and France, the United Kingdom, and the United States favoring it. On July

24, 2010, the Serbs received a blow when the International Court of Justice, in an advisory opinion adopted by 10 votes to 4, found that Kosovo's declaration of independence of February 2008 did not violate international law. The case had been brought by the Serbian government.

Since 2008 the leaders of Republica Srprska in Bosnia have threatened to hold a referendum on independence. Bosnia's Serbs are in a stronger position to secede than Kosovo's Serbs because they live in a contiguous territory that they control and have exercised autonomy over since 1992. Testifying before a U.S. congressional hearing in April 2009, Paddy Ashdown, the international community's High Representative for Bosnia from 2002–2006, accused Republica Srpska prime minister Dodik of "undermining Bosnia and poising himself to lead if events trigger secession." Ashdown urged the U.S. government "to never accept secession." As for Russia's pro-Serb stance, he said, "Russia has no long-term strategic interest in the Balkans" but rather "uses it as a stick to beat the west."

In 2004 responsibility for the international military mission in Bosnia had been transferred from NATO to the EU. By early 2011 it stood at 1,600 troops. Matthew Parish, a former international administrator in Bosnia, in a November 2009 article for BalkanInsight.com, an online news service, was pessimistic about the chances of Bosnia's remaining a single country given its hardline Bosnian Serb leadership. "Bosnia's gradual disintegration would appear inevitable. The only question is how the international community will, and should, react." He described Prime Minister Dodik as "tough, shrewd, uninterested in democracy, and determined to elevate his nation's status after a decade of weakness." Given the gradual reduction in the number of international troops deployed in Bosnia, the Bosnian Serbs' financial independence from the EU, and the weakness of the Bosnian central government, secession was more likely than not, he argued. Dodik's stance would appear to be in line with that of the majority of the Bosnian Serb people. According to a March 2010 survey, as reported by BBC's Worldwide Monitoring service, 80 percent of Bosnian Serbs favored secession and subsequent annexation by Serbia. By contrast, 80 percent of Bosniaks wanted to keep Bosnia unified.

The moves by Serbs in Bosnia and Kosovo to separate themselves from their respective central governments are meanwhile having a negative impact on the efforts of Bosnia and Kosovo to join the EU. As long as the ethnic disputes remain unresolved, the chances of either state joining the EU within the next five years look remote.

Further Reading

Gros-Verheyde, Nicolas. "One eye on Belgrade, the other on Pristina," *Europolitics*, January 22, 2008, www.europolitics.info.

EU military mission in Bosnia Web site, www.euforbih.org.

EU rule of law mission in Kosovo Web site, www.eulex-kosovo.eu.

International Crisis Group. "Kosovo: Štrpce, a Model Serb Enclave?" *Europe Briefing*, no. 56 (October 15, 2009), www.crisisgroup.org/home/index.cfm?id=6346.

Minority Rights Group International. "World Directory of Minorities and Indigenous Peoples," www.minority-rights.org/directory.

Parish, Matthew. "Republika Srpska: After Independence," BalkanInsight.com, November 19, 2009, www.balkaninsight.com/en/main/comment/23797.

"Poll shows ethnic groups largely divided over future Bosnia's territorial setup," BBC Worldwide Monitoring, April 5, 2010, translation of report by Velimir Begic, "Neither Serbs nor Croats nor Bosniaks Want B-H the Way It Is Now," in *Vecernji* (Croation daily), March 30, 2010.

U.S. Congress, Commission on Security and Cooperation in Europe (U.S. Helsinki Commission). "The Western Balkans: Challenges for U.S. and European Engagement," public hearing, April 2, 2009, http://csce.gov/index.cfm?FuseAction=ContentRecords.ViewDetail&ContentRecord_id=448&Region_id=0&Issue_id=0&ContentType=H,B&ContentRecordType=H&CFID=31586282&CFTOKEN=84442689.

SOUTH OSSETIANS
(Georgia)

In the south Caucasus country of Georgia, the South Ossetian minority has governed itself autonomously since 1991. Their de facto independence was unrecognized by any country until August 2008, when its northerly neighbor, Russia, recognized it immediately after having supported the South Ossetians militarily in a week-long war against Georgia.

The population of South Ossetia is 70,000, or 1.5 percent of Georgia's 4.6 million total. South Ossetians live in a small area stretching about forty-five miles east-west and thirty miles north-south. Twenty-six thousand ethnic Georgians used to live in South Ossetia, but conflicts from 1989–1992 and in 2008 have driven most of them out and made the enclave overwhelmingly Ossetian. Most South Ossetians are Russian citizens as well and possess Russian-issued passports. Like Georgians, South Ossetians are mainly Orthodox Christian, although the Ossetian clergy, which calls itself the Alanian Eparchy, has since 1990 functioned independently from its Georgian counterpart. Ossetians speak Ossetic, an Indo-European language related to Farsi, whereas Georgians speak Georgian.

The South Ossetia–Georgia conflict is often viewed by outsiders as an extension of cold war politics because Russia has helped the Ossetians whereas the United States has supported Georgia. However, regional expert Gerard Toal, a professor of Government and International Affairs at Virginia Tech University, has argued otherwise. "This is more about the complex relationship between Georgians and Ossetians," Toal said in February 2010 during a talk at George Washington University in Washington, D.C. "The Ossetians have a long history of loyalty to Russia. Joseph Stalin and Catherine the Great are revered there. Some say Stalin himself was Ossetian," he said. Ossetians' Christian faith has helped to draw them closer to the Russians, who are also Orthodox Christians. It sets them apart from many other Caucasian minorities, such as the Chechens, who are Muslim and have historically had tense relations with Russia.

South Ossetians proclaimed their independence through referenda in January 1992 and November 2006, although the Georgian minority in South Ossetia boycotted these votes.

By early 2011, only Russia and a few Russian allies, including Nicaragua and Venezuela, recognized South Ossetian independence. The European Union, the United States, and the Organization for Security and Co-operation in Europe (OSCE) continue to oppose the secession. Georgia insists that South Ossetia can neither be independent nor unite with North Ossetia and become part of Russia. It points to the natural boundary that is the Caucasus mountain range in support of its view. The United States has provided the Georgian army with uniforms, small arms, communications gear, medical aid, and fuel. In 2003–2004 the United States trained two thousand Georgian troops in counter-insurgency and counter-terrorism techniques. Georgia deployed these troops to Iraq to support the 2003 U.S.-led invasion of Iraq. The United States has also tried to advance Georgia's bid to join the Western military alliance, NATO. However, some Western European NATO members, for example France and Germany, are reluctant to allow Georgia to join.

Russia has provided humanitarian aid to South Ossetians, taken in refugees from the Ossetia-Georgia conflict, and helped South Ossetian authorities repair the region's infrastructure, which was badly damaged in the fighting. Moscow's support for South Ossetia is partly motivated by the poor relationship it has with Georgia. Even before Moscow recognized South Ossetia's independence in 2008, Russia had refused to help reintegrate South Ossetia into Georgia, despite its opposition to secessionist movements in principle. The main international intergovernmental organization involved in South Ossetia is the OSCE, which in 1993 deployed a mission of several hundred monitors to ensure that a June 1992 cease-fire was not broken. The EU has supported peace and reconciliation efforts, too, by helping to fund the OSCE mission and by channeling $11 million (€8M) into South Ossetia from 1997–2006 for infrastructure projects such as the rebuilding of schools.

From 1992–2004 the Ossetia-Georgia conflict was referred to as a "frozen conflict"— that is, one in which hostilities had mostly ceased but no long-term settlement was in sight. The election of a more bullish Georgian president, Mikheil Saakashvili, in January 2004 heightened tensions in the region. By late 2004 Russia was vetoing continuation of the OSCE border monitoring team. The August 2008 war tilted the balance in favor of the South Ossetians in their bid for independence. The key regional power, Russia, went from discreetly supporting South Ossetians to becoming the first country to formally recognize its independence.

Looking forward, some Ossetians would like to move beyond independence, especially if the West continues to refuse to recognize it, and unify with their ethnic brethren in North Ossetia, and consequently Russia. North Ossetia lies across their border and is home to over 300,000 North Ossetians. According to Professor Kimitaka Matsuzato at the Slavic Research Center at Hokkaido University, who visited the region in 2009 and published a paper on his findings in *Demokratizatsiya*, North Ossetians may in fact not support unity with South Ossetians as they are less anti-Georgian than South Ossetians.

History

Ossetians claim to be descendents of the Alanian and Scythian tribes that migrated from Persia to the Caucasus region over five thousand years ago. South Ossetians maintain that they have lived in their current homeland since at least the 1200s; the Georgians dispute this, countering that the South Ossetians arrived some time after the 1600s. By the 1800s both Ossetians and Georgians were under the control of the Russian Empire. When the Russian Empire collapsed at the end of World War I (1914–1918), Georgia declared independence, taking South Ossetia with it. However, the South Ossetians rebelled against Georgian rule in October 1919. By 1921 the recently installed communist government of Russia had regained control of Georgia and made it a republic within the newly constituted Soviet Union. The Soviets, rather than unite North and South Ossetia into a single administrative unit, made South Ossetia an autonomous region, or *oblast,* within Georgia. Many South Ossetians resented being part of Georgia, believing they did not enjoy the autonomy to which they were entitled.

The political climate changed after 1985 when the Soviet Union elected a reformist-minded president, Mikhail Gorbachev, who introduced greater political freedoms. Gorbachev's reforms spurred a surge of nationalism among Georgians. The fact that Gorbachev's closest political ally, Foreign Minister Eduard Shevardnadze, was Georgian gave a further boost to Georgian nationalism. South Ossetians felt further marginalized after Georgia passed a law in August 1989 that strengthened use of the Georgian language. When the Soviet Union was dissolved in late 1991, the United Nations recognized Georgia's independence and considered South Ossetia part of it.

South Ossetia had declared itself a separate republic within the Soviet Union in September 1990. Georgian and South Ossetian militias, the precursors to fully-fledged armies, clashed from 1989–1992, with the South Ossetians receiving support from Russia. An August 2004 report from the International Crisis Group found that "both sides committed brutal atrocities, including decapitation of infants, executions in front of family members, and rape." About a thousand people died in the fighting. Between ten and twenty thousand Georgians fled to "Georgia proper" (that is, not South Ossetia), while a hundred thousand South Ossetians fled Georgia proper to North Ossetia in Russia.

Eduard Shevardnadze became president of Georgia in 1995. He was more conciliatory toward South Ossetia than his predecessor, Zviad Gamsakhurdia, and did not attempt to retake it by force. Regional tensions were also contained by the peacemaking efforts of Russian president Boris Yeltsin, who had a long-standing relationship with Shevardnadze. Meanwhile, Georgia grew closer to the United States, partly because Washington remembered with gratitude Shevardnadze's role in helping to end the cold war. Critics characterized this closeness as "the tail wagging the dog," meaning that Georgia had a disproportionately strong influence over U.S. policy. The U.S.-Georgia relationship served to increase tensions between Georgia, Russia, and the United States. Negotiations for a long-term settlement in South Ossetia were launched in the late 1990s, but no breakthrough was made.

Mikheil Saakashvili's replacement of Shevardnadze in 2004 marked a turning point. The new Georgian leader declared that reintegrating South Ossetia, along with two other separatist enclaves, Abkhazia (see separate essay) and Ajara, was his absolute top priority. He quickly succeeded in peacefully winning back Ajara, a region within Georgia with a history of self-government that had cut itself off from Georgia in 1991 under the leadership of Aslan Abashidze. Ajarans are ethnic Georgians, but unlike most Georgians, who are Christian, the Ajarans are mostly Muslim, having converted when part of the Ottoman Empire. Saakashvili failed to achieve a similar success with South Ossetia. Russia's relations with Georgia continued to deteriorate, with Georgia in autumn 2006 vetoing Russia's bid to join the World Trade Organization and Russia retaliating by imposing an embargo on Georgian wine.

Leadership

The South Ossetians had a legally constituted regional government during the Soviet era. Since November 1991, when their parliament declared independence, they have effectively acted as a sovereign nation. Until 2008 the Georgian government had a foothold as it governed the Georgian-populated towns in South Ossetia, while the Ossetian authorities administered Ossetian-populated towns. But during the 2008 war, most of the remaining Georgians fled, leaving the region fully under the control of the South Ossetian government, which is supported by the Russian military.

There are regular multi-party presidential and parliamentary elections in South Ossetia, but they are not recognized by most countries. The government is based in the largest town, Tskhinvali. South Ossetia has operated as a customs-free zone, which has led to the emergence of a thriving black market in diverse products, including wheat flour, dairy, cigarettes, kerosene, heroin, stolen cars, weapons, and counterfeit wine. This black market used to be based in the town of Ergneti on the South Ossetia–Georgia border, but Georgian president Saakashvili closed it down in May 2004, further isolating South Ossetia. In April 2007, Saakashvili established a rival administration, led by Dmitry Sanakoyev, to govern the Georgian-controlled parts of South Ossetia. Prior to his alliance with Saakashvili, Sanakoyev had been prime minister of the secessionist South Ossetian government in 2001.

Eduard Kokoity, leader of the Communist Party in South Ossetia, has been the president of South Ossetia since December 2001. Generally viewed as a hard-liner, by 2004 Kokoity was calling for South Ossetia to unify with North Ossetia and thereby become part of Russia. Kokoity was reelected in November 2006, winning 96 percent of the vote. Since August 2009, the South Ossetian prime minister has been Vadim Brovtsev. The political parties who support President Kokoity are Unity, the Communist Party, and the People's Party. The opposition leaders are Vyacheslav Gobozov, head of the Republican Socialist Party, called "Fatherland," and Roland Kelekhsayev, whose group is also called the People's Party.

The first prime minister and president of South Ossetia was Znaur Gassyev, who served from November–December 1991. Other leading South Ossetian politicians in the early 1990s included Alan Chochiyev, chair of one of the first pro-independence parties, the South Ossetian Popular Front, established in 1988, and Oleg Teziyav, former chair of the South Ossetian Council of Ministers. The president from 1993–2001 was Lyudvig Chibirov, who was considered a conciliator, holding direct talks with President Shevardnadze from April 1996 until he was replaced in December 2001 by Eduard Kokoity.

Current Status

In early 2008, the atmosphere in Georgia grew increasingly tense. The key leaders were using ever more nationalist rhetoric, there was sporadic ethnic violence, and Russia was warning it would intervene if Georgia attacked South Ossetia. In July Russian troops began massing on the Russia–South Ossetia border. On August 7 the Georgian army began shelling Tskhinvali. Russia responded by ordering thousands of its troops to cross into South Ossetia. After five days of fighting, the South Ossetians had, with Russian help, further cemented their separation from Georgia. The war caused more ethnic cleansing as fifteen thousand ethnic Georgians in South Ossetia fled into Georgia proper. Many villages were burned and looted by the South Ossetian militias in retaliation for the villagers having aided the initial Georgian assault on Tskhinvali. Some thirty thousand South Ossetians fled to North Ossetia. Estimates of the numbers killed range from scores to several hundred. Russia recognized South Ossetia's independence, along with that of the other secessionist republic inside Georgia, Abkhazia (see separate essay), on August 26, 2008.

By making an initial assault, Georgia was widely perceived as having wrongly gauged on obtaining stronger support from the United States and Europe than it actually got. The United States was in the midst of a presidential election campaign, and while outgoing president George W. Bush made statements backing Georgia, he gave no military assistance to help it win the war. The presidential candidate most in favor of helping Georgia, Sen. John McCain, who pronounced during the war, "we are all Georgians," lost the election to Sen. Barack Obama. As president, Obama has adopted a more conciliatory stance toward Russia, although he still refuses to recognize South Ossetia's independence.

French president Nicolas Sarkozy brokered the cease-fire agreement that ended the war. EU countries were united in not recognizing South Ossetia but were divided over what policy to take toward Georgia and Russia. Eastern European nations, such as those comprising the Baltic countries, strongly supported Georgia; France, Germany, and Italy were more cautious, keen to build good relations with Russia. In October 2008, a civilian monitoring mission, made up of two hundred EU and one hundred OSCE unarmed observers, was put into place. No military peace-keeping mission was deployed; this means that if violence does resume it will be difficult to prevent another war. Upward of a thousand ethnic Georgians who have been displaced by the conflict have not yet returned home. Russia continues to station four thousand troops in South Ossetia. A June 2010 article in *The Daily Telegraph* by Damien McElroy reported that Russia was planning to establish a radar and electronic surveillance system in South Ossetia, having received permission to do so from the South Ossetian Parliament.

Most academic regional experts believe Georgia has little chance of taking back South Ossetia, given Russia's strong military presence coupled with the fierce opposition from the South Ossetians themselves. The South Ossetia–Georgia border, which before the 2008 conflict had seen a fairly free flow of traffic, has been tightened up considerably. Georgia is still working to establish itself as a fully functional state, which makes it difficult to enforce its territorial claim over South Ossetia, despite almost all countries siding with it in principle. President Saakashvili's failures in the 2008 war have put a major dent in his popularity among Georgians,

and his dream of reestablishing Georgia's territorial integrity seems further away than ever.

According to Professor Matsuzato, South Ossetians no longer contemplate any kind of a future within Georgia. "My own four-day stay in South Ossetia convinced me that the slightest suggestion of integration into Georgia aroused an almost physiological disgust among the South Ossetians . . . in most cases [they] lose control and begin to scream." Even if on the international level most countries support Georgia's legal claim of sovereignty over South Ossetia, the major financial and military support that South Ossetia receives from its neighbor and major world power, Russia, will enable it to continue functioning as a de facto independent nation.

Further Reading

Birch, Julian. "A Caucasian Bosnia in Microcosm," *Central Asian Survey* 14, no. 1 (March 1995), www .informaworld.com/smpp/content~db=all?cont ent=10.1080/02634939508400891.

International Crisis Group. "Georgia: Avoiding War in South Ossetia," *Europe Report*, no. 159 (November 26, 2004), www.crisisgroup.org/home/index.cfm?id= 3128.

———. "Saakashvili's Ajara Success: Repeatable Elsewhere in Georgia," *Europe Briefing*, no. 34 (August 18, 2004), www.crisisgroup.org/home/index.cfm?id= 2907&l=1.

Kluwer Law International. "EU and the Eastern Neighborhood: Reluctant Involvement in Conflict Resolution," *European Foreign Affairs Review* 14 (2009).

Lynch, Dov. *Engaging Eurasia's Separatist States.* Washington, D.C.: United States Institute of Peace, 2004.

Matsuzato, Kimitaka. "The Five-Day War and Transnational Politics: A Semiospace Spanning the Borders between Georgia, Russia, and Ossetia," *Demokratizatsiya* (Summer 2009), www.demokratizatsiya.org/ issues/summer%202009/matsuzato.html.

McElroy, Damien. "Russia is preparing for new war, claims Georgia," *The Daily Telegraph*, June 4, 2010, www.telegraph.co.uk/news/worldnews/europe/ georgia/7803879/Russia-builds-listening-post-sparking-fears-of-Georgia-strike.html.

TRANSNISTRIANS
(Moldova)

Transnistria is a small, landlocked sliver of territory in southeastern Europe. A pro-Russian political leadership operates a de facto independent state there that is not internationally recognized. This has been the situation since 1992, when Transnistrians fought a war to avoid becoming part of newly independent Moldova, which is a 78 percent Romanian-speaking country.

Transnistria is separated from the rest of Moldova by the Dniester River, extending about 140 miles north-south and 10 to 15 miles east-west, with Ukraine lying on its eastern border and Moldova to the west. Transnistrians number 537,000 and account for 13 percent of Moldova's population of four million. Some 250,000 live outside the region; most of these have left since 1989. Almost 32 percent of Transnistrians identify themselves as Moldovan, 30 percent as Russian, and 29 percent as Ukrainian; the remainder are a mix of Bulgarians, Gagauz (a Turkic people), Jews, Poles, and Germans. Over 90 percent of Transnistrians are Orthodox Christian.

Transnistria's survival as a secessionist enclave is heavily contingent upon Russia's support. Although Moscow does not officially recognize Transnistria's independence, it has about a thousand Russian soldiers deployed there who help ensure its security. Russia has bolstered the Transnistrian economy by selling it gas at cheaper rates, which enables Transnistrian factories to produce goods more cheaply than their Moldovan counterparts. Moldova would like to regain control of Transnistria both because the region is an important industrial center and because it is home to a 177,000-strong Moldovan community. The loss of Transnistria has deprived Moldova of a major source of wealth and tax revenue and, as a result, has made Moldova Europe's poorest country. Moldova relies heavily on its agricultural sector and imports almost all its energy, mostly gas, from Russia.

No country in the world recognizes Transnistria's independence. This pariah status has encouraged the development of a lucrative market in goods-smuggling. Goods are typically brought from the nearby Ukrainian ports of Odessa and Illichivsk to Transnistria and re-exported to other countries without duties being paid on them. This illicit trade has enriched many Russians, Transnistrians, Ukrainians, and even Moldovans. It has also created a disincentive for finding a resolution to the conflict, given that many people profit from maintaining the status quo. Transnistria also possesses legal enterprises, including the manufacture of arms, machinery, textiles, cognac, and wine. Much of this is exported to ex-Soviet countries, Western Europe, and the United States. The Transnistrian government has tried to preserve the social safety net that existed when it was part of the Soviet Union, providing state pensions and state-subsidized public services.

A 1998 poll carried out by Moldovan, Transnistrian, and Russian researchers and cited in a June 2004 report from the International Crisis Group (ICG) found that 83 percent of Transnistrians supported statehood for Transnistria. In a March 1995 referendum, 93 percent of Transnistrians supported the retention of Russian troops in Transnistria. However, the Transnistrian leadership has been widely accused of suppressing internal political opposition and restricting the rights of its Moldovan minority, notably to a Romanian-language, Latin alphabet–based education. While thousands of Transnistrian children go to Romanian-language schools—some of which use the Latin alphabet, others of which use the Cyrillic alphabet—the U.S. State Department concluded in a March 2010 report that these schools were inadequately funded. The school attendees are also faced with occasional harassment, such as having classes interrupted by unknown persons smashing windows.

The main international body trying to broker a long-term settlement between the Moldovan and Transnistrian leaders is the Organization for Security and Co-operation in Europe (OSCE). The European Union is the other key player. The United States, which refuses to recognize Transnistria's independence, has largely taken a back seat to the EU and OSCE's efforts to resolve the conflict. The Moldovan government, which has been forging closer ties with the EU and would eventually like to join it, uses what leverage it has with the EU to push for Transnistria's reintegration. The EU would like to avoid having to admit a partitioned country, although there is a precedent: Cyprus joined the EU in 2004 while lacking unification between its Greek and Turkish regions (see separate entry). Moldova lags behind its neighbors in its EU membership bid: by April 2010, it was the only country in southeastern Europe that was not either already a member or a candidate or potential candidate for membership.

Moldova's westerly neighbor, Romania, which joined the EU in 2007, supports Moldovan efforts to reintegrate the region. Similarly, Transnistria's easterly neighbor, Ukraine, is wary of the pro-Russian leadership in Transnistria and tends to side more with Moldova, favoring an autonomous status for Transnistria within Moldova. Some Ukrainians, distrustful of Russia, would like the Russian troops in Transnistria to leave. They hope this might set a precedent that could spur a Russian fleet that is based in Sevastopol, a Ukrainian port city, to leave, too. Ukraine is keen to avoid a resumption of hostilities, mindful that the 1992 war triggered an influx of 100,000 refugees onto its territory.

History

The Transnistrian region has been populated by many different peoples and ruled by many different powers for thousands of years. By the late 1700s Russia had become the dominant power, taking control in 1792–1793 and establishing a fortress in Tiraspol, the present-day de facto capital. In 1812 Transnistria was joined to the rest of modern-day Moldova when Russia annexed Moldova. At the end of World War I (1914–1918) Moldova and Transnistria became separated when Moldova was given to Romania and Transnistria became part of the newly constituted Soviet Union. In 1924 the Soviet leader, Joseph Stalin, created an autonomous administrative region called Moldavia, which included Transnistria. Tiraspol was its industrial center, and many Russians and Ukrainians immigrated there.

When World War II (1939–1945) broke out, the Soviets seized Romanian-governed Moldova and joined it with Transnistria to form the Moldavian Soviet Socialist Republic. In 1985 the reformist-minded Mikhail Gorbachev became leader of the Soviet Union and instituted greater political freedom, triggering a surge in nationalism in Moldova. Keen to distance itself from the rest of Moldova, specifically from the Romanian-speaking and more Western-oriented Moldovans, the regional parliament of Transnistria in September 1990 proclaimed Transnistria an independent republic. As the Soviet Union disintegrated in 1991, the Transnistrians established state structures including a judiciary, police force, prosecution service, and banking and taxation system. They received a significant boost in May 1991 when the Soviet army gave them weapons. Meanwhile, Moldova declared full independence from the Soviet Union on August 27, 1991, and claimed Transnistria as its territory. The Transnistrian leadership responded in December 1991 by declaring their independence from Moldova.

The newly independent state of Russia, led by Boris Yeltsin, was initially reluctant to support Transnistria. Yeltsin was keen to establish harmonious relations with Europe and the United States; moreover, as a staunch opponent of communism, he felt little affinity with the hard-line communist leadership of Transnistria. However, when a war between Moldovans and Transnistrians broke out in spring 1992, Moscow deployed several thousand Russian soldiers to the region and in so doing helped the Transnistrians repel the advances of the Moldovan army. A cease-fire was agreed to in July 1992 that was enforced by Russian peace-keepers. Russia henceforth placed itself more firmly on the side of Transnistria, aware its military presence gave it a useful regional foothold and made it less likely Moldova would unify with Romania, which Moscow opposed. In a 1994 referendum, 95 percent of Moldovans voted for Moldova to remain an independent country. Thus, while Romania pivoted itself decidedly westward, joining NATO in 2004 and the EU in 2007, the Transnistrian conflict to some extent hindered Moldova in following the same path.

Russian troop levels declined from 9,250 in 1992 to 2,600 by 1999. From the late 1990s gradual progress was made in talks for a settlement between the Moldovan and Transnistrian leadership. Russian president Yeltsin pledged to withdraw Russian troops at the end of 2002, although the deadline came and went and Russian troops stayed. In Moldova, the election of the communist Vladimir Voronin to the presidency in 2001 raised hopes of a rapprochement. Voronin vowed to guarantee Russian-language education in Moldova; however, in spite of his pro-Russian rhetoric, he failed to achieve a major breakthrough in the settlement talks. Relations had soured by 2003 after Voronin unsuccessfully tried to force Transnistrian businesses to register and pay taxes in Moldova. In 2003 Russia outlined a solution in its Kozak Memorandum, which would have reunified Moldova, but Voronin did not accept its terms. The EU grew more involved in Transnistria in the 2000s as a result of its strengthened ties with Moldova. In November 2005, the EU deployed a Border Assistance Mission to the region to support the Moldovan and Ukrainian border guard services.

Leadership

The Transnistrian government is isolated internationally, the EU having imposed a travel ban on the leadership since 2003. Despite this, Transnistria has succeeded in creating all the trappings of an independent state. It has its own currency, anthem, postage stamps, police, military, executive, and legislature. The president and dominant figure in Transnistria since 1991 has been Igor Smirnov. He was reelected in 1996, 2001, and most recently in 2006, when he won 82.4 percent of the vote. The Transnistrian army has 4,500 full-time officers, 15,000 reserves, and 18 tanks. As for the government's political goals, the ICG's 2004 report concluded that the leadership, "recognizing that international recognition is unlikely . . . has focused on preserving de facto independence through a loose confederation with Moldova." The ICG said that the Transnistrian authorities had repressed opposition parties from 2000–2002, denying one group, the Transnistrian Unity, the right to run candidates and banning three leftist groups in late 2001 and early 2002.

However, a subsequent ICG report published in August 2006 indicated that the political climate had become somewhat less restrictive. The report noted that the December 2005 parliamentary elections were won by a group of business leaders led by Evgeny Shevchuk, who had formed the Obnovlenye (Renewal) movement in 2000 and registered it as a political party in 2006. His group won twenty-three seats out of forty-three, defeating President Smirnov's Respublica party, and Shevchuk became speaker of the parliament. Shevchuk, like Smirnov, supported Transnistrian independence, but unlike Smirnov Shevchuk was pro-business and pro-Western and favored a parliamentary-based system of government over a presidential one.

There is also a pro-Russian party and youth movement in Transnistria called Proryv, which in 2006 protested against the proposals of Shevchuk's Renewal party to reform Transnistria's land-leasing system. The Ukrainian community is represented by the Union of Ukrainians of Transnistria, which the ICG described in June 2004 as a front organization for the Transnistrian government "designed to lobby Kiev [that is, Ukraine] over its 'one-sided' approach to the crisis." Other parties to have emerged since 2006 include the Patriotic Party, led by Oleg Smirnov, son of President Smirnov; the Social Democratic Party, led by Alexander Radchenko, which supports an autonomous Transnistria within Moldova; and the Communist Party, whose candidate for president in 2006 was Nadezhda Bondarenko. Transnistrians in theory can also participate in the Moldovan elections, but in practice there is little contact between the two sides.

Current Status

In Moldova, President Voronin's communist party was defeated in the July 2009 elections, with four opposition parties forming a coalition and Voronin stepping down as president in September 2009. The new government seems more willing to engage with the Transnistrian leadership, although there has not thus far been any major breakthrough. The EU seems to be softening its stance on Transnistria slightly, deleting three names from its travel ban list in February 2010 "to encourage progress" in the talks. The international mediation process takes place within the so-called 5+2 framework, meaning that officials from Moldova, Transnistria, Russia, Ukraine, and the OSCE negotiate, while the EU and United States act as observers.

In March 2010, the U.S. State Department reported that the Transnistrian authorities had carried out "torture and arbitrary arrest" in 2009 and "continued to harass independent media and opposition lawmakers, restrict freedom of association, movement, and religion, and discriminate against Romanian speakers." An anti-government protest in the city of Dubasari planned for November 2009 was stopped by the local authorities two days before the event, it noted. In July 2009, Transnistrian customs officials confiscated Romanian-language dictionaries and encyclopedias from a group of 160 students and teachers returning from summer camp in Romania. The Moldovan police were not immune from criticism either, having reportedly harassed the chair of the Transnistrian youth movement, Proryv, when she was travelling back to Transnistria in May 2008.

Despite continuing tensions, a resumption of hostilities between Moldova and Transnistria does not seem likely within the next five years. The EU Border Assistance Mission, whose mandate has been extended until November 2011, appears to have helped stabilize the situation. By January 2011, the mission had a staff of more than two hundred officials from twenty-two EU countries. The mission has not unearthed as extensive a black market in Transnistria as expected, for example, in illicit drugs or arms trafficking. But it has helped to clamp down on the lucrative goods-smuggling trade. The EU Commission reported that from January–May 2009, large quantities of chicken meat was being sent from the Ukrainian port of Illichivsk through Transnistria to be re-exported as part of a racket aimed at avoiding customs duties. The scheme had deprived the Ukrainian government of an estimated $40 billion (€30 billion) in tax revenue.

Transnistria continues to be pro-Russian, with a government that is often described as a relic of the Soviet era. This orientation was highlighted in a November 2009 article by Peter Wilson for *The Australian* newspaper. "Hammer and sickle emblems on street corners, photos of model workers are lined up outside the town hall, and Lenin juts his chin atop his pedestal outside a parliament that is called the Supreme Soviet," he wrote, reporting from the Transnistrian capital Tiraspol. There were Russian soldiers and tanks manning the roads. The largest company in the region, Sheriff Corporation, was the brainchild of former Soviet security officers, and Transnistria's steelworks were controlled by a Russian business tycoon. Many Transnistrians had been given Russian passports by Moscow. Wilson cited a Transnistrian doctor asserting that "when we separated, Transnistria was richer than Moldova but too many authorities and government officials have been looting our economy. Ordinary people got poorer and the quality of life is now better in Moldova."

Transnistria's small size makes it difficult for it to establish itself as a viable independent country. Yet as time passes and it continues to function, even as it is completely cut off from Moldova by operating its own Russia-oriented administration, the more difficult it will become to reintegrate into Moldova. And as Moldova draws itself closer to the West, notably through its ongoing, long-term campaign to join the EU, the chasm between Moldova and Transnistria seems likely to only grow wider.

Further Reading

Council of the European Union. "Conclusions on Moldova and Transnistria," February 22, 2010, www.consilium.europa.eu/uedocs/cms_data/docs/pressdata/EN/foraff/112952.pdf.

European Union Border Assistance Mission to Moldova and Ukraine Web site, www.eubam.org.

International Crisis Group. "Moldova: Regional Tensions over Transnistria," *Europe Report*, no 157 (June 17, 2004), www.crisisgroup.org/~/media/Files/europe/157_moldova_regional_tensions_over_transdniestria.ashx.

———. "Moldova's Uncertain Future," *Europe Report*, no. 175 (August 17, 2006), www.crisisgroup.org/~/media/Files/europe/175_moldova_s_uncertain_future.ashx.

U.S. State Department. "2009 Human Rights Report: Moldova," March 11, 2010, www.state.gov/g/drl/rls/hrrpt/2009/eur/136046.htm.

Wilson, Peter. "Bare survival in land that reform forgot," *The Australian*, November 7, 2009, www.theaustralian.com.au/news/world/bare-survival-in-land-that-reform-forgot/story-e6frg6so-1225795166328.

TURKISH CYPRIOTS
(Cyprus)

The ethnic Turkish people living on the eastern Mediterranean island of Cyprus have operated a de facto independent state since 1974, when an invasion by Turkish troops allowed them to carve out their own region in the north. Many years of negotiations with the Greek Cypriots in the south, aimed at reunifying the island in a federation where Turkish Cypriots would have broad autonomy, have failed to lead to a political settlement. The island's partition appears to be hardening.

Turkish Cypriots live in a de facto independent state called the Turkish Republic of Northern Cyprus (TRNC), which no other government apart from Turkey recognizes. It comprises 36 percent of the territory of Cyprus. The Greek Cypriots have their own state, called the Republic of Cyprus, which is the internationally recognized government for the whole island. The Turkish Cypriots' nearest neighbor is Turkey, which lies just forty miles to the north; Israel and Lebanon lie to the east, Egypt to the south, and Greece to the west.

The TRNC population is 264,000, or 24 percent of the Cypriot population of 1.1 million. At least half the Turkish Cypriots have moved there since 1974 when the Turkish troops invaded. The newer arrivals are called "settlers" by Greek Cypriots, but Turkish Cypriots avoid using this term, not wishing to draw a distinction between the pre- and post-1974 Turks. Turkish Cypriots speak Turkish and are Sunni Muslim; Greek Cypriots speak Greek and are Greek Orthodox Christian.

The Turkish Cypriots separated themselves in response to repeated attacks by Greek Cypriots coupled with a fear the Cypriot government was about to unify with Greece. The period from 1963–1974 was a turbulent time for all Cypriots. Greek nationalism was on the rise, manifested through an *enosis,* or unity movement, aimed at annexing Cyprus to Greece. Violence between the two communities was widespread, resulting in the destruction of property and the deaths of thousands. Turkish Cypriots bore the brunt of the violence.

In an October 2007 face-to-face interview, the Greek Cypriot ambassador to the United States, Andreas Kakouris, highlighted a major legacy of the 1974 invasion: dramatic population movement. Some 160,000 Greek Cypriots fled southward, leaving behind homes and property, 88 percent of which has since been sold, Kakouris said. Hundreds of monasteries and churches were converted to mosques, barracks, and hotels by the Turks. Forty-three thousand Turkish troops occupied the north, making Cyprus one of the most militarized places in the world.

Ergun Fikri, a Turkish Cypriot electronic engineer said in an April 2010 telephone interview that Greek Cypriots had demolished most of his village, Arodhes, in southern Cyprus. Arodhes' Turkish Cypriot residents had moved northward en masse in 1976 under a relocation agreement, he said. Fikri, who has lived in the United States since 1980, said demolition of abandoned Turkish Cypriot villages had taken place across the south.

There is much residual resentment between Greek and Turkish Cypriots. Social contact is limited; however, there has not been any major outbreak of violence since 1974. Because the TRNC is not internationally recognized, Turkish Cypriots encounter difficulties trading with—and to a lesser extent, traveling to—foreign countries. They are unable to export goods directly to countries other than Turkey; instead, they must be routed through southern Cypriot ports.

Travelling presents challenges, but Turkish Cypriots do have various options. For example, those who lived in Cyprus before 1974, or whose parents did, can get an internationally recognized passport from the Greek Cypriot government. All Turkish Cypriots can obtain a Turkish passport relatively easily. The TRNC issues its own passports, but only the United Kingdom—which ruled Cyprus from 1878–1960—the United States, and Turkey accept them as a valid form of identity. Neither the United Kingdom nor the United States will affix visas to them; Turkey does not require visiting Turkish Cypriots to obtain a visa. Turkish Cypriots have been able to travel freely to and from southern Cyprus since 2003 when the border, known as the Green Line, was opened. North-south trade in goods is growing but remains limited. Turkish Cypriots use the Turkish lira as their currency, whereas Greek Cypriots adopted the euro in 2008.

Turkish Cypriots have developed links beyond Turkey; for example, they have developed ties with other Islamic and Turkic countries, such as Azerbaijan and Pakistan, although neither of the latter has formal diplomatic relations with the TRNC. The TRNC is an observer member of the Organization of the Islamic Conference, an association of fifty-seven Islamic states that promotes Muslim solidarity. The Greek Cypriots, meanwhile, joined the European Union in May 2004. They have used their EU membership to obstruct Turkey's efforts to join the EU, in retaliation for Turkey's support of the TRNC and for Turkey's refusal to allow Greek Cypriot ships to use Turkish ports. The United States favors reunifying the island but has allowed the United Nations to take the lead in brokering a unification settlement; it has also taken a back seat to EU efforts to end Turkish Cypriots' economic isolation.

History

Turks first moved to Cyprus in significant numbers in the sixteenth century after the Ottoman Empire took control in 1571; prior to this, the island had experienced a host of diverse rulers, including Venetians (1489–1571), Franks (1192–1489), and Byzantines (965–1191). Although the Ottoman rulers and Turkish Cypriots were Muslim, the Greek Orthodox Church survived and played a major role in preserving and shaping Greek identity among Greek Cypriots. In 1878 the United Kingdom occupied Cyprus and in 1914 annexed it. The Greek Cypriots, who formed 80 percent of the population, launched a violent insurgency against British rule in 1956. The rebellion culminated in the handing over of power from Britain to a unitary, independent Republic of Cyprus in August 1960.

An attempted military coup in the Greek Cypriot–dominated government in July 1974, which was supported by the government of Greece, led Turkey to intervene militarily. On July 20, the Turkish government dispatched thousands of troops, who took control of the northern part of the island where most of the Turkish Cypriots lived. Four thousand people were killed in the fighting, and thousands of Greek Cypriots were detained in camps by the Turkish army. Whereas before the invasion there were many Turkish Cypriots living in the south and many Greek Cypriots living in the north, the conflict triggered large-scale population movements that led to the sharp division of the island along ethnic lines. The capital city, Nicosia, was divided, too, with the new border separating the north from the south cutting through it.

After the conflict, Turks from Turkey began immigrating to Turkish-occupied northern Cyprus in large numbers. These immigrants were a mix of commercial entrepreneurs and agricultural workers seeking jobs and land. Many of the new arrivals came from religiously conservative areas where women tended to wear Muslim headscarves. This distinguished them somewhat from the pre-invasion Turkish Cypriots, who tended to have a more secular, European outlook.

The Turkish Cypriots declared an independent state on November 15, 1983, and confirmed their status in a May 1985 referendum, which passed by 70 percent. In 1990 the Greek Cypriot government applied to join the EU, launching a negotiation process that culminated in May 2004 in Cyprus being admitted, minus de facto the Turkish Cypriot part. The EU would have preferred to admit a unified Cyprus, but a unification plan brokered by the UN failed to secure the necessary approval of the two sides. The Annan Plan, named after former UN Secretary General Kofi Annan, would have given the Turkish Cypriots a generous degree of autonomy within a federal state. In the April 2004 referendum on the plan, 65 percent of Turkish Cypriots voted in favor; however, 76 percent of Greek Cypriots voted against.

The Greek Cypriots objected to the Annan Plan because it would have allowed 650 Turkish troops to remain in Cyprus. In addition, it permitted the Turks who had moved to Cyprus after 1974 to stay, instead of forcing them to give back their land and properties to the Greek Cypriots who had fled the invasion. Rejection of the plan was a significant blow to the Turkish Cypriots because they could not enjoy the benefits of EU membership that the Greek Cypriots had gained. The EU tried to remedy the situation by adopting the Green Line Regulation, which permitted Turkish Cypriots to export goods via Greek Cypriot ports such as Limassol and Larnaca. But the TRNC was not satisfied with this arrangement and continued demanding that it be allowed to trade directly with the EU. The UN, after the 2004 failure, continued to try to promote a unification settlement—and continued to fail.

Leadership

The TRNC has a fully functional government, which like the Greek Cypriot government, is based in Nicosia. In addition to the Turkish military stationed there, the TRNC is also protected by five thousand Turkish Cypriot troops. The founding father of the TRNC was Rauf Denktash, who served as president from 1983–2005, having been elected four times. Denktash was generally viewed as a hard-liner, who sought to consolidate the Turkish Cypriots' independence. He was succeeded in April 2005 by Mehmet Ali Talat, who was considered more moderate. A prominent figure in the TRNC government is Ozdil Nami, who was appointed TRNC Special Representative to the EU and UN in November 2007.

In the TRNC parliamentary elections of April 2009, the largest political party to emerge was the National Unity Party, led by the hard-line nationalist Dervish Eroglu. The party won 44 percent of the vote and secured twenty-six seats in the fifty-seat legislature. The other political parties that won seats were the Republican Turkish Party, led by Ferdi Sabit Soyer; the Democrat Party, led by Serdar Denktash (son of Rauf); the Communal Democracy

Rauf Raif Denktash (1924–   )

RAUF RAIF DENKTASH, the founder and first president of the Turkish Republic of Northern Cyprus, was born on January 27, 1924, in the city of Paphos, Cyprus. While Denktash grew up, Cyprus was under British control. He was educated at the English School in Nicosia and then went on to receive a Barrister-at-Law degree from Lincoln's Inn, London. In 1947 Denktash began to practice law in Cyprus and became a prosecutor for the crown in 1949; he held this position until 1957. During his time working for the British, Denktash was charged with prosecuting several individuals affiliated with the EOKA (Ethniki Organosis Kyprion Agoniston, or National Organization of Cypriot Fighters), a Greek Cypriot activist group attempting to bring an end to British control of the island and initiate unification with Greece. Denktash was notably successful in his prosecution of EOKA members, many of whom were executed.

In 1957 Denktash assisted in the founding of a rival paramilitary organization, the TMT (Türk Mukavemet Teşkilat, or Turkish Resistance Organization). The main goal of the TMT was to prevent *enosis*, or the unification of Greece and Cyprus.

In 1960 the British signed the Zürich agreement granting Cyprus independence. The agreement provided a constitution that divided up power within the newly constituted Republic of Cyprus along ethnic lines. Denktash was elected to serve as president of the legislative body created by the constitution for the Turkish Cypriots, namely, the Turkish Communal Chamber.

By 1963 the independent Republic of Cyprus began to experience hostilities between its Turkish and Greek citizens, as the latter pushed for unification with Greece. Later that same year Greek paramilitary groups began initiating violent attacks against ethnic Turks. Consequently, the Turkish Cypriots withdrew from the nation's government; Denktash traveled to Ankara, Turkey, to consult with the Turkish authorities on how to handle the situation. Denktash ended up spending four years outside of Cyprus when the Greek Cypriot government refused to permit him to return. This was largely the result of Denktash's involvement with the TMT. After Denktash finally received permission to reenter the country in 1968, he began to play a key role in negotiations between the Greek and Turkish Cypriot communities. However, a 1974 Greek Cypriot coup backed by the Greek government caused the dialogue between the two groups to break down.

Turkey responded with force to the Greek Cypriot coup and took control of approximately 36 percent of the island. With this newly secured territory, the Turkish Cypriots formed an autonomous entity, the Turkish Federated States of Cyprus, and elected Denktash president for two terms.

Denktash led negotiations for reconciliation with the Republic of Cyprus from 1975 to 1983. Then, late in 1983, Denktash and the Turkish Cypriots were angered by Greece's move to bring the situation in Cyprus to the UN General Assembly. As a result, Denktash declared that the Turkish Cypriots were forming an independent nation, the Turkish Republic of Northern Cyprus (TRNC). Denktash was subsequently elected president of the TRNC and went on to serve four five-year terms. Denktash chose not to seek another term in office in 2004, as his party was losing constituent support. This effectively ended his political career.

From 1963–2004 Denktash acted on behalf of the Turkish Cypriot community as the primary negotiator with the United Nations and the Greek Cypriots. In this capacity Denktash endeavored to reach a resolution with the Greek Cypriots, one contingent on the Greek Cypriots' recognition of the TRNC as an independent state. Had the Greek Cypriots met this prerequisite, it would follow as part of Denktash's plan that the TRNC and the Republic of Cyprus would come together as a single country organized into two loosely confederated entities. Denktash's refusal to accept any proposal that fell short of this requirement led the international community to blame him for the absence of a peace agreement for many years. However, by 2004 the Turkish Cypriot community signalled an increased desire for reconciliation when it approved a referendum that would have merged the TRNC with the Republic of Cyprus. The referendum failed, however, when it was voted down in a separate poll by the Greek Cypriots. From that point forward, the face of the Cyprus problem was no longer Denktash's; it was now the Greek Cypriots who were viewed as intransigent.

Since leaving office Denktash has pursued writing and photography; he has written more than fifty books and his photographs have been displayed throughout the world. Denktash is married and has two daughters and one son. His son, Serdar Denktash, is currently a prominent politician in the TRNC and has served as Deputy Prime Minister as well as Minister for Foreign Affairs.

Party, led by Mehmet Cakici; and the Freedom and Reform Party, led by Turgay Avci.

When Cyprus gained independence in 1960, the Turkish Cypriots were guaranteed 30 percent representation in a unified island government. But relations between the Greek and Turkish Cypriots quickly deteriorated, and in December 1963 the Turkish Cypriot leadership quit the government. The Greek Cypriots argue that the Turkish Cypriots departed voluntarily and that the current Greek Cypriot–dominated government is the legitimate representative body for the whole island. The Turkish Cypriots insist they were ousted by force, in breach of the constitution, and that the official Cypriot government is consequently illegitimate because it does not have Turkish Cypriot representation.

The TRNC government supports reunification with the south on principle and is willing to form a bi-zonal, bi-communal federation that gives Turkish Cypriots a great deal of autonomy. The Turkish Cypriots oppose any settlement that involves large-scale population transfers between the north and south. In a face-to-face interview in October 2007, the TRNC's representative to the United States, Hilmi Akil, said, "we are willing to cede some territory to the Greek Cypriots, allow some to return, and compensate the rest." But Akil was adamant in stating that the Turkish Cypriots had no desire to move back to the Greek Cypriot areas they left because "they have already suffered so much."

Current Status

In May 2008, Turkish and Greek Cypriot leaders agreed to resume unification talks. Speaking at a seminar at Georgetown University in Washington, D.C., in April 2010, TRNC representative Akil stressed that any future unification deal had to respect Turkish Cypriots' separate identity. "We would like to have two constituent states in one country," he said. Turkish Cypriots will not accede to a unitary state, wary that such an arrangement

could lead to unification with Greece given Greek Cypriots' status as the majority. Akil hinted that unification might never happen. "If Cyprus is going to be divided forever, it will happen by default. It will happen if too much time passes. Greek Cypriots are aware of this, which is why they have resumed negotiations."

In April 2010, hard-liner Dervish Eroglu was elected president of the TRNC, winning 50 percent of the vote and defeating his more moderate rival, Talat, who won 43 percent. In an article in the *Irish Times* newspaper, journalist Michael Jansen reported that Eroglu received the votes of many Turkish settlers who did not want a political settlement with the Greek Cypriots, concerned that such a deal would force their return to Turkey. Jansen attributed Talat's loss to his failure to make progress in his reunification talks with the Greek Cypriots.

By January 2011, Turkey had thirty thousand troops stationed in northern Cyprus. Most Turkish Cypriots are content to have the Turkish military stay, even if there is a unification settlement, because their presence makes them feel more secure. The Turkish government seems flexible on the issue. A March 2010 article in *The Economist* magazine reported that Turkey's prime minister, Tayyip Erdogan, told a group of visiting Greek Cypriot journalists that Turkish troops would leave if there were a settlement. There are upward of a thousand UN peace-keepers on the island who help maintain the buffer zone separating the north and south.

Turkish Cypriots remain isolated from the south. They use Turkey's dialing code for telephone calls, which means that any north-to-south telephone calls are routed internationally; they receive their mail service via Turkey as well. There are still no direct international flights to the TRNC from any country other than Turkey. A private airline in Azerbaijan, a fellow Turkic nation, tried to establish a route from 2000 but abandoned the plan in response to international pressure. People-to-people contacts between north and south are growing; however, isolated attacks on Turkish Cypriots have been reported. The EU is trying to promote north-south trade. In June 2008, the EU removed customs tariffs on agricultural products from the TRNC and increased the value of goods TRNC travelers may bring back from southern Cyprus customs duty free. In an August 2008 report, the European Commission voiced concern about a growing number of illegal immigrants crossing from north to south, mostly Syrians, Palestinians, and Iranians. The commission attributed this flow to a direct ferry link between the Syrian port of Latakia and the Turkish Cypriot port of Famagusta. An increasingly contentious issue is how Turkish Cypriots will benefit financially if oil and gas is discovered off the Cyprus coast. The Greek Cypriot government undertook oil exploration in February 2007, but it is unclear how much of any future revenues it intends to give to Turkish Cypriots.

There remain a myriad of legal disputes over land and property ownership between Turkish and Greek Cypriots that stem from the 1960s and 1970s population shifts. The Strasbourg-based European Court of Human Rights (ECHR) is a key player in adjudicating these disputes. *The Economist* magazine reported in March 2010 that a recent ECHR ruling gave a boost to the Turkish Cypriots by requiring Greek Cypriots seeking land restitution or compensation to first apply to an immovable property commission in the TRNC. As for the broader issue of unification, according to Turkish Cypriot Ergun Fikri, "the best solution would be a loose federation for now. In time people will mix more and maybe in forty years they can reunify. But unity should not be forced on them within the next five years."

Further Reading

European Commission. "Annual Report on the implementation of Council Regulation EC 866/2004 of 29 April 2004 and the situation resulting from its application," August 27, 2008, http://eur-lex.europa.eu/LexUriServ/LexUriServ.do?uri=COM:2008:0529:FIN:EN:PDF.

"A fillip for Talat?; The Cyprus talks," *The Economist*, March 13, 2010, www.economist.com/world/europe/displaystory.cfm?story_id=15663646.

Jansen, Michael. "Nationalist Dervis Eroglu wins Turkish Cypriot election," *The Irish Times,* April 19, 2010, www.irishtimes.com/newspaper/world/2010/0419/1224268630458.html.

Ministry of Foreign Affairs of the Government of the Turkish Republic of Northern Cyprus (TRNC) Public Information Web site, www.trncinfo.com.

National Unity Party Web site, www.ulusalbirlikpartisi.com.

Randoux, Fabrice, and Olessia Lougaskova. "Cyprus seeks new measures against Ankara," *Europolitics*, December 4, 2009, www.europolitics.info/cyprus-seeks-new-measures-against-ankara-artr256850–40.html.

Speech of TRNC President Mehmet Ali Talat at luncheon for UN Secretary General Ban Ki Moon, Nicosia, February 1, 2010, www.kktcb.eu/index.php?tpl=show_announ&id=195.

West Europe

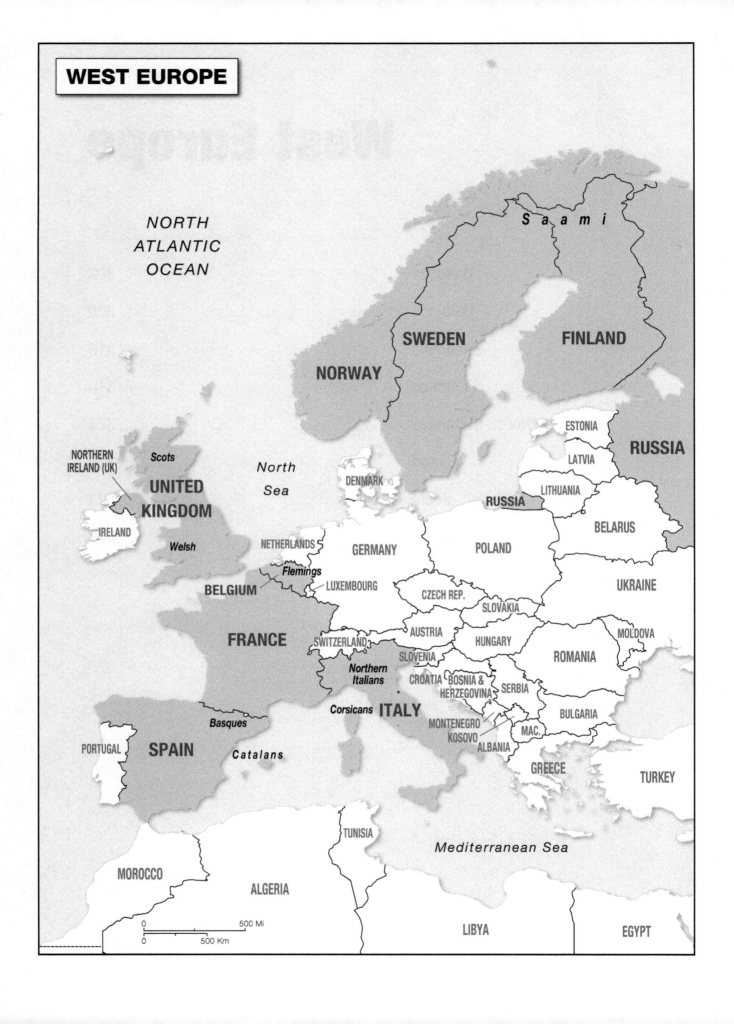

WEST EUROPE

NORTH
ATLANTIC
OCEAN

Saami

SWEDEN

FINLAND

NORWAY

RUSSIA

ESTONIA

LATVIA

LITHUANIA

RUSSIA

Scots

NORTHERN
IRELAND (UK)

UNITED
KINGDOM

North
Sea

DENMARK

BELARUS

IRELAND

Welsh

NETHERLANDS

GERMANY

POLAND

Flemings

LUXEMBOURG

UKRAINE

BELGIUM

CZECH REP.

SLOVAKIA

FRANCE

SWITZERLAND

AUSTRIA

HUNGARY

MOLDOVA

SLOVENIA

ROMANIA

*Northern
Italians*

CROATIA

BOSNIA &
HERZEGOVINA

SERBIA

Corsicans

ITALY

BULGARIA

MONTENEGRO
KOSOVO

MAC.

Basques

ALBANIA

PORTUGAL

SPAIN

Catalans

GREECE

TURKEY

TUNISIA

Mediterranean Sea

MOROCCO

ALGERIA

0   500 Mi

0   500 Km

LIBYA

EGYPT

BASQUES
(France, Spain)

The Basque people who live in north-eastern Spain and southwestern France have one of the most well-known separatist movements in Europe. Basque separatists are divided into militant and democratic wings. The main militant group, ETA, has led a violent campaign since 1968 in which over eight hundred people have been killed. Basques already enjoy cultural and territorial autonomy in Spain, but many would like an independent Basque country. The Basques in France, much smaller in number, do not have an autonomous government.

There are 2.1 million people in the Basque autonomous territories of Spain. They make up 5 percent of the Spanish population of 40.5 million. Many of these are descendents of non-Basques who immigrated to the Basque region in the 1800s. The Basques live in the Spanish provinces of Alava, Guipuzoca, and Vizcaya and the region of Navarre. They come from Spain's industrial heartland, which is also the wealthiest part of the country. France counts seventy thousand Basque-speakers, mainly located in the regions of Labourd, Lower Navarre, and Soule, an area the Basques call Parralde.

The Basque homeland is called "Pais Vasco" (Basque Country). The Basques have their own language, Euskara, which has three dialects in France and three in Spain. Euskara does not derive from the Indo-European linguistic family, and as such it is very different from other European languages. In Spain 600,000 speak Basque as their first language; another 1.2 million have some knowledge of it. Basque is an official language in Spain's Basque autonomous region and in the Basque-populated parts of the neighboring Spanish region of Navarre. The Basque language is spoken by far fewer people in France, a legacy of the French language having been imposed for a longer period and with greater intensity. The Basques are predominantly Catholic, the majority religion in both France and Spain.

For much of the twentieth century Basques in both France and Spain were living under highly centralized administrations that offered little in the way of self-government and stifled both the preservation and development of the Basque culture. The situation was particularly repressive in Spain under the fascist dictator Francisco Franco, who ruled the country from 1936 until his death in 1975. The rise of separatism among Spain's Basques was in part a reaction against the political repression and centralization they endured in Franco's Spain. In the post-Franco era, Spain's Basques have gained a large degree of autonomy as the country has introduced a democratic and decentralized system of government. The Basque autonomous government established in 1979 can, for example, raise taxes and has its own police force called the *Ertzaintza* (Peoples Guard).

The central Spanish government based in Madrid has since the late 1970s been sympathetic to Basque demands for autonomy, although it consistently opposes the Basques' right to secede and establish their own state. Under Spain's proportionally based electoral system it is rare for a single political party to gain an absolute majority in the national parliament. The central government therefore often relies on the support of regionally based, pro-autonomy political groups such as the Basque Nationalist Party (Partido Nacionalista Vasco, or PNV) to stay in power. This has given the non-violent Basque pro-autonomy parties in Spain strong political leverage. By contrast, the Basques in France are more isolated and not as well organized politically; as a result, they exert little influence over the French government. They have consequently not been able to obtain autonomy.

Spain opposes the formation of an independent Basque state because it does not wish to lose a large and wealthy piece of its territory. Its opposition is also motivated by the fear that a Basque secession could cause the entire country to break up by encouraging other autonomous communities in Spain, such as the Catalans (see separate essay), to secede as well. This fear of disintegration explains why Spain was one of the five European Union member states that refused to recognize Kosovo as an independent country when Kosovo seceded from Serbia in February 2008.

Basque separatists, despite a strong leadership and sense of cohesion, have been hampered in their campaign for independence by a lack of support from neighboring European governments. The EU, in a show of solidarity with Spain, a member of the EU since 1986, has taken a zero tolerance approach toward the militant Basque separatists. The EU classifies all Basque militant groups as terrorist organizations, including the political wings of the militants. The best known of these armed groups is ETA (Euskadi ta Askatasuna, which means "Basque Homeland and Liberty"). Some in the Basque country still support ETA's violent campaign for independence, but as the conflict has dragged on and killed ever more people with little sign of a lasting settlement, many Basques have grown hostile to ETA. In August 2008, for example, there was public outrage when ETA member Inaki De Juana Chaos was released from prison after serving twenty years for carrying out terrorist attacks that killed twenty-five people. Declining support for militancy has left ETA increasingly marginalized even though many Basques support its goals.

History

The Basques have lived in their homeland for thousands of years. When the Romans invaded in 194 B.C.E., the Basques managed to retain autonomy. In the seventh century C.E., the Duchy of Vasconia was established in the surrounding area; by the ninth century the duchy had shrunk in size to an area broadly corresponding to the Basque country. In 1200 the Basques became part of the Kingdom of Castile, whose domains lay west of the Basque country. Castile gradually merged with other kingdoms, and by 1492 it encompassed modern-day Spain. The Basques were split between the French and Spanish kingdoms in 1513.

The French Basques initially enjoyed autonomy, but the French Revolution of 1789 triggered a process of governmental centralization that also led to the suppression of regional cultures, including that of the Basques. In Spain the Basques enjoyed autonomy until 1839, when it was revoked during the Carlist wars of succession for the Spanish throne. A mining and ship-building industry developed in the Basque region in the 1800s, attracting people from other parts of Spain to the area. This population influx helped spawn a Basque nationalist movement as local leaders grew fearful of losing their identity through intermarriage and assimilation.

A republican government in Spain approved an autonomous statute for the Basques in 1936, but it had not yet been implemented when civil war broke out. The Basque town of Guernica, a republican stronghold, was bombed in 1937 by the German Air Force; Nazi Germany had allied itself with Franco's nationalist forces, who opposed autonomous movements. By 1939 the nationalists had defeated the republicans. After World War II (1939–1945), the Basques endured severe repression under the Franco government. Twenty-one thousand people were killed and thousands more exiled and imprisoned during Franco's regime. Basque militancy in Spain increased in the 1960s. In December 1973, ETA assassinated Spain's prime minister, Luis Carrero-Blanco.

After Franco died in 1975, the Basques saw their territorial autonomy restored as Spain became a democratic, constitutional monarchy. A Basque cultural revival got under way in the 1980s. Euskara was introduced into the educational system, and Basque radio and television channels proliferated. Meanwhile, ETA's militant campaign against the Spanish government intensified. In April 1995, fourteen former Spanish political and security officials were indicted on charges of having run a secret death squad that targeted ETA members in the 1980s. ETA declared a cease-fire in September 1998 but ended it in December 1999 when its core demands—the release of 450 imprisoned operatives and a referendum on independence—were not met.

The deadliest terrorist attack on Spanish soil, the Madrid train bombings of March 2004 that killed 193 people, was initially attributed to ETA by the Spanish government. In fact, the Islamist group al Qaeda had carried out the bombings in retaliation for the Spanish government's support of the United States in the U.S.-led wars in Afghanistan and Iraq, launched in 2001 and 2003,

respectively. The government was defeated in elections three days after the attacks, following a public outcry over its attempt to blame ETA. The new prime minister, Jose Luis Zapatero, was initially conciliatory to ETA, signing a peace agreement in March 2006. The cease-fire ended in December 2006, however, when ETA detonated a bomb at the Madrid airport. The Zapatero government became more hard-line thereafter, banning political parties, such as Batasuna, suspected of being ETA fronts. In France, the Basques have made some advances in the area of cultural autonomy, with the Basque language allowed as an optional subject of study at French schools. Nevertheless, even in Basque-populated areas it is the French language that dominates in education, law, and public administration.

Leadership

Founded in 1959, ETA advocates the establishment of an independent country for the Basque people. It has a socialist political ideology and operates as a militant organization. Leaders of ETA include Francisco Xabier Garcia Gaztelu, Ignacio Gracia Arregui, and Felix Alberto Lopez. By January 2011 there were approximately seven hundred ETA operatives in jails in France and Spain. Public revulsion at the destruction and killing by ETA led to the emergence in the late 1990s of an anti-ETA grassroots group called Basta Ya, which means "Enough is Enough."

ETA has a political wing that has renamed itself several times to try to circumvent the government's attempts to ban it for supporting terrorism. Its longest-lasting incarnation was Batasuna, which means "Unity," established in 1978. Batasuna competed in elections in the 1980s and 1990s; however, in 2003 Spain designated it a terrorist organization, which meant that it could no longer receive state funding, compete in elections, or organize public demonstrations. The party's assets were subsequently frozen. The Strasbourg-based European

Iratxe Sorzabal (1972?–)

REUTERS/Ho New

IRATXE SORZABAL, whose birth year is presumed to be 1972, came from a community that had strong affiliations to Basque traditions, language, and nationalism. Not much has been reported about Sorzabal's life before she became involved in ETA, but her record with them spans almost two decades and is filled with allegations of attacks, legal battles, and jail time as she rose through the ranks of the violent organization.

In the 1990s Sorzabal's "commando," or the ETA-affiliated team with which she worked, allegedly was responsible for twenty attacks, including three murders. She was sentenced to three years in prison in France, beginning in 1997, and was expelled from France to Spain in 1999.

In Spain, she was arrested in March 1999 and held without communication for five days—the maximum permitted under Spanish law at the time. Sorzabal claimed that during her time in Spanish custody she was systematically tortured. For example, after arriving in the Spanish capital Madrid, she reported being beaten by six or seven officers and being hit around the head with a rolled-up magazine or telephone directory. She also reported that she was forced to undress and had a plastic bag placed over her head and another forced into her mouth, which restricted her breathing and made her vomit. Sorzabal lodged a complaint over her alleged treatment. In September 1999, she was released due to lack of evidence. She was arrested again on March 30, 2001, for alleged links to ETA's Galicia commando, but was cleared of charges for three murders, again due to a lack of evidence. She subsequently made further allegations of torture while in Spanish custody. In 2003 a French court refused to extradite a suspected male ETA terrorist due to the fact that his extradition was requested on the basis of statements made by Sorzabal, allegedly while being tortured.

In 2001 Batasuna, a now-outlawed Basque nationalist party that provided funds for ETA, took up Sorzabal's cause, distributing press releases and graphic photographs to corroborate her claim that she had been tortured while in Spanish custody. Another warrant for her arrest was issued in 2005, and she has been pursued since then for alleged involvement in terrorism.

In April 2009, the top-tier ETA leaders were arrested. Thirty-seven-year old Sorzabal and 33-year-old Izaskun Lesaka subsequently assumed leadership positions within the ETA organization. Sorzabal, who is presumed to have been named the new political head of the organization, has been called "the most significant" member of ETA's ideological structure by the Spanish police. Both Sorzabal and Lesaka are thought to have links with the Irish Republican Army (IRA), a militant group seeking to end British rule in Northern Ireland and unite the northern and southern parts of Ireland. This was in part because Sorzabal has been connected with Thomas "Slab" Murphy, the IRA's former chief of staff.

In June 2009, a senior anti-terrorist police officer was burned to death in Bilbao; his murder is believed to have been ordered by either Sorzabal or Lesaka. In August 2009, a car bomb killed two Spanish Civil Guards, an action that was blamed on two other female ETA leaders. In 2010 photos of Sorzabal with a young child surfaced, prompting speculation that she is both a mother and a terrorist leader. Sorzabal's prominence in ETA is emblematic of a demographic shift that has taken place in the organization. Whereas in earlier days women associated with ETA tended to be the mothers of ETA prisoners who would stage protests with signs emblazoned with photos of their children, today, as more of ETA's male leaders are being killed or arrested, the operating leadership has become increasingly dominated by women such as Sorzabal.

Court of Human Rights in June 2009 upheld the ban. Batasuna's leader is Arnaldo Otegi. Batasuna subsequently renamed itself Iniciativa Internationalist II and took part in the European Parliament elections in June 2009, winning 1 percent of the vote but no seat. Batasuna has also been named at various times Partido Comunista de las Tierras Vascas (PCTV) and Accion Nacionalist Vasca (ANV).

Although ETA is more well-known internationally, the Basque nationalist PNV has consistently won more votes than ETA-affiliated parties. The PNV advocates for increased Basque autonomy, and even independence, but espouses only peaceful means to achieve its goals. The party was established in 1895 by Sabino Arana-Goiri. In 1980 the PNV's Carlos Garaikoetxea Urriza became the first prime minister of the Basque autonomous community. The current leadership includes Inigo Urkullu, Juan José Ibarretxe, Josune Aristondo, and Josu Erkoreka. A PNV splinter group was established in September 1986 called the Eusko Abertzaleak (Basque Patriots), later renamed Eusko Alkartasuna (Basque Solidarity). Led by Pello Urizar, the party is left-leaning and non-violent. It won 3.6 percent of the vote in the March 2009 Basque regional elections.

In France, a Basque political party called Iparretarrak, which means "Those of the North," was established in 1973 but was banned in July 1987 after leader Philippe Bidart was convicted of murder. The organization Irrintzi has been responsible for most of the attacks in the French Basque region since 2005. French Basque autonomy campaigners focus their efforts on preserving their culture; only a few demand independence. The Basque in France maintain a cultural association called Ikastola.

Current Status

In Spain, ETA carried out thirty-five attacks in 2008 and fourteen in 2009, a report published in April 2010 by the Hague-based European Police Office Europol found. ETA obtains most of its income through extortion, demanding that local businesses pay a "revolutionary tax," Europol reported. Dozens of ETA operatives were arrested in France, Portugal, and Spain in 2008 and 2009, and thousands of pounds of explosives were seized. In February 2010, French police, working with their Spanish counterparts, arrested a top ETA figure, Gogeascochea Arronategui, along with ETA members Aguinagalde Ugartemendia and Gregorio Jimenez Morales. Responding to the killing in March 2010 of a French police officer by ETA, the French authorities further escalated their clampdown on ETA, and in May 2010 arrested another top ETA leader, Mikel Kabikoitz Karrera Sarobe. France has long been a logistical base for ETA. With French and Spanish police increasingly cooperating with one another, however, ETA tried to set up a base in Portugal but by late 2010 that too was being dismantled. ETA in September 2010 announced another cease-fire but the Spanish government immediately rejected it, dismissing it as a sign of desperation from an organization on the verge of collapse.

In France, the number of French Basque militants continues to decrease, according to Europol, and the attacks they carry out are of low intensity. French Basques only account for 3 percent of the overall Basque population. Europol noted that in December 2009 the founder of Irrintzi was arrested. The nature of attacks in France differs from Spain, Europol noted. Whereas in Spain Basque militant attacks tend to be on government buildings, businesses, and critical infrastructure, in France private property and individuals are often targeted. There were eight attacks by Basque separatists in France in 2009, directed mostly at the tourist sector.

A July 2009 article in the British newspaper *The Observer* by Giles Tremlett revealed that "as ETA's old guard is rounded up, a new generation of ruthless female fighters is taking over." The two suspected killers of Eduardo Puelles, a counterterrorist specialist in the French police force who was killed by a car bomb in the Basque city of Bilbao on July 19, 2009, were women: Iratxe Sorzabal and Izaskun Lesaka. Whereas in 2002 12 percent of ETA prisoners were female, by 2009 this share had risen to 25 percent. ETA's most notorious female operative, Idoia Lopez Riano, known as "the tigress," is serving a thirty-year jail sentence for twenty-three murders. Journalist Tremlett noted that political groups identified with ETA still typically garner about 100,000 votes in elections.

The PNV has been demanding a referendum on independence. Its efforts have been stymied by the Spanish constitutional court, which blocked a vote on self-determination planned for October 2008. There is resentment among some Basques that the Basque autonomous government's borders do not extend to parts of the neighboring region of Navarre where many Basques live. In the Basque regional elections of March 2009, the PNV lost power for the first time since 1980 after winning 38 percent of the vote and thirty seats, eight short of an absolute majority.

In an April 2009 article in the *Irish Times* daily newspaper, journalist Victor Mallet said the results "suggest that ethnic nationalism on the Iberian peninsula is in retreat." He added that "many Spaniards, including those who voted for the unionist parties that won the latest regional elections, say the pendulum has now swung too far in the direction of autonomy. There is a whiff of centrist counter-revolution in the air, a sense Spain will fall apart if Madrid is too lenient with the regions." Spanish-speaking residents in the Basque country were opposed to the Basque government's efforts to impose Basque in schools and the civil service. "Investors, domestic and foreign, complain bitterly about the extra bureaucracy imposed by regional governments," Mallet wrote. Basque is increasingly used by young people, both in the administration and in the media, and there are many Basque-language radio stations and television channels. Basque is compulsory at all school levels in the Basque autonomous region and is a language of instruction in some universities.

Basque support for violent struggle against the Spanish government has diminished. And while many Basque continue to support the creation of an independent Basque state by peaceful means, there is little indication the Spanish government will ever agree to this.

Further Reading

Europol (European Police Office). "2010 EU terrorism and trends report," April 2010, www.europol.europa .eu/publications/EU_Terrorism_Situation_and_ Trend_Report_TE-SAT/TESAT2010.pdf.

Goodman, Al. "Spain: Basque ETA chief arrested," CNN, February 28, 2010, http://edition.cnn.com/2010/ WORLD/europe/02/28/spain.eta.arrest/index.html.

Human Rights Watch. "Counter-Terrorism Laws and Procedures in France," July 1, 2008, www.hrw.org/en/ reports/2008/07/01/preempting-justice.

———. "Setting an Example: Counter-Terrorism Measures in Spain," January 26, 2005, www.hrw.org/en/ reports/2005/01/26/setting-example.

MacCormaic, Ruadhán. "Suspected military leader of Eta arrested," *The Irish Times,* May 21, 2010, www.irishtimes.com/newspaper/ world/2010/0521/1224270806227.html.

Mallet, Victor. "Revolution in air over Spanish nationalism," *The Irish Times,* April 16, 2009, www.irishtimes.com/ newspaper/world/2009/0416/1224244810601.html.

Miller, Judith. "The Other Terrorism," *City Journal,* spring 2008, www.city-journal.org/2008/18_2_ basque_terrorists.html.

Tremlett, Giles. "Deadlier than the male," *The Observer* (England), July 26, 2009, www.guardian.co.uk/ world/2009/jul/26/basque-eta-independence-female- fighters.

CATALANS
(Spain)

The Catalan people of Spain have long aspired to the self-governance of their region, Catalonia, rather than rule by the Madrid-based Spanish government. Since the late 1970s they have made great advances in securing autonomy, but a sizable minority would like to go further and make Catalonia an independent state.

Living in northeastern Spain, the Catalans number seven million, forming 17 percent of Spain's population. Catalonia, comprised of the provinces of Barcelona, Girona, Lleida, and Tarragona, is one of Spain's wealthier regions. About half of the area's inhabitants speak Catalan, a Latin language closely related to Spanish, on a daily basis. There are 500,000 Catalan-speakers in the Balearic Islands south of Catalonia, and another 45,000 Catalan-speakers in the Aragon region west of Catalonia. The Catalans are predominantly Catholic, as are the overwhelming majority of Spanish people.

Ever since Spain transformed itself from a centralized autocracy to a decentralized democracy in the late 1970s, the Catalans have been increasing their autonomy through peaceful means. With Catalans sharing the same religion and ethnicity as most other Spanish people, it is their language that has been their primary identifier. Catalan is an official language in the administration and judiciary and a medium of instruction at all school levels in Catalonia. In the Balearic Islands, while Catalan is commonly used, Spanish is dominant. In Aragon, Catalan can only be learned as a second language.

A "potent symbol of Catalan identity," wrote Lisa Abend and Geoff Pingree in a May 2006 article in the *Christian Science Monitor,* is their world-renowned soccer team, FC Barcelona. Established in 1889, the team adopted the slogan "more than a club" and has consistently been associated with Catalan efforts to maintain a distinct identity. "Even when it was illegal to speak Catalan during the nearly forty-year Franco dictatorship that overshadowed twentieth century Spain, cheering for Barcelona was a way to express support for Catalan national identity," the authors noted. Catalonia has a national soccer team, too, that plays non-competitive matches with top international teams such as Argentina. The Catalans have not thus far persuaded the world's soccer governing body, FIFA, to allow Catalonia to compete in the FIFA World Cup.

Catalans continue to debate whether to be satisfied with maintaining autonomy inside Spain or to push for full independence. Recent polls and election results indicated that a sizable minority of Catalans favor independence. The largest political party campaigning to split from Spain is the Republican Left of Catalonia (ERC). Banned during the Franco era (1939–1975), the ERC was legally recognized in 1977. It typically has garnered between 8 and 16 percent of the Catalan vote. No European government, including Spain's, supports independence for Catalonia. The Catalans have, however, forged strong links with like-minded autonomy movements in Europe, such as the Flemings in Belgium and Corsicans in France (see separate essays). In 1981 these various movements came together to form the European Free Alliance (EFA), a Europe-wide group of regionally based, pro-autonomy parties that operates out of Brussels, the seat of the European Parliament. In the June 2009 European Parliament elections, EFA candidates from Catalonia, Corsica (France), Flanders (Belgium), Latvia, Scotland, and Wales (United Kingdom) won seats.

History

The Catalan tradition of independence stretches back to a founding father, Wilfred the Hairy, who in the ninth century C.E. repelled Muslim Moors to the south and the forces of the Christian king of France, Charles the Bald, to the north. In the 1200s and 1300s Catalans were part of the Kingdom of Aragon and Catalonia, a major trade center whose domains extended to the Balearic Islands, Sardinia, and Sicily in the Mediterranean. In 1516 they were merged with the Kingdom of Castile to the west. The Catalans enjoyed self-government until it was revoked by Spain's King Philip V in 1714 during a war of succession for the Spanish throne. Military rule was imposed, and Castilian, the form of Spanish spoken in Castile, replaced Catalan in public administration and commerce.

The Catalan language and culture were revived from the late 1800s as the region industrialized. In April 1931, a Catalan nationalist, Francesc Macia, proclaimed a Catalan Republic. Soon after, he made an agreement with Spain's republican government, settling for autonomy. But Catalonia became neither independent nor autonomous; in 1936 a civil war broke out, which Spanish nationalists, led by Gen. Francisco Franco, an opponent of Catalan nationalism, won in 1939. Franco abolished Catalan autonomy, suppressed the Catalan language, and forbade Catalans from forming their own political parties.

After Franco died in 1975, a separate Catalan identity began to reemerge. In 1979 the Catalans, along with the Basques (see separate essay), were granted autonomy. The Catalan autonomous community held its first regional elections in March 1980. Catalan politicians in 1993 and 1996 managed to increase the Catalan government's budget by making deals with Spain's two main parties, the Popular Party (PP) and Spanish Socialist Workers Party (PSOE), who needed their votes to form governments. In June 2006, Catalans approved by referendum a new statute boosting the Catalan government's powers to make judicial appointments and set immigration and transportation policy. The statute recognized Catalan as a preferential language over Castilian Spanish and defined the Catalans as a nation. Spain's center-right PP opposed the statute, fearing it would encourage similar demands from other regions and deprive the central government of authority and revenue.

Leadership

The ERC was established in March 1931. It initially supported autonomy inside of Spain but since 1989 has advocated full independence. The ERC president is Joan Puigcercos i Boixassa. Party leader from 1996–2008, Josep-Lluis Carod-Rovira quit his post as first minister in the Catalan government in 2004 when it was revealed he met with leaders from the militant Basque separatist group ETA. The ERC led the Catalan government from 1931 until Franco came to power in 1939.

The ERC usually wins fewer votes than its more moderate rival, Convergence and Union (CiU), which supports autonomy but not independence for Catalonia. Established in November 1978, CiU is led by Artur Mas i Gavarro. It is an alliance of the Democratic Convergence of Catalonia (CDC), led by Mas, and the Democratic Union of Catalonia (UDC), led by Josep Antoni Duran i Lleida. CiU won 21 percent of the Catalan vote in the March 2008 Spanish elections, securing ten seats in the Spanish parliament; this compares to the ERC's three seats.

Some of the nationwide political parties of Spain have affiliates in Catalonia that are autonomous, including the Socialists' Party of Catalonia (PSC), led by Isidre Molas i Batllori, and the Initiative for Catalonia Greens (ICV), led by Joan Saura i Laporta. A militant separatist group, Free Land (Terre Lluire), operated in the 1980s and early 1990s but disbanded in 1995.

Current Status

An abundance of Catalan-language newspapers, magazines, radio, and television stations is indicative of the degree to which the Catalans have succeeded in preserving and promoting their culture. The Spanish government accepts that Catalonia should be allowed a broad degree of political autonomy but will not contemplate granting it full independence. In February 2008, when Kosovo seceded from Serbia, Spain was one of a handful of European countries not to recognize Kosovo, fearful it would foment separatism in Spain. The conservative PP is more opposed to further increases in Catalan autonomy than the center-left PSOE. Some PP members believe too much power has already devolved to Catalonia.

While the ERC did poorly in the March 2008 national elections, it did win a seat in the June 2009 European Parliament elections, competing on a joint platform with autonomy parties from the Basque and Aragon regions. CiU became the third largest party in the Spanish Parliament after the PSOE and PP following the March 2008 elections. In December 2009, the ERC and some CiU dissidents held an unofficial referendum on independence in predominantly Catalan-speaking areas. While 95 percent of those who voted backed secession, the turnout was only 30 percent. Organizers had hoped more would vote, believing this might put pressure on political leaders to organize an official referendum. The Spanish government did not recognize the vote, pointing to the Spanish constitution's ban on such referenda.

A December 2009 article by Giles Tremlett in the British daily newspaper *The Guardian* noted that Joan Laporta, president of FC Barcelona, had emerged as a figurehead in the Catalan separatist movement. "We are a nation and I want us to have a state of our own," Laporta was cited as proclaiming. The article noted that the conservative PP had petitioned Spain's constitutional court, questioning the legality of the 2006 autonomy reforms and specifically the designation of Catalonia as a nation. In July 2010, the court ruled that Spain was one nation and curtailed some of the powers devolved to Catalonia in 2006. In response, over one million Catalans took to the streets of Barcelona in protest, many waiving Catalan independence flags. Later in July, in a further bid to distance itself from the rest of Spain, the Catalan parliament voted to ban bullfighting, a sport of huge cultural importance to Spain.

In the November 2010 elections for the Catalan parliament, parties favoring either full independence or greater autonomy won 49 percent of the vote. The pro-autonomy CiU entered government, winning 38 percent, while the pro-independence ERC's vote dropped to 7 percent. A new pro-independence party, Solidarity for Independence, founded in July 2010 by FC Barcelona's Laporta, won 3 percent of the vote, securing them four seats in the parliament. Catalan separatism seems to be on the rise, although the likelihood of secession within the next couple of years seems low.

Further Reading

Abend, Lisa, and Geoff Pingree. "In Barcelona, soccer wins mean more," *Christian Science Monitor,* May 16, 2006, www.csmonitor.com/2006/0516/p07s02-woeu.html.

Pericay Coll, Gaspar. "Catalonia sends a strong message and changes political landscape," *Catalan News Agency,* November 29, 2010. www.catalannewsagency.com/news/politics/catalonia-sends-strong-message-and-changes-political-landscape.

Ranachan, Kate. "Cheering for Barca: FC Barcelona and the shaping of Catalan identity," McGill University (thesis), August 2008, www.digitool.library.mcgill.ca:8881/thesisfile22036.pdf.

Republic Left of Catalonia Web site, www.esquerra.cat.

Toibin, Colm. "Bullfighting ban is sweet revenge for Catalonia," *The Guardian* (London), July 31, 2010, www.guardian.co.uk/world/2010/jul/31/bullfighting-ban-is-sweet-revenge-for-catalonia.

Tremlett, Giles. "International: Catalans vote in emblematic referendum on independence," *The Guardian,* December 14, 2009, www.guardian.co.uk/world/2009/dec/13/catalonia-unofficial-independence-vote.

CORSICANS
(France)

The French-governed Mediterranean island of Corsica has since the late 1970s been home to a violent separatist movement aimed at making Corsica an independent country. While most Corsicans do not support independence, many feel that the limited amount of self-government they have obtained from the French government since the 1980s is insufficient.

Corsica lies approximately 100 miles south of the southeastern French coast and 50 miles west of the northwestern Italian coast. The 300,000 Corsican inhabitants make up 0.5 percent of the population of France. Thirty percent of the island's residents are not of Corsican ancestry but are a mix of people who moved there from mainland France and immigrants of Algerian, Italian, Moroccan, Portuguese, and Tunisian origin. Corsica is one of France's poorer regions, with incomes below the national average. One of its primary sources of revenue is tourism, which typically provides the island with over a billion dollars a year. Corsicans are predominantly Roman Catholic, as are the majority of French people.

Corsicans have their own language, Corsu, which is a Latin-based language related to French and Italian. The number of Corsu speakers is estimated at 170,000. Almost all Corsicans can speak French, which is the dominant language in official life throughout Corsica. Corsu tends to be used more in homes and in social contexts. As of 2002, 5 percent of schools in Corsica were bilingual. Where Corsu is taught, it is considered a minority language of instruction; 5 percent of Corsican children had bilingual courses that exceeded three hours a week. As one of France's twenty-two regions, Corsica enjoys its own regional government, which is based in the city of Ajaccio. Corsica is also divided into two administrative departments of France, Upper Corsica and South Corsica, each one with its own prefect who represents the French state.

In a May 2010 telephone interview, Francois Alfonsi, a member of the European Parliament and representative of the pro-autonomy Party of the Corsican Nation (PNC), was critical of the current system of government. "We have our own parliament but it has very limited powers. The most powerful person in Corsica remains the Prefect." The prefect is a government official appointed by the French president. Alfonsi, who has been mayor of the town of Osani in Corsica since 2002, has campaigned for autonomy since the 1970s and served as a member of the French parliament from 1987–1998. He regretted that Corsicans, in a referendum in 2003, narrowly rejected a proposal to expand Corsican autonomy. "The two extremes on either side of the debate voted the same way, which is why the referendum failed," he explained. Corsicans are, as a result, governed by a weaker autonomy statute granted to them in 1992. "My party, the PNC, would like more self-government. We want something similar to what the Catalans enjoy in Spain, or the Scots in the United Kingdom," he said (see separate essays).

The group responsible for most of the separatist-motivated violence in Corsica since 1979 has been the Corsican National Liberation Front (FLNC), which supports the establishment of an independent Corsican state. The FLNC's tactics involve the bombing of buildings, including banks, hotels, and post offices. Their attacks have caused extensive damage to property, although they have rarely caused fatalities. Attacks are occasionally directed at empty holiday homes in Corsica, noted Angelique Chrisafis in a January 2009 article in the British newspaper *The Guardian.* "While tourists are welcome, mainland French 'foreigners' acquiring land are not," the author said. In December 2008, pro-independence activists broke into and occupied the ground surrounding the holiday villa of Christian Clavier, a friend of France's President Nicolas Sarkozy. Journalist Chrisafis reported that "fighting to defend the law is not easy on a Mediterranean island where clans, mafia, godfathers and armed separatists crisscross in a nebulous atmosphere of omerta (code of silence)."

The highly centralized structure of the French government, put in place following the French Revolution of 1789, lies at the root of the separatist tensions. While France is a democracy where Corsicans are free to campaign peacefully for autonomy or independence, France's administrative structure is more centralized than neighboring states of comparable size such as Germany and Spain. Since the 1980s, successive French governments have taken steps to enhance self-government for Corsicans, although they have firmly opposed independence for Corsica.

In August 2000, France's interior minister, Jean-Pierre Chevenement, resigned in protest over an agreement his government had made the previous month to devolve some lawmaking powers to the Corsican parliament. In an article published by the German press agency DPA, journalist Siegfried Mortkowitz wrote that Chevenement feared "that a spark of Corsican independence could lead to brush fires all over France, such as in Brittany, where small separatist groups have been active for years, and in France's Basque country." The article cited an opinion poll that found 83 percent of Corsicans were opposed to independence. More recent election results indicate that a growing minority of Corsicans, at least a third, favor either substantially enhancing the amount of autonomy Corsica has or making it fully independent.

History

Corsica has a long history of settlement and rule by other Mediterranean nations. Among the earliest to arrive were the Greeks, who established a naval base in the sixth century B.C.E. The Romans came in 260 B.C.E., building cities, introducing the Latin language, and—several centuries later—the Christian religion. As a province of the Roman Empire, Corsica retained some autonomy. After the Roman Empire fell in 476 C.E., Corsica was invaded by various peoples, including the Vandals and Visigoths. From the eleventh century it came under the influence and control of Italian city-states, notably Pisa from the mid-1000s and Genoa from the mid-1300s. In 1755 a Corsican independence movement led by Pasquale Paoli succeeded in ending Genoese rule and establishing a Corsican state. Independence was short-lived, however, as France annexed the island in 1769. Under French rule, the French language became the sole and compulsory language in the courts, administration, and schools, with Corsu surviving predominantly as an oral language.

Poverty on the island led many Corsicans to migrate to mainland France and Italy from the 1950s. Eighteen thousand French people who were living in France's North African colony of Algeria were resettled in Corsica in 1962 when Algeria became independent. Many became wine growers, and they gradually came to dominate Corsica's wine-growing industry. Their resettlement, coupled with immigration by non-French North Africans, triggered a revival of Corsican nationalism as islanders grew fearful that their language and culture was under threat. A militant separatist movement emerged in the 1970s. Following the election in 1981 of a socialist president in France, Francois Mitterrand, Corsica was granted its own parliament under a decentralization program. In 1992 the French government increased the Corsican regional government's powers to set education policy.

The separatist insurgency continued through the 1980s and 1990s, peaking from 1995–1997. On January 9, 1996, there were thirty-seven attacks on government buildings, although no one was injured in them. On February 6, 1998, the prefect of Corsica, Claude Erignac, was shot dead by Corsican separatist Yvan Colonna. The assassination marked the high watermark of the violence, after which there was a steady decline, although a low-intensity campaign continued. The militants declared a cease-fire in December 1999 but ended it in August 2000 when a car bomb exploded outside the headquarters of the Agency for Economic Development of Corsica. The line between political and non-political violence in Corsica was not always clear. A former separatist leader, Jean-Michel Rossi, writing an article in August 2000 for the French magazine *Marianne*, claimed "political violence has encouraged, even fostered common-law violence which the new caste of racketeers intends to exploit in order to establish its domination." Rossi and his bodyguard were shot dead on August 7, the morning after his article was published; rival Corsican separatists were believed to be responsible for the killings.

The French government began negotiations on autonomy with Corsican leaders in December 1999. These culminated in the Matignon Accords of July 2000. These agreements gave Corsicans greater control over their finances, tourism, environment, education system, and culture. They were subsequently watered down by the French Parliament and French Constitutional Council. The council ruled that a clause that permitted Corsicans to opt out of laws enacted by the French Parliament was unconstitutional. The devolution plan provoked tensions within the French government. France's center-right president, Jacques Chirac, was reluctant to support it whereas France's socialist prime minister, Lionel Jospin, was its principle architect. When the slimmed-down plan was presented to the Corsican electorate for approval in July 2003, it was defeated by 51 to 49 percent. In November 2003, the FLNC called a cease-fire, but ended it in August 2004 in protest over the trial of twenty-two Corsican nationalists.

Leadership

The political leadership of the Corsican separatist movement is fragmented. New factions and alliances are constantly springing up as older groups split apart or reconstitute themselves. The largest pro-autonomy party in Corsica by early 2011 was the U Partiu di a Nazione Corsa, or PNC. Founded in December 2002, the PNC drew members from three other Corsican nationalist parties that supported greater autonomy but opposed violence. The PNC won its first ever seat in the European Parliament in June 2009 by forging an electoral alliance with other regional parties in France, including the Breton Democratic Union and Occitan Party and the Ecological Party. These parties placed all their candidates on a common list, which secured

24 percent of the vote in Corsica, the alliance's highest result across France. Francois Alfonsi was elected for the South East Region of France that encompassed Corsica and southeast France. The first Corsican nationalist to be elected to the Brussels-based European Parliament was Max Simoni, who served from 1989–1994.

Corsican separatism is notable for its strong militant strain. Established in 1976, the pro-independence FLNC's focus at first was to secure the removal of French mainlanders who had been resettled there in 1962. The FLNC from 1982 began targeting people born in mainland France who had moved to or worked in Corsica. The group split into two factions in 1990: FLNC-Historic Wing, which later became known as FLNC-Union of Combatants, and FLNC-Canal Habituel, which was dissolved in 1997. The surviving faction split again in 1999 when dissident Francois Santoni established a rival group, Armata Corsa. In August 2001, Santoni was murdered. Other militant groups that have claimed responsibility for separatist attacks include Resistenza Corsa, the FLNC des Anonymes (FLNC of the Unnamed), and the FLNC 1976.

It is legal in France for parties to campaign for an independent Corsica provided they are nonviolent. Jean-Guy Talamoni has been a dominant figure in the many pro-independence political parties to have emerged from Corsica. He led the Corsican Nation (CN) party, which in November 2004 joined with another pro-independence group to form Independent Corsican Nation (CNI).

Current Status

Separatist violence continues intermittently, albeit at a much lower level than in the mid-1990s. According to an April 2010 report from the European Police Office (Europol), Corsican separatist attacks accounted for the vast majority of the eighty-nine separatist-motivated attacks carried out in France in 2009. The report said that 63 percent of those attacks were directed at private property, 26 percent at businesses, and 10 percent at government. Corsican militants were the second most violent separatist group in the European Union, after the Basques (see separate essay). France was the European country that made the most arrests of suspected separatist militants in 2009, Europol's figures show. Many of these arrests were of Basque militants.

The Corsican language is taught as a second language in Corsican primary and secondary schools, and there are some bilingual schools where it is used as a medium of instruction. However, Corsican pro-autonomy campaigner Alfonsi complained that "the teaching in schools is badly-organized. As a result, it is mostly only older people who speak Corsu." There are magazines in Corsu, a weekly newspaper, and a radio station. But despite the enhanced legal powers granting Corsicans the right to promote their language, two centuries of living under a French-language dominated administration has taken its toll, and Corsu remains vulnerable. Corsican traditional music is flourishing, however, and there are many Corsican cultural associations.

The Corsican separatist movement remains politically fragmented. There is a strong rivalry between the parties favoring an independent Corsica and those who favor greater autonomy inside of France. In February 2008, the pro-autonomy PNC joined up with another group, A Chjama Naziunale (National Call), to compete against the pro-independence CNI in the upcoming local elections. In February 2009, the pro-independence faction, led by Jean-Guy Talamoni, became more unified when Talamoni's CNI merged with three other smaller separatist groups, Corsica Nation, Rennovation, and the Corsican Nationalist Alliance, to form Corsica Libera.

In regional elections in March 2010, a coalition of Corsican pro-autonomy parties increased their share of the vote. In the first round of voting, the PNC scored 18 percent and in the second round 26 percent, their best ever performance, which secured them eleven seats in the fifty-one-seat regional parliament. "We did better than the pro-independence parties who got 10 percent. This was very positive because our score used to be lower than the pro-independence parties," said the PNC's Alfonsi. The combined second round vote of Corsica's pro-independence and pro-autonomy parties was 36 percent.

A January 2009 article in the British newspaper *The Guardian* reported that the militant separatists in Corsica had forged an alliance with ecologists centered on their mutual opposition to plans to develop the island. The Corsican authorities had proposed a twenty-year plan, called Padduc, that would herald the construction of more buildings, which environmentalists fear would create "a concrete nightmare" such as that seen on mainland France's southern coast, the Cote d'Azur. The secessionist Corsica Libera opposed the plan, too, complaining that it threatened the island's national identity. The FLNC "made death threats against the island's ruling political class," warning them not to proceed with the plans. The article cited a former fisherman and environmental activist Gerard Bonchristiani, saying, "there is a visceral attachment to the land here. We like to say: 'you don't live in Corsica, Corsica lives in you.'"

The likelihood that Corsica will become independent by 2020 is low given where Corsica public opinion now stands and given how staunchly opposed the French government remains to secession. But the prevailing climate of uncertainty arising from a lack of consensus over how much autonomy the island should have underlines the unlikelihood of a complete cessation of violence.

Further Reading

Chrisafis, Angelique. "Corsica: Armed separatists and ecologists unite against fears of a paradise lost," *The Guardian* (United Kingdom), January 26, 2009, www.guardian.co.uk/world/2009/jan/26/corsica-development-campaign-protect-coastline.

Europol (European Police Office). "2010 EU terrorism and trends report," April 28, 2010, www.europol.europa.eu/publications/EU_Terrorism_Situation_and_Trend_Report_TE-SAT/TESAT2010.pdf.

Fusina, Jacques. "The Corsican Language in Education in France," 2000, Mercator Education, Leeuwarden, Netherlands.

Kimmelman, Michael, "Cultures United to Honor Separatism," *New York Times*, November 11, 2010, www.nytimes.com/2010/11/14/arts/14abroad.html?pagewanted=1&_r=1.

Mortkowitz, Siegfried. "Corsican violence threatens plan for limited independence," Deutsche Presse-Agentur, August 17, 2000.

U.S. State Department, "Country Reports on Terrorism 2008—France," April 30, 2009, www.state.gov/s/ct/rls/crt/2008/122432.htm.

Van der Schaaf, Alie. "Developments Of Bilingual Education In The EU," seminar presentation at the Fryske Akademy, Netherlands, April 2002, www.linguapax.org/congres/taller/taller4/Alie.html.

FLEMINGS
(Belgium)

The Flemish people of Belgium, called Flemings, have a strong separatist movement that since the 1970s has greatly expanded the level of autonomy they enjoy. Rooted in a tense relationship with the other main community of Belgium, the French-speaking Walloons, Flemish separatism has brought the Fleming's region, Flanders, close to becoming an independent country. However, a majority of Flemings still support remaining part of Belgium, albeit a Belgium where Flanders has greater powers of self-government.

Flemings account for 58 percent of Belgium's 10.4 million inhabitants. They live in the small, densely populated northern half of Belgium. They mostly speak Dutch, unlike the residents of Belgium's southern region, Wallonia, who speak French. Belgium also has a German-speaking community of 73,000 that lives in Wallonia. Flemings are predominantly Catholic, like most Belgians.

The Flemish community obtained autonomy through a series of constitutional reforms enacted from 1962. The Belgian government's responsibilities have consequently been confined to fewer and fewer areas, including defense, foreign relations, monetary policy, taxation, and social security. Most Flemish political parties would like either greater autonomy within Belgium or a fully independent Flanders. The most controversial party is the Vlaams Belang (VB), or Flemish Interest party. Typically winning between 15 and 25 percent of the Flemish vote, the VB is secessionist and very opposed to immigration. Its opponents openly call the VB a racist, extreme right, or even neo-Nazi party.

Other Flemish autonomy and independence activists distance themselves from the VB. "This is such a sensitive issue. European journalists try to demonize us," said Gunther Dauwen, a Flemish political activist working for the European Free Alliance (EFA), a Europe-wide group of regionally based, pro-autonomy parties based in Brussels. "My party calls itself regionalist because the word nationalist has a negative connotation," said Dauwen in a telephone interview in January 2008. Dauwen said he was "not campaigning for an independent Flanders yet," but added, "maybe we will have to separate if the two communities cannot live together."

While Flemish separatism has caused a great deal of tension in Belgium, this tension has not led to a single death to date. Flemish separatists concentrate their energies on supporting political parties that campaign for greater autonomy or independence.

In a July 2009 article for the Scottish newspaper *The Herald*, Iain MacWhirter remarked that, despite the tensions, "Belgium certainly doesn't look like a failed state. Travelling between picturesque cities such as Bruges and Ghent with their chocolates and dentelles [lace], you pass through endless neat suburbs and orderly villages of restored cottages. Bosnia, it isn't." He added, "there are no pogroms or street fights, just the occasional flag-burning."

Flemings are very pro-active in promoting their language, Dutch, which is the dominant language in Flanders. Flemish culture is thriving, and there are many Flanders-based, Dutch-language television and radio stations, newspapers, and magazines. French is still taught in Flemish schools, and many Flemings can speak it—although they increasingly prefer to speak English. Language is a divisive issue, and Flemings and Francophone Belgians will sometimes converse with one another in English to avoid having to favor one language over the other. Flemings often criticize Walloons for being less proficient in Dutch than Flemings are in French. The Walloons have made efforts to correct this deficiency by setting up bilingual schools; this contrasts with Flanders, where classes must be taught in Dutch.

According to a May 2010 article in the British newspaper *The Observer*, the language divide has deprived Belgium of a sense of cohesion. "The country operates on the basis of linguistic apartheid, which infects everything from public libraries to local and regional government, the education system, the political parties, national television, the newspapers, even football teams. There is no national narrative in Belgium, rather two opposing stories told in Dutch and French. The result is a dialogue of the deaf," journalist Ian Traynor wrote. He noted how a Francophone, Damien Thiery, was elected mayor of the Flemish town of Linkebeek, which is 85 percent Francophone, after winning 66 percent of the vote. But Thiery was barred from performing his duties by the Flemish interior minister because he sent out election literature to his French-speaking voters in French instead of Dutch. Several other Francophone mayors in majority French-speaking municipalities of Flanders face the same predicament. Traynor wrote of Linkebeek: "Separatists deface bilingual street names. The language police show up at monthly meetings of the local Council. If the proceedings are conducted in French—thirteen of the fifteen councilors are French-speakers—the session is deemed invalid."

The biggest obstacle to Flemish independence is in fact a city: Brussels. Home to one million people and situated in the heart of Dutch-speaking Flanders, French is the dominant language of Brussels, with only 5 percent being Dutch-speakers, although the city is officially bilingual. Brussels serves as the capital of a number of governments: of the Brussels Region, of Flanders, of Belgium, and of the European Union. According to Traynor, "Brussels sucks in tens of thousands of commuters from both sides and makes a negotiated unraveling of Belgium virtually impossible."

One of the few unifying forces in Belgium has been its monarchy. The king since 1993, Albert II, often acts as mediator in disputes between the Flemish and Francophone political leadership and has helped to resolve impasses. But the monarchy can be divisive too. Many Flemings resent that the royal family is predominantly French-speaking and that Belgium's Italian-born queen, Paola, has poor proficiency in Dutch, the language of 60 percent of her subjects. Crown Prince Philippe has caused controversy, too, by speaking out against the Flemish separatist VB party.

History

The division between Dutch-speaking Flemings and French-speaking Walloons can be traced as far back as the first century B.C.E., when the Romans established a province called Belgica. At the same time, Germanic tribes began settling in the region, leading to the gradual emergence of a Flemish culture. The golden era for Flemings was the medieval period when Flanders, a patchwork of autonomous provinces, became a prosperous center of industry, commerce, and culture, and cities like Antwerp, Bruges, and Ghent developed. In 1648 the northern parts of Flanders became part of the newly independent Netherlands, while southern Flanders and Wallonia remained under the rule of the Hapsburg monarchy. Many of the Flemish elite moved to the Netherlands at this time, causing Flanders to fall into decline. Belgium was administered initially by Spain and then Austria. France ruled Belgium from 1794, when Napoleon's forces invaded, until 1815 when his forces surrendered at the Battle of Waterloo on the Flanders-Wallonia border. Between 1815 and 1830, Flemings and Walloons were ruled by the Netherlands.

In 1830 the Flemish became part of the newly created independent country of Belgium. Despite a constitution guaranteeing the right to speak Dutch, in practice French was the dominant language in public life. Many in the Flemish aristocracy spoke French, too. In 1898 a law was passed recognizing Dutch as a Belgian language; this paved the way for Dutch to gradually become the dominant language in schools, courts, and government in Flanders. In 1932 Dutch became the sole language of Flanders. In the 1930s some nationalistic Flemings formed the Vlaams National Verbond (VNV) and embraced fascist ideology. The invasion of Belgium by Nazi Germany during World War II (1939–1945) aggravated inter-community tensions as the Nazis favored the Flemings over the Walloons, viewing them as more closely related ethnically to Germans.

From the 1950s a reversal in economic fortunes occurred as petrochemical and manufacturing industries developed around Antwerp, helping to transform Flanders from the poorer to the richer half of Belgium. Wallonia meanwhile became economically depressed as much of its wealth had come from heavy industry, including coal-mining,

which went into decline. In 1970 some powers were devolved from the central government to three regions: Brussels, Flanders, and Wallonia. In 1977, following another devolution agreement, Flanders obtained its own parliament and government.

Tensions between the communities grew from the 1980s as the mostly French-speaking capital Brussels expanded and more French-speakers moved to Flanders. Brussels had historically been a Dutch-speaking city but had become predominantly French-speaking after Belgium gained independence. To emphasize that the outskirts of Brussels remained part of Dutch-speaking Flanders, Flemings began organizing an annual bicycle tour circling the perimeter of Brussels, called De Gordel (the belt), in which up to 100,000 people participated. In response to rising public support for the VB, the other Flemish parties adopted a policy called the Cordon Sanitaire (sanitary cordon), under which they pledged to exclude the VB from government. Despite this exclusion, the VB continued to win more votes and seats until the 2007 elections. Critics of the Cordon Sanitaire claimed that it actually helped the VB by allowing it to portray itself as the anti-establishment party.

Following the June 2007 national elections, Belgium went without a government for nine months as the Flemish and Francophone parties could not agree on a program for governing. The coalition talks were dominated by the autonomy question, with Flemish parties insisting that more power be devolved to the regions. The Francophone parties, whose consent is needed for any constitutional changes, were opposed to further devolution. This unprecedented delay in forming a coalition government added to existing doubt that the country would survive in the long term.

Leadership

Since 1994 Flemings have had their own directly elected parliament, which is made up of 124 members and based in Brussels. The Flemish government

Filip Dewinter (1962–   )

FILIP DEWINTER was born on September 11, 1962, and is notable for his leadership in the far-right Flemish political party Vlaams Belang (Flemish Interest) and subsequent contributions to the Flemish separatist movement.

Since his teenage years, Dewinter has been involved in organizations that promote nationalism, fascism, separatism, and the agenda of Flanders' political extreme-right. The first of such groups that Dewinter became a part of was called Jongerenfront (Youth Front). This was a Flemish militia-style organization with both neo-Nazi and neo-fascist ties.

AP Photo/Geert Vanden Wijngaert

In 1979 Dewinter founded the Flemish Student Action Group to promote nationalist ideology in response to an increase in immigration to Belgium; this group evolved into the Young Nationalist Student Union. In addition, Dewinter became a member of the Nationalist Student Association and served as president of its Antwerp chapter in the early 1980s. All of these groups have employed Nazi symbols and white supremacist rhetoric in their activities.

In 1982 Dewinter completed his studies in economics at the St. Francis Xavier Institute, Bruges. In 1985 he earned a degree in journalism from Erasmus University.

After completing his studies, Dewinter quickly moved into politics. Having joined Vlaams Blok (Flemish Bloc), or VB, in 1983, Dewinter established strong ties within the party and was elected to the provincial council of Antwerp in 1985 with its support. In 1987 Dewinter went on to be elected to the federal parliament and at twenty-five became the youngest serving MP. That same year Dewinter became a board member of VB and the chairman of Vlaams Blok Jongeren (Flemish Block Youth), or VBJ; he went on to lead the VBJ for the next two years. One year later, in 1988, Dewinter became a Flemish council member. At around the same time, Dewinter was criticized for attending a tribute at a military cemetery in Lommel, Belgium, to those Flemish individuals who volunteered for the SS and collaborated with the Nazis.

Dewinter played a prominent role in VB from the late 1980s and witnessed the party's expansion firsthand. Support for VB increased dramatically from the late 1980s until recently, reaching a 2003 high point of twenty-three seats in the Belgian Parliament. When Dewinter first joined the party, VB was only able to secure one or two seats. Additionally, it has become typical for the reformed version of VB, Vlaams Belang (Flemish Interest), to obtain approximately one-third of all votes in Antwerp; this is the city where Dewinter leads the local VB chapter.

Since 1995 Dewinter has served as party leader for VB in the Flemish Parliament. He chose to utilize his political abilities in this setting rather than in the federal parliament in order to focus on local and regional issues.

Dewinter has been a key figure in the drive for an independent Flemish nation; it is his belief that the existence of such an entity would offer the only means of safeguarding Flemish identity. Moreover, Dewinter and his supporters in VB are dissatisfied with the current makeup of Belgium; they believe that Flanders is subsidizing Wallonia, the French-speaking half of Belgium with a weaker economy. In order to advance the goal of creating an independent Flemish state, Dewinter regularly employs anti-immigrant and anti-Muslim rhetoric. It is Dewinter's contention that immigrants, especially those originating from Muslim countries, are unable or unwilling to adapt to the Flemish lifestyle.

Currently, Dewinter continues his struggle to break apart the Belgian nation; however, he saw his support drop markedly in the 2010 elections. Voters decided to move away from his party, the extreme VB, in favor of the more moderate New Flemish Alliance (N-VA). The N-VA, which won the election overall, advocates a gradual separation and exhibits neither racism or xenophobia in its rhetoric. Although his party lost seats in the election, Dewinter congratulated the N-VA, as he and other VB members view the N-VA win as a sign that the desire for the creation of a separate Flemish state has become more mainstream.

has wide-ranging powers (as does Wallonia's regional government), extending even to foreign relations. Since the early 1960s, political parties in Belgium have been organized predominantly along linguistic lines. There are seven main parties in Flanders. Apart from the VB, those most in favor of greater autonomy or independence are the New Flemish Alliance (NV-A), the Dedecker List (LDD), the Christian Democrat and Flemish party (CD&V), and the Flemish Liberals and Democrats (VLD).

The VB, initially called Vlaams Bloc (Flemish Block), was established in 1978 by Karel Dillen. The party renamed itself Vlaams Belang (Flemish Interest) in 2004 after the Belgian Supreme Court outlawed the Bloc for being a racist party. Public support for the VB grew consistently in the 1980s and 1990s and peaked in 2004 when it won 24 percent of the Flemish vote in regional elections. The VB stronghold is the city of Antwerp, where it typically wins about a third of the vote. The leading VB figures are Bruno Valkeniers, Filip Dewinter, and Gerolf Annemans.

The N-VA supports a gradual move toward an independent Flemish state. Unlike the VB, the N-VA does not have racist or anti-immigrant policies. The N-VA's leading figures are Bart de Wever, Jan Peumans, Frieda Brepoels, and Geert Bourgeois. The party was created in October 2001 as the dominant faction within the Volksunie (Peoples Union), or VU, which had split in two. The smaller faction, Spirit, was disbanded in 2009. The VU was created in 1954 to campaign for an autonomous Flanders within a federal Belgian state. At its height in the late 1970s, the VU won over 10 percent of the Flemish vote and had representatives in the Belgian government. By the 1990s, the VB had eclipsed the VU as the largest Flemish separatist party.

In the spring 2007, Jean-Marie Dedecker, who was formerly a member of the VLD, established a new group, Dedecker List (LDD). Dedecker differed from other Flemish politicians by refusing to rule out the formation of a coalition government with the VB. The LDD scored 4 percent of the Flemish vote in the June 2007 national elections. Other prominent figures in the party include Ivan Sabbe and Jurgen Verstrepen. The CD&V, which has its roots in the Catholic Party established in 1830, tends to be the most pro-devolution of the other Flemish parties. Its leaders include Steven Vanackere, Marianne Thyssen, and Kris Peeters.

Current Status

The Flemish and Francophone parties in March 2008 finally succeeded in forming a national government. The new prime minister, Yves Leterme, was a Fleming who had campaigned on a platform of extending Flemish autonomy and changing the electoral districting to prohibit French-speakers living in Flanders from voting for Francophone parties. Having failed to deliver further devolution as promised, Leterme resigned in December 2008. He was replaced by another Fleming, Herman Van Rompuy. Belgium was meanwhile badly affected by a global economic recession, which led political leaders in late 2008 and early 2009 to focus energies more on fixing the economy and less on amending the constitutional framework.

In the European Parliament elections of June 2009, the hard-line Flemish separatist party, the VB, saw its support drop by 7 percent to 15.9 percent. In November 2009, Van Rompuy resigned as prime minister after being appointed president of the European Council, which is a branch of the EU government. Leterme returned as Belgian prime minister but in April 2010 resigned and fresh elections were called for June 13, 2010. The pro-independence N-VA won the most votes of any Flemish party, taking 28.2 percent of the Flemish vote, while the combined score of N-VA and VB (which also favors Flemish independence) was 40.8 percent. As of January 2011, the Flemish and Francophone parties had failed to agree on the formation of a coalition government. The talks were foundering over the issue of the funding for the Brussels region.

Given the persistent political instability, many Flemings and Walloons are increasingly doubtful about the prospects of Belgium surviving as a single country. A pro-autonomy Flemish activist, who did not wish to be named, said in a May 2010 telephone interview that many Flemings had an emotional attachment to an independent Flanders. Others, however, supported greater autonomy or independence because "they see it as a means to build a better society." The activist added that "the French-speakers are very anxious not to let go of Belgium because they would lose the social security system, which currently benefits them financially." However, Flanders has a more rapidly aging population than Wallonia, and in the coming years this could make Flemings net beneficiaries of the Belgian social security system as their pension payments increase.

With the Brussels suburbs extending further into Flanders, Flemings are determined that Dutch remain the sole administrative language in these suburbs. Given that the Brussels Region is only separated from Wallonia by a few miles of Flemish territory, many Flemings are also worried that the French-speakers will build a linguistic bridge linking Brussels to Wallonia. Brussels is a key battleground for Flemish separatists because they would like the city to become the capital of an independent Flanders. Some Flemings believe they made a mistake in 1993 in agreeing to the creation of a regional government for Brussels. This has led to a fragmented system of government, which has been exacerbated by the strong concentration of power at the local level in Brussels' nineteen municipalities.

Some question whether Flanders could be economically viable given its small size. However, there are wealthy and functional countries in Europe that are smaller in size and population than Flanders, notably neighboring Luxembourg. As EU membership guarantees the free movement of labor, goods, services, and capital across a market of five hundred million people, an independent Flanders would not be economically isolated. Europe would be faced with something of a political conundrum if Flanders acquires independence, as no EU member state has split in two to date. EU member state governments are unlikely to be enthusiastic about this prospect, especially given its potential domino effect on some other members, such as Spain and the United Kingdom (see separate essays), who are contending with their own separatist movements.

While pro-independence political parties in Flanders are still a minority, typically winning between 30 and 40 percent of the vote, separatist sentiment is on the rise. There is a strong likelihood that the Flemings—along with the Wallonians—will gain more autonomy and possibly independence within the next five years.

Further Reading

MacWhirter, Iain. "Lessons to be learned from a potentially messy divorce," *The Herald* (United Kingdom), July 13, 2009.

Ravenne, Eric. "Council of Ministers: Dark Clouds Gather Over Belgian EU Presidency," *Europolitics* (Brussels-based EU affairs daily newspaper), April 28, 2010. www.europolitics.info.

Sciolino, Elaine. "Belgians, Adrift and Split, Sense a Nation Fading," *New York Times,* September 21, 2007, http://query.nytimes.com/gst/fullpage.html?res=9805 EFDB1639F932A1575AC0A9619C8B63&sec=&spon =&pagewanted=all.

Traynor, Ian. "The language divide at the heart of a split that is tearing Belgium apart," *The Observer* (United Kingdom), May 9, 2010, www.guardian.co.uk/world/ 2010/may/09/belgium-flanders-wallonia-french-dutch.

NORTHERN ITALIANS
(Italy)

In northern Italy between 10 and 20 percent of the population support a party that advocates either secession or greater powers of self-government. This party draws from a reservoir of resentment felt by northerners over having to financially support the south of Italy, which is poorer.

For the most part the movement has been peaceful and democratic, although its leaders are prone to inflammatory rhetoric. It is based in eleven northern regions comprising half of Italy's population of sixty million and half of its territory. These regions are Aosta Valley, Emilia-Romagna, Friuli–Venezia Giulia, Liguria, Lombardy, Marches, Piedmont, Tuscany, Trentino–South Tyrol, Umbria, and Veneto. Most of Italy's major cities are situated here, including Bologna, Florence, Milan, Turin, and Venice. The north, separated from the rest of Europe by the Alps, does not reach as far south as Rome, Italy's capital.

Northerners speak Italian, as do southerners, with variations in dialect and culture among the eleven regions. The north has French-, German-, and Slovenian-speaking minorities living in, respectively, Aosta Valley, Trentino–South Tyrol, and Friuli–Venezia Giulia, next to the Austrian, French, Slovenian, and Swiss borders. In northeast Italy, about 500,000 people speak Friulian, a Romance-based language. Northerners, like southern Italians, are overwhelmingly Catholic. The north is more industrial and wealthier than the south. Its inhabitants are mostly ethnically Italian, but it has a growing number of immigrants from Africa, Asia, and Eastern Europe who have moved there since 1990.

The separatist movement is led by a political party called the Lega Nord (Northern League), or LN. Some LN supporters would like the north to have its own state, which would be called Padania, which means "lands of the Po," in reference to the main river flowing through the north. Others would be satisfied with extensive autonomy, whereby the central Italian government remains responsible only for foreign policy and defense. The separatists argue that the north has been subsidizing the less productive south for too long, that there is little sign the wealth gap is disappearing, and that the south is dragging the north down economically. Northern Italy does not have autonomy, although the three northern regions populated by French-, Slovenian-, and German-speaking minorities—Aosta Valley, Friuli–Venezia Giulia, and Trentino–South Tyrol, respectively—are currently autonomous.

The LN has participated in the Italian government on several occasions since 1994 as a minority party, having allied itself with right-wing coalition governments led by Silvio Berlusconi. While it began as a secessionist movement, the LN has diversified its political platform and is now as identifiable as much for its passionate opposition to immigration and hostility toward immigrants as for its separatism. Northern Italian separatism is not supported by any foreign government. The LN has forged links with political parties in Europe that share its political ideology, especially parties that are hostile to the European Union. In the European Parliament, where the LN has nine elected representatives, the party is affiliated with a political group jointly led by the UK Independence Party. The latter is campaigning for Britain to withdraw from the EU.

History

Northern Italy has never been ruled independently. All of Italy formed part of the Roman Empire until the Western Roman Empire collapsed in 476 C.E. Over the next fourteen centuries, Italy was a constantly changing patchwork of city-states, kingdoms, duchies, papal territories, and republics. The northerners came under the control and influence of neighboring regional powers: first Spain, then France, and finally Austria. All of Italy was reunified in 1870 following a series of wars; the northern-based Kingdom of Piedmont-Sardinia was a driving force behind unification. Poverty led millions of southerners to immigrate northward. The north's territory was expanded at the end of World War I (1914–1918) when Austria ceded the South Tyrol and Trieste regions to Italy.

A separatist movement among northerners developed from the mid-1980s. The LN, the party spearheading the movement, won 10 percent of the nationwide vote in the April 1996 elections, making it the largest party in northern Italy. LN leader Umberto Bossi convened a self-declared parliament in the city of Mantua, Lombardy, in May 1996 where he asserted northerners' right to secede. The LN organized an unofficial referendum on secession in May 1997 in which 4.5 million people voted. In January 1998, Bossi received a one-year suspended jail sentence for criminal incitement. The LN's support dropped to 4 percent in the May 2001 elections.

In January 2004, Bossi resigned as a government minister in protest over lack of progress in obtaining self-government. By this time, the LN had embraced anti-immigrant policies and was being accused of racism. For example, the Council of Europe, a Strasbourg-based intergovernmental institution that promotes democracy and human rights, criticized the LN in a May 2006 report. The council said LN representatives had "intensified the use of racist and xenophobic discourse in the political arena," adding this discourse targeted "essentially non-EU immigrants but also other members of minority groups, such as Roma and Sinti." After the LN's poor showing in the April 2006 Italian elections, in which it won 4 percent of the vote, it softened its separatist rhetoric, calling for the establishment of a federal Italian state rather than for northern secession.

Leadership

The northern Italian separatist movement is led by LN, which is allowed to campaign peacefully for secession. Some LN supporters have styled themselves as the party's militant wing, donning green shirts at rallies. The LN first entered the Italian government in March 1994 as a junior partner in a coalition led by Prime Minister Silvio Berlusconi. That coalition government collapsed seven months later as a result of divisions between the parties. Apart from Bossi, the key figures in the party include Angelo Alessandri, Maurizio Balocchi, Federico Bricolo, Roberto Calderoli, Roberto Castelli, Roberto Cota, Roberto Maroni, and Francesco Speroni.

Umberto Bossi (1941–   )

UMBERTO BOSSI, the leader of the Northern Italian separatist movement, was born on September 19, 1941, in Cassano Magnago, Lombardy.

Following the completion of his high school education, Bossi went on to hold an eclectic mix of jobs, including rock singer, brick layer, and math tutor. Eventually, Bossi enrolled at the University of Pavia, where he studied medicine; however, he failed to finish his medical studies and as a result never received a degree from the university.

It was not until 1979, the year he met Bruno Salvadori, a leader in the Valdotanian Union, that Bossi began to garner political notice. Salvadori acted as a mentor to Bossi, teaching him that people have a right to make their own decisions and that they should be able to secede from their country if they want to. Also, Salvadori taught Bossi about the importance of extensive autonomy for local governments; it was Salvadori's view that local authority should not be given over to a strong federal entity. These principles formed key components of Bossi's ideology.

When Bruno Salvadori died in a car accident in 1981, Bossi vowed to promote his ideals. This led Bossi to establish the Lombard League, a group that endeavored to gain autonomy for the northern Italian regions. Along with this new movement, Bossi founded a newspaper, *Lombardia Autonomista*, and used it to disseminate his views.

In 1991 Bossi changed the name of the Lombard League to the Northern League as the movement consolidated its support, uniting several factions from around the various northern Italian provinces. In 1992 Bossi and his supporters in the Northern League took advantage of a series of political scandals and proclaimed themselves the party that would clean up corruption in government; this claim resulted in a significant gain in popularity.

Ironically, Bossi and the Northern League's treasurer were convicted of accepting a bribe at around the same time; Bossi received a suspended prison sentence. Bossi's Northern League expanded its base by expressing disapproval over the fact that the wealthy north paid high taxes, allegedly to subsidize the economically weaker south.

In 1994 Bossi and the Northern League entered into a coalition with Silvio Berlusconi. Bossi's support helped Berlusconi win in the national elections. However, a few months later, with his base of support voicing clear disapproval of Berlusconi, Bossi left the coalition. The national government subsequently disintegrated. Bossi used his newspaper to criticize Berlusconi and suggested that people should sabotage Berlusconi's media networks.

In 1996 Bossi declared that the independence of northern Italy, in the form of a country named Padania, was the ultimate goal of the Northern League. Bossi and his Northern League supporters created a Padanian parliament in the northern Italian city of Mantua. Bossi's actions, however, lost him the support of moderate northern Italians, and the Northern League subsequently stepped back and stated that a federalist arrangement that provided the north significant autonomy would be acceptable overall.

In 2001 Bossi renewed ties with Berlusconi's government in exchange for financial aid to the Northern League. Later that year, Bossi once again assisted Berlusconi in winning the national election. In recognition, Berlusconi appointed Bossi Reforms Minister.

On March 11, 2004, Bossi experienced a serious stroke that left him paralyzed on one side of his body and severely compromised his speaking ability. Bossi abandoned his post as Reforms Minister in July and thereafter became a member of the European Parliament. Disregarding his impairments, Bossi made the decision to continue as leader of the Northern League.

In 2006 Bossi commemorated the tenth anniversary of his pledge that the nation of Padania would one day come into existence as an independent entity and called for the reopening of the Padanian parliament.

Bossi is married to a Sicilian woman, Manuela Marrone, and has four sons, one of whom is named after an ancient god of the river Po, which runs through the north. He continues his involvement in Italian politics and promoting the causes of the Northern League.

Inside the European Parliament, the LN is affiliated with the far-right, anti-EU group Europe of Freedom and Democracy. In ideology, the LN differs from several other regionally based, pro-autonomy parties from Western Europe, including those representing Catalan, Scottish, and Welsh nationalists. Unlike the LN, these parties are affiliated with a left-wing group, the Greens–European Free Alliance, which is dominated by the Green Party. The LN was formed in February 1991 when six regional parties merged. The regions represented were Emilia Romagna, Liguria, Lombardy, Piedmont, Tuscany, and Veneto. The dominant party among them was the Lombardy League, which had been established in 1979 and named after a twelfth century federation of northern Italian cities.

Other pro-autonomy parties in northern Italy remain regionally based. They often form alliances with the LN in elections while remaining formally distinct from it. In the 2006 elections, pro-autonomy parties that stood independently included the Venetian Republic League, the Lombardy Alliance League, and the Northeast Project, which is a Veneto-based party. In the March 2010 regional elections, the Venetian League won 35 percent of the vote in the Venice region, their best showing ever.

Current Status

The Italian separatists have seen a revival in their political fortunes. In the April 2008 Italian elections, the LN scored 8 percent nationwide, securing 60 out of 630 seats in the Chamber and 25 out of 315 in the Senate. The party once again entered a Berlusconi coalition government, obtaining four cabinet posts. In the June 2009 European Parliament elections, LN won 10 percent and took 9 of the 72 seats allotted for Italy. In the regional elections of March 2010, the LN further increased its share of the nationwide vote to 13 percent and took control of two regions, Veneto and Piedmont.

LN leader Bossi, who helped raise the party's profile with his theatrical style and fiery rhetoric, has not been as dominant a figure in Italian politics since suffering a stroke in 2004. In recent years, when Bossi and other LN party leaders have made the headlines, it has been more often than not because of remarks they made criticizing immigrants rather than demands made for greater

autonomy or independence. An article on the BBC News Web site reported that in the 2008 election campaign, for example, the LN used a campaign poster that depicted an American Indian and the words: "They suffered immigration: now they live in reserves." A November 2009 article in the British newspaper *The Independent* reported that the LN mayor of the town of Coccaglio in Lombardy, Franco Claretti, was spearheading a campaign against illegal immigrants called "White Christmas." Journalist Michael Day cited an LN official who said: "For me Christmas isn't the holiday of hospitality, but rather that of the Christian tradition and of our identity."

Despite the prominence of the LN on the political scene since the 1990s, all indications from election results and opinion polls are that the overwhelming majority of northern Italians do not wish to secede. One of the early concerns raised by the northern separatists—that the south's weak economy would scupper Italy's chances of being allowed to adopt the euro as its currency—has not materialized. For now, northerners' priorities seem to be to strengthen their control over their tax revenues and enhance the powers of local government. There is little sign that the Italian government is planning to turn the country into a federal state.

Further Reading

"Berlusconi's bounce; Italy's regional elections," *The Economist*, April 3, 2010.

Day, Michael. "Italy's Northern League in 'White Christmas' immigrant purge," *The Independent* (United Kingdom), November 19, 2009, www.independent .co.uk/news/world/europe/italys-northern-league-in-white-christmas-immigrant-purge-1823231.html.

European Commission against Racism and Intolerance. "Third Report on Italy," Council of Europe, May 16, 2006, http://hudoc.ecri.coe.int/XMLEcri/ENGLISH/ Cycle_03/03_CbC_eng/ITA-CbC-III-2006–19-ENG .pdf.

Lewis, Aidan. "Italy's Northern League resurgent," BBC News, April 17, 2008, http://news.bbc.co.uk/2/hi/ europe/7350691.stm.

Northern League Web site, www.leganord.org.

SAAMI
(Finland, Norway, Russia, Sweden)

The Saami are an indigenous people in the Arctic region who inhabit a large and sparsely populated swathe of territory that cuts through northern Finland, Norway, Russia, and Sweden. Despite their small numbers, the Saami have been remarkably effective in organizing themselves politically. Their main priority has been to gain greater control over their homelands' natural resources rather than to create an independent Saami country. While some Saami are frustrated with the limited progress they have made in achieving their goals, their movement has at all times been peaceful.

The total Saami population is just under 100,000, with 60,000 living in Norway, 25,000 in Sweden, 7,500 in Finland, and 2,000 in Russia. They are not classified as a separate nation in Russia because their population does not exceed fifty thousand. The only country where they comprise more than 1 percent of the population is Norway (1.3%). Most of Norway's Saami live in Finnmark County; the Swedish Saami community lives predominantly in the municipalities of Kiruna, Gallivare, Jokkmokk, and Arvidsjaur. Finland's Saami are concentrated in three northern municipalities in the province of Lapland; Russia's Saami live on the Kola Peninsula, which lies at the northwestern tip of Russia.

The Saami call their homeland "Sapmi." In the past, the Saami lands have been called "Lapland" and the Saami people referred to as "Lapper" in Norway, "Lappalaiset" in Finland, and "Lappar" in Sweden; these terms are no longer in use. The Saami have their own language, which has nine dialects. It is related to the Finno-Ugric linguistic family that also includes Estonian, Finnish, and Hungarian. Since the 1980s the number of Saami-speakers has been increasing. Saami is now an official language in six municipalities in Norway; however, in the southern Saami homelands, there are dialects that are at risk of dying out.

The reindeer occupies a central role in the Saami culture and economy. Reindeer are used for producing meat and fur, transport, and racing. "The reindeer is our cultural carrier. It is part of our language," said Gunn-Britt Retter, in a telephone interview in July 2008. She is a Saami from Norway who works for the Saami Council, a non-governmental body representing the Saami. She noted that Saami used to live a nomadic lifestyle but not anymore. Those involved in reindeer husbandry do maintain winter and summer houses, however, as they move their reindeer between coastal and inland regions with the seasons. In Norway and Sweden, reindeer husbandry is a legally protected Saami livelihood—one in which only the Saami may engage. Fishing and berry-picking are two other activities central to the Saami way of life.

The Saami have their own parliaments in Finland, Norway, and Sweden, but these bodies do not have lawmaking powers. There is no autonomous Saami region either within any of the host countries or transnationally. The granting of such territorial autonomy would help the Saami to regain control of the ways in which their homelands' natural resources are exploited. Many Saami do not accept that the Finnish, Norwegian, Russian, and Swedish governments own the land on which the Saami have historically lived.

Saami political leaders assert their right of self-determination as a distinct nation; however, there is no agreement between them and their governments as to what this means in practice. At a February 2008 conference on self-determination in the town of Alta in northern Norway, the president of Norway's Saami Parliament, Egil Olli, said that the Saami "have never expressed any desire to secede from existing national states." Olli said his people were more interested in the "right to determine their own economic, social, and cultural development, and, for their own ends, to freely dispose of their natural wealth and resource." A Norwegian government official attending the conference said that self-determination did not entail either the establishment of a new state or of an autonomous Saami territory.

The legal rights of Saami vary from country to country. In Norway, where the Saami are most numerous, the constitution recognizes them as a distinct people. By contrast, in Russia, where the Saami population is smallest, their status is more precarious. They do not have special rights over their historic lands, something many of Russia's larger indigenous populations do have. The lack of recognition in Russia makes it difficult for Saami concerns to be addressed, in particular, how oil industry infrastructure, including mines and pipelines, is developed. Pipelines can have a negative impact on reindeer husbandry as they hinder the free movement of herds. In Finland, the Saami area, which is called Lapland, is exploited as a popular tourist destination—it is, most notably, the "home" of the legendary Christmas character Santa Claus and his reindeer. Sweden has attempted to develop tourism in the Saami regions by constructing ice hotels and model Saami villages and by organizing reindeer and dogsled tours that follow the reindeer migratory patterns.

History

The Saami have lived in their present homeland for at least five thousand years. Originally subsisting from reindeer hunting, from the 1400s they increasingly turned to reindeer husbandry as a means of subsistence. This led them to adopt a more nomadic lifestyle in response to reindeer grazing patterns. Moving freely became more difficult from the 1700s as the northern borders of Scandinavia and Russia became set. These newly formed borders had the effect of splitting up the Saami among several countries. The different governments in the region gradually extended their control. Norwegian Saami Gunn-Britt Retter noted, "We used to pay taxes to four different kings: Sweden, Norway, Denmark and Russia."

In 1751 a Lapland region was created and the borders between Norway and Sweden were demarcated. In 1809 a border separating Sweden from Finland was set. The Saami's homeland became further fragmented in 1905 when Norway, which was ruled by Sweden in the 1800s, became independent. The Saami's identity was threatened by policies Norway adopted from 1905 until the 1970s aimed at assimilating them into Norwegian society. In Sweden, from 1913 to 1920 the Saami were segregated from Swedes, and the Saami language was prohibited in schools. Despite these challenges, the Saami culture endured: the first radio broadcast in Saami occurred in 1946, and the first Saami-language television newscast was aired in 2001. A Saami-language newspaper was established as early as 1873; however, Saami print publications have struggled to sustain themselves financially and tend to rely on government subsidies.

A watershed event in the emergence of the Saami autonomy movement occurred in Norway in 1970, when the Norwegian government unveiled its plan to build a large dam in the river Alta for a hydropower plant. The government's plan provoked fierce opposition among the Saami. Their opposition was founded on the belief that the plant would seriously adversely affect salmon-fishing and reindeer grazing. Saami protests, which included hunger strikes in front of the Norwegian Parliament, culminated in January 1981 when police forcibly removed demonstrators from the planned site. The project went ahead, and the dam was completed in 1987.

In Finland, the government in 1995 extended the definition of "Saami" to include people previously identified in state registers as "Lapp," even if neither they nor their parents or grandparents spoke Saami. The Saami Parliament opposed this change, fearing it would dilute the Saami population. The Finnish Supreme Administrative Court in 1999 decided to exclude from the Saami designation those whose registered Lapp ancestors were more distant than grandparents.

In Sweden, a law was adopted in 2000 enhancing the rights of the Saami to use their language when interacting with the administration and courts in Saami-populated areas. The law provided for Saami-language education in Saami areas, although Swedish also had to be taught. Saami children were allowed to participate in reindeer-herding exercises for four weeks during the school year. In autumn 2002, the Norwegian, Swedish, and Finnish governments appointed a group of experts to begin drafting a Nordic Saami Convention codifying Saami rights. The experts submitted a fifty-one article draft text in November 2005. Norway, meanwhile, in June 2005 adopted the Finnmark Act, which created a new body, the *Finnmarkseiendommen,* composed of six elected officials who were given the task of administering Saami lands. The law established a special court for adjudicating land rights disputes.

In Russia, the Saami community struggled to maintain their way of life. A March 2006 article in *China Daily,* a Beijing-based English-language newspaper, reported that reindeer husbandry was in danger of disappearing. The article noted that of the forty herders trained in the previous twenty-nine years, only ten had graduated; at the same time, the reindeer population was experiencing decline in the face of wealthy foreign hunters and poachers.

Leadership

The Saami Parliament in Norway is the most influential of the three Saami parliaments. The Norwegian Saami Parliament is formally consulted in advance of the drafting of Saami-related Norwegian laws. It was established in October 1989 and has forty-three members who are elected every four years. Finland set up a Saami Parliament in November 1973 and increased its powers in 1996 in the areas of spending, language, and cultural policy. The Swedish Saami Parliament, which was established in August 1993, has advisory status. Russia does not have a Saami parliament. An organization that promotes Saami culture and communal rights is the Resource Center for the Rights of Indigenous Peoples, or Galdu, which is funded by the Norwegian government and is based in Guovdageaidnu-Kautokeino in Norway.

Before their parliaments were set up, the Saami Council, established in 1956, was the Saami's main representative body. Known initially as the Saami Nordic Council, it was renamed the Saami Council in 1992 when Saami representatives from

Russia joined. The council has fifteen members, and its secretariat is based in Utsjoki, a small town in the northern tip of Finland bordering Norway. The council members come from nine Saami organizations, including the Saami Association of Kola Peninsula, the Saami Reindeer Herders Association of Norway, Saami Association of Sweden, and Saami Association of Finland. It participates in United Nations' processes that relate to indigenous peoples. It is also a permanent participant on the Arctic Council, an intergovernmental body created in 1996 that brings together Arctic governments to discuss issues of common concern.

The Saami Council campaigns to bolster the rights of the Saami and limit the adverse effects caused by their division among four countries. In a declaration adopted in October 2004 at a conference in Honningsvag, Norway, the council stated that "the Saami have the right to self-determination as a distinct people." The declaration stressed the right of the Saami "to develop their own language, culture, ways of subsistence," and "to possess, manage, and use [their] own land and sea areas and utilize their natural resources." It called for the Saami customary legal traditions to take precedence in disputes about use of natural resources. On hunting rights, it demanded that Saami be empowered to "marshal and control the predatory population in Saami areas." It urged that governments' legislation be harmonized to allow the Saami to run their own education system. And it demanded that reindeer husbandry be maintained as an economic activity reserved exclusively for Saami.

Current Status

While the Saami have made progress in protecting their language and cultural rights, many would like greater autonomy. "Our parliament in Norway is underfunded. We do not have our own budget and cannot make laws. We can only give advice to the Norwegian government," said Gunn-Britt

Retter. She said the Saami would prefer a direct share of revenues from oil and gas reserves extracted from their region, instead of benefiting indirectly via subsidies from the national budget. According to Retter, "we are not against development of our resources like oil, gold, and iron. But we need to resolve the land rights issue."

In July 2008, the Saami brought together autonomy movements from around the world to Gallivare in northern Sweden where they hosted the Viva World Cup, a soccer tournament organized for groups that do not have their own country. Teams representing the Saami, Padanians (Italy), Iraqi Kurds, Provencais (France), and Suryoye (Turkey) participated. In August 2008, the UN Committee on Racial Discrimination made recommendations to the Swedish government on Saami land rights. The committee recommended that the government provide legal aid to the Saami in land use–related disputes and suggested the burden of proof in these disputes be shared equally rather than lying solely with the Saami.

The 2005 draft Nordic Saami Convention has still not been ratified. In October 2008, the Saami Council adopted a resolution urging the four governments involved to ratify it. By doing so "the states will hence fulfill their obligation to take effective measures to facilitate the Saami people's right to maintain and develop relations across national borders," the resolution said. The council voiced its concern over the fact that Finland indicated in 2008 that it would not ratify the convention.

In Russia, Saami efforts to preserve their identity are being supported by neighboring Norway. The BBC Monitoring Service reported in March 2009 that a Saami radio station based in Lovozero on the Kola Peninsula was receiving subsidies from the Norwegian government and Saami Journalists Association. The article, a translation of a newscast from a Russian local television station, Blitz TV, noted that the Kola Saami radio station was the only Saami-language station in Russia.

In August 2009, a groundbreaking land use dispute was resolved when two reindeer herding brothers, the Paadars, made an agreement with Finnish forestry company Metsahallitus over the brothers' grazing lands in Nellim, in Finland. Metsahallitus agreed not to log on 90 percent of the brothers' lands and accepted restrictions on logging on the other 10 percent. Welcoming the move, the Saami Council's Mattias Ahren said, "they have not only secured their future as traditional Saami reindeer herders but have also contributed to an important precedent for the Saami people as a whole." Ahren hoped other forestry companies looking to operate in Saami areas would make similar agreements.

At the December 2009 UN Summit on Climate Change in Copenhagen, Denmark, Gunn-Britt Retter made a presentation on behalf of the Saami Council. "Efforts to mitigate climate change cause almost as great a problem to the Saami people as climate change itself," she noted. "The exploding interest in renewable resources such as windmills, hydro-electric dams, and nuclear power plants intensify pressure on our lands never seen before." As an example, she mentioned a new Swedish-Norwegian project to install 417 windmills on Saami winter grazing lands in Jingevaerie in Sweden and explained that windmill parks can prevent Saami communities from pursuing reindeer husbandry.

The Saami are likely to continue to use peaceful, democratic platforms such as the UN, where they already have a voice, as well as the national and Saami parliaments to pursue their aspirations for autonomy.

Further Reading

"Reindeer Children a Dying Breed in Russia's Arctic Tundra," *China Daily,* March 15, 2006, www.china daily.com.cn/english/doc/2006–03/15/content_ 536789.htm.

Henrikson, John, ed. "Saami self-determination: Scope and implementation," *Galdu Cala—Journal of Indigenous Peoples Rights* no. 2 (2008), www.e-pages.dk/ grusweb/43.

Resource Centre for the Rights of Indigenous Peoples Web site, www.galdu.org.

Retter, Gunn-Britt. "UNFCCC COP 15—WWF Arctic Tent—Indigenous Day, Copenhagen 08.12.09," Saami Council, December 9, 2009, www.saamicouncil.net/? newsid=2693&deptid=2192&languageid=4&news=1.

Saami Council. "The Saami Council applauds historic settlement between Paadar brothers and Metsähallitus in Nellim!" press release, August 24, 2009, www .saamicouncil.net/?newsid=2688&deptid=2192&lang uageid=4&news=1.

———. "The United Nations strongly criticizes Sweden for violating the Saami people's right to land and natural resources," press release, August 19, 2008, www.saamicouncil.net/includes/file_download.asp?d eptid=2215&fileid=2893&file=200808CERDPress .pdf&pdf=1.

SCOTS
(United Kingdom)

The people of Scotland in the United Kingdom (UK) have since the 1960s been campaigning for greater powers of self-government from the London-based UK government. Although they gained autonomy in 1999 when a Scottish parliament and executive were inaugurated, many Scots would like to go further and make Scotland independent.

Scotland numbers five million people, accounting for 9 percent of the total UK population, and comprises a third of UK territory. While the overwhelming majority of Scots speak English, a small minority speak either Gaelic, a Celtic language closely related to Irish, or Scots, a Germanic language closely related to English. The area where Gaelic is spoken most widely is the western isles of Scotland. Scots is most commonly spoken in the lowlands and the Orkney and Shetland Islands off the north coast of Scotland. Like the rest of the UK, Scots are mainly a mix of diverse Protestant denominations; a minority are Catholic. While religious differences have caused conflict within Scottish society over the centuries, they do not figure in the debate over independence.

Because the UK has no written constitution, Scotland's system of self-government is instead enshrined in legislation enacted by the UK Parliament. The Scots' head of state since 1952 has been Queen Elizabeth II, who lives in Scotland for part of the year and who has on several occasions opened the Scottish Parliament in the city of Edinburgh. Scotland has historically maintained a separate legal and educational system from the rest of the UK. Scottish secessionism has remained largely peaceful, with Scottish nationalists competing in elections. The secessionist Scottish National Party (SNP) has since May 2007 held power in Scotland's autonomous government. Since taking power, the SNP refers to the administration as the "Scottish Government," preferring this term to its formal title, "Scottish Executive."

Among the UK's three main political parties—Labor, the Conservatives, and Liberal Democrats—Labor and the Liberal Democrats tend to be more sympathetic to Scottish demands for self-government. Labor governments have passed legislation to install devolved government in Scotland in 1978 and 1999. The center-right Conservatives have historically been opposed to autonomy, fearing it would lead to the breakup of the UK. However, the Conservatives are not demanding a repeal of the autonomy that Scotland gained in the late 1990s.

Scots have over the past fifty years taken steps to preserve and promote their culture and indigenous languages, Gaelic and Scots. There are 60,000 Gaelic speakers, while estimates of Scots speakers range from 100,000 to a million. Gaelic and Scots are taught in some schools, literature is published in these languages, and since September 2008 a Gaelic-language television channel called BBC Alba has been broadcasting. In 2005 the Scottish government passed legislation requiring public bodies to prepare Gaelic language plans. Despite such efforts, the Gaelic language is in danger of extinction because fewer and fewer people speak it in areas where it has been traditionally spoken.

While Scots have since 1999 assumed responsibility for a wide range of policy areas, responsibility for setting economic policies is still shared with the UK government. This has caused some tensions, notably over how to manage Scotland's natural resources. Scottish territorial waters—specifically, in the North Sea—contain the majority of the UK's generous offshore oil reserves. There is much debate—but little consensus—on the question of whether the Scots overall are net contributors to, or beneficiaries of, the UK government budget. According to Bill Wilson, an SNP member of the Scottish Parliament, Scots should be given control of economic and monetary policy because the Scottish economic cycle is out of sync with that of the English economy. Wilson, in a May 2010 telephone interview, claimed Scottish people tended to favor more left-of-center policies than the average Briton.

In foreign affairs, Wilson said that many Scots opposed the policies that the UK government has adopted over the decades. Scots, if left to their own devices, would steer a very different course, he maintained. "We reject much of our imperial past. I do not believe in nuclear weapons. I did not support the Iraq war," he said. As a further example of Scots' opposition to the policies of the UK government, he cited the 1982 war between Argentina and the UK over who should govern the Falkland Islands.

The Scottish separatist movement is not sponsored by other foreign governments. However, the SNP has forged links with pro-autonomy and pro-independence regionally based political parties across Europe. In the Brussels-based European Parliament, the SNP's elected representatives are affiliated with the left-leaning Greens–European Free Alliance group, which includes Catalan, Corsican, Flemish, and Welsh autonomy activists (see separate essays). The Council of Europe, a Strasbourg-based intergovernmental institution that promotes democracy and human rights, has helped bolster the status of the Gaelic and Scots languages. The council in 1992 adopted a charter to protect and promote Europe's lesser-used languages. The UK government ratified the charter in 2001 and applies it to both Gaelic and Scots, with Gaelic ranking a higher level of recognition than Scots.

History

The name "Scots" has its origins in the Gaelic-speaking Celtic people, the *Scoti*, who migrated from the island of Ireland to western Scotland from the fifth century C.E. While the Romans by this time had established settlements in England and Wales, they had failed to take Scotland. The Gaelic language and culture spread through Scotland, although never dominated. After the French-speaking Normans invaded England in 1066, English people who fled northward to Scotland brought the English language with them, dispersing across the region. From the 1300s to the 1500s, successive English monarchs sought to conquer Scotland, sometimes encountering fierce resistance from Scottish leaders such as William Wallace (1272–1305).

When Queen Elizabeth I of England died in 1603, the English throne passed to her cousin, King James VI of Scotland. As a result, England and Scotland were united under a single monarch and James moved his court from Edinburgh to London. In 1707 Scotland and England were merged to form

Great Britain, which became known as the United Kingdom in 1801 after Ireland was joined to it. A Scottish nationalist movement developed from the late 1800s, with small organizations springing up demanding that Scots be given greater control over their affairs. In the early 1900s there were numerous unsuccessful attempts to push bills through the UK parliament aimed at restoring Scottish independence.

From the late 1950s, efforts to preserve the Gaelic language and culture intensified, with Gaelic radio and television broadcasts launched in 1959. Pro-Scottish independence political activism experienced a significant resurgence in the 1960s. In 1968 the UK government, led by Labor, proposed the establishment of a commission to examine the country's tradition of strong central government, launching a process that thirty years later would culminate in Scots' gaining self-government. In the October 1974 UK elections, the SNP won 30 percent of the Scottish vote, their best showing ever in a general election. This success inspired a UK Labor government to pass legislation in 1978 providing for the creation of a Scottish Assembly. But Scottish separatists suffered a setback in March 1979 when a referendum to approve the devolution plan failed. Although 51 percent of those who voted supported the plan, the turnout, at 64 percent, was too low for passage.

The 1980s and early 1990s were a difficult time for the separatists; the UK was led by a Conservative government that opposed autonomy for Scotland. UK prime minister Margaret Thatcher (1979–1990) was unpopular among Scots. According to SNP parliamentarian Wilson, this heightened Scots' sense of alienation from the London-based government. Wilson cited Thatcher's refusal to devolve power, support for privatization, imposition of a regressive "poll" tax that went into effect in Scotland before the rest of the UK, and even her "patronizing" personality as the causes of her unpopularity. Added Wilson, "She's still hated here."

When Labor's Tony Blair became UK prime minister in May 1997, he quickly moved to devolve power to Scotland; in September 1997, he organized a referendum on the creation of a Scottish parliament that 74.3 percent of Scots voters approved. The same day, 50.3 percent of voters in Wales, a nation west of England, approved the establishment of a Welsh Assembly, which did not possess the same degree of power as the Scottish Parliament (see separate essay). The first Scottish Parliament elections were held in May 1999. The secessionist SNP won 28.7 percent of the vote, coming in second place to Labor. The electoral system, a form of proportional representation, allowed the SNP to win a bigger share of seats than it would normally win in the so-called first-past-the-post system, which favors larger parties and that is employed in UK national elections. In response to devolution, the British government between 2000 and 2002 abolished some of the functions of its Scottish department, which sets and implements UK government policies for Scotland.

Leadership

The Scottish government is comprised of a 129-seat parliament and an executive led by Scotland's first minister. Its remit extends to policies on health, education, local government, social work, housing, planning, tourism, economic development, law and home affairs, police, the environment, agriculture, sports, and transportation. The dominant Scottish separatist party, the SNP, advocates a peaceful, gradual transition to an independent Scotland. In the May 2007 Scottish elections, the SNP won the most seats, 47 compared to Labor's 46, which enabled it to form a minority government. The leader of the SNP since September 2004 has been Alex Salmond. He took over the leadership in May 1990 from Gordon Wilson. Salmond resigned in 2000 and was replaced by John Swinney, who resigned in June 2004. Swinney's resignation led to Salmond's reelection. Other

Winifred Margaret "Winnie" Ewing (1929–   )

David Cheskin/PA Photos/Landov

WINIFRED MARGARET EWING (née Woodburn) was born in 1929 in Glasgow, Scotland, where she attended Queen's Park Senior Secondary School and then attended Glasgow University. While there, Ewing was a member of the university's Scottish Nationalist Association. She earned an MA and LLB, and then in 1956 started her career as a practicing solicitor, as well as a notary public. That same year she married Stewart Ewing. Ewing served as the secretary of the Glasgow Bar Association from 1961 to 1970 and held the position of president in 1970.

In 1967 Ewing ran as a candidate to become a Member of the British Parliament for Hamilton, a constituency southwest of Glasgow, where the sitting Labor MP had resigned. Ewing won the election for the pro-independence Scottish National Party (SNP), taking 46 percent of the vote and giving the SNP its first seat in the British Parliament. Ewing's election was a huge victory for the SNP and one that marked the rise of its political fortunes. The issue of devolution for Scotland, specifically the creation of a Scottish parliament, was placed firmly on the political agenda from this point. Ewing's victory speech included the now-famous utterance, "Stop the world—Scotland wants to get on," which later served as the title of her autobiography.

Her landmark victory notwithstanding, Ewing lost her seat in 1970. However, in 1974 she defeated the sitting Tory in Moray and Nairn, winning a seat and joining six other members of the SNP in Parliament. She held that seat until 1979. During that time she became vice president of the SNP.

In 1975 Ewing became a Member of the European Parliament (MEP), representing the Highlands and Islands of Scotland. During her term, she was nicknamed "Madame Ecosse," or Madam Scotland, by the French newspaper *Le Monde*. When the European Parliament became a directly elected institution in 1979—it had previously consisted of MEPs who were appointed by national governments—Ewing stood for election and won a seat. She held onto her MEP's seat until 1999. In 1984 she was made vice president of the European Democratic Alliance. Over the years she picked up yet another nickname—"Mother of the European Parliament." In 1988 she became president of the SNP.

In 1999 Ewing resigned her seat in the European Parliament and was instead elected a member of the newly established Scottish Parliament. As the Scottish Parliament's oldest member, it was her duty to preside over its historic opening. She began the first session by saying, "I want to begin with the words that I have always wanted either to say, or hear someone else say—the Scottish Parliament, which adjourned on March 25, 1707, is hereby reconvened."

Her husband, Stewart Ewing, died in an accidental fire in 2003. He had also been politically active and had always supported his wife's Scottish nationalism. Stewart and Winnie had two sons and one daughter, passing on to them a passion for Scottish politics. Their son, Fergus Ewing, serves as an SNP Member of the Scottish Parliament in Edinburgh, as did his late wife, Margaret Ewing. Their daughter, Annabelle Ewing, served as a Member of the British Parliament, although she has been out of office since 2007.

Ewing retired from her position as president of the SNP in 2005 to spend more time with her grandchildren. She enjoys fishing and is interested in the preservation of minority languages such as Gaelic. She currently serves as the vice president of the charity Parity, which works for equal gender rights in the United Kingdom.

---

leading figures in the party include Nicola Sturgeon, Ian Hudghton, Fergus Ewing, Michael Russell, and Angus Robertson.

The SNP was established in 1934 as a merger between the National Party of Scotland and the Scottish Party. The SNP became a significant presence in Scottish politics from the 1960s. A breakthrough moment for the party came in November 1967 when its candidate, Winifred Ewing, won a by-election for a UK Parliament seat after winning 46 percent of the vote. This victory was quickly followed by the May 1968 local elections in which the SNP won over a hundred seats, with strong performances in the cities of Glasgow and Aberdeen.

One of the earliest pro-autonomy groups was the Scottish Home Rule Association, which was established in 1886—the same year the UK Parliament was debating draft legislation to give autonomy, or "Home Rule," to Ireland, then part of the UK. In 1891 the Highland Association was founded to promote the Gaelic language. There has not been a significant militia group fighting for independence in Scotland. In the 1990s radical groups, including one called Settler Watch, registered a marginal presence, but there has been little activity since 2000.

Scotland has 59 elected representatives in the 650-member British Parliament. The main parties in the UK—Labor, the Conservatives, and Liberal Democrats—each field distinct Scottish branches that are operating with increasing autonomy. Since the mid-1990s, the SNP has been competing with Labor to be the largest party in Scotland. The Conservatives and Liberal Democrats compete for third and fourth place. Gordon Brown, the UK prime minister from 2007–2010, is Scottish. Brown, in line with the official position of his Labor party, was opposed to an independent Scotland.

Current Status

Scotland has a fully functional, devolved government with a busy legislative agenda. The SNP has pushed through legislation by securing support from other parties, generally the Conservatives, Liberals, or Greens. It has abolished medical prescription charges, moved to phase out privatized healthcare, banned smoking in public places, and passed the Climate Change Act that aims to reduce Scotland's greenhouse gas emissions.

In a January 2008 article for the British newspaper *The Guardian,* political commentator Iain MacWhirter remarked that Scots were adopting different policies from the rest of the UK on education, healthcare, and taxation. The UK Parliament "has yet to come to terms with it, but legislative dissonance is likely to become one of the defining features of U.K. politics," he said. Politicians in Scotland seem to be embracing this new reality. Even the Conservatives no longer oppose devolution. UK prime minister David Cameron has floated the idea of creating some form of an English assembly to vet legislation that applies specifically to England.

The Scots language, which has struggled to attract as much government support and recognition as Gaelic, is beginning to garner more attention. According to SNP parliamentarian Wilson, Scots has previously lost out because "Gaelic is not politically dangerous. Scots is. Scottish people were told for hundreds of years that Scots was an inferior language, a bastardization of English." Wilson, a Scots-language speaker and advocate, welcomed the decision, for the first time, to ask Scottish people on the census form if they could speak Scots.

In August 2009, the world spotlight fell on the Scottish government after it released a Libyan man convicted of killing 270 people by blowing up Pan Am flight 103 over Lockerbie, in Scotland, in December 1988. The release of Abdelbaset Ali Mohmed al-Megrahi, justified on the grounds that he was suffering from terminal cancer, sparked a firestorm of criticism, especially from the United States where most of the bomb victims were from. Reporting for *Newsweek* magazine in September 2009, William Underhill cited a poll of Scots, which found that while 69 percent accepted the release had damaged Scotland's reputation abroad, 43 percent supported the move. "There are signs that rather than making Scots doubt their move, the international mudslinging may have had the paradoxical effect of stiffening Scottish spines," Underhill wrote.

In November 2009, the Scottish government published a white paper outlining the options for Scotland's future constitutional structure. They ranged from continuing the status quo to extending autonomy to fiscal and energy policy to full independence. In a January 2010 speech at the

Edinburgh International Conference Center, SNP leader and Scottish first minister Alex Salmond said, "we need to move from financial and economic policy that vitally affects Scotland being decided outside Scotland, to a position where such key decisions are taken in Scotland."

The SNP remains a strong force in Scottish politics. It won 29 percent of the Scottish vote in the June 2009 European Parliament elections, although it saw its support dip to 20 percent in the May 2010 UK parliamentary elections. The party remains committed to holding a referendum on independence. According to Wilson, the result of a referendum "would depend on how the question was phrased. If the word 'independence' was stressed it would attract greater support than if the word 'separation' was used," he said. In September 2010 SNP leader Salmond announced a postponement of the referendum bill until after the May 2011 Scottish parliament elections. The decision was taken following mounting fears from within the SNP that such a referendum would fail to pass in the current political climate and that a no vote would be a serious setback for their independence hopes.

Many Scots have doubts about whether independence would be the wisest move economically for Scotland. For example, there is uncertainty about Scotland's ability to sustain itself given that the reserves of oil off the Scottish coast in the North Sea are diminishing. Should a clear majority of Scots desire independence, however, it is unlikely that the UK government would use force to prevent Scotland from seceding.

Further Reading

Bogdanor, Vernon. "The era of two tribes is over, whoever wins," *The Times* (United Kingdom), April 16, 2010, www.timesonline.co.uk/tol/comment/. columnists/guest_contributors/article7099069.ece.

Jeffery, Charlie, and James Mitchell, eds. *The Scottish Parliament 1999–2009: The First Decade.* Edinburgh: Luath Press Limited, 2009.

MacWhirter, Iain. "The break-up of the union now appears inevitable," *The Guardian* (United Kingdom), January 10, 2008, www.guardian.co.uk/commentis-free/2008/jan/10/scotland.politics.

———. "They shelved independence and got away with it. Nice work, Alex," *Sunday Herald*, September 12, 2010, www.heraldscotland.com/comment/iain-mac-whirter/they-shelved-independence-and-got-away-with-it-nice-work-alex-1.1054409.

Peterkin, Tom. "War Of Independence Erupts Within Ranks Of SNP," *The Scotsman*, June 26, 2010, http://news.scotsman.com/news/War-of-independence-erupts-within.6385585.jp.

Salmond, Alex. "Edinburgh Lecture: Choosing Scotland's Future," January 12, 2010, www.scotland.gov.uk/News/This-Week/Speeches/First-Minister/Edinburghlecture.

Scott, Paul Henderson. *Scotland Resurgent.* Edinburgh: The Saltire Society, 2005.

Scottish Government Web site, www.scotland.gov.uk.

Scottish National Party Web site, www.snp.org.

Underhill, William. "Braveheart Stands Up to the Globe," *Newsweek* (International Edition), September 7, 2009.

WELSH
(United Kingdom)

The Welsh people of the United Kingdom (UK) obtained limited powers of self-government in the late 1990s. While only 10 to 20 percent of Welsh want their nation, Wales, to become fully independent, a much larger percentage would like Wales to acquire greater autonomy.

The Welsh people number three million and account for 5 percent of the UK population. Their native tongue, Welsh, is a Celtic language that about a quarter of Welsh people can speak. The Welsh inhabit the western part of the island of Great Britain. There is also a Welsh community of twenty thousand in the Patagonia region of Argentina, descendants of Welsh who founded a colony there in 1865. Like the rest of the UK, the Welsh are predominantly Christian of various Protestant denominations; a minority are Catholic.

A semi-autonomous government has operated in Wales since 1999. It can adopt measures (they are not called laws) in various policy areas, although it must first obtain the consent of the UK government. The Welsh government's powers are weaker than those of Scotland's autonomous government, which was established in 1999 to represent the Scottish people. Scotland is the UK's northernmost nation.

The Welsh independence movement has been predominantly peaceful. In the 1960s it had a strong civil disobedience component to it, with Welsh language activists pulling down many signs for place names that were written in English. The main political party campaigning for Welsh independence is Plaid Cymru (The Party of Wales). Since May 2007, Plaid has been in power in the Welsh government as the minority partner in the One Wales coalition it formed with the Welsh Labor Party. Plaid typically wins 10–15 percent of the vote in UK parliamentary elections and as much as 20–30 percent in Welsh and European elections.

In a May 2010 telephone interview, Plaid Member of the European Parliament Jill Evans said, "we support full independence as a long-term goal but we see it as a gradual process." Evans' view remains a minority one in Wales. The head, or first minister, in the Welsh government, Labor's Carwyn Jones, is strongly opposed to independence. Cited in a December 2008 article by David Williamson for the Welsh newspaper *The Western Mail,* Jones claimed, "Wales would be financially worse off if it was independent," adding, "Devolution? Absolutely. Independence? Absolutely not."

Preserving and promoting the Welsh language is a cornerstone of the Welsh autonomy movement. A leading organization in this campaign has been Cymdeithas yr Iaith Gymraeg (The Welsh Language Society), established in 1962. Chairwoman Menna Machreth, in a May 2010 telephone interview, said the society faces a significant challenge. According to Machreth, "many in Welsh-speaking rural communities [are] moving to cities where English is dominant, while non-Welsh speakers buy homes in Welsh-speaking areas." This, she worried, could threaten Welsh's survival as a living language. Machreth also favored creating more Welsh-medium schools; bilingual English/Welsh schools in practice did not produce fluent Welsh-speakers because English dominated in them.

History

Until the Romans arrived in Great Britain in the first century B.C.E., Celtic peoples dominated the island. The Anglo-Saxons, who were Germanic, invaded from the sixth century C.E., which caused many natives to flee westward. The Anglo-Saxons called these Celts *Wealas*, meaning "foreigners," from which the terms "Wales/Welsh" were derived. Wales came under Norman-English rule in 1284 after being conquered by King Edward I of England. An uprising by Welsh leader Owain Glyndwr in 1400 did not stem the advance of the English, nor did the accession to the English throne in 1485 of a king with Welsh origins, Henry Tudor. In 1536 Wales was formally annexed to England when an Act of Union was passed that pledged "utterly to extirpate" Welsh culture. The Welsh language was repressed but it nevertheless managed to survive, helped in no small part by the fact that the Bible had been translated into Welsh in the early 1500s.

When the coal-mining and iron industries developed in Wales in the 1800s, many English, Irish, and Scottish workers immigrated there. The 1960s witnessed a major revival in Welsh nationalism. Plaid candidate Gwynfor Evans became the party's first Member of Parliament in July 1966 when he won a by-election. In 1969 Welsh separatists planted bombs to protest a ceremony marking the investiture of Prince Charles as Prince of Wales, a title given to male heirs to the English throne since 1301.

The UK Labor government held a referendum in March 1979 to grant limited self-government to Wales, but it was rejected by 80 percent of Welsh voters. Despite this setback, support for Welsh autonomy grew in the 1980s, according to Menna Machreth, largely because the UK government under Margaret Thatcher was so unpopular in Wales, especially after Thatcher shut down the Welsh coal mines. In 1993 a law was passed that gave Welsh people the right in principle to receive public services through the medium of Welsh language. After Labor was elected to government in May 1997, it held another referendum on devolution for Wales. The referendum passed, but only barely, with 50.3 percent voting in favor. The first Welsh Assembly was elected in May 1999.

Leadership

Plaid is a left-leaning party that receives most of its support in Welsh-speaking areas. Founded in 1925, the leader since 2000 has been Ieuan Wyn Jones. Other prominent party figures include Jill Evans, Dafydd Iwan, and Elfyn Llwyd. In the 2007 Welsh Assembly elections, Plaid emerged the second largest party after Labor, winning fifteen of sixty seats. The party has an elected member in the European Parliament, where it affiliates with the left-leaning Greens–European Free Alliance group, a coalition of environmental and regionally based pro-autonomy parties that includes the Catalans (Spain), Corsicans (France), Flemings (Belgium), and Scots (UK) (see separate essays).

The main UK-wide parties, the Conservatives, Labor, and Liberal Democrats, have sister parties in Wales whose members increasingly favor more autonomy for Wales, a sentiment not shared by many of their non-Welsh party colleagues. Welsh Language Society's Machreth claimed that Labor, the largest party in Wales, had historically been hostile to the Welsh language campaign, viewing it as part of a nationalist agenda at odds with Labor's socialist ideology. Plaid parliamentarian Jill Evans said some Labor politicians in Wales campaigned against devolution in the 1979 and 1997 referenda, despite the fact that Labor governments had proposed devolution.

The Welsh government is based in the city of Cardiff. The Welsh Assembly, the Senedd, is directly elected every four years. Welsh first ministers to date have been Alun Michael (1999–2000), who was called "First Secretary," Rhodri Morgan (2000–2009), and Carwyn Jones (2009–present). The government's policy remit extends to education, healthcare, local government, transportation, planning, economic development, social care, culture, the environment, and agriculture. In 2010 it had a budget of $20 billion (£14B).

Current Status

The Welsh government's effort to expand the teaching of Welsh in schools has met with some success: increasing numbers of young people have knowledge of the language. In addition, a growing number of government services are available through the medium of Welsh, although not as many as Welsh language activists would like. There are also numerous Welsh-language radio and television broadcasts.

In the May 2010 UK elections, Plaid won 11.3 percent of the Welsh vote, a drop of 1.3 percent from the 2005 election. The party came in fourth place in Wales, after Labor, the Conservatives, and the Liberal Democrats. Plaid's top priority in the short term is the holding of a new referendum to strengthen the Welsh government's powers by allowing it to enact laws independent of the UK government. According to parliamentarian Jill Evans, "the current procedure is time-consuming, complicated and is not

working. We would much prefer autonomy along the lines of the Scottish model." The Welsh affiliates of all the main political parties supported having a referendum, she noted, and newly elected UK prime minister David Cameron has pledged to hold a referendum in 2011.

The tide of Welsh public opinion seems to be turning in the direction of greater autonomy. According to an opinion poll cited in a March 2010 article in the UK's *Guardian* newspaper, 56 percent of Welsh people want the Welsh Assembly to be granted full lawmaking powers. "First fearful, then skeptical, Welsh opinion is now embracing not merely the principle of devolution, but a richer reality," the article said. Plaid's Evans explained that "Welsh people were not originally convinced devolution would improve their everyday lives. But they have changed their minds now that they have seen it in operation."

The devolved government that Welsh—and Scottish—people have enjoyed since 1999 appears to be encouraging pro-autonomy sentiment among English people, too. Writing in the British newspaper *Daily Mail* in May 2010, right-wing English political commentator Richard Littlejohn said, "we can no longer tolerate a system which forces an overwhelmingly Tory [Conservative Party] England to bankroll separatist administrations in Edinburgh and Cardiff, while England . . . is deprived of its own parliament."

Further Reading

"Devolution: Wales points the way," *The Guardian* (United Kingdom), March 2, 2010, www.guardian.co .uk/commentisfree/2010/mar/02/wales-devolution-opposition-support.

Littlejohn, Richard. "The New Politics? More Like Brokeback Mountain," *Daily Mail* (United Kingdom), May 11, 2010, www.dailymail.co.uk/debate/article-1278266/COALITION-GOVERNMENT-The-new-politics-More-like-Brokeback-Mountain.html.

Williamson, David. "Carwyn starts setting out stall for leadership with attack on independence," *The Western Mail* (Welsh daily), December 15, 2008.

Self-determination
in International Legal Instruments

SEPARATIST MOVEMENTS often cite international legal instruments, including several that have been adopted by UN member states, in support of their case. The following are examples of such instruments. While they enshrine the right of peoples to self-determination, they do not enshrine the right of peoples to secede, nor do they define who the "peoples" are that enjoy this right. Consequently, there is often sharp disagreement between separatist movements and their governments over how to apply the principle of self-determination.

Excerpts

Charter of the United Nations, signed by founding UN members on June 26, 1945, in San Francisco, Article 73

Members of the United Nations which have or assume responsibilities for the administration of territories whose peoples have not yet attained a full measure of self-government recognize the principle that the interests of the inhabitants of these territories are paramount, and accept as a sacred trust the obligation to promote to the utmost, within the system of international peace and security established by the present Charter, the well-being of the inhabitants of these territories, and, to this end:

to ensure, with due respect for the culture of the peoples concerned, their political, economic, social, and educational advancement, their just treatment, and their protection against abuses;

to develop self-government, to take due account of the political aspirations of the peoples, and to assist them in the progressive development of their free political institutions, according to the particular circumstances of each territory and its peoples and their varying stages of advancement....

Source: www.pfcmc.com/en/documents/ charter/index.shtml

International Covenant on Civil and Political Rights, adopted by UN General Assembly on December 16, 1966, Article 1 (1)

All peoples have the right of self-determination. By virtue of that right they freely determine their political

status and freely pursue their economic, social and cultural development.

Source: www2.ohchr.org/english/law/ccpr.htm

Declaration on Principles of International Law Concerning Friendly Relations and Cooperation among States in Accordance with the Charter of the United Nations, adopted by UN General Assembly on October 24, 1970

... By virtue of the principle of equal rights and self-determination of peoples enshrined in the Charter of the United Nations, all peoples have the right freely to determine, without external interference, their political status and to pursue their economic, social, and cultural development, and every State has the duty to respect this right in accordance with the provisions of the Charter....

Source: www.un.org/documents/ga/ res/25/ares25.htm

Final Act, adopted by Conference on Security and Cooperation in Europe on August 1, 1975, in Helsinki, Principle VIII

The participating States will respect the equal rights of peoples and their right to self-determination, acting at all times in conformity with the purposes and principles of the Charter of the United Nations and with the relevant norms of international law, including those relating to territorial integrity of States.

By virtue of the principle of equal rights and self-determination of peoples, all peoples always have the right, in full freedom, to determine, when and as they wish, their internal and external political status, without external interference, and to pursue as they wish their political, economic, social and cultural development.

The participating States reaffirm the universal significance of respect for and effective exercise of equal rights and self-determination of peoples for the development of friendly relations among themselves as among all States; they also recall the importance of the elimination of any form of violation of this principle.

Source: www.hri.org/docs/Helsinki75.html

Universal Declaration of the Rights of Peoples, adopted by a group of non-governmental participants including jurists, academics, trade unions, political parties, and liberation movements on July 4, 1976, in Algiers, Article 5

Every people has an imprescriptible and unalienable right to self-determination. It shall determine its political status freely and without any foreign interference.

Source: www.algerie-tpp.org/tpp/en/declaration_algiers.htm

African Charter on Human and Peoples' Rights, adopted by the Organization of African Unity on June 27, 1981, Article 20 (1)

1. *All peoples shall have the right to existence. They shall have the unquestionable and inalienable right to self-determination. They shall freely determine their political status and shall pursue their economic and social development according to the policy they have freely chosen.*

2. *Colonized or oppressed peoples shall have the right to free themselves from the bonds of domination by resorting to any means recognized by the international community.*

3. *All peoples shall have the right to the assistance of the States parties to the present Charter in their liberation struggle against foreign domination, be it political, economic or cultural.*

Source: www1.umn.edu/humanrts/instree/z1afchar.htm

Full text

United Nations Declaration on the Rights of Indigenous Peoples, adopted by the UN General Assembly on September 13, 2007

Source: www.un.org/esa/socdev/unpfii/en/drip.html

The General Assembly,

Guided by the purposes and principles of the Charter of the United Nations, and good faith in the fulfilment of the obligations assumed by States in accordance with the Charter,

Affirming that indigenous peoples are equal to all other peoples, while recognizing the right of all peoples to be different, to consider themselves different, and to be respected as such,

Affirming also that all peoples contribute to the diversity and richness of civilizations and cultures, which constitute the common heritage of humankind,

Affirming further that all doctrines, policies and practices based on or advocating superiority of peoples or individuals on the basis of national origin or racial, religious, ethnic or cultural differences are racist, scientifically false, legally invalid, morally condemnable and socially unjust,

Reaffirming that indigenous peoples, in the exercise of their rights, should be free from discrimination of any kind,

Concerned that indigenous peoples have suffered from historic injustices as a result of, inter alia, their colonization and dispossession of their lands, territories and resources, thus preventing them from exercising, in particular, their right to development in accordance with their own needs and interests,

Recognizing the urgent need to respect and promote the inherent rights of indigenous peoples which derive from their political, economic and social structures and from their cultures, spiritual traditions, histories and philosophies, especially their rights to their lands, territories and resources,

Recognizing also the urgent need to respect and promote the rights of indigenous peoples affirmed in treaties, agreements and other constructive arrangements with States,

Welcoming the fact that indigenous peoples are organizing themselves for political, economic, social and cultural enhancement and in order to bring to an end all forms of discrimination and oppression wherever they occur,

Convinced that control by indigenous peoples over developments affecting them and their lands, territories and resources will enable them to maintain and strengthen their institutions, cultures and traditions, and to promote their development in accordance with their aspirations and needs,

Recognizing that respect for indigenous knowledge, cultures and traditional practices contributes to sustainable and equitable development and proper management of the environment,

Emphasizing the contribution of the demilitarization of the lands and territories of indigenous peoples to peace, economic and social progress and development, understanding and friendly relations among nations and peoples of the world,

Recognizing in particular the right of indigenous families and communities to retain shared responsibility for the upbringing, training, education and well-being of their children, consistent with the rights of the child,

Considering that the rights affirmed in treaties, agreements and other constructive arrangements between States and indigenous peoples are, in some situations, matters of international concern, interest, responsibility and character,

Considering also that treaties, agreements and other constructive arrangements, and the relationship they represent, are the basis for a strengthened partnership between indigenous peoples and States,

Acknowledging that the Charter of the United Nations, the International Covenant on Economic, Social and Cultural Rights (2) and the International Covenant on Civil and Political Rights, as well as the Vienna Declaration and Programme of Action,(3) affirm the fundamental importance of the right to self-determination of all peoples, by virtue of which they freely determine their political status and freely pursue their economic, social and cultural development,

Bearing in mind that nothing in this Declaration may be used to deny any peoples their right to self-determination, exercised in conformity with international law,

Convinced that the recognition of the rights of indigenous peoples in this Declaration will enhance harmonious and cooperative relations between the State and indigenous peoples, based on principles of justice, democracy, respect for human rights, non-discrimination and good faith,

Encouraging States to comply with and effectively implement all their obligations as they apply to indigenous peoples under international instruments, in particular those related to human rights, in consultation and cooperation with the peoples concerned,

Emphasizing that the United Nations has an important and continuing role to play in promoting and protecting the rights of indigenous peoples,

Believing that this Declaration is a further important step forward for the recognition, promotion and protection of the rights and freedoms of indigenous peoples and in the development of relevant activities of the United Nations system in this field,

Recognizing and reaffirming that indigenous individuals are entitled without discrimination to all human rights recognized in international law, and that indigenous peoples possess collective rights which are indispensable for their existence, well-being and integral development as peoples,

Recognizing that the situation of indigenous peoples varies from region to region and from country to country and that the significance of national and regional particularities and various historical and cultural backgrounds should be taken into consideration,

Solemnly proclaims the following United Nations Declaration on the Rights of Indigenous Peoples as a standard of achievement to be pursued in a spirit of partnership and mutual respect:

Article 1

Indigenous peoples have the right to the full enjoyment, as a collective or as individuals, of all human rights and fundamental freedoms as recognized in the Charter of the United Nations, the Universal Declaration of Human Rights (4) and international human rights law.

Article 2

Indigenous peoples and individuals are free and equal to all other peoples and individuals and have the right to be free from any kind of discrimination, in the exercise of their rights, in particular that based on their indigenous origin or identity.

Article 3

Indigenous peoples have the right to self-determination. By virtue of that right they freely determine their political status and freely pursue their economic, social and cultural development.

Article 4

Indigenous peoples, in exercising their right to self-determination, have the right to autonomy or self-government in matters relating to their internal and local affairs, as well as ways and means for financing their autonomous functions.

Article 5

Indigenous peoples have the right to maintain and strengthen their distinct political, legal, economic, social and cultural institutions, while retaining their right to participate fully, if they so choose, in the political, economic, social and cultural life of the State.

Article 6

Every indigenous individual has the right to a nationality.

Article 7

1. Indigenous individuals have the rights to life, physical and mental integrity, liberty and security of person.

2. Indigenous peoples have the collective right to live in freedom, peace and security as distinct peoples and shall not be subjected to any act of genocide or any other act of violence, including forcibly removing children of the group to another group.

Article 8

1. Indigenous peoples and individuals have the right not to be subjected to forced assimilation or destruction of their culture.

2. States shall provide effective mechanisms for prevention of, and redress for:

   (a) Any action which has the aim or effect of depriving them of their integrity as distinct peoples, or of their cultural values or ethnic identities;

   (b) Any action which has the aim or effect of dispossessing them of their lands, territories or resources;

   (c) Any form of forced population transfer which has the aim or effect of violating or undermining any of their rights;

   (d) Any form of forced assimilation or integration;

   (e) Any form of propaganda designed to promote or incite racial or ethnic discrimination directed against them.

Article 9

Indigenous peoples and individuals have the right to belong to an indigenous community or nation, in accordance with the traditions and customs of the community or nation concerned. No discrimination of any kind may arise from the exercise of such a right.

Article 10

Indigenous peoples shall not be forcibly removed from their lands or territories. No relocation shall take place without the free, prior and informed consent of the indigenous peoples concerned and after agreement on just and fair compensation and, where possible, with the option of return.

Article 11

1. Indigenous peoples have the right to practise and revitalize their cultural traditions and customs. This includes the right to maintain, protect and develop the past, present and future manifestations of their cultures, such as archaeological and historical sites, artefacts, designs, ceremonies, technologies and visual and performing arts and literature.

2. States shall provide redress through effective mechanisms, which may include restitution, developed in conjunction with indigenous peoples, with respect to their cultural, intellectual, religious and spiritual property taken without their free, prior and informed consent or in violation of their laws, traditions and customs.

Article 12

1. Indigenous peoples have the right to manifest, practise, develop and teach their spiritual and religious traditions, customs and ceremonies; the right to maintain, protect, and have access in privacy to their religious and cultural sites; the right to the use and control of their ceremonial objects; and the right to the repatriation of their human remains.

2. States shall seek to enable the access and/or repatriation of ceremonial objects and human remains in their possession through fair, transparent and effective mechanisms developed in conjunction with indigenous peoples concerned.

Article 13

1. Indigenous peoples have the right to revitalize, use, develop and transmit to future generations their histories, languages, oral traditions, philosophies, writing systems and literatures, and to designate and retain their own names for communities, places and persons.

2. States shall take effective measures to ensure that this right is protected and also to ensure that indigenous peoples can understand and be understood in political, legal and administrative proceedings, where necessary through the provision of interpretation or by other appropriate means.

Article 14

1. Indigenous peoples have the right to establish and control their educational systems and institutions providing education in their own languages, in a manner appropriate to their cultural methods of teaching and learning.

2. Indigenous individuals, particularly children, have the right to all levels and forms of education of the State without discrimination.

3. States shall, in conjunction with indigenous peoples, take effective measures, in order for indigenous individuals, particularly children, including those living outside their communities, to have access, when possible, to an education in their own culture and provided in their own language.

Article 15

1. Indigenous peoples have the right to the dignity and diversity of their cultures, traditions, histories and aspirations which shall be appropriately reflected in education and public information.

2. States shall take effective measures, in consultation and cooperation with the indigenous peoples concerned, to combat prejudice and eliminate discrimination and to promote tolerance, understanding and good relations among indigenous peoples and all other segments of society.

Article 16

1. *Indigenous peoples have the right to establish their own media in their own languages and to have access to all forms of non-indigenous media without discrimination.*

2. *States shall take effective measures to ensure that State-owned media duly reflect indigenous cultural diversity. States, without prejudice to ensuring full freedom of expression, should encourage privately owned media to adequately reflect indigenous cultural diversity.*

Article 17

1. *Indigenous individuals and peoples have the right to enjoy fully all rights established under applicable international and domestic labour law.*

2. *States shall in consultation and cooperation with indigenous peoples take specific measures to protect indigenous children from economic exploitation and from performing any work that is likely to be hazardous or to interfere with the child's education, or to be harmful to the child's health or physical, mental, spiritual, moral or social development, taking into account their special vulnerability and the importance of education for their empowerment.*

3. *Indigenous individuals have the right not to be subjected to any discriminatory conditions of labour and, inter alia, employment or salary.*

Article 18

Indigenous peoples have the right to participate in decision-making in matters which would affect their rights, through representatives chosen by themselves in accordance with their own procedures, as well as to maintain and develop their own indigenous decision-making institutions.

Article 19

States shall consult and cooperate in good faith with the indigenous peoples concerned through their own representative institutions in order to obtain their free, prior and informed consent before adopting and implementing legislative or administrative measures that may affect them.

Article 20

1. *Indigenous peoples have the right to maintain and develop their political, economic and social systems or institutions, to be secure in the enjoyment of their own means of subsistence and development, and to engage freely in all their traditional and other economic activities.*

2. *Indigenous peoples deprived of their means of subsistence and development are entitled to just and fair redress.*

Article 21

1. *Indigenous peoples have the right, without discrimination, to the improvement of their economic and social conditions, including, inter alia, in the areas of education, employment, vocational training and retraining, housing, sanitation, health and social security.*

2. *States shall take effective measures and, where appropriate, special measures to ensure continuing improvement of their economic and social conditions. Particular attention shall be paid to the rights and special needs of indigenous elders, women, youth, children and persons with disabilities.*

Article 22

1. *Particular attention shall be paid to the rights and special needs of indigenous elders, women, youth, children and persons with disabilities in the implementation of this Declaration.*

2. *States shall take measures, in conjunction with indigenous peoples, to ensure that indigenous women and children enjoy the full protection and guarantees against all forms of violence and discrimination.*

Article 23

Indigenous peoples have the right to determine and develop priorities and strategies for exercising their right to development. In particular, indigenous peoples have the right to be actively involved in developing and determining health, housing and other economic and social programmes affecting them and, as far as possible, to administer such programmes through their own institutions.

Article 24

1. *Indigenous peoples have the right to their traditional medicines and to maintain their health practices, including the conservation of their vital medicinal plants, animals and minerals. Indigenous individuals also have the right to access, without any discrimination, to all social and health services.*

2. *Indigenous individuals have an equal right to the enjoyment of the highest attainable standard of physical and mental health. States shall take the necessary steps with a view to achieving progressively the full realization of this right.*

Article 25

Indigenous peoples have the right to maintain and strengthen their distinctive spiritual relationship with their traditionally owned or otherwise occupied and used lands, territories, waters and coastal seas and other resources and to uphold their responsibilities to future generations in this regard.

Article 26

1. Indigenous peoples have the right to the lands, territories and resources which they have traditionally owned, occupied or otherwise used or acquired.

2. Indigenous peoples have the right to own, use, develop and control the lands, territories and resources that they possess by reason of traditional ownership or other traditional occupation or use, as well as those which they have otherwise acquired.

3. States shall give legal recognition and protection to these lands, territories and resources. Such recognition shall be conducted with due respect to the customs, traditions and land tenure systems of the indigenous peoples concerned.

Article 27

States shall establish and implement, in conjunction with indigenous peoples concerned, a fair, independent, impartial, open and transparent process, giving due recognition to indigenous peoples' laws, traditions, customs and land tenure systems, to recognize and adjudicate the rights of indigenous peoples pertaining to their lands, territories and resources, including those which were traditionally owned or otherwise occupied or used. Indigenous peoples shall have the right to participate in this process.

Article 28

1. Indigenous peoples have the right to redress, by means that can include restitution or, when this is not possible, just, fair and equitable compensation, for the lands, territories and resources which they have traditionally owned or otherwise occupied or used, and which have been confiscated, taken, occupied, used or damaged without their free, prior and informed consent.

2. Unless otherwise freely agreed upon by the peoples concerned, compensation shall take the form of lands, territories and resources equal in quality, size and legal status or of monetary compensation or other appropriate redress.

Article 29

1. Indigenous peoples have the right to the conservation and protection of the environment and the productive capacity of their lands or territories and resources. States shall establish and implement assistance programmes for indigenous peoples for such conservation and protection, without discrimination.

2. States shall take effective measures to ensure that no storage or disposal of hazardous materials shall take place in the lands or territories of indigenous peoples without their free, prior and informed consent.

3. States shall also take effective measures to ensure, as needed, that programmes for monitoring, maintaining and restoring the health of indigenous peoples, as developed and implemented by the peoples affected by such materials, are duly implemented.

Article 30

1. Military activities shall not take place in the lands or territories of indigenous peoples, unless justified by a relevant public interest or otherwise freely agreed with or requested by the indigenous peoples concerned.

2. States shall undertake effective consultations with the indigenous peoples concerned, through appropriate procedures and in particular through their representative institutions, prior to using their lands or territories for military activities.

Article 31

1. Indigenous peoples have the right to maintain, control, protect and develop their cultural heritage, traditional knowledge and traditional cultural expressions, as well as the manifestations of their sciences, technologies and cultures, including human and genetic resources, seeds, medicines, knowledge of the properties of fauna and flora, oral traditions, literatures, designs, sports and traditional games and visual and performing arts. They also have the right to maintain, control, protect and develop their intellectual property over such cultural heritage, traditional knowledge, and traditional cultural expressions.

2. In conjunction with indigenous peoples, States shall take effective measures to recognize and protect the exercise of these rights.

Article 32

1. Indigenous peoples have the right to determine and develop priorities and strategies for the development or use of their lands or territories and other resources.

2. States shall consult and cooperate in good faith with the indigenous peoples concerned through their own representative institutions in order to obtain their free and informed consent prior to the approval of any project affecting their lands or territories and other resources, particularly in connection with the development, utilization or exploitation of mineral, water or other resources.

3. States shall provide effective mechanisms for just and fair redress for any such activities, and appropriate measures shall be taken to mitigate adverse environmental, economic, social, cultural or spiritual impact.

Article 33

1. Indigenous peoples have the right to determine their own identity or membership in accordance with their customs and traditions. This does not impair the right of indigenous individuals to obtain citizenship of the States in which they live.

2. Indigenous peoples have the right to determine the structures and to select the membership of their institutions in accordance with their own procedures.

Article 34

Indigenous peoples have the right to promote, develop and maintain their institutional structures and their distinctive customs, spirituality, traditions, procedures, practices and, in the cases where they exist, juridical systems or customs, in accordance with international human rights standards.

Article 35

Indigenous peoples have the right to determine the responsibilities of individuals to their communities.

Article 36

1. Indigenous peoples, in particular those divided by international borders, have the right to maintain and develop contacts, relations and cooperation, including activities for spiritual, cultural, political, economic and social purposes, with their own members as well as other peoples across borders.

2. States, in consultation and cooperation with indigenous peoples, shall take effective measures to facilitate the exercise and ensure the implementation of this right.

Article 37

1. Indigenous peoples have the right to the recognition, observance and enforcement of treaties, agreements and other constructive arrangements concluded with States or their successors and to have States honour and respect such treaties, agreements and other constructive arrangements.

2. Nothing in this Declaration may be interpreted as diminishing or eliminating the rights of indigenous peoples contained in treaties, agreements and other constructive arrangements.

Article 38

States in consultation and cooperation with indigenous peoples, shall take the appropriate measures, including legislative measures, to achieve the ends of this Declaration.

Article 39

Indigenous peoples have the right to have access to financial and technical assistance from States and through international cooperation, for the enjoyment of the rights contained in this Declaration.

Article 40

Indigenous peoples have the right to access to and prompt decision through just and fair procedures for the resolution of conflicts and disputes with States or other parties, as well as to effective remedies for all infringements of their individual and collective rights. Such a decision shall give due consideration to the customs, traditions, rules and legal systems of the indigenous peoples concerned and international human rights.

Article 41

The organs and specialized agencies of the United Nations system and other intergovernmental organizations shall contribute to the full realization of the provisions of this Declaration through the mobilization, inter alia, of financial cooperation and technical assistance. Ways and means of ensuring participation of indigenous peoples on issues affecting them shall be established.

Article 42

The United Nations, its bodies, including the Permanent Forum on Indigenous Issues, and specialized agencies, including at the country level, and States shall promote respect for and full application of the provisions of this Declaration and follow up the effectiveness of this Declaration.

Article 43

The rights recognized herein constitute the minimum standards for the survival, dignity and well-being of the indigenous peoples of the world.

Article 44

All the rights and freedoms recognized herein are equally guaranteed to male and female indigenous individuals.

Article 45

Nothing in this Declaration may be construed as diminishing or extinguishing the rights indigenous peoples have now or may acquire in the future.

Article 46

1. Nothing in this Declaration may be interpreted as implying for any State, people, group or person any right to engage in any activity or to perform any act contrary to the Charter of the United Nations or construed as authorizing or encouraging any action which would dismember or impair, totally or in part, the territorial

integrity or political unity of sovereign and independent States.

2. *In the exercise of the rights enunciated in the present Declaration, human rights and fundamental freedoms of all shall be respected. The exercise of the rights set forth in this Declaration shall be subject only to such limitations as are determined by law and in accordance with international human rights obligations. Any such limitations shall be non-discriminatory and strictly necessary solely for the purpose of securing due recognition and respect for the*

rights and freedoms of others and for meeting the just and most compelling requirements of a democratic society.

3. *The provisions set forth in this Declaration shall be interpreted in accordance with the principles of justice, democracy, respect for human rights, equality, non-discrimination, good governance and good faith.*

(2)   *See resolution 2200 A (XXI), annex.*

(3)   *A/CONF.157/24 (Part I), chap. III.*

(4)   *Resolution 217 A (III).*

Bibliography

Academic articles

Baker, Bruce. "Separating the sheep from the goats among Africa's separatist movements." *Terrorism and political violence* 13, no. 1 (Spring 2001): 66–86.

Bhatia, Michael V. "Fighting words: naming terrorists, bandits, rebels and other violent actors." *Third World Quarterly* 26, no. 1 (March 2005): 5–22.

Gurr, Ted, and Monty G. Marshall. "Peace and Conflict 2005: A Global Survey of Armed Conflicts, Self-Determination Movements, and Democracy." Center for International Development and Conflict Management, University of Maryland, May 2005. www.systemicpeace.org/PC2005.pdf.

Hamilton-Hart, Natasha. "War and other insecurities in East Asia: What the security studies field does and does not tell us," *The Pacific Review* 22, no. 1 (March 2009): 49–71.

Renan, Ernest. "What Is a Nation?" Lecture presented at the University of Paris–Sorbonne, March 11, 1882. www.cooper.edu/humanities/core/hss3/e_renan.html.

Books

Anderson, Benedict. *Imagined Communities: Reflections on the Origin and Spread of Nationalism.* London: Verso, 1983.

Benedikter, Thomas. *The World's Working Regional Autonomies: An Introduction and Comparative Analysis.* New Delhi: Anthem Press, 2007.

Cheetham, Tom, and Christopher Hewitt. *The Encyclopedia of Modern Separatist Movements.* Santa Barbara, Calif.: ABC-Clio Inc, 2000.

Gurr, Ted. *People Versus States: Minorities at Risk in the New Century.* Washington, D.C.: United States Institute of Peace, 2000.

Hale, Henry. *The Foundations of Ethnic Politics.* New York: Cambridge University Press, 2008.

Macedo, Stephen, and Allen Buchanan, eds. *Secession and Self-Determination: Nomos XLV.* New York: New York University Press, 2003.

O'Leary, Brendan, Ian S. Lustick, and Thomas M. Callaghy. *Right-sizing the State: The Politics of Moving Borders.* New York: Oxford University Press, 2001.

Spencer, Metta. *Separatism: Democracy and Disintegration.* Lanham, Md.: Rowman & Littlefield, 1998.

Databases

Center for International Development and Conflict Management, Minorities At Risk Project, University of Maryland, www.cidcm.umd.edu/mar/data.asp.

CIA, *World Fact Book*, www.cia.gov/library/publications/the-world-factbook.

CQ Press, *Political Handbook of the World Online Edition*, www.cqpress.com.

Minority Rights Group International, World Directory of Minorities and Indigenous Peoples, www.minorityrights.org/directory.

U.S. State Department, Country Reports on Terrorism, www.state.gov/s/ct/rls/crt/index.htm.

U.S. State Department, Human Rights Reports, www.state.gov/g/drl/rls/hrrpt/index.htm.

Journalistic articles

"Gorbachev's bolshie republics (the possible dissolution of the Soviet Union)," *The Economist*, January 13, 1990.

"In quite a state: Defining what makes a country," *The Economist*, April 10, 2010, www.economist.com/node/15868439.

"Self-Determination a Double-Edged Sword," *China Post*, July 30, 2009, www.chinapost.com.tw/editorial/taiwan-issues/2009/07/30/218338/Self-determination:-A.htm.

Reports

Carley, Patricia. "Self-Determination: Sovereignty, Territorial Integrity, and the Right to Secession." United States Institute of Peace, *Peaceworks* 7 (March 1996). www.usip.org/files/resources/pwks7.pdf.

Hannum, Hurst. "The Specter of Secession: Responding to Ethnic Self Determination Claims." Council on Foreign Relations, *Foreign Affairs* 77 (March/April 1998). www.foreignaffairs.com/articles/53801/hurst-hannum/the-specter-of-secession-responding-to-claims-for-ethnic-self-de.

Tuminez, Astrid S. "Ancestral Domain in Comparative Perspective." United States Institute of Peace, Special Report 151, September 2005. www.usip.org/files/resources/sr151.pdf.

UNESCO. "The Implementation of The Right to Self-Determination as a Contribution to Conflict Prevention," Barcelona (conference), November 21–27, 1998. www.unpo.org/downloads/THE%20IMPLEMENTATION%20OF%20THE%20RIGHT%20TO%20SELF.pdf.

Unrepresented Nations and Peoples Organization. "Self-Determination in Relation to Individual Human Rights." The Hague (conference), January 22–23, 1993. www.unpo.org/downloads/Self-determination%20conference%201993.pdf.

Index

Bold page numbers indicate principal treatment. Names starting with al- are alphabetized by the next part of the name (e.g., al-Houthi is in the H's).